PREFACE

Hopefully this book will help visitors and temporary residents of the Netherlands feel at home quickly and answer some of the inevitable questions about how someone else's system works. With this 6th Edition of Roaming 'Round Holland, the touring section has been expanded once again so that most of the important places to visit throughout the Netherlands are included. Fun places such as zoos and recreational parks have been listed for parents traveling with children. Educational exhibits such as Evoluon at Eindhoven and the Delta Plan Works in South Holland and Zeeland are given, as well as nature reserve areas like the Biesbosch and the Waddenzee Islands. The sportsminded visitor or resident can check the Yearly Events and Sports sections to see what is going on, where and when. Museums big and small, castles, remote villages, big cities and interesting places to eat are indicated in the hopes of titillating the reader's interest. The directions given, with the aid of the new provincial site plans and a good commercial map should make touring as easy and foolproof as possible. Temporary residents can find many answers to their questions about how to settle in happily in Part 2.

The Netherlands is probably the most rewarding holidayland for families in the world. Come and see for yourselves.

HOW TO USE THIS BOOK

In order to make reading the book systematic, the places to visit are usually in order going clockwise; i.e., west, northwest, north, northeast, east, southeast, south and southwest. If a family decides they want to go in the general direction of Arnhem, for instance, they can look up Arnhem in the Index, read what is available there, but also by reading before and after that section, they will get ideas of what else can be seen in the general vicinity.

With the addition of so much new material, some provinces do not allow us to adhere strictly to directions given in a clockwise fashion; however, that is explained as it occurs and should cause no problems.

Special headings have been added to the cities and villages, such as Markets, Eating Out, Staying Over, Yearly Events, and In The Neighborhood. We hope the dining out and hotel suggestions will be tried and enjoyed both in the big cities and at places on the road. Many fascinating but often overlooked villages or special sites are included in this expanded edition.

Please bear in mind that while every effort has been made to be accurate in all details, times of openings and closings of public places often vary and it is safer to call ahead to verify that the object of your excursion will be open rather than to arrive and be disappointed. Prices also have a way of skyrocketing so please do understand if there is some variance in this direction. Prices are not quoted for museums, churches and castles because for the most part there is only a minimal charge. Whenever the price is high enough to cause some families to hesitate about going, we have indicated the amount. Most of the places recommended have been visited personally, and when this has not been possible, the listings were screened thoroughly.

Our age guidelines for children are meant to be helpful in eliminating places obviously not suitable for the youngest ones. On the other hand, every child varies and his or her parents are obviously the best judges of what will interest them.

Roaming 'Round Holland

ACKNOWLEDGEMENTS

A special note of thanks is due the Netherlands Board of Tourism and the VVV provincial tour offices for their continuing support and assistance in compiling much of the information in this new, expanded edition. In particular, we should like to thank the NBT New York office and Sandra Obma for her patience, help and efficiency in tracking down details "at the source." All the VVV-i offices in the Randstad have been called upon for their expert advice. With this new edition, the VVV offices which gave us special attention and personal guidance were Leeuwarden (Fr), Groningen (Gr), Haarlem (NH), Middelburg (Z), Valkenburg (L) and Maastricht (L). We are grateful to them all.

We would also like to thank the Stichting Bevordering Van Volkskracht in Rotterdam for its continued encouragement.

Two private corporations known for their support of public-interest ventures have included us in their generosity, enabling us to expand this edition, thereby giving a deeper view of the Netherlands:

Mobil Oil BV Netherlands
Nederlands Unilever Bedrijven BV

IN RETROSPECT...

ROAMING 'ROUND HOLLAND (The Book), previously *Roaming 'Round Rotterdam;* the City of Rotterdam (The City); The American International School of Rotterdam (The School); and the William K. Gordon Fund (The Fund), have had a fruitful relationship for more than sixteen years.

Through proceeds of sales of The Book, The Fund was established in 1973 by the author, Patricia G. Erickson, to give financial assistance to deserving students of The School who needed to follow an English-language curriculum in education. The original publishers, The City, supported The Book and The School as a public service to the foreign community of Rotterdam. Over the years, The School has prospered, offering quality primary school education to English-speaking children of all nationalities; The City has retained its interest and support of The School; The Fund, under the chairmanship of Mrs. Gazaleh since 1974, has provided 75 partial scholarships; and The Book has been expanded to cover the entire Netherlands.

This sixth edition continues the original concept: clear and complete guidance to introduce the best of the Netherlands to temporary residents and holiday guests from abroad. We extend our welcome to tourists and new arrivals of all ages!

I would like to compliment the author and the publishers with this new and updated issue of *ROAMING 'ROUND HOLLAND*, a very useful guide book which will be welcomed by all tourists to our fascinating and varied country.

This book provides the reader with a host of background information about cities, museums, castles, events, trips, travel suggestions and a great deal more.

The Netherlands Board of Tourism's adage, "Holland for all Reasons" is clearly reflected in this guide.

I would wish the visitor to Holland a very pleasant stay and hope that all the information given in this book will contribute to making his or her visit a pleasant and memorable one indeed.

J. A. T. Cornelissen, General Director
Netherlands Board of Tourism

DEDICATION

With love to our traveling companions
for their unwavering support and patience

TABLE OF CONTENTS

PART I

Sightseeing, museums & amusement centers

CHAPTER 1

TOURING HOLLAND

Have you just arrived? Why not take a commercial tour to get acquainted? The children—not to mention the adults—will love going on a Rotterdam boat tour 'round the biggest harbor in the world; or taking a tour by coach—The Royal Tour—in The Hague; or a canal tour of Amsterdam. During the summer, what could be more pleasant than a day-long boat trip or a special bike tour? It's all available and more! Any travel agency, or the well-known quasi-official tourist information agency for the Netherlands, the VVV, will be happy to sell you a tour of the city in which you are visiting or living. Most conducted tours will have guides who speak English, French, German, Dutch (naturally)—and maybe a few other languages as well.

Section Two of this book covers information of prime interest to foreign residents of Holland; however, visitors might also be interested in the sections on babysitting, summer camps for children, Dutch food specialities, movies, the dance, symphony, opera, legitimate theaters (including puppet shows), shopping, pets, biking (rules of the road), boating, fishing, horse shows and horseracing, medical care and churches. There are also chapters on beaches and where to see things being hand-made, as well as one on evening entertainment. Check the Table of Contents.

But first, there are visitors or newly assigned business people who want information before they leave home. Where do they get it? If they happen to live in their nation's capital, they can contact the Dutch Embassy for information regarding business matters; they can read some of the books listed under "Recommended Reading" at the end of this book; and they can write or call the Netherlands Board of Tourism for travel information.

13

NBT - Netherlands Board of Tourism

HEAD OFFICE (The Netherlands): Nederlands Bureau voor Toerisme,
Vlietweg 15, 2266 KA Leidschendam, tel. (070) 705705, after
Dec. 1989 dial 370 5705. Telex: 32588.
BRITAIN AND IRELAND: Egginton House, 25-28 Buckingham Gate,
London SW1E6LD, tel. 01-630-0451.
CANADA: 25 Adelaide St., East, Toronto, Ont., M5C1Y2, tel. (416)
363-1577.
UNITED STATES:
New York: 355 Lexington Ave., N.Y. 10017, tel. (212) 379-7367.
Chicago: 225 N. Michigan Ave., Suite 326, Chicago, Ill. 60601, tel.
(312) 819-0300.
San Francisco: 90 New Montgomery St., Suite 305, San Francisco, CA
94105, tel. (415) 543-6772.
■ *Other NBT overseas offices are listed in "Quick Reference," just*
before the Index.

Planning your trip is really half the fun so before doing anything else, write one of the NBT offices listed above and ask for their current Holland magazine. There are also publications on camping, biking, boating, windmills, museums, hotels (description and general prices for the current year), and a new 636-page booklet entitled "Budget Hotels, Holland" written in four languages with hotel pictures, prices and facilities indicated. If you say where you want to travel and something about your special interests (sports, cultural events, folkloric towns, etc.), they can send you the most pertinent material.

The NBT office personnel abroad will welcome you in fluent English eager to provide you with all the information you may need to plan an outstanding trip to Holland. A new service has recently been added. They can reserve theater tickets for cultural events in Amsterdam at the Concertgebouw or other theaters. Tour group travel arrangements (hotels, restaurants and tourist guides) can also be made.

One section of the magazine is "The Holland Shop," a shop-by-mail section with an order form so you can obtain books, maps, a video on Amsterdam, general guide books such as "Roaming 'Round Holland," and last but not least, the Holland Leisure Card, including the Museum Card which sells for $25.00. The Holland Leisure Card packet is only available from NBT offices overseas and entitles the holder to special services, privileges and savings on air, train, tram and subway travel. If you are visiting family or friends, you might not need the Leisure Card, but if you are on your own, it could be a money saver.

■ **The Museum Card** can be purchased separately in the Netherlands: adults, Fl. 30, seniors, Fl. 20, children to 14 years, Fl. 15. This is truly a good buy for museum lovers.

The NBT also puts out a brochure entitled "Useful Hints for Your Stay in the Netherlands" which gives extensive information about frontier formalities, medical assistance, transport, use of the telephone and so on. Available at the NBT offices abroad.

NRC - Netherlands National Reservation Center

*ADVANCE RESERVATIONS AND INFORMATION: POB 404, Vlietweg
15, 2260 AK Leidschendam, tel. 31 70 202500 (from overseas),
tel. (070) 202500 (from Holland), Telex 33755, Telefax (070)
202611; Mon.-Fri., 8am-8pm, Sat. until 2pm.*

Advance reservations for hotels, apartments, certain camping huts, boats, bungalows, theaters, tourist group guide service, can be made through the NRC. Established by the Dutch hotel keepers and the NBT, this organization has the latest information about what facilities are available . . . and their service is free. They recommend sending a telefax as the most efficient way of reserving. When making your request, give the dates you will be traveling, what price hotels you need, the number of people and rooms required, with or without a bath, shower, what cities you wish to visit. You can also ask for assistance from the NBT offices abroad.

VVV - National Dutch Tourist Offices in Holland

*AMSTERDAM: VVV-i, Stationsplein 10, tel. (020) 266444. There is
also a VVV office on Utrechtseweg and Leidsestraat, 106.*
*THE HAGUE: VVV, Koningen Julianaplein 8 (Central Station), tel.
(070) 266200.*
SCHEVENINGEN: VVV-i, Gevers Deynootweg 126, tel. (070) 546200.
*ROTTERDAM: VVV-i, Coolsingel 67 (across from the City Hall), tel.
(010) 413 6000; there is also a VVV office in the main hall of the
Rotterdam Central Station.*
*SPECIAL NOTE: After December 1989, all telephone numbers in
The Hague, area code (070), will add a '3' before local numbers.*
■ *For a more complete list of VVV offices throughout the Netherlands, refer to "Quick Reference," just before the Index.*

In Holland, this organization is the travelers' "guardian angel" when it comes to travel arrangements and knowing what's going on. Look for the sign in blue and white:

 **Verenigingen voor
Vreemdelingenverkeer**

Each VVV is a private company, partially supported by the city or village in which it operates. Therefore, there are small fees for some services, information brochures, pamphlets and maps; others are given away. The VVV knows everything about the city in which it is located, as well as the surroundings. Extremely helpful, they can answer questions in English, French and German . . . and possibly other languages as well.

15

In the larger cities, you will find the sign with an "i" added like this:

VVV-i offices have information about the whole country so you can reserve a hotel room, book theater tickets, etc., in any city in the Netherlands. Look for the magazine entitled "Gidsen voor Vakantie en Vrije Tijd" (Guide for Vacations and Leisure). About 30 of these magazines cover each province in detail . . . in Dutch, however. Ask about special package tour arrangements which can include luncheon vouchers, rental bikes, the possibility of a horse-drawn wagon arrangement, 3- or 5-day hotel with excursions at special prices, etc.

ANWB - The Royal Dutch Touring Club

AMSTERDAM: Museumplein 5, tel. (020) 730844.
THE HAGUE: Wassenaarseweg 220, tel. (070) 147147.
ROTTERDAM: Westblaak 210, tel. (010) 414 0000.
MAASTRICHT: Koningsplein 60, tel. (043) 620666.
UTRECHT: Van Vollenhovenlaan 277-279, tel. (030) 910333.

The ANWB is Holland's answer to the American AAA or England's AA or RAC. Members in these clubs are accorded reciprocal privileges by the ANWB. This can be very useful so check it out.

The ANWB offers two services to non-members and members alike: blue and white highway directional signs indicating recommended hotels, restaurants, campsites and waterway sites; and rescue on the highways if you have car trouble (see Road Service below).

Long-term visitors or permanent residents will find membership in the ANWB more than pays its way. A plethora of services is available to motorist, cyclist, boater, camper and tourist in general. Unfortunately almost all ANWB literature is only in Dutch. Representatives in their travel stores in most big cities do speak English so you can get tour guidance in person or by phone. They offer tour information, travel documentation, legal assistance and insurance. For a fee, they will inspect any used car you may wish to buy, providing you with a detailed report listing any defects.

Road Service: Last but not least are their 750 "Wegenwacht" patrol cars which travel the highways around the clock. Ready on-the-spot repairs can be made or they will tow you to the nearest service station. There are also roadside emergency phones located along all Dutch motorways . . . just press the button and you will be connected to the nearest Road Service Station. You can telephone 24 hours/day to find out about road and sea conditions in Holland and abroad (snow, ice, fog, storms).

Maps: The ANWB maps, NOORD, MIDDEN and ZUID NEDERLAND to the scale 1:200,000 are invaluable for touring, especially by automobile. They can be purchased through the NBT overseas or through their stores in Holland.

TIPS FOR TRAVELERS

DUTCH MONEY is based on the decimal system. One hundred cents make one guilder. A guilder (een gulden) is also known as a florin and by the abbreviations "Dfl," or "Fl." If you need to exchange foreign money, the "Change" (exchange bank) located in Central Railway Stations of major cities are open weekdays from 8:30am-9pm; Sat. until noon. For more details, see "Banking," Chapter 16. American Express, Visa and Diners Club credit cards are accepted in most cities.

U.S. travelers worried about dollar devaluation can purchase prepaid tour packages; or obtain Dutch guilders or cash through some banks and money exchange offices before leaving home. Even a few dollars in change, including 1 guilder pieces, can be invaluable upon arrival if you wish to use the telephone, tip, pay for a taxi, before you can get to an Exchange office. If you arrive in the wee hours at the airport, the Exchange is not open.

CUSTOMS: You will need a valid passport, but not a visa if you are a U.S., Canadian, British, Australian or New Zealand citizen. You should carry one other item of identification such as a valid driver's license. If you plan to stay longer than three months, check with the NBT or Dutch Embassy for legalities.

TELEPHONES: Foreign telephones are always a bug-a-boo for travelers. The cost for a local call is 25 Dutch cents (een kwartje) but it is well to have several 1 guilder pieces at hand, and for long-distance calls, a handful of change is advisable. Read the instructions displayed in the phone booth. It will depend on your quick-learning ability if you understand them since they are in Dutch with illustrations. If you're having trouble, snag a passerby to help.

Warning: In Europe, international calls made from your hotel room can be double (or more) than calls from a phone booth. Arrange to have family phone you at pre-agreed times if possible, as calls from the U.S. are always cheaper than to the U.S. There's a six-hour time difference from the U.S. East Coast . . . 6pm is midnight in Holland. Cost of calls to the U.S. is lower at weekends and after 7pm local time.

HELPFUL HINTS ABOUT TELEPHONING:

Information: Inside Netherlands, dial 008; for numbers outside the Netherlands, dial 060418.
Telegrams: To send a telegram, dial 009.
Credit Card Calls: Dial 06, wait for tone, then 0410, U.S. Direct (AT&T, Bell, GTE credit cards only, or calling "collect"), dial 06, then 022-9111.
International Access Code: For calling outside the Netherlands, dial 09. To call the U.S. dial 09, wait for the tone, then 1, the U.S. area code, then local number; for UK dial 09, wait for the tone, then 44, then local code and number.

> *Other country codes are: Belgium 32; Canada 1; France 33; Luxembourg 352; West Germany 49; Switzerland 41.*
> *Repairs: Dial 007.*   *Customer Service: Dial 004.*

MAIL: The Post Office puts out a brochure with symbols giving current prices, weights, etc. Post Office hours are 8:30am-5pm. For off-hours, stamp machines are usually just outside the P.O. entrance. Weight allowance for letters within Europe is 20 grams, for North America, 10 grams . . . better buy lightweight paper and write small!

CAMPING IN THE NETHERLANDS: There are approximately 2,000 campsites in Holland! Generally, it is not allowed to camp outside official campsites. Sometimes a daily charge is levied and sometimes a 24-hour charge is made, so ask for rates upon arrival or when making reservation by letter. You will need proof of identity such as a passport. It is wise to have another piece of identification in case they want to hold it for the duration of your stay. You can purchase the ANWB book "ANWB Camping Sites" (for the current year) through NBT offices abroad or ANWB offices in the Netherlands . . . symbols in English. The VVV puts out "Holland Camping."

Transportation to Holland

FROM THE U.S. AND CANADA: The most likely choice will be by air, although a leisurely ocean voyage aboard the QE2 or by freighter to Amsterdam or Rotterdam can't be beat. Some carriers to check out are Pan American, TWA, KLM, Air Canada, British Air. Try Martin Air for direct-flight round-trip fares that are hard to beat; tel. 1-800-847-6677.

FROM THE U.K.:

By ferry: One of the most popular ferry connections is between Harwich-Hook of Holland by Sealink British Ferries or the Zeeland Steamship Co. The crossing takes about 7 hours by day and 8 hours by night. Another is Hull-Rotterdam (Europoort) by North Sea Ferries . . . takes about 13 hours overnight. Other possibilities are from Great Yarmouth-Scheveningen by Norfolk Line; Felixstowe-Rotterdam by Townsend Thoresen; and if you're going to southern Holland, Sheerness-Vlissingen by Olau Line. There are also ferry services to Belgian and French ports.

By air: There are daily flights from Heathrow-Amsterdam by British Airways and KLM; flight time, one hour. NLM has daily flights from Heathrow to Rotterdam, Eindhoven and Maastricht. From Gatwick, Rotterdam Airlines and British Airways have flights to Amsterdam and Rotterdam. From London's new City Airport, there are also *Brymon and Eurocity Express* flights to Amsterdam and Rotterdam. In addition, there are a number of airlines flying to Holland from provincial U.K. airports.

Onward by train: Ongoing air travelers arriving at Schiphol Airport can scoot downstairs from the Arrival Lounge, buy their train tickets at the ticket counter there, get directions to the train platform (spoor) and wait for their train—all within a few minutes' walk. During normal hours, local trains go to Amsterdam, The Hague, Leiden and Rotterdam about every 15 minutes. Trains to other parts of Holland also stop here but less frequently. There are also trains to France, Belgium and West Germany (among other European destinations); non-stop to France and Belgium.

Transportation in Holland

BY DOMESTIC AIR SERVICE: NLM (an off-shoot of KLM) operates the following services: From Amsterdam to Eindhoven, Maastricht, Groningen and Enschede; from Rotterdam to Maastricht and Eindhoven; from Groningen to Enschede. They also organize charter trips for groups.

BY TRAIN: Roaming 'round Holland by train—from early morning 'til late at night, 4,300 NS trains transport 600,000 passengers to and from work and play. Train services are frequent and on time. During rush hours on commuter lines, it can be a matter of minutes between trains. Even for long-distance trains, there is rarely more than an hour's wait. Trains run from 5am (Sundays and public holidays from 7am) until about 1 am.

Major train stations have an Information Office which serves a multitude of purposes. They act as a travel bureau for those interested in special-priced Netherlands Railways organized outings, sell tickets for long-distance trains and make seat reservations if those are desired. These general sales and information offices will also assist foreigners with their travel arrangements, direct them to the correct window for short-distance train tickets, etc. English, German and French are spoken.

MAJOR RAILWAY STATIONS WITH INFORMATION AND SALES OFFICES:

Amsterdam: Central Station, hours, Mon., 6:30am-10pm, Tues.-Fri., 7am-10pm; weekends, 8am-10pm.

The Hague: Central Station (CS) and Hague Station (HS), hours weekdays, 8am-8pm, Sat.-Sun., 10am-6pm. Reduced price tickets can also be purchased at Post Offices in The Hague.

Rotterdam: Central Station, Stationsplein, hours Mon.-Fri., 6am-11pm; Sat., 7am-11pm; Sun., 8am-11pm. Metrostation Zuidplein, open same hours as above.

■ *Railway Information: Dial 06-899 1121 for inquiries of all kinds such as schedules, arrival and departure times, lost items, price of tickets and more. Toll free; English is spoken.*

For clear and comprehensive information about travel by train, get the excellent English-language pamphlet, "Touring Holland by Rail" ... can be obtained from NBT overseas offices and from the VVV. In the meantime, following is a bird's eye view.

Fares: There are first- and second-class tickets; one-way and return tickets (must be used on the same day); season tickets; reduction and family tickets. Children up to 3 years, travel free; from 4-11 years, they pay Fl. 1.00 when accompanied by an adult over 18 years. One adult may take 3 children at most. If you travel often, in a group, for long trips and avoid rush hours, you can benefit from cheaper fares. It is explained in the Dutch brochure "Treinprijzen," available free from NS ticket offices and information desks (not in English). There is even a ticket the whole family can use on bus, tram and train for an entire year called the "OV Jaarkaart." There are student tickets for children 4 to 9 years, as well as special fares for people over 65 years and dogs too big to be carried in a basket!

Holland is well organized to encourage tourism and to make it affordable to all. A series of Rail Ranger tickets includes the choice of:

SPECIAL FARES FOR OUTINGS:

One-day, 3-day and 7-day Rail Rangers: Allow the holder unlimited travel on 1, 3 or 7 consecutive days, commencing any day, over all NS lines.

Public Transport Link Ranger: Can be purchased in conjunction with the day Rail Rangers, above, for unlimited travel on subways, trams, city and provincial buses.

A Multi Ranger: (Meer Man's Kaart) entitles 2-6 passengers to one day's unlimited travel on all NS lines.

The Teenager Ranger: (Tienertoerkaart), available June, July, August, and during autumn and Christmas school vacations, entitles the holder to unlimited 2nd class travel on any 4 days within a specified period of 10 consecutive days. Issued only to people up to 18 years.

The Family Ranger: (Gezinstoerkaart) is available June, July and August and entitles an entire family to unlimited travel over the NS network on any 4 days within a specified 10 days.

A Senior Ranger: This ticket allows you to travel 1st or 2nd class with 45% reduction on single fares and 40% reduction on return trips.

Evening return tickets: Valid from 6pm-on, which cost the one-way fare plus 4 guilders.

Weekend return tickets: Valid on Saturday and Sunday and cost the price of a day return plus 2.50 guilders.

The Benelux Toerrailkaart: Available during the summer, Christmas and New Years holidays allows unlimited travel to Belgium and Luxembourg as well as the Netherlands.

Day trips by train: What do you have in mind for today's outing? Perhaps, a visit to see Rembrandt's paintings, the Delta Plan, or a boat trip around Rotterdam's harbor sound interesting. One especially good way to see the tulips blooming in springtime is to buy a combined ticket which includes rail/bus travel and admission fees to the Keukenhof at Lisse. The train travels right

through the large beds of multi-colored bulbs, and passengers can smile smugly as they see the jammed highways with cars crawling aong the roads. These are four of the 200 suggested day trips listed in the National Railways booklet, "Er op Uit," which is available at train stations and post offices.

Hiking and Biking trips: There are many beautiful walking and cycling tours listed in the "day trip" booklet which will take you into all the scenic corners of the Netherlands. When you purchase your ticket, you will also get an appropriate map. If you choose a biking trip, when you arrive at your destination, ask to be directed to the "Fietsenstalling" which is where you rent a bike. On some of these delightful tours through open country, it is hard to believe Holland ranks among the most heavily populated in the world.

PUBLIC TRANSPORTATION IN TOWN: In town, there is a choice of electric tram, bus or metro (the latter in Rotterdam and Amsterdam). To simplify and unify the national public transportation ticket system, the "Nationale Strippenkaart" was instituted. It divides the nation into zones with one fare system. These tickets are good on all trams, buses and underground lines, and on certain 2nd-class trains. There are 6-strip and 10-strip tickets which are sold on trams and buses as well as at Post Offices and official ticket offices. The 15-strip ticket is only sold in advance through authorized ticket agencies. Strip tickets cost less per trip than individual fares; a 15-strip ticket is cheaper per trip than a 6-strip ticket.

Commuter Tickets: You can buy a weekly, monthly, or year ticket from the authorized ticket offices and post offices. When applying, you will need a passport photo and one piece of valid identification such as a passport.

TO GET IN AND OUT OF TRAMS AND METRO:

To get in the tram or Metro, look for the "deur open" button at the front, middle or back of car. You must press it for the door to open: it will close automatically. In trams, the lowermost step controls the closing of the door and locks the door in position.

BY BUS: Bus travel is coordinated with trains to provide complete access to all towns and villages. The Netherlands railways puts out a guide, the *Nationale Buswijzer*, listing bus routes, times, zones, map, etc. Can be obtained at NS sales outlets. For more information on bus travel, you can write Streekvervoer ESO, POB 19222, 3501 Utrecht, Holland. The VVV can also provide information on special bus sightseeing trips. Always board the bus by the front door near the driver where you can purchase or show him your ticket.

BY AUTOMOBILE: Holland is a perfect country to tour by automobile . . . the roads are outstanding, down to the smallest country road (which we recommend highly for true scenic beauty). The rules of the road are honored; drinking-and-driving laws are strict with heavy fines/jail sentences for violators; the Wegenwacht (see ANWB) is on hand to rescue drivers in distress: and you can travel according to your own interests and timetable. If you are coming from abroad, check with your auto club for their advice on documentation or with help in renting a car. If you are already in Holland, the ANWB and VVV can help. The NBT offices in the States and other overseas offices can also supply you with information about driving in Holland.

Maps for the road: Dutch large-scale maps are among the best in the world, and they can be obtained from most bookstores which specialize in travel books, or they can be ordered from the NBT offices abroad, the VVV or the ANWB. Everything is indicated: scenic roads, castles, biking and walking paths, ruins, Stone Age burial tombs, recreational areas, lighthouses, swimming pools, picnic places, nature reserves, wind and water mills, etc. The ANWB road maps we have used most extensively are for Noord (north), Midden (middle) and Zuid (south) Nederland to the scale 1:200,000 entitled "Toeristenkaart." They are also available from the NBT and book shops. The VVV puts out maps and sells the excellent Michelin maps, also in three parts and to the scale 1:200,000. Falk, another major mapmaker, produces easy-to-read large-scale city maps.

Dutch guide books and pamphlets: There are specialized pamphlets available through the NBT, the VVV and the ANWB on biking and boating holidays, windmills, flowers and flower parades, and special events. Some are in English but most are in Dutch. Ask for the VVV's "Fietsen (Biking) in Holland"; the ANWB's book about Dutch castles and museums. The NBT sells "Holiday Atlas of the Netherlands," a unique map production showing holiday centers and campsites; cycling routes; castles and mills; and other maps. Available in English, German and Dutch.

EATING OUT

Holland has not always been known for its gastronomy. Recently, however, the cuisine throughout the Netherlands has taken a mighty leap for the better and having a delightful dining experience can easily be had with a little research.

Dutch restaurants like to tempt your appetite in many ways. One particularly successful idea is the children's plate: smaller portions at low cost. The set "kids" menu is usually chicken, french fries and applesauce. If you don't see "Kindermenu" listed, ask the waiter if they have one. Chapter 17 describes many Dutch foods which seem to appeal especially to children.

The Holland Tourist Menu offers good food—often Dutch specialities—at a fixed all-in price . . . Fl. 19.50 in 1989. The VVV has an updated yearly list of restaurants which feature the Tourist Menu. There is a yearly competition among the participating restaurants to see who can produce the best meal for the price. The idea for a yearly competition to encourage high quality came from Nestle's, the RAI, Misset's Horeca and the NBT.

Romantische Restaurants. Who could resist trying out a Romantic Restaurant? Some specialize in regional cooking and some offer mainly classic dishes. Each restaurant has its own character, excellent food, atmosphere, gives personal attention and warm hospitality to ensure a "special night out." Their latest pamphlet can be obtained from the VVV, or by calling (023) 291777.

Nederlands Dis. Dutch home-cooked specialities at reasonable prices. Some of our favorites are new herring at the beginning of summer; asparagus with ham and chopped eggs; smoked eel; pea soup in winter, etc. All Dutch ingredients are used in the preparation of these meals so seasonal dishes are particularly popular. The pamphlet is available from the local VVV or tel. (070) 320 2500.

Michelin has traveled north and five new Dutch restaurants received Michelin Stars bringing the total to 47 One Star and four Two-Star restaurants . . . these figures are probably increasing as you read. A complete list of these restaurants can be obtained by writing any office of the Netherlands Board of Tourism. We have indicated those which have come to our attention in the Randstad area, see Chapter 17.

The Alliance Gastronomique Néerlandaise comprises 30 leading Dutch restaurateurs who represent the peak of culinary art. They exact the highest standards and each restaurant has its special ambiance.

Relais du Centre, a relatively new group of 22 restaurants with moderate prices is aiming to offer a quality product in its price field.

STAYING OVER

Hilton, Marriott, Holiday Inn, Best Western, Novotel and Crest are all represented in the Netherlands. However, there are several Dutch hotel chains listed below which are not so well known, offering a choice of price and formality of surroundings. Many chains will offer special weekend and off-season packages which can be very attractive, such as, a weekend in Brussels with the Crest Hotels at half price; or to Medemblik for hotel/dancing/dining and sightseeing at the Holland Hotel Het Wapen Van Medemblik.

Very good hotel brochures are put out by the VVVs, NBT and the ANWB. The VVV magazine entitled "Hotels 1989, 1990, etc." lists even small towns throughout the country. The NBT has just issued a 600+-page "Budget Hotels, Holland," with pictures, prices and amenities described in four languages. Lasschuit's "officieel adresboek" lists hotels, motels and restaurants for the current year; gives all specifics including a photo of the establishment.

Golden Tulip Hotels: These hotels are located in some of the most interesting areas in the country ... they are generally in the top-price category, offering outstanding services and accommodations, including health and recreational facilities with swimming, saunas, etc., available. Their Familie Hotel in Paterswolde (Groningen) is a delightful experience. Another noteworthy member of this group is the Doelen Hotel in Amsterdam, 750 years old and boasts Rembrandt painted "The Night Watch" in one of their rooms! For their brochure, write POB 619, 1200 AP Hilversum; for reservations, call (035) 232390. From the U.S. or Canada, write 140 East 63rd Street, New York 10021 or telephone 1-800-344-1212.

Crest Hotels: Very comfortable hotels in the moderate-expensive category. They are part of the largest hotel chain in the world which includes the Quality Inns in the U.S. For their brochure, write POB 528, 2270 AM Voorburg; for reservations, tel. (020) 262922.

Holland Hotels: The hotels in this group are often in quiet scenic stops with generally moderate prices. You can reserve directly or from one Holland Hotel to another for your next night's stop. For information, write Bureau BSG, POB 432, 1400 AK Bussum. You can also reserve through the National Reservation Centre, tel. (070) 202500 ... after December 1989, 320 2500.

Postiljon (Postillion Hotels): Also highly regarded. For information, POB 720, 7400 AS Deventer, tel. (05700) 38900. One of their special services is to organize bike tours, transporting your luggage from one hotel to the next.

The Bilderberg Group: Twelve first-class "Gourmet" hotels which offer distinctive accommodations in unique settings (lakeside suites, forested surroundings, and even a turn-of-the-century castle. Leisure activities include swimming pools, health clubs and tennis clubs. For information or reservations, write Robert Reid Associates, Inc., 845 Third Avenue, New York 10022, tel. toll-free in U.S., 1-800-223-6510.

All hotels in the above groups can obtain a doctor at short notice if such an unhappy need should occur, as well as make reservations ahead for you within their chain for the next night's stop.

CHAPTER 2

THE PROVINCE OF SOUTH HOLLAND

South Holland, along with North Holland and Zeeland, form the western boundary of the Netherlands bordered by the North Sea. Its southern boundary follows from Brouwersdam, along the Hollands Diep to Gorinchem; east past Gouda and north to include the bulbfields as far as the southern edge of Haarlem. This coastline has been buffeted by storms and inundations throughout time, changing the face of the map with each new onslaught. In recent years, modern technology has led to the building of huge protective barriers, adding greatly to the land mass and allowing formerly unstable waterways to become protected recreational watersports areas.

Not the largest province in size, South Holland nevertheless is one of the most influential because of Rotterdam, The Hague, Leiden and Dordrecht, cities of major importance to the Netherlands economically, commercially and culturally. Europe's most important commercial waterway is the Rhine River which, in Holland, eventually becomes the Maas River with its outlet to the North Sea. Historically, this vital transportation and communication link has fostered the development and prosperity of Maassluis, Vlaardingen, Schiedam, Delfshaven, Rotterdam, and Dordrecht. Today, the ports along the "New Waterway" of the Maas, are abuzz with tankers loaded with oil, grain, minerals and chemicals, as well as container vessels and hundreds of inland waterway barges carrying goods of all kinds.

■ The most heavily populated area in the Netherlands is the triangle formed by Amsterdam, Haarlem, The Hague, Rotterdam, Dordrecht and Utrecht (city) and is commonly known as the Randstad.

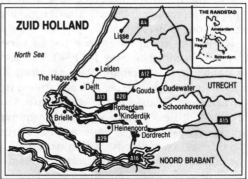

INFORMATION: VVV-i, Rotterdam, tel. (010) 413 6000.

ROTTERDAM

A dynamic modern city

GETTING THERE: By car, Rotterdam is 45 minutes south of Amsterdam and about 20 minutes from The Hague. Major autoroutes from the north are A4 (Amsterdam), A13 (The Hague); from the east A12, A20 (Utrecht), or A15, A16 (Nijmegen) and from the south, A16 (Breda). Zestienhoven Airport is minutes from downtown as are cargo and passenger vessels berthed in the inland waterway or at the passenger terminals. Trains are constant from other parts of the Netherlands and from abroad.

INFORMATION: VVV Rotterdam, Coolsingel 67, across from the City Hall, tel. (010) 413 6000.

Rotterdam of 1779 was a typical Dutch town with many canals, graceful architecture and open markets. There were cheese, butter, fish, flower and cattle markets. Big trees shaded its streets; old windmills stood in the center of town as did many small and large bridges and numerous 17th- and 18th-century houses with gabled roofs. In short, the epitome of an old-fashioned, charming Dutch town.

Today, most of these are gone. However, by losing its old-world look in the bombing of 1940, Rotterdam had to develop differently, and in today's modern world, it has proven itself to be a dynamic and fascinating city. Now, you see wide-open streets, large pedestrian shopping areas, modern architecture in all directions, the most elegant and graceful being the International World Trade Center building. Closely planted flower beds create splashes of color throughout the downtown area to soften the modern view. Pedestrians have elbow room to walk without fear of being pushed into a street of speeding traffic. There are excellent concert and convention facilities; a choice of hotels; and restaurants in all categories. There are fine museums, an outstanding zoo, and—don't forget— the busiest and most exciting port in the world.

The events which have resulted in an up-to-date philosophy, a strong work-oriented mentality, and a dogged determination to succeed were inherited by Rotterdammers from independent and innovative men such as Erasmus. A native son, this humanist urged basic rights for the common man at a time when this was considered heresy. Calvinism, too, had its influence here, as it did throughout Holland.

Rotterdam faced its greatest test of survival when the harbor and the open city were bombed on May 14, 1940. The port and the city center were completely obliterated. Rotterdam was enveloped in darkness for three days—the sun was blotted out by the dense black smoke from hundreds of fires, some of which burned from the days of the attack until August of that year. At first, rebuilding seemed hopeless. There was neither money nor materials for such an overwhelming task. But the leaders in the community lost no time in making plans for the day when reconstruction work would be possible. The city fathers knew the port had to be the first priority of business because without the port, the city could never function economically. The city's attention had to be focused on the new—the modern. This is evident today just by walking the city streets, or by talking to the progressive Mayor of Rotterdam. It is evident in the continued encouragement of city planning in all sectors which in turn has produced a dynamic economy generated through the exciting business of international commerce. If you want a taste of modern Europe, come to Rotterdam.

But Rotterdam is more than a business community. It is also a town with children in mind. There are the well-known Blijdorp Zoo; the Buffel Museum (an old ram-turret steamship); the "Toy Toy Museum;" "Tropicana," a health and swimming complex; the harbor with international ships of all types; boat tours from Rotterdam up and down this tremendous port; and a ride to the top of the Euromast—all children-oriented pleasures.

On Leuvehaven, look for Rotterdam's most dramatic—most stark—statue, Zadkine's Monument for a Devastated City. It's not a pretty thing to see perhaps but its message is clear, and may remind us of the cruel destruction of war. Happily, there are many statues sprinkled around Rotterdam and not all are in such a serious vein. Some of the more whimsical ones are The Drummer (young boy with drum located on the Lijnbaan), Young Boy with Turtle (in Plaswijck Park), Haasje-over (statue of a boy playing leapfrog) and the Bears (two bears frolicking—on the Lijnbaan).

Rotterdam has never been afraid of trying something new and different. An example is the "cube houses" located in the area where the Blaak and the Groenendaal meet (Metro stop, Blaak). You will either be entranced or dismayed by this avant-garde architecture. These cube houses come in a variety of colors and seem to pivot on one corner of the cube with windows looking downwards to the street or upwards to the sky but not straight ahead as is normal. They represent a very experimental style of living, to say the least. One of the nicest features of living here is their convenient location to the center of town; they are close to the big open-air market (Saturday and Tuesday mornings), the Central Municipal Library and Koningspoort harbor. On our recent visit, one of the cube apartments was open to view (small entrance fee). It's worth having a look.

At the foot of the cube houses, there's a docking area on the oldest harbor of Rotterdam where owners of historic—as well as just "old"—vessels can be brought by their owners for repairs or reconstruction with technical assistance in order to keep their ships "alive and well." Koningspoort was established as a foundation by lovers of old Dutch ships in order to keep historic vessels from disappearing because their owners lacked the funds for repairs. The wide open public walking and sitting area gives a close-up view of the ships. Sidewalk cafes, restaurants, outdoor concerts and festivals make this a lively spot.

A short walk along the "terraces" will bring you to the Witte Huis, once Holland's only skyscraper, where you can also have something to eat or drink under the trees!

The Central Library is almost next door to the cube houses, built in an architectural style somewhat reminiscent of the Pompidou Center in Paris. The interior is very pleasant with its multi-story-high lobby, green plants hanging from each floor from the very top of the building. Foreign users give the library rave reviews for its wide selection of books and easy access to the stacks . . . it is

27

wonderful to get lost in this world of books. Those homesick for a look at an English, French, German or Turkish newspaper can visit the newspaper reading room (separate entrance). Proceeds from the gift shop in the lobby go to charity. The Central Market is also in the neighborhood.

■ **Tropicana**, a new attraction to Rotterdam, is a subtropical (in Northern Europe yet!) swimming and relaxing paradise. Built alongside the Maas River, this mostly glass structure encloses a decor of rocks, tropical vegetation, rapids and water chutes—a most attractive addition to Rotterdam's social and physical well-being. Even when clouds scuttle across the sky, the indoor temperature is a constant 29°C (84°F) so one can swim leisurely, be swept along by turbulent rapids or enjoy a tingling massage in one of the hot whirlpools. There's a solarium, a wading pool for the little ones and terraces for relaxing.

Special treatment facilities are available such as Aqua Sana (body care), saunas, a salt-water buoyancy pool for relaxation, the Karwendel bath (uses a special fossil oil with high mineral content which produces a relaxing effect), Thalasso baths for cosmetic and body-care, and rapid tanning facilities.

The revolving restaurant offers first-class cuisine while you enjoy extensive views over the port and the Maas River. Less formal eateries within the complex include an Italian espresso bar with an ice-cream corner and an area where a cup of tea can be savored to the strings of a small orchestra; also a Pizzeria— low-moderate priced. The atmosphere is old-world charm in a super-modern setting.

For information, call (010) 402 0700 or write Maas Boulevard 100, 3063 NS Rotterdam. Hours: Mon.-Fri., 10am-10pm, Sat. and Sun., 10am-6pm.

Don't miss Delfshaven–formerly an independent town but a part of Rotterdam since 1886–with its fine reconstructed church, town hall, warehouse (De Dubbelde Palmboom), the Zakkendragershuisje (formerly headquarters for the longshoremen's union) and several small shops which have also been restored.

MUSEUMS: Two outstanding museums in Rotterdam are the Boymans-van Beuningen and the Prins Hendrik Maritime Museum. A new wing was added to the Boymans in 1972 which is one of the best-designed modern art facilities in Europe. Well-known artists are exhibited regularly. The original section of the museum is not to be overlooked either with Brueghel's "Tower of Babel," Rembrandt's portrait of his son, Titus, and a series of preliminary drawings by Rubens is on view. When the area where the Prins Hendrik Maritime Museum

and Buffel Museum are located is completed as a museum area, it will show a broad-spectrum picture of ships and shipping—past and present—as a vital part of Rotterdam's history. More information on these and other museums follows.

Among the small "neighborhood" museums are:

The **Steam Train Museum**, Giessenweg 82, tel. 462 2337, not far from Zestienhoven Airport, is all about steam locomotives and industrial steam engines with a photo exhibit on industrial archeology. Tram 1, 8 or Bus 38 . . . only open on Saturdays, 10am-5pm.

Professor Dr. van der Poel Tax Museum, Parklaan 14-16 (not far from the Euromast), tel. 436 6333. Open Mon.-Fri., 9am-5pm. Metro or Tram 5. Free. The section on smuggling is attention-getting. (Mostly in Dutch.)

Henry Chabot Collection, located in a private residence at Berglustlaan 12, Hillegersberg, northeast of the city center. Call in Dutch 422 4274 for info. The museum is devoted exclusively to the work of Henry Chabot, a Rotterdam painter born in 1894.

Nature History Museum in Villa Dijkzicht, Westzeedijk 345, tel. 467 8115 . . . a permanent collection of birds and mammals of Holland, as well as temporary exhibitions of regional nature and landscapes.

MARKETS: A nice change of pace from museum-viewing is a browse through Rotterdam's open-air market, held 9am-5pm Tues. and Sat. on the Mariniersweg near St. Lawrence Church. Interesting items can sometimes be found in the flea market section. There is also a small daily market on the Schouwburgplein (except Sundays). The weekly stamp market is held on the Grotekerkplein on Tues. and Sat., 10am-4pm.

For handicraft lovers, pewter-making from old molds is demonstrated by appointment and on Sundays every hour from noon to 4pm at the Zakkendragershuisje, Voorstraat 13-15, Delfshaven. Pewter items are for sale. Tram 9. Check with VVV for specifics.

WINDMILLS: Rotterdam's De Ster Windmill, located on the Plaszoom in Kralingen can be visited; call 452 6287 for info. Plasmolens restaurant next door is a delightful lakeside stop before or after.

Distilleerketel Windmill at Delfshaven is an added attraction for this old part of town. Check with VVV for possible visits.

De Speelman Windmill (1712 A.D.) is an old corn mill. Located at Overschiese Kleiweg 175, tel. 452 0336 for information on demonstrations, Wed.-Sat., 9:30am-4pm. Groups by appointment only. Tram 4; Bus 40.

EATING OUT: Rotterdam's long-time favorite restaurants include The Pijp, In Den Rustwat, the Chalet Swiss, the Old Dutch, the Coq d'Or, De Herberg, and Portofino. Less expensive are any of the Chinese-Indonesian restaurants (Kam Sang in Hillegersberg is a good family restaurant), or even more informal, pancake restaurants in the Kralingse Woods. In Rotterdam Park (Euromast location), a number of new restaurants will satisfy most moods and price brackets . . . especially fun is the Chinese floating restaurant Ocean Paradise, berthed across the street from the Euromast, at Parkhaven 21, tel. 436 1750;

great with children and moderate-priced. For a complete list, see Chapter 16.

South of Rotterdam in the town of Rhoon, "Kasteel van Rhoon" was constructed in 1433, rebuilt in 1598, and is now a restaurant which can also be rented for special parties. Guided tours are offered on Sundays, 2-5pm, all year. Saturday evenings at 9:30pm (when it gets dark), there is a sound and light show (end August-beginning October). For information, call Mr. Vente (01890) 43383; for the restaurant (01890) 48896.

YEARLY EVENTS: Rotterdam's yearly events start in mid-Jan. with a six-day indoor cycling event at Ahoy Hall followed by the World Indoor Soccer Championships. Feb./March the Ahoy Hall is the place to see the ABN World Tennis Tournament; in mid-April, there's the International Marathon, in mid-June, "Poetry International" is held in the Doelen Concert and Conference Center. All July there's "Youthland," indoor recreational facilities all month at the Ahoy; in Aug. there's the International Football Tournament at Feyenoord Stadium, and the CHIO Horse Show in Kralingsebos. Sept. is time for the Jazz Festival and to wind up the year in style the end of Dec., there's a Christmas market, circus, and performances by the Holiday on Ice in the Ahoy Hall.

COMMERCIAL TOURS: Daily tours (in season) of Rotterdam leave the Central Station at 1:15pm and last about 2½ hours. Included are the harbor and Delfshaven. Also in summer, from the Central Station, you may hop a special tourist tram that takes you around town. A "must" is a tour by Spido Boat which leaves from the Spido pontoon at Willemsplein. Tours available all year but hours vary so tel. (010) 413 5400 for info. Plenty of parking or take Tram 5 to Willemsplein, or the Metro to Leuvehaven Station. Evening tours available in summer. Duration, 1¼ hours. Sit on right-hand side for best view. The VVV can advise on all the above.

For a self-guided tour by car, obtain the ANWB map with English text from the VVV and follow the ANWB Rotterdamse Havens Route (distinctive road markers).

Royal Rotterdam Zoo (Blijdorp Zoo)

LOCATION: Van Aerssenlaan 49 (on the corner of Van Aerssenlaan and Bentincklaan, at the entrance to the Heemraadssingel tunnel). For those desiring public transportation, Tram 3 and Bus 39 will get you there.
INFORMATION: Tel. 465 4333. All zoos have baby buggy rentals, play areas and guides to the zoo; Blijdorp has a guide in English.
HOURS: Daily 9am-7pm.
ADMISSION: Adults, Fl. 11.00; Children under 10 years, Fl. 6.00.
■ *Of interest to children all ages.*

All kids—and most adults—love a zoo and the Rotterdam zoo is one of seven best in the Netherlands with approximately 2,234 animals and 532 species. It is too big to cover thoroughly in one visit (unless you dash from place to place) but

there are good maps of the zoo available at the entrance and with this guide in hand, you can decide which animals you want to see and where they are located. The feeding times are posted at the entrance to the zoo on a large billboard so remember to look for the schedule in order to make the most of your visit. A drowsy lion isn't nearly as exciting as one who is striding back and forth roaring eagerly for his forthcoming meal.

Visit the reptile hall, take a ride on the safari train or let the youngsters loose in the Lunar Jungle Park. The Natural History Museum is also located in the zoo.

Euromast (Space Tower)

LOCATION: Parkhaven 20 (near entrance to the Maas Tunnel).
Motorists should follow the special EUROMAST road sign; those requiring public transportation can take Tram 6 or 9.
INFORMATION: Tel. (010) 436 4811 (English spoken)

31

HOURS: Open mid-March to mid-Oct., 10am-9pm; mid-Oct. to mid-March, 10am-6pm; Jan.-Feb., Space Tower open only on weekends. Should you decide to visit the Euromast when the weather is stormy or when there are high winds, the Space Tower may not be in operation. If in doubt, verify that the tower is open before buying your tickets so that you won't be disappointed. (Space Tower open until 10pm in summer; until 5pm in winter.)
ADMISSION: To 100-meter platform: Adults: Fl. 8.00, Children to 15 years: Fl. 4.00. To 185-meter tower: Adults: Fl. 11.00, Children to 15 years: Fl. 6.00.
■ *Of interest to children of all ages.*

On a clear day, the Euromast offers a magnificent view in all directions and one can appreciate to the fullest extent the tremendous scope and vitality of the busiest port in the world, or simply the lovely scene of the public gardens below showing the formalized plantings in riotous colors, depending on the season. Even on a dull day, it is interesting to see the subdued colors of the city landscape—the city then has a most unusual, almost dreamlike quality which is quite contrary to its normal character. And to see a snow-laden Rotterdam from this height is a dazzling experience.

Start the tour by asking to be let off at the Crow's Nest, a true replica of the bridge of a 30,000-ton ocean liner (elevation 102 feet or 32 meters), where two retired sailors will explain the modern navigational instruments.

The ride to the top in the Space Tower is not to be missed (full fare). One enters a round elevator and is seated on a circular bench facing outwards—the tower spirals as it ascends and descends so everyone has a complete view of the city and its surroundings. If heights give you a thrill, it can be guaranteed that you will find it exciting to see the garden, 185 meters (605 feet) below the tips of your toes. Never fear, it is completely safe since the tower is constructed of the finest steel and glass and there are no openings for any possible accidents.

For refreshments, one can have a juice or a full meal while continuing to enjoy the scenery at one of the several restaurants 300 feet (90 meters) in the air. The Ballon and Bar (gourmet meals, expensive) and the self-service cafe are open until 10:30pm.

As you leave the Euromast, there is a very nice gift shop for anyone desiring to purchase a souvenir.

The Parkkade, Maas Tunnel and Parkhaven

LOCATION: South of the Park, near the Euromast. Motorists should follow the special EUROMAST road signs; those requiring public transportation can take Tram 6.

What a colorful sight it is when foreign military and commercial ships are tied up at the Parkkade. The public may stroll from one end of the street to the other, almost touching the ships. Children often exchange greetings with the foreign sailors, and sometimes friendships are made instantaneously.

Information about arrivals of foreign ships can be obtained through the VVV, or the appropriate Consulate General or Embassy in The Hague.

For a bit of a lark, you might try walking (or taking your bike) under the Maas River ... the entrance is in the green-roofed structure where the tunnel begins.

At the northern end of the Parkhaven, there is usually a large concentration of river police boats; it's the headquarters of the River Police and one can always hope to be on the spot when an alert is given.

St. Lawrence Church, Erasmus' Statue

LOCATION: The church and Erasmus' statue are located on Grote-kerkplein. There are no trams or buses that go directly; closest public transportation is by Tram 3. The area is difficult to find so check your map.

HOURS: Tues.-Sat., 10am-4pm; Oct.-May, Thurs., noon-2pm. Sundays (Religious services are held in Dutch) 10:30am and 5pm first Sun. of the month.

CONCERTS: Free lunchtime concerts are held every Thurs. and Fri. from 12:45-1:15pm. Evening concerts are held two or three times a month on Mon. from 8:15pm-9:15pm; also, some Fri. evenings and Sat. afternoons. Program schedules can be obtained from the VVV.

CARILLON: Sat., 10:30-11:30am; and every two weeks on Thurs., 12-1pm (by Addie de Jong).

■ *Of interest to children from 14 years.*

Sint Laurens Kerk (St. Lawrence Church) was built between 1449 and 1525 and destroyed by fire during World War II. Restoration was started in 1952 but not completed until the end of 1968.

The Church itself is very simple in its construction. Notice the wooden roof which is so typical for Dutch church buildings. Ask the children why they think a wooden roof was used instead of the commonly seen stone vaulting. If they think a minute, they might come up with the right answer, which is that stone would be too heavy for the soft soil in this part of the country.

The three organs are internationally famous because of their unrivaled beauty of tone. One is in the choir, one in the southern transept, and the chief one is in the nave. The instruments are new (constructed by Marcussen en Son, Aabren-raa, Denmark); however, the cases of the first two organs date from the 18th century. Look for the marble tombs of the Dutch naval heroes who fought many battles against the English from 1650-1688 and the wooden model of a 17th-century vessel which is located in one of the chapels.

Delfshaven

LOCATION: Delfshaven is located in the Harbor area west on the
Westzeedikj from the Euromast and encompasses an area from
the Hudsonplein to the Schiedamseweg. Trams 6 or 9; also the
Metro.
■ *Of interest to children 10 to adult, although on a warm, sunny*
day, even smaller children might enjoy a visit to the area.

It is hoped that Delfshaven in its restored state will show the architectural beauty of the past, and also, that it will become a new Arts Center with workshops for all kinds of artisans. Modern artists work here alongside men recreating some of the old crafts, such as the pewter makers who are already working at Delfshaven.

As you would imagine from its name, Delfshaven originally was the port of the city of Delft. Why, then, is this restoration being done by Rotterdam instead of Delft? To answer that question, one must delve a bit into history. In 1340 Delft was an important city while Rotterdam was just a village. Even then, however, Rotterdam was looking for ways to expand its port and share in the profits of the export trade from Delft so they dug a canal from the Maas River to Delft. The merchants of Delft were delighted to have a cheap method of transporting their goods via this canal to the ships which would take their merchandise abroad, but they were not so keen on letting the Rotterdam shipowners and merchants make a profit on their trade. In order to make some money on this transport and still not lose the benefit of the canal, the city of Delft constructed a dam with a spillway across the waterway in 1375 and levied a toll on all boats passing through. This state of affairs lasted about 5 years by which time the hew and cry from Rotterdam had created enough pressure that Delft was forced to abolish the dam.

Delft was determined not to share her profits, however, and when Albrecht replaced his brother as Count of Holland the city of Delft presented him with a very lavish gift of 4,000 florins. He was most grateful and granted Delft permission to construct its own canal—the Delfshavense Schie, which was completed in 1404.

A town grew up at the point where this new canal ran into the Maas and it became the town of Delfshaven. First, Delfshaven was the home port for herring boats and whaling fleets; then, distilleries were established, and in the 16th century, the East India Company established its warehouse and dockyard there. The authorities and merchants of Delft wanted to keep Delfshaven under their thumbs, but the descendants of the men who had created this new prosperous port would have none of it. The revolt started with the herring fishermen who moved their ships, crews and families to Rotterdam in 1638. This was the beginning of Rotterdam's growth, while Delfshaven continued to decline—gradually at first—and then much faster after the arrival of Napoleon's armies which closed down the East India Company's settlements and most of the distilleries. All of Holland suffered from the French occupation, but Delfshaven never recovered. They struggled along until 1841 and then asked to be incorporated in the Municipality of Rotterdam. At first, Rotterdam turned them down, but when Delfshaven became an eyesore and health hazard because of the jerry-built houses without sewage, drainage, etc., which were being constructed right on their doorstep, the city authorities of Rotterdam decided they had better step in and do something. It was during this period that Rotterdam was growing by leaps and bounds and needed to expand its boundaries, so in 1886, Delfshaven became incorporated into the larger Rotterdam Municipality.

Perhaps the fact that Rotterdam lost so many of its historic buildings in 1940 had a bearing on the decision to restore Delfshaven. Maybe a city—just as a person—needs a sense of history to give it balance. Whatever the reason, the city of Rotterdam has embarked on a very extensive project—some 110 houses are marked for restoration—which will take much time and money. What you see today is just the beginning.

Delfshaven has a particular significance to Americans as this was the port from which the Pilgrims sailed for the New World in July 1620. The original "pilgrims" were called English Separatists—they came from England and belonged to William Brewster's "Separate Church." The Act of Uniformity, passed in 1559, allowed the Church of England to take severe measures against all other religious sects. To escape persecution, the Separatists fled to Holland about 1608 and settled in Amsterdam where they lived almost a year. They found the life too pleasurable there and moved to Leiden where the Church Fathers felt the group could establish itself in a more strictly religious and intellectual way of life.

They lived in Leiden until—again—it was decided that they should move on before they became completely absorbed into the Dutch way of life. They came to Delfshaven to board the Speedwell, the ship which they hoped would take them to the New World. Some say they spent their last night in the Old Church—now called the Pilgrim Fathers' Church—but this has not been verified. They did worship in this church just before their departure, however. The church has now been completely restored and is most beautiful during evening

35

services when the candles are lighted and the lovely brasswork reflects their warm glow. The church can be visited on Sat., 2-4pm or by appointment. tel. 477 4156. Services are held in Dutch on Sundays. Organ concerts are given the first Sat. of the month from 4-5pm. Also carillon concerts from time to time.

The former Delfshaven Town Hall has been restored as well; its lovely old yellow bricks were cleaned by hand and then replaced in reverse order so that the better preserved side of the bricks facing the interior are now the exterior bricks. This explains to some degree the new look of the bricks. The interior has been modernized by using much of the original materials such as the beams for the ceilings, etc. In 1990, it is expected to house a new museum of Naif paintings.

The first of the Delfshaven buildings to be restored was the Zakkendragershuisje built in 1653, the Guild House which once belonged to the Sack Carriers' Guild. The sack carriers of those days were similar to longshoremen of today. They would gather in front of the Zakkendragershuisje when the bells above the house would be rung indicating a ship needed to be unloaded. If there was work for everyone, there was no problem; but when there wasn't, an ingenious system was used to decide who would work. In the niche at the bottom left-hand side of the stairs inside the house, an old tin pot holding dice was kept in order to settle the matter. A throw of the dice could decide who worked and who didn't. The address is 13 Voorstraat and there is a pewterer working here daily casting pewter items from original 18th-century molds belonging to the Rotterdam Historical Museum. Demonstrations are held on Sundays throughout the year every hour on the hour. The items made here are exceptionally accurate copies and may be purchased as gifts or as a souvenir of your visit.

At the end of the Voorhaven towards the Maas River, there is an old reconstructed windmill which once processed grain for some of the 34 distilleries in and around Rotterdam during the Golden Era. It has had a dramatic past, having burned three times and been restored three times. During World War II, the Dutch Marines set fire to "De Distilleerketel" because they thought it was the hideout for collaborators. It remained a shell until, thanks to a foundation called the Stichting Restauration of Historic Rotterdam, efforts were put forward to rebuild this cherished landmark. One million guilders were needed to complete the work. To get these funds, it was cleverly decided to issue shares in the amount of Fl. 100 each so the general public could own a symbolic piece of the mill. Even visitors can take home a piece of Holland as a souvenir par excellence—after all, how many people own even a little part of a windmill? For specifics, contact Mrs. Wenink, tel. 413 1106, Jan Evertsenplaats 39, Rotterdam. Additional funds will be needed for continued maintenance.A handsome stock certificate is issued the buyer; an interesting souvenir gift of Holland. The shareowners will be invited by the foundation to participate in ceremonies involving the Mill and Delfshaven.

Working in the area is an artist in stained glass, a silversmith and perhaps Holland's foremost expert in antique clocks and watches. He restores precious pieces for Dutch and international museums and collectors, including the royal household. Mr. F. Kats' charming shop is located at Voorhaven 4, tel. 476 4475.The former distillery is still in the process of being restored; however, artists are working and welcome visitors to their galleries—another good place to buy a little treasure.

There's a Dutch Inn in 17th-century style and several antique shops in the area, and it is hoped to have an apothecary's shop from the 19th century established in the near future. An old warehouse is now a museum, the Dubbelde Palmboom which shouldn't be missed. See "museums" which follow.

If you cross over the little bridge, you will come to the Gasterie Delfshaven Restaurant, a most pleasant place to recharge one's batteries. The food is good and moderately priced.

On the street behind the Old Church and the Town Hall, you will find Piet Heyn Plein and a statue of Piet Heyn who was born in Delfshaven in 1577, grew up to become Lord Admiral of the Dutch Fleet and who became world famous. Another famous man born in this area was Kees van Dongen, the painter.

Boymans-Van Beuningen Museum

LOCATION: Mathenesserlaan 18-20, Tram 5, Metro, "Eendrachtsplein."
INFORMATION: Tel. 436 0500 (English)
HOURS: Tues.-Sat., 10am-5pm; Sundays and public holidays: 11am-5pm; closed Mondays, January 1 and April 30.
■ *Of interest to children of school age.*

This is the only museum in the Netherlands which, with its own collection, covers the 14th century to the present. The original building houses the museum's collection of traditional paintings, old clocks, glass, pewter, silver, lace, furniture and prints. While the Boymans is known as the Mecca of modern ceramics, it also has an impressive collection of old Delftware. The paintings in this section of the museum include works by Peter Brueghel "Tower of Babel";

Rembrandt (of special note, the portrait of his son, Titus); Rubens' "Achilles" series; Hieronymus Bosch's "Prodigal Son," as well as works by Hals, Van Eyck, Jan Steen, Teniers, Van Goyen and Brouwer, to name just a few. One of the earliest pieces in the museum, dating from about 1420 is the Norfolk Triptychon, originating from the valley of the Meuse.

The new wing is considered to be one of the most outstanding showcases for modern art in Europe. Children will perhaps enjoy this part of the museum best where they can find "spoofs" in every form and where all the well-known modern artists are represented, including Dali, Delvaux, Segal, Rothko, Ernst, Picasso, Jongkind, and Van Gogh. The desire of the museum staff is to make this place a living thing. They want the man on the street, as well as the intellectual, to feel involved. For example, there is an imposing information desk with several experts on hand ready to answer all questions. There are continuous video programs relating to special exhibits (sometimes in English). The usual films and lectures are offered and the museum continues to sponsor special classes for children: some are art appreciation classes, while others are introductory tours to the museum. Regarding tours, they are usually conducted in Dutch, but if a group were to ask for an English-language tour—or even perhaps a series of lectures—they will do their best to provide it . . . call the museum and ask for the Educational Service.

Shoppers are encouraged to come into the museum and enjoy a sandwich and a cup of coffee in the most agreeably situated coffee shop in the new section. It is a very relaxing place to sit with its huge picture windows making you feel you are in a natural parkland setting in the shade of the large trees outside.

Maritime Museum "Prins Hendrik"

LOCATION: Leuvehaven 1, near Zadkine's "Monument for a Devastated City." At the corner of Schiedamsedijk and Blaak and at the end of the Coolsingel. Public transportation, Metro from the Central Station to Beurs/Churchillplein, Trams 3 or 6.
INFORMATION: VVV Rotterdam, tel. (010) 413 2680.
HOURS: Open Tues.-Sat., 10am-5pm; Sundays and holidays, 11am-5pm. Closed Mondays, Jan. 1 and April 30.
■ *Of interest to children 12 to adult, although younger children will like the many ships and ships' models.*

The location of the Maritime Museum at the end of the Coolsingel where the city center meets the Maas River couldn't be more appropriate for a museum dealing with shipping and the Rotterdam harbor. This was the site of Rotterdam's first manmade harbor and historically, one of the city's busiest. The ground floor of the museum is devoted to educational displays dealing with ships, waterways, navigation, etc. Upstairs, there are more displays, a coffeeshop, a library, documentation center, and a real periscope you can look through to see the harbor basin close up. The souvenir shop has books about shipping, nostalgia posters, and much more. This is also an information center with a computer to answer all questions, as well as a three-dimensional "shipping handbook" entitled "The Vademecum" to explain the business of transporting goods and materiel by water.

■ The outdoor museum is the highlight of a visit here. A number of real ships dating between 1850 and 1950 are tied up at the quay with the museumship "Buffel" the treat of the day since it can be visited. Also on view are the barge "Annigje"; an old-fashioned peat boat; the Frisian spiritsail barge "Gruno," which sailed the Zuiderzee as a tramp; the marketboat "Voorwaarts," an early ship propelled by an internal combustion engine. Others are steamtugs, "tjalks" (sailing barges), a "Kraak" (Salmon Drifter), a "Zalmschouw" and a "Wherry," an elegant pleasure rowboat; all typical Dutch river and inland waterway craft.

Changing exhibits are planned covering many topics of interest. Pavilions have been built between "De Buffel" and the lighthouse on the embankment designed to show the shipping business in action.

Museumship "Buffel"

Built in 1867 in Scotland, this ram-tower steamship (2nd class of the Dutch Royal Marines) houses drawings, models, machines and other material on the subjects of steam-power and iron ship construction. In addition, it has been outfitted to explain Dutch Naval history and to show how sailors lived in the second half of the 19th century. The officers' quarters installed in the style of the period may well captivate the ladies; however, today's no-nonsense navy would never allow such frivolity!

There is a small restaurant and souvenir shop on board.

The Schiedlandshuis-Municipal Museum

*LOCATION: Korte Hoogstraat 31. Going north from Churchill Plein,
take the first right-hand turn on the Coolsingel (Bulgersteyn).
The museum is on the right-hand corner one block up. Tram 3,
6; Buses 32, 49, or Metro "Beurs."*
INFORMATION: Tel. (010) 433 4188.
*HOURS: Tues.-Sat., 10am-5pm; Sun. and holidays, 1am-5pm. Closed
Mondays except Easter Monday, Whit Monday, Boxing Day,
New Year's Day and April 30.*
■ *Of interest to school-age children.*

The Schiedlandshuis stands on the site of a medieval castle, Castle Bulgersteyn,
and is the only 17th-century building in the center of Rotterdam that was spared
in the bombing of May 1940. Completely restored, it gives, once again, a varied
picture of Rotterdam's history, including its rich art period of the 17th and 18th
centuries. The city's development and the daily life of its inhabitants are well-
documented in an inviting, well-ordered fashion.

The top floor deals with birth, death, fashion costumes, textiles and toys from
the 18th-20th centuries. The first floor covers city history as depicted by period
paintings, models, glass artifacts, carvings and coins. An audio-visual film shows
the bombing of Rotterdam.

There are lovely style rooms with original furniture and decor of the 17th-
19th centuries, and displays of porcelain, silver and curiosa on the "mezzanine."
The ground floor has statues, tiles and fragments of buildings.

There is a museum shop and a charming restaurant, the "Poppagay" with a
view on the garden.

The building also houses the Atlas Van Stolk collection of prints and drawings showing the history of the Netherlands; an important research source for
scholars.

Folk Art Museum (Museum voor Volkenkunde)

*LOCATION: Willemskade 25. Tram 5 or Metro "Leuvehaven." There
is parking for private cars along the quay.*
INFORMATION: Tel. (010) 411 1055.
*HOURS: Tues.-Sat., 10am-5pm, Sun. and holidays, 11am-5pm.
Closed January 1 and April 30.*
■ *Of interest to school-age children.*

The museum building is beautifully located right on the Maas River—a visit
here can easily be combined with watching the ships on the river or a stroll
along the Parkkade. The exhibits represent primarily the folk art of primitive
peoples and ancient cultures. In addition to traveling exhibits, there is a permanent collection—including the instruments of an entire Indonesian orchestra.

Children of all ages are fascinated by masks and primitive carvings, etc., so
even the young ones can find something of interest. In addition there are film

shows held regularly (check with the attendant upon entering the museum for time of showing). Films are in Dutch but it is possible—depending on the subject— that even without the language, one can benefit from seeing the film. Other added attractions are a library, restaurant, and theater with live shows from all over the world.

The directors of this museum have been extremely helpful and cooperative when asked to arrange an English-language museum tour for children.

Historical Museum The Double Palm Tree

LOCATION: Voorhaven 12, Delfshaven. Trams 4 and 6, and Metro "Delfshaven."
INFORMATION: Tel. (010) 476 1533 or the Rotterdam VVV. Hours: Tues.-Sat., 10am-5pm. Sundays and public holidays, 1-5pm. Closed Mondays, New Year's Day and April 30.
■ *Of interest to children of school age.*

This beautifully renovated warehouse opened in 1975, deals mainly with Delfshaven, harbor work, early Dutch daily life, applied art and old trades. Notice the wonderful ship's prow entitled the Nieuwe Noordzee (New North Sea) which represents Neptune in all his strength and glory. It had been in the cellars of the former Historical Museum since 1870 when it was rediscovered in 1975, dusted off, and put on display. For instance, much archeological material is displayed to illustrate the first signs of industrial activity in the area from the end of the Middle Ages until approximately 1900 A.D.

The interior of this charming old building has been arranged in a unique and most attractive fashion by using natural materials throughout. The museum pamphlet suggests visitors take the elevator to the top floor and walk down, stopping at each landing to view the artifacts displayed. Also, at the top level you will find a comfortable and informal coffee corner, as well as a small museum shop.

"Toy Toy" Museum

LOCATION: Groene Wetering 41, in the Kralingen area. Trams 7 and 9—get off at the "Essenlaan" stop. Walk (or drive) down Essenlaan to the end, turn left. The museum is well marked at the drive entrance—it's the large brick house on the left.
INFORMATION: Tel. (010) 452 5941. English, German, French and Dutch are spoken.
HOURS: Sun. through Thurs., 11am-4pm. Closed Saturdays, July and August.
NOTE: School as well as adult groups are welcome. There is a coffee shop but groups who desire refreshments should make reservations ahead. A puzzle paper is handed out to young visitors—the person wins who finds all the items listed in each display case.
■ *Of interest to children young and old.*

41

This superb collection opened to the public in 1984. Mrs. Mars, a woman of taste and energy has created an oasis of color and cheer in this museum, located in an exclusive residential area of Rotterdam. While off the usual route for tourists, a visit to this part of town is a special treat with its lovely old trees, large traditional Dutch homes, and charming ponds.

The special treasures of the museum are the dolls created by famous French and German dollmakers, such as Steiner, Casimir Bru, Bourget and Jumeau. There are also two types of rare "A.T." dolls—look for them or ask to have them pointed out to you. Their features are exquisite. Also interesting are "sand babies," dolls made in 1923 and filled with sand; the poured wax dolls from 1870; a French fashion doll complete with painted toenails (one shoe and sock is off so you can see), binoculars, comb, scissors and eyeglasses; the life-size Jumeau doll; a boy with great brown eyes; and a number of "character dolls," i.e., dolls whose faces were created from those of real children.

The boys, too, have much to explore with all sorts of mechanical toys: airplanes, antique international cars, hot-air balloons, planes, transport vehicles, etc. Then throughout the museum, there are model rooms and doll houses depicting the style and way of life in France, Germany, England and the U.S. in the 1800's and 1900's. Not just homes are represented. There are also models of a wine shop, perfumery, barber shop, grocery store and more. One model shows a teacher with all his students at their desks in a school room in Nuremberg in 1870.

Dutch Marine Corps Museum (Mariniers Museum)

LOCATION: Maaskade 119. This is on the island across from the Leuvehaven and Boompjes. If you're driving, take the Willems-brug (bridge)—the Maaskade runs along the water on the city-side.
Bus 49.
INFORMATION: Tel. (010) 413 7505, or Rotterdam VVV.
HOURS: Open Tues. through Sat., 10am-5pm; Sundays and public holidays, 11am-5pm; Closed Mondays, December 25, 31, January 1 and April 30.
■ *Of interest to older boys and men.*

Making a visit to this museum will take you to an area of Rotterdam you would not normally visit. The underground was well entrenched here during WW II and there are many oldsters who can tell you tales of watching the city burn from the vantage point of the windows of the flat-fronted buildings, or who, as mere children then, scurried across the river, dodging German troops, to carry a message to other resistance workers.

The museum collection portrays the history of the Dutch Marine Corps from 1665, the year it was founded, to the present; it includes paintings, prints, photos, uniforms, weapons, equipment, official documents and true-to-life dioramas.

Old newsreels are shown in the cinema which is also the coffee shop.

SCHIEDAM

A "spirited town"

GETTING THERE: From The Hague and Amsterdam, take highways A4 south to the outskirts of Rotterdam. Then, west on A20, exit at the "Overschie" turnoff. From the south and east, take A29 until it crosses A15, then continue west to "Hoogvliet" follow the signs to the Benelux Tunnel. When you exit the tunnel, you'll be in Schiedam.

INFORMATION: VVV Schiedam, Buitenhavenweg 9, tel. (010) 473 3000, open Mon. through Fri., 9am-5:30pm; closed Sat. and Sun.

Just to the west of Rotterdam, the very old town of Schiedam is to be found. It received its municipal rights in 1275 and owes its origins to Countess Aleida van Henegouwen who had a dam built on this spot in 1260. A town developed and the "Schie" was the center of city life until 1850 when it burst its old ramparts and moats, extending in all directions until it now blends into the landscape between Rotterdam and Vlaardingen—its boundaries ill-defined.

Interesting places to visit in Schiedam include the Grote Kerk (also known as St. John's Church or the Great Church), at Lange Kerkstraat, tel. (010) 426 6241. There's a unique baptistry screen from 1642 and magnificent enameled windows made by the artist, Richters, as well as chandeliers of Venetian glass, and walls covered with gold-leather wallpaper. Call for an appointment if you want to visit.

The Town Hall, on the Grote Markt, is not open to the public; however, you might just happen to see a wedding party entering or exiting. It was originally made of wood but was partly destroyed by fire in 1604. The facade is typical Dutch Renaissance style from about 1782.

The court of the 18th-century Almshouse on Proveniersplein is open to the public. This building with white rococo facade was originally a leper-house and later a home for the elderly.

The National Spirits Museum is one sightseeing stop the men won't complain about; located at Hoogstraat 112, tel. (010) 426 9066. It and the Town Museum (in the same building) are open Tuesday to Saturday, 10am-5pm; Sundays and holidays, 12:30-5pm. The building itself was constructed in the 18th century by Giudici and was originally used as a home for the elderly (then called St. Jacobs Gasthuis) and as a hospital with a men's wing, women's wing and in between, the church. The contents of the two museums included ancient tools concerning the spirits industry, coopery and dioramas (Spirits Museum); and town antiquities, archaeological discoveries and modern art (Town Museum).

Also look for the "Zakkendragershuisje" (Porters Guild House) of 1275. The porters were warehousemen who carried bags of grain from the ships to the warehouse for the munificent sum of Dfl. 10.00 (approx. $5.00) per week. As soon as a ship arrived, the tower bell was rung and all the workers who lived in the Distillers quarter came to their guild-hall to work.

Other structures of interest are the "Appelmarktbrug" (Apple Market bridge), one of three cast-iron drawbridges in use still and drawn up by hand by

43

the bridge-masters; and the Korenbeurs (Corn Exchange) where the grain for distilleries was formerly traded. The harbor has been restored and a stroll along the waterway, the Maasesplanade, offers a good view of the great activity on the Maas River.

WINDMILLS: Schiedam has four windmills which make it proud: De Vrijheid (The Liberty)-1785; De Noord (The North)-1794; De Drie Koornbloemen (The Three Cornflowers)-1770; and De Walvisch (The Whale)-1794. Only De Vrijheid and De Noordmolen can be visited.

De Vrijheid at Noordvest 40, tel. 473 3000, is open Saturdays from 10:30am-4:30pm. Conducted tours are offered every half hour in season and every hour out of season. It is also possible to arrange for special tours by calling the Schiedam VVV, see above. One can purchase flour ground by this mill or bread baked locally of flour milled here.

De Noordmolen is located at Noordvest 38, tel. (010) 426 3104. It is owned and operated by the well-known Dutch gin people, Lucas Bols, and has been a bodega and restaurant since 1973 . . . why not combine a visit with a pick-me-up beverage and lunch?

EATING OUT: There are many good restaurants in the area. Our favorite is Bistro Hosman Frères on Kortedam 8, tel (010) 422 4096 . . . half a block of red awnings, smart male waiters, antiques, candlelight, and careful French cuisine! Hard to get to but persevere. Upstairs is the exspensive, even more elegant, section of the restaurant, Auberge Hosman Frères.

VLAARDINGEN

From herring port to containers

GETTING THERE: Driving from Rotterdam, take A20 towards the Hook of Holland until you see the Vlaardingen turnoff; follow the "Centrum" signs while looking for indications to the "Stadhuis" (City Hall) or "Visserijmuseum" (fishing museum). From The Hague, take A13 south then A20 west. From Amsterdam, again, A4 south towards Den Haag, Rotterdam and A20 west. There are numerous charming back roads, trains or buses from all parts of Holland.

INFORMATION: VVV Vlaardingen, Town Hall, Westnieuwland 6, tel. (010) 434 6666. Hours: Mon.-Fri., 8:45am-12:30pm and 1:30-5:15pm. Closed Sat., Sun. and public holidays.

Vlaardingen received its city charter from Count Floris V on the 14th of May, 1273—over 700 years ago. It seems, however, that people have lived here much longer. Recent excavations for the foundations of the new addition to the Town Hall unearthed pottery and other material which indicate this place was the site of a settlement approximately 2,500 years before Christ. Those early residents sought their livelihood primarily by fishing and hunting. Eventually, like so many other Dutch towns along the Maas River, Vlaardingen developed as a

center for trade and fishing. It was the biggest Dutch home port for herring fishing in the 18th century. Digging of the New Waterway caused new harbors and docks to be created which made Vlaardingen a commercial port. Today, more than 2,500 ocean-going ships and more than 20,000 inland navigation ships call at the local harbor every year. Vlaardingen boasts of being third among the important Dutch ports, surpassed only by Rotterdam and Amsterdam. In addition to the port, this city is expanding its horizons and has encouraged establishment of many new industries within its boundaries. In keeping with this effort, Vlaardingen has been extremely progressive in providing modern housing facilities in order to attract and hold its new residents.

This town is truly a mixture of the old and the new— although it is becoming more and more difficult to find the old today because of the intensive amount of new construction going on! It is even a bit surprising when you finally do burst upon the old town center, hidden behind winding streets and the modern facades of "new" Vlaardingen. Suddenly, you could be in the 17th century. You will find the entrance to the Town Hall (present building dates from 1650) across the street from the small central market place upon which stands the lovely old church.

The Great Church, a reformed church originally of late Romanesque style, consists of a nave with choir-like extension and two side aisles. There is a tower which dates from 1745 housing the well-known Oranje Chime, and inside the building you will see a famous organ (1763), guild plates, a copper lectern (1778) and stained glass windows. Lining the small street which encircles the market place are many old buildings to give you a glimpse of Vlaardingen's historical atmosphere. The Town Hall, which can be visited by appointment only, tel. (010) 435 5888, is a blend of traditional and modern architectural styles and exemplifies nicely the history of this very old town.

You should not miss the old port of Vlaardingen where you will find some restored houses and the very fine Visserijmuseum (Fishing Museum), described immediately following.

EATING OUT: Recommended are two quite different places to eat. The first is just around the corner from the Fishing Museum—a charming small restaurant, the Bistro 't Strattje, Rijkestraat 10-12, tel. (010) 434 1156, where you can have

45

a simple meal or a full-course dinner by candlelight. The owners have added something extra: a cosy coffee or aperitif drinking-area you step down into, the focal point being the fireplace—so inviting in wintertime. The second place to eat is the Delta Crest Hotel, Maasboulevard 15, tel. (010) 434 5477, located practically in the Maas River—part of the hotel is built out over the water on piles—and the view of passing river traffic is really splendid. For a private party, you can rent the Crow's Nest, several stories high where your guests can guess the nationality of the passing ships as they sip their drinks or dance.

Fishery Museum (Visserijmuseum)

LOCATION: Westhavenkade 53, Vlaardingen.
INFORMATION: Tel. (010) 434 8722.
HOURS: Mondays through Saturday: 10am-5pm; Sundays and holi-
*   days: 2-5pm. Closed—Christmas Day and New Year's Day.*
NOTE: Conducted tours and films possible on request.
■ *Of interest to children from 6 years.*

The small pool of fish at the entry is so fascinating it is tempting to spend the whole time trying to figure out the name of the different fish, or to locate another bigger eel, crawfish, or whatever, which is hiding under the sand or in the rocks. But don't stop there. The dioramas are well done and give an excellent idea of the many techniques used in commercial fishing. Fishing for shellfish is done differently from the method used when fishing for eel, cod, halibut or sole.

In the "ships' hall," you can see the development of the Dutch fishing boats from earliest times to the present. There is a simulated bridge of a cutter which can be inspected along with its complicated electronic navigational and fishing equipment. The history of fishing exhibit includes costumes and jewelry from fishermen's families throughout the ages.

The building itself is the former home of Mayor van der Linden dating from 1740. There are a couple of "stijlkamers" (model rooms) from the 18th century which will interest the girls, and upstairs, there is a small movie studio where films on fishing are shown every Wednesday, Saturday and Sunday afternoon. English-speaking visitors can request to see an English-language film when the theater is not already scheduled to show a Dutch film.

For the older and more serious visitor, there is a library and documents center (open Monday through Friday from 10am-12:30pm and from 1:30-5pm). Everyone will be interested in seeing the auction room where demonstrations can be arranged for (in advance) showing how commercial fish sales were handled.

DELFT

The town of blue and white porcelain

GETTING THERE: From Rotterdam, take Highway A13 northwest.
There are several charming small roads leading to Delft, especial-
ly the Rotterdamseweg along the Delfshavense canal. From The
Hague, A13 south; from Amsterdam, A4 south.
INFORMATION: VVV, Delft, Markt 25, tel. (015) 126100.
NOTE: For guided tours of Delft museums, call (015) 130100.

Delft is a charming town of medieval origins (founded in 1075). More intimate than Amsterdam, its splendid Gothic and Renaissance houses lining tree-shaded canals, easily transport one to another period in time. It boasts of a number of famous native sons, including the painter Vermeer, and Hugo the Great, a famous lawyer and scholar. It is the last resting place of William the Silent (and his loyal dog who died of grief). Over 40 members of the Royal family are buried beneath the mausoleum in the Royal Burial Vaults of the New Church. Delft is of special significance because of its historical role in the development of The Netherlands as a country free of foreign domination.

The best way to see Delft is to walk away from the busy Market Square with its myriad gift shops into the quiet, narrow, primarily residential, streets. The VVV guided walking tour pamphlet will help you spot places of note, but don't let facts interrupt your pleasure of personal discovery.

One of the landmarks of Delft is the Oude Kerk (Old Church) which dates from the 13th century. Contrary to one's first impression, the stained glass windows are modern; they were done by a master in this field, Joep Nicolas, between 1955 and 1972. It is recommended you purchase the small guidebook on Joep Nicolas at the entrance. The first part is in Dutch but the last half is in English and gives a good explanation of each window.

Other places of note include the early 17th-century Town Hall with its 14th-century tower; impressive monuments of Admirals Piet Heyn and Pieter de Keyser as well as lesser historical figures; Museum Paul Tetar van Elven, a 19th-century painter's home and collection; the East gate, one of the original 7 gates into the city (15th cent.); the Weigh House (De Waag) now used as a small theater; the Boterhaus adjacent to the Town Hall which dates from 1765; three almshouses: Klaeuw's Hofje (1605), 58-77 Oranje Plantage, Hofje van Pauw (1707), 55-62 Paardenmarkt (visit the horse market while here) was founded for married couples, and Hofje van Gratie (1575), Van den Mastenstraat, founded for god-fearing spinsters.

■ Delft is known for its blue and white pottery, copied originally from Chinese porcelain imported by the East India Company in the 17th century. The Delft potteries' existence was threatened by the popularity of the Chinese imports so, in order to preserve their livelihood, they imitated Chinese, Japanese and Italian pottery designs. Today, there are wonderful original Dutch motifs to choose from in multi-colored ware as well as the traditional blue and white known worldwide. Plates can be ordered for special gifts such as weddings or births showing dates of the event, time of birth, weight of baby, etc. You choose the basic design and give the specifics of what is to be added. Three potteries are working and open to visitors:

The Royal Delft Ware Factory (De Porceleyne Fles), established in 1653, is the best-known. It is located at the southern end of town at Rotterdamseweg 196, tel. (015) 560234. Visitors may see demonstrations of pottery making on the wheel as well as decorating plates by hand, April-October, Mon. through Sat., 9am-5pm; Sun., 10am-4pm; October-April, Mon.-Fri., 9am-5pm; Sat., 10am-4pm, Closed Sundays.

De Delftse Pauw, Delftweg 133 is open April-mid-October, daily 9am-4pm; mid-October-March, Mon.-Fri., 9am-4pm, Sat.-Sun., 11am-1pm, tel. (015) 124920 for info. "Modcrate prices."

Atelier de Candelaer, Kerkstraat 13, April-September, Mon.-Fri., 9am-6pm, Sat., 9am-5pm, Sun., 10am-6pm; October-March, Mon.-Fri., 9am-12:30pm and 1:30-6pm, Sat., 9am-5pm., tel. (015) 131848. It's easy to find this small family operation—just off the main market square. "Moderate prices."

■ **Antique Fair and General Markets**: A not-to-be-missed affair in October is the annual Antique Dealers' Fair held in the Prinsenhof Museum . . . most items are museum-quality with prices accordingly but it's a real treat to see a broad scope of such fine pieces on sale.

The General Market on the Markt Square is held every Thursday; the Flower market on Hippolytusbuurt is also on Thursday; Merchandise and Flower market at Brabantse Turfmarkt and Burgwal are held on Saturday; and the Flea Market is held on various canals and town squares Saturdays, May through October.

EATING OUT: Delft has a wide choice of small places to eat along the canals, off or on the market place, or near the various museums. The Stads-Koffyhuis at Oude Delft 133, just down the canal from Huis Lambert van Meerten and not far from the Prinsenhof is an old favorite . . . it's a typical students' coffee house serving 12-inch pancakes with a wide selection of fillings or toppings. The tables are the metal base of old-fashioned sewing machines . . . the shop has been a bakery since 1881 . . . tel. (015) 124625.

For a different night out, try a medieval inn dinner with wenches in costume, entertainment, and food served in the fashion of the times—you eat your chicken with your fingers—the Stadsherberg de Mol, Molslaan 104, tel. (015) 121343 . . . 3½ hours eating and carousing. Closed Mondays.

COMMERCIAL TOURS: From April 1 through September, Canal Cruises depart from the Koornmarkt (corner Wijnhaven, daily 10:30am-5:30pm, every 30 minutes). For information, telephone Mr. Brands, (015) 126385. Mr. Brands also rents canal bikes.

Also daily during the summer season, Horse-drawn Carriage Tours depart from the Markt Square near the Town Hall . . . no set times. Usually there is a poster giving departures. Colorful and obvious when they're "operating"—you cannot miss the "klomp-klomp" of the horses' hooves on the cobblestones!

New Church, with Royal Mausoleum (14-15th century)

LOCATION: On the main market square. Go to the VVV and get a detailed map for visiting the town.
INFORMATION: VVV, Markt 85. Tel. (015) 126100.
HOURS: April to Sept. 30, Mon.-Sat., 9am-5pm; other months, Mon.-Sat., 10-noon and 1:30-4pm.
TOWER: May 1 to mid-Aug., Tues.-Sat. from 10am-4:30pm; entrance fee.
■ *Of interest to older children, although when the tower can be visited, it's a treat for all. Take your camera*

The black and white marble sarcophagus of William the Silent, surrounded by allegorical statues representing Fame, Valor, Religion, Justice and Liberty, is most impressive. His little dog who died because he refused to eat when his master died, adds a poignant note to the tomb. The Burial Vaults of the Royal family are not accessible but there is a diagram showing locations and identifying coffins.

Municipal Museum "Het Prinsenhof"

LOCATION: 1 Agathaplein.
INFORMATION: Tel. (015) 602357. Tickets purchased for the "Prinsenhof" Museum, are also valid for the Volkenkunde Museum Nusantara and the Rijksmuseum "Huis Lambert van Meerten" (see next page), and vice versa.
HOURS: Open all year, except on holidays. Tues.-Sat., 10am-5pm; Sun,, 1-5pm June, July, Aug., also Mon., 1-5pm.
■ *Of interest to children 12 years or older.*

The former convent of St. Agatha was founded toward the end of the 14th century. In the 16th century this beautiful building was the residence of William of Orange from 1572 until 1585 at which time he was assassinated in this very building. The museum houses objects dealing with the history of Delft and the Eighty Years' War—art works, such as paintings, tapestries, silver items and beautiful antique Delftware. Included in the "Prince's Court" is the Oranje-Nassau Museum with portraits of the Royal Family from William the Silent to the present day. There are often special exhibits of note.

To make this period more lively, look for the chest in which the scholar, Hugo Grotius, with his wife's help, escaped from Loevestein Castle where he had been sentenced to life imprisonment because of his moderate stand in the political-religious disputes of 1612-18. It is located in the passage approaching the Soup Kitchen and the Historical Hall. At the far end of the Hall, a fanatical Catholic assassinated William the Silent at the foot of the stairs leading to his private chambers . . . the bullet holes are still visible.

This splendid building is the perfect setting for the truly outstanding annual Antique Dealers' Fair held in October. (Crowds are heavy and make maneuvering small children in strollers very difficult). The former cellar has been redone into a most attractive dining room with a vaulted ceiling. Full meals are the general rule here, however, the inner courtyard just outside is a most relaxing and restful spot to enjoy a cup of coffee.

Ethnographic Museum "Nusantara"

LOCATION: 4 Agathaplein.
INFORMATION: Tel. (015) 602357. Special tours can be arranged in
English upon request for children or for adults.
HOURS: Open all year, except holidays. Tues.-Sat., 10am-5pm; Sun.,
1-5pm; also on Mon., 1-5pm June through August.
■ *Of interest to children from the age of 8 years.*

A small museum located just across the square from the entrance to Het Prinsenhof. There is a fine display of Indonesian culture, arts and crafts, textiles, musical instruments, artifacts, masks, etc., which are colorful and attractive to children. There are special exhibits on Third World Problems also.

Tile Museum "Huis Lambert Van Meerten"

LOCATION: 199, Oude Delft.
INFORMATION: Tel. (015) 121858. Special arrangements can be
made for school children to decorate "tiles" (by appointment).
The City of Delft can also arrange for an English-language guide
for this museum, the Prinsenhof and the Ethnographic Museum
if written request is made in advance.
HOURS: Open all year, except holidays Tues. through Sat., 10am-
5pm. Sun., 1-5pm; also on Mon., 1-5pm, June through August.
■ *Of interest to school-age children.*

In addition to being a showcase for an extensive display of tiles, the building, which dates from 1893, provides an enchanting mixture of the neo-Renaissance style and older architectural fragments, among which are the splendidly carved windows with the date 1537. Its spacious rooms serve as a perfect background for the many Van Meerten treasures which are displayed here. The tiles are especially noteworthy dating from the earliest Delft and including specimens of Italian and Spanish tiles.

Royal Netherlands Army Museum

LOCATION: Korte Geer 1.
INFORMATION: Tel. (015) 146041.
HOURS: Open Tues.-Sat., 10am-5pm; Sundays, 1-5pm. July, Aug.;
daily 10am-5pm.
■ *Of interest to boys and men!*

The museum is housed in Delft's 17th-cent. armory. The visitor is guided in historical sequence through Holland's military and national events, starting in the earliest times. Highlighted are the Eighty Years' War for independence, Napoleon's annexation of Holland, and its eventual unification as the Kingdom of the Netherlands. World War I and World War II are depicted, the latter with displays of the years of occupation, the underground resistance and Dutch forces raised abroad. Of special interest are the models dressed in the uniform of the times, armored vehicles, field guns and weaponry down the ages, etc.

IN THE NEIGHBORHOOD OF DELFT:

't Woudt, 3 km west of Delft, is a charming small village whose church, pastoral buildings, farms and laborers' cottages are just as they were centuries ago. Delightful for cycling in the area.

THE HAGUE ('s Gravenhage or Den Haag)

The elegant town

GETTING THERE: The Hague and its neighbor, Scheveningen, are located along the North Sea on the west. Rotterdam is 20 minutes southeast via autoroute A13; Amsterdam, about 40 minutes northeast via A4.

INFORMATION: VVV The Hague, Central Station, Koningen Julianaplein, or VVV Scheveningen, Gev. Deynootweg 126, tel. (070) 546200 (for both addresses).

SPECIAL NOTE: By December 1989, ALL The Hague telephone numbers will add the prefix "3," i.e., (070) 354 6200.

The Hague is the seat of the Dutch Government and has been compared in temperament and atmosphere to Washington, D.C. It is a charming town ... town of many contradictions—small and intimate, while at the same time, exclusive. Don't forget, your country's Embassy will be located in The Hague. While not a "tourist" stop, it's nice to know where it is, so at least go and show your family their country's flag flying.

"Den Haag" or " 's Gravenhage" ("The Hague" in English) translates into "count's enclosure" or "hedge" and was so called because this was the hunting area of the Counts of Holland. In the area of the Vijver ("fish pond")—just a few blocks from the American Embassy—you will find the Binnenhof, the most interesting and historic cluster of buildings in Holland. It has been the seat of diplomacy and government since the 13th century when Count William built a palace here in 1250. His son, Floris V, enlarged it in 1291 and made The Hague his capital. He also had the Ridderzaal (Hall of Knights) constructed as part of the Binnenhof. However, it was not until the early 19th century, after Louis Bonaparte was named King of Holland, that The Hague received its city charter. Also within the Binnenhof are the Chambers of the States General, Parliament and other Government offices (can be visited/ see below).

Because The Hague is the seat of Parliament and the home of career Dutch civil servants as well as diplomats from all over the world, the character of the town is much different from Amsterdam or Rotterdam with their emphasis on commercial/port developments. Its wide, tree-lined avenues, lovely shopping streets, stylish traditional architecture, give it a grace and serenity . . . even a bit of snobbishness perhaps . . . that sets it apart.

■ **The Dunne Bierkade**, an old section of The Hague, is in the process of being restored to its 17th-cent. character. Famous names from The Hague's past have lived and worked here—especially many famous artists such as Jan van Goyen (1596-1656) who built the house at Spinozastraat 74, in 1646. Jan Steen (died 1679) married Van Goyen's daughter and rented the house from his father-in-law who lived just around the corner. Other well-known artists who lived in the area are Paulus Potter (1625-1654), Pieter Post (1598-1665), architect, and Joh. P. Bosboom (1817-1891). Later, the philosopher, Benedictus de Spinoza lived and died in Jan Steen's former residence. The house is a private home but is open occasionally to students of Spinoza's works. Just down the street at Paviljoensgracht 72, "Het Heilig Geest Hofje" was restored and modernized. If you look through the main entrance gate, you will see quite a large interior garden surrounded on four sides by small alms houses typical of old nuns' or church lay-women's homes. Another charming building and garden is at Dunne Bierkade 17; Pieter Post was responsible for the interior and garden, as well as co-designer of the Huygens-Museum "Hofwijk." There remain a few "red-light" houses along the canal—a bit unsettling if one comes upon them unprepared.

■ **"Hofjes" or Alms Houses** can be found in many towns of the Netherlands, all of them unique, restful, usually hidden away from the hurly-burly of city life. Some were built to house needy religious persons (there is often a chapel within the enclosed walls) and in the 19th century in The Hague, some were built to alleviate a housing shortage. Anyone was eligible who was church-going, decent, and could pay a nominal rent. The VVV puts out several walking tours, among them, the "Hofjes Walk"—only in Dutch. Still, it could act as a map. Some of note are:

Hofje Javalaantje, Javastraat nos. 99-161 (19th cent.);

Hofje Mallemolen (across the street, first street to the right)—from Napoleon's time;

Lammerstichting, founded in 1875 for "decent" women over 55 years in financial straits on Schelpstraat 5-43 . . . open Mon.-Fri., 10am-5pm;

Heilige Geest Hofje (mentioned above), Paviljoensgracht 51-125 (1616);

Geefhuisjes on Hoge Zand 2-24, some of the oldest in The Hague . . . open daily 10am-5pm;

Hofje van Wouw, Lange Beestenmarkt 49-85 (1674);

Hofje Floris van Dam, Lange Beestenmarkt 21-47 (1649) . . . open 8am-11pm;

Hofje van Nieuwkoop, Warmoezierstraat 36-5 and 92-202 (via Prinsengracht) is one of the most beautiful, built in 1660 by Pieter Post, the Dutch architect, and frequented by artists of the Haagse School . . . open 9am-6pm; and

'T Hoofts Hofje, Assendelftstraat 53-89 (via Westeinde) (1756) with a unique upper and lower living area . . . open sunrise 'til sunset.

HISTORIC CHURCHES:

St. Jacobs Kerk, Rond de Grote Kerk 10-12, tel. (070) 658665, dates from 1539 and is open Mon.-Sat., 10am-4pm. Tram 3.

The **Kloosterkerk**, (1403), Lange Voorhout 2, tel. (070) 461576, a conventional church, is open April-October, Mon.-Fri., noon to 2pm. Trams 3, 7, 8, 9, buses 4, 5, 22.

Nieuwe Kerk (New Church) (1656), Spui 175, tel. (070) 634916, Wed., 1:30-3pm. The De Witt brothers and Spinoza, the philosopher, are buried here.

Schuilkerk (Clandestine Church), Molenstraat 38, tel. (070) 463912; open Wed., 1:30pm, 2:30pm and 3:30pm. Groups by appointment only. Trams 3, 7, 8, 9, Buses 4, 5, 22.

Abdijkerk (Abbey Church) located at Willem III-straat 40 in Loosduinen is the oldest church (ca. 1240); open July and August, Sun., 3-4:30pm. Other months by appointment, tel. (070) 974182. Trans 2, 3, Buses 27, 121.

A new addition to the old town is the ultra-modern home for The Hague Philharmonic and the Netherlands Dance Theater in the downtown center. The architecture is startling in its still raw landscape—hopefully, soon to be corrected. Within the complex, there's a restaurant and coffee shop, and a new hotel adjacent.

PARKS: The Hague is blessed with 26 parks with a minimum total acreage of just under 1,000 hectares! The three parks which have been specially recommended by foreign families are:

Clingendael Park (54 hectares) boasts a lovely formal Japanese garden dating from 1896 with tea house, lanterns, bridges, typical and rare Japanese plants with an especially lovely show of azaleas. This part of the park is only open from the beginning of May to the middle of June, 9am-8pm. The main garden is open all year, of course, and has an exciting display of rhododendrons when in bloom. For further information, call the VVV. The park can be entered from Van Alkemadelaan, not far from the main ANWB office on Wassenarrseweg. Bus 18.

Westbroekpark (with a mere 20 hectares), Kapelweg, can be entered from the

Cremerweg, Nieuwe Parklaan, Nieuwe Duinweg and Kapelweg. Along with its many attractions geared to families (midget golf, playground), the gourmet cook of the family can arrange to pick some special herbs. All that needs to be done is to ask the gardener where they are. Oh yes, you can pick them every day but Wednesdays. In addition, Westbroekpark is famous for its smashing display of 20,000 roses from early July 'til the end of September. Open from 9am-9pm.

Zuider Park (110 ha.) is probably less well known to foreigners because of its location on the south side. It has many attractions of special interest to families, however, including a recreation park, bird park, small animal center, swimming pool, mini-golf, children's farm, open-air theater, walking and biking paths, a restaurant, a miniature steam train with child-sized train cars for riding, and an herb garden with free picking privileges! The Park is open all year but all the facilities are not. Everything works during school summer vacations, but for specific information, call the VVV. The kinderboerderij entrance is on Renswoudelaan, open Mon. through Fri. from 8am-4pm and most weekends. Miniature Railway information: tel. (070) 802660. Operates April-October, including Sat. and Sun., 11:30am-4:30pm and during school holidays. Tram 8, 9, Bus 129.

PALACES AND CASTLES:

Huis Ten Bosch (17th century) is the home of Queen Beatrix and her family. Located on the north side of the Hague Woods at Bezuidenhoutseweg, it is not open to the public. The castle was built in 1645 for Amalia van Solms, the wife of Frederik Hendrik, by the architect, Pieter Post; it is considered an important architectural building of the period. Buses 4, 43, 91.

The Noordeinde Palace (16th cent.), is located across from the Old Catholic Church (entrance Prinssesewal), and serves as the Queen's offices. Not open to the public. The garden, however, is a public park. At the north end, you will find the Royal Stables and the Queen's Royal Coach . . . Trams 3, 7, 8, 12, Buses 4, 5, 22.

Palace Lange Voorhout (18th century), just down the street from the American Embassy . . . not open to public . . . Trams 3, 7, 8, 9, 12, Buses 4, 5, 22.

Palace Kneuterdijk (18th cent.), former winter palace of Queen Emma . . . Not open to public.

■ **Duivenvoord Castle**, about 10 km north at Voorschoten, Laan van Duivenvoord 4, has been restored to its original state as an 18th-century country manor. The brass chandeliers, hand-painted rafters, flowered wall hangings and oriental rugs are worth seeing. In addition, it contains a fine collection of antique furniture and porcelain. Guided tours are given April-October, Tues.-Sat., 2pm and 3:30pm. For info, check with the VVV or tel. (01717) 3752.

MUSEUMS: Each year, The Hague seems to add something new on the museum-scene. The outstanding places not to miss are the Mauritshuis; Prince William V Picture Gallery; the Parliament Buildings and Knights' Hall; and a trio comprising an important overview of Dutch cultural and recreational life, The Hague Municipal Museum (Museon) and the Hague Historical Museum. The Peace Palace is the seat of the International Court where legal decisions with far-reaching significance have been reached; of interest to all nationalities.

Some smaller museums or those located in the suburbs include:

Spinoza House, the home of the Dutch philosopher, open only by appointment, Paviljoensgracht 72, tel. (070) 605008;

Museum Loosduinen "De Korenschuur," Marg. v. Hennenbergweg . . . open, Sat. 1-5pm, July/August, also Sun., 1:30-4:30pm;

Museum Rijswijk "Het Tollenshuis,"(same area as the amusement park, De Vliet Canal, see below) . . . history of the town, Rijswijk, with occasional exhibitions . . . Herenstraat 67, Rijswijk, tel. (070) 903617; open, Tues.-Fri., 2-5pm, Sat., 11am-5pm, Sun., 2-5pm;

Museum Swaensteijn, Herenstraat 101, Voorburg, tel. (070) 861673, open Tues., Thurs., Sat. and Sun., 2-5pm (Roman archeology, town history);

Museum van Zwerfsteen tot Diamant, Hoekenburglaan 1, Voorburg, tel. (070) 994766, open 10am-4pm, telephone for appointment (minerals, stones, fossils and shells).

The Huygens Museum "Hofwijck," the former country seat of the poet and statesman Constantijn Huygens, is also in Voorburg. Jacob van Campen and Pieter Post designed this charming building together. It contains memorabilia of Constantijn and his son, Christiaan Huygens, physicist and astronomer . . . open, Wed., Thurs., Sat., 2-5pm at Westeinde 2, Voorburg, tel. (070) 872311. Tram 10, Buses 23, 26, 45, 46.

The Scheveningen Museum, Neptunusstraat 92, tel. (070) 500830, deals with fishing and fisherfolk. Displays include the Scheveningen distinctive costumes, gold and silver jewelry; exhibits about the fishing industry; ship models, etc. Open in summer, Mon.-Sat., 11am-4:30pm; in winter, Tues.-Sat., 10am-4:30pm. Trams 1, 7, 8, 9; Buses 14, 23.

MARKETS: The General Market is held on Herman Costerstraat, Mon. and Fri., 8am-6pm, Sat., 8am-5pm; the indoor Markthof at Gedempte Gracht/Spui, Mon., 11am-6pm, Tues.-Sat., 9am-6pm, Thurs. until 9pm.

Antiques, Curio, Book and Picture Market: Lange Voorhout, May 15-Sept. 30, Thurs., 9am-9pm; Plein, Oct. 1-May, 14, Thurs. noon-6m.

Stamp Market: Amicitia Building, Westeinde 15, Sat. noon-5pm; Paleisstraat/Noordeinde, Wed. afternoon and Sat. am.

Fish Auction: Visafslagweg 1, Mon.-Sat., 7-10am. For more information, call the VVV.

EATING OUT: In the center of town off the Buitenhof and along the small shopping streets are various places to get a snack. McDonalds is located across from the entrance to the Binnenhof. But for a more historic stop, go to "De Boterwaag" (butter weighing house) at 8a Grote Markt, tel. (070) 659686. Built in 1681, it was restored in 1983 . . . coffee or lunch. Sometimes there are concerts and exhibitions. Great fun to get weighed on the original butter scales and receive a certificate telling "all." The best Indonesian food in town is at Tampat Senang, 6 Laan van Meerdervoort, tel. (070) 636787. Lovely romantic garden setting . . . good with children but expensive. For a night out and still a favorite, try Saur (one Michelin star) across from the U.S. Embassy, 51 Lange Voorhout, tel. (070) 463344 . . . expensive. A recent discovery is "Le Mouton," Kazernestraat 62, tel. 643263, with a moderate-priced excellent menu, old-world atmosphere but too sedate for children; romantic, leisurely, and good food. In the neighborhood, there are a number of other restaurants in the moderate-inexpensive range worth exploring.

YEARLY EVENTS: Some special events include Flag Day (Vlaagetjes Dag) and the Fishing Festival, end of May; the International Rose Show in Westbroek Park, June-Sept.; Scheveningen North Sea Jazz Festival, early July; the Hague Horse Days the end of July; the Flower Parade, last Sat. in Aug.; and Opening of Parliament the 3rd Tues. in September. Other events are listed in Chapter 20.

COMMERCIAL TOURS. The VVV operates a Royal Tour and a combination Bus/Boat Tour.

The Royal Tour (by bus) operates daily only May 1-Sept. 30 (but not Sunday). For the rest of the year, check operating days with VVV. Departs from the Central Station at 1:30pm and from the VVV Tourist office in Scheveningen at 1:45. The three-hour tour will take you past the Queen's residence, offices, and other points of interest dealing with the House of Orange. A half-hour visit to the Ridderzaal (Hall of Knights) within the Parliament complex is also included. Tel. (070) 546200 for specific dates, prices and reservations.

The Combitour starts by bus and shows you the important sights in The Hague and the fishing port at Scheveningen. You board the boat in front of "De Pauw" Delft pottery plant. Tours daily in July and August, 1:15pm from the Central Station. Group tours only in May, June and September. Same telephone as above for information.

Rondvaartbedrijf RVH operates another boat/bus tour, Spui 279A, tel. (070)

462473 . . . brochures also available at the VVV. Lasts 3 hours and takes you to many highlighted spots in and around The Hague. They also have a Candle-light tour to Leidschendam and package day trips to the Kaag, Avifauna, Delfshaven and Rotterdam. Clubs may rent boats throughout the year for receptions/tours, etc.

BOAT TOURS. Lovers of boat tours will like a tour or fishing expedition from Scheveningen. Call Sportviscentrum Trip, 3 Dr. Lelykade, Scheveningen, (070) 540887 or 541122 re June-September trips, daily at 4pm . . . Trams 10, 11, Bus 23. The sightseeing tour by boat shows you the fishing port of Scheveningen as well as a panoramic view of the boardwalk, pier and so on. Sport fishing can start with breakfast served at 6am (!) returning about 3pm. You can catch mackerel in summer and cod or sprat in winter. Fishing rods, reels and bait can be rented.

Madurodam

LOCATION: Haringkade 175, Den Haag. This is well sign-posted once one gets near. On a map it is about midway in a line drawn from the Binnenhof to the Scheveningen Pier. Bus 22, Trams 1, 9.
INFORMATION: Tel. (070) 553900.
HOURS: Vary during the year. Open Easter through beginning Jan., 9am-6pm; in June, July and Aug., usually 9am-10:30pm.
ADMISSION: Adults, Fl. 8; children to 2 yrs, free; 2-13 years, Fl. 4.
■ *Of interest to children and adults alike!*

Madurodam is a special tribute from loving parents of George Maduro to commemorate their son's life ... look for the memorial plaque left of the entrance gate. George served with honors during the WW II (May 1940) invasions by the Germans; later interned, he died at the Dachau concentration camp.

Even if you have seen model towns before, this is well worth a visit. It is advisable to have a supply of 10 cent coins, because these placed in various slots will make a band play, an organ grinder grind, a parade march past, etc., while supporting worthy charities.

Most of the buildings are copies of existing Dutch ones from different towns in Holland. Much is mechanized: ships are launched, cable cars work, railways and motorways buzz with activity—only the planes do not fly. If possible go at dusk; it is fun to see the lights turn on, and an enchanting sight in the deepening twilight.

A Sound and Light presentation, "Madurodam Moonlight Miracle," has been added ... separate hours and prices. Open daily, May 1-Sept. 30 (except May 4); in May, 10:30pm, June-August, 11pm, September, 9:30pm. Admission: adults Fl. 10, children under 13 years, Fl. 5. The walls and rocks talk, entrancing the audience with an evening's fairy tale. Refreshments, souvenirs, guide books (also in English) are available.

Binnenhof, Ridderzaal (Government Buildings)

LOCATION: The heart and center of The Hague, 81 Binnenhof.
INFORMATION: Tel. (070) 646144.
HOURS: Mon.-Sat., 10am-4pm. Closed Sundays and public holidays
except July and August. Conducted tours take three-quarters of
an hour. Groups are limited to a certain number. If you arrive
too late to join the ongoing tour, obtain your tickets for the next
scheduled tour to be sure you get in. Last tour is at 3:55pm.
■ *Of interest to older children and adults. Young children will love*
the Queen's Procession.

The Binnenhof is a group of buildings comprising the "Inner Court" of the former castle of the Counts of Holland. It is the seat of the Dutch Parliament and of political life in The Netherlands. The Gothic Knights' Hall is of particular interest. It was constructed by Count Floris V in the 13th century. The First and Second Chambers, some apartments, and the Knights' Hall (Ridderzaal) may be visited when not in use. Conducted tours begin with a 13-minute slide-show (in various languages) illustrating the story of this historic place. The last tour is at 3:55pm.

On the third Tuesday of September, Queen Beatrix drives in her golden coach from her offices in the Noordeinde Palace, on the Lange Voorhout, through the streets of The Hague to the Binnenhof, where she opens Parliament. Ask the VVV for details of the route.

There are times when, because of special events, one of the buildings in the Binnenhof is not open to visitors.

Mauritshuis Museum

LOCATION: 8, Korte Vijverberg, just outside the complex of buildings that make up the Binnenhof. One side of the building borders the Hof Vijver (lake) and the Vijverberg Plein is on the corner along another side of the Museum. Trams 3, 7, 8 or Buses 5 and 22.
INFORMATION: Tel. (070) 469244.
HOURS: Open Tues.-Sat., 10am-5pm; Sun. and holidays, 11am-5pm.
ADMISSION: Adults, Fl. 6.50; children, Fl. 3.50. Note: Admission fee is paid on leaving the museum.
■ *Of interest to school-age children.*

Originally, a nine-room "palace," the Mauritshuis was designed by Jacob van Campen for Count Johan Maurits van Nassau-Siegen, nephew of the ruling Prince Maurits van Oranje-Nassau. It was built by Pieter Post on grounds (obtained by special permission) next to the Binnenhof Court; a near neighbor was Constantijn Huygens, politician, poet and Secretary to the Prince of Orange. Completed in 1645, it is architecturally noteworthy for its perfect balance and proportions and is one of the most beautiful examples of Dutch classical architecture. Fire destroyed it in 1704. Eventually rebuilt, the State of Holland leased it to house high-ranking officials. From 1807-1819, it was used as the Royal Library. In 1819, the State bought it for 35,000 florins and then designated it as a museum. It has been renovated and modernized a number of times. After the latest reconstruction, the reception, cloakroom, museum shop, coffee shop and educational facility are located in the basement. Mauritshuis has produced a video-disc to introduce the museum contents to the visitor.

The basic collection includes outstanding paintings contributed by Orange-Nassau families, Stadholders, and the Princes William IV and V. During his military occupation, Napoleon sent all the best works to France; during WW II the treasures were hidden underground in one of the Northern Provinces—eventually, all the paintings were returned.

Today, 350 canvases, selected from its 860, are on display. Highlights of the permanent collection are 17th-century works by Rembrandt, Jan Steen, Vermeer, Frans Hals, Van Goyen, Ruisdael, Hobbema, Dou, Metsu, etc. In addition, there are important 15th-16th-century Flemish masters represented such as Rubens, Van Dyck, and Jordaens.

While the recent renovations were in progress, many of the paintings were cleaned. In 1968, a Dutch professor of art history studying the works of Rembrandt concluded that only 400 paintings out of 650 known Rembrandts are genuine. In the Mauritshuis, three Rembrandts were determined to be fakes and one is questionable; these are all in storage.

This museum is highly recommended as an introduction-museum to the early masters because of its compactness and the outstanding quality of its collection. It is probably the richest small museum in the world.

Prins Willem V Exhibition of Paintings

*LOCATION: Buitenhof 35. Take Buses 4, 5, 22; Trams 3, 7, and 8.
   Parking difficult as this is in town center.
INFORMATION: Tel. (070) 469244.
HOURS: Tues.-Sun., 11am-4pm.*
■ *Of interest to older children.*

Prince Willem V (1748-1806) collected something like 200 paintings which formed the nucleus of the "Picture Gallery" housed in the Mauritshuis for many years. The present group of paintings includes those in the original collection during the period 1774-1795. There are works by Jan Steen, Paulus Potter, Rembrandt, Philips Wouwerman and Jacob Jordaens.

Gevangenpoort (The Prison Gate)

*LOCATION: Buitenhof 33. Very near the Binnenhof in the town center. Buses 4, 5 and 22 stop nearby; also Trams 3, 7 and 8.
INFORMATION: Tel. (070) 460861.
HOURS: Open all year, Mon.-Fri., 10am-5pm. May-Sept., also open Sat., Sun., and public holidays, 1-5pm. All parties are guided. Tours take place every hour. Last tour at 4pm. If you find the door locked when you arrive, it is probably because a tour is in progress, and when they are let out, you will be let in.
NOTE: Children under 6 or unaccompanied children not admitted.
   6th class pupils (primary school) free entrance on application.*
■ *Of interest to children 7 years to adult (provided not easily frightened!).*

This is a medieval prison building with heavy wooden doors and narrow stairs and passages. There is a well-equipped torture chamber, and a variety of unpleasant methods of imprisonment described or demonstrated (you may be locked in a black hole while the guard goes away, turning out the lights as he does so!). You also visit the section where the rich and noble were imprisoned including Cornelius de Witt, who was tortured and then murdered by a mob in front of the gate. There was a women's section where they also kept sick prisoners.

The building is very small, but the half-hour tour, though not tiring, is likely to leave a vivid impression.

Printed sheet in English lent; the guide also spoke English.

Gemeentemuseum - Municipal Museum

LOCATION: Stadhouderslaan 41. Tram 10, Buses 4, 14.
INFORMATION: Tel. (070) 514181.
*HOURS: Open all year. Tues.-Fri., 10am-5pm; Sat., Sun. and public
    holidays, noon-5pm. Closed New Year's Day.*
*NOTE: Sundays, children from 4 to 12 years may stay at the "Kin-
    derwerkplaats" while their parents visit the museum. They work
    under adult supervision doing all types of handwork. Suitable for
    children of all nationalities.*
■ *Of interest to children from 4 years.*

This Municipal Museum is extensive and includes a very special Music Section (described in detail below), a library and a print section, in addition to displays of Italian ceramics, Venetian glass, Delft pottery, Dutch silver and glass, period rooms, Islamic ceramics and glass, Chinese ceramics, Indonesian art and a charming old doll's house. Modern art of the 19th and 20th centuries is well represented in sculptures and paintings including The Hague School and the world's largest collection of paintings by Piet Mondriaan. There is also a collection of ancient paintings, prints and objects illustrating the eventful history of The Hague. Many changing exhibitions, mostly of modern artists, can be seen year-round.

The **Music Section** contains two vast and varied collections—one of European and the other of non-European musical instruments. Tape recorders may be rented for a small fee which give an illustrated guided tour lasting about 50 minutes in several foreign languages. To hear the sounds of the various instruments is most interesting—and (sometimes) amusing. The European instrument collection is world-famous, ranging from tiny dancing-masters' fiddles (which had to fit in the pocket of a tail-coat) to a chamber organ, or a piano with music cupboard above. There are serpents (wind instruments just that shape); a huge one-string fiddle that sounds like a trumpet; a keyboard instrument built into a lady's dressing table; a flute carved into a walking stick to help while away the miles; and innumerable other beautiful and curious instruments right up to more modern musical boxes.

The non-European section contains African drums carved from whole tree trunks; a Javanese Gamelan (orchestra consisting of gongs, drums and other instruments); brass and horn instruments; and hundreds of other exotic and exciting makers of noise. There is a taped guide available for this section too.

The Music Section is of interest to children from 10 years; younger ones (unless particularly keen on music) may not be able to sustain their interest throughout the whole 50 minutes of the tape.

Music Library: For older children only—and adults, of course. This is a large library of manuscripts and books (English included) on all aspects of music (no actual scores) which seem to be freely available to those genuinely interested.

The Nederlands Kostuummuseum (Costume Museum) now is part of this museum. There is an introductory slide projection program and changing exhibits on the theme of costumes through the ages. There are showcases with displays and accessories dealing with such subjects as emancipation, sport, social status, fashion photography, jewelry, and so on.

National Book Museum Meermanno Westreeianum

LOCATION: Prinsessegracht 30. A few blocks away to the right (on the map) of the Binnenhof. Trams 1, 9, and Buses 18, 65, 88.
INFORMATION: Tel. (070) 462700.
HOURS: Mon-Sat., 1-5pm. Closed Sun. and public holidays.
■ *Of interest to older children and adults.*

The real work of the museum goes on, of course, behind the scenes. Based on the collections of two 19th-century gentlemen, it contains ancient manuscripts, rare books, as well as examples of modern experimental typography and limited editions. The section on numismatics is renowned.

On the other hand, there are antiquities: Egyptian statuettes, Roman lamps, Greek vases, Chinese dolls, etc., which are displayed in the small museum. There are also special exhibitions from time to time in collaboration with the Koninklijke Bibliotheek (Royal Library).

A booklet (illustrated) in English and Dutch is available at moderate cost. The staff spoke good English.

Museon - Modern Education Museum

LOCATION: Stadhouderslaan 41, next to the Municipal Museum, above. Tram 10, Buses 4, 14.
INFORMATION: Tel. (070) 514181.
HOURS: Tues.-Fri., 10am-5pm; Sat, Sun. and holidays, noon-5pm. Closed New Year's Day.
■ *Of interest to the whole family . . . even walking pre-schoolers.*

Combining in close proximity the Municipal Museum, the Space Theater Omniversum and Museon, museum officials have created an environment where families can study the world, its people, their development and the changing pattern of education. Upon entering, purchase the "Small Guide for Visitors" (various languages); it will help enormously in viewing the exhibits which are explained in Dutch, either written or spoken. Videos are throughout the museum . . . one small 5-6-year-old was all alone, mesmerized by a tape on watermelons! The length of the film is indicated below the screen . . . some a few minutes; the one on Turkey, 41 minutes.

The ground floor permanent display is entitled "The Earth Our Home"; one's attention is quickly directed to the glass cases displaying unusual creatures such as a host of cockroaches and shrimps, streaming their way from top to bottom of the case, viewable from either side, top and bottom. Another eye-catcher was a display of masks—wild and woolly, and costumes from East Greenland, Tibet, North Thailand. Upstairs, displays are all within view—few walls, so it's easy to decide what exhibit to see first. There was an Indian temple entrance with explanation of Indian culture; an Egyptian section (with one real mummy); a section on Turkey showing life-sized "people"...a man drinking tea and a woman preparing food. Another vibrantly-colored doll display entitled "The Mirrors of People" shows native costumes from 'round the world.

Serious scientific subjects are treated in easy-to-understand fashion, and sociological issues are discussed such as freedom of peoples. There are five major sections: history, geology, biology, physics and ethnology explained in 53 numbered displays. There's a restaurant, library, 300-seat auditorium and an inventory of 100,000 items . . . many in storage for future exhibits.

Omniversum - Space Theater

LOCATION: President Kennedylaan 5, The Hague, next to Museon and the Gemeente Museum. Tram 10, Buses 4, 14, 65 and 89.

INFORMATION: VVV Scheveningen, tel. (070) 546200; Reservations (070) 547400.

HOURS: Open daily with shows at 2, 3, 4, 7, 8 and 9pm. Holiday periods hourly performances from 11am-9pm. Reservations recommended.

ADMISSION: Fl. 12.50 p.p., School groups Fl. 4.00 per child; be sure and rent the sound track in your language . . . plugs are just behind your chair.

■ *Of interest to the whole family.*

This cylindrical building houses a 300-seat amphitheater with a 23.2-meter tilted dome forming an 840-sq.-meter screen for 70 mm omnimax films (about three times the size of normal 70 mm films). Films are shown on astronomy, space science, oceanography, geology, meteorology, biology, etc. Special films on culture, countries, space, can be beautiful as well as exciting; however, some shows are better done than others. For special planetarium programs, a computer-controlled cathode ray tube (Digistar) allows you to see stars as they were a million years ago and more.

Netherlands Postal Museum

LOCATION: Zeestraat 82. Zeestraat runs into the Laan van Meerdervoort at the point where this changes its name to Javastraat. Buses 4, 5, 13 and 22 stop within walking distance, also Trams 7 and 8.

INFORMATION: Tel. (070) 624531.

HOURS: Mon.-Sat., 10am-5pm. Sun. and holidays, 1-5pm. Closed December 25 and January 1.

NOTE: By previous arrangement you can have an English-speaking guide on a very worthwhile tour lasting about an hour.

■ *Of interest to children from 7 years to adult. Specially recommended for birthday party outings.*

This collection covers all aspects of Dutch Post Office history, from the boots worn by the early horseback messengers, to modern telephone systems, telex, radio, TV, etc., with many working, and in some cases, usable models. For example, it is fun to make a modern sorting machine sort letters. The stamp collection not only has thousands of Dutch and international stamps, but also shows how a stamp is designed and printed.

On sale are souvenir postcards and current stamp issues of The Netherlands.

Panorama Mesdag

LOCATION: Zeestraat 65b. Zeestraat runs into the Laan van Meerdervoort just at the point where this changes its name to Javastraat. The Postal Museum is just down the street. Trams 7 and 8; Buses 4, 5 13 and 22.

INFORMATION: Tel. (070) 642563.
HOURS: Mon.-Sat., 10am-5pm. Sundays and holidays, noon-5pm.
Closed Christmas Day.
■ *Of interest to children 7 years to adult.*

Through a gallery of paintings by Mesdag and his wife and via a spiral staircase, one suddenly emerges at the top into the world of Scheveningen in 1880. The immense panorama (circumference 394 ft., 46 ft. high) was painted from this spot. The town is on one side and the beach on the other, with fishing boats drawn up, and cavalry exercising, just as if one were standing on a sand dune a century ago.

The concept was H. W. Mesdag's, a prominent Marine painter, assisted by his wife, Sina Mesdag-Van Houten, Th. de Bock, G. H. Breitner, and B. J. Blommers. This is one of the last of the cycloramas (panoramic paintings) which were enormously popular in the 19th century as well as an important example of the work of The Hague School.

Our guide spoke good English; there is a 4-language tape available. The museum is on the same street as the Postal Museum and the Scout Shop.

National Museum H. W. Mesdag

LOCATION: 7 F, Laan van Meerdervoort; Trams 3, 7 and 8; Buses 4
and 13 stop within walking distance.
INFORMATION: Tel. (070) 635450.
HOURS: Open Tues.-Sat., 10am-5pm. Sunday and public holidays,
1-5pm.
■ *Of interest to older children.*

This museum, established by the Dutch painter, H. W. Mesdag, contains a collection of The Hague Romantic School (Maris, Breitner, Israels, etc.) and a unique collection of French 19th-century paintings of the Barbizon School (Delacroix, Corot, Courbet, Millet, etc.).

The Vredespaleis - Peace Palace

LOCATION: 2 Carnegieplein. Near the center of town, just off the
Laan van Meerdervoort at its eastern end. Buses 4, 13; Trams 7
and 8.
INFORMATION: Tel. (070) 469680.
HOURS: Open all year. No tours when court is actually sitting. Guided tours Mon.-Fri., at 10, 11am, 2 and 3pm; also at 4pm from
June 1-Sept. 1. If requested in advance, special opening days or
hours for groups of more than 50 people may be possible.
■ *Of interest to children 8 years to adult.*

The permanent home of the International Court of Justice, the Permanent Court of Arbitration, and the International Law Library was donated by the American, Andrew Carnegie. Notice the many interesting and valuable gifts from different nations such as Ming vases from China, leaded glass windows from Holland.

All tours are guided; each guide usually assembles a party of one language They speak excellent English, and enjoy relating amusing incidents of Court happenings to suit the nationalities represented in their party. The gardens surrounding the Palace are lovely in season.

Puppet Museum

LOCATION: Nassau Dillenburgstraat 8; Trams 1, 9; Buses 13, 18.
INFORMATION: Tel. (070) 280208.
HOURS: Open Sundays, noon-2pm. Performances given Oct.-June:
   Sat., Sun., 2:30pm (for children); Fri., 8:30pm (for adults).
■ *Of interest to most children.*

This museum has 1,000 antique hand puppets and marionettes, some over 200 years old. There are explanations of how they are made; also interesting articles, photos and programs from Holland and abroad.

The Hague Historical Museum

LOCATION: Korte Vijverberg 7. Trams 3, 7, 8; Buses 4, 5, 22.
INFORMATION: Tel. (070) 646940.
HOURS: Tues.-Fri., noon-4pm. Closed New Year's Day.
■ *Primarily of interest to residents.*

This museum is devoted to the history of The Hague and its citizens. In addition to the collection, which includes paintings of the town and prominent former citizens, models, commemorative medals and Hague silverware, there are video facilities and "Do-it-yourself" activities.

Zeebiologisch Museum - Marine Biological Museum

LOCATION: Dr. Lelykade 39, Scheveningen. From The Hague, follow
   the signs for "Scheveningen Zeehaven." There is plenty of park-
   ing. Tram 11, stop Statenlaan; Bus 23, stop Datheenstraat. (Good
   free parking)
INFORMATION: Tel. (070) 502528.
HOURS: Open daily from 10am-5pm; Sun., 1-5pm. Closed Christmas
   and New Year's.
NOTE: There is an English-language flyer explaining what is in each
   showcase. School groups are welcome.
■ *Of interest to school-age children and their parents.*

This small museum has plans to expand. Assuming they do as good a job as they have already, this could become a major marine museum in Holland.

Over 25,000 shells from the seven oceans of the world are on display including, for instance, shells from Atsumi Bay, Japan, and Miami Bay, Florida. For the grisly-minded visitor, there is a display of deadly poisonous shells, and for the lover of beauty, there is a display of gorgeous mother-of-pearl shells as well as shells made into jewelry.

A particularly interesting item is a mask of the Kuba tribe from Zaire in Africa, made of monkey hair, leather, raffia, beads, cowry shells, brass, seeds and textiles. The wearer looks out through the nose openings. A bit of real life can be seen in the five fish tanks containing types of fish caught in and around the North Sea and the coast of Britain.

Other interesting items on display are fossilized sea-animals millions of years old, shells on stamps, exposition of seaweed compositions, and a systematic study collection for the avid collector. There is a library and information center for those interested in further study. Seashell collectors will also have a ball in the gift shop.

IN THE NEIGHBORHOOD OF THE HAGUE:

■ **Scheveningen** is an extension of The Hague and considered officially as a part of The Hague for tourist planning. Therefore, we will mention here some of the attractions at Scheveningen of interest to visitors of The Hague. In addition, read Chapter 14 for information about Scheveningen as a beach and pleasure resort. There are many amusement arcades.

Scheveningen Casino, located in the old Kurhaus dating from 1885. Open all year, 2pm-2am. Moderate entrance fee. In its early days, this hotel was an elegant establishment for those wanting to "take the cure." Today, the Kurhaus remains a fine hotel with restaurants, convention facilities, shopping mall, outdoor cafe, entertainment (in summer) on the boardwalk, etc. The games played are French and American roulette, Blackjack and Baccarat. There are also one-armed bandits.

Drievliet Recreation Park, 16, Jan Thyssenweg, Rijswijk, tel. (070) 999305; restaurant, 903893; boat trips, 462473. Hours vary during year so check first. Practically in town, Trams 1, 10, and Bus 23. This 25,000-square-meter park includes a monorail, dodgem cars, moon rocket, ghost train, pedalos, hall of mirrors, children's farm and more as well as a restaurant for 250 people. Fl. 10 all-in for amusements.

Duinrell Recreation Park in Wassenaar

GETTING THERE: 1 Duinrell, Wassenaar. From Rotterdam, highway A13 towards The Hague, following signs for Scheveningen, then north on N44. From Amsterdam, take A4, then A44 south until turnoff for Duinrell (it will be on the sea side) at the intersection of 's Gravesandeweg and Katwijkseweg or follow the signs "Camping Duinrell."

INFORMATION: Tel. (01751) 19212/19314: Park, 14765; Tikibad, 11698; Camping, 14004.

HOURS: Open Oct.-March, daily, 9am-5pm; April-Sept., 9am-9pm.

ADMISSION: Varies, from Fl. 12-17.00 depending on season; lower evening rates.
■ *Of interest to all.*

Duinrell Recreation Park with most attractions included in the entrance fee, offers a large play garden, trampolines, canoeing, gondola, midget golf, slimming track, animated frog show, water play garden, "Duinrell Fairy Tale" (a wonderland during the day), monorail cycles, sports grounds, and a tower on the highest point of North and South Holland. The antique carousel covered by a glass cupola is lovely. There's a giant Niagara water slide, 500 meters long for the adventurous, as well as special shows of high diving from 30 meters into a pool 10 meters in diameter. For an additional fee, there are: space/wobble cycles, Punch and Judy show "Rozebons," bowling, mini-scooters–and more.

The "Tiki-Wavepool" is an all-season tropical wavepool which is becoming so popular in the northern climes. Four covered waterslides (total length 400 meters) are the longest in the world. There are many other water attractions and a complete sauna department. The Tiki-Wavepool is open daily from 10am-10pm from April-August. Call number above for information about open times during other periods of the year.

In winter, the Café-Restaurant, "De Schaapskooi" (The Sheep Hut), is available for parties from 50-500 persons. The park is open weekends all winter, at which time the permanent playgarden, trampolines and midget golf are available. Something special does go on at Duinrell in wintertime, however . . . skiing on pine needles!!! Since 1931 skiing lessons have been held on this estate every winter under the auspices of the Nederlandse Reis Vereniging. Beginning skiers learn the finer points of the sport and experienced ones can improve their technique. The school has qualified instructors (who can speak English), slopes of approximately 100 meters–also a special slope for children–and artificial lighting for night classes. Classes start the beginning of October and are held until about mid-March. In general, two courses of lessons are offered, the first group starting Oct. 1 and the second in mid-January. You may decide to take a set of three, five or ten lessons.

Camping Facilities: Duinrell's camping facilities are considered tops . . . three stars and 5 flags from the ANWB. This large campsite and bungalow park is a good headquarters for visitors but it is not open in winter; for details write or tel. (01751) 14004.

LEIDEN

Home of Holland's oldest university and of the Pilgrim Fathers

GETTING THERE: Two major autoroutes "encircle" Leiden, the A4 and A44; however, many country routes are possible. A particularly lovely drive from Rotterdam is through Hillegersberg, along farmlands to the Gouwe Canal, Alphen a/d Rijn and then follow the Oude Rijn river into the city. Leiden's canals, narrow and one-way streets, make getting about somewhat difficult. Look for "P" signs and leave the car.
INFORMATION: VVV, Stationsplein 210, tel. (071) 146846.

Leiden's known history goes back to the year 1200. Then, as now, it was a crossroads for travelers and commerce. The Breestraat lies on an old Roman road; in the 11th century, the Burcht—part fortification, part control of the old and new Rijn rivers—was built at a major north/south crossroads. Political development can be seen between 1200-1300 when the "Gravensteen," a residence for the Counts of Holland was built. It later became a prison and is part of the University complex today. The town's earliest period of prosperity was in the 14th century when it was a center for cloth-weaving (see the Lakenhal Museum). By 1500, Leiden's impressive churches were supported by a population of some 10,000 persons, about the same number as Amsterdam and Haarlem.

The Spanish laid seige to the city during 1573-74. More than half the population died of sickness and starvation but refused to surrender. The Dutch Navy was finally able to free them in 1574 after breaking down dike after dike to reach them. In 1575, in recognition to the townspeople of their tremendous resistance and suffering, William the Silent granted Leiden the right to establish the first University in the Netherlands. Ten years later, prosperity returned aided by the many immigrants from Belgium who brought skills as well as manpower to supplement the greatly depleted work force. They were textile workers, beer brewers, and exporters of parchment, books, cheese, pewter, etc.

During the late 1500's, early 1600's, Leiden was the birthplace or workplace for many famous men. Rembrandt was born here in 1606, as were the painters Jan van Goyen in 1596, Gerrit Dou, 1613, Jan Steen, 1625, and Gabriel Metsu,

1629. Scholars in Leiden included Hugo Grotius, statesman Rene Descartes, and theologian John Robinson who was pastor to the Pilgrims.

WALKING TOURS:

Leiden's streets are filled with history. In recognition, the VVV has put together four walking tours in major languages entitled, "Leiden, a true Dutch heritage," "Leiden, a town full of monuments," "Rembrandt Walk," and "The road of Freedom," the latter deals with the Pilgrims and their time. Each folder includes a map and each tour is color-coded. Arrows in appropriate colors have been made in the sidewalks to help guide you.

Some places to look for are where Rembrandt was born on the Weddesteeg (stone plaque in wall, his statue); the Weigh House designed by Pieter Post at the confluence of the Oude and Nieuwe Rijn rivers; the Korenbeursbrug, bridge housing the corn market which dates from the 15th century; the windmill museum "De Valk" (1743); Municipal Art Gallery, "De Lakenhal," along docking areas for summer boat trips; the Rapenburg, an area of old patrician houses; Leiden University and its botanical garden laid out in 1587 (see below for hours); Saint Peters Church (Sint Pieterskerk) and sites frequented by the Pilgrim Fathers; the Blue Stone where executions once took place; the Town Hall (17th century, restored after fire in 1929); Hooglandse or St. Pancras Church (1377); St. Lodewijkskerk (1538); and the Burcht with its ornate gate (1658) from where one can get a splendid view of the city.

Of special interest to Americans are the Pilgrim Fathers who made Leiden their home from 1609-1620. Their arrival was hardly noted as they coincided with the hundreds of immigrants from the south. From 6,000 survivors of the siege in 1574, immigrants swelled the population to about 40,000 by 1620.

The Pilgrims lived in the neighborhood of Sint Pieterskerk (St. Peter's) built in the 15th century on foundations of a parish church already recorded in 1121. At No. 17-A Pieterkerkchoorsteeg (near the church), there is a plaque at the site of the "Pilgrim Press," run by William Brewster who published leaflets criticizing the Church of England until his press was closed down through pressure applied by James I. At Kloksteeg 21, another plaque marks the property, "De Groene Poort" (the Green Close ... now called the Green Gate) where John Robinson, the Pilgrims' leader and pastor lived and where services were held. Twenty-one small houses were built around the garden for other members of the congregation ... eventually, the Pilgrims lived in other parts of town. Today, the "Jean Pesijnshofje" almshouse is on the site (built in 1683, some years after Robinson's death in 1625).

The story of the Pilgrim movement is fascinating and there are a number of documents in English for those interested. In addition, the Leiden Pilgrim Collection (previously, the Leiden Pilgrim Document Center) has an excellent video giving the flavor and history of the times. Unfortunately, the present museum building is being closed and a new museum/office space is being prepared (due to open in 1991) at Boisotkade 2a, 2311 PZ, Leiden, tel. (071) 120191 or 134421. The VVV will be able to inform visitors where the exhibits can be seen in the meantime and how to obtain literature. Ask for "The Pilgrims in Leiden, 1609-1620," by N. Leverland and J. D. Bangs, "Leiden, the City the Pilgrims Knew," by J. D. Bangs; the Document Center's walking tour, "In the

Footsteps of William Bradford," and "The Pilgrim Fathers in Leiden" by Dr. J. W. Verburgt.

Leiden is said to have some 30 almshouses . . . three of special note are the "Jean Pesijnshofje" mentioned above, the "Eva Van Hoogeveen Hofje" (1659), and "St. Anna Hofje" (1507) with its own chapel.

MUSEUMS: Six national museums are located in Leiden; the Rijksmuseum Van Oudheden, the Rijksmuseum voor Volkenkunde, the Museum for the History of Science, and the Municipal Museum "de Lakenhal" are discussed in detail below. In addition, there are:

Molenmuseum "de Valk" (Windmill Museum), 2e Binnenvestgracht 1, tel. 254639, open Tues.-Sat., 10am-5pm, Sun. and holidays, 1-5pm. This brick windmill, dating from 1743, was used for grinding corn. On the ground floor, you will see how a miller lived in about 1900, his working tools and smithy. Upstairs is an exposition of windmill models, parts and accessories. On top is the complete windmill-mechanism.

National Museum of Geology and Mineralogy, 17 Hooglandse Kerkgracht, tel. 146846, open Mon.-Fri., 10am-5pm, Sun., 2-5pm. The building was a former orphanage dating from 1607. There is a treasure room of precious stones and, always a favorite, a display under fluorescent lighting where normally lifeless stones come brilliantly alive.

University History Museum, 73 Rapenburg, tel. 272742, open Wed.-Fri., 1-5pm; its Print Room, 65 Rapenburg, might appeal to photography buffs, open Tues.-Fri., 2-5pm. The Botanic Garden attached to the University is one of the oldest in Europe and a delight to budding botanists, open Mon.-Sat., 9am-5pm; Sun., 10am-5pm.

The Museum Boerhaave (Museum for the History of Science), St. Agnietenstraat 10, will be reopening in the Spring of 1990 in the completely restored building where Dr. Boerhaave worked in the Middle Ages. Call 214224 for info; hours, Tues.-Sat., 10am-5pm; Sun. and holidays, 1-5pm, closing at 4pm in winter. One of the first surgeons in the world, scientists came from all over the world to study with him. This will be the foremost museum in its fields of surgery, medicine and dentistry with additional display rooms and a lecture hall in the old style.

Museum of Clay Pipes. Pipe smokers might enjoy a visit to a collection from more than 40 countries. Open Sundays 1-5pm.

Municipal Cartwright's shop, Oude Varkenmarkt 13, tel. 120072, open Sundays, 1-5pm, an original shop recently restored.

MARKETS: Five times a week there are colorful markets and a very active shopping center in the city center (Breestraat, Haarlemmerstraat and area). An old-fashioned cattle market is held Mon. and Tues., 7-11am, as well as a special horse market at a nearby village, Valkenburg . . . see below.

EATING OUT: Like all university towns there are numerous inexpensive places to eat such as the Pannekoekenhuisje (annex of the best restaurant in town, the Rotisserie Oudt Leyden) which specializes in pancakes like wagon wheels served on Delft-blue plates . . . Steenstraat 51, tel. 13314. De Grote Beer, Rembrandtstraat 27, tel. 121719 is another place to try. Tourist menus can also be had at Bernsen, Breestraat 57, and the Nieuw Minerve, Boommarkt 23. A delightful spot is the Cafe-Restaurant, "Koetshuis," located at the foot of the Burcht Burgsteeg 13, tel. 121688. It was built in 1692 as a carriage house for a large private home across the way, the "Herenlogement" which is now a library. You can even find a McDonald's at Beestenmarkt 6.

YEARLY EVENTS: Several special events occur in Leiden yearly. The first takes place the third weekend in January, the very famous Keytown Jazz Festival. On Good Friday (also evening before), the famous Matthew's Passion is performed by the Bach Choir in Sint Pieterskerk. The beginning of July is time for the big summer festival celebrating Rembrandt's birthday and Leiden's Cloth Festival. A big party is held on October 3rd to commemorate "Leiden's Ontzet," the town's liberation from the Spanish after suffering months of siege. William III of England came to their rescue by flooding the surrounding countryside. At the deserted Spanish campsite, a casserole of white beans, carrots and onions (hutspot) was found. The same day, the waterbeggars (pirates) sailed into Leiden bringing with them raw herring and loaves of bread. These have become the three traditional foods of the day. Festivities begin at 7am with "reveille": at 7:30, "haring and wittebrood" (herring and white bread) are distributed and "pirates" make their entry into town. There are fireworks and exhibitions . . . check with the VVV for details.

Another historic event of note is celebrated the last Thursday in November, American Thanksgiving Day, in honor of the Pilgrims. The U.S. President's Thanksgiving Day Proclamation is read in Sint Pieterskerk by the American Ambassador. There is usually a guest speaker, choir singing by students, and a coffee hour after the service. Included in the ecumenical service are a Catholic priest, Protestant ministers and a Reformed Jewish rabbi. For details, call the VVV.

COMMERCIAL TOURS: Boat trips 'round the moats and canals are available (seasonally), as are sightseeing tours across the Lakes . . . tel. 134938/413183. Rowboats and canoes can be rented near the Rembrandtbridge, info, tel. 149790.

National Museum of Antiquities "Van Oudheden"

LOCATION: Rapenburg 28.
INFORMATION: Tel. (071) 146246.
HOURS: Tues.-Sat., 10am-5pm; Sun. and holidays, 1-5pm. Closed
    January 1 and October 3.
NOTE: Guides are available on request; many English subtitles.
■ *Of interest to school-age children.*

Strange as it may seem, the museum seems to appeal very much to young children . . . Perhaps it isn't so strange, when you realize that it has a most complete collection of mummies!

Founded in 1818, the museum has been enhanced over the years. The most rcent collection to join the museum is the Royal Coin Collection (Koninklijk Penningskabinet) from The Hague, which includes coins, precious stones and stamps. A new Near East department is in the works as well.

National Museum of Ethnology "Voor Volkenkunde"

LOCATION: Steenstraat 1.
INFORMATION: Tel. (071) 132641.
HOURS: Tues.-Sat., 10am-5pm; Sun. and holidays, 1-5pm. Closed
  January 1 and October 3.
■ *Of interest to children from 6 years.*

This museum is entitled to call itself the first scientific ethnological museum of Europe. King William the First was deeply interested in spreading learning throughout his kingdom and he personally acquired important collections which were the basis for the national museums.

This large, airy museum has an informal atmosphere in which children are quite at home. The collection is too extensive to describe in detail but you will find displays on prehistoric art, Africa, the Islamic culture of the Middle East, India and the culture of Ceylon and Further India, Buddhism and its Art, Tibet, China, Japan, Indonesia, New Guinea, Oceania, Australia, the culture of the polar peoples of Asia and America, Central America, North America and Mestizo cultures, and Suriname.

The American Indian display is of particular interest to American children.

The museum's new (1988) wing will add much, expanding and allowing for better viewing of the collection.

Municipal Museum "de Lakenhal"

LOCATION: Oude Singel 28-32.
INFORMATION: Tel. (071) 254620.
HOURS: Tues.-Sat., 10am-5pm; Sun. and holidays, 1-5pm; Closed
  January 1 and December. 25.
■ *Of interest to children 12 years and older.*

The building housing the museum was used in the cloth-weaving trade which has flourished since the 14th century, bringing great prosperity to the town of

Leiden. The collection includes paintings by Lucas Van Leyden, Rembrandt, Jan Steen, Van Goyen, Bakker Korff and Verster, as well as a large collection of old furniture and old silver. There are rooms depicting life in the 17th, 18th and 19th centuries which are especially interesting to the ladies.

IN THE NEIGHBORHOOD OF LEIDEN:

Valkenburg, a village just west of Leiden, is where a horse market has taken place for over 1,000 years. Village history began in the first three centuries after the death of Christ when the town developed on a mound along the banks of the old river Rhine. One of the earliest Christian chapels was built here in the 9th century. To help support the chapel, a market selling flax and linen was established, and about 840 A.D., a horse market started. The high point for sales was in the 16th century when 3,000 horses were brought to market. After the Franco-Prussian war in 1872, numbers dropped to 1,100 horses and today, there are just a few. The sale price is determined by the dealer and buyer hitting each other's hand. Market days are Wednesday and Thursday, more enthusiastically enjoyed by tourists and families than serious traders, perhaps. But the big event takes place on the second Wednesday in September. Children have been excused from school. People awake to the sound of bicycle bells ringing and tin cans being dragged along the streets. The bright lights and bustle of the fair await! Not to mention the many attractions and market stalls to tempt one's purse.

Avifauna in Alphen a/d Rijn

GETTING THERE: From The Hague or Amsterdam, take Highway A4 toward Leiden until the turnoff for Alphen a/d Rijn; from Rotterdam, the scenic route is to follow the small back roads from Hillegersberg to Bleiswijk, Kruisweg Hazerwoude-Rijndijk, and then along the Oude Rijn River to Avifauna. There is adequate parking for private automobiles. For those without a car, they may go by boat from The Hague, Leiden or Amsterdam.
INFORMATION: Tel. (01720) 31090.
HOURS: Open all year, April-Oct., daily 9am-9pm; Nov.-March, 9am-6pm.
■ *Of interest to all ages.*

Avifauna is really a wonderful day's excursion for the entire family . . . it even boasts a widely known motel-hotel with a first-class restaurant. As you have noted from the above information, it is possible to go by boat from The Hague, Leiden or Amsterdam. In addition, there are cruising boats (from April 1- September 30) which may be boarded at Avifauna itself and it is possible to hire motor boats for private groups. At night, Avifauna is illuminated to add a romantic touch.

The unique aspect of Avifauna is the collection of exotic birds from all parts of the world. They are in enclosed areas set among a most attractive garden.

The children will naturally make a beeline for the recreation park with its funny mirrors, high slide, trampolines, scooter ball, skelter, swimming pool (open April-Sept.) and canoes to rent. There is also a fishing pond and children's farm and ponies to ride.

For the weary, hungry or thirsty, the Park-Café-Restaurant (upper room) serves large meals; lower room is self-service and offers popular prices) and an outer-café-restaurant for snacks.

LISSE

Springtime riot of colors ...

GETTING THERE: *The fields of many-colored tulips are located north of Leiden between Sassenheim and Lisse. Take "Nieuw Vennep" turnoff from Autoroute A4 or N208 from A44 and follow signs.*
INFORMATION: VVV Lisse, Grachtweg 53, tel. (02521) 14262/15263.

All stops are out with glorious colors and scents, and tourists by the droves from the end of March, to the middle of May when the bulb season is at its peak. The Keukenhof, described below, is the mecca and offers an unforgettable show every year ... in a class of its own.

To complement the visual experience, there's a new museum in Lisse, Museum Lisse, Heereweg 219, tel. (02521) 17900, located in a historic building.From Leiden station, Buses 50, 51; from Nieuw Vennep station, Bus 94. Hours, April and May, Tues.-Sun. 10am-5pm; June-March, Tues.-Fri., 1-5pm. A small but interesting museum giving the history of the bulb and describing the bulb life cycle. The museum is run as a private concern with English, French and Dutch guides. Their shop is full of goodies.

You can also visit an old donjon, Dever House, once a fortified private house, now a ruin. Probably built about 1375 by Reinier Dever, a member of a very old family of Dutch nobles. There is a detailed pamphlet describing the house and its history. For directions, hours, etc., check with the VVV. They also have car and bike routes to follow through the bulb fields.

Boat trips on the Kagerplassen lakes are available every half hour from the Lissebrug (summer).

The Keukenhof

Offering a festival of spring flowers

LOCATION: During the season, "Keukenhof" will be clearly indicated on the major highway signs. Or take a train from the Leiden or Haarlem train stations; check into the all-in ticket which includes train, bus fares and entrance to the Keukenhof at reduced rates.
INFORMATION: Tel. (02521) 19034, or VVV above.
HOURS: Open March 30 until the middle/end of May, daily, 8am-6:30pm.
ADMISSION: Adults, Fl. 10.00, children (4-12 yrs), Fl. 5.00 (Wednesdays, free).
■ *Of interest to all.*

The Keukenhof should not be missed during the bulb blooming season, and it sometimes seems the whole of Europe is determined to go the very day you have chosen. It is least crowded early in the season. Every year the plantings in this 66-acre park are differently arranged so the show is always a new one. When you go early, you see the crocuses, hyacinths and narcissi; when you go later, you will see narcissi, early tulips and then, the late-blooming tulips. Don't be discouraged if the weather isn't perfect—you can see the complete range of bulbs in the large greenhouses where you are protected from rain and wind. Two greenhouses are laid out as an indoor Spring garden, and the other greenhouses are planted to show you the full range of bulbs.

During the hyacinth blooming, you are likely to be overpowered with their heady aroma. Many growers are represented at the Keukenhof, all eager to provide you information, or take your orders for delivery abroad to relatives and friends. Don't worry about taking the toddlers—there are small push-cars available at the entrances for those too young to cover the garden on their own, as well as wheelchairs for older persons who might find the walk around these extensive grounds a bit too much.

Also, there are sculptural exhibits throughout the gardens, flower arrangement displays, two indoor pavilions, three self-service cafe-restaurants in different parts of the garden, flower shops, a small animal enclosure, a working windmill open for exploration, and comfort facilities.

There is a yearly flower parade on the main road between Haarlem and Noordwijk, via Sassenheim. For information about exact dates, check with the VVV. Another similar flower show can be seen in Bovenkarspel (outskirts of Enkhuizen) in February. See Chapter 3. At the end of April or beginning of May, flower mosaics are exhibited in Lisse, Haarlem, and towns in the area.

GOUDA

Cheese, and a special Christmas celebration

LOCATION: From Amsterdam, take A2 south to A12 west; from The Hague, take Highway A12. From Rotterdam, take A20 northeast. Trains or buses are also possible.

INFORMATION: VVV, Gouda, Markt 27, tel. (01820) 13666. The
VVV Guided Walkman tour (1½ hours) takes visitors through
the old city center past all the major points of interest.

Gouda is synonymous with "cheese" (except the American visitor has known it as "Goo-da" and not "How-da"!) but cheese is only one of the interesting things going on here. It's a great place to get the true flavor of Holland in a short time and without too much driving which can be tiring (especially for children).

Situated on the banks of the rivers Gouwe and Hollandse IJssel, this historic town received its town charter July 26, 1272 from Count Floris V. The story is told in pantomime and sound by the clock on the east side of the Gothic Town Hall. Every half hour when the clock strikes, colorful parading figures can be seen by the castle door—there are two groups of spectators and two standard-bearers on either side. Five seconds after the first chime of the bells, the spectators turn their faces towards the door and the standard-bearers swing round to form a guard of honor. Then the castle door opens and Count Floris emerges, accompanied by a representative of the townsfolk, to whom he hands the charter. The Town Hall is open 9am-noon and 2-4pm; closed Saturday and Sunday and for official functions. Situated on the largest market square in Holland, it is the oldest Town Hall in the country, dating from 1450. The Trouwzaal (marriage room) on the first floor is worth a visit. Its tapestry-covered walls are great works of art, and the atmospheric Council Chamber just under the beams of the roof should be seen.

To enhance your visit of Gouda, the VVV's guided stereo "Walkman Tour," (1½ hrs.) takes the visitor through the old city center past all major points of interest.

■ **The Waag or Weigh House**, built in 1668 by the redoubtable Pieter Post, is, like the Town Hall, a fine subject for photographers. The cheese and craft markets are held here in July and August on Thursdays, 9:30am-noon. The local "Boerenkaas" or farmers' cheese, is made from full-cream milk, not skimmed milk as is the case with other type cheeses. In the Weigh House, you can sample the cheese, which comes from about 1,500 farms in the vicinity. On view are the huge cheese-weighing scales and a film is run describing how cheese is made. If you want to buy a big round, yellow cheese for a huge party, check with the VVV for the name of a local distributor—or if you're there on cheese market day, this is your chance to make contact with some of the buyers or sellers. Another delectable Gouda speciality is Gouda waffles (stroopwafels . . . treacle cookies—delicious).

ST. JANSKERK AND MUSEUMS: Head for the spires of St. Janskerk walking through the back streets and browse through the stores of the little shopping sreets. St. Janskerk is known for its splendid stained glass windows. It, the Catharina-Gasthuis Museum, and De Moriaan Museum (Pipe, Pottery and Tile Museum) are discussed in detail below. There is also a new museum, the Zuid Hollands Verzetsmuseum (Resistance Museum) dealing with the resistance movement in South Holland during WW II. Located on Turfmarkt 30, tel.

(01820) 20385, open Tues.-Sat., 10am-5pm; Sun., noon-5pm.

Pottery demonstrations are given at Pottery "Adrie," Moerings, Peperstraat 76, tel. (01820) 12842, or go to the Goedewaagen factory and ask to see their "mystery pipe"—white when you purchase it, it turns brown and a pattern appears as the pipe is smoked . . . but you don't know what the pattern will be when you buy it.

Windmill enthusiasts will want to see the completely restored and working "De Roode Leeuw" (the Red Lion) Windmill (1727) . . . Vest 65, tel. (01820) 22041, open Mon.-Sat., 9am-5pm.

YEARLY EVENTS: Gouda has a special pre-Christmas event which takes place in mid-December. It has become so popular that the main square is densely jammed with people but it is such a lovely experience, we highly recommend going. (Be prepared to carry small children, however.) You must park your car before the approach to the square because it is cordoned off to general traffic. If you use a little imagination, you can believe yourselves in the 16th century. The lights have been extinguished—no electric lights are allowed in any of the buildings facing the square. Instead, they and the City Hall are illuminated only by candles. It takes literally thousands of candles to light up the City Hall alone! Suddenly, the Mayor and his guests appear—only it's too dark to really see them—and then he throws the switch which illuminates a huge dazzlingly white Christmas tree which seems to reach to the top of the City Hall itself. The tree is a gift from Gouda's sister-city in Norway. This occasions a few speeches, but not too long because at that time of the year, it's pretty crisp standing outside and the officials are thoughtful of the little children in the audience. Then, everyone joins in singing Christmas carols— if you don't know Dutch, you are asked to sing in your own native tongue. A word of warning, DRESS WARMLY. After the singing, you are invited to St. Janskerk where a special concert is given for the general public. You can get an idea of the size of the church and see some of the structural points of interest but this is not a good time to see the stained glass windows. Details follow on the church and the museums of Gouda. Other churches are also open during that evening.

COMMERCIAL TOURS: Also available from the VVV is information about summer boat tours to the Reeuwijk Lakes where you can see typical polder landscapes. The area has the largest expanse of tree, plant and rose nurseries which are worth a visit; info VVV Boskoop (01727) 4644 (just outside Gouda).

EATING OUT: Sightseeing always makes the family thirsty— if not hungry!!— and usually there is a need for a restroom as well, so stop at one of the following places for a respite: De "Zes Sterren" (Six Stars) at the Catharina-Gasthuis is a convenient place to get a bite to eat. If it's a winter visit and you need warming up, order a hot chocolate for the children and a hot spiced wine for the adults. Also, for those huge Dutch pancakes (pannekoeken) which the children usually love, you can eat at the charming, small, old restaurant close to St. Janskerk, de Goudse Winkeltje, Achter de Kerk 9a. On the Oosthaven, there is a small tavern which has white frilly curtains at the windows, and an old Dutch atmosphere in the interior. It's called the Malle Molen. There are other restaurants giving onto the Market Square which are worth a try as well . . . or if you go during Market Day, one can always buy patats (French-fried potatoes) or sausages at one of the stands.

St. Janskerk

LOCATION: "Achter de Kerk." East of the Market Place on a small winding back street. Look for the Church tower as a guide.
INFORMATION: Tel. (01820) 12684.
HOURS: Closed to visitors on Sundays. Nov.-March: Mon.-Sat., 10am-4pm. March-Nov.: Mon.-Sat., 9am-5pm.
NOTE: Guided tour on request.
■ *Of interest to older children (from 12 years).*

It's not always easy to see churches in Holland as they are never open to the public on Sundays, which is the day the whole family so often does its sightseeing. If you want to see the church in Gouda, you must therefore plan your visit for a Saturday or a weekday.

The church is very large (123 meters long) and contains 70 beautiful stained glass windows—some as high as 20 meters! The windows tell a great deal about Dutch history as well as depicting events in the Bible and are definitely worth a visit for older children. Children from Spain or England will be interested to find the window which shows Philip II, King of Spain, and Mary Tudor, Queen of England.

There is an excellent descriptive pamphlet in English, French or German which should be purchased upon entering the church. Then, take the time to read the guide as you stand before the windows. The numbers in the pamphlet relate to individual windows which are clearly marked for easy reference. There is a notation in the beginning of the pamphlet advising which windows should be seen by visitors with little time at their disposal.

As mentioned earlier, the church is open on the evening of the Gouda Christmas Tree lighting, but this is not a good time to see the windows as the colors must be seen with light reflecting through them—preferaby on a bright, clear day.

The Catharina-Gasthuis Museum

LOCATION: Achter de Kerk 32 ("Behind the Church" street), or Oosthaven 10.

INFORMATION: Tel. (01820) 13800, ext. 269.
HOURS: Mon.-Sat., 10am-5pm; Sun. and public holidays, noon-5pm.
■ *Of interest to children from 8 years.*

There are two entrances to the Catharina-Gasthuis but the most atmospheric way to enter is via the small street which runs along the south side of St. Janskerk and which is really the back entrance. One crosses over a little bridge, then under a lovely ornamented gate, The Lazaruspoortje, through a charmingly planted garden and finally to the Museum entrance itself. If you feel like a cup of coffee or a coke before or after your visit, there is a partially subterranean restaurant (used to be the location for the hospital laboratory in olden days) just to the left of the entrance. It is called De Zes Sterren (the Six Stars) and has quite a history of its own since it is located in the oldest section of the building and dates from the 14th century.

The present building dates from 1542. In a sense, it is two buildings; the rear half being the older part which housed the Hospital proper, and the front half which was the Governor's Building (the Regent's building). It should be noted that originally a gasthuis was an old-peoples' home and not necessarily a hospital. The gasthuis of Gouda is known to have existed as early as 1310—it became a hospital sometime later and remained so until 1910.

The large and small sick wards are interesting, but even more so is the dispensary which leads off these rooms and which houses all sorts of equipment and supplies from mortar and pestle to herbs used for the treatment of various diseases. Point out to the children the tools which used to be necessary for pulling teeth and remind them how much better it is today! Another grisly scene is the large painting located in the Surgeon's Guild Room called the "Anatomy Lesson" by Chr. Coevershof. To make it more realistic, there is also a case containing old surgical instruments and a cupboard for storing the skeleton.

The girls will be particularly interested in the period rooms, the Gasthuis kitchen (which is extremely well furnished), the pantry cellar, and the special collection of dolls and antique toys dating from the 18th and 19th centuries. The boys, however, will much prefer the "torture" room. You can see a rack, and all sorts of terrible instruments of torture. One item looks like a huge wooden sawhorse and it seems a sinner was put astride this thing and then heavy weights were attached to his feet. There's another contraption for stretching the neck, etc.

These are just some of the highlights, but it is a fine museum with things of interest for the whole family.

Pipe, Pottery and Tile Museum "De Moriaan"

LOCATION: Westhaven 29, diagonally opposite the front entrance of the Catharina-Gasthuis.
INFORMATION: Tel. (01820) 13800, ext. 216.
HOURS: Fri., 10am-5pm, Sat., 10am-12:30pm and 1:30-5pm. Sun. and public holidays, 2-5pm.
■ *Of interest to children from 8 years.*

The building itself has historical significance and has been beautifully restored. Note the facade which dates from 1617. The building was originally used as a sugar refinery and later spices, coffee, tea and tobacco were sold here. It got its name "De Moriaan" during the time when tobacco was sold.

Upon entering the building, you will see an antique tobacco shop completely fitted with wall cupboards containing tobacco jars and tin boxes, and an antique wooden counter with the old ingredients of a shop. In the small room to the left as you enter, there are glass cases filled with pipes of all descriptions depicting the history of pipes of Gouda. There are tiles throughout the museum of many styles and designs—a good many dealing with pipes. In one of the back rooms, is the built-in strong box and some very interesting antique furniture. Take the small winding staircase upstairs and you will find yourself in a most charming room where an old pipemaker could have been working just a few days ago. There are old models of pipes, casting molds, cases, tobacco boxes, guild boxes, a mural board with pipemaker's trademarks, etc. There's yet another floor upstairs which has been made into a modern display hall for pottery of today.

You may ask questions of the person who shows you through the Museum or you may wander around on your own.

IN THE NEIGHBORHOOD OF GOUDA: To visit a cheese farm, call the Gouda VVV for their recommended addresses of those open to the public. For example, there is one at Kamerik, a village near Woerden (just off the A12 route, direction Utrecht) where visitors can make cheese. (Reservations at least 24 hrs. in advance.) The address is Kaas Boerderij Hoogendoorn, Mijzijde 6, Kamerik; tel. (03481) 1200; open daily from 8-9:30am, except on Sundays. Group visits can be arranged by appointment. English, French, and German spoken. Another possibility to see cheese being made is "De Driesprong," Zuidbroek 154, tel. (01826) 314 in Bergambacht, a little village south of Gouda. If you reserve, you can have a farmer's cheese lunch; moderate priced.

HAASTRECHT

Mrs. Van Vliet's beautiful 17th-century home

GETTING THERE: Take Highway A12 following the signs for Gouda. At Gouda, take the bridge crossing the IJssel River. Immediately after crossing, you will come to a large intersection with indications north, south and east. Haastrecht is on the road heading east . . . look for the signpost. There are buses from Gouda, Utrecht and other major cities.
INFORMATION: Tel. (01821) 1354.

This area which encompasses Gouda, Oudewater, Haastrecht, and the IJssel and Vlist rivers is exceptionally scenic . . . a lovely day's drive. The stop at Haastrecht is suggested because of the Museum Bisdom Van Vliet, described fully below.

Worth noting for canoe buffs and bikers, there's a Kanocentrum Haastrecht, east of town, offering a number of trips by canoe or in combination with biking.

Some canoe trips are 26 kilometers and take 6 hours; one is only 7 kilometers taking 4 hours. Or, you can do a trip from Haastrecht to Oudewater or Schoonhoven and back, 3 hours by canoe and 3 hours by bike. Call (01821) 2245 or write Julianalaan 2, 2851 XK Haastrecht for information.

Museum Bisdom Van Vliet

LOCATION: Hoogstraat 166. The museum is a large private-looking residence which will be on your left, coming from Gouda. Parking is difficult; you should go beyond the museum, turn left into the village and squirrel your way back looking for a likely parking spot . . . it's only a couple of blocks.
INFORMATION: See above.
HOURS: Open April 15-Oct. 15, Guided tours only, Tues.-Wed.-Thurs. and Sat. at 10:30am, noon, 1:30 and 3pm; Sun., 2pm and 3pm.
■ *Of interest to older children and adults.*

You might call this a sort of "non-museum" if there were such a word! Just a minute ago the lady of the house could have stepped out to go shopping. Everything is maintained just as it was when Mrs. Van Vliet was alive. The curators, Mr. and Mrs. Uenk, are very cordial and will guide you through the house, giving explanations in English, Dutch—and probably French and German as well.

Built between 1874 and 1877, the house was the official residence of the Mayor of Haastrecht, Bisdom Van Vliet.

The Van Vliet family has a long and interesting history but there were no sons or daughters to inherit so Mrs. Van Vliet decided the nicest memorial she could leave was to turn this lovely house with its treasures into a museum so others could see what a home of this style and period looked like. She stipulated that all must be maintained just as it was, and today, the visitor feels he is walking into someone's home—not into an institution. Mrs. Uenk might open one of the desk drawers upstairs and show you a slip of paper with groceries listed on it. Since the Van Vliet house was the richest and biggest in this area, there were often poor people coming to the door to ask for money. Mrs. Van Vliet didn't believe in giving away money which could be dissipated foolishly and not help a man's family. She made an arrangement with the local grocer, butcher, etc., which worked like this: When someone came to the door and asked for help, she would give him a paper listing items she felt his family really needed addressed to the grocer or whomever. Her signature was at the bottom. When the merchant had filled the order, he could then return the paper to Mrs. Van Vliet and she would pay the bill. Mrs. Van Vliet died in 1923.

The house is filled with treasures—some fine paintings, for instance—but the most impressive possession is the extraordinary collection of Chinese blue porcelain mounted on the walls of one room.

In the adjoining Coach House (1879), there is a craft museum, "Verlorg." The building is in the Renaissance and Baroque styles.

OUDEWATER

. . . and its witches weighing scale!

GETTING THERE: In the province of Utrecht, but just a few miles east of Gouda along the IJssel River.
INFORMATION: Oudewater VVV, Kapellestraat 5, tel. (03486) 1871.

Once a moated and fortified town, Oudewater received its citizens rights and town privileges in 1265. Its rich history is evident in its beautifully restored 17th-century houses with fancy gables and many charming bridges. This was a rope-making town and especially known for the honesty of its merchants. During the witch-hunting mania in the 16th century, Oudewater began to lose business because of its reputation for being overly enthusiastic in its persecution of witches. To solve their problem, the people of the town hit on the idea of weighing the persons accused of witchcraft. The accused would be put in the scales and it was up to the weighmaster to indicate whether or not they were too heavy to be able to fly on a broom! It is to the credit of the governors of those days that they always weighed honestly, although they believed in the existence of the evil influence of witches. Freed from a heavy burden and with their Certificate of Proof of Innocence of Witchcraft in hand, the victims would return home, pleased about keeping their lives and property.

In addition to the Weighing House, there is a historic Town Hall, destroyed by the Spaniards in 1575 and rebuilt in 1588. You may see the beautiful hall, council-chamber and Mayor's room by special appointment.

Look for the stork's nest on the roof of the Thalia Theater near the Town Hall; storks have been returning here to nest for over 300 years.

Dominating the skyline is the unique Friesian-style tower of St. Michael's Church, Noorder Kerkstraat 27, with saddle-back roof, visit by appointment. When it was restored in 1960, remains of a Roman church dating from 1100 were discovered.

The Weighing House - De Heksen Waag

LOCATION: Leeuweringerstraat 2, on the main street in Oudewater.
INFORMATION: Tel. (03486) 3400.
HOURS: April 1 to Oct. 30, Tues.-Sat., 10am-5pm. Sun., noon-5pm.
■ *Of interest to children 5 years to 95!*

This museum deals with the history of witch hunting, but the best part of the visit from the children's point of view is the weighing ceremony and the special Certificate of Proof of Innocence of Witchcraft which they will receive to take home.

SCHOONHOVEN
The "silver city"

GETTING THERE: From Amsterdam, one route would be south on A2 towards the Lek River, then take small road turning off the main highway just before crossing the Lek. The drive along the river is slow but very scenic. From The Hague, take A12 to the turnoff for Gouda. From Gouda, you might stop at Haastrecht enroute, then south along the Vlist River to Schoohoven. From Rotterdam, you can approach Schoonhoven along the Lek River, past Kinderdijk, and across the Lek by car ferry; or via Gouda and down the small country road bordering the Vlist River (slightly longer but lovely scenery). If you are not pressed for time, go one way and return the other.
INFORMATION: VVV Schoonhoven, tel. (01823) 5009. Hours open vary according to season. Usually, Tues.-Fri., 10am-noon or 2-5pm.

Famous for its silver artisans, Schoonhoven is no less noteworthy for its scenery and architecture.

If your approach to Schoonhoven is via the Lek River you will enter the town through the 17th-century Veerpoort, a narrow gateway through which kings, merchants, bishops and pilgrims have passed for hundreds of years. If you come from Gouda, you will pass through lovely polderland, farms and meadows, and your first view of the town will be St. Bartholomew's Church with its tower which leans 4½ feet; it was last restored in 1972. In the choir of this 13th-century place of worship is the tomb of Olivier van Noort, the first Dutchman to sail around the world. The Church can be visited in the summer on Wednesday and Saturday afternoons by contacting the sexton at 84 Haven.

As you thread your car along the narrow main street (north/south) bordering the town canal, you will find the Town Hall with a most unusual town square. The canal is directly in front of the Town Hall so a very wide bridge was constructed to form a square in order to provide the necessary space for the arrival of wedding parties or for other ceremonies. A not so happy occasion was when Marrigje Ariens, condemned as a witch, was burned at the stake—a circle of white and grey cobblestones on the bridge marks the spot.

The Town Hall, easily identifiable because of its hexagonal cupola tower and facade of white Goberting stone, was built in 1452 and renovated in 1775 and 1927. The VVV and an exhibition hall are located in an old peat cellar ("turfkelder"); see above for hours open. Ask for their flyer in English describing the places of special interest to visit and their useful map of the town with explanations in Dutch, French, German and English.

Schoonhoven was once a walled town with an inner and outer moat; the buttress located on Kortedijk,to the east of the ferry landing, dates from the 17th century. The only one remaining of five original gates built in 1601 is the charming Veerstraat Ferry Gate located at the southern (river) approach to the town. The first ferry-gate, called Veerstalpoort, was built about two hundred years earlier in 1396.

The Dutch Reformed Church at 84 Haven was built in 1354 as a cruciform church. In 1653, it was rebuilt in Doric style and after restorations in 1927 and 1935, it acquired its present appearance. The church can be visited on Wednesday 2-4pm, and Saturday from 2-5pm. Another interesting church is the Roman Catholic parish church at 23 Wal, which was built in 1873. Services are held on Saturdays at 7pm, and Sundays at 9 and 10:30am.

The Assay Office on the Doelenplein, not far from the Clock Museum, is also worth noting. Built in 1780, the building was later used as a shooting range for the militia, accommodations for the civil guard, an inn, boarding-school and canton court. On December 26, 1813, King Willem I enacted provisions ensuring Schoonhoven the right of assay for gold and silverware. From 1908-1984, it was the Assay Office.

The Weigh House on the Dam, tel. 2959, is now used as a pancake restaurant during the summer season . . . closed Mondays. Facilities for weighing products were offered by Jan Van Blois in 1356 and the first weigh house was built between 1616 and 1617. The stone pillars were added in 1756. The weighing rights were farmed out to burghers (citizens) for a few florins per year. Agricultural products, such as hemp which was grown locally, were the primary items weighed here.

A commercial silver shop, A Rikkoert & Zonen, Haven 5 and Toll 11, has a wide selection of gift items for sale as well as a superior collection of antique silver. Demonstrations of silver-making for small groups can be arranged at Lapidary "Gemma," 52 Haven, tel. 5747. Another old workshop, the St. Andreshuis, 28 Oude Haven, tel. 5827, will demonstrate how filigree is made; the shop specializes in making authentic buttons from Zeeland. Open weekdays, 10am-12:30pm, and 1:30-5pm. Closed Sundays.

EATING OUT: A nice restaurant for lunch, dinner or just a cup of coffee is the Belvedere Restaurant on the dike overlooking the Lek River. Another recom-

85

mended restaurant in town is de Hooyberch. There is also a wide range of coffeeshops.

The Gold, Silver and Clock Museum

LOCATION: Haven Kazerne, Oude Haven 7.
INFORMATION: Tel. (01823) 5612.
HOURS: Tues.-Sat., 10am-5pm. Sundays and holidays, 1-5pm.
   Closed Mondays.
■ *Of interest to school-age children.*

This interesting collection is housed in a former barracks, built in 1861 on the site of an earlier structure, the St. Elizabeth Convent dating from 1412.

Among its treasures, the museum boasts of clocks spanning five centuries, among them the oldest turret clock (Gothic) in the Netherlands, and a particularly beautiful collection of Dutch silver dating from 1650. This museum combines the old collection of timepieces of the Dutch Company of Clock- and Watchmakers with the collection of antique silver, hallmarks and guildhall documents of the Dutch Assay Office.

On the first floor, clocks from the Dark Ages to the present outline the development of this craft. The 18th century was the Golden Age of clockmaking in Europe. Some fine examples are to be found of the Frisian stool-clock, the Amsterdam longcase clock, the English bracketclock, and the French pendule.

The gold and silver departments are on the second floor with special attention being given to the 19th century.

Museum of Antique Silverware (Edelambachtshuis)

LOCATION: Haven 13.
INFORMATION: Tel. (01823) 2614, ext. 2651.
HOURS: Mon., 1:30-5pm, Tues.-Sat., 10am-5pm, closed Sunday.
■ *Of interest to school-age children.*

When a former synagogue along the town canal was restored in 1983, a museum with the largest collection of antique Schoonhoven silver from its "Golden Era" to 1948 was established. The crafting of fine silverware at Schoonhoven was well known for centuries, spreading the fame of this small "Silver City" even beyond Holland's borders. The first two floors of the museum are devoted to an enormous and unique collection of old Dutch silver objects. There is also an extensive collection of present-day gold, silver and jewelry on display, and a replica of an old workshop where a silversmith demonstrates how silver is crafted. For details, check with the Schoonhoven VVV.

A state school for gold and silversmiths, jewelers, clockmakers and engravers has been established here. There are at present 850 students.

IN THE NEIGHBORHOOD OF SCHOONHOVEN:
If you have a 1,200,000 scale map from the ANWB, you will note that there

are many green markings indicating scenic roadways along the Hollandse IJssel, the Vlist and the Lek rivers—all within easy exploring distance. Gouda, Oudewater, and Schoonhoven are centrally situated in this flat polderland, a land of water and meadows, surrounded by willow trees, small lanes alongside winding creeks, narrow roads running on tops of dikes and nice as well as ugly villages. You might follow the winding road along the Lek River towards Vreeswijk where you can look for a good spot to enjoy a picnic and visit the Princess Beatrix Locks, one of the largest lock gates in Europe. It is here the Amsterdam Rijn Canal joins the Lek River. You can see the boats going through and the lock gates working at very close quarters which is extremely interesting. The drive to the locks along the northern dike of the Lek from Schoonhoven is very beautiful.

KINDERDIJK

Nineteen working windmills

LOCATION: Along the Lek River, southeast of Rotterdam (east of IJsselmonde and north of Alblasserdam).
INFORMATION: Tel. (078) 132800 VVV Dordrecht, Stationsweg 1.
HOURS: The mills work on Saturday afternoons from 1:30-5:30pm during July and August. From April to October, a windmill is open daily. One can see them at any time during the year, of course. They are illuminated the second week of September, Mon.-Sat., every year. There are tours of the windmill area by open boat (only in good weather).
■ *Of interest to all ages.*

Kinderdijk really doesn't need much introduction. A visit here is included on almost all the tours that cover the area and is probably one of the first places a new arrival will visit. Still, it is nice to have a little background information as well as to know when the windmills are in operation.

There is a legend about the name of this area. It appears that following the very destructive and traumatic St. Elizabeth's Flood of 1421, a crying baby and a meowing cat in a cradle were washed ashore at this point and thereby saved from drowning. From then on, the area was known as Kinderdijk—"kinder" means "childs" in Dutch. Of course this is only a legend. The second (probably true) story is that the dike alongside the river was built by the children of the families who lived in the village of Giessen.

Plan your visit—if at all possible—for a Saturday during July and August between 1:30pm and 5:30pm. These are the "Windmill days" when, if the wind and water are suitable, the windmill banks of the Nederwaard and Overwaard (upper and lower polder) which are normally closed to visitors, will be opened. The 19 mills in the area, which usually work only in times of emergency, and the Wip watermill of Blokweer, will be put into operation, and the second mill of the Nederwaard will be open to visitors. Of course, it is possible to pass this area by driving along the Lek (on top of the dike) and see the windmills any day of the year.

There is a special note in the VVV information pamphlet about these windmills that on "other weekdays as well as on Saturdays" the above-mentioned mill can be visited on payment of a small fee. If a group desires to see it in operation for 30 minutes, this can be arranged by calling (01859) 14118.

In addition to walking around the windmill area, during the summer months, one can take advantage of a pleasant open-air boat tour among the mills which departs every half hour (for a modest fee).

DORDRECHT

Where three rivers meet

GETTING THERE: Dordrecht is served by A16 (via Brienenoord Bridge) from the north, A15 from the east and A16 from the south.
INFORMATION: VVV Dordrecht (078) 132800.

In Dordrecht one can find the old and the new, including plenty of new ideas. Take a look at the modern City Hall for a starter— inside you will see the works of young contemporary artists from Dordrecht, including a vivid red ceramic wall which was done by an American working in Dordrecht.

Dordrecht's earliest beginnings go back to 837 A.D., but it wasn't until Count Dirk III built a castle here in 1010 that a town began. The Count and the town prospered because they controlled the river traffic and could levy tolls from passing ships. Upon receiving their town rights in 1220 from Count William I, "Dordt" (as it is familiarly known) became the first town of Holland. In 1572, an assembly of the twelve towns comprising the first Free States Assembly was held here under authority of William of Orange. It marked the beginning of the Eighty Years' War with Spain. In this same time period, Dordrecht was the most important and powerful town in the country.

Anyone interested in Dutch architecture, ancient gables and historic carvings should wander around the inland harbor to see the many beautiful houses and warehouses built in the 17th and 18th centuries. An interesting story is told about No. 18 Engelenburgerkade, "Het Bever-Schaep" (the Beaver-Sheep) house. Three brothers made a wager to see who could build the most beautiful house with the most controversial decorations. The first brother presented a mermaid on display who possessed an uncomplicated love for her mate for more than three centuries. The second brother built his house in the Wijnstraat (Wine Street) and he displayed a statue of a young naked boy in front of his house . . . the residence became known as "De Onbeschaamde" (the Impudent). The third brother won the wager. He decorated his house on the Grotekerksplein (Large Church Square) with something so indecent that the people had no desire to preserve it . . . nor do they say what that "something" was!

Notice the charming sayings on various gables, such as, "inde weelde siet toe" (When you're well off, take care). De Sleutel (the Key), Groenmarkt 31, was built in 1540. Don't miss the "Hof," historic square in the city center, and the States Hall where the Free States Assembly met.

Dordrecht was known as the Wine Town until late in the 17th century; it never produced wine, but under the Staple Rights received from Count Jan I, all wine brought to Holland by ship had to be first unloaded in Dordrecht . . . even French and German wines.

Some well-known natives of Dordrecht include the brothers Cornelius and Johan de Witt (murdered in The Hague), and artists Ferdinand Bol, Albert and Jacob Cuyp and Nicholaes Maes.

Dordrecht's Great Church (Grote Kerk, 15th century) with its square, slightly leaning, grey tower, can be seen for miles. In summer, the church is open from about May-September, Tues.-Sat., 10:30am-4:30pm, Sun., noon-4pm (small entrance fee). The rest of the year, tours are given the first and second Saturday of each month at 10:30am. The interior with its white marble pulpit (1756) and gleaming bronze screen, keep it light and cheerful. Look for the Renaissance choir stalls, built between 1539-1542 which predate the time the Church became Protestant, and the stained glass window showing the disaster of the great flood of 1421. And climb the Tower for wonderful views.

Another view-point, from the Groothoofd (Large Head's Gate) where the Merwede and the Oude Maas rivers meet, is said to be the busiest river junction in the world; located at the northern end of the Wijnstraat. Dordrecht is also very proud of its beautiful almshouse, the Arend Maartenshofje, where little old ladies have always lived (entrance Museumstraat). Nothing has changed since 1625. Two outstanding museums in town are the Museum Mr. Simon Van Gijn and the Dordrechts Museum, described below.

EATING OUT: To complete the day, why not go out to lunch or dinner? On the waterfront there is an excellent restaurant in the Bellevue Hotel, Boomstraat 37, tel. (078) 137900. It is quite expensive, but the Coffeeshop has moderate prices, and the same impressive view. It is said 1,500 ships pass this point every day. Obviously, children are enchanted by the view.

COMMERCIAL TOURS: For information about the various boat trips, boat and bike rentals, city sightseeing tours, parks and recreation areas, etc., check with the VVV. Their monthly publication lists all that is going on. Movies are listed under "Films," and activities at the Grote Kerk, museums and art galleries can be found under "Tentoonstellingen."

Simon Van Gijn Museum

LOCATION: Nieuwe Haven 29. (Ring the bell for admittance)
INFORMATION: Tel. (078) 133793.
HOURS: Open Tues.-Sat., 10am-5pm, Sundays 1-5pm. Closed Mon-
days, Christmas Day and New Year's Day. The Toy Section is
only open on Wed., Sat. and Sun. Children free on Wednesdays.
■ *Of interest to school-age children*

The Simon Van Gijn Museum is located on a canal in a most attractive and ancient part of Dordrecht. It dates from 1729 and was a gift to the city from Mr. Van Gijn, a prominent banker in town. The house contains a number of delightful period rooms which are beautifully furnished in various styles. There is, for instance, a Louis XIV drawing room, a neo-Renaissance dining room and a study and kitchen of around 1800.

Children would be most interested in the superb collection of antique toys, model ships, arms, coins and medals (see special hours, above). In addition, there are tapestries, costumes, guild silver, antique furniture, glass, clocks, pottery and china. Other exhibits include a selection of local antiquities, while a unique collection of 24,000 prints and drawings is available for inspection upon request.

Dordrecht Art Gallery (Dordrechts Museum)

LOCATION: Museumstraat 40.
INFORMATION: Tel. (078) 134100.
HOURS: Open Tues.-Sat., 10am-5pm; Sundays and holidays, 1-5pm.
Closed Christmas Day and New Year's Day.
■ *Of interest to school-age children.*

The collection consists mainly of Dutch paintings (many from the Dordrechts School) dating from the beginning of the 17th century to the present time. The paintings from the 17th century include a collection by well-known pupils of Rembrandt, such as— Ferdinand Bol, Aert de Gelder and Nicolaes Maes—in addition to works by Aelbert Cuyp, Jan van Goyen and Samuel v. Hoogstraten. Artists representing the 18th and 19th centuries are: A. H. Bakker Korff, D. Bes, G. H. Breitner, J. Bosboom, H. J. T. Fantin Latour, Vincent van Gogh, Joseph Israels, B. C. Koekkoek, J., M. and W. Maris (three brothers), A. Mauve, A. Scheffer, A. Schelfhout, A. Schouman, C. Springer, A. and J. van Strij, Fl. Verster, J. and J. H. Weissenbruch, etc. Among the better-known names representing the 20th century, one will find Alechinsky, Appel, Chabot, Constant, Corneille, Israels, J. Sluijters, etc.

HEINENOORD

Location of an 18th-century farm residence and estate

GETTING THERE: Heinenoord is south of Rotterdam on A29 at the southern end of the Heinenoord Tunnel. Following autoroutes to Rotterdam, cross the Maas River either at the Maas Tunnel (A13 to A29) or over the Brienenoord Bridge (A16) then west on A15. From the east, A15 west; from the south, A29 north.
INFORMATION: Rotterdam VVV, tel. (010) 413 6000 or tel. below.

This quiet area between Rotterdam and Dordrecht, two commercially active cities, is more similar to the open lands, never-ending skies and salubrious atmosphere of Zeeland. The island of the Hoeksche Waard is primarily agricultural land, and benefits as well from the recreational facilities which have developed around its neighboring island, Voorne-Putten. Close by, there's a nature preserve and bird sanctuary. The recreational area, Mijnsheerenland, is just a few kilometers south.

Streek Museum Hoeksche Waard

LOCATION: Hofweg 13. As you exit the Heinenoord Tunnel, take the 's-Gravendael turnoff then follow signs. In the village, keep a sharp eye out for the left-hand turn with sign, "Streek Museum." Ample parking.
INFORMATION: Tel. (01862) 1535, or VVV Rotterdam, see above.
HOURS: The house is open Tues.-Fri., 2-5pm. The farm is open Sat., 10am-noon and 2-5pm. Closed Sundays and Mondays. If you call 2-3 days ahead, an English-language guide will show you around.
■ *Of interest to children from 6 years.*

't Hof van Assendelft is a lovely former private residence and meeting place for the rent collectors and polder officials of the surrounding area. Some rooms have been restored to reflect the style of the period . . . primarily those on the ground floor. The house itself dates from 1768. Look for the small window giving a view from the second room you visit into the kitchen. The guide said, in former days the wall bed was situated in that corner of the room and the window permitted the lady of the house to supervise the housemaid working in the kitchen right from her bed! (Now this room houses a collection of antique toys.)

The first room you visit is called the Polder Kamer. This was where the Government officials met to deal with administrative matters of importance to the District. On the walls you will see large panels depicting the Greek-Turkish War of 1820; this type of wall decoration was not unusual in wealthy farmers' homes . . . you can see similar decorative panels in the little house which has now been fitted out as an old bakery—more about that later.

In 't Hof van Assendelft, you will see a very complete and interesting kitchen, including the wine cellar. Just off the kitchen, the former stable is now used as a display room for old sleds and all sorts of farm implements and machinery.

Upstairs there are several model rooms with live-looking dummies dressed in various types of dress, a collection of old tobacco pouches, pipes, ladies' lace caps, old sewing machines, sewing baskets, ironing press, a collection of doctors' tools, old watches, old eyeglasses, and so on. One interesting item is a "clacker" from about 1800. During the night someone would go throughout the town signaling the time with the clacker. Also on this floor, you will see some modern art shows displaying work of local artists.

The attic is one of the most interesting parts of this museum. It has been fitted to resemble a town square. There is the town pump in the middle of the room, a dummy-lady with her water buckets, and surrounding this town square you will peer into the lighted windows of several reconstructed former shops.

On Saturdays, you will also probably see a number of volunteers working hard cataloguing, cataloguing, cataloguing. What are they doing? They are trying to trace the histories of families who have lived on this island—14 villages—from the year 1500 to the present day.

You have now seen the first building of the Streek Museum, but there is more to tempt you. Take your car through the village (back the way you came in) to the second building of the Museum:

De Hofstede Oost Leeuwenstein—a lovely old farmhouse and barn. The house itself is occupied and not open to tourists but the barn is outfitted similarly to 't Hof van Assendelft.

At the entrance to the barn, an old shop built in 1911 and actually in operation until 1970 in Oud-Beijerland, has been transported intact.

Across from the barn is another small house—the bakery. A peek into the room next to the bakery will show you more panels decorating the walls similar to those you saw earlier.

IN THE NEIGHBORHOOD OF HEINENOORD:

Not far away, in the recreation area at Mijnsheerenland (south of Heinenoord a few kilometers), there is a café-restaurant worth mentioning: Binnemaas, tel. (01862) 1629; an attractive place with good food at reasonable prices.

BRIELLE (Den Briel)

First town liberated from Spanish occupation (1572)

GETTING THERE: Brielle is on N218, bordered by the North Sea (west), the Haringvliet (south) and parallel waters (including the Maas River) approaching Rotterdam. From the north, take A13 to Maas Tunnel then first left towards Rozenburg (signs "Pernis") and Brielle. From the east, A15; from the south, A29 to Barendrecht, then A15 west, or N57 north.

INFORMATION: VVV Brielle, Venkelstraat 3, tel. (01810) 13333.

This small town has an interesting past and still retains some vestiges of its original walls, fortifications, old residences, etc. An important historical event is celebrated on April 1st. It was on this day in 1572, that the Gueux ("water beggars" or pirates) who were encouraged financially and otherwise by Dutch nobles and burgers opposed to the Spanish occupation and religious intolerance successfully routed the Spanish from the town. This first victory became the signal for renewed battles throughout the land against the oppressors who had occupied the Netherlands soon after Philip II inherited the territory and became King of Spain.

Today, the town is best known as a water sports center because of its proximity to the Briellse Meer. There is a small museum in the old weigh house, dealing with the town's history and honoring Admiral Tromp, a native son. The Trompmuseum, Venkelstraat 3, tel. 3333, since opening times vary, call ahead or check with the VVV.

A visit can also be made to St. Catharijnekerk (15th century) where William of Orange married his third wife, Carlotte de Bourbon.

Golfers might like to try the 18-hole public course, "Kleiburg," Krabbeweg 9, tel. (01810) 17336 for reservations.

One of our favorite family beaches is located south of Brielle at Rockanje (see Chapter 14).

YEARLY EVENTS: Mark your calendars for April 1st if you like local historic festivals. The town will be decorated "to the nines" presenting a Medieval setting for the many stalls displaying old crafts (chiseling wooden shoes, weaving chair bottoms, wool spinning, etc.). The aroma of roasting meat comes from the Dutch barbecue set up in the center of the town. In the afternoon, actors dressed in the style of the times reenact the battle with the Spaniards. No traffic in town but parking places well indicated on the outskirts.

CHAPTER 3

THE PROVINCE OF NORTH HOLLAND

North Holland encompasses the arm of land bordered by the North Sea on the west, the IJsselmeer on the east, as far north as the island of Texel, and south including Schiphol Airport.

The Province of North Holland is rich in many treasures: its natural beauty includes great sandy beaches, lakes of all sizes and ancient woodlands; its fine historical buildings and world-class museums can be found in small towns as well as big cities; there is recreation for all ages; sports opportunities as well as cultural offerings abound; and it is the site of Holland's international airport, Schiphol. All of these things and more can be discovered while "roaming 'round" North Holland.

In its early history, the west coast of Holland was considerably smaller in territory than today. The main towns of importance were Haarlem, Hoorn and Amsterdam . . . the rest were villages surrounded by marshlands and islands. Still mostly below sea level, the land has been greatly enlarged through extensive land reclamation. Amsterdam is the foremost city with an emphasis on politics, international finance, and port activities. In addition, since the 17th century, it has been the hub of artistic and cultural activity with a tradition of tolerance and hospitality.

INFORMATION: VVV-i Amsterdam, tel. (020) 266444.

AMSTERDAM

GETTING THERE: From The Hague or Rotterdam, the quickest way is via Highway A4.
INFORMATION: Amsterdam VVV, Stationsplein 10 or Leidsestraat 106. Daily from 9am-5:30pm. In the summer, the Central Station office is also open until midnight; tel. (020) 266444.

Amsterdam's history begins sometime in the 12th century (or perhaps even before)—a swampy area on the edge of the Old Zuider Zee and the Amstel River. Count Floris V granted Amsterdam her city charter in 1275; she became a member of the Hanseatic League in 1369. The people were seafarers, tough and ambitious . . . they went as far as Portugal for salt and the Baltic for wood. The city, built on piles, took on its unique character and shape when the city fathers decided to build three principal semi-circular canals; in all, there are at least 100 canals crossed by over 1,000 bridges. A town of immigrants, it reached its Golden Age in the 17th century with the influx of many talented artists, artisans and businessmen fleeing the rigors of Spanish rule in Belgium and the south. Prosperity knew no bounds as is reflected in the elegant patrician houses and great warehouses along Amsterdam's canals. Amsterdam was a storehouse of international goods, with a great merchant and banking class which grew and helped support the artistic and cultural life that was unsurpassed in Europe at the time.

Amsterdam—and most of Holland—suffered under Spanish rule (16th century), French rule (Napoleonic period, 1795-1814), and the German occupation (WW II, 1940-1945). It has an active stock exchange, and is a diamond-cutting center, as well as a busy port and air traffic center. In addition, it is a city of great tolerance which is reflected in the number of young people who flock here from all over the world to breathe the atmosphere! The Amsterdamer has a great sense of humor and loves elegance. In fact, ask a Dutchman how he would rate the three big cities of Holland and ten-to-one, he would say: "Rotterdam is the city to work in; The Hague is the city to live in; but Amsterdam is the city to play in."

The first stop for visitors should be the VVV for information and current brochures listing what's going on; some are free, some for sale. If you plan on visiting Amsterdam often, buy a good large-scale map—you won't regret the investment. Ask also about the various ways to tour Amsterdam. You can see it by canal boat, by bicycle, and so forth.

Bike Tours are available through the VVV (two tours through typical landscape . . . Fl. 2.75 each) . . . You will soon note this is the way the Dutch get around and if you are secure on wheels, 20 or 30 minutes gently pedaling will make you feel a real part of the scene. A 70 km bike ride (starts behind Central Station) takes you as far as the small village of Monnickendam and return.

WALKING TOURS: And for those who like to keep their feet on the ground, there are 7 VVV walking tours. Brochures are available in four languages and take you through different parts of the city center. The different walks include:

"Architecture as Sculpture in Amsterdam South" which emphasizes typical Amsterdam architecture between 1915 and 1925; "The Jewish Walking Tour of Amsterdam"; "Voyage of Discovery through Amsterdam"; "A Walk through the Jordaan," an area famous for its gables, cafes, bars, shops, architecture and history; "Sculptures of Amsterdam I and II"; and "Maritime Amsterdam."

To help the tourist on foot, Amsterdam has instituted a series of sign posts at strategic points downtown which show a map of the area and give directional signs to the important tourist attractions, museums and public buildings in the vicinity. The locations of these maps are marked on the VVV Tourist Information pamphlet (downtown map and restaurant guide). Look for them; they will help you.

Another aid to the tourist are the special tram/bus/metro tickets which one can buy for the day . . . just ask the tram or bus driver (enter by front door) for a day ticket in Dutch, i.e., "dag kart." Tickets for several days can be obtained from the Central Station at Leidseplein or at the Amstel Station. With the day ticket, you can travel all day into night. A regular tram ticket allows you to travel for one hour. For more information about the public transportation system in Amsterdam, pick up the tram/bus/metro "Welcome" folder put out by GVB Amsterdam Municipal Transport at ticket/info points. In season (mid-April-Sept.), there is a 70-minute tram ride through the historic center of Amsterdam, with commentary in various languages . . . free snack. Ask for tickets for "Touristram" from VVV. This tour can be combined with "Museum-boat" tour.

There are two towers with interesting histories.

The Cryer's Tower (Schrijerstoren), located at the corner of Prins Hendrik and Geldersekade, was part of an old wall around the town where sailors' wives came to wave goodbye to their husbands as they sailed for parts unknown. Look for the bronze plaque put up by the Greenwich Village Historical Society commemorating the spot where Henry Hudson departed on the Half Moon, April 4, 1609, heading for Nieuw Amsterdam, today's New York.

The Mint Tower (Muntplein) was a city gate tower until 1672 when the French occupiers determined to have money previously minted in Utrecht printed here.

■ **The Beguijnehof** is centrally located in the heart of the busiest shopping area on the Spui. The 164 small houses for lay sisters open into a courtyard bright with flowers and strangely peaceful in spite of the hubbub just over the walls. In 1346, the Sisters of St. Begga came to Amsterdam from a nearby village to found a religious community. They built their own small houses instead of living in a monastery or cloister, but they had to abide by strict rules: sober manner, simple living and dress, no men allowed at night, no animals to disturb the peace; they were to engage in charitable works and they were not allowed to spend the night away from home. All was well until the Reformation; in 1578 their church was confiscated and in 1607 it was turned over to the English Reformed (Presbyterian) Community. The Sisters were allowed to remain but since Catholicism was forbidden, they had to practice their religion in secrecy. At first mass was held clandestinely in different houses until 1655 when the parish priest bought two adjoining houses and converted them into a permanent chapel for the Beguines. It became one of the "House Churches" (see also Amstelkring Museum), a hidden place of worship. The present Catholic Chapel is the unobtrusive structure across from the English Church.

As indicated, the English Church, dedicated in 1419, was the original chapel of the Beguines. Two serious fires—1421 and 1452—damaged the structure severely and it was rebuilt in more elaborate form. In the passing years, other innovations have been made. The flags on display are interesting; there are the flags of the Scottish Church, the Union Jack, the Orange Flag, and the American Flag. The latter as well as the stained glass window over the exit of the choir were presented by the Pilgrim Fathers Society. Church services in English are held every Sunday. Reputedly, the oldest house in Amsterdam is No. 34 dating from 1475. Front and back gables are made of wood and the wooden interior skeleton is Gothic (hence the name "Houten Huis," wooden house). When it was restored, a beautiful painting was found on one of the wooden partitions. Just after the Reformation, the house was used as a chapel for the Beguines and even a hospital ward.

In time, those living in the Beguinage were no longer lay sisters; today, they are primarily self-supporting single women of strong moral character. Visit the Orientation Center at House No. 35 for details about the facades, gable stones and history.

MUSEUMS: Amsterdam is said to have over 40 museums . . . a few too many for all to be included here. We will discuss below the three major museums: the Rijksmuseum, Van Gogh Museum, and Stedelijk Museum (Modern Art Museum). They will be followed by the Amsterdam Historical Museum, Anne Frank House, Rembrandt House, Amstelkring Museum, Netherlands Shipping Museum, the Aviodome (Air Museum) and the Wax Museum. Also described in detail are the Nieuwe Kerk (New Church) where the Queen's investiture took place, the Zoo and the Zeiss Planetarium. Other museums of special note are listed below . . . for the resident there are even more to be discovered "on his own."

■ Avid museum-goers should avail themselves of a Museum Card permitting entry to 16 museums in Amsterdam alone. Available from the VVV, the cards are good for one year. Most museums in Amsterdam are open Mon.-Sat., 10am-5pm, Sundays and holidays, 1-5pm. There are exceptions, so do check.

Of interest to boat lovers is a museum boat tour which would make getting culturally indoctrinated much more palatable to the family than going by tram. It has the advantage of giving everyone's feet a rest and the chance to breathe fresh air in between museums. From April through September, a special canal boat operates a transport service between the Anne Frank House, Madame Tussaud's, Amsterdam Historical Museum, Rijksmuseum, Rembrandt House, Maritime Museum and the pier in front of the VVV Tourist Office at the Central Station.

Allard Pierson Museum: 127 Oude Turfmarkt, Trams 4, 9, 16, 24, 25, tel. 525 2556; open Tues.-Fri., 10am-5pm, Sat. and Sun., 1-5pm. The highlight of this museum is a Roman house with an exhibition of furniture depicting the way of life in ancient Pompeii . . . Greek, Egyptian and Roman antiquities.

Jewish Historical Museum: Jonas Daniël Meijerplein 2-4, Metro., tel. 269945; open Mon.-Sun., 11am-5pm. Closed Yom Kippur. Religion and life of the Jews in Holland since 1600.

The Royal Palace: Dam Square, Trams 1, 2, 4, 5, 9, 13, 17, 24, 25, tel. 248698; only open during the summer months (check w/VVV). State rooms are impressive; of note are the main reception hall, the galleries and the courtroom.

Resistance Museum (Verzetsmuseum): 63 Lekstraat, Trams 4, 25; open Tues.-Fri., 10am-5pm, Sat., Sun. and holidays, 1-5pm.

Botanical Garden of the University of Amsterdam: 2 Plantage Middenlaan, Tram 9; open, Mon.-Fri., 9am-4pm, Sat., Sun. and holidays, 1-4pm.

Botanical Garden of the Vrije Univesiteit: 8 Van der Boechorststraat, Buses 171, 172; open Mon.-Fri., 8am-4:30pm, Closed Sat., Sun., public holidays, Dec. 25, Jan. 1.

Willet Holthuysen Museum, 605 Herengracht, tel. 264290, Trams 4 and 9; open Mon.-Sun., 11am-5pm. 17-18th-century patrician mansion with lovely garden.

Museum Van Loon, 672 Keizersgracht, tel. 245255, Trams 16, 24, 25; only open Mondays, 10am-5pm. 17-18th-century canal house with furnishings and French-style garden.

Theater Institute, 166 Herengracht, tel. 235104, Trams 13, 17; open Tues.-Sun. and holidays, 11am-5pm. Located in three beautiful canal houses, relates history of Dutch theater.

Shipyard 't Kromhout and Dockyard Museum, 147 Hoogte Kadijk, tel. 276777, Bus 22; open Mon.-Sat., 10am-4pm, Sun. 1-4pm. Exhibition and demonstration of 19th-century shipbuilding.

Fodor Museum, 609 Keizersgracht, tel. 249919, Trams 16, 24, 25; open Mon.-Sun., 11am-5pm. Exhibitions by contemporary artists, including Americans.

Geological Institute of the University of Amsterdam, 130 Nieuwe Prinsengracht, tel. 522 2830, Metro; open Mon.-Fri., 9am-5pm. Fossils, minerals and geological models.

Tropical Museum (Tropenmuseum), 2 Linnaeusstraat, tel. 568 8200, Tram 9 or Bus 22; open Mon.-Fri., noon-5pm, Sat., Sun. and holidays, 2-5pm. Ethnographical collections.

Film Museum, Paviljoen Vondelpark 3, tel. 831646, Trams 1, 2, 5; open Mon.-Fri., 10am-5pm. Exhibits and film shows.

Netherlands Institute for Industry and Technology, 129 Tolstraat, tel. 664 6021, Tram 4; open Mon.-Fri., 10am-4pm, Sat., Sun. and holidays, 1-5pm. Exhibitions dealing with modern technology (energy, telecommunications, computers), especially designed to interest young people.

National Money Box Museum (Spaarpotten Museum), 20 Raadhuisstraat, tel. 221066, Trams 13, 17; open Mon.-Fri., 1-4pm. 12,000 money boxes from all over the world.

Electric Tram Museum, Amstelveenseweg 264, tel. 272727. Departs from 44 Karperweg behind the Haarlemmermeer Station or the Amstelveen Station in Amsterdam to the Amsterdam woods. Operates on weekends in summer. The trains were built between about 1910 and 1950 and come from cities like Amsterdam, The Hague, Rotterdam, Groningen, Kassel (Germany) and Vienna (Austria). They have the original wooden seats, colored destination boards, and a conductor who walks up and down the aisle selling tickets. All members of the museum tramway are volunteers; they restore the cars and maintain the tracks.

■ Plans are in the works for an exciting new attraction to be completed in the 1990s. A historical, nautical district will be constructed in the harbor area near the Maritime Museum (1 Kattenburgerplein) and on either side of the IJ Tunnel pier (Prins Hendrikkade). So pedestrians can easily view the historic crafts gathered here, new piers will be constructed. Berthed at the Maritime Museum will be a special treat; a 3-masted replica of an East India Company 18th-century Dutch merchant ship.

CHURCHES: The city's historic churches shouldn't be overlooked either. The Nieuwe Kerk (New Church) is described in detail below. In addition:

The Oude Kerk (Old Church), 23 Oudekerksplein, tel. 249183, is within walking distance of the Central Station. Built between 1300 and 1566, it is the oldest parish church in Amsterdam. Between May and September it is possible to climb the Tower for one of the best views in town. Organ recitals are often given (summer).

The Westerkerk (West Church), 279 Prinsengracht, Trams 13, 17, tel. 247766. Rembrandt is buried here; this tower can also be climbed from June-September.

Zuiderkerk (Southern Church), Zandstraat, Tram 9 and Metro, tel. 552 2255. Built between 1603 and 1614, its architect, Hendrik de Keyser, is buried here. The tower can be climbed between June and September.

There's a full-blown discussion of theaters, the symphony, dance, etc., in Chapter 17, but it should be noted here that Amsterdam has a full gourmet selection of cultural activities which can be booked directly at the theaters or through the VVV Box Office, Stationsplein 10, open Mon.-Sat., 10am-4pm . . . not by phone.

■ **Artis Zoo,** 40 Plantage Kerklaan, tel (020) 231836; open all year from 9am-5pm (summer 'til 9:30pm): Tram 9 or Bus 56. The zoo has more than 6,000 animals, including 2,000 fish in the largest aquarium in Holland; dozens of penguins, a house for nocturnal animals called the "Twilight World"; and a beautiful hippo house which also has tapirs and manatees!

Amsterdam's Zoo is unique among zoos—one can arrive by boat at their own landing dock. Regular service is possible from Woltheus Cruises in Zaandam (Prins Hendrikkade) Mon., Tues. and Wed., leaving at 10am and returning by 4pm. The route takes you via the Zaan, the North Sea canal and the IJ, through some of Amsterdam's canals to the back entrance of the zoo. Check with the Zaandam VVV, Gedempte Gracht 76, tel. (075) 162221 for specifics.

The Zeiss Planetarium moved to Artis Zoo in 1988, same address and telephone as above. Hours in summer, daily, 9:30am-5:30pm; other times, Wed. noon-5:30pm; Sat., Sun. and school holidays, 9:30am-5:30pm. What could be more interesting than star-gazing and space travel? While you sit comfortably in your seat, the stars shine brightly as they would on the clearest night. In just a few moments, the moon will go through its various phases as day changes to night. The large Zeiss projector in the middle of the room looks like a veritable robot and is a technical miracle made up of more than 29,000 elements. With this instrument, it is possible to imitate reality in the most minute details.

SHOPPING: Amsterdam is a shopper's delight. One can shop for diamonds, modern art, antiques, and "little treasures" at open-air markets. Even the kids will enjoy a visit to the diamond merchant—their natural fascination with anything that glitters will surely hold their attention. Amsterdam's diamond industry began in 1586 and has been flourishing ever since in large part because of the fine craftsmen working here. The largest diamond in the world, the Cullinan, weighing over half a kilogram, was cut by Jac Asscher, and the largest of the stones is now in the sceptre of the British Crown Jewels. Some reliable establishments with guided tours are the Amsterdam Diamond Center, 1-5 Rokin, tel. 245787; Coster Diamonds, 2-4 Paulus Potterstraat, tel. 762222; Van Moppes Diamonds, 2-6 Albert Cuypsstraat, tel. 761242, or A.S. Bonebakker, 86 Rokin, tel. 232294.

The VVV puts out a packet of five shopping guides in Dutch (all 5, Fl. 10) giving a selection of the best addresses, routes, and maps entitled "Amsterdam Markets"; "Looking for Art and Antiques"; "Looking for Smart and Chic"; "Around the Canals"; and "Around the Jordaan." The busy shopping areas are found along the Kalverstraat, Nieuwendijk and Leidsestraat as well as many small shops along the canals in the Jordaan district.

MARKETS: Historically, antiques have been sold near important museums so explore the P. C. Hoofstraat and Van Baerlestraat near the Rijksmuseum . . . also the Spiegelgracht and the Rokin.

Sotheby's of London has regular auctions during the year; a bit of Dutch is helpful here.

Amsterdam Art, Antique and Collectors' Corner (A.A.A.C. Centra), 38 Looiersgracht, tel. 249038; only open during specialty fairs.

Antiekmarkt de Looier, Elandsgracht 109, tel. 249038, Sat.-Thurs., 11am-5pm.

Waterlooplein Flea Market. If flea markets are your joy, this famous market in the heart of Amsterdam's former Jewish section is for you; Valkenburgerstraat, Mon.-Sat., 10am-5pm. You can find anything from cracked toilet bowls to small treasures, dusty and unpolished.

Book Market, Oudemanhuispoort, Mon.-Sat., 10am-5pm.

Textile Market, Noordermarkt on Westerstraat, Mon. 9:30am-1pm.

Bird Market, Noordermarkt, Saturday mornings.

Stamp Market, Nieuwezijds Voorburgwal opposite 280, Wed. and Sat., 1-4pm.

Plants and Flower Market (garden supplies), Amstelveld, Mon., 10am-noon.

Floating Flower Market, along the Singel is not to be missed . . . Mon.-Fri., 9am-6pm (Thurs. 'til 9pm).

Amsterdam "swings" at night especially on the Leidseplein, Rembrandtplein and Reguliersdwarsstraat. Popular with the young are "white" or "art deco" cafes. Also try the "brown" cafes, so-called because of their dark paneled walls, nicotine-stained ceilings and old-world atmosphere.

Amsterdam's Casino is at the Hilton Hotel, Apollolaan 138, tel. 789789, open daily 2pm-3am, except May 4 (closed all day) and Dec. 31 (closed at 6pm). Minimum age for entry is 18 years; there is an obligatory dress code. Entry tickets: Fl. 7.50/day, Fl.20/month, Fl.125/year. French and American roulette and Blackjack are played. Conducted tours are possible by prior arrangement, Mon.-Fri., 11-11:30am and 12 noon.

EATING OUT: Amsterdam has an endless variety of restaurants, cafes, pubs, etc. For some tried and true quick stops one of many McDonald's is located at Muntplein 9, or for more typical Dutch fare, try pancakes at the Pancake House on Damplein. For sandwiches, Broodje van Kootje has two outlets, Leidseplein 20 and Spui 28. For more atmosphere, Heineken Hoek at Kleine Gartmanplantsoen 1-3, is a relaxing stop. Or try one of the aforementioned "white" or "brown" cafes. For evening dining out, a number of restaurants are mentioned in Chapter 17. Some special restaurants which have been on the scene a long time with well-established reputations are 't Swarte Schaep (The Black Sheep), 24 Korte Leidsedwarsstraat, tel. 223021 (dates from 1687); 'Vijff Vlieghen (Five Flies), 294 Spuistraat, tel. 248369; Dikker en Thijs, 438 Prinsengracht, tel. 267721; and the 100-year-old "die Port van Cleve," N.Z. Voorburgwal 178-180, tel. 240047. All but the latter are expensive.

STAYING OVER: Hotels start from Fl. 50 (single w/breakfast, simple) to over Fl. 500 per night. Check with the VVV for their hotel listing, write the NBT for their pamphlet on hotels or buy a copy of Lasschuit's "Hotels, Motels en Restaurants" for the current year . . . in Dutch but with pictures. Fifty youth hostels are listed by the Netherlands Youth Hostel Center, Prof. Tulpplein 4, tel. 264433. Also available from the NBT is a 637-page "Budget Hotel Guide" for the current year.

YEARLY EVENTS: To know what's going on in town during your visit, get a

102

copy of "Amsterdam This Week," available through your hotel or the VVV. Some yearly events of special note are: March, "Hiswa" boat and watersports show; Easter at the Royal Concert Hall; April 30, the Queen's Birthday celebration; May, international marathon; June-August, the Holland Festival (international and national cultural events); September, flower parade (Aalsmeer-Amsterdam), antique car parade, Jordaan Festival (typical Amsterdam event); Jazz Festival; October, toy exhibition; Oct./Nov., international horse show; November, international cat show, and the St. Nicolas parade. There are also many theatrical performances held around town in the summer, and carillon concerts in the Western Church, Mint, Southern Church and Old Church.

COMMERCIAL TOURS: For the first-time visitor, an overall conducted tour by bus will give the highlights of the city.

The **Amsterdam City Sightseeing Tour** (no smoking), daily 10am and 2:30pm; duration 3 hours. Drive past the Royal Palace and the "Skinny Bridge," then a stop at the Rijksmuseum to see the famous painting, "Night Watch" and other works of art, and a visit to see the cutting and polishing of diamonds. Substitutions possible on Sunday morning and Mondays.

The **City Tour** (Anne Frank House and Diamond Cutting Factory) also takes 3 hours and departs daily at 10am during the summer season.

A **Sunday Morning Drive** tour lasts 3½ hrs traveling along the banks of the former Zuider Zee, as well as offering a wide choice of tours into the hinterlands.

CANAL TOURS: Everyone must take one of the canal tours. Eight operators offer similar trips which usually take about 1¼ hours. Depending on the starting point of the operator, route and price of the tour may vary, so try a different one from time to time to see which you prefer.

For adults (or "adult" children), there are romantic evening tours in the summer through illuminated canals, under bridges and past historic buildings, offering you candlelight, cheese and wine, and lasting about three hours— reservations are necessary. Commentary is given in several languages describing the elaborate architecture. Notice in particular the gables . . . they were used as the home owner's identification before houses were numbered . . . some indicated the owner's occupation, his place of origin or his religion. The VVV can give you a list of tour operators.

Or, try something original—sightsee by "Canal bike," a stable, dry pedalboat that seats two or four. The operators provide a detailed brochure with map, suggested routes, description of the places you will pass and some background on Amsterdam's history. And for romantics, do the tour by night . . . the canal bikes are equipped with Chinese lanterns to rival the beautifully illuminated canals themselves. There are four possible starting points: at the Leidseplein between the Marriott and American hotels; between the Rijksmuseum and the Heineken Brewery; Prinsengracht at the Westerkerk near the Anne Frank House; and on the Keizersgracht near the Leidsestraat. Operates all year but hours vary; weather conditions can also affect availability. Easter, June-August, Mon.-Sun., 9am-11pm; Oct.-end March, by appointment; April-May-Sept., Mon.-Sun., 9am-6pm. Cost, Fl. 16.50/hr. for 2; Fl. 24.50/hr. for 4 pers. Deposit.

Nieuwe Kerk

LOCATION: The Dam; Trams 1, 2, 4, 5, 9, 13, 17, 24, 25.
INFORMATION: Nieuwe Kerk, Gravenstraat 17, tel. (020) 268168, or
    the VVV.
HOURS: Open Mon.-Sat., 10am-4pm; Sun., noon-3pm. Ecumenical
    services are held one evening a week.
■ *Of interest to older children and adults.*

Under restoration since 1959, this Gothic church dates from 1408, the second church to be built in the city of Amsterdam. In January 1645, the interior was completely destroyed by fire and as unfortunate as this must have appeared, the timing could not have been more perfect since this was the period of Holland's greatest artistic glory. Outstandingly talented artists and artisans of the Dutch "Golden Age" were available to restore and enhance the interior of the damaged church, coordinating the whole in a uniform fashion; the Royal Palace is of the same period. Recent restoration was carried out in the same 17th-century style by equally famous artists of today, costing something like fifty million Guilders (approximately $25 million)!

There is no altar—the monument-grave of one of Holland's heroes, Admiral de Ruiter, is located in its place. The organ, one of the most beautiful in Europe, is used for concerts and special musical evensong services on Sundays.

Queen Beatrix's investiture took place in the Nieuwe Kerk as did those of her predecessors. This event is the official sitting of both chambers of Parliament where the Queen takes her oath and Parliament, in its turn, swears allegiance to her. The plans for this church reflect the development in modern church thinking in the Netherlands. Originally a Roman Catholic church, it now belongs to the Dutch Reformed Church who are handing it over to the Nationale Stichting Nieuwe Kerk, a non-denominational Trust which (helped by a subsidy) will "run" it. The Board is made up of prominent people: artists, writers, TV personalities, politicians, etc., and it is hoped to make the church a lively meeting place, as it was in the Middle Ages, where non-political meetings and discussions can take place ... "a place which will evolve into a center of Christian thought, and participation."

Rijksmuseum National Gallery

LOCATION: Stadhouderskade 42. Public transportation is available
    by Trams 1, 2, 5, 16, 24 and 25.
INFORMATION: Tel. (020) 732121.
HOURS: Tues.-Sat., 10am-5pm, Sun. and holidays, 1-5pm. Closed
    January 1.
■ *Of interest to school-age children.*

This world-famous museum must not be missed, even if you have small children along. Ask for directions to the wing which has the Rembrandts, Vermeers and Frans Halses, and take a quick tour stopping especially to see "The Night

Watch." The most complete collection of Dutch paintings from the 15th to 19th century is located in this museum if you want to spend more time or for "in depth" study.

In addition, there are some very nice period rooms displaying old Dutch silver, porcelain and other objets d'art.

For those living in the Netherlands, it is highly recommended sightseeing in this museum be done during the off-tourist season . . . especially with children.

Rijksmuseum Vincent Van Gogh

LOCATION: Paulus Potterstraat 7 (a few steps from the Modern Art Museum). Trams 2, 5, 16.
INFORMATION: Tel. (020) 764881.
HOURS: Tues.-Sat., 10am-5pm; Sundays and public holidays, 1-5pm; closed January 1.
■ *Of interest to school-age children.*

This collection has been donated by Van Gogh's family and contains many sketches, early paintings during his Holland period, and other paintings which have not been viewed previously except in one or two special exhibitions in major cities of the world. It gives a broader understanding of this strange man's life and development, and should be especially appealing to children because of Van Gogh's strong colors and primitive approach to his subjects.

The building itself was specially constructed to house this collection with the nephew of Vincent Van Gogh acting as advisor. It is a very special addition to the many fine museums to be found in the Netherlands. The collection of 600 paintings and drawings also includes works by Van Gogh's contemporaries, Gaugin, Bernard and Monticelli. Visitors may also use the library and work studio.

Modern Art Museum

LOCATION: Paulus Potterstraat 13, about two blocks from the Rijksmuseum; Trams 2, 5, 16.
INFORMATION: Tel. (020) 573 2737.
HOURS: Mon.-Sun., 11am-5pm. Closed January 1.
NOTE: In June, July and August, there are special art tours in French and English. For information, ask at the entry desk or phone number above.
■ *Of interest to school-age children.*

In the Stedelijk Museum, you will find a collection of international paintings and sculptures dating from 1850 to the present day. During the high tourist season (July-September), the works of special artists are highlighted such as Cezanne, Van Gogh, Malevich, Picasso, Chagall, Matisse, Dubuffet, Appel and representatives of the current trends in European and American art. From September to June, there are constantly changing exhibitions of contemporary international art as well as samples of the permanent collection on view. Some of the contemporary artists represented are pretty far-out, but the younger generation seems to appreciate them. Photographic and video exhibits are held as well as courses in applied art (design of furniture, textiles and posters). There is a library, reading room, garden with sculptures, a Reproduction Department and a restaurant.

Anne Frank House

LOCATION: 263 Prinsengracht; Trams 13, 17, Buses 21, 67.
INFORMATION: Tel. (020) 264533.
HOURS: Open Mon.-Sat, 9am-5pm; Sun. and holidays, 10am-5pm
... June-Aug. also Sat., 9am-7pm. Sun., 10am-7pm. Closed December 25, January 1, and Yom Kippur.
■ Of interest to children from 6 years.

Anne Frank and her family lived in the upper floors of this building from 1942 until 1944, hiding from the Germans. During this period Anne grew up from a little girl to a teenager and described in detail and with great honesty and clarity her thoughts and feelings. Eventually, the Germans did find the hiding place and Anne and her family were put into concentration camps ... she was exterminated shortly before the end of World War II.

Anne's diary was found still hidden where she had left it and it was published after World War II. Children twelve or older would enjoy reading the book before or after the visit.

Amsterdam Historical Museum

LOCATION: Kalverstraat 92 or 357 O.Z. Voorburgwal, in the center
of Amsterdam. Trams 1, 2, 4, 5, 9, 16, 24, 25.
INFORMATION: Tel. (020) 523 1822.
HOURS: Open Mon.-Sun., 11am-5pm; Closed January 1.
■ Of interest primarily to older children.

The building housing the museum has an interesting history going back to the Middle Ages when it was the Convent of Saint Lucian. In 1578 the convent was confiscated by the supporters of the Prince of Orange against the town's governors who had been supporting the Spanish. It later became an orphanage and remained so until 1960 at which time the children were moved to more modern quarters.

Visitors can quickly grasp an insight into the history of Amsterdam by following the chronological order of the rooms. The subject matter is pretty serious for most children; however, there are some interesting methods of presentation such as video-tapes, a glass showcase in the open containing armor and a "singing" picture. The entrance and courtyard are charming and visitors on a warm day can join students or business people on their lunch hour relaxing at the pleasant restaurant.

Amstelkring Museum "Our Lord in the Attic"

LOCATION: 40 O.Z. Voorburgwal (center of Amsterdam). Trams 4,
*   9, 16, 24, 25, or walk from the Central Station, also Metro.*
INFORMATION: Tel. (020) 246604.
HOURS: Mon.-Sat., 10am-5pm; Sun. and holidays, 1-5pm. Closed
*   January 1.*
■ *Of interest to children from 4 years.*

This 17th-century merchant's house is not what it appears to be—in actual fact, in addition to being a merchant's residence, it also served as a place of worship with the chapel extending over the attics of three houses. There are many different ways to approach the "secret" chapel and the children will enjoy trying to figure them out, and also seeing the organ, church pews, etc.

There are good descriptive brochures for sale in English, French, German and Dutch.

Madame Tussaud's Wax Museum

LOCATION: Kalverstraat 156 in the center of the shopping district.
*   Trams 1, 2, 4, 5, 9, 16, 24 and 25.*
INFORMATION: Tel. (020) 223949.
HOURS: Mon.-Sun., 10am-6pm. July-Aug., also open 'til 7pm. Closed
*   December 25.*
ADMISSION: Adults, Fl. 7.50; Children, Fl. 4.75.
■ *Of interest to all.*

World figures—historical figures—Dutch painters, artists, commentators, all are represented in this exhibition in wax which will enthrall the children. They will see President Kennedy, Winston Churchill, President De Gaulle and during their "tour" they may even be photographed with these personages or others, such as Mata Hari or Mr. Mao. At the end of the visit, you will have a chance to buy any pictures taken of you during your visit.

An easy museum to enjoy—not too big, colorful and fun.

National Maritime Museum

*LOCATION: 1 Kattenburgplein; Buses 22, 28. Worth the good walk
from Central Station.
INFORMATION: Tel. (020) 262255.
HOURS: Tues.-Sat., 10am-5pm; Sun. and holidays, 1-5pm. Closed
January 1.*
■ *Of interest to children from about 10 years.*

This beautifully appointed, rightfully very popular museum, with its wealth of model ships, prints and paintings, countless flags, navigational instruments, maps, globes, weapons and books, should interest all the boys and men.

Particularly interesting are the magnificent ship models and the beautiful world maps showing also the Americas in the 17th century. Take a look at the cities which were indicated at that time and at California, which was thought to be an island!

The exhibits spread over three decks, each one representing more or less a century. There is a guide book to help you around the 445 exhibits which trace the evolution of this seagoing nation and its ships. Pleasant coffee ship-deck terrace.

Rembrandt's House

*LOCATION: 4-6 Jodenbreestraat; Tram 9 or Metro.
INFORMATION: Tel. (020) 249486.
HOURS: Mon.-Sat., 10am-5pm. Sundays and holidays, 1-5pm. Closed
January 1.*
■ *Of interest to children 12 years and older.*

Rembrandt lived here for 20 years during the period in his life when he was most successful financially. There are 250 original etchings, drawings and curios from Rembrandt's period.

Aviodome (Air Museum)

*LOCATION: Schiphol Airport. You can take the train from the Cen-
tral Station or Buses CN 143, 144, 145.
INFORMATION: Tel. (020) 173640.
HOURS: daily, 10am-5pm (Nov. 1-April 1, closed on Mon.). Closed
December 26, 31, January 1.*
■ *Of interest to most children, especially boys.*

This varied and interesting small museum, showing the development of air and space travel, is located inside the futuristic domeshaped gold aluminum structure easily visible as one approaches the airport building. If you're meeting someone at the airport, why not go a little early and take the children along? Show them the museum, letting them climb in and out of old planes and space craft, then take them to the airport viewing deck to see everything from private planes to modern jumbo jets taking off and arriving. One restaurant works on the automat system which is sure to be a hit. Even difficult eaters can be tempted if they can put a coin in the slot!

AALSMEER

Largest flower auction in the world

GETTING THERE: Aalsmeer is at the crossroads of Highways A4 and N201, south of Schiphol Airport. The large-scale ANWB map "Midden" shows the "Bloemenveiling" (auction hall). Trains, buses or commercial conducted tours are ways to get there.
INFORMATION: Aalsmeer VVV, tel. (02977) 25374.

This trip is for the early riser as you should be in Aalsmeer before 10am if you are going to take advantage of the flower auctions. Aalsmeer is the center of flower-growing in the Netherlands and at the auction complex (22-hectare site with 320,000 square meters of buildings) you will see cut flowers being sold before transshipment abroad. Each year three *billion* roses, carnations, freesias, lilacs and other flowers are auctioned.

The Cut Flower Auction Hall is located at Legmeerdijk 313, tel. (02977) 34567, open to visitors from 7:30-11:30am, Mon.-Fri. Recorded tapes explain the proceedings. Flowers arrive early for auctioning before noon and then they are packed for shipping to such far places as America, France, Norway, Sweden and many others. The Potted Plant Market (Auction) is open four days a week, Mon-Thurs., 8am-noon.

Another flower auction to be visited is between Rotterdam and The Hague—Flower Auction Westland. Open year-round between 8-10am, Mon.-Fri. For information, call the Rotterdam VVV.

YEARLY EVENTS: The annual Flower Parade from Aalsmeer to Amsterdam and back takes place the first Saturday of September. There are gorgeous floats, a Flower Queen, bands, drum majorettes, etc. Floats can be seen the Friday before and the Sunday after the parade in the auction hall.

Flower parades are held around the country. In August, there is the "Delta Flora" parade Rijnsburg-Oegstgeest-Leiden-Noordwijk, as well as the flower parades in Rijnsburg, Katwijk aan Zee, Breda, St. Jansklooster, Leersum, Winterswijk, and Vollenhove. In the fall, besides the parade in Aalsmeer/Amsterdam, there are parades in Zundert, Eelde/Paterswolde, Tiel (fruit parade), Valkenswaard, Vledder/Frederiksoord, Lichtenvoorde, Almelo, and Winkel. In early November, Aalsmeer hosts "the largest flower show on earth." And preparations are already underway for Floriade 1992, a horticultural event held every ten years. Zoetermeer (outskirts of The Hague) will welcome thousands of tourists between April and October for the event.

HAARLEM

Home of Frans Hals

GETTING THERE: Located on the Spaarne River, Haarlem can best be reached from Amsterdam by N5/A5 autoroute; from points south (The Hague and Rotterdam) via A4, taking the Haarlem turnoff at N201 or A5 going west. Trains go regularly from major train stations.
INFORMATION: VVV, Stationsplein 1, tel. (023) 319059.

Haarlem is 900 years old and a veritable architectural "treasure house" with buildings dating from the 13th century to the present. Count William II granted the town its charter in 1245 and built a hunting lodge (begun 1250) which became the Town Hall in the 14th century. In front of the lodge on what is today the Market Square, regular jousting events were held. The Great Church was built between 1390 and 1520 (approx.); however, the largest number of historic buildings extant date from the 17th century, Haarlem's period of greatest prosperity.

In 1572, Haarlem joined Leiden and other nationalistic Dutch towns to oppose Spanish rule, an action which spurred the interlopers to besiege the town for seven months until July 1573. After great suffering, Haarlem agreed to surrender provided the townspeople would not be punished. Frederick of Toledo, the Spanish commander, agreed but went back on his word, killing the Governor, all the Calvinist ministers and others totaling almost 2,000 people. Three years later, a fire destroyed most of the town, and in 1577, the Dutch army returned without opposition. The war against Spain and the religious battles between Protestants and Catholics ruined the Town Hall and the monastery complex lying behind it, and brought hardships to Haarlem's citizens. By the 17th century, all of Holland (including Haarlem) was enjoying the prosperity brought by an influx of skilled workmen and artists from Spanish-occupied territories to the south.

Today, Haarlem is the capital of North Holland. It fosters some heavy industry, and is known as the center for Dutch bulb export, primarily tulips. It is a good-sized town with residential areas in all directions; however, most of its touristic sites are centered within a one kilometer radius. Walking is not only the best way to get around but it allows time for the town's atmosphere to envelop and seduce the visitor. With the VVV map of Haarlem in hand, you can explore in orderly fashion. Places of interest are numbered with explanations on the back of the map in Dutch, French, German and English.

■ **The "Hofjes," or almshouses**, might be a good place to start. Haarlem has some twenty of these homes formerly built for lay persons connected with the church but which are lived in today by anyone of good moral character. About half of them are listed on the map. The oldest almshouse in the Netherlands dating from 1395, the Hofje van Bakenes, is located just off the Bakenesser Gracht (canal), not far from the Grote Kerk and Teylers Museum. Following the canal, east of town, you might have to search for the entrance which is off one of the small back streets. As you enter, you will find yourself in a hushed world of quiet dignity. The courtyard garden is lined with two-story, white-washed houses with dark green shutters and red-tiled roofs. Flowers and green grass are embellished with a jet of water splashing in a small pond surrounded by reeds, bushes and more flowers. An ancient pump (renovated in 1985), brought alive by masses of geraniums under its white-painted, square-roofed portico, adds an interesting architectural dimension.

On the opposite (west) side of the Grote Markt, you will find the Hofje van Loo at Barrevoetestraat 7. Dating from 1489, these houses lost their courtyard when the street was widened in 1885. Not far away is the Brouwershofje (1586) with its distinctive red and white shutters. Another almshouse with an elevated central area and elegant appearance is located near the Central Station, the Hofje van Staats (1730). It's fun to find your own favorites.

The "Grote Markt" (Great Market square) is one of the finest in Holland and a good place to use as "home base" for visiting the town. At one end of the square is the famous Great Church, formerly St. Bavo Cathedral. Next to it is the Vleeshal (former meat market, also known as the Butcher's Hall), at the northwest corner of the church is the Vishal (fish market), and at the far end is the ornately-gabled Town Hall (Renaissance). The Great Church is not to be confused with the much newer St. Bavo Basilica.

St. Bavo Basilica, located on the Leidsevaart, was built between 1895 and 1906. This latter church has beautiful stained glass windows, sculptures, and interesting treasury. It can be visited April-Oct., Mon.-Sat., 10am-noon and 2-4:30pm; Sun., 2-4:30pm.

The Great or St. Bavo Church, entrance 23 Oude Groenmarkt, tel. (023) 324399, is open Mon.-Sat., 10am-4pm, Sept.-March, closes at 3pm. This is the church of interest to music lovers. It houses one of Europe's most famous organs, the Müller organ, which has three keyboards, 68 registers and 5,000 pipes. Built in 1738, it has been played by Mozart, Handel and many others. Look for the early 16th-century rood-screen and its wonderful animal carvings at the base, the choir-stalls from 1512, three colorful sailing ships hanging from the rafters, and the tomb of Frans Hals. Free organ concerts are held during the year in the evenings, and, also in the afternoons during June-September . . . check times with VVV. Attached to the exterior of the church building is a series of little houses in which you will find some interesting small shops. The area also has a number of places to grab a bite to eat . . . more on that later.

The Butcher's Hall dates from 1602, built by the architect, Lieven de Key. Sure to catch the eye—and the photographer's lens—with its highly ornamented step-gables, it alternates with the Fish Market in hosting changing art exhibits. Open Mon.-Sat., 11am-5pm, Sun. and holidays, 1-5pm.

As you cross the market square on the way to the Town Hall, imagine the many jousting tournaments that were once held here.

The Town Hall consists of a number of original structures and additions. The oldest parts are the remains of Count William II's hunting lodge (built in the mid-1200s) and part of a medieval Dominican monastery which was behind the hunting lodge. Visitors are welcome during the week; however, permission to visit must be requested as the rooms may be in official use. In the destructive fire of 1351, much of the town and building were leveled. Shortly afterwards, Count William V built the Count's Hall which now serves as the "gala" reception hall. In the 15th century, several rooms were added along the Zilstraat as well as the public high court, the "Vierschaar," where judgments were pronounced. A gallows erected in 1633 was torn down in 1855. The religious battles during and after the Spanish period, along with another serious fire in the 16th century, destroyed much of the Town Hall and the buildings of the monastery. The property came into the hands of the city and a Prince's Court was added where members of the House of Orange and other important guests could stay. During the French occupation, the building was used as the Departmental Court of Law. There were changes and renovations over the years, described in a Dutch brochure with English insert.

Other buildings to look for as you walk around town are: the Guard House (Hoofdwacht), one of Haarlem's oldest buildings located on the northeast corner of the Grote Markt and Smedestraat; the former Janskerk, originally a 14th-century monastic church, corner Janstraat and Begijnesteeg); the oldest church in Haarlem, the Waalse Kerk (Walloon Church), 14th century, near Janskerk in the Begijnhof; the late 15th-century Bakenesserkerk with its elegant sandstone tower, across the Bakenesser Gracht on Bakenesserstraat; the Amsterdamse Poort (ca. 1400) only remaining town gate with parts of the city wall; and the Gravenstenenbrug, a most picturesque drawbridge across the Spaarne River.

MUSEUMS: Of Haarlem's three museums, the Frans Hals Museum rates the highest priority; however, the Teylers Museum's original drawings by some of Holland's great masters also shouldn't be missed, and the Corrie Ten Boomhuis Museum offers a valuable insight into modern wartime history.

SHOPPING: Always a pleasurable part of sightseeing, Haarlem has its fair share of attractive boutiques and pedestrian-only shopping areas . . . look for the little shops on the Cronjestraat. The major shopping streets are north, south and southeast of the Grote Markt; they are marked in yellow on the Haarlem map.

EATING OUT: A number of attractive cafes and restaurants can be found on the southern side of the Great Church on the Spekstraat. Look for the historic "De Karmeliet" coffee shop on the site of an old Carmelite Cloister (1249-1578) . . . good salad plates, hamburgers, soup, etc. Forty-four kinds of pancakes can be had at 't Pannekoekhuis, Kruisweg 57; or South American beef in various guises at Gauchos, Kruistraat 9 (not open 'til 5pm); and the ever-popular McDonald's is located at Grote Houtstraat 75. The Kroon Restaurant on the market square is recommended as is the Confucius Restaurant where you could try a Rijsttafel, the Indonesian meal which comes in the form of many little dishes and is a treat to eat . . . often spicy, so specify if you don't want it "hot."

YEARLY EVENTS: Haarlem has a number of events during the year, including a "Houtfestival" (plays, music, folk dancing and art market) in the Spring (Whitsun), and a Barrel Organ Festival in June followed by an International Organ Festival the beginning of July. From the end of April to September, there are guided tours and special organ concerts at the St. Bavo Church and the St. Bavo Basilica. Zandvoort, the nearby seaside resort, has a special motor car race circuit at Easter and the end of May with jazz on the beach the beginning of August. In November, there's an Antiquarian bookseller's market. Check with the VVV for details on all the above, verification of times, etc.

Frans Hals Museum

LOCATION: Groot Heiligland 62. The museum is not so easy to locate and you should check a map before starting out. Park your car in a "P" area or along the Gasthuis Vest before turning into Grote Heiligland street leading to the entrance of the museum.
INFORMATION: Tel. (023) 319180.
HOURS: Mon.-Sat., 11am-5pm, Sundays and public holidays, 1-5pm.
■ *Of interest to school-age (primarily older) children.*

Frans Hals (1580-1666) was a native of Antwerp, but spent most of his life in Haarlem. He painted many very large canvases depicting Boards of Governors who directed almshouses or banquet scenes of officers from various regiments, such as the Corps of Archers of St. George, etc. This latter painting brought him great success when he was only 36 years old. At first, one would think seeing one large canvas after another showing stuffy citizens or self-important military

113

officers would be pretty dull stuff. But Hals painted differently than his colleagues. If someone had too much to drink, he portrayed him that way. If he saw meanness or pettiness in their eyes, he painted that. This must have created quite a stir among his clients because it must be remembered that, according to the custom of the day, each person appearing in a painting paid for his own picture, i.e., he paid his percentage of the artist's fee for the whole painting.

In addition to the Frans Hals works, the museum shows paintings by a number of Holland's "old masters"—17th-century portraits, still lifes, genre scenes and landscapes. Of special note is the collection of Haarlem silverware and 18th-century Delftware found in the reconstructed pharmacy. Little girls will especially enjoy the 18th-century doll's house and the paper-doll tableaux showing cut-out scenes of old-fashioned homes which are behind glass and lighted to give a third dimensional impression. Period rooms are always fun . . . there are two: an 18th- and a 19th-century room.

The modern art collection consists of paintings, graphic art, sculpture, textiles and ceramics by such well-known Dutch artists as Isaac Israëls, Jan Sluyters, and Karel Appel.

The museum building dates from 1608. During Frans Hals' time, it was an almshouse for old men . . . he lived here at the end of his life. Later, it became an orphanage and around 1913, it was transformed into a museum, retaining the historic core built by the 17th-century architect, Lieven de Key. In 1981 a wing was added to house the modern art section.

Some twenty exhibitions a year are held in the museum and its annexes, the Vleeshal and the Vishal on the Grote Markt. Guided tours can be had in English, German and French but must be arranged for in advance. Concerts are held every third Sunday of the month. A very special treat to look for are the times the museum is open for candle-lighted evenings.

Teylers Museum

LOCATION: Spaarne 16, at the corner with Damstraat.
INFORMATION: Tel. (023) 320197.
HOURS: March-Oct., Tues.-Sat., 10am-5pm, Sundays, 1-5pm; Nov.-
    April, closed at 4pm. Inquire about concerts given on the Fokker
    organ . . . the first Sunday of each month at 3pm.
■ *Of interest to scientific-minded and older children.*

Within easy walking of St. Bavo Church and the historic market place, Teylers Museum, built in 1778, is Holland's oldest. This was the Age of Enlightenment in Europe and Peter Teyler van der Hulst (1702-1778), a trader and manufacturer of cloth and silk, was much interested in promoting the Arts and Sciences. Upon his death, his fortune was used to establish a foundation for this purpose, and the museum was born. The idea was "avant garde" at the time since museums were only to be found in a few major cities like Paris and London.

In 1790, an important nucleus of the collection was established when a group of 2,000 drawings, previously part of Queen Christina of Sweden's private collection, was acquired. In this group were works by Raphael, Michelangelo,

Guercino, Claude Lorrain and Hendrick Goltzius. Dutch artists of the 19th century represented in the collection of paintings include Springer, Schelfhout, Koekkoek and Weissenbruch.

Before reaching the section on art, however, the visitor passes through an incredible variety of fossils, minerals and instruments as well as displays of coins and medals. The fossils and minerals section includes "Diluvian Man," "Archaeopteryx," the primeval bird, and "Mosasaurus," a gigantic lizard. The group of physical instruments was purchased as the most advanced equipment available for experiments and demonstrations which were carried on for the purpose of research and education in the early days of the foundation.

The Oval Room, a splendid wood-paneled room built in 1780, retains its serene historical atmosphere. It is here the visitor can imagine himself in an earlier day where encyclopedic knowledge was sought in both the arts and sciences.

Corrie Ten Boomhuis Museum — The Hiding Place

LOCATION: Barteljorisstraat 19 on the Schuilplaats, a shopping area, just north of the Grote Markt.
INFORMATION: Tel. (023) 310324. Tours are given by volunteers, some of whom speak English.
HOURS: Mon.-Sat., 10am-4:30pm; Nov.-March, 11am-3:30pm. Closed Sundays and public holidays.
■ *Of interest to all ages.*

This museum, officially opened April 15, 1988, is devoted to the story of a family with great courage and strong religious beliefs. Watchmaking was the family business since 1837. Casper Ten Boom (1859-1944) was a watchmaker as was his daughter, Corrie; she was the first woman watchmaker in Holland. The 4-meter- (13 ft.+) wide house is still a shop downstairs where you enter the museum. Upstairs was the family living quarters. If it hadn't been for WW II and the persecutions under the Nazi regime, the Ten Boom family probably would have lived and died ordinary lives. Instead, Father Casper and his children Betsie, Willem, Corrie and Willem's son, Christiaan, undertook to hide Jews and others whose lives were in danger. As a result, all but Corrie died in prison. Casper was 84 years old when he was arrested and sent to Scheveningen . . . he died a year later. Betsie died in Ravensbrück in 1944; Willem died in Hilversum in 1946; Christiaan was tortured and died in April 1945, place unknown. Corrie survived Ravensbrück. Before she died, Betsie asked Corrie to go out and preach that the Lord is always there, no matter how dire the situation.

The Germans came into Holland on May 10, 1940; the Gestapo entered the house and arrested those present on February 28, 1944. Father Casper, Corrie and Betsie lived in the house during that time . . . 4 long years.

A guide will take you up the stairs to show you the house and its hiding places. Just outside Corrie's bedroom, the ration cards were hidden in a false step. In order to provide a hiding place, a carpenter built a false wall with a trap

115

door and air hole against the outside wall in Corrie's room. The Gestapo would often come and search the house; Corrie would sit on her bed and pretend nothing was amiss. Once seven people were kept in this very small space for 2½ days.

Several other bedrooms just large enough to hold a bed and perhaps a dresser were under the eaves towards the front of the house. A space was fitted in one of these for others to hide, high in the wall between it and the roof.

When Corrie was freed from the concentration camp at age 52, she remembered her sister's words. She wrote many books and visited over sixty countries giving lectures and preaching. She died in 1983 at the age of 91 years.

The house was bought by an American foundation. A Dutch organization was needed, however, to manage the museum. Corrie's doctor was instrumental in the establishment of the Dutch "connection" which resulted in the Corrie Ten Boom Museum Foundation. Private loans helped with restoring the house and volunteers have guided some 7,000 visitors per year.

IN THE NEIGHBORHOOD OF HAARLEM:

Zandvoort has plenty to offer in the way of recreation and natural beauty with miles of sandy beaches, 38 pavilions with changing facilities, food, drinks, umbrellas, etc., and special sections of the beach for nudist bathers as well as a deserted stretch for those seeking peace and quiet. You can walk all the way to IJmuiden if you want. Bikers can contact VVV Zandvoort, Schoolplein 1, tel. (02507) 17947, if 3-, 4-, or 5-day arrangements including routes, hotels, discounts on restaurants, etc., sound appealing.

The Casino offers another kind of sport at Badhuisplein 7, tel. (02507) 18044, open, noon-2am (armed bandits), 2pm-2am for Roulette, Blackjack, Baccarat, Punto Banco.

Zandvoort Racetrack, Boulevard Paulus Loot, tel. 18284, has regularly scheduled bike and motor car races.

The Kennemer National Park, between Haarlem and the coast is a beautiful natural scenic area with bird habitats, lakes, woods, beaches and dunes sure to appeal to environmentalists. The visitor's center is open mid-April to mid-Sept., 9am-4:30pm. Located on Zeeweg in Overveen, tel. 257653 for information.

Museum Beeckestijn, Rijksweg 136, east of IJmuiden at Velsen-Zuid, tel. (02550) 12091, open June-Oct., Wed.-Fri., 10am-noon and 2-5pm, Sat. and Sun., noon-5pm; Oct.-June, 2-5pm, is a beautiful manor house furnished in the style of the 18th century. This house was once the property of rich merchant families from Amsterdam. Then as now, it was not uncommon for wealthy men to have a country place.

Brederode Castle (13th-century ruins) at Velserenderlaan 2, south of Santpoort, tel. (023) 378763, can be visited March-Dec. daily except Sat., 10am-5pm.

Linnaeushof Recreation Park, Rijksstraatweg 4, south of Haarlem at Bennebroek, tel. (02502) 7624, includes a playground with over 300 attractions and midget golf. Open April-Sept., 10am-6pm.

Museum de Cruquius, Cruquiusdijk 27-32, Vijfhuizen, Heemstede, tel. (023) 285704, is an interesting museum with steam-driven pumping station. In operation from 1849-1933, the original steam engine is on view. A scale model of Holland at storm tide shows how the low land was reclaimed from the sea and then kept dry. Open April-Sept., Mon.-Sat., 10am-5pm, Sun. and public holidays, noon-5pm; Oct. and Nov., closes at 4pm; closed Dec. through March.

Pumping Station Halfweg, Haarlemmermeerstraat 4, halfway between Haarlem and Amsterdam, tel. (02907) 4396, open April-Sept., Wed.-Sun., 10am-5pm.

■ **Spaarndam** has a special meaning to readers of "Hans Brinker and the Silver Skates," the legendary boy who used his finger to stop a leak in the dike in order to save the area from being flooded. So many tourists asked about Hans that the local citizens put up a statue in his memory with a plaque which reads: "Dedicated to our youth to honor the boy who symbolizes the perpetual struggle of Holland against the water." The village is charming with a sluicegate dating from 1611 to control the water level. Spaarndam is almost an adjunct of Haarlem, but difficult to find as the way is not well marked. It's northeast of town, along the Spaarne River.

DE ZAANSE SCHANS

An old Dutch windmill village

GETTING THERE: From Rotterdam and The Hague, take highway A4 north, direction Amsterdam, through the Coen Tunnel. Take the signs for Purmerend and get off at sign "Zaandijk." Another 3 kilometers and you will see De Zaanse Schans on your right. By public transportation (train), ask for a ticket to Koog-Zaandijk. From this station, it's about an eight-minute walk to the village.

INFORMATION: VVV, Gedempte Gracht 76, Zaandam, tel. (075) 162221 or 351747.

HOURS: Open all year, weekdays, 9am-5:30pm; shops, restaurants, museums, are open various hours.

NOTE: There is a parking fee.

■ *Of interest to all ages.*

De Zaanse Schans is a living museum of old homes, buildings, windmills, dating from the 17th, 18th, and 19th centuries which have been brought together to form this "new" village. The homes are all occupied by private citizens, the intention being to eliminate any "ghost town" feeling which one instinctively feels in normal open-air museums. The houses and mills were transported from the neighboring area on boats or barges and reconstructed with loving care and attention to detail. There are a number of working windmills to visit and one where you can buy excellent mustard which has been milled on the spot.

Starting with No. 1 on the Zaanse Schans brochure, you are actually starting from the end of the village but since that is where the parking lot is located, we will follow their lead.

1. The Restaurant "De Kraai" specializes in 10 kinds of pancakes, cold snacks, and a "Koffietafel" (coffee, cookies, sandwich). Located at Kraaienpad 1, tel. 156403; open March-Sept., 9am-6pm, October, 10am-5pm.

2. Giftshop "De Bezem," Kraaienest 3, tel. 157680; open year-round, 9am-5pm . . . all kinds of gifts from Holland and abroad.

3. Photo studio where you can have a 1900s brown picture of yourself in original Dutch costume, Kraaienest 1, tel. 313204/179517.

4. Woodenshoe Workshop, Kraaienest 4, tel. 177121; open all year, 9am-5pm . . . regular demonstrations with 7,000 pairs of woodenshoes in stock.

5. Special demonstrations.

6. Catharina Hoeve, de Kwakels 2, tel. 313717; open all year, 8am-7pm (Nov. 1-March 1, 9am-5pm). Edam and Gouda cheese are made in traditional manner . . . entrance fee . . . explanations in several languages.

7. Zaanse Bakkerij Museum (old bakery and sweet shop), tel. 173522; open year-round Sat.-Sun. and holidays, 10am-5pm; March 1-Oct. 31, Tues.-Sun., 10am-5pm.

8. Antique shop.

9. Oil Mill, "De Zoeker."

10. Paint Mill, "De Kat." April-Oct., Tues.-Sun., 9am-5pm; Nov.-March, weekends, 9am-5pm.

11. Saw Mill, "De Poelenburg."

12. Mustard Mill, "De Huiseman" (1786). Built as a snuff mill; you can now buy the most delicious mustard and other spices. The mills are all open to visitors in the summer. The last Saturday in September is Zaanse Windmill Day and they will all be in operation.

13. Cruise dock.

14. Galerie "aan't Glop," a toy shop.

15. Museum "Het Noorderhuis," Kalverringdijk 17, tel. 173237 . . . outfitted to show how a rich merchant lived in the beginning of the 19th century

16. Restaurant "De Walvis" (the Whale) . . . for dinners, tel. 165540.

17. The original Albert Heijn grocery store, Museumwinkel Albert Heijn. Open to 8 people at a time, Mon.-Sat., 10am-1pm and 2-5pm . . . closed in winter, tel. 592573. Old-fashioned rock candy, cookies, postcards for sale.

18. Clock Museum, "Zaans Uurwerken Museum," Kalverringdijk 3, and

19. De Tinkoepel, pewter shop with craftsmen working.

IN THE NEIGHBORHOOD OF DE ZAANSE SCHANS:

At **Koog aan de Zaan**, there's a special Windmill Museum at Museumlaan 18, tel. (075) 215148, year-round, Tues.-Fri., 10am-5pm; Sat. and Sun., 2-5pm.

At **Zaandijk**, you can see Zaanse objects and clothing from the 17th and 18th century at Lagedijk 80. For information, tel. (075) 217626; open Tues.-Fri., 10am-noon and 2-4pm, Sun., 2-4pm.

Zaandam is the locale of the "Czar Peterhuisje" (Czar Peter of Russia's house), at Krimp 23, tel. (075) 160390; open Tues.-Sun., 10am-1pm and 2-5pm except the 1st and 3rd Sunday of the month. "Peter Michaelov was working in the shipyards . . . as a laborer and boarding with an old carpenter he had known in Archangel . . . The tsar's disguise served him only about a week: His height, his twitch, and a wart on his cheek gave him away, and it did him no good to turn his back on officials who called him 'Your Majesty' and on the crowds of the curious." . . . from "The Tragic Dynasty" by John Bergamini.

The whole area is delightfully picturesque—well worth the trip. Boat excursions (in summer) of the area last about 50 minutes.

ALKMAAR

Cheese galore

GETTING THERE: From Rotterdam (and The Hague), take A13 west, follow signs for Scheveningen, then N44 (A44) north past Haarlem and IJmuiden, all the way to Alkmaar. From Amsterdam go via Zaandam to N99 then north to Alkmaar. There are regularly scheduled trains; for information check with any Central Station.
INFORMATION: VVV Alkmaar, Waagplein 3, tel. (072) 114284.

The town of Alkmaar is an attractive old Dutch town with moats, canals, a beautiful Town Hall, stately old mansions with beautiful facades, picturesque shopping streets in the old center.

Some of the more interesting town sights include the St. Laurens Church, built between 1470 and 1516; the late Gothic Town Hall (oldest part dates from the beginning of the 16th century); the Municipal Museum; the Hof van Sonoy, a former convent, then a residence of the Governor Jonkheer Diedrick Sonoy, and now the property of the Dutch Reformed Poor-Relief Board. Also of interest are the Huis van Achten (House of Eight)—a home for eight old men since 1656 and the Hofje van Splinter which dates from 1646—an almshouse for eight old ladies.

The Town Hall can be visited when the rooms are not in use, Mon.-Fri., 9am-noon and 2-4pm. Of special interest are the council chamber, the hall with Schermer chest, the Polder Room, the room of the Mayor and Corporation, and the Nierop Room with its original wooden ceiling (1634) and antique furniture.

The Municipal Museum is to the west of the Market Square at Doelenstraat 3, tel. (072) 114284; open Mon.-Thurs., 10am-noon and 2-5pm, Fri., 10am-5pm, Sun., 2-5pm. Closed Saturdays. The collection of antique toys will titillate the interest of the young folks; history buffs will be interested in the displays relating to the town's early days, especially the siege by the Spaniards in 1573.

The Weighing House on the town square was built in 1341 as a chapel dedicated to the Holy Ghost. It was converted into a weighing house in 1582 and the tower was added about 1595. For those who love carillons, arrange to be on the square Fridays from 11am-noon (during cheese market season), or Thursdays, 6:30-7:30pm and Saturday, 1:30-2:30pm.

At noon there's sound and activity with trumpeters blowing their horns with each stroke of the clock and men on horseback charging out the doors, ready to do battle. The busy VVV office is on the ground level (stop for their map and advice on what to see and do); also, if you have time, visit the Cheese Museum in the building, open April-Oct., Mon.-Thurs., 10am-4pm, also Sat. Fri., opens at 9am.

119

The Weekly Cheese Market, which takes place from about mid-April 'til mid-September, Friday mornings 10am-noon is well known and well worth the trip. You will see big round cheeses, middle-sized round cheeses, small round cheeses, and piles of factory-made cheeses. Wholesale dealers and exporters test and taste before bidding. They bore out a long round piece of cheese with a special scoop; the cheese is smelled, tasted, and crumbled between the fingers to determine quantity of fat and moisture. The highest price offered is the winning bid which is then registered on the official board.

In the Cheese Porters' Guild, there are four Companies (or sections); a green, a blue, a red, and a yellow one. Each Company consists of 6 Porters and 1 Collector (or treasurer). Each Company also has a Foreman who is chosen by the Guild and approved by the Mayor and Aldermen; the Foreman wears a silver badge of office hanging from his neck on a ribbon the color of his Company. In addition, the Guild appoints one Provost and one Servant. The Provost waits on the Board when the Guild meets and he is also "the Executioner" because he writes the names of the porters who turn up late on the notice board in the Guild Room. The Servant does all sorts of odd jobs for the Guild.

The Porters are all dressed in spotless, white costumes with lacquered straw hats in the color of their respective company. They carry a barrow—a stretcher-like affair—which is loaded with 80 cannon-ball-sized cheeses weighing up to 160 kilos by means of a leather shoulder sling attached to the barrow's handles. The barrows are painted the colors of their company. When transporting the cheeses, the Porters have a distinctive bobbing gait which is needed in order not to spill their heavy load. The oldest and youngest of each company work together—the older of the two always at the back.

When the cheeses are sold, they are carried to the Weigh House by the Porters where the Collector weighs the cheese and marks the weight of the total load. The Weighmaster calls out the correct total weight, notes it on a blackboard, and the Porters take the cheese to the warehouses of the buyers.

IN THE NEIGHBORHOOD OF ALKMAAR:

The **Alkmaarse Hout** is a forest where you can take beautiful walks to nearby Heiloo, or if you want to see the North Sea, drive about 7 kilometers west to Egmond aan Zee, or further north to Bergen aan Zee. If you continue north past Schoorl to Groet, you will pass some most beautiful scenery. There's an artists' center on the village square of Bergen where local artists are represented.

Broek op Langedijk, north of Alkmaar just off highway N99, is the town where you can bid in a real auction . . . various foodstuffs are put up for sale in small portions in a special auction room built on wooden piles in the water. There is also an agrarian museum where you can see farm and fishing implements of former days, and you can take a motor-boat cruise to see the windmills in the area. A small restaurant specializes in coffee with "Broekerbol."

DEN HELDER and JULIANADORP

Home of the Dutch Navy

GETTING THERE: Den Helder is at the northern tip of the peninsula of North Holland. From Rotterdam and The Hague, take A4 north past Schiphol Airport; then west on A9 taking the bypass around Alkmaar (if there's time, stop and see this old town), and continue straight north. From Amsterdam, take A5/N5 to A9 and continue as above, or go via the Coen Tunnel, then northwest on A8 until the intersection with A9.

INFORMATION: VVV Den Helder, Julianaplein 30, tel. (02230) 25544. Open year-round, weekdays, 9am-6pm; Sat., 9am-5pm.

The first records of Den Helder as a town appear about 1500. Before then, only the village of Huisduinen was known which still exists, of course, and like Julianadorp, has retained its special village qualities. During the time of the French occupation, Napoleon turned Den Helder into a strong fortress town—the "Gibraltar of the North." There are still forts in the area which date from that period. Not surprisingly for a peninsula of land which juts into the North Sea on the west and the quieter Waddenzee on the east, its history has been intimately linked with the sea. Today, Den Helder is home to much of the Dutch Navy.

Den Helder is the jumping-off place for the island of Texel. But even more importantly, it is an active fishing center and Holland's largest naval port. Another important industry, of course, is tourism. Tourist officials like to say Den Helder has more hours of sunshine per year than any other city in the Netherlands and that the water is cleaner and sunbathing is better here than anywhere else.

In the springtime, you will be enchanted with the lovely colors of the many bulbfields in bloom around Julianadorp. This is the place to stay if you want to enjoy a beaching holiday in this region. There are a number of parks, and many hiking places around the dunes. People of the Den Helder-Julianadorp area are great beachcombers—after each storm, you will find any number of people

121

looking to see what fascinating things the sea may have thrown up.

The Helders Marine Museum, "Het Torentje," gives the history of the Dutch Navy from 1813 to the present. Located on the Hoofdgracht, tel. (02230) 11234; open Tues.-Fri., 10am-5pm, Sat. and Sun., 1-4:30pm, Mon. (June-Aug. only), 1-5pm. Ship models, weapons, mines, uniforms, marine paintings and the like are on view.

The Reddingmuseum, "Dorus Rijkers," Keizerstraat 1a, tel. (02230) 18320; open Mon.-Sat., 10am-5pm. Den Helder is renowned for its efficient sea rescue teams and this museum deals with lifesaving.

On a lighter vein, there's the doll museum, Käthe Krüse, Binnenhaven 25-26, Wed.-Sun., but call ahead, (02230) 16704.

IN THE NEIGHBORHOOD OF DEN HELDER:

The Afsluitdijk is about 24 kilometers east of Den Helder on N99 and will take you to Friesland. Even if there's only time to drive to the observation point on this magnificent dike (about halfway), it's an impressive sight.

TEXEL

The "sheep island" and bird preserve

GETTING THERE: Texel is the most southerly of the Wadden islands which run in a chain along the Northern coast of Holland. Or put another way, Texel is the most northerly land of the Province of North Holland, reachable from Den Helder via roll-on-roll-off vessels of the T.E.S.O. steamship company . . . cars, caravans and buses are all carried on the 20-minute crossing. Follow directions to Den Helder, and then signs to Texel or steamship terminal. Boats usually leave hourly five minutes after the hour, but in summertime, crossings are more frequent. For details, contact the VVV.

INFORMATION: VVV Texel, Groeneplaats 9, Den Burg, tel. (02220) 14741 or VVV Den Helder, tel. (02230) 14888.

Still a world apart, Texel has always been known as the "sheep island." Roughly 30,000 sheep are on the island which, along with cattle-breeding, agriculture, bulb-growing and fishing, provide an economic base. In addition, tourism has risen each year making it a very important factor in the economic health of the area.

Texel, 15 miles long and 5 miles wide, is the largest of the North Sea islands which were formed during the Tertiary period and are part of a dune area which extends to Jutland in Denmark. It is protected by its immense sand dunes on the west. Even today, it offers a relatively isolated area with some of the most beautiful sand beaches in the world. Not particularly well known by most foreigners, the island is crowded during the summer with Dutch and German vacationers. If you want to visit during this time, do make reservations ahead.

Beaches along the whole length of Texel are accessible by roads with good

parking facilities and supervised areas. The National Forestry Service, which is responsible for the protection of the dunes, offers guided walks in the nesting areas. In addition, there are many dunes marked as special walking paths for visitors to enjoy on their own. Originally planted to keep the sand dunes from blowing away, there are more than 1,250 acres of pine woods between Den Hoorn and De Koog which add another dimension to the landscape and which provide lovely picnic spots.

Den Burg is the main town on Texel; smaller villages are Den Hoorn, De Koog, Horntje, Cocksdorp, Oosterend, de Waal and Oudeschild. Den Burg has a fine shopping center with a Monday morning market (mid-May to the end of June), the interesting museum Oudheidskamer (Kogerstraat 1, tel. 3135; open, summer only, 9am-12:30 pm), and a 15th-century church on Aan de Binnenburg. The museum has a collection of Texel art works, clothing and local items.

MUSEUMS AND CHURCHES: For those determined to have their daily ration of culture, there are several museums and historic churches around the island.

Den Hoorn has a 1500-1700 church and a ship museum, the Scheepvaartmuseum, Diek 11, tel. 264.

De Koog's Texel Museum in the nature recreation center "Ruylsaa", Fuyslaan 92, tel. (02228) 741 is open mid-May to the end of September, 9am-5pm.

Oosterend can boast of the oldest church in Texel, the 15th-century Martinuskerk (can be visited . . . check with VVV).

Oudeschild is proud of its Protestant church (1650) and the windmill, De Traanroeier (1902). In an old farmer's house, De Waal, visitors will enjoy a folkloric museum, the Texels Wagonmuseum with wagons from the 1700s.

BIKING: Texel is a wonderful area for biking so bring your own if you can. Or, you can rent them on the island or at Den Helder (check with the Texel VVV). In addition, visitors by auto—as well as serious bike riders—should buy the Texel map showing the recommended Texel scenic route . . . 75 kilometers of changing views: the sea, sand, dunes, polderland, wooded areas, moors, marshes, ponds, bird sanctuaries, typical Texel sheep barns and walls of sod dividing the fields.

Just south of Den Burg in a landscape reserve area, you can see Texel's "high mountain"—all of 45 feet above sea level. At the end of the Ice Age, this little mountain was a glacial deposit which provided the original core around which

123

the action of the sea, together with typical Dutch land reclamation know-how, has produced the island as you see it today. There are more than 30,000 sheep—a breed unique to Texel—throughout the island, outnumbering the population almost 3 to 1.

We cannot leave Texel without mentioning its importance to serious and amateur students of ornithology. There are more than 100 species of birds breeding on the island and innumerable migrants stay on Texel in spring and autumn. Among the breeding birds are several rarities such as the Avocet and Spoonbill. Other interesting species include the Icterine Warbler, Golden Oriole, Blacktailed Godwit, and Ruff. One of the most important bird reserves is the small lake of the Muy in the dunes north of De Koog, where nest, among others, Spoonbill, Heron, short-eared Owls, Marsh and Montagu's Harrier, Redbacked Shrike, Grasshopper Warbler, Blacktailed Godwit, Redshank and Curlew. Near Cocksdorp in a marshy promontory crisscrossed by many creeks, is a reserve for migratory waders, ducks and Brent Geese. You can obtain a small guide book written in English from VVV which describes the bird reserves of the island.

STAYING OVER: There is an old-fashioned and inexpensive hotel right on the market square of Den Burg, the "Lindeboom," a good place from which to observe local happenings. Incidentally, be careful where you park your car the night before the market. You might wake up to find it immovable and completely integrated into the market itself. It has been known to happen. From July to mid-August, the place jumps with sheep-shearing demonstrations and market (Wed., 2-6pm), and an arts and crafts market.

Den Hoorn or De Koog might appeal to beach lovers with their miles of sandy beaches backed by high dunes and pine forests. Campers have a choice of some fourteen campsites between Den Burg and De Koog.

YEARLY EVENTS: In May and June, birdwatchers and other nature-lovers come to see a rare occurrence; various species of bird (including the spoonbills) placing their eggs in the inlets of sweet water in the middle of the dunes. Guides are available for a tour of the nesting areas.

MEDEMBLIK, TWISK and KOLHORN

Three charming villages

GETTING THERE: Medemblik is to the east of A7/N7, north of Hoorn. From points south, follow directions to Amsterdam, through the Coen Tunnel, west on A8 and then north on A7/N7. Twisk and Kolhorn can be located in the vicinity of Medemblik on a large-scale map showing small local roads.
INFORMATION: VVV Medemblik, Stationsgebouw, Dam 2, tel. (02274) 2852, or from the Hotel Het Wapen van Medemblik, Oosterhaven 1, tel. (02274) 3844.

Medemblik, a charming village now situated on the IJsselmeer, is also one of the oldest towns in West Friesland with a recorded history to the year 334. It comes alive during the summer when its harbors overflow with sailors, their crew and their boats. International sailing races are held several times a year so check ahead if you want to see or avoid the events.

Driving down the main street, note the historic architecture until you come to the hotel, Het Wapen van Medemblik, on the left-hand corner just before crossing over the bridge in the direction of the Castle. Some of the buildings of interest in town include the 15th-16th-century Bonifacius Church, former weigh house on the Kaasmarkt, former orphanage, the old widows' houses on Heeresteeg, the City Hall with 17th-century brick step-gables, and the pumping station, the "Vier Nooderkoggen." The orphanage, Die Oudtheytkamer tot Medemblik, has an interesting collection of Dutch artifacts, money, ceramics, silver and tin dating from the 14th-17th centuries.

Radboud Castle, built by Floris V in 1288 to keep an eye on his newly conquered subjects, was originally square with four round defensive towers in each corner. The portion evident today, restored in 1890 by Dr. P. J. H. Cuypers, is only about a quarter the size of the original castle. Open in summer June-Sept., daily 10am-5pm, Sun., 2-5pm; in winter, Sept.-May, only Sun. 2-5pm. For information, tel. (02274) 3844 or 1960. The castle houses a national weapons and flag museum, as well as furniture, paintings and other items dealing primarily with the history of Medemblik.

At Gedempte Achterom 5, Oosterdijk, there is a private steam machine museum which contains mid-18th- to mid-19th-century steam machines from ships and factories; open in summer, except Mondays, daily from 10am-5pm. From the old train station which has been restored, it's possible to take a steam train ride to Hoorn and back. And for a ride "on the water," you can drive to Lelystad via Enkhuizen over the new dike in about an hour. June, July and August, there's a sound and light performance at Radboud Castle . . . for other special summer festivities, check with the VVV.

STAYING OVER: One of the nicest hotel stops in this part of Holland is Hotel Het Wapen van Medemblik. The old section (now the main reception and dining room) has been a renowned hotel at least since 1897. If you can't stay overnight, at least have lunch or tea. For those who can spend a few days exploring the area, the new addition offers traditional hospitality with exceptionally comfortable modern rooms overlooking the old harbor. Off-season (October 1-March 31) special weekend rates are offered which include a cup of coffee upon arrival, a champagne-cocktail before a dinner-dance on Saturday night, a good Dutch breakfast on Sunday and Monday mornings, Sunday dinner to the accompaniment of piano music, and a visit to Radboud castle.

Twisk, just a few kilometers from Medemblik, is a small village well worth a detour. The houses are so charming, so colorful, with such original lace curtains and decorative iron work, they could almost be a stage set. The town is literally built on either side of the main road. For most of its length, there are only properties one-house deep with nothing but fields and meadows stretching to the horizon. On the canal side of the road, the houses are reached by private bridges. A unique village with practically no parking; leave the car at one end or the

125

other and walk its length so you can enjoy its vistas to best advantage.

Kolhorn is an example of a typical dike village similar to what others in the area, such as Enkhuizen, must have been before the original draining of the Wieringerwaard land in 1844. From the top of the high enclosure dike built in the middle of the 14th century, there is a beautiful view of Kolhorn, its houses and the surrounding polderland. Behind the dike, there's a ditch, and behind the ditch, are the houses. Along one side of the village, near the old church, there is a narrow paved walk running between the traditional houses and their small gardens, well planted with fruit trees, flowers and sometimes a few vegetables.

In olden times, Kolhorn was known for its peat storage sheds—peat was brought from Friesland in sailing ships—and for its fishermen. Shell fishing near Texel was one good source of income. You might even be able to still smell the tar from the old fishing boats. Ships too large to dock at Amsterdam used to bring their exotic cargoes from the East Indies to towns like Kolhorn where they transferred their goods to "coasters," smaller lighters which could navigate the shallower waters. This way of life ceased, however, when the Zuider Zee was enclosed. This area—now about 10 kilometers from the water—was pumped dry for farming. At first, this was not successful because of the high salt content. Experiments were carried out and eventually a root was discovered which, when planted, rendered the land porous so the salt could escape. You can drive into the town now and park near the church. The Kerkepad across from the church will take you to the old houses with their "projecting" gardens—houses on one side and gardens on the other side of the walk.

ENKHUIZEN

Boats, boats, boats and a very special museum

GETTING THERE: From Rotterdam and The Hague, follow directions for Amsterdam, through the Coen Tunnel, west on A8 to the intersection with A7 going north until you see indications for Hoorn and Enkhuizen. There is a boat available from the end of May to the beginning of September between Enkhuizen and Staveren, Urk, and Medemblik. Trains are available to and from Amsterdam, Alkmaar and Den Helder; buses from Lelystad, Hoorn and Medemblik. In nice weather, why not drive over the impressive dike between Enkhuizen and Lelystad, in Flevoland?
INFORMATION: VVV Enkhuizen, Stationsplein 1, tel. (02286) 13164.

Enkhuizen is a photographer's paradise. At every turn, there are old Dutch facades, ships at anchor—from small sailboats to ocean-sized two-masted sailing vessels and scenic drawbridges.

Most tourists are not aware that in the 16th century Enkhuizen actually rivaled Amsterdam. It still contains many beautiful old facades and historic buildings as memories of its more glorious days, buildings such as the famed Drommedaris, the 15th-century Zuidertoren (South Tower) with vault paintings; the 16th-century Weighhouse with surgeons' guild room and city museum; the 17th-century Town Hall with paintings and the old city prison (behind the Town Hall on Swaanstraat); the Koepoort (1649), a city gate; the 15th-century Westerkerk with its wood carvings and choir screen; and the Vestingwal (1590), city walls with bulwarks and water gates.

The Zuiderzee Museum is one of Holland's most exciting museums with the completion of the outdoor section (Buitenmuseum). There is an excellent brochure in Dutch, English and German entitled "Het Buurtje" (the neighborhood) which visitors should buy in order to understand how the Zuiderzee Museums came into being and what they are all about.

If there's time, why not treat the kids with a visit to the recreational center "Enkhuizer Zand." There you can enjoy a sandy beach, heated pool, playground, mini-golf course and water sports facilities for small craft.

Another attraction sure to delight the younger set is "Sprookjeswonderland" (fairy-tale land), Wilhelminaplantsoen 2, tel. (02280) 17853, located in the heart of Enkhuizen very near the Open Air Museum. There are dolls' houses, "motor cars" to drive yourself, fairy-tale characters, as well as a children's zoo. Summer hours (from the first Sun. in May through the second Sun. in Sept.) are: Mon.-Sat., 10am-3:30pm; Sundays, 1-5pm.

STAYING OVER: This part of Holland deserves an overnight stay at least. If you decide to enjoy the local, rural atmosphere, try "Het Wapen van Enkhuizen" or the "Die Port Van Cleve," both moderate-priced. For lovers of atmosphere, the latter has old-world charm. There are also a number of camping sites in the neighborhood—check with the VVV or the Camping Council.

YEARLY EVENTS: On the outskirts of Enkhuizen at Bovenkarspel, there is a yearly happening in February worth mentioning. It's called the Westfrisian Flora. You will find more information about this flower show/country fair immediately following the description of the Zuider Zee Museum.

COMMERCIAL TOURS: For a totally relaxing way to sightsee as well as learn about the polders and land cultivation of this fertile area, you can take an open flat-bottom boat, the Rijo, from Lutjebroeker Laadplaats (between Enkhuizen and Hoorn) for a tour of the **Streekbos** and the **Grootslag**. There are exhibits and displays showing cultivation of the blooming flowers common to the area, dairy production (and the cows, of course), and a polder museum showing the working life of people who have lived in the area for the past 500 years. For information, tel. (02285) 16789 or 16925, or the VVV. Tours run from May through October, Tues., Wed. and Fri., 1:30pm returning at 4:30pm. On Sundays, the boat leaves at noon and returns at 3pm. If you need public transportation, the bus stop is St. Nicolaas Church on the Enkhuizen-Hoorn line.

Zuider Zee Museum

LOCATION: Indoor Museum: Wierdikj 18—in the Peperhuis— Enk-huizen. Outdoor Museum: Look for signs directing you to the "Zuiderzeemuseum" parking area, from where you will board the ferry to the outdoor museum.
INFORMATION: Tel. (02280) 10122 or VVV Enkhuizen, tel. (02280) 13164.
HOURS: Both museums are open from April 5-Oct. 20, 10am-5pm ev-ery day. Closed Oct. 21-April 4.
ADMISSION: Indoor Museum: Adults, Fl. 5.00; children to 6 years, free; 6-18 and over 65 years, Fl. 3.00. Outdoor Museum (includes parking): Adults, Fl. 9.00; children to 6 years, Fl. 4.00; 6-18 and over 65 years, Fl. 7.00 .
NOTE: Dogs are not allowed. Admission tickets to the Outdoor Muse-um can be bought at the car park before boarding the boat. One can return by boat to the car park, or one can walk into town to see the Indoor Museum and then take a boat from the jetty near the station to return to the car park.
■ *Of interest to all.*

The Indoor Museum is located in a historic building, the Peperhuis, once the headquarters of the Enkhuizen Chamber of the Dutch East India Company. In it are national costumes in authentic period interiors, painted furniture from the Hindeloopen and Zaan areas, models of typical ships, maps, paintings, prints and all sorts of nautical ornamentation. There are old-style anchors, fishing nets, farm implements and farmhouse utensils including things like cheese presses, a ropemaker's wheel and a sailcloth loom. Particularly unique is the fleet of Zuider Zee and inland ships lying moored at the quay, and the covered hall of ships where old ships can be viewed from a walkway around the area.

The Outdoor Museum plans were announced in 1943 by S. J. Bouma, then director of the Netherlands Open-Air Museum at Arnhem. His concept was to establish a living museum on the open waters of the IJsselmeer where all the activities characteristic to the culture of the area could be retained. The result is described in the booklet, Het Buurtje, which can be purchased at the museums:

"What one now sees when approaching by water from the direction of Staveren and Medemblik is the silhouette of a town consisting of a complex of buildings which fit into the landscape in a natural and harmonious way. This landscape, the confines of the museum area, is encircled by a sea-dike merging into natural vegetation beyond the dike.

"The complex consists of a collection of buildings representing aspects of Flevian culture and comes from a great number of places round the IJsselmeer. A common factor is that they fit in stylistically with the town of Enkhuizen, which forms a background to them a little way off."

One hundred thirty houses have been built along streets, canals and alleys to provide a picture of life between 1880 and 1932. As you stroll along, you can pretend one of them is "your house." For instance, you might choose an urban

128

farm from Harderwijk, or a commercial fisherman's house, or the house of the Van der Kamp family who ran a steam laundry. There are displays showing traditional trades as well. But mostly, breathe in the atmosphere, look across the still waters of the IJsselmeer, and enjoy a quick visit into the past.

Westfrisian Flora

LOCATION: On the approach to Enkhuizen at Bovenkarspel. After you turn off A7, follow the signs to Enkhuizen until you see indications for the Westfrisian Flora. You will be directed to park your car just outside the village where buses will transport you, free of charge, directly to the door of the exhibition halls . . . it is done very efficiently. For those desiring public transportation, there are NZH bus services from the major cities in North Holland, as well as special train service every half hour. Many railroad stations sell a combined train/entrance ticket which is more economical. From the Flora stop (Bovenkarspel-Grootebroek) it is only a 3-minute walk to the exhibition entrance.

INFORMATION: Correspondence address: Hoofdstraat 233, POB 23, 1610 AA Bovenkarspel, tel. (02285) 11644 (4 lines).

HOURS: Open for 11 days, about mid-February. Those interested should call the above number for precise opening and closing dates each year.

ADMISSION: Adults: Fl. 10.00; Children (to 14 years): Fl. 5.00. (Multiple-entrance card, Fl. 25.00.

■ *Of interest to everyone, except infants.*

This yearly happening of extremely short duration is worth mentioning because it's a preview of what you'll be seeing at later flower exhibitions such as the Keukenhof, but also because it's a fascinating, hurly-burly, old-fashioned country fair with a real Dutch touch! There's 14,000 m" of covered and heated exhibition space, a "Flora Fair," a children's farm; an original auction room where the public can buy flowers with the help of an auction clock; and an exhibit of bulb-growing machinery.

Each year, there's a different theme. In 1988, it was a tribute to airborne transport. Dutch flowers and bulbs are sold successfully all over the world because of rapid air transportation. Special platforms were constructed so visitors could see the exhibits from on high—an interesting and very effective perspective.

HOORN

Land, water and an interesting past

GETTING THERE: Hoorn can be reached by land or by water— it's a natural locale for sailors of all kinds. From Amsterdam and other points south, take highway A7 north until you see signs for the turnoff to Hoorn.
INFORMATION: VVV Hoorn, Nieuwstraat 23, tel. (02290) 18342.

It is easy to see that Hoorn was once a very rich—and even an international—city. Daring adventurers started from here to brave the hazardous seas in search of merchant treasures such as spices, gunpowder and all manner of exotic items from the Baltic, the Levant and even the West Indies.

Hoorn was founded in the 14th century at the site of a natural harbor which was to bring its citizens wealth and power during the 17th century. In this "Golden Age" it became the central administrative and commercial center of all Holland north of Amsterdam.

Hoorn was the birthplace of Willem Schouten (1580-1625) the man who discovered the passage around the southern tip of South America in 1616. He named it "Cape Horn" after his native town.

There are some interesting historical landmarks worth seeking out. Facing the old church, St. John's Hospital (1563) is now used for exhibitions and other city functions. If you take the Kerkstraat to the left in front of the hospital, you will come to the heart and most picturesque part of Hoorn, the Rode Steen (town square) with its statue of J. P. Coen, the founder of the East-Indies empire.

Opposite the Westfries Museum is the Weigh House (17th century), its lovely edifice and interesting construction the work of Hendrik de Keyser. If you follow the Groote Oost, you will pass the Oosterkerk with its 17th-century facade, and at the corner of Groote Oost and Slapershaven, you will see the Bossuhuizen with their ornamental Frisian sculpture. From here the citizens watched the great naval battle of October 1573 when the Spaniard, Admiral Bossu, Stadholder of Holland, was vanquished by the Netherlanders. If you continue along the Slapershaven, look at the architecture of buildings 17, 19, 21 on the Oude Doelenkade, then, the old warehouses at Veermanskade 2, 3 and 6. At the end of the Veermanskade, you will see the romantic, white Hoofdtoren which has stood guard at the port entrance for many years.

In the beautifully renovated Noorderkerk at the Kleine Noord near the railway station, a large model of Hoorn in the 1650s is exhibited. The glorious past of the town is depicted in a 20-minute audio-visual program . . . English is spoken. Open May through September and during school holidays. For specifics, contact the VVV, tel. 18342 or Maquette Hoorn 1650, tel. (02290) 31128.

To tempt the ladies, there are many nice small shops in town, but in particular, there are also some outstanding antique shops to be discovered.

YEARLY EVENTS: In February, just a little further along the road towards Enkhuizen, there's a wonderful tulip festival, the "Westfries Flora." Throughout the summer, Hoorn organizes a number of folkloric and market events on and around the former market place. There are folk dancers, old-fashioned handicrafts and all sorts of goings on.

COMMERCIAL TOURS: What could be nicer than a train ride along the North Holland countryside? The Steamtrain Museum Hoorn-Medemblik is open from the beginning of May 'til the middle of September. Unique to this movable museum is that the steam locomotives are all working trains; operates July and August, check with the VVV for specifics.

If a trip on the water is more your style, there's a restful boat excursion from Hoorn-Medemblik and Enkhuizen on "De Stad Enkhuizen" (City of Enkhuizen); buffet on board. The National Railways also offers a combined steam train, boat trip with stops at the towns . . . an all-day expedition. The visit to the Open Air Museum at Enkhuizen is not included in the price.

Westfries Museum

LOCATION: Rode Steen 1 (city square).
INFORMATION: Achterom 2-4, Hoorn, tel. (02290) 15597, if no answer, 15748.
HOURS: Mon.-Fri., 11am-5pm; Sat.-Sun. and public holidays, 2-5pm.
■ *Of interest to most children over five years.*

The present West Frisian Museum is housed in the former State Council building—a beautiful baroque structure constructed in 1632. It stands on even older foundations—the vaults are now used for exhibiting part of the museum collection.

In the 17th century Hoorn was a most important and prosperous town. Delegates representing Alkmaar, Hoorn, Enkhuizen, Medemblik, Edam, Monnickendam and Purmerend used to meet in this building to formulate a common position before sessions of the States of Holland in The Hague. Voting in a block gave them a stronger voice than they would have had individually. That meeting room is the showpiece of this museum.

The collection has something to attract everyone—period rooms for the girls and ladies; coins, coats of arms, prison cells for the men and boys. In addition, there are models of mills, ships, houses; firefighting equipment, archaeological finds, and so on. There is a small pamphlet in English for a modest fee which will make a visit to the museum more interesting.

EDAM

The round-red cheese town

GETTING THERE: Edam is just north of Volendam. From points south, A7 will take you to the general area. Purmerend is the biggest town and right on the highway. Rural roads to the east will take you to Edam.
INFORMATION: VVV Edam, Speeltoren, Kleine Kerkstraat, tel. (02993) 71727.

131

Edam didn't receive its city rights from Count Willem V until 1357. Still a most picturesque town, it was once a bustling port and like its neighbors, reached its greatest prosperity in the 17th century. It had several shipyards, but its fame today has been spread more by its round red balls of cheese than its buildings or museums.

St. Nicolas Church (the 15th-century late Gothic Grote Kerk), in the center on the Damplein, is open to visitors in season from 2-4:30pm. Look for the fine choir screen and stained glass windows (mostly 1606-24). On the other side, the 16th-century Proveniershuis was formerly the home of the Beguine sisterhood. The Town Hall (1737) is also worth a visit with its beautiful Council Chamber, magnificent wedding room, antique furniture, hand-painted wallpaper, and sand on the floor—ask permission from the VVV.

Near Breestraat and Achterhaven, the wooden house, Houtenhuis (15th century) is the oldest in town. A late Gothic house with a floating cellar is the local museum ... open Easter-September, Mon.-Sat., 10am-4pm; Sun., 1:30-4:30pm. Also don't miss the Captain's House across from the Town Hall with its paintings depicting characters in folktales of the region. Just seeing the house is an experience "curiouser" and "curiouser." Another old structure is the Speeltoren of the former "Onze Lieve Vrouwe" Church, weekdays, 9am-6pm ... the carillon dates from the 15th century. The tower threatened to topple but in 1972 it was restored. The Cheese Weigh House, built in 1778, has a permanent cheese exposition from April-Sept., daily, 10am-5pm.

Walk around this old town and enjoy the old bricks, canals, tea houses set in charming gardens, and the French Garden.

PURMEREND

A cheese and cattle town

GETTING THERE: Purmerend is just off Autoroute A7 between Zaandam and Hoorn.
INFORMATION: Municipal Information Center and VVV, Kaasmarkt 20, tel. (02990) 52525.

Purmerend has been a market town for 500 years. The primary markets today are the cheese market and the cattle market. The Cheese Market is held in June 'til the end of August on Thursdays from 10am-1pm. Old handicrafts are demonstrated and there is music as well as special activities. The Cattle Market is held on Tuesdays, 7am-noon as is the general market, 9am-noon. Drivers will be glad to know Purmerend has no parking problems!

The centuries-old cheese market is held at the foot of the Town Hall in the center of Purmerend. Cheese porters dressed all in white and wearing straw hats trimmed with blue or red ribbons to indicate their guild, carry the cheese to the weigh-house; then, it is tasted, bought and weighed. See "Alkmaar" for more details on the guilds, etc. Also on Thursday (Cheese Market Day), the Historical Museum in the Town Hall is open to the public.

Purmerend's "touristic international shopping center," the Willem Eggert Center, sounds too good to pass up.

YEARLY EVENTS: Special events during the year, in addition to the cheese, cattle and general markets mentioned above, are town celebrations, a cattle show and steeplechase held in September—check with the VVV for details.

The following three villages, Volendam, Monnickendam and Marken, clustered together just north of Amsterdam, along with Zaandam, Broek in Waterland, Edam and Purmerend, are among the most charming and scenic places in the Netherlands. Their old-world character has been noted by visitors for years, and their proximity to Amsterdam has made them popular. If you can, try to visit the area just before or after the heaviest summer traffic. If you have no choice, never mind, touring is well organized and the area should not be missed.

VOLENDAM

A Roman Catholic fishing village

GETTING THERE: Volendam is north of Amsterdam via the Coen Tunnel towards Leeuwarden. You will pass Broek in Waterland and Monnickendam before arriving at Volendam. From The Hague and Rotterdam, A4 to Amsterdam then follow directions above. In summer, you can make boat trips to the island of Marken on the "Marken Express."
INFORMATION: VVV Volendam, Zeestraat 21, tel. (02993) 63747.

Originally a fishermen's village, Volendam is a Roman Catholic town as opposed to Marken which is Protestant. The villagers in both towns continue to wear their very colorful traditional dress—at least on Sundays for the tourists! Since the draining of the Zuider Zee, Volendam's 17,000 inhabitants make their livelihood from tourism and by working in some recently established local industries.

There are various things to see. For instance, if cigar bands have always fascinated you, you can see such a collection at "De Gouden Kamer," Oude Draaipad 8, open in season from Mon.-Sun., 10am-5pm. Something more traditional is the Volendams Museum, Kloosterbuurt 5, tel. (02993) 64564.

At the Hotel-Restaurant Spaander, 15 Haven, there's a collection of more than 100 old masters, artists who worked in Volendam . . . a good stop for a cup of coffee or more.

The ceramics factory at 1 Ventersgracht is open Mon.-Fri., 8am-5pm, tel. 64564. Then, there's the cheese farm "Alida Hoeve," Zeddeweg 1, open daily from 9am-6pm. And finally, the fish auction on the Haven . . . sale of eels takes place Mon.-Fri., 10-11am and 4-6pm.

Then last but not least, you can go to one of the photographers on the dike and have your picture taken in traditional Dutch costume to send back home.

MONNICKENDAM

Fishing, smoked eels and wooden shoes

GETTING THERE: From Amsterdam, take the Coen Tunnel going north, A10, then A8 towards Leeuwarden. You will pass the turn-off for Broek in Waterland about 4 kilometers before Monnickendam. From The Hague and Rotterdam, take A4 to Amsterdam then follow directions above.

INFORMATION: VVV Monnickendam, De Zarken 2, tel. (02995) 1998.

This small town dates back to the 13th century when Frisian monks built a dam in the sea and a lake was formed. Before the Afsluitdijk was built and the Zuider Zee became the IJsselmeer, fishing was the life's blood of this town and its neighbors.

Grote Kerk, the 13th-century Great Church, is one of the important sights in Monnickendam; open June 6-Sept. 6, Mon.-Sat., 10am-4pm, Sun., 2-4pm.

The Town Hall, Noordeinde 5, dates back to 1746. Originally a patrician mansion, notice the town symbol on the facade—the figure of a monk. Visits are possible by appointment, tel. (02995) 3939.

The Speeltoren, Noordeinde 4, has an 18th-century carillon which chimes on the hour while two knights perform a slow parade. It houses the Archaeological Museum, open mid-June-Aug., Mon.-Sat., 10am-4pm, Fri. eves., 7-9pm, Sun., 1-4pm.

At the Clogmaker, Irene Hoeve, Nogedijk 1, Katwoude, tel. 2291, you can see wooden shoes being made. The Weeshuis (orphanage 1638), Weezenland 16, tel. (02995) 3642, has an herb garden and changing exhibitions. Or you can visit a cheese farm, "Jacobhoeve," Hogedijk 8, Katwoude, by calling 1597; open daily, 9am-6pm. The "Speeldozenmuseum" on the Haringburgwal is all about music boxes.

An unusual stop is "De Oude Visafslag" where one can see the eel smoking rooms as well as pottery being produced. Open in summer from 9am-5pm; in winter, only on weekends.

EATING OUT: The ancient weighing house, De Waag, is now a pancake restaurant, tel (02995) 1241. Another restaurant, The Nieuw Stukenburg, also houses a musical box museum. For a more formal meal, try the famous Stuttenburgh restaurant, Haringburgwal 2, tel. (02995) 1896.

MARKEN

An "island" village

*GETTING THERE: On a peninsula (once an island) to the east of
Monnickendam and south of Volendam.*
*INFORMATION: VVV Monnickendam-Marken, De Zarken 2, Mon-
nickendam, tel. (02995) 1998, or c/o the Clogmaker at the car
park, tel. (02996) 1630. If you drive, leave your car at the car
park. The Clogmaker can provide you with a map showing a
walking or cycling route.*

Monks in the 13th century constructed a dam around the Isle of Marken. As in
Monnickendam, fishing was the main source of income until the closing of the
Zuider Zee. The wooden houses formerly built on piles of wood now have stone
basements.

Approaching Marken by boat gives every impression it is still an island and is
much more picturesque than driving over. Also, you are dropped off right in
town, a nice convenience. The traditional costumes you will see here are quite
different from those in Volendam.

Be sure and visit the Dutch Reformed Church, open May-Oct., Mon.-Sat.,
10am-5pm . . . notice the six ships in full sail, constructed by local craftsmen,
hanging from the ceiling . . . one is a herring boat.

The Marken Home will show you how the old seamen and their wives lived;
open every day except Sunday. The house is cosy, as compact as the interior of a
ship's cabin.

The Marken Museum, Kerkbuurt 44-47, tel. 1904, shows the history and way
of life in Marken from beginning to present. Open Easter-October, Mon.-Sat.,
10am-4:30pm, Sun., noon-4pm.

Pottery is made at Havenbuurt 1, open all year, Tues.-Sun., 10am-6pm and
the Clogmaker is also open all year, 9am-6pm, except Sundays.

YEARLY EVENTS: Take your cameras with you on the Queen's Birthday
(April 30) when the citizens of Marken all dress in orange clothing. In August
and September you can see sailing competitions for fishing boats . . . Info, VVV.

BROEK IN WATERLAND

Brook in water land!

*GETTING THERE: By private car from Rotterdam and The Hague,
take highway A4 towards Amsterdam, turning off at the Coen
Tunnel. Immediately upon exiting the tunnel, continue following
A8/A7 signs (Leeuwarden). Normal driving time from Rotterdam
is approximately one and a half hours; distance from Amsterdam
is 10 kilometers. N247 goes right through Broek in Waterland;
turn left off the main highway to see the old part of the village
described below. Immediately after turning off the highway, you*

135

will cross a bicycle path; turn right and follow the Parking signs.
INFORMATION: VVV Monnickendam, Nieuwpoortslaan, Loswal,
   Tel. (02995) 1998.

What a fantastic name! You will quite agree the town is aptly named as you drive past its picturesque small lake and walk along its many canals. This attractive old village is full of surprises and has something to offer everyone in the family from a gourmet-type restaurant to a small home-style children's farm.

The best way to see Broek in Waterland is on foot—it's a small village and everything is very close by. Notice the lovely old homes which have been restored or are in the process of restoration, many of them with the upper stories leaning forward—a unique feature in this area. Some say the houses were built like this because of the harsh storms and the overhang would protect the windows from bearing the brunt of full-force winds; another explanation is that since many upper stories were used as storage areas, it was easier to get whatever was being stored into the house with this type construction. No matter what the reason, these houses with their green and white exteriors and unusual architectural design are lovely to look at and give the village a special charm.

■ **The Protestant Church** should be your first stop—don't be diverted by the klompen-maker, children's farm, antique shops or cheese farm. It is open all day during the summer season (May to Sept.) except when there is a funeral or a wedding. Off-season, you can ask the Rector for permission to visit; he lives alongside the church itself. The church was built before 1400 and was consecrated to Santa Claus . . . that bit of information should intrigue the younger set. The church was destroyed by fire in September 1573 by Spanish soldiers, and in 1628, rebuilding was started. When completed, the townspeople gave many of the objects which you can still see in the church. Especially interesting is the hour-glass at the pulpit—everyone could watch to see how much longer the sermon was going to last! Incidentally, the arrangement of chairs and benches goes back to the period of the Hedge-sermons. Armed men used the benches which were placed in a protective ring around the chairs where the women and children sat. There is a printed paper available in English which gives more information about the church . . . a small donation to the church is appreciated.

As you walk into town from the parking area, you will be drawn to De Swaen, Havenrak 21, tel. 1432, one of the most attractive and interesting wooden shoe factories in Holland. Here the shoes are actually floating from the ceiling. The owner is a gregarious host and will demonstrate how they are made.

Walking along the main street, the Havenrak, which goes along the side of the little lake, you will pass two antique shops. The cheese farm, Cheesery De Domme Dirk, Roomeinde 17, tel. 1454; open Mon.-Fri., 6am-6pm, is organized to receive visitors.

Before returning to your car, stop (if you haven't already) at the children's farm. The squawking and honking of the geese, cackling of the chickens and turkeys, grunting of the pigs and sundry sounds from the animals is almost deafening when they spot their supper on the way . . . about 4:30 or 5pm is the usual time.

136

EATING OUT: The pancake house on Dorpsstraat, de Witte Zwaen, is a rustic and informal place with moderate prices. For something a bit more dressy, try the "Neeltje Pater," tel. (02903) 3311. This small, tastefully decorated restaurant has a lovely view over the lake. The present owners also specialize in high teas. On Sunday afternoons between 3-5pm, you can luxuriate in the taste delights of homemade sandwiches, hot scones, tarts and a variety of delicious cakes. Reservations recommended.

IN THE NEIGHBORHOOD OF BROEK IN WATERLAND: There's a recreation area "Het Twiske" west of the village, Ilpendam . . . the area is wonderful for biking. And a small museum at Landsmeer, Museum Grietje Tump, Kadoelenweg 69, tel. (020) 313455, open Sun., 2-5pm.

NAARDEN

An ancient fortified town

GETTING THERE: From Amsterdam take A1 east to Naarden. From The Hague and Rotterdam, A20 northeast to A12 east, around Utrecht to A27 going north, then A1 northwest to Naarden, OR for a specially scenic route, take A12 east to A2 north to turnoff for Maarssen. Then follow the Vecht River past the castles at Nijenrode, Oudaen and Gunterstein, and past Breukelen (Brooklyn, N.Y. was named after this town), Loenen, Hilversum, Bussum and finally Naarden.
INFORMATION: Naarden VVV, Adriaan Dortsmanplein 1B, tel. (02159) 42836.

Naarden's history is a bit hazy, since most of the town records were destroyed during many years of regional fighting. However, the name of the town does appear as early as 968 when it became part of the possessions of the Abbey of Elten. In 1280, Count Floris acquired Naarden through conquest; he was later dramatically murdered at Muiderslot Castle, not far away. One of the most traumatic historical episodes occurred in 1572 when the Spaniards burned the town to the ground and killed most of the inhabitants as an example to other Dutch rebels. This event is depicted in the carved stone facade which can be seen above the doorway of the present Comenius Museum.

Naarden is a medieval fortified town with a design so beautiful it seems more make-believe than real. But the exciting thing at Naarden are the fortifications themselves which are something to stir the imagination of any small (or large) boy or girl . . . it's like having a sand castle suddenly come to life—only better. The kids won't drag their feet going to the museum here, either, because it is actually located underground inside the very bastions of earth which form the ramparts. But, more about that later.

As you approach the town of Naarden, you can see the architectural layout of the fortifications; you cross the moat and enter the city through one of the three entrances. Originally there were two entrances—the lovely Utrecht Gate, and the Amsterdam Gate which disappeared in 1915. It is easy to believe yourself in the 17th or 18th century as you drive through small city streets lined with interesting private and commercial houses, historic monuments such as the Utrecht Gate (1870), Weigh House (1808), Arsenal (1688), not to mention the lovely Town Hall (1601), St. Vitus Church (built between 1380 and 1440), and the Spanish House (1615). Reconstruction of the fortifications, begun in 1965, still goes on.

The VVV offers a "Gable Tour," a walking guide folder, which points out the remarkable building facades and other interesting features not to be missed in Naarden. Also interesting to know for active youngsters (and oldsters, too, of course) there's a footpath which runs on top of the inner wall around the entire fortress. Check with the VVV for the access point. Another help in your orientation is a pamphlet entitled, "History of the Fortified Town of Naarden Holland"...from the VVV.

St. Vitus Church, the Netherlands Reformed Church, on St. Annastraat, underwent extensive restoration and was re-opened in 1979 by the Queen. The tower of the church (no elevator) is open in summer for a smashing view of the town and its surroundings. Inquire about the church festival featuring Bach's St. Matthew's Passion.

In the meantime, there is plenty to be seen which makes a visit worthwhile. In addition to the places one can enter such as the Vesting Museum (description follows), the Spanish House (presently the Comenius Museum), Comenius' Mausoleum, and the Town Hall, there are also places worth seeing from the outside, such as the Arsenal and the many restored houses listed on the VVV map of Naarden.

The Naarden Town Hall, located at Marktstraat 22, is a fine Renaissance building which was restored in 1950. It is open May-Oct., Mon.-Fri., 8:30am-noon and 1:30-4:30pm. There are exhibitions in the Town Hall from April through September, at which time it is also open to the general public on Saturday.

The Spanish House, which now houses the Comenius Museum, was the Town Hall until 1601. It got the name "Spanish House" when the citizens were murdered there by Spanish soldiers in 1572. The present collection honors the great Czechoslovakian philosopher, Jan Amos Komensky. It is located at Turfpoortstraat 27; for information, tel. (02159) 43045. The museum is open mid-Feb.-Dec. 15, 2-4pm, closed Mondays, or by special appointment. There is no entrance fee but a donation is appreciated. After a visit here, the Comenius Mausoleum, Kloosterstraat 29, tel. (02159) 40312, may be visited; daily except Mondays, from 4-5pm.

EATING OUT: If possible, pick a sunny, picnic-type day to visit Naarden and enjoy eating on the ramparts or in the lovely countryside. There are many local restaurants.

Vesting Museum

LOCATION: Westwalstraat, Naarden.
INFORMATION: Tel. (02159) 45459, or Naarden VVV (02159)
42836.
HOURS: Open Easter through October, Mon.-Fri., 10am-4:30pm;
Sat.-Sun., noon-5pm. Out of season, open for groups by appoint-
ment.

■ *Of interest to children from 6 years.*

As previously mentioned, the Vesting Museum is built right into the ramparts of
the Turfpoort bastion of the fortifications of Naarden. The smallest child might
not be fascinated with some of the more serious displays inside, but he will love
running up and down the ramparts and in and around the 19th-century guns
which are placed realistically in positions of defense on top of the high wall.

Inside this authentic 17th-century building, you can see a scale model of the
Turfpoort bastion which explains the ingenious system of defense; there are
model figures ready to fire a cannon; other models show the means of transport
on water and land; there is a gunpowder room where you will see old engravings
of the town of Naarden; and for gun enthusiasts, there is an arms collection
showing gun development from flintlock, percussion, to breechloading and
repeating rifle.

Incidentally, the fortress was in active status through World War I until 1926;
it became a national monument in 1964. There is a reconstructed WWI ma-
chine-gun nest including model soldiers in uniform, and a big Krupp 75-mm
field gun. You can visit the listening gallery which was actually used by sentinels
in time of war to listen through holes in the ceiling for the enemy who might be
trying to approach stealthily. There's more, but this is just a sample of what's to
be seen in this very unusual museum.

IN THE NEIGHBORHOOD OF NAARDEN:

Muiden Castle is located at the mouth of the Vecht river about 7 Kilometers
northwest of Naarden and 12 Kilometers southeast of Amsterdam, A1 going
east. For information, tel Amsterdam VVV or the Castle, (02942) 1325. Open,
Mon.-Fri., 10am-4pm, Sun., 1-4pm. Closed Saturdays, December 25, 26 and
January 1. All tours are conducted, and take about 1 hour. The last tour leaves 1
hour before closing. English-language tours are possible.

Muiderslot looks like a castle should! It's a massive red brick structure topped
with pointed towers, step-gables as well as a crenelated wall—all set within and
protected by its water-moat.

The origins of the castle date back to 1280 and Floris V. Its history has been
checkered and the castle has suffered heavy damage down the ages. It was at its
zenith in the 17th century when the well-known Dutch playwright and historian
P. C. Hooft repaired the castle and lived in it until his death in 1647. During this
period, important and influential men such as Hugo Grotius came to visit. With
Hooft's death, the castle lost its splendor and at the time of the French occupation
had received its death blow. The domain itself was put up for sale with the
intention of demolishing it entirely. King Willem I intervened to save it and it was
restored by Victor Stuers in 1883-1909 and again, later in this century.

Snacks are available at the Castle Tavern, or pack a lunch to enjoy at the picnic tables on the estate.

LAREN

Home of many former Dutch planters

GETTING THERE: The charming town of Laren is on A27 north, just off A1, a few minutes east of Hilversum.
INFORMATION: VVV Hilversum, Emmastraat 2, tel. (035) 11651.

Laren is located in an area full of ancient woods and imposing residences of former wealthy Dutch people. Coupled with the attraction the town has had for artists since the early 1900s, one cannot help but react favorably to its special charm.

The Singer Museum (see below) is more than a museum. It is the center of cultural activities in the area including musical presentations from the classics to jazz.

YEARLY EVENTS: There are flower shows and competitions as well as visiting art shows during the year. For instance, the "Herfstflora" (autumn flower exhibition) takes place in October. A folkloric event of ancient origin occurs in June with the St. John's procession in the center of Laren, ending at the "Old Cemetery" where once-upon-a-time, human sacrifices are said to have taken place.

Singer Museum

LOCATION: Oude Drift 1, Laren (follow the signs; it's just off the main town square; you may have to ask). Buses 134, 136, 138 stop at the museum.

INFORMATION: Museum tel. (02153) 15656.
HOURS: Tues.-Sat., 11am-5pm; Sun. and holidays, noon-5pm; closed Mon., except during the Fall Flower Show.
■ *Of interest to children from 8 years.*

The Singer Museum is a delightful place to come any time but especially during the summer and autumn when a show of exotic flower arrangements will be competing with nature's gently regulated blooms in the museum garden. It's this time of year when people come from far and wide to sit outside surrounded with gaily colored blooms while having tea, coffee and cake. In winter, the indoor restaurant is cosy and welcoming.

The museum's permanent collection is devoted to the works of the American artist, William H. Singer, Jr. (1868-1943), who lived and worked in Laren. In addition to his romantically impressionistic canvases, there are portraits by Jacob Dooijewaard and Indonesian scenes by William Dooijewaard as well as works of other international painters of the 19th and 20th centuries, many of whom lived in the area. Today, Laren continues to be a flourishing artists' colony and special exhibitions of their works are often presented at the museum.

CHAPTER 4

THE PROVINCE OF UTRECHT

Centrally located, Utrecht is the smallest of the 12 provinces. It has had a long and influential history; in particular, the role it played during the Eighty Years' War against the Spaniards. The Provinces of Holland tried to offer mutual resistance but disputes developed between the Catholic South and the Protestant North. The Northern provinces refused to deal with the occupiers while the Southern group wanted a reconciliation with the Spanish Duke of Parma who was Governor of the Netherlands at the time. The Northern provinces signed the Union of Utrecht on January 23, 1579. There followed a long war but the Spaniards were finally ousted in 1648, and the Union of Utrecht then served as the basis for the Netherlands State.

The history of the area can be found in the Province's ancient towns such as Utrecht and Amersfoort and the famous Het Loo Palace at Soestdijk. And all around, the countryside offers corners of relaxation: the southeast with fruit orchards which, when in flower, will send visitors into a euphoria of delight, and castles galore to titillate the imagination; the southwest with polder lands hiding behind the dikes along the charming twisting IJssel and Lek Rivers; the northwest with the Loosduinen Lakes where aquatics of all kinds are plentiful; and the northeast with its old forest-lands, grand country hotels and restaurants and the former hunting grounds of the Dutch Royal family. It is indeed a small province but with a great variety of natural beauty and explorations to appeal to everyone.

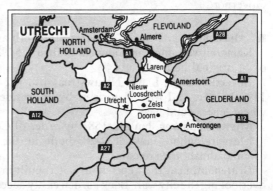

INFORMATION: VVV Utrecht,
  tel. (030) 314132.

UTRECHT

A city with a Medieval past and active present

GETTING THERE: From Amsterdam, take highway A2 south until you see signs for Utrecht Centrum. From The Hague and Rotterdam, take highway A12, then follow signs, "Centrum."
INFORMATION: VVV-i, Vredenburg 90, tel. (030) 314132.

The fourth largest town in the Netherlands, Utrecht's known history dates back to 48 A.D. when the Romans built a fort on the spot now called "Domplein" (Cathedral Square).

In an old city like Utrecht with its narrow (but picturesque!) streets, difficult parking and unending one-way streets, the VVV tour by foot-power is highly recommended. For residents or visitors here for an extended holiday, there are lovely parks, gardens, wharves and wharf cellars, the old Fish Market, Town Hall, Van de Poll Workhouse, and a number of churches to explore. Look for the "Paushuize," 's Rijks Munt, Leidseweg 90, tel. 910342, the Provincial Government building constructed in 1520 by Adrianus VI, the only Dutch Pope, which is reputed to be the most beautiful house in Utrecht. Other interesting places to seek out follow:

Academy Building of the University, Domplein 29, tel. 394252, where the Union of Utrecht was signed in the auditorium in 1579, contains coats of arms, organ, Gobelin tapestries (visit by appointment).

St. Bartholomew's Hospital, Lange Smeestraat 40, tel. 310254, a home for the aged, has large Gobelin tapestries (1642) in The Regents Room (open by appointment).

The Buurkerk (local church) which houses the Musical Clock to Street Organ Museum, ... dates from 10th century, in heart of merchants community opposite a long-established ecclesiastical district.

De Doelen, Doelenstraat 12, dates from 1337. Originally a convent for lay sisters, it became a prison and then a workhouse for vagrants and prostitutes.

Flora's Hof (Flora's Court), part of a psychiatric hospital, next to the Dom Tower, is the court of the former Episcopal Palace and now a restful and attractive flower garden. Entrance gate dates from 1634 and was built for the Governor.

■ **Almshouses** in Utrecht date from the 16th and 17th centuries:

Kameren van Jan van Campen, built in 1579, Schalkwijkstraat 6-14; remains of 14 original houses.

Beverskameren, Lange Nieuwstraat 108-132 and Agnietenstraat 4-6, built in 1597 by Mr. and Mrs. Andriaen Beyer; residents received a yearly supply of wheat, cheese and peat.

Mieropskameren, built in 1583 by order of Cornelis van Mierop.

Margaretenhof, Jansvelt 4-20, built in the 16th century; nine of twenty original almshouses remain.

Brutenhof, near the Lepelenburg, was built in 1622 on the least expensive land overlooking the city wall. Back garden easily accessible. Statue is of novelist Crone.

Pallaeskameren, Agnietenstraat 8-30 and Niueuwegracht 205, built in 1651. Above the gate: "Maria van Pallaes, Driven by God's Love, Being a Widow of Mr. Schroyestein, Has Founded These Almshouses/Not Heeding the Favour of the World/But a Place in Heaven's Square."

The Botanical Gardens of the University, Fort Hoofddijk Budapestlaan 17, tel. 531826. These freely accessible walking areas and gardens offer a splendid show of flowers and shrubs all year. Open Mon.-Fri., 8:30am-4:30pm, Sat.-Sun., 10am-4:30pm. At its peak from April-August.

Also, "Nieuw en Oud Amelisweerd" estates, Koningsweg, 47 hectares of footpaths, sand pits, bridleways; "Rhijnauwen" Estate, Laan van Rhijnauwen, Bunnik, 13 ha., footpaths, playing field, tennis court, pancake restaurant; Julianapark, Amsterdamsestraatweg . . . playing field, ponds with fountains, aviaries with tropical birds, deer park, flamingo pond.

MUSEUMS: In addition to the Domkerk, the Museum Het Catharijneconvent (Catherine Convent), the National Museum from Musical Clock to Street Organ, the Centraal Museum, and the Dutch Railways Museum, all described below, the following are worth a look:

The Phonographic Museum, Gildenkwartier 43, tel. 318107; displays from Edison's first sound recording instruments to the compact disc . . . also, a recording studio from 1890.

Kruideniersmuseum Betje Boerhave (Grocery Shop Museum), H⊂ ⌐ot 6, tel. 316628. Sells items typical of the 19th century.

Universiteitsmuseum (University Museum), Biltstraat 166, tel. 731305, contains important medical equipment and apparatus used in the natural sciences . . . portraits, photos, etc., regarding history of the museum.

Historisch Kostuum Museum (Historical Costume Museum), Loeff Berchmakerstraat 50, tel. 315397; open Wed.-Sun., 1-5pm. Dress of the 18th century worn by people from various social backgrounds . . . also textiles.

's Rijks Munt, Leidseweg 90, tel. 910342, National museum with a collection of Dutch coins from 7th century to present . . . also military insignia and medals. Visits by groups only.

MARKETS: Markets in Utrecht have an irresistible pull:

General markets: at Smaragdplein, Tues., 10am-3pm; at Oppenheimplein, Wed., 9am-1pm; at Vredenburg, Wed., 9am-5pm, Sat., 8am-5pm; Zamenhofdreef, Thurs., 9am-1pm.

Antique market: "De Ossekop," Voorstraat 19, Fri., 9am-5pm.

Flower markets: at Janskerkhof, Sat., 7am-4pm; on Oude Gracht between Zakkendragerssteeg and Bakkerstraat, Sat., 8am-5pm.

Drapery and Ragbag Market: Breedstraat, Sat., 8am-1pm.

Horse Market: Veemarkthallen, Sartreweg, Mon. 7am-noon.

Stamp trading: Vismarkt, Sat., noon-5pm.

Flea Market: Willemstraat, Sat., 8am-2pm.

Cattle, poultry and small animal market: Veemarkthallen, Sartreweg, Thurs., 7am-1pm.

You can also visit a Bric-a-Brac market in Haarzuilens; an art and curio market in Loosdrecht; as well as general markets in Maarssen, Nieuwegein-Vreeswijk, Oudewater, and IJsselstein.

Handicrafts can be seen by appointment, such as candle making at De Waskit, Donkerstraat 23; pottery, ceramics, tile at "Schoppen Drie," Schalkwijkstraat 8, and even wrought iron at J. C. Nebbeling & Zn., Sofialaan 5. In the outskirts of Utrecht, you can visit a cheesemaker, a carriage builder, a wine merchant ... info from VVV.

On the business side, Utrecht is the locale for the Royal Netherlands Fair which organizes annual commercial fairs. The exhibition center is the largest in the Netherlands. For information, Jaarbeursplein, P.O. Box 8500, 3503 RM Utrecht.

WINDMILLS: One windmill in Utrecht, "Rijn en Zon," Adelaarstraat, open Saturdays, 10-11am and by appointment, is one of the five largest brick tower grain mills in the country. There are windmills also in the surrounding little towns of Breukelen, Kockengen, Loenen, Lopik, Maarssen, Montfoort, Tienhoven, Vreeland and Wilnis. For info about the windmills, write Stichting De Utrechtse Molen p/a Provinciehuis, Achter St. Pieter 25, Utrecht, or tel. 582361.

EATING OUT: Sightseeing is hungry-making-work so you might like to try some food specialities of the area such as Domtorentjes (chocolate cup with whipped cream and mocha and chocolate topping), Utrechtse sprits, a brittle kind of shortbread, and Utrechtse theekantjes, a local cookie. In Vreeswijk, try the Vreeswijkse zandschuitjes, a special butter cookie.

Utrecht is full of good and varied restaurants, especially along the Oude Gracht. Try Stads Kasteel Oudaen, Oude Gracht 99, tel. 311864,a beautifully restored medieval castle. Opposite the Utrecht Central Station, the luxury shopping, restaurant and relaxing center the "Hoog Catharijne" offers a great choice of cafeterias, snack bars, cafes and restaurants ... there's even a McDonald's. The adjoining Holiday Inn also has a choice of eateries. Another recommended shopping area is La Vie at the corner of Lange Viestraat and Vredenburg.

YEARLY EVENTS: There's an Old Music Festival the end of August-beginning of Sept.; Windmill Day, beginning Sept.; Film Festival of Dutch and international films, and Horse and Cattle shows in Sept.; Annual International Collectors' Market in November. Contact the VVV for the current year's events. Every Sunday, there's a VVV-conducted tour of the city, from mid-May to the end of September.

COMMERCIAL TOURS: Boat trips are always great fun and popular with families. They are relaxing and romantic as well so why not try one of the following? A one-hour tour of the Utrecht canals (departure from the wharf under the Viebrug (Vie bridge) on the Oude Gracht) and an eight-hour boat trip on the Vecht River and the Loosdrechtse Plassen (lakes near Loosdrecht) are offered from June to mid-August by Utrechts Rondvaartbedrijf, Mr. B. H. Schuttevaer, Vogelaarsweide 2, Nieuwegein, tel. (030) 319377.

In Loosdrecht, Rondvaartbedrijf Wolfrat also offers a one-hour boat trip on the Loosdrecht lakes. For information call (02158) 3309. Also, De Driesprong at Veendijk 1, tel. (02158) 3230, or Piet-Jan Weijs with his old oak fishing boat—groups only—tel. (02943) 1284.

Domkerk, Domplein and Domtoren

LOCATION: On the Domplein in the old part of town. The one-way streets make getting here about as sure as a win with one roll of the dice. From the Vredenburg, driving east, take the third right you can after crossing the Oude Gracht.

INFORMATION: Tel. (030) 310403 (Church) or 919540 (Tower).

HOURS: The Cathedral: open Mon.-Sat.: May-Sept., 10am-5pm; Oct.-April, 11am-4pm;Sun. and public holidays, 2-4pm.

The Tower: open April 1-Oct. 21, Mon.-Fri., 10am-5pm; all year, Sat., Sun. and holidays, noon-5pm. Carillon concert performances can be heard on Saturdays, 11am-noon, and in May, June, July and Aug. on Thurs., 8-9pm. On public holidays, extra performances are given between noon and 1pm.

■ *Of interest to all, especially a visit to the Tower.*

The earliest record of a church on this site is in the 7th century. Like so many of its kind, it has seen both good and bad times. Built in stages between 1254 and 1517, the nave of the Cathedral was destroyed by a hurricane in 1674 and was never rebuilt. The remaining tombs and a 15th-century wall painting are impressive. The Cathedral is connected to the University by beautiful 14th-century cloisters.

Inside the Cathedral there is a sepulchral monument for Admiral Baron Van Gendt, the canon of the Cathedral in 1672. Also, look for the "holy sepulchre" (1501) in the choir gallery and at the specially fine leaded windows. The Bishop of Avesnes is buried in the black marble tomb.

The Dom Square was created in 1826. An interesting way to show visitors the site of the original church nave before its collapse in 1674, is in the use of grey bricks which outline the contours of the nave as it once was. The plan of the chapel of the Holy Cross and St. Salvator Church is indicated by heavy basalt rocks. A bronze plaque on the south wall of the Cathedral shows the location of the Roman castellum.

The Gothic Dom Tower was built from 1321-1382 as a self-supporting campanile-like tower. Inside the tower, there are two chapels—the Chapel of St. Michael (the bishop's private chapel) and the Egmond Chapel, the private chapel of Bishop George of Egmond. There are thirteen bells, all named after Saints, which weigh from 880 lbs to 18,000 lbs; they were cast in 1505 by Geert van Wou.

There are conducted tours almost to the top of the Tower. Only children and those with strong hearts should try the 465 steps to the top from which you can see (on a clear day) the church steeples of Amersfoort, Rhenen, Montfoort, Oudewater, Woerden and even Amsterdam itself.

Just behind the Cathedral is St. Pieterskerk from the 11th century, which has frescoes and a crypt containing the mortal remains of Bishop Bernold.

"Het Catharijneconvent" State Museum

LOCATION: Nieuwe Gracht 63. From the Domplein (Cathedral Square) take Nieuwe Gracht.
INFORMATION: Tel. (030) 313835.
HOURS: Tues.-Fri., 10am-5pm; Sat.-Sun. and holidays, 11am-5pm.
■ *Of interest to adults and older children*

For many years, this building (1528-1562) was the town hospital. Later it served as a way-station for military troops and then as a museum. This museum won the European Museum of the Year Award (1987) for its exceptional collection of Medieval Art. The religious art depicts how Christianity developed in the Netherlands and explains how Church, State and community have interacted historically as well as how they continue to influence each other today.

From Musical Clock to Street Organ Museum

LOCATION: Buurkerkhof 10. A bit difficult to find due to the narrow old streets in this part of the city, but look for the Domtower (the tall steeple) in the very center of the city and the museum is on the other side of the Oude Gracht in a medieval church.
INFORMATION: Tel. (030) 312789.
HOURS: Open Tues.-Sat., 11am-5pm; Sun., Boxing Day, Easter Monday, Whit Monsay, 1-5pm; closed on public holidays.
NOTE: Guided tours every hour; last tour at 4pm.
■ *Of interest to children from 6 years of age.*

This National Museum from Musical Clock to Street Organ contains an international collection of automatic musical instruments from the 18th-20th centuries which is fascinating.

The tour, which takes about an hour (and can be given in four languages, one of which is English), is full of surprises as demonstrations are given of many of the exhibits, ranging from simple music boxes to mechanical singing birds, a machine which plays violin and piano both at once, large complicated orchestrations, and—of course—lots of gorgeous, noisy dance and fairground organs, all of which play music to set you dancing.

As a backgrounder, you might like to know that there is quite a history to the development of the music box and that Holland pioneered this form of musical entertainment. Such well-known composers as Beethoven, Mozart, Handel and Haydn composed music especially for barrel organs and music boxes—these boxes were often in the form of musical clocks, snuff boxes, candy boxes, jewel boxes, drinking glasses, etc.

146

Visitors are asked to operate some of the exhibits from time to time and there is one special chair which a child in the audience is asked to "try-out." You can undoubtedly guess what happens when the child sits in the chair, but keep it a secret and enjoy the look of surprise on the moppet's face. Another surprise is when big brother, Dad or Mom tries to operate one of the big organ grinders and finds he'd better go back to eating Wheaties for breakfast if he wants to make the sound come out right.

If you want to take a group to the museum out of the usual hours—say, for a birthday party—it may be possible if you write or telephone the Conservator-Directeur. There are two portable barrel pipe organs with a wide selection of music rolls which can be rented overnight or for a weekend in case you are having a party and you would like an unusual added attraction!

Unfortunately, there is no descriptive guide book in English; however, there is one in Dutch if you can manage that. For sale are souvenir postcards, slides, records, books and even musical key-hangers playing Bach or Mozart!

Railways Museum (Spoorweg Museum)

LOCATION: Maliebaanstation, Johan van Oldenbarneveltlaan 6.
INFORMATION: Tel. (030) 318514.
HOURS: Open Tues.-Sat., 10am-5pm; Sun. and public holidays,
*   1-5pm. Closed December 25, Easter Sunday, Whit Sunday and*
*   January 1.*
   ■ *Of interest to all children . . . and adults.*

Did you remember that Utrecht is the headquarters of the Netherlands Railways? Naturally, you would expect to find the best railway museum in this city and you wouldn't be disappointed. The Spoorweg Museum is well worth a visit with a fascinating collection of old trains, railway objects, accessories of the past, present and future.

Outside, there are all sorts of real locomotives. The driver's cab of one, the "Longmoor," can be climbed into for a look inside. Indoors, you will find working models in two sizes; one small and the other about 12" high. The trains can be seen zipping along a track with modern signals, barriers and the Rotterdam Koningshavenbridge during the demonstrations which are held several times a day. There is even a simulated train ride where you drive the train from the cab of a modern express train.

Central Museum

LOCATION: Agnietenstraat 1. Bus 2 from the train station. The museum is located at the south end of town. Follow Korte and Lange Nieuwestraat, starting at the Domplein, until you come to the Agnietenstraat.
INFORMATION: Tel. (030) 315541.
HOURS: Open Tues.-Sat., 10am-5pm; Sun. and public holidays, 1-5pm. Closed December 25, January 1.
■ *Of interest to children from 8 years.*

The outline of the Agnieten Convent can be seen in the center of this museum which is best known for its collection of paintings mostly from the 15th-16th-century Utrecht School. Boys will probably be more interested in the authentic "Utrecht ship" which dates back to the 12th century. Another sure-to-please item is a scale model "doll house" of 1680. As was common in those days, this was not built as a toy, but a scale model for a rich merchant's home. In addition, the Decorative Arts Section and the Period Rooms give a bird's eye perspective of life in early Utrecht.

Serious art buffs will also find much to interest them, such as sandstone statues dating from the second half of the 15th century which are in the Antiquities Collection.

Also, part of the Central Museum is the "Rietveld-Schröderhuis," Prins Hendriklaan 50, tel. 517926 (open only by appointment). Designed in 1924 by the architect Gerrit Rietveld, this house reaches the peak of the "De Stijl" architecture popular in the early 20th century. Appears on the world list of protected buildings and monuments.

IN THE NEIGHBORHOOD: Utrecht's past can be discovered by visiting the castles in its vicinity, but it might take some time to do them all—there are 63 of them! If you're still undaunted and want to discover them, check with the VVV or the ANWB. A special castle booklet can be obtained from the VVV.

The most interesting and outstandingly beautiful castles are De Haar Castle and Zuylen Castle—descriptions follow. In addition, however, there are two scenic castle manor houses near the village of Breukelen:

Nijenrode, along the left bank of the Vecht River, is historically interesting but cannot be visited. It is worth driving past because of its true castle-like setting within a filled moat, and its gate with wooden drawbridge.

Gunterstein Manor House is on the east side of the Vecht. For information or to arrange a visit, contact Jhr. Mr. Quarles van Ufford, Zandpad 48, Breukelen. The original house probably dates from the 13th century. Johan van Oldenbar-neveldt used it as a summer house from 1611 to 1619. In 1673, the French troops left it in ruins but it was rebuilt in 1681. It is now a two-story building, the lower story dating from the end of the 17th century In the interior, there are Gobelin tapestries, documents about the history of the house and portraits.

Oudewater, about 20 kilometers southwest of Utrecht, with its rich history and 17th-century. character, is covered in Chapter 2, South Holland, because of its proximity to Gouda, Haastrecht and Schoonhoven. Its Witches Weighing Scale is worth experiencing!

De Haar Castle at Haarzuilens

LOCATION: Eight kilometers west of Utrecht off north-south highway A2. Take Maarssen turnoff and follow small road to Haarzui-lens, then bear northwest until you come to the castle.
INFORMATION: Kasteel de Haar, Haarzuilens, tel. (03407) 1275.
HOURS: March 1-Aug. 15 and Oct. 15-Nov. 15, Mon.-Fri., tours every hour from 11am-4pm (closes 5pm); Sat.-Sun., 1-4pm.
■ *Of interest to all.*

The original castle on this site was built in the 12th century, but it was demolished, rebuilt, demolished again, and rebuilt until it was totally destroyed by the French soldiers serving under King Louis XIV. About 90 years ago, the castle was rebuilt by Baron Etienne Van Zuylen van Nijevelt, a descendant of the family which has owned the castle since 1434.

The structure itself is very special—fairy-like almost—with its beautiful grounds, moat, and spikey turrets reaching skyward. Among the curiosities is a small carriage in which King Louis XIV (the Sun King) rode as a child. There are also enormous Gobelin tapestries, Persian carpets, paintings by Spanish primitives, Louis XVI furniture, Chinese and Japanese porcelain, and a Japanese litter.

The red and white colors of De Haar Castle are repeated in the town of Haarzuilens showing the influence of the castle on the village which is still the Baron's property. Every September, the owner lives in the castle for the month. Worth a look is the antique pump in the middle of the town square.

Zuylen Castle in Maarssen

LOCATION: Tournooiveld 1, Oud-Zuilen, Maarssen. On the Vecht River, near the Vecht bridge. From Utrecht, take any small road going north towards Maarsseveen or Maarssen. The castle is hid-den by trees and bushes and a bit difficult to find. Look for a tree-lined road followed by a serpentine brick wall. The castle should be behind it.

149

INFORMATION: Tel. (030) 440255. There is an illustrated guide, postcards and slides for sale at the castle.

HOURS: May-Sept., Tues.-Sat. on the hour, 10am-4pm; March 15-April and Oct.-Nov. 14, conducted tours on Sat. on the hour from 10am-4pm; Sun. afternoons, tours at 2, 3, and 4pm; closed Mondays.

NOTE: The castle can be rented for special occasions; call the number above.

■ *Of interest to castle lovers.*

Zuylen Castle offers an overview of five centuries of living. The old castle was destroyed early in medieval times. The present palace dates from approx. 1300. In the 18th century, the fortress was partly altered into a stately country house with a magnificent garden. The Gate dates from the 16th century

The collection includes porcelain, glassware, paintings, furniture and tapestries. There are books and writings by the feminist, Belle van Zuylen (Isabella van Tuyll, 1740-1805), who spoke out against the hypocrisy of the social mores of her day. She maintained an active correspondence with such prominent men of letters as Voltaire and James Boswell. It was the latter who admonished her to hold her tongue which was too quick to criticize normal conventions. She married but found her husband dull and she had an eight-year "intensive friendship" with Benjamin Constant. She wrote several books under the pseudonym "Abbe de la Tour."

The main feature of the garden is the famous serpentine wall, ideally suited for growing citrus fruits. The public has free access to the garden.

NIEUW-LOOSDRECHT

The land of lakes

GETTING THERE: Between Hilversum and Utrecht, along the Loos-drechtse lakes. Via highway A2, then take the Vinkeveen exit to-wards Hilversum; look for a small road going south to Loos-drecht.

INFORMATION: VVV, Oud Loosdrechtsedijk 198, Loosdrecht, tel. (02158) 3958.

This conveniently located community about 8 kilometers north of Utrecht, surrounded by seven lakes, is a family and sportsmen's paradise ... fishermen, swimmers, water-skiers, and boaters find the area "heaven." For the non-activist, summer days are filled with sailing meets or waterskiing exhibitions. Encircled by woods and moors, there are wonderful walking and cycling tours and plenty of tennis opportunities. You can rent a rowboat to enjoy the "Vuntusplas" next to a nature reserve where you can see both familiar and unfamiliar birds and plants.

In Nieuw Loosdrecht, stop to see the picturesque church with its 14th-century chapel. And you can't miss Sypesteyn Castle, just across the way (see following).

This part of Holland has been popular with the rich as well as not-so-rich throughout the centuries. As you drive along the Vecht River, you will see an endless succession of imposing dwellings, castles and manor houses built by rich merchants at the zenith of their wealth and power in the 17th and 18th centuries. Most large houses are now used as offices and conference centers. Today's residents are often descendants of ancient families; however, there are many new families who live here and work in Amsterdam, Hilversum or Utrecht.

For those not fortunate enough to live in this region, everything is available to make a great family vacation with a particularly good selection of cottages and camp sites. For more information, write or call the VVV.

Sypesteyn Castle

LOCATION: Nieuw Loosdrechtdijk 150. (South of Hilversum)

INFORMATION: Tel. (02158) 3208.

HOURS: Open May 1-Sept. 15, Tues.-Sat., conducted tours at 10:15, 11:15am, 2, 3, and 4pm. Sun. and holidays, at 2, 3, 4pm. For vis-its during the rest of the year, call the Administration.

■ *Of interest to adults and older children.*

This castle is famous for its beautiful garden laid out in 16th-century style with a maze, and should be visited during the rose-blooming season if possible. Built on what were thought to be the remains of a 13th-century castle, it was the home of Sir Catharinus van Sypesteyn until 1937. There are twelve rooms furnished in the style of the 16th, 17th and 18th centuries as well as an irreplaceable collection of Chinese, Loosdrechts and other Dutch porcelain. There is also a large collection of valuable furniture, copper, iron-work, clocks, glassware, arms and old pictures.

AMERSFOORT

With a Middle Ages atmosphere

GETTING THERE: Amersfoort is served by major and minor roads, located about equidistant from Arnhem and Amsterdam with Utrecht just a few kilometers southwest. From The Hague or Rotterdam go east on highway A12 to Utrecht, then A28 direction Zwolle; from Amsterdam, take A1 southeast.
INFORMATION: VVV Amersfoort, 28 Stationsplein, tel. (033) 635151.

The earliest settlers of Amersfoort established themselves at a shallow place on the Amer River, now the Eems River, which could easily be forded. The name Amer was no longer in use in the year 777 so it is believed the settlement must have been founded long before that time. In 1259, Amersfoort was enfranchised by Henry of Vianden, the Bishop of Utrecht. The first wall was built at this time. Another wall was started around 1389 and finished in 1451. When the second wall was built, the first and oldest ramparts were probably destroyed and the ground sold. This is also when the "Muurhuizen" (wall houses) were built on the site; they were commonly used as living quarters and warehouses. The lanes and squares of the old inner city are there today, just as they were, giving the visitor a true feel for what the original town was like. Wall houses, archways, canals, wall segments and crooked alleyways combine to give a beautiful picture of a medieval town.

■ **The Kamperbinnenpoort** is the only gate remaining of the first wall. Two other surviving gates were part of the second wall. The Koppelpoort, a water and land gate built over the river, is said to date from before 1427. Years ago, a wooden door could be lowered into the river by a wooden wheel in order to close off the town from marauders. The other old gate, the Monnickendam, spans the Eems River on the south side of town. Its old towers were used for defense purposes. The "Tinnenburg" is the oldest-known wall house dating from before 1414. Check with the VVV for a conducted tour of these gates and the wall.

A highlight on the horizon is the tower of the Church of St. Mary (O. L. Vrouwetoren) (1445). In the center of town, St. Joriskerk (1442-1534; base of church, 1243), is worth a look, as is the Marienhof (1480) a former convent with a beautiful garden. It is possible to visit (through VVV) one of the oldest institutions for charity, St. Pieters and Bloklands Gasthuis.

The Museum Flehite is within walking distance at 50 Westsingel, tel. (033) 619987, open Tues.-Fri., 10am-5pm, Sat.-Sun., 2-5pm. The collection is housed in three wall houses, two of which have been beautifully restored. Many interesting exhibits give Amersfoort history from early times to the present.

Amersfoorters are often teased about their unique boulder. The story goes: In the 17th century an eccentric man bet his friends he could get the gullible people of Amersfoort to drag a 9-ton boulder from Leusderhei to the locale of his new house. We are told he succeeded but not how he succeeded. And that's why the people of Amersfoort are sometimes called "boulder haulers" . . .

The Amersfoort Zoo, Barchman Wuytierslaan 224, tel. (033) 616658 is located in lush Birkhoven forest on the western edge of town . . . 700 animals with over 90 species, including lions, tigers, elephants, chimpanzees, wolves, antelopes and many birds. Open 8:30am-6pm in summer, 9am-5pm in winter. Get the free trail sheet at the zoo entrance so you don't miss anything.

IN THE NEIGHBORHOOD OF AMERSFOORT: The entire Eemland district is extremely scenic with beautiful farms, a unique avifauna, extensive polders, and impressive lakes such as the Eemmeer, the Gooimeer and the Veluwemeer. In addition, there are some small towns to the east and north worth investigation:

Baarn, just north of Amersfoort on North/South highway N221, was the home of many kings and queens. Soestdijk Palace was awarded in 1816 to King Willem II of Utrecht by the Diet, when he was still Prince of Orange, in recognition of his bravery at the battle of Waterloo.

The Oranje Museum, Luitenant Generaal van Heutzlaan 7, tel. (02154) 22776 or 13898, open Tues.-Sun., 10am-5pm. The collection comprises memorabilia of the House of Orange. Two scale models of former family castles can be seen: Slot Dillenburg was the original family castle and Soestdijk Palace, the former residence of Princess Juliana. The 21-meter-long coronation cavalcade, including the Golden Carriage, is something to see.

Groeneveld Castle, Groeneveld 2, tel. (02154) 20446, open Tues.-Wed.-Fri., 10am-5pm, Sat.-Sun., noon-5pm. Closed Mon. and Thurs. The castle, built about 1703, contains information about the history of the Dutch woods and Dutch landscape.

Spakenburg, straight north to the Eemmeer waterway, is a former fishing village which celebrates Spakenburg Days, the last two Wednesdays of July and the first two Wednesdays of August. A bonanza for shutterbugs, the whole village turns out in their traditional dress, the only costume in the Netherlands in which parts of the medieval dress are preserved. In addition to its historic restored building along narrow streets, there is a folkloric market, fun fair, and displays of arts and crafts. For specifics, write the Amersfoort VVV, above.

An exhibition of traditional costume and fishing boats can be seen at the Klederdracht- en Visserijmuseum (Museum of Traditional Costume and Fishing), Kerkstraat 20 (behind the Noorderkerk), tel. (03499) 81685 or 81589; open May-Aug., Mon.-Sat., 10am-5pm.

Spakenburg Museum 't Vuurhuis, Oude Schans 47, tel. (03499) 83319, open May-mid-Oct., Mon-Sat., 10am-5pm, is worth a stop to see the Bunschoten and Spakenburg traditional costumes, shops and the living-room of a fisherman's family set in 1915, fine china, jewelry including the "spiervangers," gold decorations on traditional dress.

Barneveld, east of Amersfoort via A1, also celebrates old traditions in costume, a market with more than 100 stalls and all sorts of events reenacting history from the Middle Ages. See "Gelderland" for details.

153

AMERONGEN

A castle town and a tobacco museum

GETTING THERE: From Amsterdam and points north, take A2 south to the crossroads with A12, then east to Maarsbergen turnoff, south on N226 to N225, then 8 km east to Amerongen. From Rotterdam and The Hague, start east on A12 and follow above directions. Amerongen Castle is on the south side of the town at Drostestraat 9, tel. (03434) 54212.

INFORMATION: VVV Amersfoort, (033) 63151 or VVV Amerongen, Drostestraat 20.

Amerongen itself is a historic village with some old arcades and structures, and an original moated feudal castle (little evidence of the original structure) dating from 1166.

Historically, tobacco-growing has been the agricultural crop for the region. The Amerongen Historical Museum, Burg. Jhr. H.v.d. Boschstraat 46, tel. 56500 or 51196; open April, Tues-Sun., 1-5pm, May-Oct., Tues.-Fri., 10am-5pm, Sat.-Sun., 1-5pm; closed Monday. Located in a former tobacco shed, the museum gives the history of tobacco-growing in southeast Utrecht from 1640 to 1965 . . . drying shed, tools, tobacco-grower's living room, carpenter's workshop.

Between Amerongen and Utrecht, there are roughly 17 castles shown on the map . . . a challenge to anyone wanting to cover them all. The area of these castles is called the Langbroeker Wetering. Aristocracy chose to settle here because of the Utrecht Ridge Woods where hunting was good and where there was sufficient land to lease out farms. The Duke of Gelder and the Bishop of Utrecht were constantly battling over territory, which explains the number of "fortifications." Most cannot be visited; however, Amerongen Castle and Doorn House are open to the public, covered in detail following.

Amerongen Castle

LOCATION: Drostestraat 20.
INFORMATION: Tel. (03434) 54212.
HOURS: Open April-Oct., Tues.-Fri., 10am-5pm, Sat.-Sun. and holidays, 1-5pm. Closed Mon. and Nov.-March.
■ *Of interest to older children.*

The castle belonged to the powerful Bishop of Utrecht and later to the Counts of Holland. In 1672, Louis XIV slept here. Not long afterwards, the castle was completely destroyed by the French. In 1676 it was rebuilt according to the designs of Maurits Post, son of Pieter Post.

Over the moat there is a double bridge of interest. The upper entrance went to the reception rooms whereas the lower entrance was for the use of servants who were supposed to be not heard but also not seen, it seems.

The original castle had two towers. Unfortunately, today it is lacking any outer decorations. Ex-Kaiser Wilhelm II of Germany stayed here from November 1918 to the summer of 1920 when he moved to Huis Doorn.

In 1876 Count van Aldenburg-Bentinck inherited the castle, and it is still owned by a member of that family.

The interior of the castle is filled with priceless objects, including Delft and Imari (Japanese) procelain, silk wall coverings, portraits, et cetera.

EATING OUT: To the east of Amerongen on the main road through town, where "Koningin Wilhelminaweg" changes name, there's a very nice Pannekoekhuis for pancakes.

DOORN
With a special Manor House

GETTING THERE: East/West on autoroute A12 past Utrecht. Take the Maarn turnoff going south. Doorn is just outside Driebergen-Rijsenburg. North/south, take autoroute A2 past Utrecht, then A12 going east to Maarn turnoff.
INFORMATION: VVV Doorn, Dorpsstraat 4, tel. (03430) 12015.

Doorn, just a few kilometers from Amerongen, has a similar story. It, too, is located along the Langbroeker Wetering and has as its main attraction a manor house, Huis Doorn. It is located in the midst of a wooded area but an area influenced by two rivers, the Rhine and the Lek. It's a wonderful area for hiking and biking. Garden lovers will enjoy seeing the Van Gimbornarboretum.

Moersbergen Castle, Moersbergselaan 17, lies in a 75-hectare estate with trees 140-150 years old.

Huis Doorn

LOCATION: Langbroekerweg 10.
INFORMATION: Tel. (03430) 12244.
HOURS: Mon.-Sat., 10am-5pm.

This manor house is impressive, shaped like a "U" with a round tower which gives the building a warlike appearance.

The house was used as the summer residence in the 14th and 15th centuries by the dean of the Utrecht Cathedral. It became a manor house in 1536 and underwent radical changes in 1780.

Exiled Kaiser Wilhelm II of Germany lived there from 1920 until his death in 1941.

Now a museum, there is information and mementoes about Kaiser Wilhelm's stay as well as antique furniture, porcelain and a famous collection of snuff boxes which belonged to Frederick the Great. A number of these snuff boxes plus 14 antique gold watches and gold chains were recently stolen. The missing items were valued at two million guilders.

IN THE NEIGHBORHOOD OF DOORN:

Driebergen: The Dutch Toy Museum, Prins Hendriklaan 1, tel. (03438) 13626, open only by appointment, unfortunately. The collection consists of historic and modern toys, dolls, doll houses, trains, games, stuffed animals, tea sets, sewing machines, planes, etc.

The Museum of Military Traditions, Hoofdstraat 94, tel. 17588, open April-Sept., Tues.-Fri., 2-6pm, Sat., Sun. and holidays, noon-6pm; Oct.-March, Wed., 2-6pm, Sat., Sun. and holidays, noon-6pm. The collection includes uniforms of all kinds, equipment, dioramas, as well as a model of part of the Battle of Waterloo.

Wijk bij Duurstede: This town, south of Doorn on N229, has a Castle and a Municipal Museum worth exploring.

Duurstede Castle, Langs de Wal 7, tel. (03435) 72053/71869, open mid-May to mid-Sept., Tues.-Fri., 11am-6pm, Sat., Sun., 10am-8pm. Closed Mondays. The Burgundian tower traces its name to Bishop David of Burgundy who lived in Duurstede in 1459. The rest of the complex is the dungeon. Free access to the park.

Municipal Museum, "Kantonnaal en Stedelijk Museum," Volderstraat 15, tel. (03435) 71448; Open Tues.-Sun., 1:30-5pm, closed Mondays. The permanent exhibition deals with the birth, growth and decline of an early medieval settlement, Dorestad, the precursor of Wijk bij Duurstede.

The winding Rhine River passes through Wijk bij Duurstede with its unique alleys, arches and restored buildings, all the way to Utrecht. If you're a canoer, you can go up the river to Utrecht and moor your boat in the shadow of the Central Tower.

On the other side of the Rhine River in the Province of Gelderland, the moated town of Culemborg is worth a visit, as well as are Buren and Zaltbommel.

ZEIST

Old woods, private mansions, and Air Force Headquarters

GETTING THERE: From Amsterdam take A2 south, then east bypassing Utrecht (A12) to Zeist turnoff; from The Hague, east on A12, north on A27, east on A28; from Rotterdam, A20 north to A12 east, A27 north, A28 east.
INFORMATION: VVV-i Zeist, Steynlaan 19a-b, tel. (03404) 19164.

Zeist is on the main highway between Utrecht and Amersfoort in a lovely wooded area. There are many large homes once owned by rich Dutch planters from Indonesia. In 1746, the town of Zeist was the refuge of the Evangelical Brotherhood (Moravians) who had fled from Czechoslovakia. In 1950, the Zeist City Council took over the houses on the Brothers and Sisters Square which flanks the Zeist Palace.

Zeist Palace

LOCATION: Zinzendorflaan 1. The palace is on the western outskirts of Zeist.
INFORMATION: Tel. (03404) 21704.
HOURS: Guided tours, June-Aug., 2:30 and 4pm.
■ *Of interest to older children.*

This superb castle is worth a detour both on its own merits and to learn something of its unusual history involving the Community of the Moravian Brethren who occupy buildings located on the castle property.

The front and back facades of the present structure carry the date 1686. In 1676, William Adrian of Nassau (the son of Prince Maurits) petitioned for and received virtually infinite powers within his territory. The castle became his headquarters, he made laws, levied taxes, coined his own money, et cetera. The castle has superbly furnished and restored period rooms—a delight to the ladies' eyes. In addition, changing exhibitions are held here throughout the year.

IN THE NEIGHBORHOOD OF ZEIST:

Soesterberg is the home of the Netherlands Royal Air Force at Camp Zeist. Its Military Air Museum is just north of Zeist (Huis ter Heide turnoff), then east to Camp Zeist, Kampweg 2. For information, tel. 34222, ext. 2270; open April-Jan 4, Tues.-Fri., 10am-4:30pm, Sun., noon-4:30pm. Easter Monday, Whitmonday, April 30, Ascension Day and May 5, 1-5pm. Closed December 25, 26, and January 1. The museum, which would be of special interest to men and boys, contains documents, photos, paintings, uniforms, airplanes, and clothing depicting the history of military aviation since 1913.

CHAPTER 5

THE PROVINCE OF GELDERLAND

This province covers an enormous amount of territory with "fingers" of land going as far west as Gorinchem, north to Flevoland, east as far as the German border and south to the Waal River. In the interest of a logical progression, the following material is laid out according to locations north, central (The Hoge Veluwe, Apeldoorn and Arnhem), east (to the German border) and south and west along the Waal River.

The beginnings of Gelderland are complicated indeed, not least because it was made up of four areas: Zutphen, Arnhem, Nijmegen and Roermond. For much of its history, it was under the control of German counts who battled for power, signed treaties, lost power, changed allegiances, until three of the "four quarters," Zutphen, Arnhem and Nijmegen signed the Union of Utrecht in 1579 and became part of the United Provinces (of the Netherlands). Roermond remained loyal to Spain. In 1713, under the Treaty of Utrecht, Venlo became a part of the United Provinces and Roermond went to Austria. With the end of the Napole-onic era, Venlo and Roermond returned to the fold as part of the Province of Limburg. Today, the three geographic districts are the Betuwe, the Achterhoek and the Veluwe.

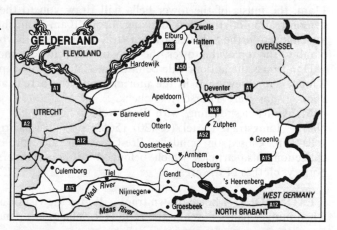

INFORMATION:
VVV-i, Arnhem,
tel. (085) 420 330.

159

Our explorations will begin with a folkloric event which takes place in Barneveld—the Old Veluwse Market.

There are many castles in Gelderland . . . a number covered here. To explore on your own, get the VVV folder about castles or write Stichting Geldersche Kasteelen in Arnhem, Zijpendaalseweg 44, 6814 CL Arnhem, tel. (085) 420944.

In the Betuwe, there's a Spring treat each year . . . about mid-April to mid-May depending on the weather, all kinds of fruit trees—plum, cherry, pear, then apple—are in bloom.

Early in September, the fruit garden of the Netherlands presents its Harvest and Fruit Show (details, Tiel VVV, tel. (03440) 16441).

BARNEVELD

The old Veluwse Market

GETTING THERE: Barneveld is just east of Amersfoort. From Amsterdam, take A1 to intersection N30, then south to Barneveld. From The Hague and Rotterdam, A12 to N30, then north to Barneveld.

INFORMATION: VVV Voorthuizen, Smitsplein 19, tel. (03429) 1301.

■ *Of interest to children of all ages.*

Every Thursday in July (plus the first two in August), EVERYTHING seems to happen in Barneveld, an old market town in the Oud Veluwe. The yearly program differs from time to time, so if this sounds interesting, call the VVV and get the current schedule of events.

There is a market with more than 100 stalls where antique and modern articles can be purchased, people in national costume can be photographed, and you can see old-fashioned crafts being done such as clog-making, spinning with ancient spinning wheels, pottery or basket-making, horse-shoeing and "cake beating," which has to be seen to be believed.

At about 10am a procession of costumed residents pushing antique baby carriages or riding old-time bikes makes its way through the streets. About 11am, the music of the tower bells will draw you to the Town Hall to see a demonstration of street folk dancing. From 10am-2pm, there are puppet shows for children in the Schaffelaartoren (tower) area and if you have the energy to climb to the top of the tower, the view of the Veluwe is most rewarding.

Don't miss the antique sale behind the Café Het Schaap in the Burgemeester Kuntzelaan. Viewing is in the morning and the actual auction takes place at 2pm . . . not every Thursday so check.

Many articles dealing with Barneveld's history can be seen at Museum Nairac, Langstraat 13, tel. (03420) 15666; open, Tues.-Fri., 10am-12:30pm and 1:30-5pm. Closed on holidays. Pre-Christian and 15th-century archeological collection; also articles which belonged to householders such as tin, glass, pottery, clothes of the area.

EATING OUT: A horse-drawn tram will give the visitor a tour of the town and when hunger pangs develop, the Café Het Schaap has pancakes on their menu!

IN THE NEIGHBORHOOD OF BARNEVELD:
't Ouwe Hoefslag, a cheese farm between Barneveld and Voorthuizen offers visits, Mon.-Sat., 9am-6pm; demonstrations between 9:45 and 11:15am. By train, get off at Barneveld North station, then follow signs.

HARDERWIJK

A Veluwse town with the largest Dolphinarium in Europe

GETTING THERE: From Amsterdam, east on A1 and then north on A28 to Harderwijk; from The Hague and Rotterdam, east on A12, north on A27 around Utrecht, then northeast on A28. The Dolphinarium is located at Strandboulevard-Oost 1. By train: to station, then Buses 107, 144, 145, 147 (stop, Dolfinarium).
INFORMATION: Tel. (03410) 16041 or VVV Arnhem, tel. (085) 513713.
HOURS: Early March-end Oct., daily, 10am-6pm. No entry after 4pm.
ADMISSION: Adults, Fl. 13.00; children 2 yrs-12 and seniors, Fl. 11.
■ Of interest to adults and children ... who doesn't like dolphins?

Harderwijk is splendidly located for easy access by road or by boat. It's an old Hanseatic town which now caters to holiday seekers. There's a small Veluwse Museum (info from VVV), but the big show in town is the Dolfinarium.

There are six shows per day in this largest marine mammal zoo in Europe. Among the offerings are: 1. Dolphin show in the largest covered stadium. 2. Educational show with sea lions in the "Robben" theater. 3. A brand new program specially written for the sea lions in Zeeleeuwen theater. 4. A comic and educational walrus show in the "Nova Zembla" theater. 5. Seals feeding in their natural surroundings, "'t Wad." 6. False Killer Whales can be seen eyeball to eyeball through large glass windows.

ELBURG

A town with historic architecture and charming streets

GETTING THERE: From Amsterdam, take A1 east to intersection with A6/E232 north toward Dronten, then follow signs to Elburg. From Rotterdam and The Hague, east toward Utrecht and Amersfoort, then north on A28 as far as 't Harde and follow indications for Elburg (going west). The Flevohof is only 6 km away in Flevoland.
INFORMATION: VVV Elburg, POB 47, tel. (05250) 1520. They speak good English and are very helpful.
■ Of interest to all who love old architecture and charming villages ... also fishermen, swimmers, hikers ...

Elburg, once a town of some importance as a member of the Hanseatic League, is today a quiet village hidden from the open fields and moors which surround it by its moat and old city walls. To be there in the early evening and see its main street twinkling with tiny white lights clustered in its espaliered trees and outlining the old Fish Gate is a delightful beginning to a romantic adventure.

This town is a treasure-trove of historic architecture with structures still in use dating from the 14th through the 18th centuries. For instance, the Fish Gate was built in 1392-94; the former St. Agnes Cloister (now the City Hall and Municipal Museum) dates from 1418; St. Nicolas Church was first built in 1396; sides and back gables of the Castle date from 1396; and the first Town Hall dates from about 1200. You can see some widows' almshouses (1650) and houses built in 1687 and 1616 (restored). The step and bell gables, facades, and 18th-century houses are worth the trip alone.

The best way to visit Elburg is on foot. The streets are narrow and there is little parking, so put on your most comfortable walking shoes and strike out. Your first stop should be the VVV where you can obtain their walking map of the town . . . in English too. A few stops worth mentioning are:

The St. Agnes Cloister dating from 1418, now houses the Town Hall, Gothic Chapel and Municipal Museum (local history). Open, Tues.-Fri., 9:30am-noon and 2-5pm.

The Fish Gate (an annex to the Municipal Museum) is open in summer: weekdays, 9:30am-noon and 2-4:30pm.

St. Nicolas Church and tower, are open weekdays, 10am-noon and 2-4:30pm.

STAYING OVER: Elburg is a small town with few "fancy" facilities; however, how many chances are there to stay overnight in a moated and walled town? If the romance of the situation attracts you, investigate the Smeede Hotel—modest and inexpensive but it has a room fit for a princess with four-poster bed draped in gauzy white material! There are also pensions and campsites in the near vicinity. Or, stay at Kampen, 10 km north; the Herberg d'Olde Brugge, IJssel-kade 48, tel. (05202) 12645, overlooks the IJssel River.

This is a good family stop. Flevohof is just across the bridge, there is swimming and all water sports within minutes—anglers can fish to their hearts' content, and if you don't know how to sail, there's a sailing school.

APELDOORN

Playground of royalty

GETTING THERE: Apeldoorn is easily accessible via a series of high-ways. North/south autoroute A50 bypasses the town on the east and east/west, A1 bypasses it to the south. There are a number of turnoffs for the town center, depending on your destination.
INFORMATION: VVV, 16 Stationsplein, tel. (055) 788421.

Apeldoorn is located in a wooded area embracing 50,000 acres full of huge trees, brooks, lakes, wild animals and birds of many species. Its beginnings as a town date from the 700s but it has been known for several centuries principally as a royal summer residence and hunting preserve. The story of Het Loo Palace follows below.

Apeldoorn, a holiday and convention center, has charming inner-city streets with outdoor cafés, old facades, and many shops. In the summertime, the Market Square (you can park underneath) is active almost daily with goods for sale and special events.

In town, the Historical Museum Marialust gives the history of Apeldoorn and the Municipal Van Reekum Museum offers modern art exhibitions.

In addition to the national forests and the Palace's Royal Park (within walking distance of the town center), Apeldoorn's oldest park, the "Orange Park" is a lovely restorative place. The gorgeous colors in the fall are worth a special visit to this area.

■ **"Berg en Bos"** a new-type zoo, Schelmseweg 85, has become famous for its 250 monkeys which move freely among the visitors, swinging in the trees, and generally creating "monkey-fun," especially for children. A special island is reserved for gorilla families. Open all year, but hours vary; usually 9:30am-5pm.

The "Koningen Juliana Toren" recreation park has motor boats, a big dipper, caves, lookout tower, etc. Apeldoorn also boasts a children's farm, "Malkenschoten" and a planetarium, "Kuiper's Planetarium." Train rides to the village of Dieren are popular as well as excursions by boat or covered wagon. Gliding, parachuting and plane rides can be arranged at Teuge airfield.

Of special interest are bus trips through the Royal Forests to the game vantage post in the State Game Sanctuary. Check with the VVV for specifics.

SPECIAL YEARLY EVENT: Beginning of June, a Jazz in the Woods Festival.

Het Loo Palace Museum, Royal Stables and Gardens

LOCATION: Follow directions for Apeldoorn, above. Turnoff A12 heading north to Nieuw-Milligen, then right on the Amers-foortseweg until you see indications for Het Loo Paleis. There is plenty of parking. From railroad station, take Bus 102, 104.

INFORMATION: VVV Apeldoorn, tel. (055) 788421 or at the Museum, (055) 212244.

HOURS: Palace: Open all year, Tues.-Sun., 10am-5pm. Closed December 25. Stables, East and West Wing of the Palace: April-Oct. only. The Park is open 9am-6pm.

NOTE: The tour of the Palace is self-conducted. A color brochure in English, French and German is for sale, as well as a flyer in each language describing the furnishings room-by-room. Groups can make arrangements in advance for conducted tours. The tour of the Stables is guided. In summer, there is a 30-minute audiovisual program (English, French, German and Dutch). A restaurant in the West Wing is open April-Oct., and a self-service teahouse near the entrance is open all year.

■ *The Palace is of interest to older children; the Royal Stables of interest to children from 7-8 years.*

Het Loo Palace was one of the favorite residences of William I and William III. When William III and his wife, Mary Stuart, were crowned King and Queen of England in 1689, the Palace was enlarged; however, it has been used primarily as a hunting and summer residence by the Dutch Royal Family. From 1806 until 1810 while he was King of Holland, it was the residence of Louis Bonaparte, brother of Napoleon Bonaparte.

Queen Wilhelmina retired to Het Loo after her abdication in 1948 and after her death, Princess Margriet and her husband lived at the Palace from 1967 to 1975. Queen Juliana renounced further use of the Palace by the royal family in 1971, and it became a national museum. It was then decided to remove all the 19th- and 20th-century "improvements" and restore the Palace and the French Gardens in the 17th-century style. The stucco was removed from the exterior to reveal the beautiful bricks of an earlier construction. The restoration took seven years to complete; it was opened in 1984 with great fanfare as an important royal family museum commemorating the House of Orange.

The self-conducted Palace tours start with rooms decorated in the style of the earliest residents (complete with portraits and memorabilia appropriate to each time period) depicting the mode of living for the 300 years the House of Orange used the house. This gives a long view to the past but also leaves the impression of a very mixed bag of interior decoration. The children will probably like Wilhelmina's playroom best.

Do take time to visit the French Gardens before you leave the Palace. Ancient records and prints were used to replant the gardens in their original 17th-century style . . . There is a sunken lower garden, an upper garden and two side gardens. Look for the King's Garden and the Queen's Garden, and, hopefully, the King's Fountain in the upper garden will be in operation—it spurts almost 14 meters high.

The Royal Stables are immaculate and it is hard to imagine that horses ever sullied these surroundings. Children are expected to be kept under surveillance; this is NOT an informal stable. All groups are guided so you will have ample opportunity to learn all about the various types of Royal conveyances which are on view . . . one of the most endearing is Queen Wilhelmina's painting wagon.

Two, five and seven kilometer color-coded walks are included in the price of admission. For those with unlimited energy, they can see how much of the 650 hectares which comprise the grounds they can cover.

IN THE NEIGHBORHOOD OF APELDOORN:

Other places in the neighborhood of importance are: the Hoge Veluwe, just south of Apeldoorn, is a nature-preserve area but also the location of the not-to-be-missed Kroller-Muller Museum. To the east are the towns of Zutphen and Deventer, historic town centers and lots of local color. To the north enroute to Zwolle, De Cannenburgh Castle can be visited, see below. West in Flevoland, there's the Flevoland Recreation Park, a fun, learning experience in agriculture.

A visit to the ANWB is recommended in order to purchase their large-scale map of the Veluwe area indicating scenic routes for walking or driving and showing locations of castles, windmills, etc.

De Cannenburgh Castle in Vaassen

LOCATION: The village of Vaassen is approximately 6-8 kilometers north of Het Loo Paleis (Apeldoorn). The castle is on the north side of the village, on Maarten van Rossumplein.
INFORMATION: Stichting Vrienden der Geldersche Kasteelen, Vaassen. Tel. (05788) 1292.
HOURS: Easter Mon. to last Sun. in Oct., Tues.-Sat., 10am-6pm; Sun., from 1-5pm. The restaurant and garden are open all year.
■ *Of interest to most.*

Originally built in 1365 this right-angle building with square towers was rebuilt about the middle of the 16th century with medieval remains, and in 1661 more additions were made. The original main entrance was the natural stone tower with Renaissance ornamentation until 1751 when another entry in the style of Louis XIV was added.

In the 18th-century hall there are portraits of the ancestors of the owners. The museum includes such items as antique furniture, paintings, porcelain, handicraft items and portraits.

't Smallert Fish Hatchery and recreation park, located at Smallertsweg, is open daily from 9am-6pm.

EATING OUT: A good place for a restful cup of tea—or lunch, or dinner—is in the restaurant of the castle, "Het Koetshuis."

165

ZUTPHEN
Ancient city of towers

*GETTING THERE: Zutphen is some distance from our three major
cities. From Amsterdam, A1 around Apeldoorn to intersection
with N345 south, then follow signs to Zutphen; from The Hague
and Rotterdam, east on A12 until N345 south, then ditto above.*
INFORMATION: VVV, Wijnhuis, Groenmarkt 40, tel. (05750) 19355.

A town of many battles and rulers. The original Counts of Zutphen lost their
inheritance when the land passed to Count Henry of Gelder in 1131. The
Spanish wreaked havoc during the years it was under their rule. The French
occupied Zutphen twice and there was a great deal of destruction during WW
II. In spite of so much damage, the town retains some gates and towers of
historic interest. For instance, an inn dating from the 14th century became part
of the fortifications as the 17th-century Wijnhuistoren (wine house tower). The
Berkel Gate (ruin), the Bourgonje Tower (1457), the Drogenaps Tower (1444), a
rampart tower, can be seen as well as the Spanish Gate and Gunpowder Tower.

Zutphen as a member of the powerful Hanseatic League, allied herself with
towns in north Germany and Holland to protect themselves from Baltic and
North Sea pirates. The members of the League signed commercial treaties
among themselves and undertook joint improvements in the field of navigation.

Just walking the streets is a treat for those interested in architecture. On the 's
Gravenhof, you will see the 15th-century Town Hall and a complex of buildings
with fine Gothic and Renaissance facades. Saint Walburga Church (also, Grote
Kerk), is the church of greatest significance in town, described below.

An unusual feature in such a small town is its three large market squares: the
Groenmarkt (vegetable market), the Houtmarkt (wood market), and the Zaad-
markt (seed market).

The Municipal Museum, open, Tues.-Fri., 10am-5pm, Sat., 10am-12:30pm,
Sun., 2-5pm, is housed in the cloisters of the 13th-century Broederenkerk
(Dominicans).

Saint Walburga Church (Sint Walburgiskerk)

*LOCATION: The church is on 's Gravenhof. From the Groenmarkt,
take the Lange Hofstraat to 's Gravenhof. The church and the
City Hall are both there.*
INFORMATION: VVV Zutphen, see above.
*HOURS: May 15-Sept. 15, Mon.-Sat., guided visits at 11am, 2 and
3pm. In winter (Oct.-May), ask at the Church Office (Kerkelijk
Bureau) on Kerkhof 3, tel. (05750) 14178. Closed Sundays.*
■ *Of interest to older children.*

This Protestant church dates from the 13th C. but was transformed in the 15th
century to its present Roman-Gothic style. Damaged in 1945, it was accidentally

burned in 1948. Its exterior decoration using many different building materials adds a most picturesque look. The Door of the Virgin on the north side was entirely redone from 1890 to 1925. St. Walburga is richly endowed with impressive ceiling and wall frescoes, fine wrought iron work, and an important library.

Library: (Entry fee). The library has existed since 1561 virtually without change. There are 400 books with some especially rare and valuable, such as the Bible printed in the Dutch language; the Logic of Aristotle, printed by Henri Estienne; two volumes of the Encyclopedia of Vincent de Beauvais (1494); and "l'Homère" by Erasmus.

GROENLO

An old town with a folkloric museum

GETTING THERE: Almost to the German border, Groenlo is on the main highway N319, going southeast from Zutphen and makes an intersection with north-south highway N18.
INFORMATION: VVV Groenlo, Notenboomstraat 10, tel. (05440) 61247.

This part of Holland is so beautiful, a drive or picnic on a warm day is pleasant indeed. Give the boys a fishing pole and they can join others along any canal to try their luck.

But first, visit the town to see its Medieval city walls and ramparts with its old Spanish cannon (1627) and the Callixtus Church (Protestant) which dates from 1234 (wall paintings, stained glass windows, carillon).

The Grolisch Museum, Notenboomstraat 15 (buses from Zutphen, Enschede, Doetinchem, Winterswijk and Lichtenvoorde) is worth a special visit. For information, tel. (05440) 63271; open, Mon.-Fri., 2-5pm or by special appointment. Pottery, weapons, cannon balls, a fire engine, loom and paintings of the region form the collection. Until a foundation for the museum was established in 1935, there was a small school here.

's HEERENBERG

Windmill and castle country

GETTING THERE: 's Heerenberg is located just a few kilometers southeast of Arnhem on the German border off the main east-west highway A12. Take the Emmerich turnoff heading north (N316).
INFORMATION: VVV, De Bleek, tel. (08346) 63130, or (08363) 1486.

The Bergh Castle is the important cultural stop but take a look around the town itself. The steeple of the town hall is of Roman origin and the church is Gothic. The "Gouden Handen" (golden hands) is an arts center in an old monastery. In addition, there are a few houses dating from the late Middle Ages and a small castle, Boetselaarsburgh, which can be seen quite well from the outside. This old patrician house was named for Willem Jacob van Boetselaer van Toutenburg, bailiff of Bergh from 1617 to 1646. The northwest wing and the tower are most likely 16th century while the major part of the rest of the building is 18th century.

Bergh Castle (Huis Bergh)

LOCATION: Hof van Bergh 2—in the southwest part of town.
INFORMATION: Tel. (08346) 61281.
HOURS: Hours vary according to season. One-and-a-quarter-hour
tours are offered Sat. and Sun. at 2pm and 3pm: March-June
and Sept.-Dec. In July and Aug., open, 11am-4pm, Sat., 1-4pm,
Sun., 11am-4pm on weekdays.
ADMISSION: Adults, Fl. 5.00; seniors, Fl. 4.00; children, Fl. 3.00.
■ *Of interest to school-age children.*

Built as a fortress in the 1200s for the Counts of Bergh who were strict Catholics, the oldest part was a round tower which no longer exists. The middle of the building dates from about 1600 while the northeast side addition dates from the 17th century with a classical entry (1679). The upper entrance and stairway are dated 1701.

The Counts lived in the castle from about 1200-1712; Oswald III was the last. His successors were the royal dynasty of Hohenzollern-Sigmaringen. In the 19th century the castle was used as a seminary and in 1912 it was bought by Dr. J. H. van Heek who restored it entirely. A disastrous fire in 1939 did considerable damage; however, the valuable art collection was saved.

There are medieval artifacts, paintings by Dutch, German and Italian masters of the 14th- to 18th centuries, old weapons, coins, maps, and a priceless collection of Delft and Japanese Imari porcelain.

DOESBURG

15th-century trading town in the Achterhoek

GETTING THERE: Doesburg is eleven kilometers northeast of Arnhem
on A48. From Amsterdam, The Hague and Rotterdam, follow di-
rections to Arnhem, bypassing to the north on A12. At Velp, turn
off north on A48 to Doesburg.
INFORMATION: VVV Doesburg, Kerkstraat 6, tel. (08334) 72409.

This attractive, historic trading town of the 15th century on the IJssel River, has a number of sites worth seeing, an arts and crafts center, picturesque shops, a mustard factory which can be visited—one of the last in Holland—and a mustard restaurant.

Places of interest are the large Gothic Martini Church and Gasthuis Chapel (15th century); an original 16th-century town hall built of brick with a renaissance entrance; a 16th-century Weigh House, "De Waag"; ruins of a former fortress and ramparts from 1607; and some interesting buildings along the

Koepoortstraat.

The Museum Stad en Ambt Doesburg, De Rood Toren, 9-11 Roggestraat, tel. (08334) 74265 is open Tues.-Fri., 10am-noon and 1:30-4:30pm; Sat., 1:30-4:30pm. In July and Aug., Sun., 1:30-4:30pm. The museum deals with the town history and is part of the arts and crafts center.

ARNHEM

Capital of the Gelderland, great national forests to the north

GETTING THERE: From Amsterdam, south on A2 then east on A12. From The Hague or Rotterdam, east on A12.
INFORMATION: VVV Arnhem, Stationsplein 45, tel. (085) 420330 or 426767.

Arnhem, capital of the Province of Gelderland, is situated on the slopes of the Zuid-Veluwe hills and the Rhine River, one of the most wooded and scenic areas of the Netherlands. Once it was a flourishing Roman settlement, and according to the first-century historian, Tacitus, the region was called Arenacum. Its location has blessed it with great scenic beauty, but also cursed it through the ages as a strategic military prize. During World War II the area was heavily damaged during the Battle of Arnhem. Luckily, many historic sites have been preserved.

For the tourist, Arnhem's attraction is undoubtedly three-fold: the Burgers' Zoo, Safari Park and Bush, the Open Air Museum, and the nearby Hoge Veluwe National Park with the Kröller-Müller Museum.

Oosterbeek is also "in the neighborhood" with its city boundaries practically overlapping Arnhem's western approaches. It will be the focus primarily for a view of this area during WW II when it was the center of many heavy battles, beginning with an explanation of "Operation Market Garden."

In town, you can see the House of the Province, the Town Hall and the Municipal Museum.

The Municipal Museum Arnhem, Utrechtseweg 87 (5-min. walk from NS railroad station, Buses 1, 6), tel. 512431, is open Tues.-Sat., 10am-5pm, Sun. and public holidays, 11am-5pm, Christmas and Easter Sun., 1-5pm; closed January 1. The museum offers an outstanding view of the Rhine River as well as a garden with statues of famous citizens. It is famous for its collection of "Magic Realistic" paintings by Carel Willink, Pyke Koch and Wim Schuymacher. It also has a good collection of contemporary art, industrial and applied art, Delft and Chinese pottery, original Gelderland silver, archeological finds and changing exhibitions.

"De Witte Molen" (15th century) watermill, Zijpendaalseweg 24, tel. 424095, 450660, is still in operation during the week. Hours open, Tues.-Fri., 9:30am-4:30pm, Sat., Sun., 11am-4pm.

Papendal—National Sports Center, Papendallaan 3, tel. (08308) 7911, is a sports center offering facilities galore for sports groups, including a 254-bed hotel with basic accommodations but including three restaurants and lounges as well as two campsites. Some of the facilities are a gymnasium with power-sports

169

center, swimming pool, field and track facilities, four tennis courts, seven soccer grounds, a hockey field, a cycling track, two midget golf courses, and a 9-hole golf course.

COMMERCIAL TOURS: For boat rides on the Rhine River, see Rederij Heymen, Office Ship Rhijnkade, tel. 515181, operates May-September. There's also something for bike riders. Check with the VVV or railway station about a rent-a-bike system through the National Railways. You can pick up the bike at one station and drop it off at another.

EATING OUT: Like all good-sized cities in Holland, there are any number of quick-stop restaurants for a hamburger or sandwiches; the VVV will have them listed and even make suggestions if you ask. For something a bit special, go to one of two nearby farm restaurants. The closest one to town is the Boerderij, 2 Parkweg, a 19th-century farm in Sonsbeek Park, tel. 424396. Highly recommended is the Boerderij-Restaurant Rijzenburg, Koningsweg 17, tel. 436733. It is situated at the entrance to the Hoge Veluwe Park amid trees and meadows. Known for its cuisine, you can dine here in style or choose something light from their luncheon menu.

STAYING OVER: For a quiet rest overlooking the Rhine River, try the Rijnhotel at Onderlands 10, tel. 434642 . . . or stop for their Dutch lunch.

Netherlands Open Air Museum

LOCATION: Schelmseweg 89, Arnhem (north). From Amsterdam, A2 to A12 east; from The Hague and Rotterdam, A12 east, then look for signs directing you to the Openluchtmuseum. If you arrive by train, take Bus 3 from Arnhem Railway Terminus at Alteveer.
INFORMATION: Tel. (085) 576111.
HOURS: Open April-Nov., daily, 9am-5pm, July and Aug., 'til 6pm. Closed in winter.
ADMISSION: Adults, Fl. 7, seniors and children to 18 years, Fl. 4.
■ *Of interest to children from 6 years.*

In this park of about 100 acres, one must be prepared to walk a great deal, so if you bring babies or toddlers, be sure to have a stroller for them and comfortable shoes for yourself. This open-air museum is a fascinating collection of authentic architecture from all over Holland brought together to give a picture of the traditional culture and life of the rural population. Farms, dwelling places, windmills, watermills, a church, etc., from all over the country are represented. All buildings are originals, furnished as far as possible in a traditional manner, so one can even smell the smells that come with living among the animals, as was common in the early days.

In the Costume Hall, you will find an important collection of Dutch dress; there is a Bee House, an Herb Garden, a Cart Hall (farm wagons, carts, sleighs, bikes, etc.), a souvenir shop in the Merchant's House and much else to discover.

Plenty of space for running and playing in the woody areas should help keep the "cultural kinks" from forming. Handicraft demonstrations in summer.

EATING OUT: In the park grounds, there are two places for rest and refreshments. The specially charming Museum Restaurant serves warm and cold meals, and by the herb garden, there's a pancake restaurant, formerly an old inn, "de Hanekamp."

Burgers' Zoo, Safari Park and Bush

LOCATION: Take A12 east from points west, following indications for Arnhem. By car, follow the blue signs for Burgers' Zoo along the approach roads to Arnhem. By rail (Day trip No. 10), take trolley line 3 from the station. Plenty of parking at entrance.
INFORMATION: Tel. (085) 424534 or 450373.
HOURS: Summer hours: 9am-8pm, last safari train ride, 5pm; Winter season: 9am-sunset, last train, 4pm.
ADMISSION: (Includes ride on train through Safari park) Adults, Fl. 15, seniors (65+) Fl. 13, children (2-9 yrs.), Fl. 11. Make Safari train reservations in advance by phone.
■ *Of interest to all children.*

Four hundred free-running animals are bound to be popular with most everyone. The Zoo, with over 2,000 animals, including the famous chimp colony and gorilla island, can be studied from special observation posts. There is also a wolf-inhabited wood and large attractive bird collection.

Burgers' Bush was officially opened in 1988 on the 75th anniversary of the original Burgers' Zoo and Safari. It will continue to expand with completion expected in the 1990s. The Bush is the largest covered tropical forest in the world. Visitors can follow three routes (different degrees of difficulty) to explore plants and animal habitat from Asia, Africa and South America ... swamps, waterfalls, trees, flowers and palms intermixed with big and small game.

171

EATING OUT: The Bush Restaurant can seat over 300 people. There's a roof terrace with a nice overview of the forest and park; you can have a cup of coffee, exotic lunch and "tropical buffet."

The Safari train departs from the restaurant. It seats 200 people, traveling over the "African" savannah, among cheetahs, giraffes, rhinos, ostriches, etc.

IN THE NEIGHBORHOOD OF ARNHEM:

Three castles in the area are worth mentioning:

Rozendael Castle, located northwest of town at Rozendaal. The road to the Openlucht Museum heading west, will get you there. For information, tel. 634853 or the Arnhem VVV. Open, mid-June-mid-Sept., 10am-5pm, Sun., 1-5pm. The castle is the home of the International Castles Institute, and a fund of information about castles in Holland and elsewhere. The model castles on display from other countries are worth a look.

This 14th-century museum has the largest brick dungeon in Holland. Try imagining yourselves in its small, low-ceiling prison chamber, chained to the wall—it's enough to make your scalp crawl.

First built in 1314, the castle was rebuilt in 1615 using the old foundations. The massive round stone tower surrounded by water, dates from 1350.

The park of the castle is large (618 ha.) and very popular with its French-style, well-manicured garden, grotto with rare inlaid shells, lawns, trees, suspension bridges and waterfalls.

Doornenburg Castle, south of town in the vicinity of the old village of Gendt and the Pannerdens Canal. It's about 20 km south at the confluence of the Rhine and Waal rivers, east of the crossroads A15 and A52. Follow country roads to Bemmel, Gendt and then Doornenburg. For information, call the Castle Foundation, tel (08812) 1456. Hours vary during the year. In July and Aug., tours are generally offered Sun., 2:30 and 4pm; Tues.-Thurs., 11am, 1:30 and 3pm; Fri., Sat., 1:30 and 3pm. This is not just a castle but a moated complex of buildings with courtyard and stables. Built in the 14th and 15th century, this impressive castle gives an excellent impression of how feudal lords were able to defend themselves from attack by hostile forces.

Doorwerth Castle (Hunting Museum), West of Oosterbeek and east of Heelsum, the castle is on the Bac River. For public transportation, check with the Central Station. Tel. (085) 335375 or VVV in Arnhem. Open all year, April-Nov., Tues.-Fri., 10am-5pm. Sat.-Sun., 1-5pm; Nov.-April, Sat.-Sun., 1-5pm.

The castle (really a manor house) originates from the 13th century; however, during the attack on Arnhem it was largely destroyed. In 1947 the restoration was begun and today it houses the Hunting Museum. The oldest part of the building is the area of the right-hand corner of the building.

The day the family decides to explore this area of Holland, the men and boys will have "lucked out." In addition to the two war museums in Oosterbeek and Overloon, there is the interesting hunting museum, Het Nederlands Jachtmuseum (The Netherlands Hunting Museum) which opened in 1973. It is filled with fascinating displays and stuffed wild animals. In addition, there are often special exhibitions of interest. Inside the courtyard, there's a rustic café to soothe the "inner man."

172

The **Zuid Veluwe Nature Reserve** is the largest national park in Northwest Europe—240 square miles, virtually uninhabited. To the east, are the Posbank and the Imbos and adjoining them, is Deelerwoud and the Hoge Veluwe. You can picnic, camp, sightsee, swim, ride—there's something for everyone. You can lose yourself pretending for a short while that you aren't living in the most densely populated country in the world.

"DE HOGE VELUWE" NATIONAL PARK

GETTING THERE: Apeldoornseweg 250 between Otterloo, Hoenderloo and Schaarbergen, just north of Arnhem. In season there are special tour buses and trains from major cities (check with the information counter at any Central Station), or regular bus service from Stationsplein in Arnhem.
INFORMATION: Tel. (05768) 1441.
HOURS: Open all year, 8am 'til sunset.
ADMISSION: Cars, Fl. 6; Adults, Fl. 6.25; children 6-15 yrs., Fl. 3.

This large nature reserve with over 13,000 acres of woods, heath, dunes and fens includes hundreds of red deer, mouflons, roes and wild boar to see . . . if you're lucky. Motorists can park the car and explore the park on bikes (no charge) over 40 kilometers of track. Upon entering the park, ask for a map and get directions to the Kröller-Müller Museum, St. Hubertus House, the deer-feeding area—or whatever else you are interested in seeing—as the park is a large one and it is easy to get lost the first time around.

The St. Hubertus House can be seen by special appointment in groups of 20-40 persons, but everyone can and should see the Kröller-Müller Museum (description follows).

The Spring or Fall when the leaves have fallen from the trees is a good time to watch the deer being fed. This is done from a special enclosure raised six feet or so from the ground. You must be very quiet—sitting on wooden benches while waiting patiently for the animals to come into the clearing from the woods some distance in front of your viewing place. In the Spring, they are especially wary and you will see the Buck leading the pack, examining the ground and the general area thoroughly before he allows the rest of the group to follow him. Once he is satisfied there is no danger, they start to eat and then the bucks will fight with one another for the best food.

Otterlo, on the outskirts of the Hoge Veluwe, the tile museum "it Noflik Ste," is worth a visit if you have time. Once a private collection, it was presented as a gift to the Dutch Government. Tel. (08382) 1519 for info; hours, Tues.-Sat. 10am-noon and 2-5pm, Sun., 2-4pm. The museum shows the development of tiles in the Netherlands from 1550 to 1850.

EATING OUT: In addition to De Koperen Kop, tel. (08382) 1289, a rustic restaurant in the park which is very nice for a snack, the farm restaurant Rijzenburg located near Schaarsbergen at Koningsweg 17, tel. (085) 436733, is known for its good cuisine.

The Kröller-Müller Museum

LOCATION: In the National Park, De Hoge Veluwe, at Otterlo. From Amsterdam, take A2 south to A12 east towards Arnhem. From The Hague and Rotterdam, A12 east until the turnoff for the Hoge Veluwe.
INFORMATION: Tel. (08382) 1241 or (085) 420330.
HOURS: Tues.-Sat., 10am-5pm, Sun. and holidays, 11am-5pm. Nov.-March, 1-5pm only. Sculpture Garden is open April-Oct., 10am-4:30pm, Sun. and holidays, 11am-4:30pm.
ADMISSION: Included in entry price for the park.
■ *Of interest to all children from 10 years.*

Located in the scenic wooded parkland of the Hoge Veluwe, visitors feel the museum is a continuation of their walk in the garden and woods. Sculptures are displayed indoors against a background of greenery seen through large picture windows and one moves quite naturally from this to other rooms leading to Van Gogh's brilliantly colored canvases depicting the flowers and landscapes of Southern France. It is only a few steps from the indoor sculpture exhibits to the outdoor Sculpture Garden where the children can run on the grass enjoying the pond, ducks, or what-have-you, while the parents ponder the meanings of some modern sculptor's creation.

The museum is particularly known for its fine collection of over 200 Van Gogh paintings and French impressionists. You will find works by Seurat, Redon, Braque, Picasso, Juan Gris and Mondriaan. In the Sculpture Garden, there are works by Marta Pan, Hepworth, Rodin, Bourdelle, Lipchitz, Marini, Paolozzi, Moore and many others.

In celebration of its 50th Anniversary in 1988, the museum was renovated and the Sculpture Garden extended another 10 hectares.

OOSTERBEEK

The largest airborne battle of WW II

GETTING THERE: Southwest of Arnhem along the Bac River, between A50 and A52.
INFORMATION: VVV Oosterbeek, Utrechtseweg 216, tel. (085) 333172 or VVV Arnhem, Stationsplein 45, tel. (085) 420330.

Located in the midst of a green forest next door to Arnhem, this is the locale of the largest airborne operation of World War II. Three museums in the area deal with the subject: the Hartenstein Airborne Museum at Oosterbeek, the National War and Resistance Museum at Overloon, and the Museum of the 1944 Liberation at Groesbeek. Operation Market Garden, described below, tells about the major battles which took place throughout the area.

YEARLY EVENTS: The first Saturday in September, there's a walking tour of the battlefields; in mid-Sept, special commemorative ceremonies are held.

Operation Market Garden

If you think this is a visit to a wholesale greenhouse or a great vegetable and fruit market, you'll be very surprised upon arrival.

Operation "Market Garden" was a deadly serious and daring military operation during September and October 1944 to resist further German breakthroughs along a corridor from the Belgian border via Eindhoven to Nijmegen and Arnhem. It was hoped to cut off German troops by a pincer movement to deprive them of their sources of supply, and thus, hasten the end of the war.

The plan included the largest airborne operation of WW II in Holland with paratroopers being dropped to the west and south of Oosterbeek/Arnhem, south of Nijmegen and around St.-Oedenrode. The four groups that participated were the U.S. 101st Airborne Division, the U.S. 82nd Airborne Division, the British 1st Airborne Division and the Polish Independent Parachute Brigade Group. Three thousand casualties resulted between September 25 and October 16 when the Allies had to retreat short of their goal. A large part of Holland had been liberated, but crack SS troops held their position leaving Nijmegen in the front line for another seven months and Arnhem wasn't liberated until April 1945.

Some of the heaviest fighting took place in Overloon, including the only tank battle in the Netherlands. This aspect of the operation is explained in the National War and Resistance Museum (6 km north of Venray at Overloon) which was founded in 1946 with war materiel left behind. In Oosterbeek, there's the Hartenstein Airborne Museum, and in Groesbeek, the Museum of the 1944 Liberation. A list of the cemeteries in the area follows.

Cemeteries in the Arnhem Region

Oosterbeek	British Airborne Cemetery	1,746 graves
Nijmegen	Jonkersbos British Cemetery	1,636 graves
Groesbeek	Canadian Cemetery	2,595 graves
Mook	British Cemetery	322 graves
Milsbeek	British Cemetery	210 graves
Uden	British Cemetery	703 graves
Overloon	British Cemetery	280 graves
Ysselstein	German Cemetery	31,576 graves
Venray	British Cemetery	692 graves
Mierlo	British Cemetery	665 graves
Eindhoven	British Cemetery	686 graves
Nederweert	British Cemetery	363 graves
Valkenswaard	British Cemetery	222 graves
Lommel	German Cemetery	39,158 graves

Many of the Americans who died are interred in the U.S. Military Cemetery in Margraten, Limburg . . . for details, see Chapter 12, Limburg.

Organized battlefield tours can be arranged by writing Arnhem VVV, Group Dept., P.O. Box 552, 6800 AN Arnhem, tel. (085) 426767. Four brochures in English are available from the VVV, Arnhem, or from the museums: "After the Battle," "It Was Like This," "September 1944," and "Holts Battle Guide."

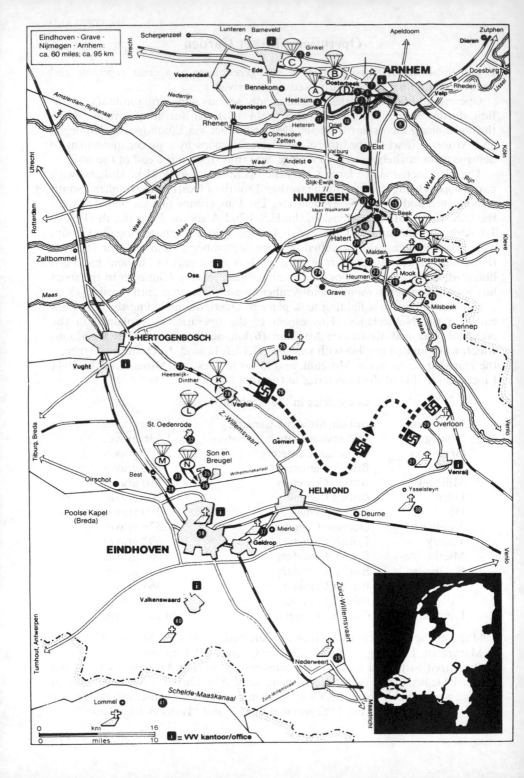

OPERATION "MARKET GARDEN" SEPTEMBER 1944
Historic spots in and around The Corridor, also known as Hell's Highway

1. Withdrawal of the paratroops across the Rhine (25 and 26 September). About 2150 Red Devils escaped. About 1200 dead and 6650 missing, wounded or captured.
2. Oosterbeek. Church at Benedendorpseweg, rendez-vous before the withdrawal.
3. Ede. Memorial airborne landing on Ginkel Heath, opposite restaurant De Ginkel.
4. Heelsum. Memorial airborne landing.
5. Oosterbeek. Airborne Museum Hartenstein, headquarters of Major-General Urquhart.
6. Oosterbeek. Monument opposite Hartenstein.
7. Oosterbeek. Cemetery containing about 1750 British graves.
8. Arnhem. Bridge across the Rhine. "A bridge too far". In spite of heavy fighting it remained under German control.
9. Arnhem. Railroad bridge. Blown up by the Germans on 17 September.
10. Driel. Monument Polish parachutists.
11. Heteren. Memorial plaque 101st US Airborne Division in town hall.
12. Elst. Allied offensive comes to a halt around 24 September.
13. Nijmegen. American parachutists cross the River Waal in canvass boats on 20 September. Railroad bridge and the northern end of traffic bridge captured.
14. Railroad bridge across the River Waal, Nijmegen, destroyed by German frogmen.
15. Traffic bridge across the River Waal, captured 20 September. Memorial cylinder buried in Hunnerpark.
16. Nijmegen. British cemetery Jonkersbos, 1636 graves.
17. Nijmegen-Groesbeek, Hotel Sionshof. Meetingpoint American parachutists and Second British Army. Memorial plaque.
18. Groesbeek, Canadian cemetery, 2595 graves.
19. Mook. British cemetery, 322 graves.
20. Milsbeek. British cemetery, 210 graves.
21. Hatert-Nijmegen. Bridge over Maas-Waal Canal. Destroyed by Germans on 17 September.
22. Malden. Ditto.
23. Heumen. Lock and bridge Maas-Waal Canal. Taken by American paratroops on 17 September.
24. Town of Grave. Bridge over the River Maas. Taken by Americans on 17 September.
25. Uden. British cemetery, 703 graves.
26. German break-through about 20 September causing severe delays.
27. Heeswijk-Dinther. Castle, chapel airborne forces.
28. Veghel. Memorial airborne forces.
29. Overloon. National war and resistance museum. Battle 25 September to 15 October. British cemetery, 280 graves.
30. IJsselstein. German cemetery, 31,576 graves.
31. Venray. British cemetery, 692 graves.
32. St. Oedenrode. Henkenshage Castle, headquarters 101st. U.S. Airborne Division.
33. Best. Joe Mann memorial in open air theatre.
34. Best. Bridge over Waal Canal. Destroyed by Germans on 18 September.
35. Son en Breugel. Memorial airborne forces.
36. Son. Bridge over Waal Canal. Destroyed by Germans on 17 September, repaired on 19 September.
37. Mierlo. British cemetery, 665 graves.
38. Eindhoven. Memorial airborne troops; memorial in British cemetery, 686 graves.
39. Nederweert. British cemetery, 363 graves.
40. Valkenswaard. British cemetery, 222 graves.
41. Nederpelt-Lommel. Bridgehead Schelde-Maas Canal. Starting point of operation Garden by Second British Army. German cemetery, 39,158 graves.
42. Museum of the 1944 Liberation.

DROPPING AND LANDING ZONES OPERATION "MARKET GARDEN", SEPTEMBER 1944

A-B-C-D
Dropping and landing zones 1st British Airborne Division (17 and 18 September) at Wolfheze-Heelsum.
Task: Bridge over the River Rhine at Arnhem.

E-F
Dropping and landing zones 82nd US Airborne Division (17 and 18 September) near Groesbeek.
Task: Bridge over the River Waal at Nijmegen.

G-H-J
Dropping and landing zones 82nd US Airborne Division (17 September) near Overasselt and Grave.
Task: Bridge over the River Maas at the town of Grave and the bridges over the Maas-Waal Canal.

K-L-M-N
Dropping and landing zones 101st US Airborne Division (17 September) north of Eindhoven.
Task: Bridges at Son, St. Oedenrode and Veghel.

P
Dropping zone Polish parachutists (20 September) at Driel.
Task: support of British troops in taking the bridge over the Rhine at Arnhem.

Hartenstein Airborne Museum

LOCATION: Utrechtseweg 232, 6862 AZ Oosterbeek. Bus No. 1 from
both Oosterbeek and Arnhem railway stations.
INFORMATION: Airborne Museum, Hartenstein, tel. (085) 337710.
HOURS: Weekdays 11am-5pm, Sun. and holidays, noon-5pm. No en-
try after 4:30pm. Closed Christmas Day and New Year's Day.
Children under 12 years must be accompanied by an adult.
■ *Of special interest to boys and men.*

The Airborne Museum was founded in 1949 as a tribute to the British and
Polish airborne troops who fought in the Battle of Arnhem in 1944. It is housed
in the former Divisional Headquarters, Hartenstein, with its large park where
anti-tank guns and a Sherman tank stand where they were left after the battle.

The course of the battle is explained with a number of visual aids. For
instance, there's a large model of the area with spoken commentary and slides,
many photographs, and dioramas (in the cellar) depicting the battles with
historical accuracy. You will also see a large collection of weapons and equipment used by both the Allies and the Germans.

IN THE NEIGHBORHOOD OF OOSTERBEEK:
The Recreation Center, "De Westerbouwing," can add a lighter touch to the
day's outing. Located on a hill overlooking the Rhine River, the amusement
park is open March to November . . . call the VVV in Oosterbeek for info.
There's a cable railway, playground, belvedere, dodge 'em tracks, scooters, a
Swan Train and restaurant.

Museum of the 1944 Liberation in Groesbeek

LOCATION: Wylerbaan 4, next to "De Oude Molen" camping site,
Bus 84 from Nijmegen Central Station. Groesbeek is south of Nij-
megen about 8 kilometers. From Arnhem take A52 south, cross
the Waal River into Nijmegen and then continue south on N271.
From Oosterbeek, A50 south, then at Knooppunt Valburg A15
east to A52 south to intersection with N271.
INFORMATION: Tel. (08891) 74404 or VVV Arnhem, tel. (085)
420330 or VVV Nijmegen, tel. (080) 225440.
HOURS: Mon.-Sat., 10am-5pm, Sun. and holidays, noon-5pm.
■ *Of interest to military history buffs and young strategists.*

This museum was founded as a token of gratitude to the men from overseas who
participated in the massive Allied operations which took place in this area.

The story of Holland's struggle for freedom starts with 1918 but quickly
passes to the 1940-45 period of German occupation and eventual liberation by
the Allies. There are scale models, dioramas, displays of all kinds, to give insight
into what happened here. First, the arrival of the Americans led by Gen. James
Gavin, the youngest Divisional Commander in "Market Garden"; then, their

departure to fight the Battle of the Bulge (mid-November 1944), leaving behind 1,800 dead. They were replaced by British, Canadian, as well as some Polish and Dutch troops, who suffered heavy casualties as well.

One of the museum's purposes is to emphasize the successful military actions of the American 82nd and 101st Airborne Divisions, the American 9th Troop Carrier Command, and of the 30th British Army Corps during Operation Market Garden.

National War and Resistance Museum at Overloon (NB)

GETTING THERE: Museumpark 1, Overloon, a small town about 30 km south of Nijmegen. From Arnhem, A52 south to Nijmegen, then N271 to small village of Bergen, then country roads to Overloon . . . about 5 miles north of Venray. From The Hague and Rotterdam, east on A15 to A52, then south on N271 to Bergen, etc. From Amsterdam, A2 south to A15 and then same directions as above.

INFORMATION: VVV Eindhoven, tel. (040) 449231 or VVV Nijmegen, tel. (080) 225440. Museum: Tel. (04788) 1250.

HOURS: April-Oct., 9am-6pm; Oct. 1-March 31, 9:30am-5pm. Closed December 24, 25, 26, 31 and January 1.

■ *Of interest to all children, but mainly to boys and fathers.*

Overloon, site of fierce tank battles, is covered here as part of the overall discussion of the World War II military operation, "Market Garden," because of its National War and Resistance Museum. It is geographically out of place, being further south than the previous towns and belongs to another province, North Brabant.

The museum consists of a 35-acre park which is the very location of one of the fiercest tank battles of World War II. Here an American Armored Division (7th) and the British Infantry, met with stubborn resistance of the Germans and fought for 20 days in 1944. There were over 300 tanks from both sides destroyed in the battle and the city was completely shattered.

One can wander through the park encountering tanks, planes, guns, antitank devices and many other remnants of World War II. There is a large building housing the documentation museum which consists of 17 rooms outlining the history of the war.

Keep in mind the possibility of a stopover in Nijmegen to see the Holy Land Foundation; or if you return via Eindhoven, you could make a short stop at Evoluon; or for a complete change of pace, you might prefer a stopover south of Tilburg to see the Beekse Bergen Safari Park.

NIJMEGEN

A Roman town called "Noviomagus"

GETTING THERE: From The Hague, east on A13, through Rotterdam to A15 and to Nijmegen; from Amsterdam, south on A2 to A15 east.
INFORMATION: VVV Nijmegen, St. Jorisstraat 72, tel. (080) 225440.

Nijmegen is an old Roman town which originated in 69-70 A.D. as a command post on top of a hill in the revolt against Rome. The rebels were defeated and Noviomagus was established as a frontier town and fortress in the year 105. Such famous names as Charlemagne (who resided here) and Barbarossa appear in the history books. Its ancient history, however, has been superseded in the minds of visitors by the military events of World War II and each year's International Four-Day Marches.

Because of the severe fighting in 1944, much of the town has been rebuilt; however, there are some historic structures left. To get an overview of the town and surroundings, one could start by going to the Valkhof, the top of the hill where that battle of 69-70 took place. Charlemagne built a palace here in 777 which was rebuilt by Barbarossa in 1155. It lasted until 1769 when the States of Gelderland demolished it. The gardens are a pleasure and the chapel built in 1045 imitating the Aachen Cathedral is worth a look.

At the town center on the Grote Markt (Market Square), there are St. Stevens Church (founded in the 13th century but mostly 14-15th century); the old Weigh House (1612); the Kerkboog, a vaulted passage; and the Cloth Hall (Lakenhal), now a restaurant. Close by on the pedestrian-only street, the Broerstraat, look for the Blauwe Steen (Blue Stone) imbedded in the ground which marks the original town center. The City Hall (Stadhuis) (1554) on Burchstraat just steps from the Blauwe Steen, can also be visited. Tours are offered May-Oct., Mon.-Fri., at 2pm and 3:30pm . . . Gobelin tapestries, paintings, porcelain and antique furniture.

MUSEUMS:

The Commanderie van St. Jan (1196) on the Fransplaats (French Square) between the Weigh House and the river, is now the Nijmeegs Museum, a local history museum. For information, tel. 229193; hours, Mon.-Sat., 10am-5pm, Sun., 1-5pm.

Rijksmuseum G. M. Kam, Kamstraat 45, tel. 220619, open, Tues.-Sat., 10am-5pm, Sun., 1-5pm . . . a museum of the Roman period with an emphasis on military matters in the former residence of amateur archeologist, G. M. Kam.

Velorama, a bicycle museum, Waalkade 107, tel. 225851; open weekdays, 10am-5pm, weekends, 1-5pm, adds a lighter note to the sightseeing.

The Liberation Museum (Bevrijdingsmuseum), 35 Keizer Traianusplein, open, Mon.-Sat., 10am-5pm, Sun., noon-5pm, takes us back to the events of Sept. 1944. An interesting collection of war items and photographs of the action.

Grandmother's Kitchen Museum is located in a former gunpowder magazine in Kronenburger Park. Open, March-Aug., Mon.-Fri., 10am-noon; Sat., Sun., 2-

4pm. It contains kitchen utensils from about 1900 . . . Granny's collection of tins, egg cups, grocery shop articles, etc.

PARKS: Nijmegen is blessed with a number of in-town parks. At Kronenburger Park there are ruins of 15th-16th-century fortifications, one of which, the Kruittoren (powder magazine) at Parkweg 99, is home to two museums: Grandmother's Kitchen, mentioned above, and a planetarium (Planetarium en Ruimtevaartcentrum) . . . VVV for details. At Parkweg 65, Het Rondeel is another fortress tower. Another park with remains of 15th-century fortifications is Hunnerpark where heavy fighting took place in Sept. 1944.

If you walk west from Kronenburger Park along Lange Hezelstraat, you will come to the Waalhaven (harbor). The site of the original Roman town, Noviomagus, is along the river at the western end of the harbor.

MARKET: There are several markets in town; an interesting one is the Luizenmarket for second-hand goods.

EATING OUT: Nijmegen has used its historic sites to good purpose in establishing restaurants in the Belvedere, an old military tower built in 1646 . . . near the Valkhof overlooking the river, and in the old Cloth Hall near the Market Square.

YEARLY EVENTS: From May through mid-Sept., many interesting events take place, the best known of which are the Four Day Marches (3rd Tues. in July . . . details from VVV) when Nijmegen is inundated with physical fitness enthusiasts from all over the world. As early as 1908 an organization with the long title, Koninklijke Nederlandse Bond voor Lichamelijke Opvoeding (Royal Netherlands League for Physical Culture) was established in The Hague. Its purpose was to encourage the Dutch to participate in some form of physical activity. At first, rowing, horseback riding and cycing were part of the program, but as time went on, these became separate groups.

The walks have never been a form of competition—the only objective was, and still is, to complete the route. In the early 1900s, the marches were primarily undertaken by the military, but civilians in greater numbers joined the trek after 1916. Nijmegen was first incorporated in the marches in 1917; from 1925 on, Nijmegen became its permanent home. Over a thousand participated in 1928; today, more than 20,000 people join in. Anyone over 12 years (no upper limit), is welcome to choose a 35-, 55-, 75- or 125-km march. If you would like to participate, you must reserve a hotel well in advance unless you don't mind sleeping in the fields! The VVV tries to arrange rooms in private homes.

In August, the well-known market in the village of Deest takes place. There are arts and crafts of today and yesteryear, antiques, clowns, puppet shows, and more. Also in August, the beautifully restored town of Heusden has a festival with flea market, music, and many attractions for young and old.

COMMERCIAL TOUR: In summer you can take a 3-hour cruise up the Rhine and Waal rivers on the paddlesteamer, "The Mississippi Queen." Leaves from the Waalorama, Oude Haven 47, tel. (080) 220617 for info. You can have lunch, listen to Dixieland music, enjoy a film, and relax on the spacious decks and lounges. Check with the VVV for times and tickets. Other boat tours leave from the same dock.

IN THE NEIGHBORHOOD OF NIJMEGEN: Two very different museums, close to one another and just a few kilometers southeast of Nijmegen, are worth exploring.

■ **Holy Land Foundation,** 3 km east of the center of Nijmegen can be reached from Rotterdam and The Hague A13 to A15 east to A52 south, cross the Waal River and follow signs via small local roads toward the "Heilig Landstichting." From Amsterdam follow route to Nijmegen and then above directions.

For information, telephone (080) 229829; hours, Easter-November, 9am-

5:30pm; admission, adults Fl. 7.50, children under 13 yrs., Fl. 4.50. There are leaflets in English. Lovely walks through the woods show Biblical scenes with palaces, inns, workshops, homes, places of worship and more . . . just as they were in Christ's time. The display is in two parts: (1) Christ's early life and public life as a grown man, and (2) the Passion and Resurrection. This is very worthwhile, regardless of your religious preferences. There are two restaurants for the hungry and a museum train for weary senior citizens and the handicapped (gratis).

■ **Afrika Museum,** about 4 km east of Nijmegen at Berg en Dal. See directions above from Amsterdam, The Hague and Rotterdam. Information, tel. (08895) 42044. Open all year, April-Sept., Mon.-Fri., 10am-5pm; Sat., Sun. and holidays, 11am-5pm. Oct.-March, Tues.-Fri., 10am-5pm, Sat., Sun. and holidays, 1-5pm. Closed December 25 and January 1.

This museum offers a unique collection of African masks displayed in a modern museum with brightly displayed artifacts, pots, warrior's shields, etc. Surrounded by woods, the children will love the open-air African village with animals. There are films, slide-tape shows, and pavilion with terrace. Various programs are held during the year, including special vacation activities . . . check with the administration for info.

TIEL

The heart of the Betuwe and castles galore

GETTING THERE: From The Hague and Rotterdam, A13, then A20
to A16, branching off at A15 and continuing east to Tiel. From
Amsterdam, A2 south to A15 east to Tiel.
INFORMATION: VVV Tiel, Korenbeursplein 4, tel. (03440) 16441.

In the Springtime, a drive in this area is a very special treat ... orchards of
blooming trees (cherry, pear and apple) tease your nostrils and herald the end of
winter.

Another very old town, Tiel is said to have existed as early as the middle of
the 5th Century. Strategically situated on the Waal River with its access from
the hinterlands to the sea, Tiel has suffered constantly from the destructiveness
of war. The most recent period was during World War II. Almost every day
from the end of October 1944 until May 1945, the town was heavily shelled by
the Allied forces while the Germans plundered and set fires to destroy the town.
One of the few surviving historic buildings is the Ambtmanshuis (1525), formerly the residence of the peace officer.

St. Martin's Church (St. Maarten's) (1400) was rebuilt in 1965. Its tower now
contains a most beautiful carillon with 47 bells. The composer Liszt visited the
church and Karl Marx worked on "Das Kapital" in Tiel. The Church of St.
Cecilia was totally destroyed but has also been rebuilt and is used as a Dutch
Reformed Church.

The Streek Museum, in the "Groote Sociëteit," Plein 48, tel. (03440) 14416, is
open Mon., Wed. and Fri., 2-5pm, and Sat., 2-4:30pm. There are many antiquities of local interest; also a watergate which can be visited during museum hours.

IN THE NEIGHBORHOOD OF TIEL:

There are a number of small towns and many castles in the close vicinity of
Tiel. The towns of Buren, Zalthommel and Culemborg have been designated
National Monument Towns and are discussed separately. Other small villages of
scenic interest are Drumpt (north of town), Kapel Avezaath (southwest), Ophe-
mert (southwest) with its ancient castle, and Waardenburg (a few km further
west) with two castles.

The largest inland locks in Europe are located just east of Tiel where the
Amsterdam-Rhine canal runs into the Waal River. A most impressive civil
engineering project.

BUREN

"Orange Town"

GETTING THERE: About halfway between Tiel and Culemborg,
along country roads. From Amsterdam, take A2 south, then east
on N320 looking for turnoff for Buren. From The Hague and
Rotterdam, A12 east to A2 south and follow directions above.

INFORMATION: VVV Buren, Markt 3, tel. Tiel VVV above.

Almost the entire town (nicknamed "Orange Town" because of its close ties with the Dutch Royal Family) has been restored. Important buildings to look for include the former orphanage founded by Maria van Nassau in 1613 (houses Museum der Koninklijke Marechausee); the Weigh house; the Culemborgse Poort, formerly part of the town ramparts; the "Prins van Oranje" Mill (grinds every Saturday); and the very old St. Lambertus Church with its interesting tower and crypt. Countess Anna van Egmond-Buren and "William the Silent," Prince of Orange, were married here and their daughter, Maria van Oranje, is buried in the crypt.

MUSEUMS:

The Boerenwagen Museum, Achter Boonenburg 1, is open May-Sept., Tues.-Sun., 1:30-5:30pm. Housed in part of the "Muurhuizen" (houses built into town walls), this museum houses many beautifuly decorated farm wagons as well as a complete wagon builder's shop and forge.

The Royal Military Police Museum, Weeshuiswal 9, is open May-Sept., Tues.-Fri., 10am-noon and 1:30-4pm, Sat., Sun. and national holidays, 1:30-5pm. This museum is in the old orphanage, includes paintings, watercolors, documents, uniforms, arms and means of transport detailing the history of the Royal Military Police as well as the civilian police.

ZALTBOMMEL

An old fortress town

GETTING THERE: From Amsterdam, A2 south to Zaltbommel. From The Hague and Rotterdam, A13 south, A15 east to Knooppunt Deil and south on A2 to Zaltbommel.
INFORMATION: Town Hall, Markt 10, tel. (04180) 18177 or 12617.

Dating from 1229, Zaltbommel is a former fortress with many old buildings. Two of the earliest are St. Maartenskerk (13-14-15th century) and the Maarten van Rossum Museum, built in 1535. St. Maartenskerk has some beautiful frescoes, the oldest choir stalls in Holland and a Louis XVI organ. The Maarten van Rossum Museum is described below.

Other sights to look for are the classical town hall (1762) with sundial and clock; the three-aisle market-hall of the Fish Market (Vismarkt) (1776); the weigh house near the market (1797), the town pump (1800) and many historical homes, some with old step-gables.

Maarten van Rossum Museum, Nonnenstraat 5, open, Tues.-Fri., 10am-12:30pm and 1:30-4:30pm, also Sat., Sun., from May 15-Sept. 15, 2-4:30pm. It houses a fine collection of furniture, utensils and ornaments, as well as items from prehistoric and Roman excavations.

IN THE NEIGHBORHOOD OF ZALTBOMMEL:

Ammersoyen Castle at Ammerzoden is south of Zaltbommel about 7 kilometers. For information, tel. (04199) 1270; open, April-Oct., Tues.-Sat., 10am-5pm, Sun., 1-5pm (last tour at 4pm). Closed December and January.

Destroyed by fire in 1590, the castle retains its "Middle Ages" facade and highy fortified character. Once renovated as a monastery, it now houses part of the town hall and a museum of antiquities located in the former moat. The restored town of Heusden just across the Maas River is worth a visit.

CULEMBORG

A moated and fortified town

GETTING THERE: Culemborg is southwest of Utrecht along the lovely Lek River. From Amsterdam, it's not far off A2; from The Hague and Rotterdam, follow the Lek River to Culemborg, or major highways A12 east to A2 south to signs for Culemborg turnoff.
INFORMATION: VVV Tiel, tel. (03440) 16441 or check with the Elisabeth-Weeshuis Museum, see below.

Culemborg obtained its municipal rights in 1318. A moated and fortified town, you can still see the moat and part of the ramparts; the Lanxmeerse or Binnenpoort (the only remaining town gate); the beautiful step-gabled town hall designed by the Belgian architect, Rombout Keldermans; the Elisabeth Orphanage (houses the museum, VVV and library); the restored Grote- or Barbarakerk (14th and 15th centuries); and the fish-auction house at the Havendijk which has been restored.

"Elisabeth-Weeshuis" Museum, Herenstraat, is open all year, Tues.-Fri., 10am-noon and 2-5pm, Sat., 2-5pm. It deals with the history of Culemborg.

WOUDRICHEM

Site of Loevestein Castle

GETTING THERE: Woudrichem is about 40 km southeast of Rotterdam and 35 km southwest of Utrecht. The castle is across from the town where the Maas and Waal rivers meet. In the summer, there's a special ferry from Gorinchem and Woudrichem.
INFORMATION: Tel. (01832) 1375 or the VVV, tel. (01833) 2750.
HOURS: The castle is open April 1-Oct. 31, daily, 10am-5pm.
■ *Of interest to all children.*

Built in 1357-1366 by Dirk Loef van Hoorne, this castle has had an interesting history. It has been a manor house, a prison, and a fortified castle. Badly damaged in about 1400, the present walls were constructed about 1576. In the 17th century when it served as a State prison, Hugo the Great escaped from here in a bookcase. Another prominent prisoner was Jacob de Witt (1650), the father of the brothers De Witt.

Loevestein Castle can be visited by a passenger-only ferry from Gorinchem or Woudrichem.

CHAPTER 6

THE PROVINCE OF FLEVOLAND

Flevoland is a brand new province. In a ceremony on January 9, 1986, in Lelystad, Queen Beatrix unveiled the new flag of Flevoland and proclaimed it the 12th province of the Netherlands. On that occasion, she also unveiled the sculpture of a "Kiekendief," a slender hawk which inhabits the area, to be the symbol of Flevoland. The province now incorporates the Noordoostpolder which used to belong to Overijssel. From Rotterdam and The Hague, take A4 to Amsterdam, bypass from the south to A1 going east, cross over to Flevoland via A6 over the Hollandsebrug bridge and you're on the polder. Four northern approaches to Flevoland are (1) via the Elburgerbrug, outside Elburg, (2) by crossing west of Kampen, (3) via A6 from Emmeloord over the Ketelbrug, and—a really special drive—from south of Enkhuizen via the Markerwaarddijk (N302) . . . it's like "walking" on water.

Everyone who travels to Holland will soon become aware of the love-hate relationship between the land and the seas that surround it. For centuries, nature won the uneven battle; farmlands, homes and towns were swallowed up time and again by violent storms. But, in more recent years, with the help of new technology, man has been the winner, literally creating new territory from the seas and oceans. Flevoland is an example.

In an effort to protect the central Netherlands from the sea, Dr. Cornelius Lely devised a plan to partially reclaim a large water mass, the Zuider Zee. When the great dike, the Afsluit-

INFORMATION: VVV Flevoland, de Meent 4, Lelystad, tel. (03200) 30500.

187

dijk, was completed in 1932, the Zuider Zee became the IJsselmeer, and, in 1965, the job of reclaiming land needed for the ever-expanding population around the Amsterdam region was begun. Expert town planners as well as seafarers and engineers, the Dutch did not allow Flevoland to grow helter-skelter.

It was created to provide "a new future," taking into consideration the desire for more agricultural land, the need for additional housing, and the need for leisure areas, while at the same time, developing and preserving the natural environment.

Flevoland has a network of foot and cycle paths, winding through forests, woodlands, orchards, meadows and farmland as well as canals, colorful bulb-fields and brilliant carpets of rapeseed. A network of huts has been built all within easy hiking or cycling distance of one another. The Flevo-Schokland Path runs from north of Utrecht city on A27 through the length of the Flevoland to Havalte in Drenthe, passing through the southern part of the Noordoost Polder. Contact the VVV for details about huts, maps, etc.

ALMERE

The gateway to Flevoland

GETTING THERE: Almere, the newest town of Flevoland and only 25 kilometers from Amsterdam and Hilversum, is growing by leaps and bounds. From Amsterdam, head east on A1 and cross the Hollandsebrug; from Rotterdam and The Hague, A4 to A1 and cross the Holland Bridge.
INFORMATION: VVV Almere, Spoordreef 20, tel. (03240) 34600.

Almere's harbor on the Gooimeer (Gooi Lake) is a natural rendezvous point for boaters, swimmers and nature lovers. Swimming beaches, the Muiderzand and the Zilverstrand by the Hollandsebrug and the beach by the harbor are crowded with bathers on sunny days.

■ Among the nature reserves around Almere are the Oostvaardersplassen which stretch along the western edge of the land mass from Almere to Lelystad, and woods with plenty of trails for walking or biking such as the Almeerder-hout, the Pampushout and the Beginbos. These and other nature reserve areas offer open lakes, swamp areas, closed reed fields, willow woods, bird protection areas (not generally open to the public), long sandy beaches, and fishing areas. In May, fields are brilliant with the intense yellow of rapeseed in bloom. In August there's the harvesting of wheat and oats which have given Flevoland the title of the "granary of Europe." Almere also has many bulbfields.

The Kemphaan Outdoor Recreation Center is southeast of the town ... fighting cocks, among other activities, tel.114223 for information.

EATING OUT: All the recreational areas have cafes but if you are hungry for pancakes, try the Pannekoekrestaurant 't Spantje, Grote Markt 82. Another inexpensive place is 't Schansje, at Deventerpad 26.

IN THE NEIGHBORHOOD OF ALMERE: At Koolzaad, a few kilometers east of Almere, a colza exhibition is traditionally held in a barn located on the Gruttoweg in Zeewold from May 4-June 3 (could vary), from 10am-5pm daily. Colza is an early, tall-growing crop very good at suppressing weeds. Over 2,800 hectares of colza is grown for the oil contained in its seed (rapeseed). The harvest starts the first half of July when it is cut and arranged in windrows. About a week after the cutting, the IJsselmeerpolders Development Authority's 40 combine harvesters, 40 tractors and 130 trucks roll into action. Quite a sight.

LELYSTAD

One of Holland's young towns

GETTING THERE: After crossing the Hollandsebrug, continue on A6 past Almere to the turnoff for the town center.
INFORMATION: VVV Lelystad, Agorahof 4, tel. (03200) 43444.

The land reclamation project in the Lelystad area was begun in 1965. The first residents came in 1967; today, about 60,000 people reside there, and it is expected that eventually 100,000 people will make Lelystad their home. Of special interest to today's visitors are the "Informatiecentrum Nieuw Land," (New Land Information Center), and the "Batavia, a Sailing Monument." Other sights include:

Nature Park, Vlotgrasweg, tel. 53643 . . . reindeer, elands, bison, przewalski-horses and Father David deer.

Lelystad Airfield and "Vliegend Museum," Emoeweg 20, tel. (03203) 328, where you can sightsee by air, learn to pilot a plane, or try gliding or parachute jumping.

Robert Morris Observatory, Swifterringweg, where you can see the sun rise through peepholes—a different view with each season.

"From Rocket to Space Shuttle" Museum, Schoener 16-79, tel. 51218. Small amateur space museum, VVV for info.

Lelystad has one outdoor swimming pool and two indoor heated pools. There are four yacht harbors, bowling alleys, squash courts, car and motorcross terrains, riding schools, tennis courts, several experimental farms and a number of camping sites. In addition to the unique nature center, Oostvaardersplassen, mentioned above, there are five woods which offer camping, barbecuing, bike and walking paths as well as day-camping.

EATING OUT: Like all towns in the Netherlands, there is a good choice of Chinese-Indonesian restaurants which have modest prices. An inexpensive place for a bite is the Pizzeria Sicilie, Agorahof 15. Two "fancy" restaurants include the Raadskelder, Maerlant 14, and Don Quichot, Agorahof 8, expensive.

STAYING OVER: A week's vacation in the area enjoying the water sports and sightseeing would fly by all too quickly. Hotel Lelystad, Agoraweg 11, tel. 42444, is a 4-star attraction, or try the budget Hotel "De Oostvaarder" on Oostvaardersdijk 29, tel. 60072.

New Land Information Center

LOCATION: At the water's edge of the IJsselmeer, just north of the
   Lelystad harbor.
INFORMATION: Write Nieuw Land Informatiecentrum, Oostvaar-
   dersdijk, 8242 PA Lelystad, or tel. (03200) 60799.
HOURS: Open April-Oct., daily, 10am-5pm; Nov.-March, Mon.-Fri.,
   10am-5pm, closed Sat.; Sun., 1-5pm.
■ *Of interest to older children and adults.*

If you were always curious about how polderland is created and how water can
be turned to mud and then mud turned to land, you will want to take time to
visit this center. The immensity of the project must be seen to be understood. In
the last fifty years, 165,000 hectares of new land have been created several
meters below sea level. The Information Center tries to show how this tremendous undertaking came about by using a number of exhibition techniques
including films, slides, models, photographs, and the display of objects which
have been discovered. They want to show how the polders were created but also
why and how they are being developed.

The Batavia, A Sailing Monument

LOCATION: Oostvaardersdijk 01-09, next door to the New Land In-
   formation Center.
INFORMATION: VVV Lelystad or write, "Batavia Lelystad," Oost-
   vaardersdijk 01-09, 8243 PB Lelystad.
HOURS: Visits possible 10am-5pm daily; exhibition and film in the
   summer months.
■ *Of interest to older children.*

If you can arrange a visit, you will see a 17th-century sailing ship under
reconstruction. The locale where the keel was laid in 1985 is the very place past
which the Batavia sailed on her first voyage to the Far East from Amsterdam.

The Batavia was built in 1628 by the United East India Company as an armed
merchantman destined for shuttle service between Holland and the Dutch East
Indies. In the beginning of the 17th century, construction of such a ship took
approximately six months; today, the rebuilding will take four years and six
months!

During "Sail Amsterdam 1990," the Batavia will lead the fleet of ships sailing
from IJmuiden to the IJ River for the special summer events. Later, the Batavia
will sail to countries in the Far East, such as Australia and Indonesia, representing Holland culturally and also for the promotion of Dutch business interests.

DRONTEN

A place with Stone-Age roots

GETTING THERE: Dronten is a bit north and to the east of Lelystad.
From points south, take A6 to Lelystad, then N309 following
signs for Dronten.
INFORMATION: VVV Dronten, De Rede 1, tel. (03210) 18250.

People lived on this site as early as the Stone Age before the land disappeared to
be replaced by swamps and lakes. Today it is a completely modern town with a
large congress center with sports accommodations, movie theater, market, cafe-
restaurant, a theater-in-the-round, exhibit halls, and the studio for the local
television station. There are a number of sign-posted touristic routes which you
can follow through bulb areas, to the Museum of Maritime Archeology at
Ketelhaven via the small local road north to the Ketel Sea, and southeast to the
Flevohof, a well-known recreational park outside the town of Biddinghuizen.

Museum of Maritime Archeology at Ketelhaven

LOCATION: North of Dronten as far as you can go before getting wet
in the Ketelmeer. If you are without a car or happen to be in the
town of Kampen, there's a special boat directly to the museum.
Ask about the combination ticket, boat and museum.
INFORMATION: Vossemeerdijk 2, Ketelhaven, tel. (03210) 13287.
HOURS: April-Sept., daily, 10am-5pm; Oct.-March, Mon.-Fri., 10am-
5pm, Sat.-Sun., 11am-5pm.
■ *Of interest to older children.*

When the Zuider Zee was drained, many ancient ships were discovered. More
than 200 old wrecks from the last 700 years were found which have provided
archaeologists with considerable information about the history of shipbuilding
as well as an insight into ancient cultures through the study of artifacts such as
household goods which have been discovered, some dating as early as the 14th
century. The wreck of a merchant ship sunk in the 17th century is on display.

Flevohof at Biddinghuizen

LOCATION: Spijkweg 30, Biddinghuizen. Follow directions given for
Lelystad, bearing in mind you can approach the Flevohof from
Harderwijk or Elburg as well. Plenty of parking. You can also
purchase train/entrance tickets from the VVV or National Rail-
ways Central Stations. Special tourist buses also bring passengers
right to the Flevohof entrance.
INFORMATION: Write Flevohof, P.O. Box 40, Dronten, tel. (03211)
1514.
HOURS: April-Oct., daily, 10am-6pm.

ADMISSION: Adults, Fl. 17.50; children, 3-12 yrs., Fl. 15.00 which includes many attractions.

■ *Of interest to children of all ages.*

A long drive, perhaps, but it can be done as a day's excursion if one starts fairly early. There are 350 acres of recreation area at Flevohof, including exhibition halls, a cattle farm of 88 acres and an agricultural farm of 165 acres. There is a mushroom nursery, greenhouses for vegetables and flowers, a children's farm, pony farm, a children's village with indoor and outdoor playground, an Indian village including cowboy saloon, etc. In the children's village, there are all sorts of activities: they can make cookies, fry pancakes, do photography, make pottery or paint.

At the model farm you see and touch the animals—lots of baby animals—which are especially appealing. In the woods, children can "shoot 'em up" to their hearts content at the Indian village or the cowboy saloon! The promenades are enclosed and heated to provide protection against bad weather and if one gets tired, there are tractor trains which carry visitors around the area for a scenic tour.

There are two restaurants with terraces on the lake which use the fresh produce from the surrounding area. Nowhere is "off limits" to the visitor—you may wander to your heart's content and explore the fields, houses or barns.

NOORDOOSTPOLDER

The Northeast Polder Land (Emmeloord, Urk)

GETTING THERE: The Northeast Polder is reached by A6 crossing from the southern part of Flevoland over the Ketelbrug. From Friesland, take A50 south at the intersection with A7.
INFORMATION: VVV Noordoostpolder, Lange Nering 12c, Emmeloord tel. (05270) 12000.

The Northeast Polder was "dried out" in 1942 providing an additional 50,000 hectares of new land. A new town was built and a very old town was incorporated into the new geopolitical unit, first as part of the Gelderland, and then incorporated into the new province, Flevoland.

Emmeloord is the largest town and the geographic and commercial center for the area. To the south is the important Schokland Museum and to the west is the picturesque town of Urk, both described below.

Museum Schokland, Archeological Museum

LOCATION: From Lelystad, cross the Ketelbrug on A6.
Follow directions to the museum shortly after crossing the bridge . . . due east of Urk and south of Emmeloord.
INFORMATION: Tel. (05275) 1396.
HOURS: April-Sept., daily, 10am-5pm; Oct.-March, Tues.-Fri., 10am-5pm, Sat.-Sun., 11am-5pm. Closed Mondays.
■ *Of interest to children from 6 years.*

Once upon a time Schokland was an island. When the Zuider Zee, specifically the northeast polder was drained, Schokland was attached to the mainland. The treasures found after the waters were drained make up this museum collection. The little village is raised from the surrounding polderland and consists of a series of colorful red-roofed houses constructed in the Zuider Zee style period 1859. The museum is in the ancient chapel of Middelbuurt.

The collection includes ship-rudders, figureheads, pieces of Roman galleys and Norman dragonships. Kids will be intrigued by the bones of prehistoric mammoths, woolly-haired rhinoceros, giant deer and wild horses. There are stone tools and weapons, Neolithic hunting gear, and pre-Christian cooking pots.

URK

An island for more than 700 years

GETTING THERE: Follow directions to the Schokland Museum, above, except take the road west as soon as possible after crossing the Ketel Bridge.
INFORMATION: VVV Urk, Westhavenkade 47, tel. (05277) 3030.

Urk has a longer history than the polder it is a part of. For at least 700 years it was an island, until 1941, when the land around it was reclaimed. It has, however, retained its traditional seaport atmosphere, and trades such as ship-building and repair.

On Sunday the local fisherfolk wear their traditional dress. It's one of the few places where men wear their extremely colorful outfits with baggy pants and wooden shoes. Walk around the old town through the small streets and notice the compact fishermen's homes with their neat front gardens behind painted picket fences. Their green facades and red and white shutters make a colorful picture. There is also a lighthouse at Wijk 3-80, tel. 1582, and a huge anchor just in front of its entrance which came from one of Admiral de Ruyter's ships.

The Fishing Museum (Visserijmuseum), Westhavenkade 44, tel. 3262, is open mid-April-mid-June, Mon.-Fri., 2-5pm; mid-June to end of Aug., Mon.-Fri., 11am-1pm and 2-5pm, Sat., 11am-1pm; check for the rest of the year. It has a collection of clothing, the inside of a house dating from 1900, and displays detailing the way of life of Urk.

COMMERCIAL TOUR: From the middle of May until about September 10th, there's a boat trip possible from Urk to Enkhuizen . . . passengers, bikes and some autos (inquire first). The boat leaves Urk at 9am and 3:15pm, and Enkhuizen at 11am and 6pm . . . not on Sundays. For information, call (05277) 3407, Friese Recreatie Onderneming b.v., Slenk 5a, Urk.

CHAPTER 7

THE PROVINCE OF NORTH BRABANT

North Brabant is one of the largest of the Dutch provinces, extending west to the Oosterschelde almost to the North Sea; east to within a few kilometers of the Dutch-German border; with its southern boundary falling just short of running the entire length of the Dutch-Belgian border. All major highways north/south pass through some part of the Brabant so check out a good map and pick the route best for you. The province has such a varied landscape, it offers a wide choice of outdoor activities. In addition, it has its fair share of castles and a fine selection of recreation parks (De Efteling, Beekse Bergen Safari and Recreation Park, and two antique car museums), not to mention historic monuments and towns. 's Hertogenbosch is the Provincial capital.

Because of its southern location, North Brabant (which includes West Brabant, The Heart of Brabant, The Meierij, Kempenland, North-East Brabant and Peelland) is a good place to visit in the Spring or Fall when the other provinces are not yet—or are no longer—at their best climatically. In addition, the province has special celebrations and folkloric events throughout the year.

North Brabant did not become a part of the Netherlands until it was ceded to the United Provinces (Treaty of Münster 1648) after it was conquered from the Spanish by Prince Maurice and Prince

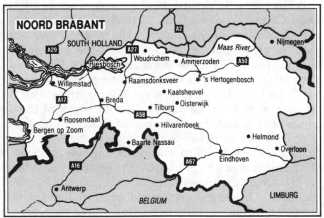

INFORMATION: VVV-i,
's Hertogenbosh
tel: (073) 123071

Henry. Earlier on, from 1190 to 1430, it was the independent Duchy of Brabant; there are still descendants from those early rulers who consider themselves apart from Belgium and Holland in their heart of hearts.

Since North Brabant is wide and narrow geographically and divides itself according to north/south designations, we will not take our visitor clockwise through the province, but west to east, city-by-city with points of interest listed clockwise around the nearest big town. We will start with Willemstad, the closest stop from the Randstad, then travel south to Bergen op Zoom before returning north to discuss the Biesbosch and then east through the rest of the province.

WILLEMSTAD

Fortress town and boating center

GETTING THERE: From Amsterdam and The Hague, drive through Rotterdam taking A13 south through the Maas Tunnel then A29 over the Haringvliet Bridge to Willemstad.
INFORMATION: VVV Breda or Gemeente Huis, Hofstraat 1, Willemstad, tel. (01687) 2350.

Most Dutch sailors know about Willemstad, but for some reason, it's not so well known to foreigners. This fortress town was named after William of Orange who ordered that it be enclosed in 1583 by Abraham Andriesz with a moat 125 feet wide and ramparts laid out in the shape of a seven-pointed star. Two openings were left in the fortress works: the Land Gate on the land side (what else?)— now replaced—and the Water Gate on the water side also now replaced.

Willemstad can vie with Naarden (in the area of Amsterdam) for the title of best-kept fortress town. It is a quieter place, however, becoming more animated primarily on weekends and during holiday periods when pleasure-craft owners come in droves to sail the Biesbosch, an area of innumerable inlets and outlets perfect for fishing or other watersports. Surfboards, boats and such like can be rented if you don't have your own.

Within its walls, the streets all converge on Church Square and the Reformed Dom Church, completed in octagonal design in 1690 as the first Protestant church building in the country. Young and those young-in-heart may (check with the church) climb the Dom tower for a spectacular view of this precisely laid-out town. Take the Hofstraat leading from the Church Square to the Voorstraat and you will find the hunting castle of Prince Maurits which is now the Town Hall (1587); its herb garden is worth a visit. Behind the Town Hall are the arsenal and the harbor. The weather-cock of the Town Hall is a mermaid which once graced the Markiezenhof in Bergen op Zoom.

A reminder of not-so-happy times is the cemetery with the graves of 134 Belgian soldiers who died when their ship was mined in May 1940 on the way to Germany as prisoners of war. On the ramparts near the water is the Oranje Mill (1734). To get the feel of this town, there are two possible walking tours on the ramparts. The longer tour would be to follow the old walls lining the large canals; those not so energetic can follow the walls flanking the small canals.

A Ceramics Museum, Raadhuisstraat 2, tel. (01687) 3357 is open April-Oct., Tues.-Sun., 9am-noon and 1-6pm; Nov.-March, Wed.-Sun., same hours.

BERGEN OP ZOOM

Asparagus, shellfish and anchovies!

GETTING THERE: A little more than halfway between Rotterdam and Antwerp, Bergen op Zoom is easy to find. It has always been on a well-traveled road as is evident by the number of times it has been under fire. The most direct road from Antwerp is N4 north; from Rotterdam, The Hague and Amsterdam, take A29 to N259 after Rotterdam.

INFORMATION: VVV, Bergen op Zoom, Hoogstraat 2, tel. (01640) 66000.

During its heyday, this fortress town was besieged fourteen times; however, it was victorious against two of the sieges by the Spaniards—once in 1588 and again in 1622. Until the French took the city in 1747 and bombarded it heavily, it had been known as the "virgin" city. There is little to be seen today of its distinguished past as a result of these military maneuvers.

Bergen op Zoom has had important economic and trade relations with England and Antwerp, Belgium. Today, it is well known for its asparagus, oysters, lobsters, and anchovies.

The Stadhuis (City Hall—17th century) on the Market place can be visited Mon.-Fri., 8:30am-12:30pm and 1:30-5:30pm. The beautiful facade of the building dates from 1611. The inscription in the front of the City Hall reads, "I have overcome thousands of dangers." Inside, there is an interesting chimney (the Christoffen chimney) with Renaissance motifs in stone designed by Ramout Keldermans. While on the Market Place, notice the Sint Geertrudis Church (St. Gertrude's), with its remarkable domed tower (the pepper box). On the interior, there is an impressive memorial to Charles Morgan, son-in-law of Marnix van St. Aldegond.

If you can take a few moments, stroll around the area. Look for the house called "de Olifant" (the elephant) built over St. Anna Street running out of the Town Hall through a late Gothic gateway. Outside the Market Square is the Marquis' Court with its 15th-century outlook and interesting grill-work on the ground floor windows. In the summer months on Wed. at 2pm there are guided walks through the old town.

On O. L. Vrouwestraat, you will see the most beautiful facade of the town. Flemish in form but Baroque in style, particularly impressive is the Vrouwepoort or Gateway with its lower walls 7 feet thick, the last remains of the former town ramparts.

MARKETS: There is an antique and curio market on the Steenen Tuin (behind the Peperbus), April-Aug. on Sat., 10am-5pm.

Other markets are held as well as special events. Check with the VVV to see what's going on when you're visiting!

197

Markiezenhof City Museum

LOCATION: Steenbergsestraat 8. Buses 1, 2, 3, and 4 from the Central Station go to the Grote Markt every 15 minutes.
INFORMATION: Tel. (01640) 42930.
HOURS: June-Aug., Tues.-Fri., 11am-5pm, Sat., Sun. and holidays, 2-5pm. Rest of the year, Tues.-Sun., 2-5pm. Closed December 25, January 1, Easter Sunday and Carnival Tuesday.
■ *Of interest to children from 5 years.*

The late Gothic palace of the Marquises of Bergen was designed by Anthonis Keldermans and built between 1485 and 1525 on the site of an earlier dwelling.

Its twelve-room museum contains many archeological finds of the area, as well as some light-hearted items appealing to children, such as toys. There are also fishing displays, prints, carpets (from about 1580), 15th-18th-century paintings, sculptures (15th-16th century), furniture (17th and 18th centuries), and display rooms furnished in the Louis XV, XVI and Empire periods.

IN THE NEIGHBORHOOD OF BERGEN OP ZOOM:
Roosendaal originated as a peat cutting village in the 13th century but today, industry is its mainstay along with plenty of shopping opportunities. It does have a museum, De Ghulden Roos (The Golden Rose), Molenstraat 2, tel. (01650) 36916; open, Tues.-Sat., 2-5pm in the pastorie of St. Jan (1762). The collection includes silver, glass, crests, pewter, toys, a little shop, print cabinet, tools, porcelain and earthenware. Within walking distance of the train station.

Wouw is about halfway between Roosendaal and Bergen op Zoom. For info, check with the VVV, Markt 14, tel. (01658) 1951. Called the Geranium Village because flowers are always blooming (in season). You can't miss the splendid silhouette of St. Lambertuskerk (15th century); inside are 17th-century choir stalls and lovely stained glass windows.

■ **The Silk Museum, Zijdemuseum "Ter Zÿde,"** Schoolstraat 3, tel. (01658) 3690, open, April-Nov., Mon.-Sat., 10am-5pm; Sun., 1-5pm, is the town's stellar attraction. If you happen by at the right moment, you might see the birth of a silkworm! You will see them live, watch their life pattern and extraordinary appetite. There's a slide show explaining it all. Many silk articles are on exhibit, past and present. And don't miss the lovely collection of materials in the museum shop.

There is also a Graphics Museum and a cornmill, "de Alvend." Located in an area of about 180 acres of woods, this is the place to enjoy the out-of-doors life. At the Wouw Plantage, there are many nature trails and good camp sites.

Huijbergen, a village southeast of Bergen op Zoom, was inhabited by monks for centuries. There is a 17th-century gate as a reminder of times gone by and a small museum, Wilhelmietenmuseum, Staartsestraat 8, tel. (01644) 2650, only open April-Oct., 2nd and 4th weekends, or by appointment–items of the town's inheritance.

THE BIESBOSCH

Largest valuable nature reserve in Holland

GETTING THERE: The Biesbosch is encircled by major (as well as minor) highways: A16 to the west, A15 to the north, A27 to the east and A59 to the south. The closest big city is Dordrecht (ZH).
INFORMATION: There are two information centers:
Info Center "Drimmelen," Dorpstraat 14, Drimmelen, tel. (01626) 2991, Wed.-Fri., 10am-5pm, Sat., 1-5pm, Sun., 11am-5pm.
Info Center, "De Merwelanden," Baanhoekweg 53, Dordrecht, tel. (01840) 18047, Tues.-Sun., 10am-5pm.

When the Haringvliet Dam was completed in 1970, what had been a fresh water tidal area was replaced by a controlled non-tidal alluvial landscape. There were vast changes with losses of certain plant and animal species, and gains when they were replaced by others ... changes and adjustments continue to take place.

The Biesbosch as a wetland (an area rich in water important as a waterfowl habitat) dates to 1421. The polder became an inland sea after a severe flood at that time and tides entered the area freely. At the same time, sludge and sand were deposited from the Meuse (Maas) and Waal rivers. With the build-up of the sludge, rush, reed and willows grew and by 1850, more than two-thirds of the former inland sea was being used for agriculture. Changes occurred with 20th-century developments, and particularly, with the completion of the Haringvliet Dam.

The area is managed by the National Forest Service; yachting is subject to navigation regulations. The flora includes osier beds, stinging nettles, willowherb, marsh marigold, bulrush, yellow iris and many others. Birds have always come to roost, feed and breed, especially migrating birds. You will find ducks, cormorants, spoonbills, swans, herons, meadowbirds, wild geese. Even rare kingfisher and the night heron are seen here. Among the mammals are bats, roe deer and polecats.

Start your visit at one of the information centers ... "Drimmelen" is on the southern shore of the Maas River; "De Merwelanden" is just outside Dordrecht. They will advise you about recreational facilities and organized day-trips. Changing exhibitions describe the area and you may experience the joys of the Biesbosch on bikes, by canoe, boat, or by swimming and walking.

The Biesbosch Museum, not far from the southern shore of the Waal River, Spieringsluis 4, Werkendam, tel. (01835) 4009; open, Tues.-Sun., 10am-5pm, Mon., 1-5pm, deals with the history of the area before 1970. In the paludarium are birds, fish and mammals, among them a 3-meter-long sturgeon. This fish has disappeared due to pollution and over-fishing. Fishing, basketmaking, reeds and thatch-making are explained. Fascinating slide show of about 20 minutes.

EATING OUT: In the same building as the museum, there's an attractive restaurant with open fireplace for cold, damp days, and an outdoor terrace for golden, sunny days ... typical Brabant food.

COMMERCIAL TOURS: Check with the VVV Dordrecht for information about boat tours around the Biesbosch.

IN THE NEIGHBORHOOD OF THE BIESBOSCH:
Willemstad, mentioned above, is within a few kilometers west of this national park. You can rent boats here for your own exploration of the waterways.

The National Automobile Museum at Raamsdonksveer, 3 km south of the Maas River near Drimmelen is a total change of pace!

The National Automobile Museum, Raamsdonksveer

LOCATION: Steurweg 8, Raamsdonksveer. From The Hague, A13 to Rotterdam, following directions for the Brienenoordbrug. From Rotterdam south via A16 to intersection with A59/N59 to Raamsdonksveer. From Amsterdam, south on A2, then A27 south exiting at Raamsdonksveer.
INFORMATION: Tel. (01621) 85400.
HOURS: All year, Mon.-Sat., 9am-4:45pm, Sun., 11am-4:45pm.
ADMISSION: Adults, Fl. 7, children to 13 yrs., Fl. 4.
■ *Of interest to children from 5 years upward, including fathers!*

This national museum covering 6,000 square meters, has a fascinating international collection of antique cars (150 of them at last count), 40 motorbikes, carriages, fire engines, an airplane and even bicycles . . . not to be missed.

Summer weekends there are films usually every hour about unusual forms of transport, inventions, and racing car history.

BREDA

Home of the Counts of Burgundy

*GETTING THERE: From Amsterdam, south on A2 to Vianen, then
A27 south; from The Hague and Rotterdam, A13 south to A20
east. At Knooppunt Terbregseplein, take A16 south to the Breda
turnoff.*
INFORMATION: VVV Breda, Willemstraat 17-19, tel. (076) 222444.

Breda is known for its friendly atmosphere, numerous ethnic restaurants, parks,
two castles, Burgundian market place, and "Begijnhof" (almshouses). Breda can
trace its origins to 1252 when it received its town rights and to a prominent
family named "Boevenjen." In 1350, the town passed as a Brabant fiefdom to
the Lords of Polanen and, in 1404 to Count Engelbert of Nassau-Dillenburg.
Specific details are somewhat lacking about those early days due to several fires
between 1490 and 1534 which destroyed most city records.

According to a pamphlet entitled *Breda,* quoted in part below, the wealthy
counts of Breda succeeded in attaining a noble position at the Burgundian Court
through introductions and alliances with distinguished noblemen. Henry III was
a personal friend of Charles V. At the beginning of the Eighty Years' War in
1568, the Prince, Charles V, and most of the noblemen left Breda:

"The Barony of Breda became a battlefield, Breda a besieged town. Nearly all
'the pearls' of the string of castles around Breda were destroyed. Only the
Bouverie remained more or less intact, although it was severely damaged too.
Under the guidance of William of Orange, the 'Father of the whole country' the
country tried to shake off the yoke of the Spaniards, which had become so heavy
under Philip II. Educated in Spain, he was a stranger in the eyes of Dutch
noblemen—he couldn't speak Dutch and he refused to acknowledge Calvinism.
The war for independence was to go on for 80 years."

According to a local legend, in 1590, seventy soldiers under the command of
Maurits of Nassau, using the old Trojan Horse ruse, were able to enter the city
hidden in a peat barge giving them the military advantage of surprise to gain a
victory over the Spaniards. Maurits' father was William the Silent, the great
fighter for Dutch liberty. When Maurits succeeded his father, the power and
wealth of the Republic rapidly increased, active hostilities were frequently taken
against the Spaniards.

An interesting walk is along the "Historic Mile." You can start with the
Great church, a fine example of so-called Brabant Gothic; then visit the Town
Hall (1768, enlarged in 1924) ... there is a copy of a painting by Velasquez
entitled, "De Overgave van Breda" (The Surrender of Breda) and portraits of
members of the House of Nassau. Breda Castle, not far from the Market Square,
can be visited (see below) as well as Valkenberg (Falcon's mountain), formerly
part of the castle grounds but now a fine public park with rare plants and
flowers. Near the castle is the Spaniards' Gate, and next to the park is the
Beguinage.

Breda Castle, north of town on Kasteelplein, not far from the VVV office, tel.
(076) 222444 for info. The castle was begun in 1536 under Henry III of Nassau

by an Italian builder, Thomas Vincidor da Bologna. It was reconstructed in 1696 by William III of England. Today, the castle houses the Royal Military Academy of the Netherlands. There are interesting tunnel vaults in the quiet inner court which still evoke memories of its warlike history.

The Spanish Gate, next to the castle, is a water gate flanked with two big guntowers. It is said this is the gate through which the peat barge with its cargo of soldiers under command of the Prince of Orange sailed into the city to do battle with the Spaniards.

The Beguinage, a quadrangle surrounded by medieval dwellings built of yellow bricks offers quite another atmosphere. The original occupants were Beguines, religious women whose status was somewhere between lay-women and nuns. Eldery women now live quietly in these small houses, protected from the hustle and bustle of the outside world. The middle of the quadrangle is occupied by a small 18th-century church and an herb garden.

MUSEUMS: There are two museums and one art gallery in Breda:

The City and Episcopal Museum, Grote Markt 19, tel. 223110; open, Wed.-Sat., 10:30am-5pm; Tues., Sun. and holidays, 1-5pm, closed January 1, Carnival Monday afternoon and December 25. Housed in the former "Vleeshal" (Meat Hall) and St. Joris Guild House, the collection contains ecclesiastical art and deals with the history of the Barony of Breda. There is also a collection of coins, prints and changing exhibits.

The State Museum for Ethnology, "Justinus Van Nassau," Kasteelplein 55, tel. (55076) 224710; open, Tues.-Sat., 10am-5pm, Sun. and holidays, 1-5pm; closed January 1, Carnival Sunday and Monday. Changing exhibitions jockey for the public's favor with the permanent collection from Indonesia and other countries such as North Africa, North and Central America, India, China.

De Beyerd Art Center, Boschstraat 22, tel. 225025; open, Tues.-Fri., 10am-5pm, Sat.-Sun., 1-5pm. Exhibits of contemporary art, photography, architecture and ceramics.

Just south of town, the manor house, Bouvigne "Castle" was probably built in the beginning of the 16th century. As early as the 13th century, a family named Boevenjen lived in the Barony of Breda. This estate was called "The Boeverie" which means pasture, village green or landed property in old French. A number of noblemen and commoners have resided here, including Prince William of Orange. At his death the property passed on to his son, Maurits. Today, it is a lovely spot for a picnic lunch looking at the reflection of this graceful brick "palace" with elegant lines and onion dome reflected in the small artificial pond.

In addition to cultural possibilities, Breda offers sports activities such as riding schools, swimming pools, bowling alleys and several parks and gardens. A relaxing way to explore is to rent a canoe from Rofra, Kraanstraat 7, near the Spanish Gate, tel. 224813—reasonable rates. For adult evening entertainment, Breda has a Casino, Bijster 30 ... roulette, jackpot machines, Blackjack and Punto Banko.

MARKETS: Weekly markets are held Tuesday and Friday, 9am-1pm on the Grote Markt; Sat., 1-6pm on the Nieuwe Haagdijk/Haagweg; Thurs., 9am-

12:30pm in the Molstraat (north Breda) and Sat. on the Vijverstraat from 9am-1pm.

EATING OUT: The wide selection of international foods available includes Portuguese, Italian, Thai, Greek, Cantonese, Yugoslav, Argentine, Hungarian and Swiss plus 19 Chinese-Indonesian restaurants. For a quick hamburger, there's a McDonald's at Karnemelkstraat 5. Two pancake restaurants are d'Oude Vest, Oude Vest 21, and Kloostertaverne, Kloosterplein 4-5. Or try a farm restaurant: De Boschwachter, Huisdreef 4, tel. 652880, or Boswachter Liesbosch, Nieuwe Dreef 4, tel. 212736.

YEARLY EVENTS: Some of Breda's activities during the year include an Art and Antique Fair and a performance of St. Matthew's Passion at Eastertime; Ascension Day, an old-style jazz festival; a military taptoe on Whitsun; Breda Flora and a National Taptoe in August, etc. Check with the VVV.

Grote Kerk (Great Church)

LOCATION: On the Market Square in the old city center. Getting into the area can be tricky because of the canals which completely surround the town. Coming in on A16, take the Prinsenbeek turnoff going east and follow signs for Centrum.
INFORMATION: VVV, Willemstraat 17, tel. (076) 222444.
HOURS: May-Sept., Mon.-Sat., 10am-5pm, Sun., 1-5pm; for other times, inquire by calling the church.
■ *Of interest to older children—especially in summer when it is possible to climb the tower.*

The church took 150 years to build and resulted in one of the most beautiful towers of the Netherlands, 97 meters high. If possible, come here on Tuesday and Friday mornings when the forty-five bells of the carillon in the church tower ring out over the heads of the stall-holders and buyers in the Square.

Originating from about 1400, this is a fine example of Brabant Gothic style. It was enlarged in the 17th century with the addition of some small chapels. There are interesting gravestones; in particular, that of Engelbert II of Nassau, a Governor of the Netherlands, and his wife.

On the lighter side, look for the satirical wooden sculptures in the choir of the church depicting vices of the clergy.

IN THE NEIGHBORHOOD OF BREDA:

Oosterhout, just north of Breda, has a Toy Museum at St. Vincentiusstraat 86, tel. (01620) 52815; open, Fri.-Sat. and first Sun. of the month, 1-5pm. Also a full-scale recreation area, "De Warande," Bredaseweg 127, tel. (01620) 53800, with all sorts of swimming pools (including impressive waterslide), lake, pedaloes, playground, midget golf, restaurant with open-air terrace.

Etten Leur, about 5 km west of Breda, has two museums and a recreation park:

The Regional Museum, "Jan Uten Houte," Markt 55, tel. (01608) 34244; open, Mon.-Fri. and first Sun. of the month, 2-4:30pm, has an old Brabant farm living room with fireplace, furniture, tiles, clothing, tools (18th-century honey press), shoe and cart-making tools, painter's shop, classroom, grocer's shop, and village inn.

The Printing Museum, Leeuwerik 8, tel. 34244, same hours as above, shows early bookprinting techniques ... setting, binding, tools and machines of the 19th century are still in use. Stone, litho and engraving techniques.

Recreation Park Basbad Hoeven, Oude Antwerpsepostbaan 81a, 4741 SG Hoeven, tel. (01659) 2366; open generally, 1-5pm ... call for specifics. A great family day out: pools for every age and purpose, a paddling pool, racing pool, diving pool, 60-meter-long super water-slide; playground with more than 50 attractions; electric motorboats, "sightseeing" train, horses, pedaloes, etc. There is a campground attached, Camping Hoeven, tel. (01659) 2570 for info and reservations.

Baarle-Nassau and Baarle-Hertog represent a unique political and economic phenomenon; twin cities, one Dutch and one Belgian deeply imbedded in the Netherlands. Located southeast of Breda and southwest of Tilburg, Baarle-Nassau is the last Dutch village enroute to Turnhout, Belgium. For information, VVV Baarle-Nassau and Baarle-Hertog, St. Annaplein 10, tel. (04257) 9921.

This situation has existed since the 15th century and has created many ridiculous situations. For instance, the Mayor of Baarle-Hertog must pass through Holland in order to go from his home to his office. Everything is doubled: there are two electrical systems, two post offices, two schools, two police departments and two Mayors with two City Halls.

There is a small museum, 't Brouwershuis (Belgian Brewery), Molenstraat 42, and the Parish House next to the Belgian Church. A "Curiosity Market," next to the Baarle-Nassau City Hall, is held May-Sept., Sat., 9am-5pm.

TILBURG

"Home" of antique and modern textiles

*GETTING THERE: From The Hague and Rotterdam, take A13, A16
south to the Prinsenbeek turnoff at Breda, then east to Tilburg.
From Amsterdam A2 to A27 to Breda then A58 to Tilburg.
INFORMATION: VVV Tilburg, Spoorlaan 416a, tel. (013) 351135.*

Tilburg is a center of education with a textile school, well-considered University of Economics, and the Brabant Academy of Music with excellent ballet training. In addition, its central location has always made it a center for the wine trade ... ships and carts that transported textiles all over Europe brought back various products, including wine.

Its "heyday" came late with the Industrial Revolution of the 18-19th centuries and the development of modern factories. They were often set up willy-nilly in the countryside. Tilburg became a center for workers' families living near the textile factory. As soon as the number of families warranted it, a church was built. Under Louis Napoleon (Bonaparte's brother), it received its town charter.

The factory owners had excellent relations with King William II who lived in Tilburg during much of his reign. He gave his palace to the town which serves today as part of the Town Hall.

The wool trade has gradually been replaced with a variety of service industries and companies specializing in modern technology. Industrial giants are often good supporters of the arts as a cultural counter-balance to factories, and Tilburg has a number of museums, art galleries, theaters, and enthusiasts of modern jazz. In addition, there are sidewalk cafes, shops, fifteen movie theaters and a wide choice of restaurants. Check out the "Kruikenmarkt" where antiques, curiosities and second-hand goods are on sale.

MUSEUMS:

The Textile Museum, Goirkestraat 88 (in an old mill), tel. (013) 422241, is open Tues.-Fri., 10am-5pm, Sun., noon-5pm. A most interesting museum. Check times for spinning and weaving demonstrations when you come in. Antique textiles from Peru, Persia, India, Japan and China; batik, old European damask, brocades, printed cloth, old costumes (especially from North Brabant), are all on display. There are also looms and other apparatus for weaving and finishing textiles.

The Wine House, Geminiweg 9, tel. 434920; open, Tues.-Fri., 10am-6pm, Sat., 10am-5pm. A little bit of France in the middle of the Brabant. Something for the adults; the kids will like it too. Enter through the Orangerie, then visit the "Cinema du Vin" (movie on wine), then follow the "Route du Vin" past a barrel or cask maker, art gallery, a glass store, wine library and a Grand Cru shop. For the thirsty or hungry, there's a French-style café and an open market with wine tasting. Fun and instructive!

The Folk Art Museum and North Brabant Nature Museum are both located at Spoorlaan 434. For info about the Folk Art Museum, tel. (013) 358655; open, Tues.-Fri., 10am-noon and 1-5pm, Sat.-Sun., 1-5pm. On display are ethnographic and practical tools from China, Japan, Indonesia, the Philippines, New Guinea, Africa, Central and South America. To see the North Brabant Nature Museum, you must call ahead, tel. 353935. The collection includes plants, animals, rocks, prehistoric fish, petrified wood, and so on.

The Writing and Typewriter Museum, Philips Fingboonstraat 3, tel. 353777; open, Mon.-Fri., 10am-4:30pm and the first Sat. of each month, 2-5pm. Over 500 typewriters, calculators, ink pots, brushes, pens, letter openers, are just a few of the items in this museum. In addition, there is interesting material on calligraphic art, ancient writing materials, and old writing styles.

YEARLY EVENTS: May-June, there's a sheep shearing festival; in July, a Fun Fair; and in Oct., a wine festival. Check with the VVV for more, especially summer events.

IN THE NEIGHBORHOOD OF TILBURG:

Two world-class recreation areas are located near Tilburg: De Efteling to the north, and Beekse Bergen, southeast of town. They are covered separately below.

At **Waalwijk**, north of De Efteling, there's a Leather and Shoe Museum, in a former shoe factory at Eizenweg 25, tel. (04160) 32738; open, Tues.-Fri., 10am-5pm, Sat.-Sun., 2-5pm. Shoes from 'round the world and from all eras. Also tools and machines used to make shoes and boots dating from 1870. Still functioning, they are used in demonstrations.

De Efteling

GETTING THERE: De Efteling is located near Kaatsheuvel, about 8 kilometers north of Tilburg on highway N261 (A261). From The Hague and Rotterdam, take A16 south then by-pass Breda (Prinsenbeek turnoff) to Tilburg, then north on N261. From Amsterdam, A2 south to Knooppunt Everdingen, then A27 south, to A59 east (Waalwijk) and south on N261. Check with the Railway Station for all-in tickets.

INFORMATION: Tel. (04167) 80505, or write POB 18, 5170 AA Kaatsheuvel. You can rent a Kodak camera or Panasonic VHS video camera; there are facilities for payment in your own currency; free wheelchairs; free dog kennels; souvenir shops and at least three restaurants with good meals to suit every budget.

HOURS: (Vary somewhat yearly) Mid-April to mid-Oct., daily 10am-6pm; summer 'til 8pm; no entry after 5pm.

ADMISSION: Adults, Fl. 19; children up to 3 yrs., free; seniors and handicapped, Fl. 16.50. Attractions are included in the price.

■ *Of interest to children of all ages.*

De Efteling had been a sports park from 1933 until after World War II when the need for more recreational areas throughout Holland became pronounced.

At that time, Anton Pieck, the famous Dutch artist and a great lover of children, designed De Efteling trying to bring to super-life-size his drawings and characters from fairy tales of Holland and around the world. It took 10 years to complete what you see today.

The Enchanted Forest is full of fascinating scenes such as the castle of Sleeping Beauty, the Dwarfs' Village, Longneck, Little Red Ridinghood, The Red Shoes, Hansel and Gretel, and Snow White's Cave. These characters are found in a woodland setting, laid out like a maze; recordings in Dutch tell their story. Most are well-known figures and the average child is already familiar with the stories.

There is also an amusement park—geared primarily for the little ones—which includes a merry-go-round, pony carts, a miniature train which the children can drive themselves, a separate playground for the very little ones with a paddling pool and an elephant which spouts water high in the air.

Also available are puppet shows, swimming pool, boating lake, mini-train ride around the whole complex, an original steam Carousel, and Diorama. The latter shows a village and country scene extending 50 meters and comprising towns, roads, miniature railway with trains moving in all directions, through craggy mountains, along lakes, in daylight, twilight, night time, and so forth.

Another important attraction is the haunted castle where an audience of 500 can watch a 25-minute spook show. It is the biggest in Europe and compares to the one in Disneyland, USA.

In fact, there are so many things to see and do, one should plan to spend all day. Something new is constantly appearing so there's always a surprise.

One of the most unique attractions is "De Halve Maen," a 3-masted sailing ship which swings its passengers at a 90° angle upending from bow to stern as it goes back and forth. The loop-the-loop is huge and scary while the Gandolettas are relaxing and wonderful family fare. Small-boat fans might like to try out the Pirana, a not-so-restful ride on turbulent waters in round, rubber-bottomed boats, passing waterfalls and other "hazards," such as simulated white water areas. Also spectacular is the Pagode which rises into the air 45 meters higher than Long Neck . . . from this height you can get a panoramic view of the Carnival.

Beekse Bergen Safari Park and Beach

*GETTING THERE: The Safari Park is about 3 km southeast of Til-
burg at Hilvarenbeek off highway N269 going south. From Amsterdam, take A2 south around 's Hertogenbosch to Vught, then
N65 southwest to intersection with N269 and follow signs. From
the Hague and Rotterdam, A13, A16 south past Breda to A58
east to N269 south.*
INFORMATION: Tel. (013) 360032.
*HOURS: Safari Park: early April-early Nov., daily, 10am-6pm; winter
hours, 10am-3:30pm. Recreation Park: mid-May to end Sept.
only, same hours as above.*
*ADMISSION: Fl.11.75 per person with their car; Fl. 14.75 per person
with safari bus; or rent a Safari jeep @ Fl. 45 for 1½ hours.
Children under 2 yrs., free.*
■ *Of interest to children all ages.*

Safari Park: Ferocious MGM lions and whimsical Wizard-of-Oz lions, leopards,
cheetahs, zebras, monkeys galore, ostriches, many strange birds, and so on, are
living at the Beekse Bergen Safari Park. It would be wise to note that they aren't
all living "free" together—or some of them would not be free long!

You approach the entrance to the Safari Park through a very high double-
fenced double-gated area into a no-man's land of about 25 meters during which
time the entrance gate has been closed behind you. As soon as the gate is closed
and you have approached the exit ahead, that one is opened and you are out of
the protected area into the park itself. From this time you are advised not to
open car doors or windows . . . even when sorely tempted because the baby
animals look so cute and cuddly or because those mischievous apes are doing a
good job of tearing off your side mirror. The monkeys are really the greatest fun
because they are so active and full of naughty tricks. They will jump on your car
for a ride—have a good fight on your car roof—peer in through the windows
showing their teeth—look at themselves in the outside mirrors—handle anything loose or interesting—(put your radio antennas all the way down unless you
want them broken off). The lions had just eaten and were quite placid the day we
went through but the cheetahs were having some sort of family squabble, and
that was exciting enough to satisfy the more bloodthirsty of the children. It is
best to try and come at feeding time.

There is an area in the heart of the park where you may walk among safer
animals and even take a boatride, "Water Safari" through the islands watching
the monkeys and other animals . . . 30-45 minutes.

A very impressive show offered several times per day in season is a demonstration of various birds of prey, including falcons, buzzards and a number
native to North America such as the American Sea Eagle.

Beach-Strand Park: Visitors will come for the day and want to spend a
weekend or longer—especially the small fry who will go out of their little minds
trying to decide which "event" they want to tackle first. There are trampolines,
water bikes, rowboats, waterskiing by cable, mini-soccer, mini and midget golf,

rollerskating, a jogging track, small cars for children to drive, sailboats, tennis courts, horseback riding, an amusement hall, a jump cushion, a maze, playground and play street, Imax film theater, and a magnificent beach to top it all off. Something for all tastes, all ages, and something new is always in the planning stage! Come by bike, car or boat; there's a fine campsite, bungalow park and yacht harbor.

's HERTOGENBOSCH

A Medieval town with a magnificent Gothic cathedral

GETTING THERE: From Amsterdam, take A2 south; from Rotterdam and The Hague, A13 then A16 south to A15 east, then A2 south.
INFORMATION: VVV, 's Hertogenbosch, Markt 77 (in De Moriaan House), tel. (073) 123071.

This medieval town is the Provincial capital of North Brabant and boasts a splendid cathedral as well as a resident Roman Catholic Bishop. Because of the many woods in the surroundings, this was once the hunting preserve of the Duke of Brabant which is how it got its name. 's Hertogenbosch means "in the Duke's Woods" ... today, it is most often referred to as "Den Bosch" (the woods).

The town grew from a village on the Duke's wooded estate along the Maas River; in 1185 Henry I, Duke of Brabant, granted the town its municipal charter. During this time, this part of the Netherlands and what is today Belgium were an independent state, the Brabant. In 1430, Brabant became part of Burgundy but was later annexed by France as part of the Spanish Empire. The Eighty Years' War held the whole country in its grip; Den Bosch was liberated in 1629. Brabant joined the United Provinces (Dutch) until Napoleon won the territory for France in 1810. The Kingdom of the Netherlands was created in 1814 including the Low Countries. Soon afterward, South Brabant separated and became part of Belgium.

The historic town center is full of atmosphere with numerous facades and architecture worthy of note. On the Market Square you will see a statue of the famous painter and native son, Hieronymus Bosch (1450-1516); opposite, is the 16th-century Town Hall (remodeled in 1671). From its tower, carillons chime every half hour while a group of mechanical horsemen ride into view—there's a one-hour concert on Wed., 10-11am. The oldest house in town is "De Moriaan House" (13th century), now the VVV offices. It was built as a hunting lodge for the Duke so he could escape the pressures of business in Brussels . . . originally, it would have been wooden.

Not far from the Kruithuis, the Citadel was renovated in 1982-85 . . . notice the ancient fortifications with moat and high ramparts. There 's unfortunately nothing left of the original city walls circa 1200. At the southern bastion, the "Oranje," the huge cannon, "de Boze Griest" (The Devil's Woman) was cast in 1511 in Cologne. The German inscription reads "Brute force I am called, Den Bosch I watch over" . . .

The Refugiehuis, corner of Spinhuiswal and St. Jorisstraat, was originally a safe place for those persecuted for their religious beliefs . . . today, it is an arts and crafts center.

If you enjoy walking, stroll along the Uilenburg Quarter to see some award-winning houses designed to replace unsafe buildings, and then look at the colorful houses at the Brede Haven along the Inner Harbor. At the corner of Hoogstraat and Kolonel Johnsonstraat there's an Airborne Memorial in honor of Colonel Johnson and the 501st Parachute Infantry Division which fought there in WW II . . . the Colonel was killed here.

Of special note are St. Jan's Cathedral and the Noordbrabants Museum, both of which are described in detail below. The Provincial House has an important modern sculpture collection . . . free entry.

MUSEUMS: The smaller museums in town include:

The Kruithuis (Gunpowder Magazine) . . . now Museum of Modern Art. Located at Citadellaan 6, is open Tues.-Sat., 11am-5pm, Sun., 1-5pm.

Museum Slager, on Choorstraat behind St. Jan's Cathedral; open, Tues.-Fri., Sun., 11am-5pm, also the first Sat. of the month. Deals with the works of the Slager family of artists.

"De Brabant Poffer" Museum, 3A Postel Straat; open Sat., Sun. all year, 1-5pm; Also Tues.-Fri. in the summer, same hours. A "poffer" is the name for the lady's bonnet in the old Brabant costume . . . this is a local museum, not just about hats.

The Zwanenbroedershuis, Hinthamerstraat 94, is open Fri., 11am-3pm. Music books, antiques, statues, pewter mugs and artifacts illustrating life in the Brotherhood of Our Lady during the Middle Ages.

MARKETS: On Wednesday morning, there's a cattle market in the Brabant Halls on the Veemarktkade and on Thurs., horses are "on the block."

The general market is held on the Market Square Wed., 8:30am-1pm and Sat., 8:30am-2pm.

EATING OUT: Informal, sometimes rustic, eateries are found in the cellars of city halls. This is not so common in Holland as it is in Germany—fewer cellars perhaps—but there is one beneath Den Bosch's town hall. The "Raadskeller" dates from 1520 . . . try it for old-world character.

YEARLY EVENTS: Den Bosch and Maastricht in Limburg have the reputation for the most colorful Carnivals in the country . . . just before Lent. When in full swing, it's quite an experience to dress the kids up, put on a crazy headpiece and join the fun! Every other Sept., there's the National Draft Horse Show; in Oct., there's the Brabant Wooden Shoe Fair at St. Oedenrode.

St. John's Cathedral (St. Jan's Kathedraal)

LOCATION: In the center of the old city on the parade grounds. Follow signs for the Central Station. Once there, and with the station behind you, take the large road directly in front, cross the Dommel canal, continue straight (unless additional one-way streets have been instituted) to Hinthamerstraat. The Cathedral will be on your right. This is also the most direct way on foot.
INFORMATION: VVV, 's Hertogenbosch, above.
HOURS: Church: daily, 10am-5pm, except when services are in progress (Sun.); Carillon Concerts, daily, 11:30am and 12:30pm.
■ *Of interest to older children.*

St. John's Cathedral is considered by many to be the most beautiful cathedral in Holland. It was constructed between 1330 and 1530 on the foundations of a previous church which burned in 1240. It suffered heavy damage during many wars which required it to be restored in 1860 and 1955.

Of particular interest are the strange grotesque creatures scampering over the flying buttresses reminiscent of the people in Hieronymus Bosch's paintings.

The spacious interior boasts 150 pillars! There are a number of superb items to see. For instance, the highly decorated stalls of the choir, a Renaissance-style chair, a copper baptismal font (1492), fine statues, a beautiful buffet and two paintings, the Virgin with Child and St. John, attributed to the School of Bosch.

There's a good view of the church from the "Parade." If you have binoculars, take them out for a good look at all the little people sitting on arched braces supporting the walls. A local tale is that each time someone drinks a pint of beer, these little characters change their position.

211

North Brabant Museum

*LOCATION: Verwersstraat 41, in Gouvernementhuis (1769), a former
residence of the Governor.*
INFORMATION: Tel. (073) 133834.
*HOURS: Open Tues.-Fri., 10am-5pm, Sat., 11am-5pm, Sun. and holi-
days, 1-5pm.*
■ *Of interest to older children.*

The museum is housed in the 18th century Government House built for the
Military Governor after Den Bosch was liberated from the Spanish rule. The
main building houses the collection of ancient art including an archeological
collection which gives an exceptional picture of North Brabant. In one of the
modern wings, there's the history of 's Hertogenbosch and the Brabant; in the
other wing, temporary modern exhibits are shown. There is also an attractive
sculpture park.

IN THE NEIGHBORHOOD OF 's HERTOGENBOSCH:

Den Bosch is ringed by some of the best family-oriented sightseeing spots in
Europe as this chapter will attest. At Rosmalen, touching Den Bosch's northeast
edge, there's a terrific car museum, Autotron, covered at the end of this section.
Northwest of town on the banks of the Maas River, the restored town of
Heusden is worth a slight detour. As for castles, they do abound . . . three are
worth mentioning. Ammersoyen Castle is about 7 kilometers north in the
Gelderland . . . see Chapter 5; Maurick Castle and Heeswijk Castle.

Maurick Castle, south in the village of Vught, may not be visited but the
garden is open during the week. For info, tel. (073) 479108. In 1601 the castle
was a military base under Prince Maurits of Orange (an ancestor of Queen
Beatrix), and used by his brother Frederik Hendrik in 1629.

Heeswijk Castle, southeast at Heeswijk-Dither. For information, call the
VVV, tel. (04139) 2884 . . . an 11th-century Medieval castle. Also at Heeswick-
Dither, you can enjoy rave-notice organ concerts on Sunday afternoons in an
abbey which has housed the oldest religious community in the Netherlands. Or,
visit a local farm museum, the "Meierijsch Museum," and Wildhorst Forest,
with midget golf, children's playground, a heated open-air swimming pool, etc.
Write "Wildhorst," Meerstraat 22, tel. (04139) 1466, for info about renting a
bungalow, pitching your own tent or renting a covered wagon.

's Hertogenbosch was also part of Operation Market Garden during WW II.
At the village of Veghel, just south of Heeswijk-Dither on N266, there is a
museum devoted to that operation:

The "Liberating Wings" Museum (Bevrijdende Vleugels), Zuidkade 5, tel.
(04130) 64994, is open Tues.-Sun., noon-5pm from June-September. You feel
you are walking the streets in 1940. A panorama, 340 square meters, shows you
the German occupation and the liberation by American parachutists. There is a
slide show and a document center with an astonishing collection describing the
rise of the Nazi movement, the resistance movement and the effect on the Jews.
There are scale models of airplanes, uniforms and large firearms collection.

Autotron, Rosmalen

GETTING THERE: Graafsbaan 133, Rosmalen. From The Hague and
Rotterdam, take A13, A16 south to intersection with A15 east,
then A2 south to Rosmalen. From Amsterdam, A2 south.
INFORMATION: Tel. (04192) 11133 or 19050.
HOURS: Open May 28-Oct. 26, Mon.-Sun., 10am-5pm, July and
Aug., open 'til 6pm.
ADMISSION: Adults, Fl. 9.75; children to 4 yrs., free. All attractions
included in entry.
■ *Of interest to all children.*

Car buffs will have "lucked out" the day the family decides on touring this area. Autotron is one of two antique car museums in Europe with a collection of more than 400 cars of which 250 are permanently on show, as well as airplanes, fire engines and a steam train. Some special added attractions include a children's train, a traffic-garden where children 10 years and up can drive themselves, a Tower of Babel, boat trams, pedaloes, a children's village and farm, botanical garden, etc.

The cars are in "mint" condition and range from the earliest models to a super-modern low-slung futuristic car built by the Vauxhall Company. Very interesting is watching the restoration of cars for the museum.

There are car makes most of us have never heard of; cars made in France, England, the United States, Germany, Belgium, Italy—and one of the most impressive groups of cars were those manufactured in the Netherlands—the Spyker. Then there are all the famous makes including the Model T Ford, the Stanley Steamer, the Pierce Arrow and many others. There are cars covered in leather, others in rattan trim, others with wooden wheels, steam-operated and electric-operated vehicles, etc.

Their brochure has explanations in English, French and German, as well as Dutch. There are attractive restaurant areas where you can get a cup of coffee or a hot meal.

EINDHOVEN

City of light, science and commerce

GETTING THERE: Located in the southeast corner of North Brabant,
not far from the Belgian border, you can reach Eindhoven from
Amsterdam via A2 south, around 's Hertogenbosch, then N2
south. From The Hague and Rotterdam, take A13, A16 south to
Breda, then east on A58 to Eindhoven.
INFORMATION: VVV, Stationsplein 17, tel. (040) 449231.

It's hard to believe this bustling industrial metropolis had barely 5,000 inhabitants in 1900. Its rise as a city of great importance with worldwide tentacles of scientific and commercial development has occurred since 1891. If the modern

213

history of Eindhoven belongs to any one person, it must belong to the man who started the "Lighting Capital" of the world, Mr. Anton Philips. As a result of his company's scientific progress, technicians from all over come here to study. The Technical University is an important polytechnical school with an outstanding reputation.

St. Catherine's Church, Stratumseind, is a neo-Gothic basilica built in 1860-67 by Dr. P. C. Cuypers. And nearby is the Monastery of the Augustine (17th century with a 15th-century wing). Mr. Philips' original factory where electric lights were first manufactured in 1891, is on the Emmasingel.

MILLS: There are three mills, two of which are open:

Collse Watermill (to grind corn), Collseweg Loostraat, tel. 111301; open, Tues., 2-8pm.

Gennep Watermill (1249), at Genneperweg 147, tel. 518551; open, Mon.-Tues., Thurs.-Sat., 9am-6pm.

Windmill De Annemie (1891) at Boschdijk 1006 (no visits).

The Prehistoric Settlement, Boutenslaan 161b, tel. (040) 522281, or (04934) 1795, open daily 10am-6pm, presents a "living" picture of an Iron Age village engaged in mixed farming. During the summer a small group of people live the life of Iron Age man every Sunday. Visitors should make an appointment for a conducted tour lasting about 1½ hours. The first weekend in October, the prehistoric days are organized during which a large range of handicrafts is demonstrated. For a small fee you can join in the activities and eat the food prepared . . . or even stay overnight. Suitable for all ages and children are most enthusiastic.

MUSEUMS: The No. 1 attraction in this area is Evoluon, Philips' top-rated scientific exhibition designed to attract, entertain and teach all ages . . . described below, as is the Van Abbe Museum. In addition, there are:

Museum Kempenland, St. Antoniusstraat 5-7, tel. 529093; open, Tues.-Sun., 1-5pm; regional cultural history.

The Natural History Museum, in the Gennep area, tel. 526665; open Tues.-Fri., 9am-12:30pm and 1:30-5pm; Sun. and Mon. afternoons.

Another children-oriented place to visit in Eindhoven is the Animali Bird and Monkey Gardens. And 10 km south of town, Eurostrand is famous for its many lakes where sailing and swimming galore is available. Check with the VVV for specifics. Eindhoven also has a luxurious ice skating center with a covered, heated figure skating and ice hockey rink, and two open-air rinks . . . skates can be rented.

In addition to the above activities, the family could take a break from sightseeing and spend the day at the Tongelreep Recreation Center, Antoon Coolenlaan 1, Eindhoven South, tel. (040) 123125. There's an open-air pool and two indoor pools, one 59 meters and one 25 meters, a subtropical wave pool with hydro slides, a paddling pool, tanning area, jacuzzi, billiard room, six bowling alleys, midget golf, etc. Hungry? Restaurant and cocktails on the premises . . . also pancakes for the little ones. Great place for a bad-weather day!

YEARLY EVENTS: Interesting activities are scheduled year-round. Recently there was "Open Day" at all the art galleries (end of August) . . . the VVV had a map with the route. Brabant Days (a cultural-historic procession) in Heeze; a Floral Parade in Valkenswaard; the September Festival; and the South-Dutch Fair in October. But check with VVV to verify.

Van Abbe Museum

LOCATION: 10 Bilderdijklaan.
INFORMATION: Tel. (040) 389730.
HOURS: Tues.-Sun. and holidays, 11am-5pm. Closed December 25.
■ *Of interest to school-age children.*

The museum was founded in 1936 when industrialist H. J. van Abbe presented the gallery to the city. Unfortunately, the city had no paintings to put in it. Eventually paintings were acquired—first, a few Dutch paintings, then a Chagall, and in the past 20 years the collection has grown to include painters representative of expressionism, cubism, orphism, neo-plasticism, cobra, matter painting and surrealism. When you now walk into the once-bare van Abbe Museum, you will find one of the most striking arrays of modern paintings to be found anywhere. There's Picasso's "Seated Woman," Braque's "La Roche-Guyon," Leger's "Accordian," Kokoschka's "The Power of Music," and action paintings and chromatic abstractions by Morris Louis, Robert Indiana and Frank Stella.

Evoluon

LOCATION: Noordbrabantlaan 1a. Situated on the "Rondweg" (Ring Road) at the junction of the road from Tilburg and Noordbrabantlaan, signs will direct you. Ample free parking. City buses from the train station will take you directly to Evoluon.
INFORMATION: Tel. (040) 512736.
HOURS: Open all year, Mon.-Fri., 9:30am-5:30pm; Sat.-Sun., 10:30am-5pm. Closed December 25 and January 1.
ADMISSION: Adults, Fl. 12.50; children under 12 yrs. and senior citizens, Fl. 10.
■ *Not especially recommended for children under 8 years, although this would depend on the child's interest in science. For the younger children, a 2-hour visit is probably long enough. For older children, all day would not be too long.*

Evoluon was founded by Philips—what is it? Evoluon is an action-exhibition (things move, light up, you participate) dedicated to the ingenuity of man, to our rapidly changing society and to the evolution of science and technology. An impressive spectacle of sound and shape; of motion and color. An exhibition where you don't just look and listen, but where you are actively involved operating the many exhibits and working models with which you can play to your heart's content. Each floor has a theme; the top floor is about food, accommodations and communications; the middle floor shows scientific developments; and the main floor, the effect industry has on society, i.e., T.V. implications, etc. For instance, you can see yourself on television; look at a microchip magnified tens of thousands of times; see how important lighting is for comfortable living by visiting the home of Mother Goose and Master Frog; see what energy consumption used to be, what it is now, and what it will be in the future; or just sit in a stereo booth listening to your favorite music from classics to pop.

Le Relais Restaurant, restrooms and a cloakroom are on the premises. Daily shows are given (documentary films) ... check the times and subject of the movie at the Information Desk when you arrive.

IN THE NEIGHBORHOOD OF EINDHOVEN:

As has been mentioned previously, this area was in the midst of military action during WW II. Northwest of Eindhoven on N2, the town of Best suffered some heavy casualties. One was an American, PFC Joe Mann who saved his buddies by throwing himself on a grenade. He is honored by a memorial east of town by the road to Son en Breugel. Best also boasts a unique wooden shoe museum, "De Platijn," Broekdijk 16, tel. (04998) 71247, which describes how clogs have been made since 1800.

Son en Breugel is thought to be the birthplace of the senior Breugel of the famous painting family. It, too, has a memorial to an anonymous soldier, in the Europalaan. The soldier is still attached to his parachute with grenade in hand.

Overloon, quite some distance northeast between the Maas River, N272 and N270, was also the scene of fierce fighting. The War and Resistance Museum is worth a visit. See Chapter 5, the discussion on Operation Market Garden.

Nuenen, northeast off A270, is where Vincent Van Gogh lived from 1883-85. His painting studio has been preserved and his home is still standing. There's a memorial in the park.

Helmond, east via A270, has a castle dating from 1402 which is now a cultural center and museum with changing exhibitions.

Deurne, east via N270, is mentioned in a manuscript dating from the year 721—a gift to St. Willibrord. Archeological finds indicate Deurne was inhabited before this, however. In 1326, the Duke of Brabant presented the town to its inhabitants.

Heeze Castle, south about 6 km at Heeze, Kapelstraat 25; open, March-Oct., Wed. and Sun., 2pm or by appointment ... 17th- and 18th-century furniture, paintings and tapestries.

There are many old and picturesque villages such as Eersel, Duizel, Steensel, Oirschot, Hulsel, Knaegsel, Netersel, Reusel and Wintersel. If you can't do them all in one day (!), do some and save some for another day.

CHAPTER 8

THE PROVINCE OF FRIESLAND

Friesland, coupled with its neighbor Groningen, are the two most northerly provinces of the Netherlands. There are so many routes to get there, it is hard to make a suggestion. One can, for instance, go to Alkmaar and then take the most direct route to Den Oever and cross the Afsluitdijk (a special experience), starting one's tour at Harlingen. Or go via Amsterdam to Almere (Flevoland), north over the Ketelbrug, past Emmeloord and start your sightseeing at Lemmer. Or, take the ferry from Enkhuizen across the IJsselmeer (only in summer) to Stavoren which has a nice hotel overlooking the water, and start your visit from there.

The Afsluitdijk deserves a word. Its length is 30 kilometers and its width 90 meters. The complete flatness of view across the IJsselmeer and the long stretch of highway before and behind are almost mesmerizing. Stop at the visitors' rest stop for a cup of coffee and the view if the weather is clear. Another special drive is across the water from Enkhuizen to Lelystad in Flevoland via N302.

Friesland is an independent place inhabited by proud, resourceful people. Fifty percent of them have retained their original Fries language with many English-sounding words due to its west-Germanic origin. In fact, the Frisians are so chauvinistic about their heritage, they issue visitors a "Friesian" (Frijske) passport which gives discounted prices on some attractions.

Friesland is one of the oldest inhabited areas of what is now the Netherlands with evidence of hab-

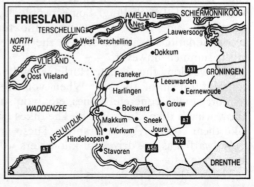

INFORMATION: VVV Friesland, tel. (058) 132224.

217

itation since 400 B.C. As long as 2,000 years ago, the Frisians built mounds upon which they established their villages in order to escape the flood waters that covered the land.

About 1,000 years ago, Frisians inhabited the entire northern and western coastline from the top of Groningen to the present Belgian border, an area then called the "Seven Frisian Islands."

Because of its watery, marshy landscape, outsiders had difficulty conquering the territory. In fact, the Romans never did control Friesland; trade developed, however, which explains the many Roman artifacts found in the province. It wasn't until the 7th century when a religious Frisian lady (whose name seems to have gotten misplaced) married Pépin d'Héristal, that Anglo-Saxon missionaries gained a foothold in the area.

The Counts of Holland were determined to obtain this rich, fertile land and many battles were fought to that end. The last battle in 1345 at Warns, a small town in the southwest corner just inland from the Rode Klif (Red Cliff), was the last. The villagers defended themselves ferociously with hay forks and clubs, killing the leader and many of the would-be invaders. There's a plaque commemorating the event at Rode Klif.

Real trouble developed from within when two rival factions, the Schieringers and the Vetkopers, weakened the country which allowed Charles V of Spain to incorporate Friesland into his empire.

In 1579, Friesland joined with Holland, Zeeland, Utrecht, Gelderland, Overijssel and Groningen to establish the Union of Utrecht; however, they insisted on retaining their hegemony by choosing an independent Stadhouder. They were able to maintain this privileged position until 1747 when the provinces came under one Stadhouder, Willem IV, son of Johan Willem Friso of Friesland, and became a centrally governed country.

If you haven't been to Friesland, don't delay. Take the first opportunity to make a trip and without a doubt, you will not find it your last. It is a charming, highly colorful area with a strong sense of individual history. It goes without saying that the most desirable time to visit is during the spring or summer months, but any time of year has its own attraction . . . the ice-skating races in winter, for instance.

Bird watchers cannot miss the northern islands. From Lauwersoog, Holwerd and Harlingen, there is regular ferry service to Schiermonnikoog, Ameland, Vlieland and Terschelling. Some people like to go off-season because it is a wonderful time to get away from the turmoil of everyday life with good accommodations available even in the winter months. Don't come for isolation in the summer, however.

A drive along the dikes to Harlingen will impress upon you and the family the constant threat of the sea. When you see those towering mounds of earth reinforced with concrete, stones, etc., you suddenly can say to yourself, "Now I know what a dike is all about." The dikes one sees normally are so ordinary we take them completely for granted. These northern dikes are tremendous—one feels dwarfed as one drives for kilometers with this great protective wall to one's immediate left.

The whole of Friesland is a summer sports paradise with camping places galore. There are pensions, sailing camps, places to rent bungalows or houses, boats, etc. Friesland offers many folkloric events during the year, some of them unique to this part of the Netherlands. The VVV is always your best point of reference to help you plan your trip, especially if you want to rent a bungalow on one of the islands.

HARLINGEN

A national historic site

GETTING THERE: From the Afsluitdijk, take the immediate left turn-off A31. Harlingen is about 8 km north.
INFORMATION: VVV Harlingen, Voorstraat 34, tel. (05178) 17222.

This seaport town is so rich in historic buildings that the old center has been declared a national historic site which will be preserved without change as an inheritance for future residents or visitors. Along with its interesting architecture, there is an attractive Town Hall at Noorderhaven 86, dating from 1730.

The Municipal Museum, Hannemahuis, at Voorstraat 56, has an excellent collection of old silver and porcelain as well as a unique tile collection and ship models. It is open, July-Aug. 15, Tues.-Sun., 10am-5pm; May, June and Aug. 16-Sept., Mon.-Sat., 1:30-5pm.

Special excursions can be made to Texel, Vlieland, and Terschelling from here . . . contact the VVV for ferry schedules and reservations.

YEARLY EVENTS: One event of special interst to sailors is the "Harlingen-Terschelling" international race which takes place the middle of June. The end of August-beginning of September, is Fishing Day—native costumes, old ships, and old-time activities.

FRANEKER

Photogenic town hall, canals, and a planetarium

GETTING THERE: Six kilometers east of Harlingen on A31.
INFORMATION: VVV Franeker, Voorstraat 51, tel. (05170) 4613.
NOTE: Unfortunately, most of Franeker's attractions are closed on Sunday and several are closed on Saturdays as well.

In 1811, Napoleon left his mark here as he did in so many Dutch provinces by suppressing a university which had existed since 1585; it was never re-established. Today's heritage are several professors' homes on the main street, the Voorstraat.

If you are lucky, you might see a wedding party leaving the Town Hall, built in 1591 in the elaborate Dutch Renaissance style. The elegant octagonal tower is worth a photo, as is the entire facade. Ask permission to see the Council Chamber and wedding hall. The Council Chamber walls are lined in tooled leather, walls painted the typical Dutch grccn, with a fine crystal chandelier hanging from the beamed ceiling and a painting of Queen Beatrix on the wall.

Across from the Town Hall is Eise Eisinga's Planetarium (1781), description follows. Just a little further east on Eise Eisingastraat along the small canal, look for the Corn Porter's house which dates from 1634. On the town side of the Town Hall, there are two medieval fortified dwellings which have been restored and the local museum, 't Coopmanshuis (1746).

MUSEUMS:

Martenahuis (1448), Voorstraat 35, tel. 3046; open, Mon.-Fri., 8am-noon and 1:30-3pm by appointment only, is now the provincial office for the district of Franeker. Visit the garden which was restored in 1970-74 according to the original plans of the French Landscape architect, Lenotre; includes a maze and an Orangerie.

Cammingahuis (14th-16th century), Voorstraat 2, tel. 3690; open, May-Sept., Mon.-Fri., 1-5 pm, houses a coin and numismatic collection.

Municipal Museum, 't Coopmanshuis, Voorstraat 49, tel. 2192; open, May-Sept., 10am-noon and 1-5pm, closed Sun., Mon. and from Oct. to May. This museum exhibits Frisian folk art including a special collection of cutout work by Anna Marie van Schurman.

YEARLY EVENTS: In mid-June, there's a competition of a special game similar to handball called "Kaatsen."

IN THE NEIGHBORHOOD OF FRANEKER:

Aeolus, Hearewei 24a, Sexbierum (take A31 west from Franeker; buses run from Harlingen and Franeker), tel. (05179) 1144; hours, April-Sept., daily 10am-6pm, Oct.-March, daily, 10am-5pm; Admission: Adults, Fl. 7.50, children 6-12 years, Fl. 6.50. The theme park was established to promote interest in the importance of this wind-powered research station . . . There's a wind simulator so you can experience a light breeze and a force 12 gale; windmills of yesterday, today and tomorrow, etc. There is also a play area with miniature windmills from Holland and abroad, model sailing boats, radio-controlled model boats, and a restaurant with terrace.

Planetarium of Eise Eisinga

LOCATION: Eise Eisingastraat across the canal from the Town Hall.
INFORMATION: Tel. (05170) 3070. Guided tours are provided in various languages.
HOURS: Jan.-April and Sept.-Dec., Tues.-Sat., 10am-12:30pm and 1:30-5pm, closed Sun. and Mon. May-Aug., open Sun., 1:30-5pm.
■ *Of interest to older children.*

This enormously popular exhibit is quite fascinating although, as one might expect, a bit technical. You will see our planetary system on the ceiling of the living room showing the orbits of the planets Mercury, Venus, Earth and Mars as well as the moon.

Mr. Eisinga, a wool comber by trade, worked on his project seven years. He lowered the ceiling of the living room to install the complicated cogs and wheels and built the central clockworks over the cupboard bed with the eight weights necessary for the operation hanging in the presses on either side of the bed. He must indeed have had a most understanding wife!

Non-Dutch speakers can buy an excellent brochure in English, French and German.

LEEUWARDEN

GETTING THERE: Coming over the Afsluitdijk, take N31 directly to Leeuwarden; from Groningen, N355 is the main road; from the south, A50 or A32 to N32 . . . just keep going north.
INFORMATION: VVV Friesland, Leeuwarden, Stationsplein 1, tel. (058) 132224. You may obtain a Culture Pass from the VVV showing the sights on a nice little map and accompanied by a series of discount tickets for shops, museums, parking garage in the city center, bike rental, etc. Also, ask for the pamphlet, "A Walk Through the Town of Leeuwarden," and you might consider getting a Frisian Passport, also with discount coupons.

Leeuwarden is the capital as well as the administrative, economic and cultural center of Friesland. It was the residence of Frisian Stadholders, the Counts of Nassau (ancestors of Queen Beatrix), from 1582 until 1747. And a famous early settler to America, Peter Stuyvesant, was born in Scherpenzeel, Friesland in 1592.

A fact little known by Americans is that the people of Leeuwarden were the first to vote for Holland's recognition of the United States in 1782, accompanied by a very substantial loan of funds to the fledgling nation. A bronze plaque on the Provincial House reads: "Memorial of Gratitude. At Leeuwarden, in the States of Friesland February 1782, the first vote was taken which led to the recognition of the independence of the United States of America by the Republic of the United Netherlands. Erected by the De Witt Historical Society of Tompkins County at Ithaca, N.Y., A.D. 1901."

Walking Tour: As mentioned above (Information), get a copy of the walking tour if you have the time for a leisurely exploration. There are many historical buildings, charming canals, shopping areas, and attractive cafés, in addition to two museums of major importance which will be covered below, not to mention four smaller museums, and a number of interesting sites to visit.

Starting with the Town Hall (1715), built upon the old cellars of the "Auckemastins," we will wend our way around town, mentioning some of the places of special interest as we go. Note the dome-shaped belfry on top of the Town Hall with carillon (1668), and the beautifully decorated Council Chamber (on the Hofplein side of the building). Nearby is the statue of Count Willem Lodewijk, the first Frisian Governor (1584-1620). Across from the Town Hall is the "Hof," a white stucco building which has served as the Governor's house and official residence of the Queen's Commissioner. Today it is used for offices and houses the official wedding chamber.

Just north on the corner of Beijerstraat and Grotekerkstraat, you will find

Mata Hari's former house, now the Frisian Literary Museum. Mata Hari (née Margaretha Geertruida Zelle) lived here when she was a young girl . . . she was born in the small house at 33 "the Kelders" near the Korfmakerspijp (bridge) where her statue stands. She became a famous dancer, was accused as a spy during WW I and shot by the French in 1917.

Follow the Grote Kerkstraat north and you will come to the Great Church (Jacobijner Kerk-15th century) which contains the burial vault of the Nassau family . . . open in summer. Further east and a bit north is St. Boniface Church (1882-1884), a good example of Dutch Neo-Gothic architecture. South along the canal and on the parallel street, Turfmarkt, there are the Frisian Museum which you should visit, and across the street, one of the loveliest buildings in town, the Chancellery (1566-1571) . . . formerly seat of the Frisian Court.

Down the street is Government House, seat of the Provincial Council, once an abbot's house (1570). If you return west on Korfmakersstraat, you will find the canal. Follow it going west to the Waagplein. Now is a good time to have a bite "al fresco" at the outdoor tables in front of the Weigh House, or go upstairs for a nice lunch.

Then head west toward the Noorder Plantage, a public park, with the Oldehove Tower (1532) at one end and the Prinsentuin Park with the Pier Pander Museum and Temple at the other end. Climb the Oldehove Tower . . . 40 meters high . . . for a splendid view (only in summer). This leaning structure was to be the tower of the church but left unfinished due to lack of funds.

The Princessehof Museum (visit) on the Grote Kerkstraat is in the former palace of Princess Maria Louise of Hessen-Kassel. The annex, "Papingastins," was formerly a warehouse for storing wine. Continuing east on the Grote Kerkstraat, you will come to the Colon House (Colonhûs) now home of the Frisian Academy, an organization established in the 18th century to promote Frisian scholarship.

Leeuwarden boasts the largest covered cattle hall in Europe, the Frieslandhall on Heliconweg, and if you're here on a Friday between 6am and noon, you might find it interesting. In spring and autumn, examinations for the Frisian Blue Book of cattle are held. Friesland's dairy cooperatives are famous. Leeuwarden claims 55% of the cheese production for the entire country, 17% milk and butter production, and 75% of the export of cattle.

MUSEUMS: The four small museums in town include:

Natural History Museum, Schoenmakersperk 2, tel. 129085; open, Mon., 2-5pm, Tues.-Sun., 10am-5pm (flora and fauna of Friesland).

Frisian Resistance Museum, Zuiderplein 9-13, tel. 133335; open, Tues.-Sat., 10am-5pm, Sun., 2-5pm.

Frisian Literary Museum, Grote Kerkstraat 28, tel. 120834; open, Mon.-Sat., 10am-noon and 2-5pm.

Pier Pander Museum and Temple, Prinsetuin, tel. 127438; open, Tues.-Sun., 10am-1pm and 2-5pm. Sculptures of Pier Pander.

MARKET: The open-air market takes place on the Wilhelminaplein, Fri., 7:30am-5pm, Mon., 1-4pm and Sat., 9am-5pm.

EATING OUT: There are three pancake restaurants to choose from, one on a 100-year-old 2-masted clipper ship tied up at the Willemskade; one at Nieuwestad 125; and one at Grote Hoogstraat 16. For an even quicker bite, McDonald's is located at Wirdumerdijk. For something a bit dressier and with atmosphere, try the dining room upstairs at the Weigh House on the Waagplein (Nieuwestad) . . . good food and moderate prices; or Onder de Luifel, Stationsplein 6.

STAYING OVER: In town there are two modern hotels, the Eurohotel, Europaplein 20, tel. 131113 and the Oranje Hotel (5 star), Stationsweg 4, tel. 126241. Something more special is the Hotel Princenhof, P. Miedemaweg 15, at Eernewoude, tel. (05117) 9206 or 9333, about 15 minutes by car just south of Leeuwarden. This tried and true (over 15 years) hotel cannot be beat for its restful site right on lake "Oude Venen." Rooms facing the lake upstairs have their own balconies; downstairs, lakeside rooms have a private terrace where you can sit out of doors soaking up the sunshine. Rooms overlooking the meadows cost about Fl. 10.00 less. From the dining-room over-sized picture windows, sunset is a special time to see the light changing from golden to rose to deep red, reflecting across the water and on the farmhouse windows opposite. Food and service are very good . . . a dressy place but comfortable with children too.

YEARLY EVENTS: Annual activities include boat and motor races during the year and in July and August, special folkloric events are held, and in the summer, arrangements can be made with the VVV to visit the 11 towns by bike or private car.

COMMERCIAL TOURS: Boat Tours are possible from July 15-Aug. 15 on the "Princehof," Spanjaardslaan 29, tel. 153737 at 2pm or on the "Stad Leeuwarden," Tijnjedijk 31, tel. 139290 or 133603, or call the VVV. Waterbikes can also be rented in the summertime from Aan Bierkade, tel. 882323, 10am-6pm.

Fries Museum

LOCATION: Turfmarkt 24.
INFORMATION: Tel. (058) 123001.
HOURS: Open, Tues.-Sat., 10am-5pm; Sun., 1-5pm.
NOTE: While there were no free flyers when we last visited, we did
    purchase a booklet in English and German with many fine photo-
    graphs of the museum collection with explanations.
■ *Of interest to all.*

A visit to this museum is urged if one is interested in better understanding the political, economic and cultural history of Friesland. Its collection of antiquities is justly famous and includes, for instance, the 1397 drinking-horn of the St. Anthony Guild of Stavoren; a chalice from Bozum, 1505; and the immense sword of the Greate Pier, the Frisian champion who drove the Saxons out of Friesland in 1515-1520. In addition, there are medieval costumes, silver, porcelain, paintings, craftwork and period rooms as well as a section on archeology.

The period rooms give a bird's-eye view into living conditions of the past, including highly decorated rooms with blue and white tiles lining the walls, a kitchen, silversmith's workshop, brightly painted Hindeloopen wallbeds, and women's and children's costumes, again, worked in the typical Hindeloopen designs. There are children's toys, including dolls, wooden trains, and games such as slot machines.

The Numismatic Cabinet dates from 1834 and gives a good survey of coins struck between 1580 and 1738. There is a significant collection of Roman coins which were found in Frisian mounds.

"Het Princessehof" Museum

LOCATION: Grote Kerkstraat 9-5.
INFORMATION: Tel. (058) 127438.
HOURS: Mon.-Sat., 10am-5pm; Sun., 2-5pm. Closed January 1 and December 25.
NOTE: There are no brochures in Dutch or English; however, excellent explanations are given with all displays (in both languages). This is a bright museum with padded window seats.
■ *Of interest to teenagers and older.*

The Princessehof Museum consists of three wings, a 15th-century east wing (formerly a convent), 17th-century central block, and an 18th-century west wing. Princess Marie Louise van Hessen-Kassel, widow of Johan Willem Friso, joined the three sections together and furnished them in the style of the day. The entrance to the museum is in the central block. This is the only part of the Princessehof where original interiors remain of the time when the Princess used it as her residence between 1731 and 1765. Her husband was the Governor of Friesland until he drowned in 1711 before his heir was born who would become the Stadhouder of all the United Provinces. The family portraits on the walls are identified so you can tell who's who.

The Town Council obtained the central building in 1917 to preserve it as a historic site and put it to use as a museum. Numerous wealthy patrons helped put a collection together. Most important was Nanne Ottema, an artist "manqué" who satisfied his deep interest in art by collecting. His own collection was spread in three locations. On August 31, 1917, Ottema moved into the Princessehof with all his belongings (including his art objects) to become the first director. After Ottema's death, the two former wings of Marie Louise's court were added.

The Princessehof's main collection of Asian ceramics can be subdivided into a number of export groups: Japanese, Chinese, Vietnamese and Siamese porcelain and stoneware manufactured for the Persian, Indonesian, Philippine and European markets. Look for the earthenware jars from Vietnam and from Thailand, dating from 3600-250 B.C.—the most sophisticated prehistoric wares in the world. Also, the Japanese kilns such as Mino (Shino and Oribi ware), Kutani and Arita are well represented. The 18th-century white marble Buddha from Burma is a lovely piece. Another interesting group are stoneware jars dating from 7th-11th centuries. Found in the ground in Central Java, they were termed Hindu-Javanese "martabans" by collectors. Leak-proof and pest-proof, they were used on ships, in temples, shops and villages to keep drink pure and grain safe. The largest examples weigh about 20 kilograms.

The tile collection in the annex forms one of the principal sections of the museum. The Dutch majolica tiles on display are one of the largest collections in Europe. Tiles became popular in the 17th century for use as an interior finish to damp walls. The wealthy used oak and leather to panel the walls; the middle-class used tiles. Early tiles were profuse in their artwork ... some using geometric designs, others, exotic fruits and flowers. After 1625 the fashion became more sober and most tiles were painted only blue on white. In the 18th century, walls were tiled in white and decorated with ornamental tiles as borders, or sparingly decorated illustrating children's games, occupations, coats of arms, etc.

Students of ceramics come here to join in study groups and to use the library. There is also a work cellar where visitors can try their hand with clay ... a way to get to know ceramics better by trying out the materials and techniques.

IN THE NEIGHBORHOOD OF LEEUWARDEN:

Popta Slot, Marssum, 5 km west of Leeuwarden off N355; open, April-Oct., Mon.-Sat., 11am, 2 and 3pm for tours. This impressive 18th-century manor house/castle (restored) is filled with typical 16-18th-century furnishings such as Dr. Popta would have had in this elegant rural home. Dr. Popta was a bachelor and the story goes that he took pity on aged women. In 1711, he founded the Popta Gasthuis, next door, and allowed the ladies to live there as long as they polished his furniture once a year.

The park surrounding the manor house is well-tended with formal gardens, big trees, flower plots, and waterlilies floating in the moat.

As you enter the Gasthuis through the elaborately carved portal, notice the handsome pump. Neat brick houses face a green square ... a lawn bordered by roses and surrounded by a white picket fence.

Schierstins, Veenwouden, about 15 km northeast, N355 to N356, is a small village with an ancient square fortified tower, the last remaining watch tower for floods in Friesland. It houses a small museum with temporary exhibits ... check with VVV.

Grouw, about 15 km south of Leeuwarden on N32, is a popular watersports center on the Pikmeer lake. The small village has a rather old-fashioned hotel, The Oostergoo, Nieuwekade 1, and a brand-new live-in sports center with modest rooms accommodating several singles or families ... meals are included and are eaten family-style in two large dining rooms. Cheerful, busy, but very much for the young! For information, write Oer 't Hout, Raadhuisstraat 18, 9001 AG, tel. (05662) 1528. A couple of sailing schools are also located here. In August, Grouw becomes a regatta town and one can see boats: big, little, commercial, sail, motor launches, et cetera.

Wieuwerd: north of Sneek and south of Leeuwarden ... stop to see the four mummies in the crypt of the mysterious sepulchral vault of the church. Dating from 1609, no artificial means have been used to preserve the bodies. There is conjecture that the cross-ventilation in the crypt (or that a gas exudes from the earth) is responsible for this interesting phenomenon. Other things—such as dead birds—hung in the crypt don't decompose either. A short visit is recommended!

SNEEK

Town with a sailing history dating back to the Vikings

GETTING THERE: Autoroute A7 goes through town east-west, and N354, north-south. Located about 21 km south of Leeuwarden. INFORMATION: VVV Sneek, Leeuwenburg 21, tel. (05150) 14096.

Before the creation of the IJsselmeer resulted in the silting up of the harbor, Sneek was an important seaport on the North Sea. The walls of the town were demolished in 1720 and the Water Gate by the Lemster bridge over the Geeuw is all that has survived of the early fortifications.

Sneek has been a sailing town since the time of the Vikings. Three-quarters of the surrounding area offers lakes for sailing, fishing, swimming, water-skiing, and so on.

Today, Sneek is best known as a watersports center but it is also an important center for trade and commerce in southwest Friesland. Much of the old city center has survived and is of interest with its picturesque buildings and streets.

The principal sights are the Watergate (1613); the 18th-century Town Hall (see the Civic Guard's Room where the town's silver is displayed); the early 16th-century Dutch Reformed Church (fine vestry and restored bell cage); and the Frisian Shipping Museum with its Chamber of Antiquities.

The Martini Church (about 1500) once had two towers which collapsed in 1681. The roof has a bell cupola with a carillon and a restored bell cage mentioned above. The famous local warrior Greate Pier's grave is in the church. Pier fought against the Saxons and the Burgundians from 1515 to 1520 "on land and on sea." His helmet is displayed in the Town Hall guard room, open in summer, Mon.-Fri., 2-4pm.

There are beautiful gables along the city streets. Behind the so-called captains' facade on the Oosterdijk promenade, look for the old Frisian refreshment room with painted and tiled Hindeloopen interior.

The Frisian Shipping Museum, Kleinzand 14, tel. 14057; open, Mon.-Sat., 10am-noon and 2-5pm, has a good collection of ships models, navigation instruments, ships' porcelain, paintings and an especially fine display of Frisian-silver.

MARKET: General market day is Saturday. A speciality in town is dribble cookies ("drabbe koeken") there's a factory on the Oosterkade.

YEARLY EVENTS: In July/Aug., finals of the "Skutsjesilen" (a series of races of traditional sailing barges, the skutsjes) are held on Sneekermeer Lake. In August, Sneek Week attracts boaters and tourists like a magnet with its international sailing regatta and fair.

IN THE NEIGHBORHOOD OF SNEEK:

On the eastern outskirts of Sneek at Ysbrechtum, the lovely Epema State manor house/castle (19th century with 1625 gate house guarded by ferocious lions) can be visited June-Aug., tel. (05134) 1592 or the VVV for information. The castle is the family home of Baroness van Eisinga and the rooms have been kept in the same fashion as when the family was living here full-time.

BOLSWARD

A starting point for the "Aldfaers Erf" Route

GETTING THERE: Located on A7, about 20 km from Harlingen
(south then east) or 9 km from Sneek (west).
INFORMATION: VVV Bolsward, Broereplein 1, tel. (05157) 2727.

One of Friesland's oldest towns and once a member of the Hanseatic League, Bolsward was settled even before 715. Originally, it was built on a mound as protection from regular flooding. It was a busy port before the Zuider Zee was silted up, reaching its most prosperous period in the 17th century. Bolsward was also the home of a number of well-known Dutch men of letters, artists, engravers and silversmiths.

■ **The St. Martinikerk** (1446-1466), open, Mon.-Fri., 10am-noon and 1:30-5pm; also Sat. in season, is worth a visit. An impressive Gothic church with carved pulpit. It has an organ and tombstones worth noting.

For a look at a fine example of Dutch Renaissance architecture, visit the

Town Hall (1614-1617) with its richly decorated facade and beautiful Council Hall . . . open, April-Nov., Mon.-Sat., 9am-noon and 2-4:30pm.

IN THE NEIGHBORHOOD OF BOLSWARD:

Bolsward can be one starting point to the "Aldfaers Erf" Route which means "Our Forefathers' Heritage." The route is well sign-posted and will take you through a number of villages which have been carefully preserved to recapture the rustic way of life found at the end of the last century.

But first, stop at Makkum to visit this charming pottery town.

MAKKUM

Town of tiles

GETTING THERE: Almost on the IJsselmeer, only a couple of kilometers south of the entry point to Friesland from the Afsluitdijk. Take turnoffs Zurich or Witmarsum going south to Makkum.
INFORMATION: VVV Makkum, Waaggebouw, tel. (05158) 1422.

This small town on the IJsselmeer has been synonymous with outstanding pottery for a couple of centuries. It is also known for its shipyard, harbor, and as a watersports center—a real surfer's paradise. Besides seeing, feeling, learning about, and buying pottery, there are canals, bridges, churches and beautifully restored houses and gables. If time permits, try to see the Netherlands Reformed Church (Hervormde Kerk) (1660) which sits in the middle of an old terp (mound) at Kerkeburen . . . check with the VVV for directions and hours.

A study of the archives revealed that Makkum was a place of great ceramic activity in the 16th century and that on the site of the present Tichelaar Factory, a ceramics workshop existed. The historical "tracking down" of where various pottery pieces originated, we leave to the specialists. For the lover of beauty, it is enough to enjoy the fine collection in the local Pottery Museum.

The Frisian Pottery Museum (Fries Aardewerkmuseum De Waag), Pruikmakershoek 2, tel. 1422; open, May 1-Sept. 15, Mon.-Sat., 10am-5pm, Sun., 1:30-5pm (also by appointment), is housed in the Weigh House (1698) and connecting dwelling. Pottery from Harlingen and Makkum dating from the 17th, 18th and 19th centuries is represented. Of particular interest is the tile picture (Room 3) of a Frisian Tin-Glaze Pottery Factory, copy of a similar tile-picture in the Rijksmuseum in Amsterdam dating from 1737. The Rijksmuseum picture is believed to have originated in a Bolsward factory which existed from 1737-1800.The picture shows 26 people working in a Fries factory using traditional 18th-century methods. The inscription on the top of the picture reads: "The Founders of this work Are the same four Whose crests with their names This wall do adorn" "Anno 1737" "Joh. Tichelaar, Hero de Jager, Jan Steensma, Wijbe Steensma."

■ Tichelaar's Royal Ceramics and Tile Manufactory, Turfmarkt 61, tel. 1341; hours for visitors: Mon.-Fri., 10am-4pm (groups by appointment); sales to visitors, Mon.-Sat., 9am-5pm. Founded in 1641 (a few years before De Porceleyne Fles in Delft), Tichelaar's has been under the same family management for over 300 years. In 1960, Tichelaar's was allowed to add "Royal" to its full title as a result of Queen Juliana's patronage. Tichelaar's tiles and ceramics have a unique luminescent quality which is a result of this company's use of what they call a "mysterious white tin glaze." In fact, they are the only remaining tinglazing factory in the Netherlands.

Manufactured Makkum pottery started as a rough, soft-baked product . . . usually cooking pots or tiles to cover the damp floors or walls of people's homes. At first, decoration consisted mostly of sculpting the clay. With the introduction of tin glazing to the Netherlands from Spain and Italy, elaborate decoration became possible. Tin glazing started in the Orient, was brought to Spain by the Moors in the 11th century, then sent to Italy via Majorca (hence the name "Majolica" ware) and then found its way north. Another explanation for the quality of Makkum pottery is the care with which it is worked using mostly hand methods in traditional fashion, the continued use of the ancient tin-glaze recipes, and the special quality of the Frisian clay.

Shopping is always a great tourist attraction. The sales display center of Tichelaar's is like a modern museum display, hours are given above. For first quality ceramics and other art work, try Tichelaar's Arts and Crafts, "De Bleek," Kerkstraat 9, tel. 1264, and for first and second quality tiles, you can go to Tichelaar's House of Tiles, Plein 10, tel. 2500.

EATING OUT: The VVV suggests De Waag (Weigh House) in town, tel. 1301, or "De Vigilante," at the beach, tel. 1333. Also, there's a well-known farm restaurant, "Nynke Pleats," at Piaam, tel. 1707.

STAYING OVER: "Recreatie Vigilante" located right on the beach at Makkum, tel. (05158) 1772, offers perfect relaxation at moderate prices, with a choice of rooms or apartments (2-4 persons) by the day, weekend or week. The dining room features complete menus, including fresh fish, but there is also a snack counter and occasionally, barbecues and fondues are offered. In addition to the beach activities (swimming, surfing, boating), billiards, bowling and other family games are available. Write Recretel Adema, Postbus 37, 8754 ZN Makkum, for their brochure showing apartment layouts and price list.

Aldfaers Erf Route "Heritage Route"

The Aldfaers Erf Route ("Our Forefathers' Heritage") extends within a triangle framed by Bolsward, Makkum and Workum. The primary villages within the triangle are Exmorra, Allingawier, Piaam and Ferwoude. The drive should be taken leisurely to allow the atmosphere to soak in. Absorb the lovely meadows, crossed by streams, polderland, narrow twisting roads through tiny villages with their tiled roofs, red brick walls, and lace-curtained windows. Stop and explore the special sights each village has to offer.

Exmorra: Here you will see an old-fashioned grocery shop, licensed spirits provisioner, and a 19th-century village school. The new Frisian Agricultural

Museum gives a clear picture of local farming methods.

Allingawier: There are a number of stops here, starting with the farm museum, "De Izeren Kou" (The Iron Cow), an 18th-century farmer's house in its original state. The living quarters are interesting with an outstanding milk cellar; there's a slideshow presentation describing life on the land at that time. There is also a pastry shop ("dribble" cookies a speciality) and a coffeehouse, "The Mermaid." Once fortified with food, you can visit the little house of "Age," a former day-laborer's cottage, a painter's workshop, and the Church in the Woods which offers an audio-visual presentation of the Creation. You might notice Mr. Y. Schakel's impressive home with onion-domed tower (cannot visit).

Piaam: The charming farm restaurant "Nynke Pleats" offers formal dining in one section or relaxed luncheon fare in the main room with brick floor, chairs with rush seats, red and white tablecloths and green and white Frisian roof decorations under the huge beamed ceiling. A folksy and fun atmosphere where you can choose a hearty typically Dutch dish such as an "uitsmijter" (a piece of bread with a slice of ham topped by two or more fried eggs), soup or et cetera.

Stop and see "It Fugelhus," a bird museum in a former church.

Ferwoude: The farmhouse-carpenter's workshop with tools and leather stacked high is worth a quick stop.

WORKUM

Lovely main street and pottery production

GETTING THERE: Take one of the small country roads from Bolsward (N359 going south); or N359 north from Lemmer.
INFORMATION: VVV Workum, Merk 4, tel. (05151) 1300.

This small town was once a center of the weaving industry and also exported eels to London. Today, it is the administrative center for Nijefurd, a new municipality, and produces centuries-old Workumer pottery in several factories. Also of interest is the old shipbuilders yard "De Hoop."

On either side of the main street there are scores of houses with stepped or necked gables. Adjoining the Town Hall (15th and 16th century) on the market square is a charming Frisian house dating from 1620. The Weigh House (1650) houses the VVV and local museum. The Saint Gertrudis Church (16th century) has a beautiful choir-screen, carved pulpit, mourning-signs with nine painted guild biers for boatmen, farmers, apothecaries, surgeons, gold and silversmiths, carpenters and their children. Also note its detached tower. The Saint Werenfridus Church has ancient wood carvings, and a 17th-century clandestine church in the outer form of a farmhouse.

Two potters to visit are: J. Altena, Noord 76, tel. (05151) 1610, and Doting, Noord 3, tel. 1718.

HINDELOOPEN

Colorful Frisian furniture and cloth

*GETTING THERE: Right on the IJsselmeer south of Bolsward just off
N359.*
INFORMATION: VVV Hindeloopen, Het Oost 12, tel. (05142) 2550.

Hindeloopen is an old town which received its charter of city rights in 1225 and joined the Hanseatic League in 1368. It carried on a flourishing trade with Scandinavia first, reaching its greatest prosperity as a seaport in the 17th century. In the 18th century trade developed with the Balkans as well, and soon Hindeloopen sailors were bringing home brightly colored materials and decorative items from the Orient.

Like all seamen around the world, many of them spent the winter months repairing sails, nets, or just whittling useful items for the house. In Hindeloopen, the whittling led to making furniture and that led to painting it the highly admired colors and designs of the East. In those days, small towns were quite isolated and it was possible for Hindeloopen to develop an independent and unique style of dress and decoration. Even the language used here was different than any other in Friesland, surprisingly incorporating words of Asiatic origin. Soon, the popularity of the Frisian designs extended beyond this village and others began ordering furniture and yardage with their unique hues. You can visit a factory producing copies of the traditional painted and carved furniture of Hindeloopen, and maybe you'll be tempted to add a small piece or two to your collection of treasures. You will be welcomed graciously at Roosje Hindeloopen, Nieuwstad 44, tel. (05142) 1251.

This small town is a maze of narrow streets and lanes, interspersed with small canals winding past traditional style homes painted in the local green with white detailed roof decorations. Boats of all kinds are tied to the small private docks at the end of green lawns and flowering gardens. The visitor may feel he has stepped back in time to another, more relaxed era.

As you walk around town, notice the summer cottages by the waterside, the Commanders' and Captains' Houses, the Liar's Bench; rest a moment on the "Ringmuorre," the wall near the harbor which used to protect the town from encroaching waters. Then admire the Westertoren—doesn't it lean just a bit? During the summer, the historical buildings are illuminated in the evening, adding a further touch of romance. The local singing and dancing society, "Aald Hielpen" makes its appearance at the Valdelingenplein, from time-to-time. Stay a bit longer for a real vacation . . . the area is known as a center for aquatics, especially attractive for windsurfers.

MUSEUMS: There are two museums in town:
Hidde Nijland Stichting—the museum of Hindeloopen, Dijkweg 1, tel. 1420; open, March-Oct., Mon.-Sat., 10am-5pm, Sun. and holidays, 1:30-5pm. Housed in the former Town Hall. Notice the statue of Justice over the side entrance and in front of the steps, a freestone pillory. The purpose of the museum, however, is to show the history of Hindeloopen. The original interiors show the style of life,

furniture and dress of the local people . . . especially interesting are the highly decorated tile walls, the women's costumes in colorful Indian chintz and checked cloth which matched the colors of the furniture. There's the reconstruction of an 18th-century Hindeloopen captain's house showing a bride trying on her bridal veil. About 1740, Hindeloopen was at the height of its prosperity with two and a half times as many inhabitants as today but by 1880, women stopped wearing their traditional dress.

Skate Museum, Kleine Weide 1-3, tel. 1683; open, March-Nov., Mon.-Sat., 10am-6pm, Sun., 1:30-5pm. This is the largest collection of skates in the world!.

STAVOREN

Watersports center

GETTING THERE: Stavoren lies on a southwest point of land project-ing into the IJselmeer, south of Hindeloopen. From May-Sept., there's a ferry service from Enkhuizen which connects with the train to Leeuwarden.
INFORMATION: VVV Stavoren, Voorstraat 80, tel. (05149) 1616, if no answer, 1818.

Famous today as a watersports center, in its heyday it was known for its shipping and trade. The haughty Lady of Stavoren is legend here; her statue in bronze stands on the harbor wall. She overlooks a harbor crammed with pleasure sailing craft instead of commercial vessels.

The largest pumping station in Europe, the J. L. Hoogland, is close to the Johan Willem Friso sluice, just south of town.

IN THE NEIGHBORHOOD OF STAVOREN:

Warns and Rode Klif, nearby, are of interest because of the famous Battle of Warns in 1345 when the army of Earl Willem IV was defeated in the vicinity (see intro above). There are beautiful views from Rode Klif (Red Cliff) with a monument commemorating the unsuccessful Dutch invasion. Warns is built on a sand ridge, 7 meters above sea level.

SLOTEN

One of the Eleven Frisian Towns

GETTING THERE: A small village north of Lemmer, about mid-way on the road connecting N359 and N354 on the Slotermeer Lake.
INFORMATION: VVV Sloten, Dubbelstgraat 125, tel. (05143) 583.

Smallest in the group of Eleven Frisian Towns on the famous ice-skating circuit, it is extremely picturesque. In the former Town Hall you can visit a small local museum, then walk along the ancient protective walls and bastions, passing many restored buildings with beautiful gables along the Diep. Next to the museum is the Dutch reformed church (1647) and parsonage with double stepped gable (Renaissance).

Boaters might consider a special route: Lemmer-Sloten-Woudsend. Lemmer is the entrance to the Polder canals, the Buma pumping station and many sluices. Woudsend's big homes remind one of the town's importance as a shipbuilding center in the 18th Century. Enjoy its waterside café terraces, its restaurant in a former clandestine church, and more. On the outskirts of town, there is the largest factory producing powdered milk in Holland.

Museum "Stedhus Sleat," Heerenwal 48, tel. 541 or 611; open, Tues.-Fri., 10am-5pm, Sat., Sun., 2-5pm; off-season, check with VVV. The collection consists of town historical artifacts, fans, clothes, costumes, jewelry, clocks, magic lanterns and their forerunners, antique cameras, etc.

JOURE

Clocks down the ages

GETTING THERE: Joure is between Sneek and Heerenveen just off A7 (at intersection with A50).
INFORMATION: VVV Joure, Kooilaan 32, tel. (05138) 16030.

Joure is synonymous with clocks. The ancient Frisian clocks—the best of their kind—came from Joure and are worth a small fortune today. However, the modern shopper can obtain good reproductions at reasonable prices. Check with the VVV for a recommended clock-maker. There is also a clock museum within a museum:

Museum Johannes Hessel Huis, open, Mon.-Sat., 10am-5pm, Sun., 2-5pm, May-Sept., also on Sat., 2-5pm. Nice collection of pipes as well as Frisian clocks galore; also, a coffee and tea cabinet on the ground floor with clocks on display.

233

HEERENVEEN

Thialf Ice Stadium

GETTING THERE: Drive straight south of Leeuwarden on N32, approx. 26 km.
INFORMATION: VVV Heerenveen, v. Havenpad 48, tel. (05130) 2555.

Heerenveen has an old manor house, a museum and the Thialf Ice Stadium to make a stop worthwhile. To visit the manor house, "Crackstate," on Oude Koemarkt, tel. 41234 for an appointment. It was built by Hypolitus Crack in 1608. The building has a classic facade surmounted by a clock tower. House and garden are surrounded by a moat with an arched bridge dating from 1776.

Museum "Willem van Haren," an old patrician house from the 17th century, serves as the regional museum. Open, Mon.-Fri., 10am-5pm, Sat., 11am-4pm.

The Thialf Ice Stadium is the locale for Holland's world skating champions. In winter when the ice is well-formed and the Eleven Towns Race is held, you could try your stamina from here . . . it's only 120 miles.

DOKKUM

The demise of St. Boniface

GETTING THERE: Take N355 east of Leeuwarden, then north on N356.
INFORMATION: VVV Dokkum, Waaggebouw, Grote Breedstraat 1, tel. (05190) 3800.

Dokkum has had a long and eventful history as a port town. Built on a "terp" (a mound), it has retained its hexagonal fortress shape with bulwarks still intact, moats and bastions. In fact, the Frisian Crusade fleet sailed from here in 1217 heading for Damietta in Egypt.

It also has the dubious honor of being where the priest of the Germanic tribes (later Saint Boniface) and his group (all 52 of them) were murdered by Frisians in 754 because they resented his attempt to convert them to Christianity. This determination to retain their independence in matters of religion, state, language and culture is well documented and the special Frisian character continues to be fostered today.

On the ramparts, there are two windmils—one from 1847 and the other dated 1862. The City Hall dates from 1608; open, weekdays from 9am-noon and 2-4pm. The ornately decorated Louis XIV Council Room is worth a visit.

MUSEUMS: There are two museums of interest.
Admiralty House Museum (1618), Laang Oosterstraat, tel. 3134; open daily April-Sept., 10am-5pm, Oct.-March, daily, 2-5pm, closed Sunday. The collection includes archeological finds, folk art and topography, pottery, silver, local dress and costumes, and items dealing with fishing and maritime events of the area.
Natural History Museum, Keereweer, tel. 2674; open, Mon.-Fri., 10am-5pm. Specializes in the flora and fauna from the northeast corner of Friesland.

IN THE NEIGHBORHOOD OF DOKKUM:

Moddergat is north of Dokkum about 10 km right on the shores of the Waddenzee. A fisherman's cottage, "It Fiskerhuske," has been turned into a museum. Open, March-Oct., Mon.-Sun., 10am-5pm.

Wierum, almost next door to Moddergat, is one of the departure places to join an organized walking tour on the tidal marshes to Engelsmanplaat and from Holwerd to Ameland; mid-May-Oct. on Saturdays. VVV for more info.

Lauwersoog on N361 east of Moddergat, right on the border with Groningen. There's a small information center, "ExpoZee," its purpose being to explain the Waddenzee (sea), how it developed 900 years ago and its environmental effect on the area. It is situated on an extensive lake, the Lauwersmeer which offers all sorts of aquatic possibilities. A new facility of possible interest to would-be sailors is the International Watersportcentrum, "de Lauwer" with group accommodations for students. It offers an ANWB-approved sailing school and windsurfing lessons. For specifics write, Noordergat 8, Postbus 1 9976 ZG Lauwersoog, or tel. (05193) 9000.

THE WADDENZEE ISLANDS

LOCATION: On the Waddenzee (sea) north of Noord Holland, Friesland and Groningen.

INFORMATION:

VVV Texel, Groeneplaats 9, Den Burg, tel. (02220) 147411.

VVV Vlieland, Havenweg 10, tel. (05621) 1357.

VVV Terschelling, Willem Barentszkade 19a, tel. (05620) 3000.

VVV Ameland, R. v. Doniastraat 2, Nes, tel. (05191) 2020.

VVV Schiermonnikoog, Reeweg 5, tel. (05195) 1233.

There are five major, and several smaller uninhabited islands located between the Waddenzee and the North Sea.

Texel in North Holland is the largest and most developed with access by ferry from Den Helder. The main town, Den Burg, is located in the center of the island, while the most developed beach is at De Koog on the east coast of the island. See Chapter 3 for details about the Texel Museum and other attractions on Texel.

Each of the islands has its special charm which you can discover for yourself. The differences in character are less pronounced than the similarities: they all have dunes, woods, bird sanctuaries, interesting architecture, sandy beaches, bracing air, soothing sunshine (in season of course) and a closeness to nature.

Information on the islands in Friesland is best obtained from the VVV Friesland-Leeuwarden, Stationsplein 1, 8911 AC Leeuwarden, tel. (058) 132224. For specific information on individual islands, write to the VVVs listed above. There are hundreds of bungalows nestled in the dunes or close to the villages which can be rented. Some are simple and will sleep two people and others are very elaborate with accommodations for eight, a hot tub and other special attractions. The VVVs are prepared to help you make hotel, bungalow, campsite, and ferry reservations.

STAYING OVER: Ameland has the largest selection of hotels followed by Terschelling, Vlieland and Schiermonnikoog. The only personal experience we have had is at the d'Amelander Kap on Ameland, Postbus 10, 9160 AA Hollum, tel. (05191) 4052 . . . a brand new facility with indoor pool, charming lounge with fireplace, excellently appointed dining room; rooms are airy and spacious . . . families can select bungalow accommodations . . . expensive. A more traditional hotel is Hotel Nobel, Gerrit Kosterweg 16, 9161 EW Ballum, Ameland, tel. 4157 . . . modern rooms in an old-world setting, moderate-priced.

COMMERCIAL TOURS: If you want to explore the Waddenzee area on board ship, there are two possibilities:
The Hollands Glorie, a typical Dutch sailing barge, sleeps about eleven. The route is planned with departure from Amsterdam—possible visits to Hoorn, Enkhuizen, Medemblik, Stavoren and Harlingen. Texel, Vlieland and Terschelling can also be visited. Write "Hollands Glorie," Postbus 2448, 300 CK Rotterdam, tel. (010) 411 4944 or 411 5880.
The Spes Mea, Bruine Zeilvloot Zoutkamp, Postbus 11, 9974 ZG Zoutkamp, tel. (05956) 2309 or 2433, accommodates 16-18 persons on a do-it-yourself vacation (under the captain's supervision!). Sailing the Waddenzee, passengers can walk across the sandbanks and mudflats looking for mussels, catching shrimp, watching seals, swimming, fishing and more.

Vlieland

The car-free island

If you want to get away from it all, try Vlieland. There is no pollution from auto, motorbike or motorcycle exhaust—they are prohibited on the island, except to local residents. Access is by boat ferry from Harlingen with three departures a day in season. The trip takes 1½ hours. Once on the island, bikes are the best way to get around . . . bring your own or rent one.

The only town on Vlieland is Oost-Vlieland but it has a nice selection of accommodations including two 4-star hotels. It is conveniently located next to 3,000 hectares of dunes and pine forest, offering easy accessibility on foot or bike to beaches, dunes and woodlands. The island has two special attractions: the longest nudist beach in Europe and seals.

The island is famous for its unique flora and fauna . . . 96 species of birds have been observed, including the eider duck which come during the breeding season. At that time, excursions are made to the breeding grounds, the woods and dunes with guides from the National Forest Service. You can also explore the "wadden" at low tide. And if you come in winter after a snowfall, you can cross-country ski your way around.

In addition to swimming or sunbathing on the 12-km-long beach, there are walking tours, tennis, windsurfing, horseback riding, midget-golf, bowling, fishing and biking. Culture-bugs will find two museums:
The Natural History Museum (part of the Visitors' Center), Dorpstraat 152, tel. 1205; open from May to Oct., 10am-noon and 2-5pm; Oct.-April, 2-5pm; Nov.-March, Wed. and Sat., 2-5pm. A nice introduction to the island.

236

Trompshuys Museum, Dorpstraat 99, tel. 1205, same hours as above. Formerly the Admiralty Building (17th century), the collection includes paintings by Betty Akersloot-Berg, a transplanted Norwegian who lived here many years. There are also interesting displays of porcelain, tile, copper, glass, tin and furniture.

Terschelling
A "National Trust Park"
The Dutch Government designated this island a "national landscape" . . . come and see why. Visitors can take a car ferry from Harlingen two or three times a day. The crossing takes about 1½ hours; reservations are a must: Rederij Doeksen, tel. (05620) 6111; price, approximately Fl. 130 per car, according to size.

People have been living here for 15 centuries, farming, fishing and seafaring. The villages reflect this rich past in their charming homes and gardens. Terschelling is the second largest island with 40 miles of duneland, woods and sandy shores. There are unique bird sanctuaries all over the island, the most important is "De Boschplaat" with enough space and tranquility to encourage a myriad collection of wild plants and dozens of species of birds numbering in the thousands. Cars are not allowed in the preserve so explore on foot or by bike. Group visits can be made in a "huifkartocht" (a covered wagon); write Douwe Spanjer, Dorpstraat 20 or check with the VVV.

West Terschelling, the largest town and the capital of the island offers some interesting sights. For instance, it would be pretty difficult to miss the 190-foot-tall Brandaris lighthouse, constructed in 1594. There is also a nautical school, a Natural History Museum, Burg. Reedekerstraat 11, tel. 2390, and the municipal museum, "Het Behouden Huys."

Het Behouden Huys is located at Commandeurstraat 30-31, tel. 2389; open, April 1 through Dec. (except closed Nov.), Mon.-Fri., 9am-5pm; also Sat., mid-June to mid-August. Before entering, notice the beautifully sculpted pavement. The interior contains furniture, costumes and practical items used by local people. In the attic there is a marine collection including items used in former whaling days.

An interesting local crop is cranberries which are also used in making cranberry wine—try it.

Ameland
A true Wadden diamond
Boat service from Holwerd to Nes takes about 45 minutes, with departures almost hourly from 6:30am-7:30pm (in season); price, approximately Fl. 81 for an auto plus Fl. 12 per person. For specifics and assistance in reserving, contact the VVV or write Wagenborg Passagiersdiensten B.V., Reeweg, Nes-Ameland, tel. (05191) 6111. Bus service on the island is very good. There is also a small airfield north of Ballum.

This island deserves an entire chapter. Not only is it rich in natural beauty—

woods, dunes, sea, beaches and bird sanctuaries—it has four village centers which have been designated national trust areas, encouraging restoration and preserving the atmosphere of its early days when navigation and whaling were the principal means of livelihood. Look for the 17th- and 18th-century Commanders dwellings and notice if the sign is out indicating the captain is looking for cargo . . . The houses themselves can be identified by an extra row of bricks forming a ledge on the gable and chiseled work on the front.

Whaling and seafaring in general used to be income-producers. Today, tourism and black and white Frisian cows (and agricultural products) support the economy. This is the only place where milk is transported by underwater tube to the mainland for processing.

Some unusual local activities worth noting: Monthly practice of the lifeboat crew and horses . . . the lifeboat is drawn by 10 horses from the boat house in Hollum (boat house open to the public on occasion) to the beach, then launched by eight horses. In 1979 eight horses drowned; they have been buried beside the dune crossing of the lifeboat track.

Then there is parachute jumping from the airfield at Ballum. Sleigh races—an exciting event—and cross-country skiing in winter when there is snow. There are 80-90 km of bike courses along the shallows and through the dunes; 27 km of beach with foaming surf (north side); tennis courts, bowling alleys, horseback riding with special routes; 2½ km from Nes (Nesser woods) along the beach; 4 km through the Hollumer woods along the dunes. In addition, you can arrange lessons for skydiving and windsurfing. And in Nes, there's a subtropical swimming "paradise" with sauna and fitness center.

Commercial tours and VVV-sponsored excursions include: Fishing trips to the Bobbenbank near Terschelling and Schiermonnikoog on the "Ameland 1," Hans Jochemstraat 3, Nes, tel. (05191) 2166; tours around the nature preserve the Oerd or in the Briksduinen; walks on the Wadden shallows; tractor trips to de Hon; and conducted bus tours of the churches.

Hollum, the most westerly village on the island has a lovely town center with a number of fine "Commanders" houses. The most beautiful, De Ouwe Polle, along with the adjacent farmhouse, houses the Museum of Antiquities, "Oudheidskamer," and Museum Farm, Oosterlaan 31; open from the beginning of May to Nov., Mon.-Fri., 10am-noon and 2-5pm; in season, also open some evenings. The collection in this 1751 commander's house includes objects of former whalers with their contributions to folk art, along with information on whaling and lifesaving. There is also a natural history museum on Westerlaan 4, open March-Nov. and during the Christmas vacation.

One outstanding landmark in Hollum, the Amelander Lighthouse, built in 1880, is 193 feet high and stands 233 feet above sea level. One of the most penetrating lights, it measures 4½ million candlepower and can be seen as far as 63 miles under favorable weather conditions. The tower can be visited daily, 9:30am-12:30pm and 1:30-4:30pm. On Wed. and Sat. evenings between 10pm and midnight, the light is put in operation . . . presumably, also in times of need.

The other landmark difficult to miss is the span roof tower (late 15th century) of the Nederlands Hervormde Church (1678) which used to serve as a beacon for sailors. The remains of three earlier churches were recently discovered on the site, the oldest dating to the 11th century.

Ballum is small but has a rich history. The rulers of Ameland, the Lords of Cammingha, had their palace here; it was demolished in 1829. The Lords Cammingha sold the island to the van Oranje family, making Queen Beatrix the hereditary Baroness of Ameland. In the present cemetery, all that remains of the castle chapel is the burial vault. The huge stone which shuts it off was made in 1552/56 by a sculptor from Franeker. The chapel itself was destroyed in 1832, at which time the present Dutch Reformed Church was built. The pulpit is among the oldest in the Netherlands . . . date of origin uncertain, it was brought to Ameland in 1771 from Harlingen.

The airfield just north of Ballum is the island's lifeline when the ferry service is canceled due to ice drifts on the Shallows. It is also used to carry the mail and sick or injured persons. In summer, sightseeing flights by small planes keep things humming. There are also parachutists who enjoy themselves and thrill onlookers. In winter, there are races with horse-toboggans.

Nes with its active VVV office will be the center of planning (along with the VVV in Hollum) for your time on Ameland. The village is charming with numerous "Commanders" houses, shops, restaurants, an old-fashioned post office, 17th-century Dutch Reformed Church on a picturesque square. The church tower, as in Ballum, stands approximately 100 meters away from the chapel because in olden times these towers were built as beacons for sailors. The windmill "De Phoenix" on Mullensduin dates from 1880. The flour milled here is conveyed by the millers to the bakers who produce the Ameland Millbread. The mill is open to the public on Saturday mornings.

The Natural History Museum is small but it will give the visitor a bird's eye view of this most important aspect of life on the island. The abundance of nature in and around the island is explained by means of dioramas, models, and displays, as well as films and programs from time-to-time. There is a small sea aquarium to interest the little ones.

Nes has a Mennonite Chapel (the oldest on the island, rebuilt in 1843), and a Roman Catholic Church (1878) designed by the master builder Dr. Cuypers.

Buren has a little square with a bronze statue representing Rixt the Witch from Het Oerd. Legend has it she lived on wreckage after she stranded ships by making fires on shore. Of the greatest importance is Buren's neighbor, the nature reserve "Het Oerd," well known for its great variety of flora and fauna. The area is protected from the casual tourist in order to preserve the ecology and to allow complete peace and quiet during the nesting season. A section of the reserve is closed to the public between April 15 and August 15. There is a biking path of about 1½ miles through some of the area with over 50 species of birds and at least 500 different plants to see or photograph. A descriptive route is available through the VVV.

Schiermonnikoog

Bird Island

This is the quietest and most natural of the inhabited Waddenzee islands. The ferry leaves from Lauwersoog on the border with Groningen and takes about 45 minutes. Departures about 7 times per day, depending on the season. For information, see "Wagenborg Passagiersdiensten B.V." under Ameland. While automobiles are not allowed, bikes can be rented on the island.

Schiermonnikoog is also the name of the island's only town which is mainly concentrated along one street with many restored houses. A walk along Midden-streek and Langestreek will take you past some of the most interesting.

The Government has declared one-quarter of the island a National Monument Park. In addition to two exceptional beaches and a small lake, the Westerplas, there is a nature reserve east of town worth a visit, De Kobbeduinen (2,400 hectares).

STAYING OVER: While hotels are few (there's a two-star possibility, the Strand Hotel, tel. (05195) 1201), there are plenty of summer houses, guest houses, bungalows, apartments and campsites for rent.

CHAPTER 9

THE PROVINCE OF GRONINGEN

Holland's most northern province is at the "top of the map" and can be reached by many super highways. On the way, depending on the route chosen, the visitor can combine it with a visit to Friesland, Drenthe, the Hoge Veluwe, North Holland or whatever your fancy. Roads are terrific; traffic is generally comfortable . . . especially on the national or provincial roads.

As mentioned in the previous chapter (Friesland), the Frisians controlled the entire coastal zone of present-day Holland. Their influence also extended into neighboring lands in Germany. In 911 A.D., Groningen (then East Frisia) demanded its independence, and in 1040, Emperor Henry III gave the city of Groningen and its surrounding area, the Gorecht, to the Bishops of Utrecht. The rest of the province remained under the control of big land owners, known as "Jonkers"; these areas were called the "Ommelanden" as separate from Groningen city and area. The Jonkers were rich, powerful and built some lovely manor houses/castles, a number of which are open to the public.

Not surprisingly, the locals and those designated by the Bishops of Utrecht to rule the area were constantly battling for control. By 1440, Groningen's independence was formalized but in 1536 Charles V united the area into greater Holland. The establishment of a university in 1614 brought learned men from around the world turning Groningen City into an important intellectual center.

The province is fertile, well drained and the chief peat region of the country with much of the land devoted to agriculture. Driv-

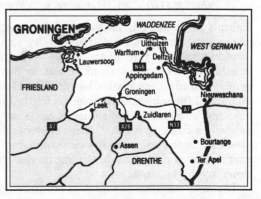

INFORMATION:
VVV Groningen,
tel. (050) 139700.

ing along, one is impressed by the huge Groningen farm buildings, unique in style to this area.

In recent years, a number of commercial products, such as cardboard, have been made from agricultural products. Also of great importance has been the discovery of one of the largest deposits of natural gas in the world in the Slochteren region. Delfzijl, at the mouth of the Eems canal and the Dollard Gulf, is a big port, ship-building and industrial center.

And for those who want to return to nature, this province can offer a wide choice of possibilities from walking the mudflat areas in the northwest, to sailing and aquatic opportunities on the Dollard Gulf in the northeast, the Lauwers Lake in the extreme north, Paterswoldse Lake and Zuidlarder Lake, all within 20 km of Groningen City. In this flat, long-view countryside, bikers of all ages can do "it" on their own or join an organized group. One special treat is an 850-km canoeing expedition through watery polderlands, past historic manor houses and windmills, and through ancient villages. Check with the Groningen VVV, tel. 139700 for information about the "Kano Plezier." Regular ferries from Lauwersoog (northwest) will take you to the smallest and quietest of the Waddenzee islands, Schiermonnikoog, where you can come close to nature, studying the migrating birds and nature reserves or take a walk through the mud-flats (in season) from the mainland to the islands. Only for the hardy!

The city of Groningen makes a good base for exploring the province as it sits in the center of a cluster of highways radiating out like a spider's web in all directions. Assen, its neighbor to the south and the capital of Drenthe, is only 20 km away and shares with Groningen some unusual sightseeing possibilities. Friesland, too, is a good sharing neighbor especially in the Lauwers Lake area.

GRONINGEN CITY

Hub of the North

GETTING THERE: The capital of Groningen Province can be reached by various highways: from Leeuwarden and points east, N355; from Flevoland north and east to the German border, A7; from Assen and points south, A28.
INFORMATION: VVV Groningen, Naberpassage 3, tel. (050) 139700.

The city of Groningen has an atmosphere peculiarly its own. Even if one weren't aware that the second oldest university in the Netherlands is located here, it wouldn't take long to figure it out—especially on Saturday nights when the weather makes it pleasant to be out in force on the Grote Markt where the principal student association has its Club House. Hundreds of bikes are gathered all around the square, their owners circulating, calling to friends from balconies, enjoying a pizza or Italian ice cream, or simply sitting at a sidewalk cafe enjoying a coffee or a Pils. College students number about 17,000; they probably aren't all on the Square at the same time, but it almost seems so. It's great fun to participate as onlookers breathing in the electric atmosphere and excitement generated by the students.

The next morning, the litter of the streets is hard to believe but look ahead—

not down—and you're sure to see one or more bikes perched precariously on street signs or other stationary supports four or more feet off the ground, a traditional joke played on one's friend during the past evening's hilarity.

Groningen's importance and wealth date from very early times. In fact, Groningen provided ships and material for the Crusades. It was a fortress town in the 12th century and became an important commercial center in 1251 with conclusion of a contract between it and the surrounding towns establishing Groningen as the central market town for the area. After joining the Hanseatic League in 1594, Groningen became an even more important trading post.

Today, Groningen ranks fourth in commercial importance in the Netherlands. Being connected to the sea by three long canals has effectively made it an active seaport where commercial vessels come to do business. Agriculture and fishing have long been traditional activities; however, the discovery of large natural gas reserves in 1946 has added to the Province's importance and has turned a number of formerly sleepy townships into busy commercial centers.

Groningen has a well-known and highly reputed university (since 1614) which continues to bring international educators and scholars to the city, greatly enhancing it culturally and intellectually.

A walking tour with map is now put out by the VVV in English, French and German. It's a useful guide and helpful in finding your way about. In addition, the VVV puts out a small flyer showing locations of special shops, galleries and antique dealers ... there's a Japanese "center" for Chinese, Japanese and Indonesian gifts and foodstuffs as well as one for North African goods. The Naberpassage has a number of shops.

The Martini Tower, 315 feet tall, on the Grote Markt in the center of old Groningen dominates the scene. Gothic in style, the church was reconstructed in the 15th century on a much earlier base. The present tower was completed in 1482, also on an earlier base. It is affectionately referred to as the "Old Grey One" which is appropriate in the daytime, but at night, there's a Jekyll and Hyde change. The Old Grey One becomes a tantalizing sprite. The top galleries were destroyed by fire in 1577 and rebuilt in 1627 and the foundation was renewed during WW II. In 1837, the city council placed a lightning-conductor on the tower to end the regular fires caused by lightning (also by bonfire in wartime). The bells of the tower are known internationally and a bell-ringer's guild, established in 1982, now has about 40 members. Access to the tower is possible Easter to mid-Oct., Tues.-Sat., noon-4:30pm; bear in mind, there are 370 steps to the top!

The St. Martin Church is Romano-Gothic in origin as can be seen from the exterior. It dates back to 1230 A.D. and has been preserved in its present form since the 15th century. The vaults show numerous 15th-century murals, and the walls of the choir are decorated with a series of exquisite frescoes. Various stained glass windows show the coats of arms of the captains of the citizen soldiery (1770). The organ dates from 1480. For visits, contact the VVV.

The glaringly modern building on the Grote Markt is an addition to the neo-classical baroque City Hall built at the end of the 18th century. Soon to be demolished, it will be replaced with a structure in keeping with the traditional architecture of the original building. Nearby is the only 17th-century house which survived the destruction of WW II. The Gold Office (Goud Kantoor), built in 1635 as the tax house, has a Latin inscription over the entrance: "Render unto Caesar that which is Caesar's."

The Grain Exchange (Korenbeurs), facing the Fish Marketplace is, the major grain exchange for domestic grains in Western Europe. Dating from 1865, the three Gods protecting this building are: Mercury, God of Commerce (over the entrance); Neptune, God of the Seas, and Ceres, Goddess of Agriculture (on either side of the entrance). You can watch the action Tuesday mornings.

Nearby between A-Kerkhof NZ and ZZ, stands the A-Kerk with its delicate Renaissance cupola (it collapsed twice). In 1247 the church was dedicated to Maria, St. Nicholas and all saints. It is presently in the form of a 15th-century Gothic church.

The Princenhof Garden (northwest of the Grote Markt) is worth seeking out . . . especially in rose-blooming time. Open from March 15-Oct. 15, this 17th-century rose and herb garden is entered from the canal side (Turfsingel). The 1731 sundial in the gate has a Latin inscription: "The past is nothing, the future is uncertain, the present is unstable, beware that you do not lose the latter which is yours." The hedges are clipped in the letters A and W for the governor of Friesland and Groningen, Willem Frederik and his wife, Albertine.

The Princenhof (23 Martinikerkhof) originally housed the friars of the Order of the Brethren of the Common Life in the 15th Century. It was converted in 1594 to accommodate the court of the Frisian Governors. Under Louis Bonaparte of France it served as a military hospital. Today, it's the home of Studio Radio North, the broadcasting organization for the north and east of Holland. The Pleinpoort (square gate) dates from 1642 and the annex, the Gardepoort (guard's gate), built in 1639, also housed the Governor's Guard.

■ **Almshouses** are to be found in all large cities of the Netherlands and are often used to house elderly church members. You will see one small gem on Peperstraat called "Geertruidsgasthuis," or "Pepergasthuis," just off Poelestraat. The gate (1640) is a masterpiece, and the sculptured sandstone pediment over the entrance door dates from 1743. There are two courtyards; the first has a water pump dating from 1829; and the second presents a very charming site with its 18th-century facades, ivy-grown in part, and the 1651 gate. Visits can be arranged by calling the matron, tel. 124092.

If you return to the Oosterstraat and walk south, the street changes names and becomes the "Rademarkt." Here, you will find another old gasthuis, the St. Anthony Gasthuis, established in 1696 to serve as a hospital for plague victims. From 1644 to 1844, the hospital served the mentally ill. The old corridor leading toward the "dolhuis" behind the Gasthuis still survives. Not open for visitors.

However, if you want to see the oldest and the biggest gasthuis, coming back from Rademarkt, take a left turn on Ged. Zuiderdiep and a right on Pelsterstraat. The Heilige Geest Gasthuis (or Pelstergasthuis) dates from 1267. Over the years it expanded gradually until today it ranks among the largest in the Netherlands. There are three inner courtyards, separated by quaint old gates and corridors. A fourth courtyard has been added and is enclosed on all four sides by small modern houses. The back exit, giving access to Nieuwstad, has a very nice

Tuscan pilaster gate, renovated in 1724. The Chapel was converted in 1600 to hold Reformed Church services. Visits are possible by contacting the matron, tel. 120703.

The Jacob en Anna Gasthuis was founded by Jacob and Etteke Grovens in 1494; also called the "tidbit" house. It is located in the northwest corner of town between Vishoek and DeLaan streets. And in the opposite corner of town (northeast) near the Princenhof there's an almshouse founded in 1766 for women over 65 years.

Beautiful buidings can be seen throughout the town such as the Provincial Government House, 12 Martinikerkhof, which dates from the 15th century. The caretaker's house (to the left) has an early Renaissance gable which was part of another house until 1893. The richly sculptured facade is called either the "Cardinaal" house or the house with the "Three Kings" after the medallions in the gable wall representing Alexander the Great, King David, and Charlemagne. Visits are possible by appointment, tel. 164911 or the VVV.

Note also the buildings along the Oude Boteringestraat which include the former residence of the Queen's Commissioner, built in 1791; the Court of Justice; the house with the Thirteen Pinnacles (ornate facade; no longer 13 pinnacles); a 1913 copy of a medieval wine house; and on the corner of Braerstraat and Oude Boteringestraat, a stone house built in the Middle Ages.

MUSEUMS: The Groningen Museum of Art and History and the Northern Shipping and Tobacco Museum are discussed below. In addition, there are:

The Natural History Museum, St. Walburgstraat 9; open, Tues.-Fri., 10am-5pm, Sat.-Sun., 2-5pm;

University Museum, Zwanestraat 33, tel. 635562; open, Tues.-Sat., 10am-4pm, Sun., noon-4pm;

Folk Art Museum (Volkenkundig museum), Nieuwe Kijk in 't Jatstraat 104, tel. 635791; open, Tues.-Fri., 10am-4pm, Sat.-Sun., 1-5pm;

The Film Museum, Ged. Zuiderdiep 139, tel. 140659, Tues., 1-5pm (also theater and cafe).

MARKETS: Markets are held Tues., Fri. and Sat. on the Grote Markt and the Vismarkt (vegetable/flea markets). A small flea market is also held on the Grote Markt on Wed. and Thurs., 9am-5pm, except Oct.-April when it closes at 4:30pm.

The City Park (Stadspark) is a wonderful place to relax or to entertain the children. Besides a camping facility at Campinglaan 6, tel. 251624, there are canoes for rent, horseback riding, midget golf, ice skating rink and a children's playground. Groningen's busy exposition hall, Martinihall, is also located here.

The Casino, Kattendiep 150, tel. (050) 123400, offers Blackjack, American and French roulette, and one-armed bandits.

EATING OUT: For a moderate-priced bite, there are two pancake and three pizza restaurants in town: 't Pannekoekschip, Schuitendiep t.o 41, (also Tourist Menu); La Creperie, Nieuwe Ebbingestraat 89; Contini, Peperstraat 12; Costa

Smeralda, Poelestraat 12; and Isolabella, Naberpassage 20 (near Grote Markt).

For a French-inspired dinner, try La Crémaillière, Zuiderdiep 58, tel. 124466 (reserve); the dining room at De Doelen Hotel, Grote Markt 36; or for a romantic atmosphere, the dining room of 't Familie Hotel at Paterswolde Lake, about 12 km south of town (Groningerweg 19).

STAYING OVER: For those who like being right in the center of things and are intrigued by the historic, De Doelen Hotel, situated at Grote Markt 36, tel. 127041, is a convenient, moderate-priced stop. The hotel dates from 1798—with modern innovations, of course. And very importantly, a private parking lot.

Families or couples who want a bit of outdoors action, elegance, and time to relax, 't Familie Hotel is an excellent choice. One of the Golden Tulip chain, 't Familie Hotel must rank as one of their best. The hotel has a tropical-like indoor pool, sauna, gift shop, several eateries including a top-rated gourmet restaurant, extremely comfortable rooms and a pavilion by the lake (short walk) where one can sail, windsurf or just take tea. Also available, walks in the woods, biking, horseback riding, golf, and parajumping. Expensive, but worth it.

YEARLY EVENTS: Groningen's Martinihall (in the Stadspark) is booked solid Jan.-March with sports events, animal shows, antique exhibitions, and textile and other commercial markets. The yearly flower market is held the beginning of April, and in late April there's a jazz festival. The City Fair is held in May; June-Sept. there are organ concerts in the Martini Church; in Aug., the town jumps with special summer programs; the International Industries Fair is held the end of Aug., beginning Sept.; the beginning of Oct., the horse and pony market; and in Dec., an Antiques Fair.

COMMERCIAL TOURS: Canal boat tours are possible 4 or 5 times a day during June, July and Aug., Mon.-Sat. Reservations are necessary: Reederij Kool, Damsterdiep 244, tel. 128379.

Groninger Museum of Art and History

LOCATION: Praediniussingel 59.
INFORMATION: Museum tel. 183343 or VVV, tel. 139700.
HOURS: Tues.-Sat., 10am-5pm; Sun., 1-5pm. Closed December 25
and January 1.
■ *Of interest to school-age children.*

The collection deals primarily with the history and culture of Groningen (city and province), including "terp culture." There are ancient and modern art works; Groningen silver and special-order 17th- and 18th-century porcelain from the Far East; antique glass and coin collections; as well as paintings and drawings by Dutch masters of the 16th to the 20th centuries. There are archeological finds from the area and a room of regional costumes.

The Oriental porcelain collection is especially fine and highly valuable—a must for any Far East "specialists."

Northern Shipping and Tobacco Museums

*LOCATION: Brugstraat 24-26 in the Gotische Huis just west of the
  Vismarkt.*
INFORMATION: Museum tel. 122202 or VVV.
HOURS: Tues.-Sat., 10am-5pm; Sun. and public holidays, 1-5pm.
■ *Of interest to school-age children.*

The two buildings in which the Northern Shipping and the Tobacco Museums
are located are wonderfully restored 13th- and 14th-century structures with
heavy beamed ceilings, and bright, well-ordered display space.

Fifteen centuries of history are represented in the superb Northern Shipping
Museum. The story is told of the ships and their captains: the voyages they
made, the far shores they visited; the cargoes they carried; the way they lived;
what they brought back to adorn their homes or for trade. There's a skipper's
model room, ship models, machinery, and a collection of art dealing with
maritime matters.

The Tobacco Museum collection is quite famous with its fine-quality objects,
engravings, and paintings depicting the history of tobacco in Western Europe
from 1500-1930; also, its healing properties, its use as a luxury item and present-
day anti-smoking campaigns. In addition, there's an outstanding American
collection from the period of Columbus.

IN THE NEIGHBORHOOD OF GRONINGEN CITY:

Paterswoldse Lake (6 km south of town) and Zuidlarder Lake (15 km
southeast) offer the complete spectrum of activities to enjoy these beautiful lakes
and the surrounding wooded countryside. Just across the border from Zuidlarder
Lake into Drenthe (2 km) two megalithic tombs can be explored. Also in Zuidlaren
and of special interest to children, there's a fairy-tale garden and recreation park,
"De Sprookjeshof" (see Chapter 10), and a 17th-century moated manor house,
Laarwood Castle, which serves as the town hall.

Haren (southeast 6 km) is the locale of the University Botanical Garden; open,
Mon.-Sat., 10am-4:45pm, Sun., 2-4:45pm. Especially interesting is the glasshouse
divided into 5 sections: tropical, subtropical, desert, savannah and monsoon. The
watermill, "De Helper" can be visited on Sun. from 2-5pm.

Noorderhoogebrug (northeast edge of town) boasts the biggest windmill in the
province, "De Wilhelmina"; in operation Sat., 1:30-4:30pm. Check with VVV to
find out when demonstrations might be given.

Our tour of the Province will begin at Leek about 14 km west of Groningen via
A7, and continue clock-wise around the province. The places highlighted will
include the Land of the Waddenzee, manor-house/castles, towns, and sites of
special historic interest.

LEEK

A carriage museum, manor house and park

GETTING THERE: From the west, just off the A7/N7 autoroute, about 20 km before Groningen. From Groningen, about 14 km east. It's in an area called Bosweg—a large park surrounded by water.
INFORMATION: VVV Leek, Tolberterstraat 39-1, tel. (05945) 12100.

A special treat for families, Leek is the home of the National Carriage Museum located in the 16th-century Nienoord Castle, more about that below. In town there's an interesting Protestant Church, the Midwolde Church, containing a 17th-century mausoleum with exceptionally fine marble sculptures; a midget golf course, and swimming pools (on grounds of the Castle Park).

Leek's origins stem from the historic manor-house Nienoord, which was founded about 1525. The house burned but in 1880 it was rebuilt in its present form on the earlier foundations. The estate—20 acres—belongs to the municipality of Leek and the park is open to the public for cycling and walking all year.

The "pleasure grounds" of the Nienoord Park offer many activities for the whole family. There's a miniature railway station and trains to the scale of 1 to 8 which are in operation. On Sundays, they are towed by a real steam engine and on weekdays by a model of a diesel-electric engine. There is also a railway model (scale h0), covering 100 square meters with 35 trains. Railroad-model fans should come during "Operating Steam in Miniature," an international show occurring Ascension Day through the following weekend.

There is also a children's zoo in the park with rare breeds of domestic pets, including more than 25 breeds of poultry, the "Lakenvelder" cows, all Dutch breeds of sheep, and the "Groningen" horse. Donkey and pony-riding or a trip by pony cart, a visit to the playground, and watching the storks in the breeding ground, an open-air theater "Podium Nienoord" and the racecourse for Greyhounds are all good reasons to spend the day here . . . there's fun for all.

EATING OUT: On the ground floor of the castle, there's an elegant-looking restaurant, Restaurant Nienoord Castle, tel. (05945) 12370. Don't worry, it's more moderate in cost than one would think; a daily special of 2-3 hot dishes, sandwiches, soup, ice creams galore; or try the pancake restaurant "Albertus Hoeve," tel. 12230.

STAYING OVER: Something out of the ordinary would be to stay in one of the two log cabins in the "pleasure grounds," tel. 12610 for info and reservations. Or try the Hotel Leek, tel. 18800, or the Campsite Westerheerdt, tel. 12059.

YEARLY EVENTS: There are all kinds of activities going on in Leek all year . . . for that list, check with the VVV. The major nationally-known events include a historic motor-bike race the last Sunday in April (Leek-Assen-Leek); an international 4-day show of train models operated by steam, Ascension Day through weekend; an open-air play performed by the Playgroup Leek in June; and a large cattle and goods market on Whit Monday, with a fair.

Nienoord Castle/National Carriage Museum

LOCATION: From Groningen, take "Leek" exit from A7 going west. Motor traffic is restricted so be prepared to walk around this green-wooded area. The castle is in an area called Bosweg—a large park surrounded by water.
INFORMATION: VVV Leek above.
HOURS: Good Fri.-Sept, Mon.-Sat., 9am-5pm, Sun., 1-5pm.
■ *Of interest to all children, especially the recreational facilities.*

The castle is the home of the National Carriage Museum and can be visited during Museum visiting hours (above). This 16th-century castle was greatly damaged by fire in 1880 which necessitated its reconstruction. It is sparsely furnished; instead, the museum collection fills the rooms.

The small goat carriages and sleds belonging to former "royal" children can put stars in many youngsters' eyes while the sleds from the 17th and 18th century will find a romantic responsive chord in the ladies.

Upstairs, notice the elegant "Diana sleds"—one luxurious German model dates from 1760. The men of the group will be interested in several coaches on display in the carriage house which belonged to the last German Kaiser. Also interesting is a "Prince Albert" coach from 1900 which bears a resemblance (on a smaller yet more luxurious scale) to the old covered wagons.

In addition, there's a summer pavilion of the 1700s completely decorated on the interior with shells, known as the "Shell Cave" . . . there's a legend which explains the origins. Be sure and ask about it.

IN THE NEIGHBORHOOD OF LEEK:

Roden (Drenthe), about 8 km southeast, has a "Child's World Museum" at Brink 31 that is worth a visit.

Grijpskerk, straight north of Leek about 16 km on country roads. This town is full of activities during the year. The ones of special interest are in mid-June when national pole-vaulting events take place, and the end of August when the national championship matches for pole-vaulting occur. In addition, there's the celebration of the Queen's birthday, April 30; a fair in May; a mid-summer evening bike race (40-75 km) in June and so on.

LAUWERSOOG

Surrounded by water

GETTING THERE: In the extreme northwest corner on highway N361, just across the border from Friesland.
INFORMATION: In summer, check with Expo-Zee, Strandweg 1, tel. (05193) 9045; in winter, VVV Zoutkamp, Reitdiepskade 1, tel. (05956) 1957. For info about the Expo-Zee center, see "Friesland."

This part of Groningen shares with Friesland the Wadden landscape where you can take a walk through the mudflats across to Schiermonnikoog (in season), or where you can visit the Expo-Zee center to learn about studies being made in the presently enclosed lake area. Or, take surfing and sailing lessons under proper supervision. You can also walk, cycle, swim or fish. There are well-equipped camp sites and comfortable bungalows. You can ply the canals via canoe or "hooded boats" spending the nights in log cabins.

LEENS

To the Manor born

GETTING THERE: From Groningen, take N361 north to Leens.
INFORMATION: VVV Lauwersmeer Oost, tel. (05957) 1957.

Leens is the home of Verhildersum Castle, now a folklore museum with period rooms, and the "Ommelander" Museum. In addition, there is a historic church in the town, Petruskerk and its 1733 organ made by Hinsz. The church is a fine tuff stone building from about 1000 A.D. with a saddle roof of the 13th century. For those interested in visiting, ask for the key at the shop "d'Olle Smidse," Zr. A. Westerhofstraat. To make arrangements ahead, tel. (05957) 1677.

YEARLY EVENT: Leens celebrates with a festival the beginning of September with street music, handicraft displays, special markets, etc.

Verhildersum Castle

LOCATION: Wierde 40, Leens, on the east side of town.
INFORMATION: Tel. (05957) 1430; restaurant, 2204.
HOURS: April-Nov., Tues.-Sat., 10:30am-5:30pm. The restaurant, open 11:30am-6:30pm, offers inexpensive lunches, tea and lovely cakes. Dinners are about Fl. 50.00—reservations are required. Closed on Mon. but open on holidays.
■ *Of interest to most children.*

Verhildersum Castle is a wonderland to explore. Not only is it beautifully maintained and furnished, its history dates back to the 14th century. What you see today, however, is more representative of the 19th century in style and decorations, as opposed to Menkemaborg Castle (just down the road a piece) which represents the 17th and 18th centuries. There used to be a couple of

250

witches in the house, but they seem to be gone now. One was in the linen closet sitting at her spinning wheel.

The original castle was repaired in 1514 and its silhouette was greatly changed about 1786. There's a painting dated 1670 which shows one of the former owners and his wife, Allard Tjarda van Starkenborgh and Gratia Susanna Clant and their ten children in the foreground, with the castle and town in the background.

The rooms are richly furnished and filled with objects of considerable value such as a splendid collection of "Familie Rose" porcelain. In the same room is a rocking horse which would have made any four-year-old boy in 1885 happy. In the dining room, the chairs and table come from a demolished manor house in Pieterburen. Notice the 19th-century highchair with its built-in chamber pot under the removable seat and a little footwarmer. A charming contrast to the formal rooms is the high-ceilinged kitchen, the vaulted cellar which dates to the 14th century, and the scullery with its peat funnel through which lumps of peat were dropped from the attic where they were kept dry.

The top floor is furnished with a variety of objects, photos, etc., relating to the history of the Shallows and the land. In the back, something is shown of the Groninger costume and what the old clothes attic might have contained.

There are often special exhibitions in the old coach-house, or you can visit the "Welgelegen," a farm house/museum with agricultural implements. The gardens offer different impressions depending on the time of year but they are always a lovely place to relax. The old storehouse is now a farm-style restaurant ... it's a pleasure to sit in the open-air enjoying a delicious tea cake and admiring the castle across its moat.

IN THE NEIGHBORHOOD OF LEENS:
If you have time, detour into this lovely countryside to see Allersmaborg Castle, Allersmaweg 64, Ezinge, tel. (05941) 1389. The two-story building dates from the 18th century but the house in the back with cellar is much older. The "castle" is open to visitors by appointment, but on Sat.-Sun., 1-6pm, there are changing exhibitions in the carriage house.

PIETERBUREN

Seals, mustard and mudflats

GETTING THERE: A northernmost village west of Warffum off N363.
INFORMATION: VVV, Bezoekerscentrum Ten Dijke, Hoofdweg 83,
tel. (05952) 522.

Here's a chance for lovers of seals to visit the Zeehondencreche, Hoofdstraat 94a, tel. (05952) 285, a research establishment where seals are studied with a view to preserving the remaining species and discovering the causes of their rapidly depleted numbers. The organization welcomes visitors—open daily, free—but it also welcomes contributions to help with their work.

Also in town is a mustard museum/restaurant, "Museum-Abraham's Mos-terdmakerij Restaurant," Molenstraat 5, tel. (05959) 1600 or (050) 122235. For

Fl. 25, you can have a special arrangement which includes a tour, coffee, slide show, lunch and a pot of Abraham's mustard. The "museum" is open 10am-10pm. If you haven't the time for the whole day outing, you are welcome to watch a demonstration of mustard-making and have lunch.

WARFFUM

An important agricultural area, "Het Hoogeland"

GETTING THERE: North of Groningen on N363, about halfway between Verhildersum and Menkemaborg Castles.
INFORMATION: VVV Warffum, Noorderstraat 7, tel. (05950) 2214.

Warffum has a Protestant Church with a tower dating from 1638 and two clocks, one from 1686 and the other from 1701. Also of interest is the collection of stone charters. For information, contact Mrs. de Groot, Kerkstraat 1.

This area is a prosperous clay-area in the important agricultural district, "Het Hoogeland." There are fine farm houses to be seen in this unusually picturesque region such as the "Groot Zeewijk" and "sibbe Kerkhoje."

"Het Hoogeland Open Air Museum," Schoolstraat 2, tel. (05950) 2233; open, April-Oct., Tues.-Sat., 10am-5pm, Sun., 1-5pm; Nov.-March, only by appointment, is of special interest. To preserve the style of living of the local rural population, this open-air museum has restored and furnished some really interesting buildings. There's a Jewish butcher's shop; an almshouse for widowed women (brought from Groningen); a double house ca. 1850 with one furnished as a sailor's home; a double-fronted house (1909) furnished in Jugenstil (art nouveau); a building ca. 1887 with two period rooms, a Biedermeier room and a King Willem III room; a barn for stray cattle (1850), a local pub and grocery ca. 1850, and a day-laborer's cottage ca. 1800.

You can get coffee, tea, soup and pancakes at a cozy 19th-century pub "bie Koboa" or at the Schutstal (The Barn) . . . reserve.

STAYING OVER: A recommended campsite in the area is "De Breede," De Breede 5, tel. (05950) 4642 . . . swimming, midget golf and two tennis courts.

YEARLY EVENT: In late June, there's an international folkloric dance festival called "Op Roakeldais" (in Frisian dialect), which means something like "Hoping for the Best," or "For Good Luck." An art and antique market is also part of the festivities.

UITHUIZEN

A lovely manor house

GETTING THERE: North of Groningen on N363.
INFORMATION: Town Hall, tel. (05993) 1555, or VVV Groningen.

The "pièce de resistance" here is Menkemaborg Castle which is described below. Also look for the 13th-century church "with a tower from the 12th century"

Inside, there are some unusual pieces of furniture, a pulpit dating from 1711, a gentleman's bench from 1702, and an organ from 1701.

An inexpensive rustic stone vacation house with accommodations for 5 people is available for a weekend or week's stay. The "Vacatiehuisje Uithuizen" is only 100 meters from the yacht and canoe port. For details, contact the Groningen VVV and mention their "Vakantiereisgids", Code X1410... Available April 1-Octrober 31.

YEARLY EVENTS: In August, there's a fair and in Sept., a celebration, "Groninger Week."

Menkemaborg Castle

LOCATION: Menkemaweg 2, Uithuizen. The castle is on the southeast side of town. There are small signs pointing the way.
INFORMATION: The castle telephone is (05953) 1970; restaurant, tel. (05953) 1858. There's a good English-language flyer.
HOURS: April-Sept., 10am-noon and 1-5pm; Oct-March, Tues.-Sun., 10am-noon and 1-4pm. Closed January.
■ *Of interest to all castle-lovers.*

Menkemaborg Castle is considered to be one of the finest restored castles of the Province. The original structure was a simple square affair dating from the 14th century. The first owners were not particularly well known and it wasn't until the house was enlarged in 1700 that it took on its present shape. By the end of the 18th century it had been modernized into an elegant fortified manor house.

It is filled with authentic furniture, paintings, porcelain, glass, silver, heavily carved oak fireplace mantels, an old and picturesque kitchen, and more, representing the 17th and 18th Centuries.

Happily, you may ask for an English-language information sheet to help guide you—you don't have to follow in sequence either. In apartment 4, there's a huge 18th-century four-poster bed. King William III of the Netherlands slept here. Also note the comfortable toilet cupboards—a vast improvement on the "outhouse" if not yet up to modern standards. The two round towers in the front garden making a corner with the moat were also "toilet facilities."

Apartment 5 is the old kitchen which is still cozy and inviting. The thick walls and low ceiling with heavy beams are an indication this is the remainder of the original house. Note the two pumps. One is for clean drinking water from the cistern; the other, for water from the moat to clean with.

The garden has been planted according to an 18th-century plan found in the house. If you're here during the rose-blooming season, you will enjoy the famous rose bowers as well as the garden maze.

EATING OUT: The architecturally interesting tea room was the former storehouse. On nice days, light lunches and drinks are offered out of doors next to the moat where one can enjoy the castle's lovely exterior and hear the noisy honking of geese and ducks. Moderately priced—pannekoeken (pancakes) a speciality.

DELFZIJL
Largest port in the North

*GETTING THERE: On the Eems estuary. From Groningen, take N41
northeast to Delfzijl.*
INFORMATION: VVV Delfzijl, Waterstraat 6, tel. (05960) 18104.

Heavily fortified in the 16th century, now Delfzijl has a look more in keeping
with its today-image as the largest port in the North with a harbor that has been
expanded six times, most recently in 1973. The estuary is 12 miles long and five
miles wide, allowing for the passage of large ships for the important shipbuilding
and shipping trade. A walk along the sea wall provides a fine view (on clear days
of course) of the German coast and of the shipping activities on the Eems.

The salt and soda production is now surpassed by chemical production,
agricultural products, an aluminum foundry, and other industrial goods, as well
as the aforementioned shipbuilding and shipping trade in bringing increased
prosperity to its citizens.

But life in Delfzijl isn't all work. There is an extensive recreation park along
the sea wall which includes a Marine Aquarium, a collection of some 4,000
different kinds of shells, a Geological Museum, swimming pool, exhibition hall,
youth hostel, campsite and open-air theater. There is also a fine yachting harbor
as well as an ocean terminal for big ships.

Georges Simenon, the well-known French author of mystery books (Maigret
series), spent some time here in 1929 and his statue by Pieter d'Hont is at the
port to greet all comers.

STAYING OVER: The Eemshotel, Zeebadweg 2, tel. (05960) 12636, sits on
piles with the swish-swish of water to lull you to sleep . . . special weekend rates.

YEARLY EVENTS: At the end of May, Delfzijl is host to a Neptune Festival
with a fair and international deep-sea sailing races; in October, the Autumn Fair
is held.

APPINGEDAM
An old sea harbor on the Damsterdiep Canal

*GETTING THERE: From Groningen, N41 going east; from Delfzijl,
N41 going west.*
*INFORMATION: VVV Appingedam, Blakenstein 2, tel. (05960)
22072.*

One of the group of VVV-designated "Beautiful Old Towns and Buildings,"
Appingedam is worth a stop. Situated on the Damsterdiep Canal between
Groningen and the Eems River, it boasted that it was the most important sea
harbor in this area until the sluice gates were built in Delfzijl in 1317. The town
received its rights in 1327.

This medieval seaport town has been greatly restored in the past years. In

particular, look for the picturesque little kitchens overhanging the Damsterdiep; the imposing Nicolai Church (1225), with a Hinsz organ (1500), a vault painted with frescoes, carved pews and a beautifully carved pulpit, old gravestones and sarcophagus; and the Town Hall with a fine antique period facade dating from 1630 which was originally the house of the Marksmen's Guild. There is a small art history museum in town, Gem. Kunsthistorisch Museum, Blakenstein 2-4, tel. 24488; open, Tues.-Thurs., 1-5pm, Fri., 1-5pm and 7-9pm, Sat.-Sun., 2-5pm.

Appingedam will be a happy stop for the children, giving them a break from adult-type sightseeing. In town there's an open-air pool, bowling alley and pony park. In addition, Ekenstein Park is a fine recreational center with a children's farm, playground, fishing ponds, deer park, aviaries, and an excellent hotel on the grounds in an elegant manor house, "Ekenstein."

STAYING OVER: As indicated above, the Hotel Ekenstein, Alberdaweg 70, tel. (05960) 28528, offers something special for the whole family. There is rest and luxury in its peaceful surroundings and elegantly appointed lounge with a roaring fire on cool evenings. There are special weekend arrangements and excursions such as sailing charters or a week on the Wadden Sea aboard a historic Frisian barge.

YEARLY EVENTS: Appingedam has a number of events during the year including festivals and markets. In June, there's the "Night of Appingedam"; in Sept., a parade with papier-mâché figures, and in Oct., a folk craft market.

COMMERCIAL TOURS: Boat trips can be arranged with 't Proat Hoeske, Wijkstraat 22/24, tel. 26039, daily, April-Oct.; reservations necessary.

Check with the Groningen VVV for special tours made through the Goeie Reisbureau, including a week on the Wadden Sea, see above.

255

IN THE NEIGHBORHOOD OF APPINGEDAM:

At **Nieuwolda,** south of Delfzijl and Appingedam on N362, there's a Baby Carriage Museum (Kinderwagen Museum), Hoofdweg West 25, tel. (05964) 1941; open, Wed., Sat., and Sun., 1-6pm during the summer months. Located in an 18th-century farmhouse, this private collection of approximately 60 old and antique baby carriages of the 19th and 20th centuries which have been beautifully restored, is worth a stop.

Nieuweschans, on country roads to the border with Germany (take N7 east from Groningen), is an old fortress town. The fortress is no longer but the Voorstraat in the town center has a parade-ground and fortress museum to visit. Of special interest is the new Spa center, Kuurcentrum Nieuweschans. Taking the waters is old stuff in more southerly countries of Europe but this was the first of its kind in the Netherlands, a competitor having recently opened in Valkenburg, Limburg. The water pumped up from the earth's depths has healing minerals such as iodine and iron. This, plus its high salinity, is extremely beneficial to mind and body. The outdoor pool is kept at a temperature of 36°C and can be entered from indoors or outdoors. There are massages, curative coiffure, manicure and hair treatments and a Thalasso-therapy center. The algae used come from the coast of Brittany. To find out all about it, contact "Kuurcentrum Nieuweschans," P.O. Box 44, 9693 ZG Nieuweschans, or telephone (05972) 2444 . . . the spa is closed Aug. 25-Sept. 2.

At **Heiligerlee,** (A7, N7 going east from Groningen, west of Nieuweschans on N7 about 12 km and south of Nieuwolda on N362) an unusual museum might be of interest. The Bell Casting Museum (Klokkengieterij Museum), Provincialeweg 46, tel. (05970) 211799; open, Tues.-Sat., 10am-5pm, Sun. and holidays, 1-5pm. The Van Bergen Foundry which closed its doors in 1980 was famous over many years for its traditional method of casting bells and excellent workmanship. They cast church bells, carillons, ships' items, and had markets in the U.S., Japan, and Brazil as well as the Netherlands. They even became known for the manufacture of brass fire hose nozzles.

The museum's purpose is to present a clear picture of the creation of the bell from the beginning (liquifying bronze or copper) to the final result (tone quality). Demonstrations show the casting of small bells, then carillon concerts are held in the garden so visitors may appreciate the sound. There are also changing exhibitions dealing with local industrial or regional history, modern production techniques, and contemporary local art. A coffeeshop is available.

FRAEYLEMABORG CASTLE

GETTING THERE: From Groningen, autoroute A7 east to the Hoogezand intersection, then north toward Slochteren. Drive through the village in the direction of Schildwolde. The castle is near the intersection toward Noordbroek.

INFORMATION: The castle, tel. (05982) 1568, the Restaurant, "De Boerderij," tel. 1940, or VVV Groningen.

HOURS: Open March-Dec., Tues.-Sun., 10am, noon, 1pm and 4pm.

Closed Jan. and Feb. In summer, 1-5pm.
■ *Of interest to most children.*

More an elegant country manor than a "castle," Fraeylemaborg was known for many years by the name, "Fraelema." The wings date from the second half of the 16th century and it was restored in 1846. Johan de Witt held a conference here in the 17th century, with Jan Oesebrant Regers. At the end of the 17th century, William III was the guest of Hendrik Piccardt, head of operations for the Ommelanden States. There are many portraits and other mementos of the Netherlands Royal Family as well as changing exhibitions from time to time.

Notice the elaborate doll's house filled to the nines with miniature silver items used in a very rich household, including a tiny tea/coffee service, child's bed, upright piano, pink brocaded walls and matching carpet.

If time permits, take a walk through the extensive park of about 60 acres.

BOURTANGE

A 300-year-old fortified town

GETTING THERE: From Groningen, N7 east to N366 as far as Stadskanaal, then follow provincial roads east toward the German border. From Assen (Drenthe), local roads to Stadskanaal then Onstwedde, Vlagtwedde to Bourtange.

INFORMATION: VVV Bourtange, Marktplein 4a, tel. (05993) 54600 or contact Groningen VVV. Note: During a special week usually the end of July, beginning of August, local people dress in costumes and special events are held.

HOURS: April-Nov., Tues.-Fri., 10am-noon and 1-5pm, Sat.-Mon., 1-5pm.

■ *Of interest to the whole family.*

Three hundred years ago, this small town in southeast Groningen was one of the most important fortified towns in the northern part of the Netherlands. The original fortification, in the shape of a five-pointed star, was built during the Eighty Years' War by the Frisian landholder, Count Lodewijk of Nassau. In 1672, the bishop of Münster, a Spaniard named Verdugo, attempted to capture Bourtange but was unsuccessful. As a matter of fact, the fort was never captured due mainly to its location on a sandy ridge in the middle of the greater Bourtanger marsh. However, these marshes slowly began to dry up, and by 1851, this fact, as well as the development of new methods of warfare, lost Bourtange its value as a fortress and it was dismantled.

When you visit Bourtange, you will arrive via the Frisian or Münster gates, both of which will lead you to the picturesque market place with its fourteen ancient lime trees. Also on the market place, notice two partially restored officers' homes dating from the 17th century. From the market square, ten little streets radiate out to the walls and bastions, and are linked to each other forming a perfect radial street pattern. The former pentagon is now completely restored. Of the reconstructed buildings of interest, you can see a number of

257

barracks, an old rectory, the little school and the school teacher's home—all in the style of the 17th Century. 's Landhuis is a beautiful large building which has now become a picturesque restaurant. Also of interest are the wooden draw-bridges, wells, guard houses and many old cannons.

Shutterbugs might like to find out the precise dates for Bourtange's special celebration week. Bourtange is a long drive from the Randstad; however, it can easily be incorporated into a general visit of Groningen. There are a number of hotels in Groningen city, Assen and Emmen, as well as the Holland Hotel Homan, Dorpsstraat 8, tel. (05992) 2206, in the small town of Sellingen just south of Bourtange.

TER APEL

Site of a medieval cloister

GETTING THERE: Ter Apel is just on the German border, about 18 km northeast of Emmen. Coming from Groningen, there is a choice of highways, including the very scenic route south of Wins-choten through the small towns of Wedde, Vlagtwedde, Jipsing-huizen, Sellingen, etc. Coming from Emmen, drive north taking either the road toward Nieuw Weerdinge or the road past Em-mer-Compascuum. If you want to see the old Terp village at Barger-Compascuum, you would follow the latter route.

INFORMATION: Lectuurhal, Hoofdstraat 42, tel. (05995) 3559, or VVV Groningen, tel. (050) 139700.

Ter Apel is the site of a medieval Dutch Cloister. First established in 1260, it was Catholic until 1603. Reconstruction was undertaken from 1931-33, and great care was taken to clean the original bricks by hand and replace them in their proper spots. As you walk around the cloisters, you will notice depressed areas in the brick walls where memorial stones were formerly imbedded.

The guide will suggest you walk along the cloisters (turn left upon entering). The first two rooms are a former meeting room and a reception room containing remnants of original stained-glass windows and other items of interest.

At the far end, you can enter left and find yourself in a large open room with high ceilings. Notice the faint wall decorations and the heavily carved stalls. There is an interesting collection box with hinged top and a great iron padlock to protect its riches. This room is divided about halfway by a barrier through which you can see where services are held today.

Retracing your steps, you can see the former dining room with its black, green and yellow patterned tiles. The adjoining room goes to the cellar and the kitchen is next. If the kids are getting bored, let them hurry along to the cellar where there are some huge stone tombstones.

Ter Apel can make a convenient day-tour including Emmen, Barger-Compas-cuum, the hunebedden, etc. Or, you start from Groningen and make the swing clockwise, taking the most scenic provincial roads south of Winschoten and through Wedde, Ellersinghuizen, etc.

CHAPTER 10

THE PROVINCE OF DRENTHE

This province "rounds out" the northeast of the Netherlands. Just south of Groningen and north of Overijssel, the major autoroutes north/south are A28, N371 and N34. Drenthe is a poorer province than either of its northern neighbors—Friesland and Groningen, which were settled by the same tribal group around 300 B.C.

For years the region was used as an object of barter by the Romans, followed by the Frankish kings and German emperors. For five centuries the Bishop of Utrecht held control over this territory. Even at the time of Confederation, Drenthe had no representation, until finally it became an official province in 1815. The discovery of oil and greater industrialization have had a most salubrious effect on the economy but, happily, it hasn't changed the rural, peaceful character of the province.

This is the region of the hunebedden (Megalithic tombs—dolmens); groups of large boulders carried to this area by ice-age glaciers thousands of years ago and then buried by the sand until early inhabitants unearthed them and used them for ready-made tombstones. It is possible these were the "Funnel Beaker" people, so-named because of the shape of the pots found in graves of their people. Out of fifty-three megalithic tombs found to date, fifty-two of them are in Drenthe. (Remember, Neanderthal Man was found in this area.) A mystery is always intriguing and mystery this is . . . All the tombs

INFORMATION: VVV Assen, tel. (05920) 14324.

259

lie in a south-west direction and can be entered from the south. The largest tomb is found not far from the small town of Borger. It has 47 stones and is 20 yards long; the heaviest stones weighing some 20 tons. 't Aole Compas in Barger-Compascuum (east of Emmen), is an open-air museum explaining the traditional commercial digging of peat for use as fuel. A fascinating stop, especially when the crafts demonstrations are given. See below for details.

Foreign travelers may be puzzled about signs indicating the "Bartje" route. Bartje is the main character in a novel by Anne de Vries which became nationally famous when the book was made into a TV series. Bartje is one of many children of a very poor and simple assistant farmer in the 1900s. The story deals with the way of life, the trials and tribulations, the folklore and the pleasures of this family. The VVV's in Drenthe have a pamphlet for sale (only in Dutch) giving the Bartje route.

There are many recreation centers—some shared jointly with Groningen in the lake regions of the Paterswolde, Zuidlaren, Midwolde and Noordlaren. The landscape is varied with clumps of dense forest land interspersed through an endless horizon of fields, heaths and grazing land.

Perhaps because Drenthe has not been a center of international trade and commerce, the old traditions have remained closer to the surface. As a result, folklore and folkloric events can be found in many parts of Drenthe, especially during the summer months.

YEARLY EVENTS: Drenthe's yearly events that "travel" from town-to-town as well as those occurring in one place, include: April, spring walking tours; May-June, sheepshearing in Westerbork, Exloo and Balloo; the TT international Motorcycle races in Assen and the bee-market in Eelde in June; the 4-day biking event with Assen, Emmen, Hoogeveen and Meppel as stops, and the trades and crafts festival in Exloo in July; July-Aug., the Shakespeare performances in Diever, also country-wedding performance in Borger, and special Thurs. events in Meppel and Hoogeveen. Hoogeveen's "Pulledagen" in summer can be traced to former times when on this day, farmers received payment for their milk production and went into town on a shopping spree. "Pulle" means milk churn. Today there are street fairs, etc. In Aug., there's a harvest festival in Dwingeloo and a pancake race is held in Gasselte. The flower processions and jazz festivals in Eelde and Assen occur in September. The largest horse market in Western Europe is held in Oct. (third Tues.) at Zuidlaren and the traditional geese market takes place in Coevorden in November.

ASSEN

Provincial capital and land of the Hunebedden

GETTING THERE: From Amsterdam, take autoroute A1 east to Amersfoort then north on A28. From the south, A50 to Arnhem and then north.
INFORMATION: VVV Assen, Brink 42, tel. (05920) 14324.

Assen's earliest history has been estimated as beginning about 3000 B.C. according to data obtained from the ancient burial chambers. The Saxons overran the land in the 5th and 6th Centuries. By 1024, the area came under the jurisdiction of the Bishops of the See of Utrecht and was ruled by a governor from the House of Coevorden.

The main street in town is the "Brink" which means an open area used as a meeting place in Old Dutch. The Provincial Hall (Provinciehuis), originally the chapel and part of the choir of the Cistercian Convent, "Maria in Campis" (13th century), was used as the City Hall until the latter was relocated to House Tetrode, a historic building on the Brink. Behind the City Hall, there's a statue of Bartje—a little boy who is the hero in one of Anne De Vries' novels.

The local woods, the Asser Stadsbos, has a sports park, tennis, swimming pool and paths for strolling. Another family-attention-getter is the young people's recreation park, "De Gouverneurstuin," Rode Heklaan 1, corner of Witterstraat and the municipal forest, the Asserbos. For general information, tel. 14500; midget golf, tel. 55141. Assen also has an indoor/outdoor ice skating rink, open mid-Oct. to mid-March.

The Auto Museum, Rode Heklaan 3, tel. 10563 is open March-Dec., daily, 10am-6pm, June-Aug., until 9pm, Jan.-Feb., Sat. and Sun., 10am-6pm and by appointment . . . antique cars and motorbikes.

The Youth Traffic Park (Verkeerspark Assen), is within easy reach via the exit Assen-Zuid from A28 (Zwolle-Groningen) and from the direction of Veendam via N33; for information, tel. (05920) 55700 or FAX (05920) 11192. The largest and most modern traffic park in Europe covering over 80,000 square meters, the park has midget-sized electrified vehicles (racing cars, autos, motorcycles) in which the kids can learn the traffic rules on a special circuit. Many of the instructors speak English and if arrangements are made ahead, English-speaking groups will be run through the course . . . good for school groups. In addition, the park has something for everyone; you can spend the day enjoying the playground, a labyrinth, several walking routes, a pond with radio-controlled boats, etc. It's possible to tour the park by boat or by train, and when hunger strikes, there's a restaurant.

EATING OUT: There's a quick lunch counter at the Nieuwe Brink Hotel, and various places to eat in town and in the recreation park and the Asserbos.

STAYING OVER: Check with the VVV for their list of hotels; the Witterzomer camping facilities at Witterzomer 7, tel. 55688, have been recommended . . . 75 hectares of space with playground and pool.

261

Provincial Museum of Drenthe (Drents Museum)

LOCATION: Brink 1 and 5. Follow signs to the VVV. There is park-
ing near the museum.
INFORMATION: Museum tel. (05920) 12741 or VVV, 14324.
HOURS: Tues.-Sat., 9:30am-5pm, Sat. and Sun., 1-5pm. Also open
Mon. in July and August.
■ *Of interest to children from six years.*

The museum building itself is fascinating with its highly ornamented walls, ceilings and fine mosaic work. The contents are rather serious dealing with such matters as the geology of the area; prehistoric remains which tell about the early residents; the oldest canoe in the world from Pesse (6800 B.C.); various exhibitions, prints, silver, old coins, pottery, etc. There is a slide show but only in Dutch.

Ontvangershuis (House Overçingel): This lovely 18th-century residence is beautifully maintained and furnished. The oldest part of the house dates from the middle ages but a serious fire in 1676 caused considerable damage and the house was rebuilt in 1693.

Some of the highlights are the blue room, paneled in romantic 18th-century scenes; the Yellow Room (reception/living room); the Red Room (bedroom) done in Louis XIV style, and a collection of early toys.

IN THE NEIGHBORHOOD OF ASSEN:
At Balloerkuil, not far from town, provincial meetings were once held in the open air. Legal cases were tried and judgments made here until 1602.

Veenhuizen west of Assen, has a museum dealing with the prison system; also horse markets several times a year.

Norg (northwest of town), Vries (off N372 north), Anloo (northeast off N34) and Roden (north, outside Leek) are all charming and authentic Drents villages with a village green, medieval church, and typical Saxon farmhouses. Norg also has two windmills; Vries has a small bell foundry museum in the bell tower of the 12th-century Roman church; and Anloo has the oldest church in Drenthe . . . Romanesque with 11th-century nave, 13th-century choir and Gothic Chapel (open by appointment). There are hunebedden in the neighborhood. There are also hunebedden at Loon (northeast city's edge) and Balloo (east).

■ **Roden: Child's World Museum** (Museum Kinderwereld), Brink 31 (the Pietershuys) . . . follow directions for the VVV; it's in the same building; tel. (05920) 18851; hours, April-Aug., Mon.-Sat., 10am-noon and 2-5pm, Sun., 2-5pm; Sept.-March, closed Mondays. This museum is of interest to all children! The collection includes old children's games, dolls and doll houses, miniature cooking stoves, tin soldiers, trains, children's books and so on. A natural sightseeing combination is to visit Nienoord Castle, the carriage museum, at Leek (only 7-8 km northwest).

262

ZUIDLAREN

A Hondsrug or ridge village

GETTING THERE: Zuidlaren is about 15 km northeast of Assen just off A28.
INFORMATION: VVV Zuidlaren (summer), Stationsweg 15E, tel. (05905) 2333 or VVV Assen.

The word "Hondsrug" refers to a ridge of hills between Groningen and Emmen where many prehistoric graves and artifacts have been found. Zuidlaren is at the northern end with a series of towns with Hunebedden along N34 such as Anloo, Gieten, Drouwen, Borger, Exloo, Odoorn, etc. The dolmens lie on the slopes of the Hondsrug, a long loam-bank dating back from the last ice age.

The "Laarwoud Estate," Laarweg 6, is a 17th-century moated house which now serves as the Town Hall. In addition, the 13th-century Dutch Reformed Church can be visited from Monday through Friday; key at Kerkbrink 8, just across the road.

■ **"De Sprookjeshof"** a fairy-tale garden with recreation park for the small visitor, at Groningerstraat 10, would be worth the long drive. Open Good Friday to Oct., 9am-6pm. A children's farm, recreation park, and boat tours on the nearby Zuidlaardermeer (Zuidlaren Lake) are possible end of May to mid-Sept., 9am-6pm. For information, call (05905) 1212.

STAYING OVER: This area has a wide choice of campsites and holiday cottages. A suggested lakeside camp is Bloemert, de Bloemert 1, 9475 TG Midlaren, tel. 1555.

YEARLY EVENTS: A household goods market in March; the largest horse fair in Western Europe in October; an international Horse Show in December; and the Zuidlaarder Lake Week, in the middle of December.

IN THE NEIGHBORHOOD OF ZUIDLAREN:
At Midlaren, there are two giants' graves.

EMMEN

Peatfields, grave mounds and woods

GETTING THERE: From Assen take N34 south about 27 km; from the south, take N34 north from Coevorden.
INFORMATION: VVV Emmen, Raadhuisplein 2, tel. (05910) 13000.

Surrounded by huge peatfields, prehistoric graves, gravemounds, "win" fields, and lovely wooded areas, with or without children, this is a fascinating folkloric area to discover.

The small museum, Oudheidkamer de Hondsrug, Marktplein 17, tel. 41709 is worth a quick stop to view its historic items and learn about the area. Upstairs, there's a radio museum, Radiotron, with a collection of early radios, TV sets, cameras, record players, telephones, etc.

■ **The Noorder Zoo** (Northern Zoo), Hoofdstraat 18, tel. (05910) 18800, is one of the most attractive and modern in Europe. Hours vary slightly according to season but generally in summer, open 9am-6pm; in winter, 9am-4:30pm. Admission, Adults, Fl. 11.00, children to 13 years, Fl. 9.00; dogs NOT allowed. Visitors are right in the midst of the animals' natural habitats with as few railings or cages as possible. You can imagine yourself in the African savannah surrounded by antelopes, zebras, gnus, giraffes, rhinos and ostriches. There are 200 exotic birds, a butterfly house, an African House with tropical atmosphere, sea lions in an immense pool, a natural history museum, folk art museum and "Biochron" where one can take a trip back in time and come face-to-face with fossils showing the evolution of animals. The little ones will enjoy the kinderboerderij where they can touch the small animals.

IN THE NEIGHBORHOOD OF EMMEN:

If you're fascinated by prehistoric matters, there are at least a half dozen hunebedden including the "Long Grave" (two big stones marking a grave) in the immediate vicinity. Originally these were probably covered with smaller stones and peat to form shelters. Look for the Valtherbos (woods) near the Westenesserbosje.

At Exloo (N34 north) there are hunebedden but also lots of sheep with a sheep fold, park and sheep market; also a museum farm.

Ter Apel (Groningen), just a little further north is worth the detour to see the magnificent Dutch Cloister . . see "Groningen" for description. There is a fine restaurant across from the church. To eat under the huge old trees while admiring the impressive architecture of this outstanding Middle Ages structure, is most relaxing.

Don't miss Barger-Compascuum (described below), a few kilometers east of Emmen. The Fen museum village, 't Aole Compas is well worth a visit.

Coevorden, about 12 km south of Emmen, is one of the oldest towns in

Drenthe. Primarily industrial, it retains some of its fortress-like qualities in the few remaining city walls and bastions. Drents Vest, the local museum, is open Mon.-Fri., 10am-12:30pm and 1:30-5pm, Sat. and Sun., 2-5pm.

On the way to Orvelte (see below), take the national road north toward Schoonoord, stop along the way to see a restored hunebed, the "Papeloze Kerk."

■ **Schoonoord's** open-air museum, De Zeven Marken, tells the story of how life was in southeast Drenthe a century ago (in some places even until 1948). There's an old country inn, a toll house peatery, miniature lime kiln, turf huts with sheds, sheep's cage with sheep, Saxon farm, old schoolhouse and carpentry shop from 1900, among other interesting things. The legend of two "giants" is explained in the cave of Ellert and Brammert. Demonstrations of crafts are held during the week starting at 10am. There's a playground and an old Drenthe Inn where you can have lunch, tel. (05918) 1579.

BARGER-COMPASCUUM

Site of the recreated village, Veenmuseum, "'t Aole Compas"

GETTING THERE: Barger-Compascuum is very close to the German border and only a few kilometers from Emmen; follow small roads using large-scale map to the village Barger-Compascuum. From Zwolle and points south, national road through Ommen, Hardenberg, Coevorden to museum, at 4 Berkenrode.
INFORMATION: 't Aole Compas, Berkenrode 4, Barger-Compascuum, tel. (05913) 49631; VVV Emmen, Raadhuisplein 2, tel. (05910) 13000.
HOURS: March 15-Oct., daily, 9am-5pm; summer months, 6pm.
ADMISSION: Adults, Fl. 10; children to 12 years, Fl. 9.
■ *Of interest to the whole family.*

This little excursion off the beaten path is highly recommended, adding another piece in the puzzle of the history of this region. The hunebedden are all around this reconstructed village which shows how the peat dwellers lived and worked. Demonstrations include the actual digging of peat; the baking of yummy bread filled with raisins, some plain and some sweetened with cinnamon and sugar; and the making of wooden shoes. Seeing the many loaves of different shaped breads being put into the outdoor oven paddle-by-paddleful will whet your appetite, making it impossible to resist buying one or more warm scented fresh loaves.

Start your tour by visiting the information center. If you have squirmy little ones, there is a small playground to the right of the entrance.

The displays in the Information Center describe the manner of digging peat in this area and how the farmers and their families lived and worked. Also, there are photographs explaining local customs, as well as a display of tools for collecting the peat. Look for the most unusual shoes made especially to cope with the soggy, wet ground—there are even special hoof-pads for the horses so they won't get bogged down in the mushy earth. You'll feel the resilience of the ground when you walk where the demonstration of peat cutting is being given.

Follow the paths as they take you to visit the tiniest, most simple one-room house for family and animals made out of peat blocks with steep thatched roof almost touching the ground, to a prosperous-looking several-roomed brick house. Upon entering even the simplest structure, one is surprised how pleasant it is because of the windows which allow quite a bit of light to enter.

Animals were kept in part of the house–the poorest houses only had a little area "reserved" for the animals; more prosperous houses had well-defined and somewhat separated areas for the family and the animals.

A large house made of brick may have been the local beer parlor. Also, there's the "Korenmolen" (grain mill) dated 1880.

Then, there's the schoolmaster's two-room house and barn. It has a stove in each room and is wallpapered. Next door is the school with space for about 15 children. "De Boete" is the former store, now filled with cast-off old furniture being stored.

There are good toilet facilities and a nice place to have a simple bite to eat.

ORVELTE

A restored Saxon village

GETTING THERE: About twenty kilometers south of Assen, 25 kilo-
meters west of Emmen, just north of east-west highway N37.
INFORMATION: Stichting Orvelte, Dorpsstraat 3, tel. (05934) 335.
HOURS: Mon.-Fri., 9:30am-5pm; Sat., Sun. and holidays, 11am-
5pm.
NOTE: There is plenty of parking outside the village; only residents
may drive in. A small contribution is requested (a "toll" just as in
olden days) which goes to help maintain the village.

■ *Of interest to everyone—a haven of rest but lots of activity too.*

The beautifully restored Saxon village of Orvelte with its thatched-roof farm-houses and barns, isn't simply an open-air museum. People also live and work here. Before it deteriorated to the point of no return, a foundation was established to preserve the village. In 1974, the year of the "European Monuments," Orvelte received international attention as a fine example of rural architecture. A surveyor's map from about 1830 was used as a guide in the reconstruction. The folder in Dutch includes a map and describes each building along your route; there's a flyer in English with corresponding numbers so you shouldn't miss a thing.

Some demonstrations usually given include the old method of threshing wheat, rope-making, lace-making, making of beehives, and ancient farming methods. During the holidays, special courses are offered in spinning, candle-making, caning chairs, dough doll-making, etc.

A couple of children-oriented pleasures include pony rides or a trip on a "huifkar," a covered wagon used formerly on farms, and a visit to the old Fire Brigade house with antique fire extinguishing equipment.

This is a quick view of what is available to the visitor of Orvelte. There are

266

also lovely organized walks with explanations by a Dutch guide or one can do the same route by covered wagon.

EATING OUT: "De Schapendrift" restaurant offers everything from a cup of coffee to a three-course meal. How about trying the herb drink (kruiden borrel)? There's also a special berry gin or brandy with raisins!

STAYING OVER: Camping is available in the area and there are three hotels in the neighboring village of Westerbork.

IN THE NEIGHBORHOOD OF ORVELTE:
Westerbork was a former transition camp for Jews in WW II. A Remembrance Center is now in nearby Hooghalen.

MEPPEL

The gateway to Drenthe

GETTING THERE: On the border between Drenthe and Overijssel.
From the Randstad, take A28 past Zwolle to Meppel; from Assen,
N371 south or from Groningen, A28 south.
INFORMATION: VVV Meppel, Kleine Oever 11, tel. (05220) 52888.

Meppel is the largest town in the southwest corner of Drenthe, situated close by an extensive group of lakes in the neighboring province of Overijssel: the Bovenwijde where Giethoorn is located, the Beulakerwijde and the Beltenwijde, just to name the largest. In addition there are six streams which converge at Meppel, providing extensive opportunities for watersports activities. The surrounding countryside has a special quality which comes when the sky and the land seem to blend, tied together by by shimmering lakes and marshlands, tempting the visitor to leave the automobile in favor of a bicycle or a canoe to explore at human-pace the beauties of the land.

Those six waterways have also contributed to Meppel's reputation as the Rotterdam of Drenthe. This crossroads of waterways has made the town a center of inland navigation over thye years, until today it is a prosperous and busy industrial, ship-building, shipping and agricultural center.

Just south of Meppel are the villages of Staphorst and Rouveen, known for their somewhat rigid traditional ways. Hoogeveen, to the east, is another straight-laced Protestant town. It is not surprising that Mepple's development as a work-ethic-oriented town has contributed to its prosperity, and that the local folks often wear their traditional dress.

The Reformed Church steeple dates from the 15th century. The Grafisch Museum, Kleine Oever 11, focuses on the history of printing and book-making: open, Mon. - Sat., 10 am-4:30pm.

STAYING OVER: Just off A28, east of Meppel, you have the chance to stay at a real castle-hotel, "Havesathe de Havixhorst" where you will be "pampered like a prince." For two centuries, the building was the home of the noble family De Vos van Steenwijk. It has recently been renovated into a 4-star hotel; for

267

info, Schiphorsterweg 34-36, 7957 NV De Wijk (Dr.), tel. (05224) 1487. There are also two moderate hotels in town; the Hotel Grupen, Parallelweg 25, tel. (05220) 51080 and the Hotel Kwint, Kerkplein 15-16, tel. (05220) 52410.

YEARLY EVENTS: Shutter-bugs shouldn't miss Meppel Day (mid-July to mid-Aug.); Thurs., 8am-6pm with folks dancing to a village band in traditional dress.

IN THE NEIGHBORHOOD OF MEPPEL:

■ **Giethoorn** (Overijssel) about 8 km west on the Beulakerwijde (lake) is a not-to-be-missed experience, especially if you're this near. This is truly the Venice of the north with charming houses perched on their own little terps around which waterways wind to get from one part of the village to another. The gardens are little jewels and when the area is illuminated during the summer months, a tour by boat is a real treat.

Havelte, about 8 km north on N371 has many beautiful traditional farmhouses as well as some interesting burial mounds. A historic estate, "Overçingel" is near here, but not open to the public.

CHAPTER 11

THE PROVINCE OF OVERIJSSEL

This province lies between the German border and the IJsselmeer, and while extensive in area, hasn't been "discovered" by most foreign tourists. Good enough reason to seek it out for your own explorations. This area was under the control of the Bishops of Utrecht until 1527. In 1579, at the signing of the Union of Utrecht, Overijssel became one of the seven United Provinces. When Flevoland became a full-blown province in 1987, the Noordoostpolder was no longer a part of Overijssel.

In the northwest corner (West Overijssel) of the province are intriguing villages well steeped in rigid religious practices (Staphorst and Rouveen) as well as lake areas with ancient peat-villages (Giethoorn) still utilizing some of the old methods of living and commerce. A typical continental climate and landscape with lovely woods, ancient towns and interesting castles/manor houses, are found in the east which extends to the German border. On our tour, we will start with the provincial capital Zwolle, and then describe the western, northern, eastern and southern sections of the province.

The center section of Overijssel is the "Salland," a lesser-known region, unspoilt and peaceful but with comfortable hotels, campsites or bungalows for those who want to spend time fishing, canoeing, swimming, visiting old villages, or taking the children to see Slagharen Pony Park and the Hel-

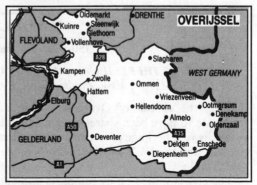

INFORMATION: VVV, Almelo tel. (05490) 18767.

lendoorn Adventure Park. On the border with Gelderland, Deventer is the biggest town in the Salland.

"Twente" is the eastern section of Overijssel, a very old land, until 200 years ago mostly marsh land. Accessibility to the area was much better from the German side which explains German influence in the language and architecture. Once there were 80 watermills, but only 8 remain (12th-15th centuries). Around the three large towns of Enschede, Hengelo and Almelo there are numerous hamlets with a country church, a cafe, few shops and houses, some of which will be discussed below.

Overijssel is proud of its network of waterways—270 km—suitable for canoeing. Canals, lakes, rivers, streams, etc., wander from the very north as far as Steenwijk through the "Beulakerwijde" to Zwolle, west beyond Hardenberg, southwest, and south to the IJssel River at Deventer. For information on organized (or not) canoe trips, contact the VVV, tel. (05490) 18767. Also, cycling tours, walking holidays, horse-drawn tilt-cart trips, and fishing holidays can be arranged by the VVV. In winter, the scenery with snow is superb; the ice skating outstanding. To ward off the winter chills, it's a perfect time to indulge in some suitable Dutch specialities such as thick pea soup, "erwtensoep," a hot pot, "hutspot," mashed potatoes, carrots and onions, or a "stamppot," mashed potatoes and cabbage.

YEARLY EVENTS: The area abounds with traditional festivals starting with events at Easter-time until the midwinter hornblowing around Christmas. Some of the more intriguing events include enormous bonfires lit at 8am on Easter Day as a sign of the coming of Spring. In Ootmarsum, on Easter Day and Easter Monday, everyone walks hand in hand through the streets singing religious songs. Denekamp celebrates Easter with "Paasstaakslepen" (see below for description), and many small communities have shooting contests ("schuttersfeesten") . . . the contestants hit a wooden bird and whoever wins is made King for the rest of the celebration. No one seems sure whether the midwinter hornblowing was devised to drive away evil spirits around Christmas or to warn churchgoers of the Inquisition during the Eighty Years' War. The meter-long horn has five notes which carry far and wide . . . the horns are blown between the first Sunday in Advent and Epiphany.

ZWOLLE

A 750-year-old market town

GETTING THERE: Highway A28 or A50 take you directly to Zwolle
INFORMATION: VVV Zwolle, Grote Kerkplein 14, tel. (038) 213900.

Zwolle, the capital of Overijssel, with a 750-year history has indeed been fortunate to have been spared major natural disasters and wars, permitting it to retain its rich heritage of important buildings and monuments. Before starting to explore, ask the VVV for their recommended walking tour, "Strolling Through Old Zwolle."

The city is walled off by ramparts and surrounded by canals, dating from the wars of independence (1568-1648). The old town center street plan hasn't changed in 500 years and since it covers less than a square kilometer, it is ideal for the walker.

St. Michael's Church (Grote Kerk), on the Grote Markt, is of special interest. Open July-mid-Aug., Mon.-Sat., 10am-noon and 2-5pm. Off season, only by appointment through VVV. This Gothic triangular hall church was started in 1406 and completed 40 years later; the tower rising 125 meters was added in 1548, however, it was destroyed by fire in 1669. Notice the fine carved pulpit dating from 1620 and the world-famous Schnitger organ (1721) with 4,000 pipes and 4 manuals.

The Town Hall consists of three buildings: the old Town Hall, the "Weehme" (formerly the 16th-century vicarage of the Grote Kerk), and the new Town Hall, 15 Grote Kerkplein, tel. 82013 or VVV. Guided tours in summer but check with the Receptionist (closed Saturdays). Be sure and see the splendid "Schepenzaal," dating from 1448, where the Council members met. The new Town Hall has a beautiful civic hall and council chamber.

Also look for the 1408 Town Gate, the Sassenpoort; the Church of Our Lady (Onze Lieve Vrouwekerk) dating from 1395 with its tower, the Peperbus, which can be climbed in season; the Karel V house at 33 Sassenstraat; the medieval Celle complex on Papenstraat; the Hoofdwacht (1614) on Grote Markt; parts of the town rampart on Buitenkant and Achter de Broeren; and two old towers being restored, the Wijndragerstoren and the Pelsertoren.

MUSEUMS: The three museums in Zwolle are:
The Provincial Museum, Melkmarkt 40, tel. 214650; open, Tues.-Sat., 10am-5pm, Sun., 2-5pm. The regular exhibits include period rooms from Gothic times to "Art Nouveau." An archeological section and regularly changing exhibits can also be seen.
The Contemporary Art Museum (Librije Hedendaagse Kunst Museum), Broerenkerkplein 15, tel. 213614; open Mon.-Sat., 10am-5pm, Sun., 1-5pm.
West-Overijssel Nature Museum, Voorstraat 32, tel. 227180; open, Tues.-Sat., 10am-5pm, Sun., 2-5pm.

MARKETS: Markets have been held from the Middle Ages to the present and have been of major importance to the city's economy. The cattle market (Fri. mornings) on the cattle market grounds on Rieteweg, is the second largest in Holland. There is also a horse fair held the same time and place. The Goods Market is held on the Grote Kerkplein in the center of town on Fri., 9am-noon; on the Melkmarkt and Grote Markt, Sat., 9am-6pm; and in Holtenbroek on Tues. from 2-6pm. Wednesdays in July plus the first Wed. in Aug., there's an Art and Antique Market at the IJsselhal. Other interesting market days are held in July such as one specializing in old handicrafts and an exotic Indonesian market-bazaar. The latter is also usually held at Easter. Check with the VVV for details.

STAYING OVER: The Wientjes Hotel and Restaurant, Stationsweg 7, tel. (038) 254254, is one good choice, however, it is closed from July-Aug. 15.

Less expensive and open all year is the Postiljon Hotel, Hertsenbergweg 1, tel. 216031.

YEARLY EVENTS: The beginning of Aug., Zwolle holds its "Blue Finger Days." There are also organ concerts, a guitar festival, the Dahlia Fair, as well as a number of trade fairs and shows.

IN THE NEIGHBORHOOD OF ZWOLLE:

At Staphorst and Rouveen, north of Zwolle about 15 km on A28, one can see the traditional dress and customs of people belonging to a strict religious sect. In contrast to other towns such as Marken and Volendam, here the people are not friendly to "outsiders" and taking pictures can be a difficult—and sometimes dangerous—affair. These people are very stern, highly religious and do not even approve of riding bicycles on Sundays. They will tolerate visitors on weekdays, but can be quite unfriendly on Sundays.

Slagharen, is about 30 km directly east. The Poneypark, Zwartedijk 39, tel. (05231) 3000; open, April-Oct., 9am-6pm and on school holidays, is a real treat which includes ponies by the score but also a huge outdoor pool, ferris wheel, merry-go-round, etc.

Ommen, about 20 km due east on N34 is in the middle of woods and on the banks of the Vecht River. Ommen is proud of its four majestic and well-preserved windmills and its local museum, "Oudheidkamer Ommen," Den Oordt 7, tel. (05291) 3487; hours, June-Sept. 15, Mon.-Fri., 10am-noon and 2-5pm, Sat., 2-4pm. "Bissingh" occurs the beginning of July—an authentic annual fair with music-making and entertainment.

Elburg (Gelderland), about 20 km southwest on the boundary with Flevoland, is a charming walled town worth exploring. When the old Town Gate and historic buildings are illuminated (summertime), this village takes on an "other-worldly" atmosphere.

Hattem Regional Museum, Gelderland

LOCATION: Achterstraat 48. Hattem is located about 6 kilometers south of Zwolle, to the east of north-south autoroute A28. From the south, take A28 north until you see the right-hand turnoff toward Hattem.
INFORMATION: VVV Hattem, Kerksteeg 1, tel. (05206) 43014.
HOURS: Mon.-Fri., 10am-5pm; closed weekends.
■ *Of interest to school-age children, and those who know Pieck's fairy-tale characters.*

This picturesque former Hanseatic town has something special to offer the visitor, archeology and works by artists Voerman and Anton Pieck.

Like many regional museums, originally the collection contained primarily local archeological finds. Later, the Voerman house was added with the collected works (1900-1940) of two well-known Dutch illustrators, Jan Voerman senior and junior. The most recent addition to the museum is the work of Anton

Pieck—one hundred and fifty illustrations which delight his modern-day followers with scenes of nostalgia. He died in 1987 leaving his scenes of Old Holland as a memorial.

Above the entrance to the museum is a wrought-iron sign depicting a Dickensian-type figure painted by Pieck, welcoming the visitor to another time. As one enters the building, one is greeted by pre-war Hattem and IJssel River landscapes of Jan Voerman senior's time. Just beyond, one enters a small courtyard with picturesque water-well designed by Pieck. One is surrounded by old roofs and ancient walls reminiscent of Holland's Golden Age. To complete the picture, there's the inevitable windmill close by. What a place for romantics! The walls of the barn (converted by Pieck) are covered with his works, capturing the period of tow barge, post coach and horse-drawn sleigh.

In the attic, there's a continuous video film about Anton Pieck.

KAMPEN

Important 15th-century seaport

GETTING THERE: Coming from Arnhem and other southern points, take A50/N50; from Zwolle, west on N337.
INFORMATION: VVV Kampen, Oudestraat 85, tel. (05202) 13500.

Kampen, a member of the Hanseatic League, reached its greatest prosperity in the 15th century before its harbor silted up and the closing of the Zuider Zee. Emperor Maximilian bestowed Kampen with the title, "Imperial Free Town," an indication of its wealth in the late Middle Ages.

Kampen has some of the loveliest gabled facades in the Netherlands as well as three city gates worth photographing: the Broederpoort on Ebbingstraat, an old defensive gate on the town moat; the Cellebroederspoort which houses the Civic Museum; and the Kroonmarktpoort on IJsselkade with two 14th-century towers. Another 1400 structure is St. Nicholas' Church on the Kroonmarkt. The New Tower on Oudestraat is also worth a look.

The Town Hall, located near the Kroonmarkt, dates from the first half of the 14th century but was largely devastated in 1543 and immediately rebuilt. Notice the statues on the facade: Charlemagne, Alexander the Great, Moderation, Fidelity, Justice and Love. There are a number of interesting antiquities in the original Aldermen's Room, the "museum" Schepenzaal Oude Raadhuis, Oudestraat 133, tel. (05202) 92999, Mon.-Thurs., 10-11am and 2-3pm, by appointment on Fri., Sat., 2, 3 and 4pm.

There is also a Tobacco Museum on Botermarkt which is worth a visit just to see the biggest cigar in the world (5 meters long).

The Stedelijk Museum, Oudestraat 158, tel. 17361 or 92777; hours, April-Oct., Tues.-Sat., 11am-12:30pm and 1:30-5pm. July, Aug., Sat., 11am-5pm. Located in the Gotische Huis, a fine merchant's home dating from Kampen's greatest period of prosperity, the museum specializes in local history.

EATING OUT AND STAYING OVER: Along Kampen's waterfront (canal), you can have a quick lunch, leisurely dinner, or stay overnight at the Herberg d'Olde Brugge, IJsselkade 48, tel. (05202) 12645, nice views of the water traffic and inexpensive.

YEARLY EVENTS: On Thurs. in July, there's a folkloric festival, an open-air market and old handicrafts demonstrations in the "town of eels and cigars."

GIETHOORN

The Venice of the North

GETTING THERE: North of Zwolle about 25 km via N331 to N334, continue north to Giethoorn; from Meppel, take N375 southwest, then north on N334.
INFORMATION: VVV Giethoorn, tel. (05216) 1248.

Popularly known as the Venice of the North, Giethoorn is located in a large lake area on the Bovenwijde. This is a very special outing for the whole family. Giethoorn has a long history, starting about 1280 when a group of flagellants (people who believed the day of judgment was approaching and who wandered throughout Europe scourging themselves) coming from regions bordering the Mediterranean settled here and then interbred with the Saxons. Most areas of Europe persecuted them, but the Lord of the Castle of Vollenhove was sympathetic to their beliefs so they were allowed to remain. They found masses of goat horns (probably dating from the 10th C.) on the land they were allowed to settle, so they called their village "Geytenhorn" (Goat's Horn), which eventually became known as "Giethoorn." In order to pay taxes to the Count of Vollenhove, the villagers dug peat and sold it. They worked in a very disorganized way, digging the peat soil wherever they pleased, mixing it in a trough and spreading it on the land to dry. The result could be cut as peat. This peat digging led to the formation of lakes and then ditches, and canals had to be excavated in order to transport the peat. Little islands were created on which the houses were located, reachable only by boat or high bridges. These canals and bridges give Giethoorn its present storybook appearance.

It isn't easy to find Giethoorn but don't become discouraged. Of course, it is not possible to drive right into the village—you will find a small parking area opposite the point for boat tour departures. These tours are inexpensive and highly recommended . . . they last about one hour or perhaps a bit longer. This area is known for its "punters"—special boats with double bottoms which transport the baker, milkman, cows, furniture, or whatever. You might be lucky and see a wedding party going by on the way to the church—all in boats. You can do the water tour first and walk around the village later, or vice versa, but do both.

MUSEUMS: Even little Giethoorn has a choice of museums:
The Minerals Museum, "De Oude Aarde," Binnenpad 43, tel. (05216) 1313, open, March-Oct., Mon.-Sat., 10am-6pm; Nov.-Feb., Sat.-Sun., and school vacations, 10am-6pm. It has a most interesting collection of primarily semi-precious stones from all over the world, from agates to zwanel! They are exceedingly well

displayed in a semi-darkened room with spotlights strategically located and ultraviolet lights being used to good advantage to show off the beauty of the crystallized rocks and the fluorescent minerals. In addition, there is an assortment of birds and strange animals such as lizards, snakes and others of that ilk that children find fascinating! As you leave this private museum, you pass through a shop where you may purchase various minerals or decorative items made from the stones, such as pins, earrings, tie clips, etc. It is an educational—as well as pleasurable—experience for the budding mineralogist.

The Speelman Museum (Street Musician), Binnenpad 123, tel. 1776; open, April-Oct. and school holidays, Mon.-Sun., 10am-6pm, Nov.-March, by appointment.

The Gloria Maris Museum, Binnenpad 137, has a display of shells and corals.

The Histo-Mobil Museum, Cornelisgracht 42, tel. 1498; is open, May-Oct. 15, daily, 10am-6pm, Oct. 16-April, only by appointment for groups.

The " 't Olde Maat Uus" Binnenpad 52, tel. 2244; open, March-Oct., 10am-6pm, Nov.-Feb., Sat.-Sun. and school vacations.

You can see how the Giethoorn punts are built at the Schreur shipyard . . . details from VVV.

STAYING OVER: Giethoorn can be done as a one-day trip even from The Hague and Rotterdam, but with small children, an overnight stay is recommended. There's a two-star hotel, Jachthaven Giethoorn, Beulakerweg 128, tel. (05216) 1216 . . . moderate.

Surrounded by water, it isn't surprising Giethoorn is famous for water sports; this is another ideal spot for camping so get a list from the VVV or ANWB.

YEARLY EVENTS: The village is illuminated in July, Aug., and on the last Sat. in Aug., a special gondola trip is available for visitors.

IN THE NEIGHBORHOOD OF GIETHOORN: This is a region of water, reeds, woods and small towns not to be missed. The towns listed below form a circle around Giethoorn:

Vollenhove, west on the border with Flevoland, was built around a bishop's hunting lodge. There are fine historic buildings and splendid facades as well as the ruins of an old castle, "De Toutenburg." The town flourished from the Middle Ages as can be seen by its old patrician houses and the many large country farms in the area. It has a busy harbor where traditional ships, fishing boats and yachts can all be found. South is Kraggenburg, where you can do some glider flying.

Kuinre, another border town off N351, has a Town Hall dating from 1776, formerly an old butter weigh-house and a number of 17th-century houses.

Oldemarkt at the top of the Province on the border with Friesland, is surrounded by water areas abounding in water fowl: the purple heron, bittern marsh harriers, and much more. Also in the neighborhood are old peat-cutters' houses. The National Forestry Service operates the nature reserve, "De Werribben." You must reserve ahead to visit: write VVV Zwolle, Grote Kerkplein 14, tel. (038) 213900. You can also take a boat trip to see hundreds of windmills irrigating the area.

Steenwijk, just off north/south A32, was once a fortified town. Its 90-meter-high tower of St. Clement's Church (15th-16th centuries) is still a beacon to the town. The countryside abounds in natural beauty. There's a deer park, "De Ramswoerthe"; and if you enjoy elegant homes, you can search for three estates in the area: "de Woldberg," "de Bult," and "de Eese."

Two museums of possible interest are the Fair and Circus Museum, Markt 64, tel. (05210) 11704; open, Sept.-June, Tues.-Fri., 10am-noon, 2-5pm, and Sat., 2-5pm; and the local museum, "Oudheidkamer Steenwijk," same address, tel. number and hours, except closed Saturdays. You can make boat trips from here, windsurf, or fish.

South of Steenwijk is Giethoorn and south of Giethoorn is Zwartsluis an aquatic paradise with peaceful surroundings.

ALMELO

An old fair town

GETTING THERE: Almelo is southeast of Zwolle and northwest of Enschede; it is served by highways N36, N35, N349 and A35/A1. INFORMATION: VVV Almelo, Wierdensestraat 49, tel. (05490) 18765.

Almelo is in the Twente region, located in one of the most scenic green areas of the country with many parks and forests for picnicking, walking, bike-riding and whatever. Twente is also a modern, industrialized area and the center of the Netherlands textile industry. The third largest town of Overijssel, Almelo was once famous for its fairs. Today, it continues its commercial tradition and the shopper can seek out its many shopping centers. Some of the town's former glory can be seen in Huis Almelo or Almelo Castle which once belonged to Count Rechteren-Limburg. Also, look for the commercial exchange on the Grotestraat built on the spot where the town hall was established in 1489. The present building is from 1690.

The local museum, "Museum voor Hemmkunde," Korte Prinsenstraat 2, tel. 16071, is open Tues.-Sat., 12:30-5pm.

YEARLY EVENTS: The end of May, Almelo has its fair throughout the center of town. Also about this same period, ask about the parade of historical carriages, "Twenterit."

IN THE NEIGHBORHOOD OF ALMELO:
Hellendoorn is best known, perhaps, for its adventure-recreation park of the same name. "Hellendoorn," Luttenbergerweg 22, tel. 55555 or 56465; open, May-mid-Sept., 9:30am-6pm (attractions "work" from 10am-4:30pm, 5pm or 5:30pm). Parrots, sea-lion shows; ride the monorail; plunge 12 meters down the Log Flume; take a dive in the dark in the Black Hole; eat at the Avontuurmaakt Hongerig (poffertjes are offered—try them for a tea or dessert treat). There's also a local museum at Reggeweg 1, tel. 54193; open, mid-May-mid-Sept. The end of July the "Heldersfeest" takes place, including an enormous fireworks display.
Vriezenveen, about 6 km north of Almelo, is an old fen colony. Look for the traditional farmhouses and the nature reserve, "De Kooyplas," and also the Museum of Antiquities with a Russian Room. Museum Oud Vriezenveen, Westeinde 54, tel. 63476; open, Mon.-Fri., 9am-5pm. The Veenmuseum Wester-haar-Vriezenveenschewijk, Paterswal 9, tel. 59127, opened in May 1988. Call for details.

DENEKAMP

Another ancient town surrounded by lovely scenery

GETTING THERE: From The Hague and Rotterdam, A12 to Arnhem; A50 to Apeldoorn, A1 to A35 following signs for Enschede. From Amsterdam, A1 all the way to A35. North of Enschede to Oldenzaal, then northeast on N342 to Denekamp.
INFORMATION: Singraven Castle, Molendijk 36, tel. (05413) 2088.

The primary attraction is Singraven Castle (Huis Singraven), Molendijk 36 (southwest of town), tel. (05413) 2088; open, April 15-Nov., Tues.-Fri., 11am, 2, 3, and 4pm, Sat. (appointment for groups), 11am, 12, 2 and 3pm. Purchase your ticket at the water mill-restaurant, "De Watermolen," (pancakes as well as other fare). The castle dates from 1381 and contains 17th- and 18th-century paintings, Gobelin tapestries and antique furniture.

MUSEUMS:
Museum Huize Kaizer, Kerkplein 2, tel. 1205/1705; hours, Mon., Wed., Fri., 9am-noon and 2-4pm, Tues., 9am-noon, Sun., 2-5pm.
Museum Natura Docet, Oldenzaalsestraat 39, tel. 1325; hours, Sun.-Fri., 10am-5pm; Dec. 25, 26, 1-5pm. This natural history museum is just across the road from Singraven Castle. There is also a 13th-century sandstone church, and a 14th-century watermill with three wheels.

YEARLY EVENTS: Denekamp joins in the Easter celebrations with "Paasstaakslepen." The town people are led by "Judas Iscariot" to Singraven. From here an Easter pine tree is dragged to the Easter meadow, its branches disposed of and the resulting pole, including a barrel of tar at the top, is burnt in the evenings as part of the Easter fires. The first Sunday in July, come join the sheep-shearing festival, and around Christmas, you might hear the sounding of the mid-winter horns.

IN THE NEIGHBORHOOD OF DENEKAMP:

Ootmarsum, straight north on N349, is an extremely old town and one of the meccas for tourists because of its town center with houses renovated in old timbered style of the 18th century. Wander through the narrow streets and enjoy the views. There's an old town square with a 12th-century church, and three watermills. On the edge of the town center, there's the Museum Het Lös Hoes, Smidhuisstraat 2, tel. (05419) 2787; hours, Tues.-Sun., 10am-5pm, a farmstead museum from 1666, complete with tools and utensils from that time as well as a geological museum on the same site. You can get anything from a light bite to a gourmet meal in Ootmarsum, and if you want to stay over, this small town has 1-star to 4-star hotels! You have a wide choice. At Eastertime, everyone goes through the village hand-in-hand singing Easter songs.

ENSCHEDE

Former Saxon town, now the biggest city in Overijssel.

GETTING THERE: From The Hague and Rotterdam, A12 to Arnhem; A50 to Apeldoorn, A1 to A35 following signs for Enschede. From Amsterdam, A1 all the way to A35.
INFORMATION: VVV Enschede, Markt 31, tel. (053) 323200.

This old Saxon town is almost to the German border and like most border towns of significance, Enschede has lost almost all its ancient buildings because of wars, invasions, and other acts of God and man. Today, it is the largest city in Overijssel due to the textile industry and the introduction of micro-electronics to further develop the economy.

The Grote Kerk (9th-century foundations ... 15th century) is one of the historical edifices left standing on the Market Square. The most important museum is the Rijksmuseum Twente and Oudheidkamer Twente, discussed below. Also visit the Textile and Industry Museum, Industriestraat 2 (corner Haaksbergenstraat); tel. (053) 319093; hours, Tues.-Sun., 10am-5pm. Big and little girls who enjoy handicrafts will like this museum! One room is devoted to lace-making and detailed explanations of how batik is made in Africa and the Far East. Natuurmuseum (Natural History Museum), located at De Ruyterlaan 2, right in the middle of town within walking distance of the Station and the Market. For info, tel. (053) 323409; hours, Tues.-Sat., 10am-12:30pm and 1:30-5pm, Sun., 2-5pm. A collection to appeal to young people: minerals, fossils, skeletons and snails from the sea. Also various dioramas, and, in the basement, a collection of precious stones. Don't miss the Vivarium—unique in the Netherlands—aquariums, terrariums and insectariums!

As for parklands and walking areas, there are thirty to choose from. Of particular interest to children would probably be the children's farm, Wooldrikspark, Gronausestraat 12, tel. 316070; midget golf at Camping Aamsveen; playground Hoge Boekel (midget golf), and Ter Riet (ponies).

For shoppers, be advised, there's a great Saturday market.

EATING OUT: You can get a tourist menu at the "Cafe Hoge Boekel," Hogeboekelerweg 410; or, if price is no object, go for atmosphere in an old coach house, "Het Koetshuis," Walstraat 48, tel. (053) 322866.

STAYING OVER: The 3-star DISH hotel, Schermerhorn Hall, Boulevard 1945 No. 2, tel. (053) 866666, has all the modern conveniences (including T.V.), but there are less expensive choices . . . check with the VVV.

Rijksmuseum Twente and Oudheidkamer Twente

> *LOCATION: Lasondersingel 129, Enschede. This is the northern section of the road and canal which encircles the town.*
> *INFORMATION: Tel. (053) 358675.*
> *HOURS: Tues.-Fri., 10am-5pm, Sat.-Sun., 1-5pm. Closed Jan. 1.*
> ■ *Of general interest.*

There are sections dealing with prehistory, religious art, secular art, a room devoted to Delftware, and a reconstructed farm of the region called "lös Hoes," in the garden. The collection of paintings is an important one with such artists represented as Holbein the Younger, Cranach, Breughel the Younger, Van Goyen. The religious art collection is of special value because of its Primitives. The modern artists include Sisley, Redon and Jacob Wagemaker.

IN THE NEIGHBORHOOD OF ENSCHEDE:

Oldenzaal, about 10 km north of town, has an impressive Basilica of St. Plechelmus dating from the 12th century, built of Bentheim sandstone and with the largest bell-tower in Europe. Its museum of antiquities is Museum Het Palthehuis, Marktstraat 13, tel. (05410) 13482; hours, Tues.-Fri., 10am-noon and 2-5pm, Sat.-Sun., 2-5pm. A second museum is the "Schatkamer" of the Basilica, Gasthuisstraat 10, tel. 12301/12808; hours, June-Aug., Tues.-Sun., 2-5pm and Wed., 2-4pm. St. Plechelm, an Irishman, converted the district and died here in 730. The textile industry developed and spread in the region.

Delden: From Enschede, take A35 north, then N346 west; from points west (Arnhem), take N48 northeast to Zutphen, then N346 west to Delden. The Counts of Twickel were very influential in this area and Twickel Castle remains a very impressive monument to their wealth and power. The interior cannot be visited; however, a walk through its grounds to admire the moats, towers and the garden (open Wed. and Sat. afternoons) is recommended. Also in Delden is a Dutch Reformed Church of Bentheim sandstone with a fine interior; notice the pulpit, the pew of the Counts of Twickel, and ancient wall paintings.

The Salt Museum, Langestraat 30, tel. (05407) 61300; hours, May-Oct., Mon.-Fri., 10am-5pm, Sat.-Sun. and holidays, 2-5pm. It was Count of Wassenaar Opdam who discovered salt underground here in the 18th century.

Diepenheim: Southwest of Delden on N346, Diepenheim can also be reached from Enschede (SW on N18 to Haaksbergen, then NW on N347 to Goor and west on N346); from Zutphen, east on N346. A lovely town surrounded by five handsome castles. Only one, Warmelo Castle (gardens) can be visited, Tues. and Thurs. afternoons. In summer, art lovers come for the unique art exhibition, a walking route past the works of well-known masters. Also ask about the VVV route which will take you past the castles, Warmelo, Diepenheim, Westervlier, Nijenhuis and Weldam. The oldest watermill in Twente, "Den Haller," 12th century, is on Watermolenweg in the direction of Hengevelde.

DEVENTER

An important Hanseatic League town

GETTING THERE: Two major highways pass through Deventer: north-south N48 and east-west N344. It is also only about 11 km from Apeldoorn, the heart of the Hoge Veluwe. Major highway A1 (east-west) passes by to the south of town.
INFORMATION: VVV Deventer, Brink 55, tel. (05700) 16200.

Believe it or not, Deventer was already an important town in the 6th and 7th centuries. As a reminder of its ancient origins, the Berg Church (St. Nicholas) and Berg Quarter have been completely restored in a medieval street pattern lined with stately patrician houses. Thanks to its location on the IJssel River, it was an early trading center and important member of the Hanseatic League. Throughout history, the IJssel has been used for trade and military advantage.

Enjoy the lovely countryside with its windmills, numerous thatched roofs, black sheep grazing in groups, and woods with sunlight dappling starlight patterns to the heavy cover of leaves on the ground. For photo bugs, the young and energetic, it is possible to climb the tower of the Romanesque Libuïnus Church, or take a trip on the IJssel River for a more relaxing experience.

MUSEUMS:
The Weigh House Museum (Museum de Waag), Brink 56, tel. 93780, 93784; open, Tues.-Sat., 10am-5pm, Sun., 2-5pm, for a peek into the town's history. The collection includes historical items such as prehistoric pottery fragments, topographical displays, bikes and interesting kitchen displays.

The Toy Museum (Speelgoed en Blikmuseum), adds a lighter touch. Brink 47, tel. 93784, 93786; hours same as the Weigh House. Not only has this private residence been furnished in period styles, it also has displays of folk costumes, toys, children's books, miniature furniture, dolls and doll houses.

STAYING OVER: There's a 3-star Postiljon Motel at Deventerweg 121, tel. (05700) 24022, just outside of town and a smaller 2-star, Hotel Royal, Brink 94, tel. 11880, in the center of town.

THE PROVINCE OF LIMBURG

Limburg is the most southerly province of the Netherlands, hugging the borders of Germany (east) and Belgium (south). The major north-south road is A2; the major road east-west, A67. The provincial roads are well-surfaced, sometimes a bit narrow, but almost always scenic, changing from farmland, heath and woods in the north; flat river-dominated land in the center; to hilly, rather undulating land in the south, wildflowers vying with cultivated fields and small forests.

Archeological explorations show that people lived in the region as early as 750,000 B.C. Roman warriors on their northern explorations built a settlement (today's Maastricht) near a ford over the Maas River which they fortified. Wealthy Romans soon followed, building villas, hot springs baths and planting vines for wine along the sunny hills. The first walled town was outgrown and abandoned toward the end of the 4th century A.D. From 380-722 A.D., Maastricht was a Bishop's seat; from 1202-1795, the Duke of Brabant controlled the area. With the Peace of Westphalia in 1648, the Netherlands became an independent country, but conflicts continued to rage between the British and the Dutch, and between the French and the Dutch. After Napoleon's defeat at Waterloo in June 1815, the Netherlands and Belgium were consolidated into a United Kingdom under Willem I. This uneasy union lasted until October 1830

INFORMATION: Provincial VVV, Valkenburg, tel. (04406) 13993.

when Belgium declared its independence.

Following the period of Spanish domination, the country, north and south, developed differently. The Dutch Republic in the north became an imperial and maritime trading nation; the people spoke Dutch and were Protestants. In the southern provinces (North Brabant, Limburg, Belgium), the emphasis was on manufacturing, coal mining, and industrialization. Here, people spoke French and Flemish, and were strongly Catholic. Limburgers, as a result, have a strong affinity to the shared past with Belgium and Germany.

Once part of the Burgundian Empire, there continues an appreciation for outstanding French cuisine, fine wines, and a "joie de vivre" as well as great warmth of hospitality. Limburg cannot help being a top-drawer holiday destination where children are entertained "to the nines" and adults are tantalized by fine restaurants, generous drinks AND entertainment from sports to cultural events to cabarets.

In the north, there are some pleasant old villages such as Gennep, Afferden and Bergen at the edge of the Leukermeer Lake, an active watersports center. Across into Germany, the Reichswald Forest reserve beckons. A fine place for walking and appreciating the countryside is in the flat land west of the Maas River, the Peel. The Maas River, itself, offers many diversions along its banks including such holiday resort stopovers as Arcen ("Chateau Arcen Gardens"), Tegelen (known for its pottery), and Steyl (Mission Museum). But this is just the beginning. Venlo is the biggest town in this area, then comes Roermond with the Meijnweg moorland nature reserve southeast of town, and the interesting villages of St. Odiliënberg, Montfort, Sgevensweert and Thorn also to the south. As you travel south, you will find many places to discover on your own, but also more congestion. Valkenburg is buzzing with visitors day and night, summer and even in winter; Maastricht is the "Big City" with all that implies . . . lots of people on the streets and a sense of electricity in the air.

In addition to the purely fun aspect of this part of the country, if possible make time to visit the large American cemetery at Margraten (outside Gulpen, near Valkenburg). Each year, Memorial Day weekend, services are held to honor those who fell. Dignitaries, including the Queen's Commissioner, the American Ambassador and ranking generals, come from The Hague, Rotterdam, Germany and the United States to participate. It's a big show with wreathlaying, planes saluting overhead, and speeches (of course).

Especially touching are the children of the surrounding villages who bring flowers and stand by "their" grave. They are representing their grandparents' generation, the Dutch who housed the U.S. soldiers and got to know them briefly before they perished in the common cause. It is heartwarming to see the continuation of Dutch remembrance when so many others have forgotten.

Because of the popularity of both Valkenburg and Maastricht, it is highly recommended that hotel, motel, and camping reservations be made well in advance. Also dining reservations if one of the five Michelin-starred restaurants is on your agenda. The VVV puts out lists of recommended hotels and restaurants. In particular, families might be interested in the special brochure entitled, "Limburgse Familiehotels" for the current year. The hotels are listed giving all particulars including a photo. A few personal recommendations are included in the following text.

Food specialities can be found all over the Netherlands and Limburg is no exception. There's a special fruit tart called Limburg Vlaai—open-faced and delicious when prepared in traditional fashion; Limburger cheese, which is best known in the U.S., sold in filled juice glasses; but the most delectable and not known generally by Americans, are the white asparagus which grow in Limburg. Supplying over 80% of the Dutch production, the season is usually from May to the end of June. Don't miss taking advantage of this wonderful vegetable if you're passing through.

Limburgers are exceedingly proud of their location with easy access to Belgium, West Germany, Luxembourg and France. They will not hesitate to point tourists to the highest spot in the Netherlands up a gentle, wooded hill at Vaals, from where one can see three countries at once: the Netherlands, Belgium and West Germany. Limburg can be reached easily by plane or train. The International Airport, located only 6 miles from Maastricht and Valkenburg, has regular services to cities in Holland, and London-Gatwick. Train service is frequent from the major Dutch cities, but also to Belgium (and then France) and West Germany.

Because of Limburg's geography, our travels will start in the north and end in the south, following the Maas all the way, beginning with Venlo.

VENLO

The asparagus capital

GETTING THERE: From Amsterdam, take A2 south around Eindhoven, then east on A67; from The Hague and Rotterdam, A13 then A16 south to Breda, A58 east to Eindhoven and A67 east to Venlo. From southern parts of Holland, take A58 east or from Antwerp, A13 to N73 east to A2 and Limburg.
INFORMATION: VVV Venlo, Koninginneplein 2, tel. (077) 543800.

Venlo's rich history started in 96 A.D. when it was founded by a legendary larger-than-life man, Valuas of the Bructeri (Bructeres) tribe. He and his wife are depicted in folkloric celebrations as great colorful giants. In 1343, Venlo received its city rights from the Duke of Gelder, including the right to charge a mandatory storage fee on all goods being transported on the Meuse River before they went on sale. Located on the border between Holland and Germany, it has been constantly overrun and repeatedy destroyed by tribal wars and armies throughout the centuries. In the 15th century, Venlo joined the powerful Hanseatic League, and thus began a period of great prosperity for the area. During WW II, Venlo suffered heavy damage and for the most part, its ancient buildings are no more.

On the plus side, its location has also made Venlo an important trade and traffic center; it handles one-fifth of all traffic across the Dutch-German border. Today, Venlo is more modern than ancient. It is a developing industrial area as well as the second most important market garden region in the Netherlands with over two millon square meters of greenhouses. In May-June, the asparagus is King. You can enjoy the marvelous vegetable in restaurants throughout the area which feature it during the season. The "asparagus route" is famous, starting and ending in either Roermond or Venlo. People flock to the markets to buy thin, fat, or in-between stalks of this white delicacy. Or you may stop at a farmer's house along the route to buy directy from the grower when you see a sign, "asperge te koop" (asparagus for sale).

Because there are so few ancient buildings remaining in Venlo, those that do exist are even more meaningful for its citizens. Of special architectural interest are the 16th-century Renaissance Town Hall (Stadhuis), and the 14th-century Gothic St. Martin's Church on the Grote Kerkstraat in the center of the town. The Town Hall is located on the corner of Lomstraat and Gasthuisstraat, near the Maaskade. If possible, see the Council Chamber with its highly ornamental Cordovan leather-covered walls. St. Martin's, constructed from 1597-1600 and redone in neo-Renaissance style between 1880-1885, was severely burned in 1955 and had to be restored. It is full of important art treasures such as a bronze baptismal font made by a famous Dutch sculptor early in the 17th century; and paintings by 17th-century artists as well as its richly Baroque pulpit and choir stalls.

Other buildings to look for are an old merchant's house, the "Romerhuis" (1521) on Jodenstraat, and an old patrician house, "Huize Schreurs" (1588), located across the street from St. Martin's.

MUSEUMS: Venlo offers three very different museums: a modern art museum, a museum dealing with local prehistory, and the Roman period up to the present, and a police museum.

The Modern Art Museum Van Bommel-Van Dam , Deken van Oppensingel 8, tel. (077) 513457; open, Tues.-Fri., 10am-4:30pm, Sat., Sun. and public holidays, 2-5pm. Closed Jan. 1, Easter Sun., Whit Sun. and Christmas Day. This famous museum deals with paintings of the 20th century, including a special Japanese print collection.

Goltzius Museum, Goltziusstraat 21 (just off the Msg. Nolensplein), tel. 42983; open, same hours as above. This museum deals with regional history including ancient archeological collections. There are displays of folkcrafts, weapons, silver, coins, topographical maps, antique porcelain, glass, tin, as well as paintings and period rooms.

Police Museum (Museum Limburgse Jagers), Rijnbechstraat 1, tel. 549944; open, Tues. afternoons. A small but interesting museum dealing with police "phenomena."

EATING OUT: Venlo has its fair share of quick restaurants in town but if you want to splurge, the Hostellerie de Hamert at Wellerloi, about 20 km north of Venlo, tel. (04703) 1260, is one of the 1988 award-winning restaurants in Holland . . . lunch menu including wine is about Fl. 70.00.

STAYING OVER: Venlo has five 4-star hotels including the Wilhelmina (one of the group of "Familiehotels"), Kaldenkerkerweg 1, tel. (077) 16251.

YEARLY EVENTS: From May to the end of June, the "asparagus route" between Venlo and Roermond is organized, a trip of approximately 100 km, which takes you past lovely scenery and the best asparagus restaurants. Also exhibitions all about asparagus from how it's grown to how it's eaten! Get current data from VVV.

IN THE NEIGHBORHOOD OF VENLO:
Chateau Arcen Gardens, about 10 km north of Venlo on N271 (exit at sign for Chateau) along the Maas River. Open, mid-May-Oct., daily 9:30am-6pm . . . the castle is open year-round for meals. Admission to gardens, Adults, Fl. 11.00; children to 15 years, Fl. 5.00. Plenty of parking; wheelchairs available at no cost.

The gardens form a permanent ornamental plant exhibition with the rosarium its focal point. There are 32 hectares of land with canals, ponds, subtropical flora, canyon of waterfalls, etc. The chateau dates from 1750 and offers a choice of restaurants or cafes.

ROERMOND

A center of commerce

GETTING THERE: Roermond is in Middle-Limburg almost on the German border. Highway A2 is the quickest way from the west, picking up A68 at Sonnsbeck intersection. N271 and N274 go through town north/south.
INFORMATION: VVV Roermond, Markt 24, tel. (04750) 33205.

Roermond is the most important commercial city in middle-Limburg, and is the center of Catholicism for the area. Its city-rights were obtained as early as 1232. In 1572, it was taken by William the Silent, but it fell to the Spaniards within a few months. Then, it was a pawn of war under Austria and France before it became a part of the Netherlands in 1815.

The Onze Lieve Vrouwe Munsterkerk is the important site to visit. This ancient church built in 1224 comprised the nunnery of a Cistercian abbey. The style of the building is transitional from the Roman to Gothic periods; it was restored in the years 1864-1897 by Cuypers, a well-known Dutch builder. Inside, there is a retable, carved and ornamented in Brabant style as well as tombs of the founders of the abbey, Count Gerard III and his wife, Marguerite of Brabant. Located on the Munsterplein, the church may be visited by appointment (groups only), tel. (04750) 92222.

Nearby at the corner of Pollartstraat, there is a former "palace" dating from the period of Spanish domination, the Prinsenhof.

The Cathedral of St. Christopher on the Markt was constructed in 1410 and restored after the damage caused during WW II. Notice the statue of the patron saint of city and church (on the tower).

The Hendrik Luyten-Dr. Cuypers Museum, Andersonweg 8, tel. 13496; open, Tues.-Fri., 11am-5pm, Sat.-Sun., 2-5pm, honors two native sons. Mr. Luyten was a painter and Dr. P.J.H. Cuypers was a famous builder. In addition to its permanent collection dealing with the history of Roermond, there are often temporary exhibitions.

The "Golfslagbad de Roerdomp," Achilleslaan 2, is open Mon.-Fri., 1-7pm, Sat.-Sun., 10am-7pm ... a huge pool with wave action, mini-golf, and games galore.

EATING OUT: If a lovely tart (cherry, apple, pear, custard or whatever) is tempting, Kemmeren Bakery at Markstraat 18 comes highly recommended.

STAYING OVER: In addition to a choice of hotels, this area abounds with camp sites and bungalow parks, the most luxurious of which offer color T.V., central heating, heated and non-heated swimming pools, and more.

IN THE NEIGHBORHOOD OF ROERMOND:

The "Maasplassen" are only 7 km from Roermond. These artificial lakes have been a well-known water recreation center for two decades with ideal conditions for surfers and swimmers. A nearby campsite is "Elfenmeer," Meinweg 1, Herkenbosch, tel. (04752) 1689.

THORN

"The White City"

GETTING THERE: Thorn is south of Roermond, east of Eindhoven and west of the Maas River, 5 km south of the crossroads of A2 and N273.

INFORMATION: VVV Wijngard 8, Thorn, tel. (04756) 2555 or 2761.

Almost overlooked in today's hustle and bustle, Thorn was once an independent principality and the location of a royal residence of this small kingdom for 800 years. It was nicknamed the "White City" because of its buildings painted white, and the "Musical City" because of the many musical societies it has always supported.

Before Christianity came to these parts, a tribe of Eburons built a temple dedicated to their idol, Thor, on the site of the present Chapel of the Virgin Mary. This may explain the derivation of the name, "Thorn."

The Abbey was built toward the end of the 10th C. by Count Ansfried and his wife, Hilsondis. Ansfried was one of the richest and most powerful noblemen of his time. He was educated by his uncle, the Archbishop of Trier, entered the service of Otto the First, and later became Bishop of Utrecht. As a reward for his faithful servic, Otto granted him many new lands. His rights were later reconfirmed by Otto III. In essence, Ansfried was given complete legal jurisdiction, the right of coinage, the right to maintain arms for the defense of his properties, and so on.

He and his wife decided to set Thorn aside and to establish a double cloister, one for men and one for women, where they could spend their last years. Their daughter became the first abbess, perhaps striking an early blow for women's lib. She was followed by women from the most noble and influential families who kept control through management of the Abbey-church in their roles as abbesses and canonesses. After the invasion of the French in 1797, the Principality of Thorn ceased to exist.

To begin your visit, go to the Abbey Church which has an "automatic guide" with color slides about the history of Thorn and the abbey church. In addition, pick up the flyer indicating points of interest to see in town ... this is also available from the VVV. The Abbey Church, the Chapel, former abbey and chapter houses are open every day, 9am-6pm. The Chapel under the Lindens was founded in 1673 by Clara Elizabeth of Manderscheidt Blankenheim.

A walk around the old town will transport visitors into another era when aristocratic ladies had everything to say about the town and its famous abbey. There are 22 suggested sites to discover as you negotiate the cobblestone streets. Incidentally, three-inch heels are not recommended if you want to wander comfortably.

EATING OUT and STAYING OVER: The restaurant of the charming Golden Tulip Thorn Hotel, "La Ville Blanche," offers excellent cuisine but our pleasure was sitting outside at the little tables watching the passing parade. This would be a charming overnight stop—the hotel building is an older structure, painted white like many of the other buildings in town. It has been completely renovated and offers all the amenities, including Sunday morning concerts once a month.

Stiftskerk—The Abbey-church of Thorn

LOCATION: Follow "Centrum" signs to the old part of town.
INFORMATION: VVV, tel. (04756) 2555.
HOURS: Thurs. before Easter-Nov., daily from 9am-6pm; other times
by appointment.
NOTE: Price of admission includes an introductory slide show in
Dutch, English, German and French. In addition, there's a very
complete guide folder describing the Abbey-church.
■ *Of interest to older children.*

The Stiftskerk has a long and early history, see "introduction." The white and gilded baroque interior accentuates the impression of great space, wealth and tranquility. The Gothic crypt under the sanctuary is interesting as well as two apartments of the 14th-15th centuries.

This complex of abbey buildings was modified structurally for various reasons throughout the years. The church is the only well-preserved structure remaining. In the 12th century it was Romanesque in style; at the end of the 13th century it was rebuilt in Gothic style; and in the 15th century, late-Baroque additions can be seen in the architecture of the priest's choir and the ladies' choir.

HEERLEN
Roman baths and former coal mining center

GETTING THERE: Coming from Maastricht, take A2 north to A79
east. From the north and west, A2 south to A76 southeast.
INFORMATION: VVV Heerlen, Stationsplein 4, tel. (045) 716200.

The Romans were here also. Two thousand years ago, two important roads crossed where the municipal library now stands; one going from Xanten to Trier, the other, from Boulogne-sur-Mer to Cologne. A settlement of merchants and craftsmen built themselves elegant homes and gave Heerlen its original name "Coriovallum." Flavius had a country seat built on what is now the center of town. The bathhouse, which was the focus of social life at the time, is incorporated as part of the Thermae Museum, described following.

With the passing of the Roman fortunes, the busy settlement soon became a small inconspicuous village. St. Pancras-church (12th century) was then, and remains today, the heart of Heerlen. In the late 1800s coal was discovered and everything changed. The sleepy town was awash in coal mines; the sky was smoke-laden; the population doubled in 10 years and by the next decade, there was a 500% increase.

When the mines were no longer economic, the pits were closed in the 1960s. To keep alive, Heerlen became an important administrative center (Dutch State Mines headquarters), developed new industries and built shopping centers "around the clock."

■ The VVV recommends three trips to see all of Heerlen. The suggestions are good. Begin with a cultural-historical tour starting with the Roman period . . . visit the Thermae Museum . . . then, jump ten centuries and visit Hoensbroek Castle (north of town), followed by visits to St. Pancras-church and the water-mills, Weltermolen and Oliemolen. The latter have been restored and can be visited on certain days. Also check out the small but charming Terworm Castle.

The next "trip" is centered on the period of Heerlen's coal industry. You can see "mine colonies" (workers' housing facilities), one of which is included on the list of protected buildings. Also, the former Oranje-Nassau Colliery winding wheel can be seen behind the General Office of Statistics (CBS). Then visit the Geological Museum, Voskuilenweg 131, open, Mon.-Fri., 9am-noon and 2-4pm. Another mine museum is in the Rolduc Abbey near Kerkrade (see following).

The last "trip" will unquestionably please the ladies. It's a shopping and entertainment tour. The largest shopping center is around St. Pancras-church; the oldest is "Sarool"; and nearby on Oranje-Nassaustraat, there's "Fashion Street." A modern covered shopping center is connected to town via a pedestrian tunnel, "Shopping Center 't Loon," Homerpassage 5. Lastly, there's more shopping in the town of Hoensbroek. The major market days in Heerlen are Tues., Thurs., and Sat.

The little ones will be intrigued by the Recreation Park "Dream Castle," Ganzeweide 113-115, north Heerlen; open, May-Sept., daily, 10am-6pm.

288

Roman Thermae Museum

LOCATION: Coriovallumstraat 9.
INFORMATION: Museum tel. (045) 764581.
HOURS: Open, Tues.-Fri., 10am-5pm; Sat.-Sun., 2-5pm, closed public holidays.
■ *Of interest to older children, especially those who appreciate Roman history.*

The Roman archeological ruins are very interesting as are the models of a potter's oven, a Roman villa, and reconstructions of Roman thermal baths. Utensils, jewelry and items made of earthenware discovered in the region from the Roman period to the present are on display. The model of a late Middle Ages fort should intrigue the boys.

IN THE NEIGHBORHOOD OF HEERLEN:

Hoensbroek Castle, located just off A76, north of Heerlen; from Maastricht, take A79 east to A76 north. Information, VVV Kasteel Hoensbroek, Klinkerstraat 118, tel. (045) 211182; open, June-Sept., daily, 10am-5:30pm; Oct.-May, 10am-noon and 1:30-5:30pm. Guided tours are usually on the hour in the morning and half-hour in the afternoon. Closed, Jan. 1 and Carnival. Hoensbroek Castle is the biggest and most impressive castle between the Maas and Rhine rivers. It was built in five successive phases between the 13th and 18th centuries. In 1927 it was leased to a Foundation which turned it into a cultural and educational center. There is a first-class restaurant in the castle complex. Just north of Hoensbroek Castle at Geleen there's a 4-star hotel ideal for a luxurious stopover, The Golden Tulip Geleen, Geleenbeeklaan 100, tel. (04490) 40040.

Kerkrade, southeast of town on the German border, is known for its botanic center highlighting facets of Limburg flora and the reminders in town, including the Mining Museum, of the days of the coal industry. In recent years, Kerkrade has engendered much enthusiasm and appreciation for its music festival held every 4 years.

Rolduc Abbey, just east of Kerkrade; open, May-Oct., Tues-Fri., 9am-5pm, Sat. (and Sun. in July), 1-5pm; Nov.-April, first Sat. of the month, is well worth a visit. Founded in 1104, the abbey became a church in 1107. An impressive Romanesque structure with many carvings, a clover-leaf crypt, it contains the sarcophagus of the young priest who was the founder.

The Mining Museum, located in a wing of the Rolduc Abbey, is open May-Oct., Tues.-Fri., 9am-5pm, Sat. (and Sun. in July), 1-5pm; Nov.-April, the first Sat. of the month. Gives the picture of the mining days in Limburg.

Kasteel Erenstein, a castle-hotel, 6 Oud Erensteinerweg, tel. (045) 561333 (expensive) is a deluxe stopover which includes a sauna, fitness center and other amenities. The 14th-century castle is situated in an extensive park and the dining room is listed as one of Holland's 75 top restaurants.

VALKENBURG

The recreation capital of the Netherlands

GETTING THERE: From points north, take autoroute A2 following signs for Maastricht, then A79 east towards Heerlen exiting at Valkenburg turnoff. Maastricht is about 11 km southwest on a local road.
INFORMATION: VVV Valkenburg, Th. Dorrenplein 5, tel. (04406) 13364.

Another ancient town, dating from 1040 when it received its city charter from Emperor Henry IV. It is believed the charter was given upon completion of the castle, the ruins of which are still visible and which can be visited in summer. Before starting your tour, drop by the VVV office and get its city-plan and English information pamphlets describing the sights. Since hours at various sights vary according to season, your stop at the VVV is imperative for planning your visit to best advantage. In addition, they will be able to make suggestions about campsites, bungalows, apartments, hotels, and places to eat according to price and category. Don't hesitate to write ahead if you like things ready-planned; they speak good English and have many brochures they can send you.

High on the hill overlooking Valkenburg, you can visit (in season only) the remains of the once proud castle belonging to Walram of Arlon, a noble and large landholder who retained his independence (under overall control of the Dutch rulers) until the French period. In spite of decades of war and various destructions, the ruins still offer a good impression of what the castle was like. A secret passageway leading to the Velvet Grotto was discovered the beginning of this century. Open approximately, April-Oct., Mon.-Sun., 10am-5pm.

Some historic buidings in town include the railway station, built in 1853, the oldest station continually in use in the Netherlands. The VVV is located in a historic building, the Spaans Leenhof, and the Provincial VVV offices are in the Kasteel Den Halder which dates back in part to the 14th century. There are two old town gates, the Berkelpoort (east) and the Grendelpoort (west).

Limburg is honeycombed with caves which have been put to good use over the years. In times of war, they have been places of refuge and in these days of peace, they are used for educational and recreational purposes. The most important caves to visit are the Town Cave and the Coal Mine Cave. They are

290

located near one another. The Town Cave is on Cauberg not far from Grendel Plein and the center of town, and the Coal Mine is at the top of Daalhemerweg which comes into Grendel Plein.

■ **Town Cave,** Cauberg 2, tel. (04406) 12271; open, Sun. before Easter until end of Oct., 9am-5pm, Sun., 10am-5pm; Nov., Sun. before Easter, one tour daily at 2pm, Sat.-Sun., 3:30pm. Wear comfortable warm clothing. The visit is conducted or you would lose yourself in the many warrens underground; it takes about an hour on foot, a half-hour by train. Most tours are in Dutch, but other language groups can also be accommodated on request. The cave is well worth a visit but a bit puzzling in its eclectic nature. You will see evidence of prehistoric fossils and layers of shells, subterranean passages that go off in all directions. The remarkable natural phenomena are the underground lake—light green and "glowing"—and the water that drips with clockwork regularity through the roof. In addition, as you go through the cave you will see sculptures, wall painting, some from the 12th century, some present-day additions. The Roman sections of the cave date from 2,000 years ago; the shells in "marl" (limestone) date from 100 million years ago.

Valkenburg Coal Mine, Daalhemerweg 31, tel. (04406) 12491 or 12950; open, one week before Easter-Oct. 31, 9am-5pm; winter hours, Sat. at 2pm. There are special openings during the Christmas and Carnival vacations. This was never a real coal mining cave, but it has been laid out to be as realistic as possible showing how coal was mined in the area before it became uneconomic. The real mining was done in diggings some distance from town. Because of the ease of cutting the marl, and because there was an already existing model coal mine dating from 1917 (the Daalhemer pit), the Mine Museum Foundation decided to extend and improve the model mine to produce one so realistic that it is viewed as a cultural and historic monument, an example of industrial archeology. Loudspeakers on the wall project the sounds one would hear under real working conditions: the thunderous roar of explosion, trains rumbling down the tracks, excavation machines at work. Well lighted and warm, you walk through at your own pace. Getting hungry? There's a cozy cave restaurant at the exit of the mine where you can get a light lunch . . . on a sunny day, sit on the terrace and enjoy the woodsy atmosphere.

The Fluwelen Grotto and the Panorama of the Prehistoric World Grotto both connected with the castle at one time. The Fluwelen Grotto was a hiding place and the Panorama of the Prehistoric World Grotto is a painted display on the walls of one of the oldest caves.

The Catacombs (in the Rotspark) is a faithful reproduction of major parts of fourteen of the best-known catacombs of Rome. They were laid out from 1909-1913 under the guidance and supervision of experts.

The Phantom Caves (in the Rotspark) show prehistoric beings in fluorescent colors amusingly depicting the development of man and beast. Electronic sounds complete the mysterious atmosphere.

And this is only the beginning. In addition there are all sorts of activities at Rotspark with the two grottoes mentioned above, an open-air theater, bobsledding and woods. There's also a cablecar to Wilhelminatoren (near Prehistoric

World Grotto), and an underground aquarium. Valkenier Fun Fair Park attractions include the Paratower, Magic mirrors, autoscooters, Rodeo Hall, Double Rollercoaster, Oldtimer track, Moonrocket, House of Horrors, Horse Track, Mini-car circuit, Merry-go-round, Big Wheel, Mississippi Boat, Cinema 2000, a playground, and restaurant.

Visit the Hermit's Park from where you can get wonderful views. Twelve hermits lived here most of their lives until 1928. There's also the Lourdes Grotto (near the Town Grotto), a copy of the famous one in France. Don't miss the Fairy-tale Wood where you may encounter Snow White and her friends. It's illuminated on summer evenings (closed in winter), and has a rustic restaurant complete with water organ and colorful display of light and water.

You will also find skittle alleys, trampoline centers, go-cart track (for the over 14's), midget golf, dance halls, swimming pools, tennis courts, boating pond, playgrounds, chair lift above the entire center and a regional museum.

MARKET: The weekly market is held Mondays, 9am-12:30pm on the Walramplein.

Adults without children might prefer making their headquarters at Maastricht, but before deciding, read on.

Thermae 2000 is an extraordinary Roman-type spa opened in early 1989. Situated at the top of the Cauberg, it is made almost entirely of glass and offers splendid views of the trees and the valley below giving one the peace of mind of Shangri-la. Two springs provide 100% pure mineral-rich warm water from an underground reservoir 40,000 years old which conforms to the highest European standards, and also to the stringent German standards for "Medizinisches Heilwasser." There are baths for different purposes: a Roman bath, Turkish bath, salt baths, baths to help sufferers of rheumatism, and indoor as well as outdoor pools for exercise ... one intriguing facet of the complex are the many corridors filled with water so one can swim from one bathing area to the next. The waters contain sodium chloride and fluorine in 30°C temperatures. This four-season complex provides adults with healthy recreation 364 days of the year between 9am and 11pm. One can take a health cure, bathe, sunbathe, keep fit, meditate, jog, or just laze around. There is a yoga-meditation center under the energy source of the glass pyramid, the highest point in the building. In addition to a botanical garden, there's a buffet-restaurant and two bars, one in the sportcafé and one in the sauna area. A cure can be arranged directly by writing Thermae 2000, P.O. Box 198, 6300 AD Valkenburg aan de Geul, tel. (04406) 14600. Or contact the VVV or individual hotels which offer all-in packages.

CASINO: One of Holland's most beautiful casinos is located at Odapark, Valkenburg, tel. (04406) 15550; open, 2pm-2am; offers Roulette, Blackjack, poker, bingo machines and "one-armed bandits." There is a simple dress code.

Gourmets and lovers of luxury will be intrigued to know that Valkenburg and vicinity have several restaurants with Michelin stars (see Eating Out), and a number of elegant chateau hotels (see Staying Over). And for those watching their budgets, there are plenty of cozy terraces and moderate-priced restaurants, as well as a list (at this writing) of roughly 49 hotels in all price ranges!

EATING OUT: This town has a café-restaurant at every turn so light- and moderate-priced meals are no problem. For that special night on the town, however, the choice is more complicated. The Restaurant Prinses Juliana heads the list with two Michelin stars, Broekhem 11, tel. 12244. The dining room is very formal and rather severe; summertime eating on the terrace is the most pleasant. Menus range in price from Fl. 75, "Alliance Menu," Fl. 110 menu, wine included, and Fl. 115, a Gastronomique Menu. Open daily except no Saturday lunch.

Restaurant Lindenhorst, Broekhem 130, tel. 13444, with one star, is small, intimate; high-style New York decor. The owner-chef, Ida van den Hurk, will bid you welcome sometime during your meal . . . you can choose the Fl. 75 menu with five courses which is excellent. At the Kasteel Wittem (Wittem Castle), Wittemerallee 28, about 10 km southeast of town, there is a cozy lounge for cocktails while waiting for your table . . . . You might want to try the "Menu Dégustation Cave et Cuisine" (Gastronomic Menu, wine included), a 7-course dinner at Fl. 160 is worth a try. The Wittem has a Michelin star and boasts a fine pastry chef as well as an excellent wine cellar. Just outside Maastricht is the Chateau Neercanne (see Maastricht).

STAYING OVER: There are so many choices in Valkenburg, the VVV can best recommend a suitable hotel according to space and price. Apartments can be rented by the week for 2, 4, or 6 persons at the Casinohotel Valkenburg. The Prinses Juliana in the top-priced category has conveniently located rooms; tel.(04406) 12244 for reservations . . . 2-star dining room. Another first-class hotel is the Parkhotel Rooding, Neerhem 68, tel. (04406) 13241 with a heated indoor swimming pool, lovely grounds, and near a wooded area. Of special note are the castle-hotels in the area. Just outside the town of Gulpen on the main highway between Maastricht and Aachen, the Kasteel Neuborg, 1 Riehagar-voetpad, tel. (04450) 1222, is complete with moat, drawbridge, quiet woody surroundings, spacious rather old-fashioned rooms (with all facilities). Formal and rather expensive but a lovely place to stay. A bit further east on N278, the Kasteel Wittem (see above) has a small private park area, a half-moat with swans and walks along country roads. The dining room is very well recommended . . . children usually eat at a special first sitting. At Kerkrade, almost on the German border, there's another castle-hotel, Kasteel Erenstein. (See "Kerkra-de" above.) And right on the Belgian border at Epen there's the 4-star Golden Tulip Zuid Limburg Hotel, Julianastraat 23a, tel. (04455) 1818. The green countrysde can be enjoyed from the terrace or balconied apartments with kitchenettes . . . special culinary weekend arrangements.

IN THE NEIGHBORHOOD OF VALKENBURG:
Margraten, site of the American Cemetery (see "introduction") is a worth-while stop to briefly honor the 8,301 American soldiers buried here who died in 1944-45 during the battles in southeastern Holland. The gardens are lovely.
We've been so busy describing organized primarily children attractions, we

haven't mentioned the beauty that surrounds Valkenburg. The town is built on the Geul River which flows through town under bridges and past outdoor cafés and parks. Explore the Geuldal, the land south of Valkenburg and Maastricht with its hidden villages, woods, small farms, castles and the high point of the whole Netherlands, Vaals. Some of the small old villages include Sibbe, Vilt, IJzeren, Oud-Valkenburg, Geulhen, Hoathem and Walem. A variety of country accommodations can be found if you want to "get away from it all". . . see VVV.

MAASTRICHT

A Lively Roman Influence

GETTING THERE: From Amsterdam, all the way on A2; from Rotterdam and The Hague, follow directions for Eindhoven, then take A67 east to Knooppunt Leenderheide intersection south of Eindhoven, then south on A2 to Maastricht. Parking is almost impossible, so look for the underground parking garage at the Vrijthof (city center plaza).
INFORMATION: VVV Maastricht, Het Dinghuis, Kleinestraat 1, tel. (043) 252121.

There is an electricity in the air at Maastricht. People are lively, hurrying, enjoying themselves. And when the fair is going on, the town really jumps. But it wasn't always as effervescent as it is today. The Roman legions founded "Mosa Trajectum," today's Maastricht, at the junction of the Meuse River (Maas River) with several Roman roads leading south to the Low Countries (Belgium, etc.) and to important Roman centers of defense at Cologne, Rheims and Trier. Merchants, farmers, traders and adventurers soon gathered at this point where business was burgeoning. The settlement was a walled castellum until about the end of the 4th century. Then, it was a bishop's seat for about 350 years. From 1202, the Duke of Brabant dominated the town as well as the region. The first outer walls were built in 1229 but the town grew so rapidly, a second wall was begun in the early 14th century. Quite a lot of city wall is extant and great fun to explore.

Maastricht was a rich prize, hence repeatedy came under siege by the Dutch, Spanish and French. In 1795, the French forces made Maastricht the capital of a French province. After Napoleon's defeat at Waterloo, Belgium and the Netherlands were united under King Willem I. They battled constantly and 9 years later a partition was agreed upon under which Maastricht remained a Dutch city.

Today, Maastricht is an industrial as well as a cultural, religious, educational and political center. Ceramics, paper, beer and cement are some of its important products. Students attending the three colleges add to the city's vitality.

You can't beat walking to really get to know a place. The Maastricht VVV has a number of detailed walking tours such as a fortifications walk, walks up Mount St. Peter and on the plateau once you have reached it. During the summer and school holidays, conducted city walks are organized. But you can strike out on your own with a little guidance pointing you in the right direction along the old city walls with parks and walks in lovely green areas, a pleasant respite from city sidewalks.

One pleasant walk is east into the Wijk area over the Saint Servaas Bridge (1280-1298), one of the oldest bridges in the Netherlands, originally a 9-arched wooden bridge. Explore some of the streets noting the old facades. As you leave the bridge, turn left on Oeverwal to St. Maartenslaan and you will pass St. Martins Church (1858). This Gothic-style church was designed by Dr. Cuypers to replace an older church. Go inside to see "The Black Crucifix," a life-size image of Christ made of walnut. Turning right after the bridge along the Stenenwal, there's a small museum, "Santjes and Kantjes," Corversplein 14, tel. (043) 251851, only open by appointment except in July and August, daily, 2-5pm ... a unique collection of objects of popular piety such as prints, prayer books, figurines. As you walk further south, along part of the first Medieval ramparts, note the Water Gate along the stone wall and the "Meuse Tower" on the Maaspuntweg, both 13th century. Walking east from the water tower along Hoogbrugstraat, you will come to the "monumentale panden," a former place of refuge of the deanery of Meerssen (1690). Across the street is Sint Gillishofje, an almshouse dating from 1759. Walking back north along Rechtstraat, note the interesting facades and gable stones. The Wycker Brugstraat is the main street leading from the bridge toward the train and bus station ... there are shops along the way and a 4-star hotel, Hotel Beaumont, where you can stop for a cup of coffee or overnight.

Maastricht is rich in ancient churches with outstanding collections of religious art. Of particular note are the Romanesque churches, St. Servatius Basilica on Vrijthof Square and the Basilica of Our Beloved Lady on O.L. Vrouweplein, both described in detail below. In addition, there are a number of Gothic churches as well as those dating from the 17th, 18th and 19th centuries. Four interesting ones are:

St. Matthias' Church, Boschstraat (visit by appointment only), dates from the 14th-16th century. Financed primarily by the cloth weavers' guild, it has a beautiful 15th-century pieta. Tel. 213303 for information.

The Dominican Church, Dominicanerplein 1, is a 13th-century sandstone church. Note remains of wall paintings on the arched roof dating from 1337 (north aisle) and 1619.

St. John's Church (14th-15th century), Henrie van Veldekeplein, boasts a beautiful 70-meter-high tower, Louis XVI pulpit and some fine tombs. Open to visitors after Sunday church services and on Fridays in summer.

The Synagogue, Capucijnengang 2, was designed by master builder Matthijs Hermans and completed in 1840. Note the semi-circular window showing the Ten Commandments and the names of the Twelve Tribes of Israel.

There are many buildings worth locating in Maastricht. Some of the most important are:

The City Hall on the Market Square, built 1659-1664 by Pieter Post, has fine proportions and an interesting double flight of stairs probaby built for the two authorities ruling the city at the time. Note the murals, archway decorations and rococo plastered ceilings as well as the paintings, and fine Gobelin tapestries. The carillon tower (1684) has 43 bells that are played regularly.

The Dinghuis, Kleine Straat 1, seat of the former Lord Chief Justice, is now the locale of the VVV. Built in 1470, notice the beautiful stone gable and timbered side wall on the Jodenstraat side of the building.

The Stokstraat Kwartier is south of the VVV just after the St. Servaas Bridge and should be explored on foot to appreciate the many fine shops and admire the notable period houses of the 17th and 18th centuries (restored). If you continue on Stok Straat heading south, you will come to the Hotel Derlon with its fascinating Roman excavations.

The Roman Baths on Op de Thermen aren't far away . . . look for the plan of the baths on the small square.

The Stads Schouwburg Theater, on Hondstraat, was formerly the Jesuit Church built in the 17th century. Since 1786, however, it has been used as a theater with a hall of mirrors (for masked balls). All that remains of the Cloister is the square tower with sundial.

The Bishop's Mill, 17th-18th century, Stenenbrug 1, is close to the first wall fortifications . . . cross the little bridge to the back of the mill where the wheel can be seen. Visits by arrangement only.

Faliezusters Nunnery (1647) is along the fortifications, just south of the Bishop's Mill . . . built in Maasland Renaissance stye.

The Plague House on Vijf Koppen (on south bank of the Jeker), is the name given to a former water-driven paper mill named "De Ancker" (1775) because of the nearby barracks which housed plague sufferers.

Leeuwenmolen, also in the vicinity at Peterstraat 29, dates from the 17th century.

St. Martin's Almshouse (1715), Grote Looierstraat 27, consisting of 13 cottages, was founded by Martinus Rencken. Notice the beautiful gable stone over the entrance . . . the courtyard can be visited.

MUSEUMS: Two museums of primary interest are the Bonnefanten Museum and the Derlon Museum Cellar, described below. In addition, there are:

Natural History Museum, De Bosquetplein 6-7, tel. 293064; hours, Mon-Fri., 10am-12:30pm and 1:30-5pm, Sat. closed, Sun., 2-5pm. As you would guess, this museum deals with the natural history and geology of Limburg and surroundings. There's a permanent exhibit of rocks, minerals, fossils, flora and fauna but also changing exhibitions. In addition, there's a traditional garden and a vivarium. You can't miss the huge quartzite boulder next to the museum.

Spanish Government House, is located at Vrijthof 18, tel. 292201; guided tours, Wed. and Thurs. at 10am, 11am, noon, 2, 3 and 4pm. This restored building dates from 1545 and was the residence of the dukes of Brabant and the Spanish rulers. There are period rooms in Dutch, French, Italian and Liege-Maastricht styles; collections of art and artifacts; crystal chandeliers; statues and figurines; and many other artifacts dating from the 17th century.

MARKETS: The markets of Maastricht draw crowds from far and near. The general market is held Wed. and Fri. mornings on the Market Square around the City Hall from 8am-1pm; the antique and curio market is held Sat. on Stationsstraat, 10am-4pm.

Some Maastricht food specialities worth discovering are the Limburgse flan, gingerbread, apple dumplings, the Maastricht beer, wine, and a hard liquor, "Els," a local cheese, "rommedou," mushrooms and trout.

■ **The Casements** will be enjoyed especially by military history enthusiasts. The Waldeck Bastion entrance is at the southwest part of town near Tongerseplein. Tours are held usually at 2pm, although there is also one at 12:30pm mid-July to mid-Aug. and for a week in Oct. during the Autumn school holiday. The normal tour is one hour but there is a three-hour tour (not suitable for children under 12 years) giving greater detail . . . must reserve with VVV . . . hours variable. Men and boys will find this an interesting expedition. Between 1575 and 1825, mining created the network of galleries which were later used in times of siege for subterranean approach and elimination of the enemy. The tour guide explains all about this military monument with its domed vaults, impressive shell-proof refuges, powder rooms, plunging steps and a variety of galleries.

Fort St. Peter, located south of the city on St. Peter Mountain overlooking the whole area. Departure for the tour is from the café-restaurant Fort St. Peter, Luikerweg 80. Check with the VVV for times, dates, and ticket sales. The fort was constructed in 1701-1702 and was instrumental in the siege of Maastricht in the battle with the French in 1748. The fort is shaped like a 5-pointed star, has two major galleries at its center and a gallery round its five sides. You will see the galleries, the shell-proof chambers, look down the water well, and climb up to see the wonderful view. The tour takes about an hour.

"Linie van Du Moulin" (complex fortifications), located on the west side of town, behind Staten Singel and between Pastoor Habetsstraat and Cabergerweg (entrance from Cabergerweg) is another treat for our military buffs. These fortifications, covering 15 hectares, were developed 1773-1777 by Mr. Du Moulin, an expert on defense. There are dry trenches, bastions with bombproof shelters and mine galleries. The guide, a historical expert, gives a one-hour tour, usually every Sun. at 3pm . . . details from the VVV.

Plays, concerts, musicals, opera, international dance productions, puppet shows, etc., can be enjoyed at:

The Stadsschouwburg, Achter de Comedie, is busy all year with "serious" productions such as plays, cabarets, musicals, opera, etc.

The Staargebouw (Concert Hall), Henric van Veldekeplein 25, offers productions ranging from jazz to Beethoven.

The Generaalshuis, Vrijthof 47, accepts reservations for events at the above theaters, tel. 293828 for the box office. The Generaalshuis has small theater halls and puts on a variety of shows, including in winter, special children's plays and puppet shows.

Podium Posjet, Vijverdalseweg 1, tel. 841777, ext. 2207, also gives performances in winter by Ruben's Puppet Theater, "De Kleine Wereld," and others.

Maastricht Exhibition and Congress Center has two theaters where congress and cultural events are given. In addition, regular concerts are held in a number of churches . . . check with the VVV. Open-air concerts on Vrijthof Square and O.L. Vrouweplein (square) are held regularly during the summer, and don't forget to check when the carillon concerts at the City Hall on the Market Square are to be held. Student performances are held at the Conservatoire Concert Hall, Bonnefanten 15, tel. 292222, and at the College of Music Concert Hall, St. Maartenspoort 2, tel. 293141.

Adults looking for a bit of glamor might try their luck at the Valkenburg Casino, Odapark, Valkenburg . . . about 11 km east of Maastricht, open 2pm-2am. French and American roulette, Blackjack, Baccarat and jackpot machines await. Bar, restaurant and lounge on the premises to offer sustenance and relaxation. Or, enjoy a night at the Limburg Race Course in Schaesberg, on the Hofstraat. Friday evenings at 7pm. Tel. 319191 for information.

EATING OUT: Around the Vrijthof, there are sidewalk cafés galore: The Monopole's menu is Fl. 15.50. A Greek restaurant, Sertaki, Kesselkade 42, offers a menu at Fl. 8.50; and at the Promenade Bistro, Maaspromenade 25, the menu is Fl. 11.00. One of the best, yet informal, places for dinner is Gauchos Grill Restaurant, Vrijthof 53, tel. 255022 (in the Hotel Du Casque) offers wonderful beef from Argentina and all-you-can-eat ribs that can't be beat. Popular so get there early or reserve . . . moderate-priced.

Gourmet dining is available at a number of restaurants: "Grandmère," Vrijthof/Helmstraat 16, tel. 252325, has old-world charm; "Le Bon Vivant," Capucijnenstraat 91, tel. 210816, is in a vaulted cave; and well recommended is "Au Coin des Bons Enfants," Ezelmarkt 4, tel. 212359.

■ The "Chateau Neercanne," Cannerweg 8000, tel. 251359, southwest of town on the Belgian border, is a must for any special occasion. This Michelin one-star restaurant offers an elegant setting in a castle brimming with history dating from 1698 sitting high on the side of a hill—the only terraced castle in the Netherlands. The Gourmet Menu is about Fl. 70; the Chateau Menu, about Fl. 100. Large mushrooms are featured in a number of dishes as well as pasta and fish. Ask about the special soup that comes bubbling under its own mille feuilles "hat" . . . delicious. As would be expected, the wine list is extensive and excellent. Wines are kept in the castle caves which served the double purpose of perfect climate-controlled wine cellars and escape route and hiding place for underground and resistance workers in WW II . . . they lead right across the border into Belgium. Tours are possible (ask ahead when making reservations), or come Tues.-Fri. and Sun., 9:30am-noon and 4-6pm. It is also possible to visit Frans Tuinstra's ceramics studio on Wed., Fri and Sun. afternoons.

STAYING OVER: You may consider staying in the Wyck section, east across the Maas River where the pace is more relaxed and the prices are generally a bit lower. The railroad station and the new Congress Center, MECC, with a Golden Tulip Hotel Barbizon ideal for conferees, are located on this side. Hotel Beaumont, Wyckerbrugstraat 2, tel. 254433, is in the heart of the Wyck shopping center . . . modern rooms in a period hotel with style; nice dining room; TV on request; rates are moderate. The Hotel Maastricht, De Ruitery 1, tel. 254171, offers rooms and "apartments"—rates are at the top end of the scale. A large, rambling establishment, totally modern, rooms along the Stenenwal overlooking the river have wonderful views of the "City."

In the center of town, there are even more to choose from, including a comfortable older hotel in the process of being refurbished, the Hotel Du Casque, Helmstraat 14, tel. 214343. There is parking in the Vrijthof underground garage and a couple of spaces in their private parking area. This hotel couldn't be more conveniently located and has the added attraction of the Gauchos Grill and a terrace overlooking the Vrijthof square where all the action is going on. Service is impeccable; prices vary according to room type— moderate to expensive. For a special treat ask if the room which also serves as a conference room is available . . . elegant, comfortable, with a small balcony. Or, choose the Golden Tulip Derlon Hotel, O.L. Vrouweplein 6, tel. 216770 with its Roman antiquities "museum" in the cellar tea room. The hotel offers all amenities, including overlooking a charming little square . . . very expensive.

Ask about holiday flats such as Paul Mertens, Heggenstraat 7, tel. 218401, which is centrally located and offers a sitting room, bedroom, shower and toilet (1-2 persons) for around Fl. 80/night. There are also campsites and a youth hostel recommended by the VVV.

YEARLY EVENTS: The special yearly activitis of note include one of the largest Carnivals in the Netherlands in February, the International Antique Market in March, St. Servatius Fair on the Vrijthof in May, Burgundian Gastronomic Festivities on the Vrijthof in August, and a three-day Jazz Festival in October.

COMMERCIAL TOURS: The VVV in Maastricht is very active and organizes a number of well worthwhile tours: City Guided Walk to the old center, 1½ hours, July and Aug. and holidays, daily at 2pm; City Guided Walk with visit to caves and treasury of St. Servatius' Basilica, 6½ hours, year-round (Fl. 32.00 each); Tour of St. Pietersberg Caves, 1 hour, year-round by appointment; Walk of City Fortifications (fortifications, churches, city walls and city gates), 1½ hours, summer and autumn holidays, daily at 2pm.

Boat Tours are offered by Rederij Stiphout, Maaspromenade 27, tel. 254151: daily one-hour tour plus: Boat trip on the Maas and visit to St. Pietersberg caves, option of lunch in caves, 3 hours, May to Sept. hourly from 10am-4pm; Moonlight Cruise with music and a glass of wine, 4 hours, May-Dec., Fri. and Sat., 8:30pm; "Vasco da Gama" night tour with buffet and drinks, 5 hours, year-round; boat trip from Maastricht to the Belgian border on the Maas River, lunch included, 4 hours, all year Mon.-Fri., 11:15am; Maastricht/Liege Boat Trip includes a visit to the Ardennes, 3½ hours mid-May to beginning Sept., 10am.

Bus Tours by Splendid Cars, will take you to Brussels (10 hours) or a Three Countries Tour to Eifel, Monschau and the Ardennes (8 hours). Or see the city of Maastricht from an old-fashioned horse-drawn hunting coach. Forty-five leisurely minutes through the oldest part of the town with comments by the coachman. Coach-hire G. Costongs, Koestraat 14-16, tel. 214812, departure: O.L. Vrouweplein and Vrijthof, May-Sept., daily, 11:30am-4:30pm (weather permitting), adults, Fl. 12, children to 12 years, Fl. 5 . . . minimum party, 2 adults.

Bonnefanten Museum

LOCATION: Dominikanerplein 5, across the street from the Du Casque Hotel and near the Vrijthof square.
INFORMATION: Tel. 251655.
HOURS: Open Tues.-Fri., 10am-5pm, Sat.-Sun., 11am-5pm. Closed New Year's Eve afternoon, New Year's Day, Carnival, Good Friday, Christmas Eve afternoon, and Christmas Day.
■ *Of interest to school-age children.*

The collection of this museum of art and antiquities includes Limburg archeological finds, Maastricht pottery, Maasland statues, Southern Dutch and Italian paintings, modern and contemporary art. In addition there's an educational exhibit detailing various world cultures with sound effects and dioramas. Of special interest to visitors is the large-scale model of Maastricht in a room of its own. Ask if they can put on the film in English, which, by sound and lights, depicts the history of the city. The original maquette was made in 1752 by the French and is at the Hotel des Invalides in Paris. Each section of the city is highlighted and its story told. The film covers the battles of 1748 between the French, Spanish and Dutch, and shows by lighting effects how the town was encircled; where it was bombarded; how Fort St. Peter figured in the assault; and the surrender.

Derlon Museum

LOCATION: Plankstraat 17 . . . go in the side entrance to the Derlon Hotel and walk downstairs.
INFORMATION: Tel. 252121.
HOURS: Open, Sundays, noon-4pm; although if you want to enjoy a nice lunch or a lovely cup o' tea, you may view the display as long as the tea room is open.
■ *Of interest to most children . . . especially if they get an ice cream while being exposed to "culture."*

Luckily, the city's archeologists were on their toes when surveying this site for the new Derlon Hotel. Upon the discovery of important 2nd-, 3rd- and 4th-century Roman finds, it was decided to build the hotel around and over them, and incorporating them into a most attractive (and practical) setting for anyone

to enjoy ... a lunch/tea room. On display are part of the 2nd- and 3rd-century square, a section of a 4th-century wall and gate, a 3rd-century well, and part of a pre-Roman cobblestone road. Artifacts are displayed in illuminated glass cabinets. There's an information sheet (not to take away) with information about the survey and the display. This is a compact "museum" in a gracious setting.

Basilica of Saint Servatius

LOCATION: Vrijthof Square.
INFORMATION: VVV Maastricht, tel. (043) 252121.
HOURS: Open, April-Nov., 10am-5pm.
■ *Of interest to high school and older children.*

This Medieval cruciform basilica is located on the site of an early Roman "sanctuary" built between 560 and 599. The heart of the basilica itself dates from ca. 1000. The crypts dating from the 6th, 11th and 12th centuries, hold the remains of the first bishop of Maastricht, St. Servatius, and Karel of Lotheringen. In the 14th and 15th centuries, the basilica was enlarged and in the 19th century, it was restored. Items of special note are the Treasury (see below), the Emperor's Gallery and Hall (impressive columns), richly sculptured Gothic south portal (Berg Portal), the 16th-century paintings and columns in the choir, and St. Servatius' tomb in the crypt. The Treasure-House visitors' entrance is from Vrijthof Square between the Basilica apse and the Military Headquarters ... visits can be arranged through the VVV. Hours: April-Oct., daily, 10am-5pm. This rich collection of reliquaries, paintings, figurines, old Eastern fabrics, ivory, is worth a visit. The most magnificent items are the 12th-century reliquary of St. Servatius, and the saint's bust done in 1579, as well as a number of his possessions.

Basilica of Our Beloved Lady

LOCATION: O.L. Vrouweplein.
INFORMATION: VVV Maastricht, tel. 252121.
HOURS: Open daily except between noon and 3pm and during
church services.
■ *Of interest to older children.*

The West wing and crypts are the oldest parts of this Medieval basilica, dating from the 12th century. The structure was built on Roman foundations and enlarged, altered and restored a number of times. Of special architectural significance are the West wing and the choir, the only ones of their kind. Notice the impressive columns, the richly sculpted capitals surrounding the choir, the cloisters and the crypts. The Treasure-House can be entered through the church on O.L. Vrouweplein; tel. 251851 for info. Hours: Easter to mid-Sept., daily, 11am-5pm, Sun., 1-5pm. Another rich collection of ecclesiastical art and artifacts, including richly embroidered garments. Ask to see the "Levite Tapestry" of the next to last Bishop of Maastricht, St. Lambertus.

Caves of Mount St. Peter

LOCATION: There are two sections of the labyrinths open to the public: Northern Passage, departure is from Chalet Bergrust, Luikerweg 71; the Zonneberg Caves, departure from Casino Slavante, 1 Slavante (near Enci Cement Works, Maastricht).
INFORMATION: VVV Maastricht, tel. 252121.
HOURS: Vary throughout the year . . . check with the VVV.
■ *Of interest to most children. Bring a stroller and warm clothing for little ones.*

This is certainly more to the children's taste than churches or museums. Visits are guided and take one hour. Dress warmly even in summer, wear very comfortable low-heeled walking shoes and bring a flashlight if possible. The caves resulted from centuries of excavation of marl, a building stone. There is an enormous labyrinth of more than 20,000 passages, more than 200 kilometers long with some sections as high as 16 meters. Throughout history these caves have been a place of refuge, and signs of habitation can still be seen. In WW I and WW II, the caves were used as escape routes between Holland and Belgium and a place to hide Allied soldiers, airmen, resistance workers, etc. Some of the emergency provisions are still there. In the Northern Passage, there are ancient writings on the walls, a baker's oven dating from the French occupation in 1794, a treasure chamber from the Second World War, and a collapsed dome. The Southern Passage (Zonneberg Caves), contains charcoal drawings, old handwritings, a water reservoir, an oven, museum and a chapel. A two-hour tour is offered in the Zonneberg Caves for those wishing a more in-depth explanation about the history of this cave. Also, on Sun., Feb.-Nov., and during Easter and Autumn school holidays, a combined boat-trip and visit to the caves is possible . . . check with VVV.

CHAPTER 13

THE PROVINCE OF ZEELAND

Zeeland can be a day's trip from Rotterdam, The Hague and even Amsterdam, but if you want to explore it all, you should plan on staying overnight. The quickest route from Rotterdam, take A13 south via the Maas Tunnel, then A29 through the Heinenoord Tunnel continuing over the Haringvlietbrug, then west following signs for Zierikzee over the Grevelingendam (N59). From Zierikzee, take N256 over the longest bridge in Europe, the Zeelandbrug (5,022 meters long), into South Beveland then west following signs for Middelburg and places south.

BUT, if you want to enjoy the seascapes along the western land mass, from Rotterdam, take A4 south through the Benelux Tunnel, west on A15 following signs for Hellevoetsluis; then cross the Haringvlietdam with its 17 sluice gates, continuing southwest following directions for the Brouwersdam and Ooster-schelde. As you cross the Oosterschelde Storm Surge Barrier, you can stop to see Delta Expo and Neeltje Jans Island (details follow). You can view the Barrier and learn how this extraordinary engineering feat was achieved at Delta Expo. Continuing south, you will come to North Beveland where you can choose your road to Middelburg, Veere, Vlissingen. After crossing by boat to Breskens, you will be in the Flemish part of Holland next door to Belgium.

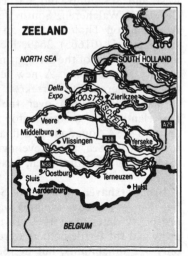

Zeeland was one of the richest and most powerful of the Dutch provinces. Middelburg, the capital, had its own East India Company. Veere was the staple port for the Scottish wool trade, and the merchants of Zierikzee were

INFORMATION: Provincial VVV Zeeland,
tel. (01180) 33000.

known at every port in the Baltic. Gradually, its commercial preeminence declined and by the 18th century agriculture had overtaken foreign trade as the most important occupation. The farming community, behind their great sea dikes, had less exposure to the outside world and life seemed to stand still until World War II.

Historically, this area of the Netherlands has always battled with the sea . . . it has been a source of wealth, but also a harbinger of total destruction, and often death. In 1000 B.C., the sea level was 127 meters lower than it is today; the North Sea was dry land. With the melting of the ice caps, north and south, the sea level has risen approximately 20 centimeters per century. Gradually dikes were built to protect the land. One of the most disastrous floods occurred in 1421; the St. Elisabeth flood destroyed 72 villages and drowned about 10,000 people. In the last two centuries, flood disasters have been recorded for the years 1877, 1883, 1889, 1894, 1896, 1911, 1916, and 1953, the last being the worst in our times. The Delta Plan was born as a result of that devastation; details of the story follow in the discussion of the Delta-Expo Oosterschelde. The Delta Plan strongly influenced the awakening of Zeeland from its deep sleep. The mouths of tidal estuaries now linking the islands together, have taken away their isolation and formed a protective barrier all along the North Sea Coast. The Veerse Meer, an inland lake 22 kilometers long, was formed with the closing of the Veerse Gat and the Zandkreek. It is now an active recreation center for aquatic sports and a new age of prosperity looks to be well on its way.

Because of the islands and peninsula-like land formations of Zeeland, we will start our exploration from north to south, beginning first with a series of smaller villages and stops of interest. Before leaving South Holland, however, an introduction to the Delta Plan can be made by visiting the small Haringvliet Expo located at the southern end of the Haringvliet dam. A more detailed story will be found at Delta Expo-Oosterschelde which is covered in full below.

The most northerly "islands" of Zeeland are Schouwen-Duiveland to the west, and St. Philipsland and Tholen to the east. They are followed by North Beveland, Walcheren, South Beveland and Dutch Flanders. The town of St. Annaland on Tholen boasts an interesting museum, "De Meestoof," Bierensstraat 6, tel. (01665) 2649, located in the former town hall. The collection includes clothes of the area, farmers' style rooms, archeological finds and a 19th-century school room. A new ferry for pedestrians and bikers opened in 1988 from Schepernisse to Yerseke.

Taking N57 south over the Brouwersdam, the first town in Schouwen-Duiveland where we might stop is Scharendijke, just east of the south exit of the dam, to see "Aquadome," a floating aquarium with many species of fish native to the North Sea, the Grevelingen and the Oosterschelde. Tel. (01117) 2038 or (01110) 3698 for info; open, Easter-July, 10am-10pm, Aug.-Nov., 10am-6pm.

Brouwershaven, just east of Scharendijke, received its town charter in 1477, but there is evidence the area was inhabited even earlier. The period of greatest prosperity dates from 1590. In the flood of 1682, many buildings were washed away and the fertile polders were covered with salt and silt. By 1822, there were only 322 inhabitants, but in 1838, things began to look up. From 1840-1860,

Brouwershaven was a busy seaport servicing Rotterdam and Dordrecht. It had international Consular representatives, solicitors, pilot services, a law court, tax office and some 27 hotel-cafés. When Rotterdam's Nieuwe Waterweg provided direct access to seagoing vessels, Brouwershaven was dealt the fatal blow.

The Town Hall (built 1599; restored in 1970-1973) is considered by some experts to be one of the most beautiful examples of the Flemish Renaissance style in the Netherlands. The inscription over the entrance reads "The Law is for the Common Good." If there is time, note the Dutch Reformed Church, St. Nicolas, which it is believed was started as early as 1293. The small local history museum, "De Vergulde Garnaal," Markt 5, tel. (01119) 1226, open May-Sept., Tues.-Sat., 2-5pm, has models of the Town Hall and the church.

To the west toward the North Sea, just south of Brouwershaven Dam, there are lovely walks between the villages of Renesse and Haamstede, as well as 750 acres of forest and 2,000 acres of beach and dunes to explore. A former 12th-century fortified castle is located just north of Renesse, Slot Moermond. It has a long and interesting history but can be visited only from mid-June to mid-Aug.; info, tel. VVV Renesse, (01116) 2120. Maps of the area are available from the VVV with walking tours indicated.

Serooskerke, on N57 south just before the Oosterschelde Sea, suffered terrible damage when the sea dike here broke in 1953 creating enormous loss of property not to mention their share of the 1,854 people who died throughout the province. After the hole in the dike named Schelphoek (shell corner) was closed, a deep inland creek remained. This area has been planted and offers fine natural scenery and provides birds and waterfowl a place of refuge.

East of Serooskerke and north of Zierikzee, there are three former terp villages built around a central square with the local church in the center. Zonnemaire is known for its illustrious citizen, Pieter Zeeman who won the Nobel Prize in 1902 for physics; Noordgouwe's church dates from 1462; but Dreischor is the most charming with an interesting 14th-15th-century church with a leaning tower, small moat and a town hall dating from 1637. The agricultural museum, "Landbouwmuseum," (Mr. Pieter Moggestraat 5, tel. (01112) 1579 or 1280 for info.) is open June-Aug., Mon-Sat., 1:30-4:30pm or by appointment. It has a large collection of farm implements including a farmer's room and kitchen.

Bruinisse, known for its oyster culture and also watersports activities has two museums. The Visserijmuseum (Fishery Museum), Molenstraat 44, tel. (01113) 1412, open, mid-May to mid-Sept., Mon-Fri., 1-4pm. The Antiquities Museum (Oudheidkamer), is located in an 18th-century home at Oudestraat 27, tel. (01113) 1251, open, June-Sept., Mon. and Thurs., 2-4pm.

Completing the circle tour of Schouwen-Duiveland, the biggest town is Zierikzee, a fascinating old town.

ZIERIKZEE

A trading town . . . salt, red dye

GETTING THERE: From the north, take N57 south then N59 east; coming from the east, N59 from Willemstad, or various roads from Bergen op Zoom.
INFORMATION: VVV Zierikzee, Havenpark 29, tel. (01110) 12450.

Zierikzee is the largest and most important town in this part of Zeeland. Eleven centuries old, it has had its ups and downs through the ages.

When Count Willem III granted Zierikzee its city rights in 1248, it was about half its present size. In 1325, the town developed on both sides of the harbor,new quays were built, and the whole quarter surrounded by a wall. Its location on the Oosterschelde and a tributary of the Gouwe, enabled it to become an important port. To a large extent, it owes its development to trade between England, present-day Belgium (then, Brabant and Flanders), and Holland. Two products much in demand which Zierikzee was able to provide were salt and madder, a root which produces a red dye used in dyeing cloth.

You can sense the Middle Ages atmosphere when visiting the town's early structures. The old church, "Gasthuiskerk," on the Havenplein can be visited by contacting Mr. L.C. Krijger, de Cranestraat 7, for the key. The 16th-century Town Hall is easily identifiable by its tall "frilly" spire. Another ancient building is the old prison, 's Gravensteen. Museums are housed in both these buildings and are described below. The heavy, square Gothic tower, "De Sint Lievens Monstertoren" was built in 1454 as a tower for a cathedral which was never finished. You can visit weekdays in summer from 11am-5pm. If you have the strength, it's a good place for an overview of the surrounding area.

Zierikzee is surrounded by a canal which encloses the original town. At the north entrance, the Nobelpoort water gate with decorative 1559 facade is worth noting. The Zuidhaven port (15th century) and the Noordhavenport are at the southeastern corner of town at the locale of the old port which leads to the Havenpark and Havenplein. This is a part of town worth exploring if you are interested in buildings with early facades. The front of the White Swan, Havenpark 1, dates from 1658. Two corn grinding watermills in town can be visited: "De Hoop" (1874), Lang Nobelstraat 43, and "Den Haas" (1727), Bolwerk. They are both open Sat.-Wed. from 9am-4pm.

MUSEUMS: The two major museums in town are in the Town Hall and the Maritime Museum, 's Gravensteen . . . both will be discussed below. The third museum is the Burgerweeshuis Museum, Poststraat 45, tel. 12683; open, mid-June to mid-Aug., Mon.-Sat. , 10am-5pm. The weighhouse dates from the 14th-17th centuries. The collection includes a Regent's room with gold and leather-covered walls, and Louis XIV wainscoting, paintings, ceramics, etc.

MARKETS: Regular market day is held on Thursday in the town center. During the high season (approx. July 8-Aug. 12), a special tourist market is held every Tues. Here, too, the carillons in the Town Hall tower give a concert on

Thurs., 10:45-11:45am (approx.). You can go to the local oyster cultivating beds and buy oysters to take home (or eat them locally, of course).

EATING OUT: The recommended pancake house is 't Zeeuwsche Pannekoekenhuis, Appelmarkt 6, tel. 16179, from 10am-9pm, closed Sun.; or you can try typical Dutch dishes "Nederlands Dis," at Restaurant Concordia, Appelmarkt 29, tel. 15122. Tourist Menus are offered at the Wegrestaurant "De Val," Weg naar de Val 10, tel. 13208; and at the Cafe-Restaurant, "De Zeeuwsche Herberghe, Havenpark 2, tel. 14118.

STAYING OVER: Two moderate hotels in town are: Mondragon, Havenpark 21, tel. (01110) 13051, and the Monique Hotel, Driekoninginnen 7, tel. 12323. For camp sites, get the VVV "Kampeergids 1989 . . . " which will give you full details on camps, prices, accommodations, etc. There are also folders on hotels, boarding houses, holiday homes and apartments. Of special interest might be the off-season rates (Sept.-June) for 3-, 5-and 8-day hotel and bungalow arrangements at very special prices.

YEARLY EVENTS: Special folkloric events include the traditional sailing race on the Oosterschelde, May 14; Expo Zierikzee from May 18-21; Yearly market, June 1; Deltaweek, July 1-10, Tourist days, every Tues. from July 12-Aug. 9; and the Funfair, Sept. 3-8. Check with the VVV to be sure of dates or possible additional events.

COMMERCIAL TOURS: Seasonal boat trips are offered by Rederij den Breejen, tel. 14995 . . . the short trip on the Oosterschelde takes you under the Zeelandbrug toward Colijnsplaat and return with a half-hour visit in Colijnsplaat. Hours: May-June and Sept., every Thurs.; July-Aug., Mon.-Fri., 10:30am departure, 12:15pm return. Adults, Fl. 8.50; children 4-12 yrs., Fl. 5.00.

The longer trip goes along the Schouwen-Duiveland coast to Burghsluis then along the Delta Works via Colijnsplaat under the Zeelandbrug and return Zierikzee. Departure Zierikzee, 12:30pm; return 5:15pm. Adults, Fl. 20.00; children 4-12 years, Fl. 15.00.

Check with the VVV for details on biking tours, hiking trips, renting a boat or whatever activity interests you. The Westenschouwen is a forested area with organized walks.

Town Hall and Municipal Museum

LOCATION: Meelstraat 6-8. Look for the tall spire.
INFORMATION: Tel. (01110) 13151 or VVV Zierikzee 12450.
HOURS: May-Sept., Mon.-Fri., 10am-noon and 1-5pm; Closed Sat.,
Sun. and public holidays. Town Hall, same hours as Museum.
■ *Kids will like the torture instruments, hangman's sword and the*
ship models.

Start your visit on the ground floor. There you will find the great hall where weddings are conducted and the Mayor's office (only possible to visit by appointment or when he's not using it) with scenes of the town as it was in 1506. The Council Room was reconstructed in 1775 in Louis XV style. The "Schutterszaal" (on the next floor up) is where the 17th-century Home Guard used to practice. Notice the open roofing constructed very much like a ship's hull but upside down.

The museum deals with local history and has a collection of silver, porcelain, earthenware, national costumes, paintings and drawings. Town and regional history is depicted in a room decorated with tiles, typical of the Schouwen area.

Maritime Museum 's Gravensteen

LOCATION: Mol 25, on the street leading from the VVV to the old
town center.
INFORMATION: Tel. 13038.
HOURS: May-Sept., Mon.-Sat., 10am-5pm.
■ *Of interest to most children.*

The original building named "Gravensteen" stood elsewhere. It was used by the Counts of Holland and Zeeland. The new "steen" was built on the Mol in 1358. When it fell into disrepair, a new building was built on the site between 1524 and 1526. The present building housed the Count's officials, the Count's High Tribunal, and the prison (until 1923).

There was a debtor's cell, a women's cell, the dormitory and infirmary. The jailer lived on the ground floor next to the room where the judges passed sentences. At the rear was the office of the "sheriff" and the cellars were the torture chambers. There were prisoners awaiting trial, those serving their sentences, those imprisoned for debts and pisoners of war. Many were sailors, detained for smuggling, theft or violence. Inscriptions were discovered in 1969 when a layer of plaster was removed. This part of the building has not been changed; notice the heavy oak reinforced with metal bands for security. There are large holding cells, and smaller rooms with iron cells for two persons each. You can look through the peep holes into the dormitories and the "window" where the food was passed to the prisoners. Spend a little time reading the graffiti and imagine who these prisoners were . . . notice the dates, pictures, etc.

The object of this museum is to portray accurately Zierikzee's centuries-old struggle with the sea. There are ships' models, maps, paintings, and items relating to the history of fishing as well as archeological finds from the Scheldt. The copper statue of Neptune which stood on top of the Town Hall spire (1554-1976) is now located here, along with the legendary Zierick with his kayak, who was brought home by whale-fishing ships.

IN THE NEIGHBORHOOD OF ZIERIKZEE:
Ouwerkerk Caissons. A drive east of Zierikzee to Ouwerkerk (follow signs, "caissons") along the coastline will take you to the break in the dike which severely flooded this area. Great concrete "caissons" were dropped into place to breach the gap. It took from February 1, 1953 when the break occurred until

November 7th to make the repairs. The spot is a quiet, secluded area—nice for a picnic while enjoying the views. There is also a small museum and a restaurant.

Leaving Zierikzee, you have a choice of taking the Zeelandbrug south (N256) or going west on N59 to Serooskerke, then N57 south to visit Delta Expo and Neeltje Jans before arriving on North Beveland. It is recommended the first-time visitor take the southwestern route on N57 in order to stop at Delta Expo and Neeltje Jans. At Delta Expo (details below), the complete Dutch hydraulic engineering history from pre-Roman times 'til today is presented. Neeltje Jans is the former construction island; Delta Expo is housed in the central service building on Neeltje Jans. There is plenty of parking.

The latest dam, St. Philipsdam (N251) was opened October 1988 from Gravelingendam (east of Zierikzee) to St. Philipsland and St. Annaland on Tholen. This new dam will save north-south travelers time as it is no longer necessary to go from Tholen via Bergen op Zoom to get to South Beveland.

DELTA EXPO—OOSTERSCHELDE

GETTING THERE: Follow general directions given at the beginning of this chapter. Once you are on N57, just continue south following signs for Haamstede. Then look for the sign, "Oosterschelde Werken" and "Middelburg."

INFORMATION: Delta Expo, tel. (01115) 12702, or Zeeland Provincial VVV, Middelburg, tel. (01180) 33000.

HOURS: April-Oct., daily, 10am-5pm; Nov.-March, Wed.-Sun., 10-5.

ADMISSION: Adults, Fl. 10 (including boat trip during April-Nov.), Senior Citizens and children to 12 years, Fl. 8.00.

■ *Of interest to school-age children and adults.*

The Information Center has many exhibits to explain the history and development of the Storm Surge Barrier. Films are in Dutch, English (ask about French and German) and give a visual explanation of the work carried out.

As mentioned earlier, the great flood on January 31, 1953 was one of the worst in history. The following weather forecasts were announced:

8am: all areas, westerly wind, Force 7; 9:30am: all areas, gale warning, west-northwest; 5pm: all areas, strong west/northwest gales; 5:15pm: "Northern and western North Sea, strong westerly-northwesterly gales imminent, spreading south and east, persisting all night. Dangerously high tides at Rotterdam, Willemstad and Bergen op Zoom."

By the next day, 1,855 Dutch had drowned and hundreds had lost all their possessions. Damage was in the millions of guilders. Rescue teams and volunteers came from all over to help. The inundations extended to most of Duiveland, Tholen, St. Philipsland, the area north of Bergen op Zoom to the Hollands Diep, Overflakkee, area around Hellevoetsluis, the Biesbosch, Dordrecht and even further east. The shock of lives lost was so great, immediate action was demanded to make sure a disaster of this magnitude could not happen again.

The Delta Act of 1958 was the result.

Before work along the North Sea inlets such as the Haringvliet, Brouwersdam and Veerse Gat could be started, however, dams had to be built inland to prevent strong currents causing further damage. The Veersgat dam was completed in 1961, the Haringvliet in 1971 and the Brouwershaven in 1972. Work was begun to seal off the Oosterschelde in 1968 but there was immediate opposition from environmental groups and local fishermen whose livelihoods would be destroyed if they could not reach the North Sea to fish. Studies were undertaken to see what compromise could be reached. It was finally decided not to close off the estuary completely but to construct a storm-surge barrier in the mouth of the Eastern Scheldt (Oosterschelde).

Details of the construction are well explained; the magnitude of the task and the solutions found—the innovations made—are enormously impressive. Sixty-five prefabricated concrete piers were placed on foundation mattresses in the three channels in the mouth of the Eastern Scheldt. Sixty-two steel gates were installed, suspended between the piers, which can be closed under dangerous conditions. Normally, the gates will be kept raised, maintaining the difference between high and low tide at roughly three-quarters of its former range. Fishermen still have access to the North Sea where they can continue their traditional fishing. If the Oosterschelde had been closed, it would have meant the end of the mussel, oyster and lobster trade, an economic loss of about 200 million guilders, not to mention the business and social problems caused the fishing industry and the fishermen. In addition, the Oosterschelde also functions as a nursery for many other species such as sole, plaice and shrimp, which live in the North Sea.

Rethinking the original plan meant a 7-year delay in completion of the overall project; however, the final result is worth the delay and extra cost. The land and inhabitants are protected; the fishing industry is saved; the Delta Plan has created new recreational watersports areas as well as the natural environment for birds which feed and nest in the protected areas and created study areas for flora as well as fauna.

The tour concludes with a visit to a section of the barrier giving visitors an appreciation of the enormous size of the works and the force of the water. From the roof of the Delta Expo building, there is a magnificent view of the mouth of the Oosterschelde.

After visiting Delta Expo and the Storm Surge Barrier, you will continue south to North Beveland island. On the northeast coast you will come to Colijnsplaat. You could also arrive here via the longest bridge in the Netherlands, the Zeelandbrug. There's a bona fide fish auction held Tues. and Thurs. afternoons, 2-4pm. But don't push a button, otherwise you might find yourself the owner (at considerable expense) of 50 tons of fish!

Again, there is a choice of routes. You can cross over to the largest "island-peninsula" of Zeeland, which includes Walcheren and South Beveland. We will go west via N57, cross the Veersgatdam, and, on our way to Middelburg, the capital of Zeeland, stop to see the historic and utterly charming village of Veere. We will visit Goes and Yerseke and then Vlissingen before crossing into Zeeland Flanders, the southernmost part of the province.

It should be noted here that the western coastline of South Beveland offers wonderful dunes and huge, white sandy beaches, with innumerable campsites or bungalows for families wanting to just relax. A Dutch concept allows you to join a program which includes walking or cycling by day and then spending the night in wooden trekking huts. The four-berth huts offer simple seating, cooking and sleeping facilities. And the best part is the price: Fl. 42 per night for four persons! For more information contact the National Reservations Center (NRC), tel. (070) 202500.

VEERE

Once the center for the Scottish wool trade

GETTING THERE: Veere can be approached from all directions via a number of small provincial roads. It borders on the Veerse Meer (lake) and is only about 7 km north of Middelburg.
INFORMATION: VVV Veere, Oudestraat 28, tel. (01181) 1365.

Veere, a quaint old town today was a very prosperous city when it was the port for the Scottish wool trade from the late 14th century until the 18th century. It was also one of the East India Company's headquarters. Today, trading ships can no longer enter the harbor and the town depends on tourists and yachting enthusiasts for its livelihood. The original fortifications are in good condition; the old tower has been an inn since 1558. An interesting point of history is how the Scots acquired their special privileges to conduct trade . . . the Lord of Veere married Mary, the daughter of James I of Scotland. This alliance prospered until the arrival of the French in 1795.

In the village, you should visit the Town Hall, dating from 1474, see the interior if possible; the Great Church (Grote Kerk) (1348) which has been restored and offers a fine view from the tower; the Scottish Houses which were once warehouses and offices of the Scottish wool merchants—now a museum; the Cistern or Town Well (1551)—interesting architecturally; the Campveerse Tower (15th century) which forms part of the fortifications at the harbor entrance; and the Ramparts which are extremely well preserved.

As you wander the streets of Veere, you will see many unusual house facades, mostly made of brick, often with step gables, usually with dark green and white used for window and shutter decorations. Around the little town square look for the houses called "The Dolphin," "The Phoenix," "The Golden Lion" and the "Pannekoekhuis Suster Anna" (Pancake house) with three sailing ships portrayed in full sail over the doorway. On the square is a fine bronze sculpture of two children playing. On the Town Hall side of the square the rustic family hotel " 't Waepen van Veere" at Markt 23, with its cluster of tables and chairs in front, is very appealing.

Beyond the town square, there's another green area, facing which are a series of alms-type houses. The gardens that can be glimpsed from the alley over the not-too-high property walls are a joy to behold with a variety of plantings—some for the table, some cutting flowers, some just decorative.

Fans of the famous author, Hendrik Willem van Loon might be interested in

311

locating the house dating from 1572 in which he lived when he wrote "The Wood Garden." Van Loon was born in Rotterdam but studied, lived and worked in the U.S. and produced many popular histories. One of his classics was "The Story of Mankind."

Along the wharf, there are many brick step-gabled houses such as the house which was once the Grain Stevedores' Guild, a former prison. A present-day antique shop appears to have been a little church once-upon-a-time. The smallest house was a ship's chandler, just 7 feet wide with one double door and one double window. Then you will come to the impressive Scottish Houses, "Het Lammetje" and "De Struys" dating from the 16th century. Continuing along the quay, you will come to the Yacht Club and eventually to the fortifications (telescopes to see the view), part of which is the hotel-restaurant, "De Campveerse Toren." Behind this structure on the quay, you will find the departure point for the boat tours (see "Commercial Tours").

Across from the wide variety of sailing yachts docked along the wharf, you will see the restaurant "The Old Wharf" (d'Ouwe Werf), well known for its fine meals. It's very relaxing and delightful to enjoy a cup of tea on their terrace "al fresco," watching the birds scuttle to and fro, and the harbor activity.

SHOPPING: Shopping and demonstrations can be found at "De Aquamarijn," Markt 37-39, tel. (01181) 1980 . . . exposition and sale of minerals and ornaments. Open, April-Dec., Mon.-Fri., 9am-6pm, Sat., 9am-5pm; Jan.-April, Mon.-Sat., 9am-5pm.

At "De Schapekop," demonstrations are given of hand work; Kerkstraat 3, tel. 1416; open, April-Dec., Mon.-Fri., 9am-6pm, Sat., 9am-5pm. Also, there are pottery demonstrations at "Potterie S," Simon Oomstraat 1, tel. (01180) 29672.

The Town Hall dates from 1477. Located on Markt 5, tel. 1455, it is open from June to mid-Sept., Mon.-Sat., 10am-noon and 1:30-5pm. Built in the Gothic style, the Renaissance tower was added in 1599. The facade is decorated with statues of Lords and Ladies of Veere (renovated in 1931-34). The interior contains a museum with interesting objects forming part of the history of Veere, including the celebrated cup belonging to Maximilian of Burgundy (1551). The Council Chamber is hung with Gobelin tapestries and paintings of note. In the tower, 47 bells ring June-Sept., Sat., 7-8pm; May-Oct., Thurs., 3-4pm; Nov.-April, every 14 days, Thurs., 3-4pm.

De Vierschaar, Markt 5, tel. (01181) 1253, open, June to mid-Sept., Mon.-Sat., noon-5pm. This former courtroom of the Town Hall is now a small local museum.

The Grote Kerk (Gothic, 15th-16th century), also known as "Onze Lieve Vrouwekerk," located on Oudestraat, can be visited April-Nov., daily, 10am-5pm, Sun., 2-5pm. It dates from 1348; unfortunately, history has not been kind to this old building. The interior was destroyed by fire in 1686; then in 1809, the British used it during the Walcheren expedition after which Napoleon took it over in 1811 as a barracks and a hospital. The stained glass windows were destroyed and five floors were built in the nave and transept—these have since been removed. There is a fine view from the 42-meter tower. Exhibitions and

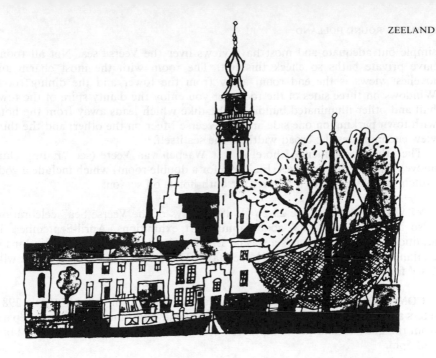

cultural programs are held here. South of the church, the Cistern or Town Well was constructed in 1551 by Maximilian of Burgundy who promised the Scottish wool merchants good water, necessary to development and trade.

The Scottish Houses, "Het Lammetje" (1539) and "De Struys" (1561) were once warehouses and offices of the Scottish wool merchants. Now they have become the Museum Schotse Huizen, Kaai 25-27, tel. 1744; open, April-Sept., Tues.-Sat., 10am-5pm. There are old Zeeland costumes, antique furniture, books, atlases, a fisheries museum and various annual exhibitions.

EATING OUT: Already mentioned are the "Pannekoekhuis Suster Anna" on the Town Hall square, and the Hotel " 't Waepen van Veere," Markt 23, tel. 1231, where you can order a "Koffietafel" (typical Dutch sandwich lunch), as well as regular lunches and dinners (seafood is the speciality). Another reasonably priced restaurant can be found along the quay in an old cellar, "Restaurant in den Strupkelder," Kade 25, tel. 1392, attractively decorated in old Dutch fashion. If you want to "step out on the town," try the restaurant of the Campveerse Toren Hotel where Prince William of Orange had his wedding supper. From your table in this former Medieval Powder Magazine you can see private yachts and even commercial fishing vessels gliding lazily past. The small circular room is beautifully appointed with silver and copper and offers top quality service and food. Expensive but worth it. Across the harbor is "d'Ouwe Werf Restaurant," another well-recommended gourmet restaurant.

STAYING OVER: Which we do recommend heartily. While dining at the "Campveerse Toren" is expensive, sleeping there is not. Accommodations are simple but adequate and most have views over the Veerse sea. Not all rooms have private baths so check this out. The room with the most charm and loveliest views is the end room away from the tower and the dining room. Windows on three sides of the room let you enjoy the dainty spire of the town hall and other illuminated buildings; the dike which leads away from the hotel with town parking on one side and the Veerse Meer on the other; and the third view encompasses the broad width of the sea itself.

The other recommended hotel is " 't Waepen van Veere (see "Eating Out" above), with moderate prices (Fl. 70-95 for a double room) which include a good Dutch breakfast. Prices are lower for both hotels off season.

YEARLY EVENTS: June 23-26 (1988), "Days of the Veerse Sea" celebration. Also inquire at the VVV about annual art exhibitions, April-September. In addition, June 23-25, there's a special ZLM agricultural show at Neeltje Jans in conjunction with the "Zeeland Horse Day." These events can vary so check with VVV for particulars.

COMMERCIAL TOUR: Rederij Dijkhuizen, Vlissingen, tel. (01184) 12981, offers a number of tours in the area. The one-hour boat tour from Veere, departs from the quay behind the Campveerse Toren Easter to mid-Sept, between 11am and 5pm.

IN THE NEIGHBORHOOD OF VEERE:

Vrouwenpolder, four miles west toward the dunes, is the place for swimming and dune-exploring.

Oostkapelle, a little bit larger town, is the center for camping and beach activities, offering a wide range of accommodations. A couple of kilometers toward the sea, you will find Westhove Castle. Its Orangerie houses the Museum of Natural History; open, Tues.-Fri., 11am-5pm, Sat.-Mon., 1:15-5pm.

Domburg, south of Westhove Castle, is the oldest bathing seaside resort of Zeeland. In the 18th century, the first outdoor bathing facilities were erected and in 1837 the first bath pavilion was opened.

MIDDELBURG

Provincial capital, Thursday market, and a miniature village

GETTING THERE: Located inland on Walcheren, Middelburg is in the center of a web of provincial roads. From the north, follow directions given previously entering town on N57; from the east (Bergen op Zoom and points north and south), A58 will lead you to town; from the south, you have a choice of two ferries, one leaving from Breskens for Vlissingen and then on to Middelburg, or the other which crosses from Perkpolder (N60) to A58 and then to Middelburg.

The Vlissingen-Breskens ferry operates weekdays from 4:50am-11:35pm, with departures every 30 minutes; Sat. and Sun., departures every

hour between 9:25am and 6:55pm—check schedule for other departures on weekends. Trip takes 20 minutes.
The Kruiningen-Perkpolder ferry operates 4:05am-11:25pm, every half hour, except Sat. and Sun., then hourly; 20 minutes one-way.
INFORMATION: VVV Middelburg, Markt 65a, tel. (01180) 16851.

Before the bridges and dams were constructed on which modern highways are built, this area of Walcheren was isolated but not so much so as other parts of Zeeland. In Middelburg there is a deep sense of history which makes the town worthy of interest. The Abdij or Abbey, which dates from 1120, had a great deal of influence both on the town and the area generally. When Middelburg became an early convert to the Protestant faith during the uprising against the Spanish, the Abbey was dissolved and the complex of buildings used for other purposes.

The town suffered greatly during WW II under German occupation. The Allies needed to eliminate the heavy German artillery barrage coming from Vlissingen and other parts of South Beveland which prevented badly needed war supplies from being off-loaded in the Belgian port of Ghent. The best approach seemed to be to bomb the dikes thus causing flooding throughout Walcheren. Furious Commando attacks followed forcing the Germans to surrender. Naturally, Middelburg came under attack, and suffered heavy damage throughout the city.

Some of Middelburg's special attractions include the 15th-century Town Hall, considered by some to be one of the most beautiful in Holland. Just next door in the old Vlees Hall (Meat Hall) there are seasonal exhibits. Another stop not to be missed is the Abdij complex of buildings (discussed below) which was destroyed in 1940 and reconstructed. Its 280-foot tower, nicknamed "Long John" (Lange Jan) offers wonderful views for anyone willing to make the climb.

The Town Hall facade dates from 1452-58; the former meat hall, now used for special exhibitions, was added in 1506-1520 as was the elaborate tower. In 1780 there were more additions but in 1940 most of the building was destroyed from German bombings. The tour times are given at the front entrance. There are info sheets in English and German and the guides speak Dutch, English and German and are prepared to answer questions. You see the Council Chamber, Mayor's private office, Reception Hall, etc. Notice the beautifully carved wooden chests all over the building from old Zeeland farms. Reconstruction of the building began even during the war. Because wood wasn't available, steel beams were used then decorated in Zeeland colors and style so you can't tell they're not wood.

The Abdij or Abbey Church complex, dating from about the 9th century, has the longest history in Middelburg. It served its designated function until 1574 when it became the seat of government. It was severely bombed in May 1940 and the burning tower crushed the buildings below, which included the Nieuwe Kerk, the Koorkerk and The Trouwkerk. The complex was restored as quickly as possible and today visits can be made of the three churches, the States Hall and the Zeeuws Museum which is located in the complex (details below). Carillon concerts from the Abdij are given on Thurs., noon-1pm; May to 1st week of Sept., Sat., 11am-noon; Fri., in May, 1:30-2:30pm; July and Aug., Wed.,

7-7:30pm; July to mid-Aug., also Thurs., 7:30-8:30pm. The Abbey serves as the meeting place for the governors of Zeeland.

MARKET: Middelburg is known for its Thursday market day ... lovely antiques; splendid local costumes are worn; 10am-4:30pm, on the main Market Square. Also on Thurs. in the summertime, a special art market is held on the Vischmarkt. And the town has a number of interesting antique shops if you happen to miss the Thurs. extravaganza.

MUSEUMS:
The Zeeuws Museum, Abdijplein next to the Abbey Church, tel. 26655; open, Mon.-Fri., 10am-5pm; (afternoons only on Easter Monday and Whitsuntide). In May, also Sat., 1:30-5pm; June-Aug., 10am-5pm, Sat.-Sun., 1:30-5pm. The museum is located in one of the oldest quarters of the Middelburg Abbey. The collection includes Roman artifacts, Zeeland costumes, Chinese porcelain and Delftware, furniture, paintings and a marvelous tapestry gallery.
National Holografie Museum, Gartstraat 36 (in the Grote Nederlandse Bank Building), tel. 38810; open, every day, 11am-9pm. Holography is a new optical technique allowing three-dimensional photography: people and places appear "in the round" rather than flat as is usual. The museum has one of the largest collections of holograms which can be viewed in special rooms.

EATING OUT: Like other big cities, Middelburg has a wide choice of places to eat inexpensively or otherwise. Tourist menus can be had at "De Huifkar," Markt 19, and the "Station Restaurant," Kanaalweg 24. Or eat at one of the food stands if you're visiting on market day (Thursday) ... a shrimp or eel sandwich is a nice change of pace from a hamburger. On the expensive side, you can choose to eat in the atmosphere of an old patrician house, "Den Gespleten Arent," 25 Vlasmarkt, tel. 36122, or if you prefer fish, try "Rotisserie Michel," 19 Korte Geere, tel. 11596.

STAYING OVER: To tempt you to stay a bit longer, the important buildings of Middelburg are illuminated during the summer months and can best be appreciated if you spend the night. Three first-rate hotels are the Best Western "Hotel du Commerce," Loskade 1, tel. 36051, the "Le Beau Rivage," Loskade 19, tel. 38060, and the 4-star "Arneville," Buitenruststraat 22, tel. 38456. Less expensive is "De Huifkar," Markt 19, tel. 12998.

YEARLY EVENTS: In May, Jazz Festival; end of May-Aug., don't miss the tilting for the ring on horseback competitions, held at Molenwater near the main city entry gate ... a very old and unusual folkloric event; in June, a "Braderie"; in July and Aug., the New Music Festival; in mid-Aug. "Steam Days"; beginning of Sept., the City Festival; mid-Sept., Music Festival, 17-22 Oct., "Present-Day Art Show."

COMMERCIAL TOURS: City tours by horse-drawn trams, approx. May-Aug.; pick-up point, Standplaats Markt ... goes to Miniature Walcheren and returns.

Boat tours: from Loskade to the Veerse Meer and back by "salon boot Madeleine"; Ascension to mid-Sept., daily departures at 1:45pm . . . 3-hour round-trip. Adults, Fl. 9.50; children, Fl. 4.50 . . . purchase tickets at VVV office.

Miniature Walcheren

LOCATION: At the town side of the main gate of Middelburg, Molen-water, Zuid Singel, and Koepoortlaan.
INFORMATION: VVV Middelburg, Markt 65a, tel. (01180) 16851.
HOURS: Easter to Nov., daily, 9:30am-5pm.
■ *Of interest to big and small people.*

Along with serious sightseeing, it's only fair to allow the squirmy generation a chance to stretch their legs and see something of special interest to them. If you take the island of Walcheren and reduce it to 1/20th of its normal size, monuments, churches, and museums which were totally deadening to the small fry, suddenly become quite enchanting. Up to now, more than four million people have seen the "Miniature Walcheren" and we suggest you do too.

This scale model of the island of Walcheren shows streets, dikes, ports, 500 of the principal buildings, ships, trains, barges and there's a good overview of the area's water-control system. In addition, trains and buses travel along their normal routes so there's something happening all the time.

IN THE NEIGHBORHOOD OF MIDDELBURG:
Veere, just a few kilometers north, shouldn't be overlooked. A charming village with an interesting history, and a photographer's delight.

Westkapelle, bordering the North Sea, as far west as you can go from Middelburg. There are still interesting WW II antipersonnel fences, tank traps, cement blockhouses and gun emplacements to be seen here. Notice the commemorative tablet in English and Dutch honoring the date, Nov. 1, 1944, when the British 4th Commando Brigade landed to liberate the area. More interesting to the average tourist, perhaps, are the little concrete "houses" sunk into the dunes with just a window exposed; they were previously used by German soldiers but are now Dutch vacation cottages.

Drive along the huge new dike of Westkapelle, completed in 1987. Normally, the sea side of dikes are dunes with no view. The exception is in North Holland and here where this dike was built twice as high as previously as part of the Delta Works. You look down on the sea, a wonderful North Sea expanse before you. If you'd like to see a pottery demonstration, " 't Draaiertje," at d'Arke 22 is open Mon.-Sat., 9am-6pm . . . not for large groups.

Before going south to Vlissingen and Flanders, we will travel to South Beveland, the eastern part of the peninsula.

At Goes, try to see the late Gothic basilica, St. Marie-Magdalenakerk, 15th-17th Centuries. Its pretty interior is open June-Aug. Mon.-Fri., 10am-noon and 2-4pm. Goes also boasts a 14th-century Gothic City Hall (open in summer, daily, 11am-4pm) and a museum for North and South Beveland located at Singelstraat 13, tel. (01100) 28883.

If you have a soft spot in your heart for steam engines, you might have to stay over so you can spend the afternoon on a very old original steam train from Goes to Oudelande ... the return trip takes most of the afternoon. The usual operating hours are Sun. from May 15-Sept. 11; also on Sat., July 3-Aug. 26. Departure from Goes is 2:05pm with stops at Kwadendamme, Oudelande and Hoedekenskerke, returning to Goes at 4:45pm. Certain days in July and Aug., there's a special trip including dinner leaving Goes at 6:30pm, returning at 9:15pm. The Goes VVV, Stationsplein 3, tel. (01100) 20577, has tickets and information about the train as well as brochures for the whole of Zeeland.

In the springtime, this area is ablaze with the blossoms (and their heady odor) of fruit trees. Most of the villages are very old with lovely landscapes, Kapelle is one and even smaller is Baarsdorp with just 10 houses, some farmers and that's all. Get the VVV "Blossom route around South Beveland" to help you enjoy your exploration.

Yerseke, just east of Goes, is Holland's center for oyster and mussel culture. Mussel seed are fished from the Wadden Islands and brought to beds in Zeeland where they are allowed to mature two-three years before consumption. They are exported in great quantity to Belgium and France where they are enjoyed to the fullest. The mussel auction sale room is in the building, "Produktsshaap van Vis and Visprodukten," Ankerweg off Julianahaven; auctions are held daily (in season) except weekends. For details, call the VVV Yerseke, tel. (01131) 1864. For shellfish lovers, there are many restaurants in Yerseke and surrounding area specializing in oyster and mussel dishes (in season, of course).

On Aug. 20th (check yearly), Yerseke celebrates with a Mussel Festival. Special tours around the oyster beds are given during the season (Sept.-April) and regular tours of the Oosterschelde depart from Julianahaven. For information about the latter, call (01131) 3339 for details.

It is now possible to cross South Beveland to Tholen without going via Bergen op Zoom, a great timesaver. The last dam from the Schelde-Rhine canal north to Tholen was completed October 1988.

VLISSINGEN

Summer resort, fishing and shipbuilding center

GETTING THERE: Vlissingen is south of Middelburg about 5 kilometers. Follow directions to Middelburg (above) or take A58 west from just south of Bergen op Zoom.

INFORMATION: VVV Vlissingen, Nieuwedijk 15, tel. (01184) 12345.

Like all port towns, Vlissingen has had a long history of naval battles and military action. It was in the forefront of activity to become free from Spanish control. It revolted in 1572 and came under British "care" from 1585-1616. It didn't begin to develop until 1872 when the railroad was built and the docks were completed the following year. More recently it suffered heavily in WW II when the harbor was bombed by the Germans in 1940. Then in 1944 the dikes were breached and the Allies were able to subdue the Germans. The defenses and bunkers of that period can still be seen. Vlissingen and other surrounding

318

towns were damaged or seriously threatened in the 1953 flood. For them, the Delta works are very important.

From Vlissingen, you can take a relaxing ferry boat across the Westerschelde to Breskens and south into Belgium. If you decide to spend the night here many hotels are located on the Boulevard along the water. From your room you may see streams of international ships passing by. These ships are heading for the Belgian port of Antwerp which explains the tremendously varied traffic.

Among the interesting sights in Vlissingen are St. Jacobskerk (1308), the new and modern Town Hall, and the city museum.

St. Jacobskerk (1308) is located on the Kleine Markt (small market). Its structure is late Gothic with a beautifully restored tower and carillon. It can be visited from mid-June to mid-Sept., Mon.-Fri., 10am-noon, 2-4:30pm, Sun., 2-4:30pm, mid-Sept.-June, Tues.-Fri., 10am-12:30pm and 1:30-5pm, Sat., 1-5pm.

The Stedelijk Museum, Bellamyplein 19, tel. 12498, can be visited from mid-June to mid-Sept., 10am-5pm, Sat.-Sun., 1-5pm. Off-season hours are, Tues.-Fri., 10am-12:30pm and 1:30-5pm, Sat., 1-5pm. The collection includes portraits, silver of the town, a room devoted to Michiel de Ruyter (1607-76) famous native-son-Admiral, a painting of Vlissingen in 1664, remains of the "Vliegend Hart," a VOC (United East India Co.) merchant ship that sank just off shore.

The City Hall is new (1965) on the Boulevard next to the Gevangentoren, 15th-century remains of the West Gate. A stroll around town should include a walk along the wide boulevard facing the Schelde River (the street changes names from De Ruyter, Bankert and Evertsen Boulevard) with its forever changing view of tug boats, sailing ships, ferry boats vying for position. Some old Vlissingen houses of interest are the Beeldenhuis (1730) at Hendrikstraat 25; the Beursgebouw (1635) on the Bellamyplein; the Lampsinhuis (1641) at Nieuwendijk 11, and Cornelia Quack's (I kid you not) hofje, Korte Zelke. The house dates from 1786, the small gate from 1643.

Vlissingen's windmill, "Oranjemolen," on Oranjedijk (dike), is open June-Sept., Wed., 1:30-4:30pm and Sat., 8:30-11:30am.

Free ponytrams tour the inner city and the Boulevard in July and Aug., Sat., 1:30-4:30pm. Data from VVV.

MARKET: The year-round weekly market is held Fri., 9am-4:30pm, at the Lange Zelke and Spuiplein. Flanders, across the Westerschelde, is a mecca for Dutch and Belgian shoppers. Merchandise is listed in the currencies of both countries and "good buys" are possible as prices fluctuate for such items as butter, cigarettes, etc.

EATING OUT: There are places to eat along the Boulevards with super views and in all price categories from small bistro-cafés to the Golden Tulip Strand Hotel which, although generally expensive, also offers a Tourist menu (set menu at modest cost).

STAYING OVER: A favorite hotel for its exceptional sea views and access to the beach is the "Britannia," 244 Boulevard Evertsen, tel. 13255 . . . spacious rooms with wide windows, the better to watch the river traffic (all rooms have

319

sea views); the Strandhotel Vlissingen, at 4 Boulevard Evertsen, tel. 12297; and a newer first-class hotel, the "Piccard," 178 Badhuisstraat, tel. 13551, moderate-priced.

YEARLY EVENTS: Boat tours on the Westerschelde are available the beginning of July to the end of Aug., every Tues., Thurs. and Fri. Departure from Koopmanshaven at 2pm. Tour lasts two hours; Adults, Fl. 12.00; Seniors, Fl. 10.00; Children 6-11 years, Fl. 7.00. Arrange through VVV office, tel. 12345. There are also bus tours possible to the Belgian coast from May through Sept., Mon.-Fri., tel. 13043 for details.

TERNEUZEN

The Belgian connection

GETTING THERE: To reach Terneuzen, one of Holland's most important harbors, cross the Westerschelde from Vlissingen by boat ferry to Breskens or from Kruiningen to Perkpolder.
INFORMATION: VVV Terneuzen, Burg. Geillstraat 2B, tel. (01150) 95976.

Terneuzen is the entry point from the Westerschelde to the Ghent/Terneuzen Canal—an active and economically important waterway for traffic to Belgium. In addition, the harbor has about 500 berths for pleasure boats and the demand is growing daily for more.

The well-known story of the "Flying Dutchman" originated here in the 17th century. According to the VVV, the story is as follows: "William van der Decken, captain from the port of Terneuzen, left with his ship for the East. He was a rough and brutal man, shouting all the time. In his many attempts to round the Cape of Good Hope, his ship was tossed by heavy storms. The crew saw a bad omen in their misfortune and begged the captain to return. But Van der Decken had not the slightest intention of returning and cursed the gods and forces of nature, until a voice resounded from heaven, condemning him and his ship to roam the cape for the rest of his days. The ship's company died and the captain did roam the seas all alone. In heavy weather, when the waves worked up high in the sky, the sailors of those days often thought they recognized the ghost of the phantom ship with the captain grim behind the steering-wheel. A confrontation with the ship carried death and destruction."

Terneuzen has an old, atmospheric town center which is bordered on one side by the sparkling harbor (its wealth and its pride), and on the other side by a modern housing complex.

Browse around the locks, watching ships of all nationalities, or wander through the old town shops. A good walk for views of the old section as well as the constantly changing pattern of international and local shipping is along the Westerscheldedijk (Schelde Boulevard). If you are here at low tide, you can see large sandbanks appear—quite a sight. The Town Hall, designed by the firm Van den Broek en Bakema, is built on a split-level system with shifting floors at the sides of the Westerschelde and the town. Carillon concerts can be heard Wed., 2:30-3pm.

If fishing is your sport, water is all around. You can choose "De Braakman-creek," the "Otheense Creek," or the "Westerscheldt." You can rent a boat and go it on your own, or join a group. There are also three river vessels especially outfitted for deep-sea sports fishing. Details from the VVV.

EATING OUT: Rather expensive but if you enjoy water-view dining, try "de Milliano," 28 Noteneeweg, tel. (01150) 20817.

STAYING OVER: If you need a place to rest your head, try the "Hotel Churchill Terneuzen," 700 Churchilllaan, tel. 21120 (pool, air-conditioning), or "Hotel 'L Escaut," Scheldekade 65, tel. 94855.

YEARLY EVENTS: The end of May the Schelde-Jazz Festival is held and in mid-June, there's the Port Celebration.

IN THE NEIGHBORHOOD OF TERNEUZEN:

Zaamslag has a picturesque town square with its former town hall surrounded by a green park and an original bandstand. Also, a small museum, Plein 3, tel. 1233.

Axel is famous for its general goods market on Saturdays . . . the stands are two kilometers long! Local costumes are often to be seen. As mentioned above, shopping in Flanders draws both Dutch and Belgians who seek bargain prices. Both Dutch guilders and Belgian francs are used. The Belgians buy whatever is cheaper in Holland (i.e., Genever (gin), butter), and the Dutch buy whatever is cheaper in Belgium (cigarettes). Prices flip-flop so sometimes one thing is cheaper in one currency and other times, it might be cheaper in the other.

Axel also has a farm museum, "The Land of Axel," Noordstraat 11, tel. (01155) 2885, and a photo and radio museum at Bastionstraat 47, tel. (01155) 3073. The tower of the Town Hall has a 35 bell carillon . . . concerts on Sat. from 2-3pm.

Hulst, east and south of Terneuzen on north/south highway N60, is almost in

321

Belgium. For information, tel. (01140) 13755. A little jewel, hidden away from normal touristic routes, Hulst is full of historical monuments.

The ramparts, in outstanding condition, are perhaps the most important thing to visit here . . . inquire at City Hall for permission to visit the nine 17th-century bastions. The four town gates are: Bagijnepoort (1704), Dubbele Poort (1771), Gentse Poort (1781) and Bollewerckspoort (land and water gate—1506).

St. Willibrordusbasiliek (Basilica) sits on 12th-century foundations but basic construction dates from 15th-16th Centuries. In its checkered career, it has been used by both Catholics and Protestants until 1929 when the Catholics bought out the Protestants. It became a Basilica in 1935. The interior is lovely and the 35-meter tower can be climbed by special arrangement with the City Hall, or call, Mr. D.M. Hollardt, tel. 13029. The City Hall was constructed in 1534 . . . you can find it by its tall tower, located at Grote Markt 21, tel. 13755. It's worth a few minutes to see the main hall with the family portraits of members of the House of Nassau.

Biervliet is one of the most charming villages of Flanders. Formerly a prosperous trading town, there are remnants of the old city ramparts; a Dutch Reformed Church (1659) with lovely stained-glass windows (1660-61), and an old corn mill, "Harmonie," Molenstraat 9, which can be visited Sat. and Sun., tel. (01150) 1462. Saturday afternoons, you can watch "Bollen" with "Krulbol," a folkloric game similar to bowling. And if you're around in mid-May, there's a Beggars' Festival (Geuzenfeesten).

OOSTBURG

District buying center

GETTING THERE: Oostburg is the largest town in the extreme western section of Dutch Flanders, located between Breskens and Aardenburg.
INFORMATION: VVV Cadzand, tel. (01179) 1298, or VVV Breskens, tel. (01172) 1888.

Oostburg is the district buying center for the western part of Zeeland. The weekly Wednesday market is an active and interesting place to shop. There's a cheese farm in town, "De Ysenagel," Bakkerstraat 58, tel. (01170) 2063 for an appointment. Also, the nature reserve "Het Groote Gat" is worth exploring.

EATING OUT: For pancakes, try "De Pottekijker," Ledelplein 3.

YEARLY EVENTS: Of special interest are the "bol" tournaments with the "krulbol," a type of bowling with round wooden cylinders . . . held on Q. van Uffordweg 10.

IN THE NEIGHBORHOOD OF OOSTBURG:
The towns of Aardenburg and Sluis offer some unusual and interesting sightseeing and recreational facilities. These towns will be dealt with individually below.

Breskens is the arrival point for the ferry from Vlissingen. Ferry schedules are discussed under "Vlissingen." A trout farm in the harbor at Kaai 2 offers a tour as well as the chance to catch your own; also a café-restaurant. Hours during May-Sept.: 9:30am-10pm; for other periods, check with the VVV.

Breskens has several markets. The Easter market is the end of May; the annual fair is the end of July; and the fish market is held the beginning of Aug., followed in mid-Aug. by the Fish Festival. Check with VVV for exact dates.

■ **Cadzand and Cadzand-Bad (Beach)** are about 10 km northwest of Oostburg and about the same distance southwest of Breskens. For info, call VVV Cadzand, Boulevard de Wielingen 17a, tel. (01179) 1298 . . . closed from noon-1pm.

Cadzand is the place to relax and enjoy the beaches, or various activities such as biking, bowling, tennis, squash; take a sauna or go dancing at the "Dancing Zeebad," Boulevard de Wielingen 4 in Cadzand.

Cadzand has an art museum, free entry, "Lucas Tack," Princenstraat 4, tel. 1426, and a windmill at Zuidzandseweg 3, open all year on Sun. from 2-6pm.

STAYING OVER: If you've come for the sand and surf, a hotel at Cadzand-Bad is what you'll want. There are several 4-star hotels including the hotel "De Blanke Top," Boulevard de Wielingen 1, tel. 2040, located on the dunes with sea views. It also boasts a fitness center with sauna, turkish bath, whirlpool, tanning area, and protected terrace. Open all year. The Strandhotel, Boulevard de Wielingen 49, tel. 2110, is above the dunes with sea views. They have an indoor swimming pool, sauna, four automatic bowling lanes, billiards and table tennis. Rooms have T.V. and video. Open all year. Check with the VVV for recommended moderate-inexpensive hotels.

AARDENBURG

With Roman sarcophagi

GETTING THERE: North-south highway N410. Aardenburg is practically on the Belgian border, about 11 kilometers west and south of Oostburg.
INFORMATION: VVV Cadzand or VVV Breskens (see above).

Aardenburg has origins dating to the Stone Age and was a Roman town as can be verified by a visit to the Gemeentemuseum, located at Markstraat 18. Hours open, June-Aug., Tues.-Fri., 9am-12:15pm, 1:30-5pm; Sun.-Mon., 1:30-5pm. It contains a collection of sarcophagi from the Roman period. Northwest of town, you can see the Kaaipoort (17th century), one of the gates of the old town walls. Attractive 17th-century buildings can be seen along the Weststraat. The 13th-century church, St. Baafskerk on Sint-Bavostraat, can be visited (and tower climbed), April-Sept., daily (except Tues.), 10am-noon, 2-5pm; Oct.-March, 2-4pm. In the restoration of the church, a number of counts' stone coffins were discovered and can now be seen in the church.

Shoppers might want to visit on a Tuesday morning—that's market day.

Along the small road between Heille and Aardenburg, the Streeklandbouw Museum has exhibits on farming, farm life, and riding equipment. Perhaps as important, there are also a children's farm, beehives and herb garden. For

323

information, tel. (01177) 1600; open daily, 10am-noon and 1-5pm; Sun., 1-5pm, closed Tues.

SLUIS

An action-filled tourist center with evening and Sunday shopping!

GETTING THERE: Located at the western corner of Dutch Flanders on the Dutch-Belgian border, Sluis can be approached from the south, east and north on N58 or from Breskens along the provincial road via Groede and Nieuwvliet.
INFORMATION: VVV Sluis, St. Annastraat 15, tel. (01178) 1569.

In 1290 Gwidje van Dampierre gave Sluis its town charter. It was already a well-known port and commercial center and together with Damme, the town of Tyll Ulenspiegel, was an outer harbor of ancient Bruges (Belgium). It declined over the years because of many wars fought in the area and also the silting up of the Zwin River. In World War II, 80% of the town was destroyed, then was rebuilt through the courage and efforts of its townspeople. Wisely, these good people didn't wipe out the old to make way for the modern; rather, they blended the two and endeavored to restore the characteristic old atmosphere as much as possible. The many visitors will attest to their success.

Today, tourism is the main commercial endeavor of Sluis although some industry and agriculture also play a part. Through special dispensation, dozens of attractive shops are allowed to remain open in the evenings and on Sundays— an unheard of occurrence in the rest of Holland. Because of this, its proximity to popular Belgian beach centers, comfortable hotels, and atmospheric cafés and restaurants, Sluis is buzzing with activity in holiday periods and on weekends.

The Town Hall was severely damaged in WW II, but has been restored. It is the only 14th-century belfort in Holland and houses all that remains of the former Museum of Antiquities. The Council Chamber is resplendent with its wood carving, ornamental ironwork, tapestries and painting by famous masters. The wooden figure in the tower of the belfort is of Flanders' oldest jaquemart, Jantje van Sluis—carved in the Middle Ages by Jacoppe van Huusse. This symbol is reputed to have saved the town from attack by Spaniards. He is colorfully dressed—a sure photobug's objective—and he indicates the time every half-hour in ingenious fashion. Special carillon concerts are given during the summer periods in addition to the regular chimings.

"De Brak," a working corn mill can also be visited . . . .Severely damaged in 1944, it has been fully restored.

The town ramparts, gates and the ruin, "De Steenen Beer," should not be missed. On the ramparts there is a statue of a Sluis schoolmaster who achieved fame for his compilation of the standard Dutch dictionary.

Then there is the rustic village green, Louis XIV pump, which together with the 17th-century church form an area known as St. Anna ter Muiden. It's located about a mile on the outskirts of Sluis and has been a part of the town since 1880. This is a favorite place of painters and authors—and ordinary people like you and me, too.

324

BEACHES: North and South Holland

Believe it or not, going to the beach in Holland can get a bit perplexing for some foreigners. Maybe the following tips will make a day at the beach more enjoyable for newcomers who aren't sure how the system works.

Most of the beaches in Europe are more developed than they are in the U.S., Turkey, Portugal—just to name a few—and it's nice to know that at the beach cafés, you may get snacks served to you whether you elect to take a table inside within their glass enclosure (when they have one) or if you choose to rent chairs, umbrella (and space) on the beach. The waiter will settle you with your chairs and umbrella wherever you choose (in front of his establishment of course), clean the area, see that you are comfortable, and wait for your drink order. Some places offer changing rooms which can be rented for the day or half-day; others have changing rooms but you must take your clothes with you; others have changing rooms and then you check them with the establishment. Some have showers, but many do not. They nearly always have toilet facilities (look for the W.C.). How you figure out which establishment has which facility when you don't speak Dutch is a matter of chance and luck. Probably, the foreigner should just simply adjust to "paying his money and taking his chances." You pay for whatever facilities you want to use, naturally, but the cost is usually minimal. You are expected to order a coffee or a coke—and later on, perhaps an ice or another drink, but they won't bother you to order something every few minutes. At the more sophisticated beaches, you will find cafés which offer a full meal, special glass-enclosed sunbathing areas, and so forth.

The first visit to a beach may present an unusual sight to the visitor, (particularly the many topless "beauties") when he sees hundreds of people huddling behind various colored tarpaulins. As the kids say, "Try it, you'll like it." You'll especially like it at any of the exposed North Sea beaches where the wind is ever present even when the sun is shining brightly. You may leave home convinced it's going to be a brilliant-hot-windless day and find when you arrive at the water's edge that as soon as you remove your clothes those goosebumps appear. The answer is a "windscherm" which may be purchased at any sports store or department store, or which may be rented along with the deck chairs.

If you go to an underdeveloped beach with your picnic lunch, you will eventually be faced wih Johnny and Suzie's desire to "go." In that case, look for the nearest beach café (there's usually at least one not too far away) and simply pay to use the facilities. If you happen to buy an ice cream or a drink, that's fine from the Management's point of view, but it isn't required.

The following will describe some of the better-known beaches in the Randstad area—try several and decide for yourself which one suits your family best. Some areas are designated as "naturist" beaches, a euphemism for nude beaches. Topless sunbathing is pretty much the norm today at Dutch beaches.

There are fabulous beaches all along the North Sea coast, including those of Zeeland, South and North Holland, the Waddenzee Islands, Flevoland, Friesland and Groningen. These are within the Randstad which boasts the greatest concentration of population and where most foreigners live. We will start south of Rotterdam and go northward to the top of North Holland.

OOSTVOORNE, ROCKANJE AND BRIELLE

GETTING THERE: Southwest of Rotterdam, these beaches are within a few minutes' drive of one another. The most direct route from Rotterdam is via the Maas Tunnel or the Benelux Tunnel. From points east, you would go over the Brienenoord Bridge, then west following signs to Spijkenisse. A good driving map is always helpful. From The Hague and Amsterdam, take A4 south, then follow signs to Benelux Tunnel, Spijkenisse, Brielle, etc.

By Metro and bus, from Rotterdam go to Spijkenisse. Transfer to bus which stops at Brielle, Oostvoorne and Rockanje (last stop).

INFORMATION: VVV Rotterdam, tel. (010) 413 6000.

Oostvoorne: The town originated as a settlement around a castle. With the development of the Europoort, Oostvoorne has grown and there is a permanent population as well as the summer visitors. The beach here is so wide and flat you can drive your car right on it. There is no boardwalk, but beach cafés spring up during the season. You will find ideal conditions for swimming and windsurfing.

There are marvelous walks to be made in the woods and dunes between Oostvoorne and Rockanje but you need a special permit. These day tickets (you can get season tickets as well) are available from the VVV in the town of Oostvoorne or Rockanje.

STAYING OVER: For those wanting to spend a weekend or longer, there are several hotels to choose from, or if you prefer staying in a private home or pension, the VVV will give you a list of names. There are hotels along the boulevard to the beach, the Badhotel Duinoord and the Hotel Het Wapen van Marion (with moderate prices).

Rockanje: Another lovely small village with a wide, safe sand beach and dunes for exploring. Rockanje has a special attraction which isn't found at most beaches. You can rent little huts, the flap doorway of which can also be made

326

into an awning. With the flap down, it is a private dressing room or a nap-time area; the flap up, your little hut opens up and allows a shady area in front for sitting and reading while the picnic lunch is protected in the interior. This beach is perfect for families with infants and young children because it is wide, the water is calm (not for surfers!), the little huts offer protection from too much sun, and since the completion of the Haringvlietdam, the area is free of shipping and its accompanying pollution. The atmosphere is definitely geared to families and not to the jet set!

EATING OUT: There is a large parking area at the main entrance to the beach for private cars and also Restaurant 't Golfie which has mini-golf, all restaurant facilities including a live band on the weekends.

STAYING OVER: There are a few beach hotels for overnighting or apartments, pensions and private homes which let rooms ... information on the latter through the VVV. About 15 minutes' walk from the beach is the Badhotel Rockanje which boasts a heated pool, and which offers housekeeping apartments, and rooms as well as hotel accommodations.

Brielle: The historic town of Brielle is best known as the first town to be liberated from Spanish rule during the Eighty Years' War. There are still some interesting old buildings to be seen: St. Catharine Church, the Town Hall, and the Weigh House (housing a small museum).

This area has recently become a first-class watersports center with the creation of the Brielse Meer, a new recreational park, which extends some 8.5 miles from Spijkenisse to Oostvoorne along the former Brielse Maas. Natural and unspoiled, it would appeal to nature lovers, campers, sailors and swimmers. There are paths for walking and biking, a large protected outdoor swimming area and enough water to satisfy waterskiers, motorboaters and sailboaters.

EATING OUT: There is a nice restaurant on the waterfront, the "in the Gouwe Geit" where you can have snacks or pancakes. They also rent boats.

HOOK OF HOLLAND AND KIJKDUIN

GETTING THERE: These beaches are on the North Sea slightly northwest of Rotterdam (Hook of Holland, Monster) and on the outskirts of The Hague (Loosduinen and Kijkduin). From Rotterdam follow A20/N20 west to the North Sea, following directions "Hoek van Holland," then signs for Monster, Loosduinen and Kijkduin (at The Hague). From Amsterdam, Directions Den Haag and then roads toward the beaches.
INFORMATION: VVV The Hague, tel. (070) 546200, after 12/89, 354 6200. VVV Rotterdam, tel. (010) 413 6000.

Hook of Holland: From the center of Rotterdam you can drive to the Hook of Holland in approximately a half hour. There is also quick and frequent public transportation (check at the Central Station) because this is the daily take-off place for the car ferry between Hook of Holland and Harwich, England. There are also daily ferry connections from Rotterdam Europoort to Hull from the

South bank of the river opposite Hook of Holland.

Besides being the closest ocean area to Rotterdam, this is the least developed—surprising, but true. This is one of those beaches that the Dutch like to call "homely" meaning a family-type beach and as a result, it isn't listed in normal tourist literature. There is no highly developed boardwalk; in fact, not really much boardwalk at all. The beach is flat and very wide; unfortunately, sometimes it gets a bit oily from the ships entering the Nieuwe Waterweg. There are sand dunes for walking, a small wood, a few places to get something to eat or where you can rent a place to change your clothes, or use the facilities. During the season, there may be donkeys and horses for hire.

From Hook of Holland there is a long stretch of sand beach and dunes bordering the North Sea as far as the Afvoer Canal which cuts through the center of Den Haag. The beach of Scheveningen begins on the other side of the canal with miles of beaches and dunes stretching northward. Because the dunes are needed to protect the inland area and because a road along the sea would be under constant repair anyway, there is no highway paralleling the beach proper. For those who wish to explore this area more thoroughly, they should turn off the main highway at 's Gravenzande, Monster, or Loosduinen.

Kijkduin: Kijkduin is Den Haag's "family beach," as is Wassenaarse Slag just to the north. Kijkduin is the quietest. You have to walk a little from the center with its sun terraces, bistros, restaurants and shops to get to the beach. In season, there are puppet shows for children in the Pavilion and music groups playing for teenagers. A covered shopping area is open 7 days a week . . . open 'til 10pm in summer. There's plenty of parking available.

SCHEVENINGEN

GETTING THERE: From Rotterdam, take A13 following signs for The Hague, then Scheveningen. From Amsterdam, A4 south to intersection with A44 (slightly southwest) to outskirts of The Hague, then signs to Scheveningen.
INFORMATION: VVV Scheveningen, Gevers Deynootweg 126, tel. (070) 546200, after 12/89, dial 354 6200.
Note: Add a "3" as a prefix to all The Hague (070) telephone numbers after December 1989.

Scheveningen is the most famous and the most developed of the North Sea beaches. It certainly deserves its reputation, especially if you want entertainment, shopping and activity along with your enjoyment of the sun and sea. The beach itself is wide, long and has good breakers for those who are not satisfied with the quieter beaches such as Oostvoorne and Rockanje. There is a special children's play garden on the beach at the foot of the pier and an area which is well patrolled by lifeguards. For young jumpers, there are trampolines, and for bathers, you will find bathhouses and restaurants galore on the beach. On the boardwalk above the beach (which is concrete tiles—not wooden boards—with glass wind protectors here and there) you can buy anything from inexpensive

328

souvenirs to fur coats or the finest crystal. You can eat from a french-fry stand or have a sumptuous meal at a hotel or restaurant overlooking the water.

Scheveningen celebrated the 700th anniversary of its fishing port in 1985. Before this century, fishermen pulled their boats onto the beach until the terrible storm of 1894 when most of the fleet was demolished. Today, there are regular piers where ships dock in a protected area, a short drive at the southern end of town beyond the Promenade. This area is full of interesting dining-out spots, see "Eating Out" below.

MUSEUMS AND ATTRACTIONS:

The Marine Biological Museum (Zeebiologisch Museum), Dr. Lelykade 39, tel. (070) 502528, open, daily 10am-5pm, Sun., 1-5pm, Tram 10, 11, Bus 23, was built in the former fish auction hall with a view on the Marina. The seashells are superb as is the collection of items from the sea, fish and sea creatures, etc. For details, see The Hague, Chapter 2.

The Scheveningen Museum, Neptunusstr. 92, tel. (070) 500830; open Mon.-Sat., 10am-4:30pm (summer); Tues.-Sat., 10am-4:30pm (winter), Tram 1, 7, 8, 9, Bus 14, 23, has a unique collection of ships' models, navigation instruments and antique costumes.

The Palace Promenade has been developed into the largest shopping, walking and entertainment center in this part of Holland. Open 7 days a week until 10pm in summer. For Bowling, there's a 24-lane bowling center along the Palace Promenade, tel. (070) 543212, after 12/89, 354 3212.

The Parade and Amusement Pier, Strandweg, tel. (070) 543677; open April-Sept., Mon.-Sun., 9am-9pm; Oct.-March, Mon.-Sun., 9am-5pm. Sometimes the attractions close early due to weather conditions. This is something special with four "islands" extending 400 meters out into the sea from the main walkway where you will find a restaurant, terraces, shops, an underwater wonderland, a 400-meter underwater walk, an aquarium and amusement arcade, cinema, cycling track, and a look-out tower 45 meters above the sea.

Scheveningen Golfbad (Wave Pool), Strandweg 13 just south of the Kurhaus, tel. (070) 542100; hours vary according to season so call ahead. Admission includes free use of all facilities with reductions for families: Adults, Fl. 12.50, children 4-14 years, Fl. 7.50. Among the facilities are an indoor and outdoor swimming pool, sports hall, underwater massage and tidal wave, a sauna, a solarium, table tennis, badminton, volleyball, keep-fit training program, and so on. There is a restaurant with menus from Fl. 17.95 (full meals), lunches, Fl. 7.95, as well as a "tropical cocktail bar."

EATING OUT: As mentioned above, the number of restaurants, snack shops, food stands on shore is nearly inexhaustible and your greatest problem will be to choose which place should receive your patronage. If you want to eat something traditionally Dutch, you should take the road toward the Lighthouse, past the Norfolk Ferry Service until you see the fishing port. At the corner of Vissershavenweg and Treilerdwarsweg you will see a food stand on the quay and people blissfully eating a whole herring, their heads thrown back, fish overhead, fish tail between their fingers, mouths open to receive the next bite. If you haven't enough courage for this delicacy, the stands also have other typical Dutch snacks, such as open-faced shrimp or smoked eel sandwiches, croquettes, frites, etc. On a Sunday, you might be lucky enough to see a fisherman's wife dressed in her traditional Sunday outfit, long black skirts ballooning along and those lovely gold ornaments in the coif quivering and sparkling with each step.

In addition to Dutch food, one of the best Indonesian, an excellent Japanese, as well as Italian, Mexican, French and fish restaurants are available. There's something for every taste and every purse. Cocktail lounges, bars, theatres, convention halls and many places of entertainment abound in Scheveningen. During the height of the tourist season, the boardwalk is fairly buzzing with activity from early morning 'til late at night and often it's all a person can do just to get through the crowds. Come and see for yourself.

In the famous Kurhaus, there are a number of restaurants: "The Signpost" with a Michelin star is at the top of the list; Saur's (from The Hague) has an "Oysterbar" downstairs (tel. 462565); "Kandinsky's" is elegant and has wonderful sea views; also a reasonable buffet in the Kurzaal, the main lounge.

STAYING OVER: Scheveningen is a favorite stopping place for families wanting to mix their sightseeing with sea breezes and swimming as well as people doing business in The Hague and at the conveniently located Conference Center. The top of the line is still the majestic Kurhaus Hotel (5 stars), Gevers Deynootplein 30, tel. (070) 520052, expensive; amenities include the Casino, fine dining, and right on the boardwalk and beach.

Less expensive is the Bel Park Hotel, Belgischeplein 38, tel. 556831 or 505000; apartments are available, 5 minutes' walk to the beach.

Another hotel worth checking into is the Strand Hotel, Zeekant III, tel. 540193; views of sea and dunes, moderate-priced.

Going north from Scheveningen, the beaches are first, the nudist beach; then Wassenaar beach (undeveloped family picnic beach); Katwijk aan Zee (family-type beach); and Noordwijk aan Zee which is similar to Scheveningen in its tourist pleasures but on a smaller and more intimate scale.

NOORDWIJK AAN ZEE

GETTING THERE: From The Hague, N44/A44 north to turnoff for Noordwijk a/Zee; from Rotterdam, A13 northwest to A4 north to A12 west, then N44/A44 taking turnoff for Noordwijk a/Zee; from Amsterdam, south on A4 to fork with A44, then south on A44 to turnoff for Noordwijk a/Zee.
INFORMATION: VVV Noordwijk, tel. (01719) 19321.

The beach is wide and extends for miles up and down the coast and there are hotels and guest houses galore either directly on the seafront or slightly behind and among the sand dunes.

There are places to rent horses for riding on the beach and in the dunes, tennis courts, a pool for indoor-outdoor swimming and a bowling alley; a slot-machine/mini-golf establishment to break the pace, and a shopping street buzzing with activity where you may run into friends or buy something you may have forgotten.

There are also bike paths along the coast, through the dunes inland to the

lakes. Bike rental info from the VVV.

MUSEUMS AND ATTRACTIONS:

The "Oud Nordwijk" (Old Noordwijk) Museum, Jan Krooslaan 4, tel. (01719) 17884; open, June-Sept., Mon.-Sat., 10am-5pm, Sun., 2-5pm. A renovated old farm with full inventory of 1880 tells the history of fishermen.

Jan Verwey Nature Center, Wetteringkade 27; open, Sat., Sun. and Wed., 2-4pm, is a permanent exhibit of flora, fauna, shells of the area, etc.

Aqualand, Koningen Wilhelmina Boulevard 20, tel. (01719) 19340, is a new indoor surfpool attached to the Hotel Oranje but open to the general public.

Less commercialized than Scheveningen, Noordwijk is especially popular with foreign tourists. Close by is the beach-dune-woods area and Noordwijkerhout. The Dune Reserve area between Noordwijk and Zandvoort is a protected waterfowl area open to walkers only (no bikes or dogs)—an oasis of peace full of flora and fauna. Passes must be obtained—check with the VVV Noordwijk.

EATING OUT: The beach and the boulevard have many pavilions with terraces for a bite or a drink, but for living it up in style, the terrace of the Grand Hotel Huis ter Duin with its lovely view from high on the dunes over the North Sea is hard to beat. They still have the high wicker beach "basket" chairs of yesteryear which protect you from the wind—rare to find these today in spite of their practicality. Also worth a try for a special meal is "Het Hof van Holland."

STAYING OVER: Away from the hustle and bustle of the seaside, there's a charming hotel-restaurant with typical Dutch atmosphere "Het Hof van Holland." Take the Noordwijk-Binnen turn as you enter town and you will find yourself just off a tree-lined square with an old city pump—a quiet old-world situation. The address is Voorstraat 79, tel. (01719) 12255. You may also have a super-duper French-style menu with white linen and crystal to grace your table (expensive), as well as an extensive wine list for an elegant dinner out.

331

ZANDVOORT AND IJMUIDEN

GETTING THERE: From Amsterdam, take one of the expressways to
Haarlem, then look for signs to Zandvoort—it's about a 20-min-
ute drive going west. IJmuiden is slightly north of Zandvoort. The
best route would probably be N5 west to A9, then north on A9 to
IJmuiden turnoff.
From The Hague, take N44/A44 and N208 north to Haarlem, look-
ing for directions to Zandvoort. For IJmuiden, continue north on
A208. From Rotterdam, take normal route to The Hague and
then follow above directions.
INFORMATION: VVV Haarlem, tel. (023) 319059.

Zandvoort: This is Amsterdam's playground—going along with Amsterdam's image of the avant-garde it boasts a nude bathing beach, an atmospheric casino, and an automobile racecourse. For more traditional types, they can enjoy 15 kilometers of superb sand beach, a national park (dunes), De Kennemer, fields of flowers in the spring, and a choice of three recommended hotels, the Bouwes Palace, a skyscraper with all facilities—right on the beach; the Concorde, a small traditional Dutch hotel with only 15 rooms; or the Zuiderbad which is in between in size and has a café-restaurant.

IJmuiden: IJmuiden is a bit further north and more traditional. Fishermen can do their thing from the jetty or take a fishing boat out to sea in search of more exciting game. Haarlem is a good place to stay and offers all sorts of tourist accommodations and attractions.

EGMOND AAN ZEE, SCHOORL, JULIANADORP

GETTING THERE: From Rotterdam, The Hague and Amsterdam,
follow directions above to IJmuiden but continue north on A9/N9
toward Alkmaar. Then look for signs indicating the beaches.

The following North Holland Beaches are similar to the family-style beaches mentioned in the outskirts of Rotterdam.

Egmond aan Zee and Bergen aan Zee: Two beaches closest to Alkmaar. The villages of Egmond aan Zee and Bergen are quietly scenic in the Boswachterij Schoorl protected national dunes area.

Schoorl: A couple of kilometers north of Bergen off north/south road N9. Schoorl beach is only accessible by foot or bike, therefore, more peaceful than other beaches on this coast. Bikes are for rent in the area.

Julianadorp: Even further north—just south of the busy harbor town of Den Helder, Julianadorp has a town-like atmosphere, see Chapter 3. One area is reserved for nudists!

CHAPTER 15

HOW IT'S MADE: Crafts and Industry

In this world of plastics and throwaways, it seemed a fine idea to remind ourselves that many products we use every day are still made by hand in traditional fashion and that many such have no peers in the "ready-made" market. This list is not comprehensive, but it is a jumping-off place to find your own "How It's Made" places. If you have children, it's a good idea they should know milk comes from a cow and not a carton-factory . . . that is easy to prove in Holland.

If you want more information about these places, the VVV of the town mentioned in our list is your contact. VVV addresses and telephone numbers are found at the beginning of each provincial chapter and also in the Quick Reference section just before the Index.

Baking and Grinding Wheat

't Aole Compas, Drenthe. Demonstrations of raisin bread being baked with all the mouthwatering odors wafting overhead.

Gouda, South Holland. Baking treacle wafers is demonstrated in Gouda during the summer months.

Schiedam, South Holland. De Vrijheid Windmill, Noordvest 40, tel. 473 3000, is open Sat., 10:30am-4:30pm . . . conducted tours every half hour in season and every hour off season. You can purchase flour ground by the mill or bread baked locally from the flour milled here.

Rotterdam, South Holland. Distilleerketel Windmill, Delfshaven, offers pancakes to eat on the spot made from their own ground wheat, but also flour and bread to buy for home consumption.

Allingawier, Friesland, along the Aldfaers Erf scenic 4-village tour of the countryside. The bakery adjoining the coffeehouse "De Meermin," next to the "Iron Cow" restaurant, demonstrates the biscuit making process. Frisian "drabbelkoeken" are made according to a secret family recipe from a kind of batter fried in boiling butter. For information, tel. (05058) 1736 or (05157) 5681. Open, April-Oct., Mon.-Sat., 9am-5:30pm, Sun., 10am-5pm.

333

Basketry

IJsselstein (west of Utrecht City). Willow and and Cane Processing Co. IJsselstein, W. Vink & Sons, Kronenburgplantsoem 30, tel. (03408) 81313. Wands and cane are processed into a product suitable for baskets and chairs. Can be visited by making prior arrangement. Demonstrations in the summer months. Wand-stripping demos only in May.

Brewing Beer

Amsterdam, North Holland. Every beer-drinker knows the name "Heineken." To see it brewed, contact the Heineken Brewery, Stadhouderskade 78 (or v.d. Helststraat 30) 1072 AE Amsterdam, tel. (020) 207 09111. Groups only.

Groenlo, Gelderland. A good brewery museum is Grolisch-Grolsch Museum, Noteboomstraat 15, 7141 AB Groenlo, tel. (5440) 3271; open Mon.-Fri., 2-5pm.

Breda, North Brabant. Ver. Bierbrowerijen Breda-Rotterdam BV, Ceresstraat 13, Breda, tel. (076) 252424 or check with the Breda VVV. Groups, 20-50 only.

Candle Making

Utrecht City. Candle making can be seen by appointment at De Waskit, Donkerstraat 23, Utrecht.

Delfshaven, South Holland. Illuminee Candlemakers, Aelbrechtskolk 39, Delfshaven; demonstrations, Tues.-Fri., 11am-5pm; Sat., 11am-4pm; Sun., 1-5pm.

Scheveningen, South Holland. Handicraft Candle-Workshop, Gevers Deynootplein 45, tel. (070) 523486, Mon.-Fri., 9am-5pm, Sat.-Sun., noon-6pm. This workshop has been organized to show all aspects of candle making in the course of a conducted tour. There's a pictorial history of candle making showing the age-old process of candle dipping and casting. At the end of the program, you can try your own hand at dipping a candle which you may take home. There is a very low admission fee which includes the cost of your personally made candle.

Gouda, South Holland. Gouda is a candle-making center as well as a cheese-producing town, headquarters for a large candle factory. Candle making is demonstrated during special crafts days in the summer . . . check with VVV.

Apeldoorn, Gelderland. Candlemaker de Veluwe, Oranjeweg 9, Emst near Apeldoorn, tel. (05787) 1632. See candles being made by hand in the traditional manner. For Fl. 3.50, make two of your own in the color of your choice; open, daily, 10am-5pm except Oct.-April only open Saturdays.

Carriage Making

Houten, west of Utrecht. Verwey Brothers, Herenweg 1, Houten, tel. (03403) 71327; open, Mon.-Fri., 8am-noon and 1:30-6pm. Maximum, 5 persons.

Cheese Making

It isn't so easy to see this being done as you might think, considering that cheese is a big export item and a full-scale industry in the Netherlands. The small farmer usually only makes cheese once a year—he keeps some for his use and that of his family and will also sell some privately, but much of it goes to be sold along with the commercial cheeses—it's called "Boerenkaas" (farmer's cheese). Cheese-making is a delicate process, requiring very controlled conditions (no drafts, for instance) or the milk will not set properly. For this reason, a large group of sightseers cannot usually be accommodated since the space is limited where the farmer must work.

You can, of course, go to the cheese markets in Gouda and Alkmaar, or to Edam and see the various kinds and sizes of cheese which are sold on the market. If, while you are there you are the type to strike up a conversation with one of the cheese dealers, they might invite you to their farm to see how it's done.

Gouda, South Holland. Kaas Boerderij Hoogendoorn, Mijzijde 6, Kamerik, tel. (03481) 1200, open, daily, 8am-6pm except Sun.; demonstrations Mon.-Sat., 8am-10:30pm . . . you can try your hand.

Bergambacht (south of Gouda). De Driesprong, Zuidbroek 154, tel. (01826) 314 . . . a cheese lunch is also possible if you reserve ahead.

Den Helder at Schagen, North Holland. Het Nederlands Kaasmuseum, about 23 km south of Den Helder shows in detail how cheese and butter are made.

Nieuwer ter Aa, Utrecht. Sterreschans, Oukoop 32, tel. (02943) 1246 . . . demonstrations possible; appointment necessary.

Vreeland, Utrecht. De Willigen, Nigtevechtseweg 40, tel. (02945) 1668 or 1582.

Zegvelt, Utrecht. W. Langerak, Hoofdweg 147, Zegveld, tel. (03489) 327; open mid-May-Oct., Mon.-Sat., 8am-11am . . . maximum 10 persons.

Monnickendam, North Holland. Jacobhoeve, Hogedijk 8, Katwoude, tel. (02995) 1597; open, daily, 9am-6pm . . . cheese farm.

Broek in Waterland, North Holland. The cheese farm, Cheesery De Domme Dirk, Roomeinde 17, tel. (02903) 1454, is open to visitors Mon.-Fri., 6am-6pm.

Zaanse Schans, North Holland. Catharina Hoeve, de Kwakels 2, tel. (075) 313717; open all year, 8am-7pm (Nov. 1-March 1, 9am-5pm), shows how Edam and Gouda cheeses are made in the traditional manner. Entrance fee.

Crystal Factory

Leerdam, South Holland. Did you know the Dutch made crystal? They do and very well, too. For information about visiting the crystal factory, contact Mr. Schillermans at Lingedijk 8, Leerdam, tel. (03451) 13141. He can tell you about visiting hours, directions for finding the factory, and so forth.

Diamond Cutting

Amsterdam, North Holland. Amsterdam is known as the "City of Diamonds" with seven well-known diamond cutting and polishing factories offering guided tours for individuals and groups. You can check with:

Amsterdam Diamond Center, B.V., Rokin 1, tel. (010) 245787; Coster Diamonds, Paulus Potterstraat 2-4, tel. 762222; Gassan Diamond House, Nieuwe Achtergracht 17-23, tel. 225333; Bab Hendriksen Diamonds, Weteringschans 89, tel. 262798; Holshuysen-Stoeltie, Wagenstraat 13-17, tel. 237601; Van Moppes Diamonds, Albert Cuypstraat 2-6, tel. 761242; and AS Bonebakker & Zoon B.V., Rokin 86-90, tel. 232294.

Rotterdam, South Holland. Diamond Centre Rotterdam, Kipstraat 7b, tel. (010) 413 4552 . . . diamond cutting and exhibition. Also the Treasure Trove (beneath the Lijnbaan) G. C. Heetman, Lijnbaan 92, tel. (010) 411 6670. Call for information about demonstrations and video presentations about diamonds and pearls. There is also a fluorescent room with semi-precious stones highlighted . . . Mon.-Sat., 10am-5pm.

Distilleries

Schiedam, South Holland. The National Spirits Museum, Hoogstraat 112, tel. (010) 426 9066, describes the whole procedure; open Tues.-Sat., 10am-5pm, Sun., 12:30-5pm. Branderij de Twerling, Noordwest 93, tel. (010) 473 4399—to see Genever-making (gin); visits and tasting, Friday evenings.

Eel Smoking

Monnickendam, North Holland. At De Oude Visafslag, you can see the eel-smoking rooms, 9am-5pm daily in summer; in winter, only on weekends.

Flower Arrangements

Vleuten, west of Utrecht. Lodder-Vleuten b.v., Utrechtseweg 21, Vleuten, tel. (03407) 1285; open Mon.-Fri., 9am-noon and 1-4pm; Sat., 9am-noon . . . Bonsai (miniature Japanese trees).

Maartensdijk, west of Utrecht. J. Rijksen & Sons, Molenweg 44a, Maartensdijk, tel. (03461) 1380, flower arrangement demonstrations preferably on Wednesdays by appointment.

Furniture and Cloth

Hindeloopen, Friesland. Call the VVV, tel. (05142) 2550 for details about visiting a factory producing Hindeloopen furniture with its unique multi-colored designs. At "Roosje Hindeloopen Holland," Nieuwstad 44, tel. (05142) 1251, Mr. E. Stallmann will demonstrate furniture being hand-painted, etc. Cloth is also dyed in a unique Hindeloopen fashion used both for garments and home accouterments, such as tablecloths, etc.

Nieuwegein, Utrecht. Studio Mill "De Batavier," Herenstraat 71A, Nieuwegein, tel. (03402) 32892. Demonstrations of wood turning, Tues.-Thurs., 1-5pm, Fri., 1-5pm and 7-9pm, Sat., 10am-4pm.

Peat Digging

't Aole Compas, Drenthe. It might come as a surprise but peat is still used for fuel in Europe and this unusual occupation is explained at 't Aole Compas during their demonstration days.

Pewter Making

Delfshaven, South Holland. The Zakkendragershuisje, 13 Voorstraat, Delfshaven, tel. (010) 477 2664 (or Rotterdam VVV, (010) 413 6000), welcomes everyone during normal working hours and also on Sundays when special demonstrations are held every hour. The craftsmen use authentic molds dating from the 18th century which are on loan from the Historical Museum. You may purchase souvenirs for a few guilders or hundreds of guilders according to the importance of the piece.

Tiel, Gelderland. Tinfabriek Metawa, Spoorsstraat 5, tel. (03440) 15254, is another place to seek out this centuries-old craft in production. Call for an appointment.

Zaanse Schans, North Holland. The Tinkoepel Pewter Shop has craftsmen working. For information, VVV Zaandam, tel. (075) 176204.

Pottery Making

There are two major manufacturers of pottery, porcelain and tiles in the Netherlands, each with a fascinating history which is discussed in the text. Makkum in Friesland and Delft in South Holland have been competitors almost since the beginning of their operations.

Makkum, Friesland. Tichelaars Koninklijke Makkumer Aardewerk en Tegelfabriek, Turfmarkt 61, tel. (05158) 1341; open to visitors Mon.-Fri., 10am-4pm for conducted tours. The Tichelaar's Royal Ceramics and Tile Manufactory has earned the right to add "Royal" to their title due to the quality of their work and the patronage of the House of Orange.

Workum, Friesland. In the near vicinity of Makkum, another town with a number of pottery factories can be visited. Call ahead for details, Workum VVV, tel. (05151) 1300.

Delft, South Holland. The Royal Delft Ware Factory is particularly famous, receiving visitors from all over the world. Located at Rotterdamseweg 196, tel. (015) 560234, open April-Oct., Mon.-Sat., 9am-5pm, Sun., 10am-4pm; Oct.-April, Mon.-Fri., 9am-5pm, Sat., 10am-4pm, closed Sunday. This factory also has Royal Family connections as can be seen in the title. Known primarily for its blue and white designs, in recent years it has produced many multicolored versions and employed artists who create works under their own title—elegant and modern.

De Delftse Pauw, Delftweg 133, tel. 124920, open April to mid-Oct., daily, 9am-4pm; mid-Oct. to March, Mon.-Fri., 9am-4pm, Sat.-Sun., 11am-1pm. Established in 1954, this manufacturer produces pottery alongside a canal a bit outside the city center . . . go to the VVV for directions. You can order plates

338

made to your own design or for special occasions at reasonable prices.

"Atelier de Candelaer," Kerkstraat 13, tel. (015) 131848, is a small family-operated shop. Designs are under the guidance of the lady of the house; the owner handles the rest of the operation. Conveniently located in the shadow of the New Church, this is an easy visit for visitors ... the selection of goods is smaller but also less expensive. Try here for a special order; they seem to be very cooperative and will ship anywhere.

Pottery "Adrie," Moerings, Peperstraat 76, tel. (01820) 12842. Demonstrations are also given here.

Gouda, South Holland. Pottery (Aardewerk) Factory de Drietland, Stavorenweg 5, tel. (01820) 16494; open all year by appointment.

Utrecht, Utrecht. At "Schoppen Drie," Schalkwijkstraat 8, pottery, ceramics and tile are produced.

Marken, North Holland. Pottery is made at Havenbuurt 1, Open Tues.-Sun., 10am-6pm.

Silver Making

Schoonhoven, South Holland. Schoonhoven is known as the Dutch "silver town" offering a number of places where you can see how silver is worked. A state school teaching center for aspiring silversmiths has about 850 students.

The Museum of Antique Silverware (Edelambachtshuis), Haven 13, tel. (01823) 2614, has two floors devoted to an enormous collection of old Dutch silver, and a replica of an old workshop where a silversmith gives demonstrations.

St. Andrieshuis, 28 Oude Haven, tel. 5827, open weekdays, 10am-12:30pm and 1:30-5pm. Here they demonstrate how filigree is made.

Gold, Silver and Clock Museum, Haven Kazerne, Oude Haven 7, tel. (01823) 5612. Silversmiths can be seen at work here as well as at the Edelambachtshuis, by appointment.

Textile Making

Tilburg, North Brabant. The Netherlands Textile Museum, Goirkestraat 88, tel. (013) 422241. Demonstrations of spinning and weaving are given during open hours: Tues.-Fri., 10am-5pm, Sat., 2-5pm, Sun., noon-5pm.

Wine Making

Nieuwegein, Utrecht. "Trouvaille" Wine Merchants, Het Fort Jutphaas 3, tel. (03402) 31708. Wine-making demonstrations but only by appointment.

Rotterdam, South Holland. "Holland Natuurwijnen," Maaskade 125, tel. (010) 433 4171. Fruit wines made in a natural way—demonstrations. Small fee; glass of wine.

Tilburg, North Brabant. The Wine House, Geminiweg 9, tel. 434920, open Tues.-Fri., 10am-6pm, Sat., 10am-5pm, offers a film about wine, displays showing wine-making and, finally, wine tasting.

Wooden Shoes

Wooden shoes are made all over the Netherlands so we will only give a few names to get you started. Other clog makers can be found at Volendam, Zaanse Schans, and at 't Aole Compas during their demonstration days, to name a few.

Broek in Waterland, North Holland. One of our favorite wooden shoe factories is De Swaen, Havenrak 21, tel. (02995) 1432, open normal business hours and on weekends (check with VVV, tel. 1998 for specifics). Wooden shoes float from the ceiling and the host is gregarious.

Schuwacht (at Lekkerkerk), South Holland. The Van Zwienen company has been in business since 1815. Sawdust flies in all directions as hundreds of clogs are turned out daily. They are dried in piles in special drying rooms before being finished off and painted. During summer vacations, children even help. Clogs, plain or colored, can be bought reasonably.

Aalsmeer, North Holland. Clogmaking can be seen in Aalsmeer at van Cleefkade 15, Mon.-Sat., 8am-1pm. (Close by you can see the flower auction at Legmeerdijk 313, workdays, 8am-noon.)

Marken, North Holland. Ask any of the merchants to direct you to the clogmaker in the center of the old village; open all year, 9am-6pm except Sundays.

Monnickendam, North Holland. "Irene Hoeve," Hogedijk 1, Katwoude, tel. (02995) 2291.

PART II

CHAPTER 16

Living in Holland

LIVING IN HOLLAND

WELCOME TO HOLLAND. To feel at home and not be threatened by an unknown system, one must understand something of the culture, social mores, the past and the future hopes of a people, the attitudes of one's hosts toward happiness, success, place in the world, and know how the system works. In this chapter, we will address the problem of where to go for advice and help in adjusting to life in the Netherlands. Adjustment is not a flat concept. Knowing the language is helpful but even verbal communication is only one aspect of "adjustment." For instance, many Dutchmen born in Indonesia or South Africa, who came to Holland as adults, were miserable when they first arrived because they were faced with an entirely different social and cultural picture than they had known. And in spite of the fact that English is spoken more often and better here than anywhere else in Continental Europe, adjusting to life in Holland is not necessarily easy. We hope we can help by pointing the way toward solving the everyday problems that arise.

Reading ahead is always helpful whether one is touring or establishing residency in a new country. The books listed in the Recommended Reading list at the end of this book can be a start. Also, before leaving home, contact the Dutch Embassy or Consulate and ask for whatever information they can give to prospective residents of their country. The Cultural Officer is a good contact and can make suggestions about a reading list. The Commercial Officer can answer business-related questions, and have information on the cost of living in the Netherlands.

The first concern of families with children is schooling. The burning questions are, what is available, where is it, and how much will it cost. As a starter, write the Ministerie Onderwijs en Wetenschappen (Ministry of Education), POB 25000, 2700 LZ Zoetermeer for their booklets. You can also write to the schools listed in the following chapter on education, asking for their brochures stipulating requirements, costs, etc. If you are in Holland, make an appointment to meet the principal and see the facilities.

Once you have arrived, your best source of help is through people you meet—Dutch and foreign. The jobholder will meet colleagues as a natural course of working; however, their wives and children must make their own way. For them, the best contacts are women's clubs and schools. Both groups are listed in this and following chapters.

After the school is chosen and the housing situation is in hand, the next thing to tackle is making friends and having fun. We hope Section I of this book will give you some ideas on having fun. This chapter and those following are written in the hopes of giving the newcomer pointers so frustrations are minimal.

The practicalities of living, such as establishing a personal banking and checking account, getting an English-language newspaper, knowing about the public libraries, etc., must not be overlooked. We will therefore start with the nitty-gritty of settling in and then move on to the fun and games in Chapter 17. The chapter entitled "The Younger Set" gives all manner of information about schools and children-oriented activities and organizations.

ENGLISH-LANGUAGE NEWSPAPERS: Most English-language newspapers are available at city railway stations, hotels and bookstores. Major Dutch public libraries carry a selection of newspapers published abroad. An example is the Newspaper Reading Room of the Central Municipal Library in Rotterdam, tel. (010) 433 8911. There you can read the *London Times, Telegraph, International Herald Tribune, Financial Times, Christian Science Monitor* and a number of French, German, Turkish newspapers as well.

Subscriptions can be arranged through:

The International Herald Tribune, printed in Holland . . . general world news with an emphasis on the U.S.; no local information except as a world news event. To subscribe, call (023) 322341 or write Edipress Int. B.V., Wilhelmina-straat 13, POB 3636, 2000 AJ Haarlem (NH).

USA Today International . . . all U.S. news; subscriptions: 184 High Holborn, London WC17AP or call 09.44.1.831 2266.

Window, monthly news for non-nationals living and working in the Netherlands. Available at newsstands. To subscribe, contact Rohong Publishers, Antwoord Nr. 93238, NL 2509WB, The Hague.

RELOCATION SERVICES: There are several organizations which help newcomers relocate to the Netherlands.

ACCESS (Administrative Committee to Coordinate English-speaking Services), Rotterdamsestraat 66, 2585 GN The Hague, tel. (070) 558551, after December 1989, 355 8551. This English-speaking referral service provides information by telephone to an English mother tongue counselor; education workshops promoting cultural adaptation, human development and family life. Also offers a counseling referral system. Staffed by volunteers.

Crossroads Newcomers Network, POB 536, 1180 RM, Amstelveen, tel. (020) 477333, offers support and practical advice to newcomers through volunteers.

EXPAT Advice Service, Backershagenlaan 40, 2243 RD Wassenaar, tel. (01751) 10143. They have just expanded their previous service to include a Personnel Package for the individual and his family on behalf of the employer.

Formula Two Relocation, 190 Stationweg, 1077 TC Amsterdam, tel. (020) 664 2759 and 455969. Run by two Englishwomen living in Holland.

Relocation Services, van Hamellaan 40, 2252 BN Voorschoten, tel. (01717) 4643, and Hilversum, tel. (01751) 10743. Run by an American and a Dutch woman.

Education for Relocation, Graafschappad 38, 5691 LX Son, (near Eindhoven), tel. (04990) 77193.

Money and Banking

The following explanation of money and banking hopefully will be useful to the new arrival. Dutch money is based on the decimal system. One hundred cents make one guilder. A guilder (een gulden) is also known as a florin in Dutch and by the abbreviations "gld," "Dfl." or "Fl." Dutch banks will handle overseas payments with very little formality. The bank employee will help you fill out an application; the bank sends the check to the addressee. As mentioned below, salaries and recurring bills can be paid automatically through your bank. Banks often have folders in foreign languages explaining the particular forms of payment and investments. If they are a small neighborhood bank and cannot answer your questions, they will call their head office for assistance. Safe deposit boxes are available at most banks.

Currency Exchange: There are 75 GWK (De Grenswisselkantoren N.V.) offices at 35 railway stations and border checkpoints. Besides changing foreign currencies, these offices can change travelers checks, arrange travel insurance, and give cash on demand for Euro-cheques, Giro Cash cards, the Eurocard, Access, MasterCard, Diners Card, Visa Card, American Express, JCB card and Air Plus Card. Offices are usually open weekdays, 8:30am-9pm; Sat., 8:30am-noon. Official agents are on trains from and to foreign destinations. The exchange rate is based on the daily quotation. Commissions can vary so it is wise to inquire, especially in big cities where there is a choice of exchange offices. VVVs at large resorts can also change money.

Credit Cards: All Dutch banks, savings banks ("Spaarbanken") and the Postgiro/Rijksspaarbank, honor the "Eurocard." It is the European version of the MasterCard, Access Card . . . valid worldwide, including the East bloc. A Eurocard costs Fl. 100 annually. It is available from the head office, Aert Van Nesstraat 45, Rotterdam, tel. (010) 414 1833; from all GWK and Change Express offices, the Algemene Bank Nederland (ABN) office at Schiphol airport and the AMRO Bank at Beek airport, Limburg. Other credit cards accepted in the Netherlands are:

American Express, Head Office, Damrak 66, Amsterdam, tel. (020) 262042
Diners Club, Head Office, Weesperstraat 77, Amsterdam, tel. (020) 557 3557
Visa Card, Rijswijk, Postbus 157, 2280 AD Rijswijk, tel. (070) 957857,
after December 1989, 395 7857.

PERSONAL BANKING: There are two ways to open a personal checking account: through any private bank or through the Dutch Government's postal banking service known as the "Postgiro." Both will allow you the same privileges. The Postgiro has the advantage that they are found in all post offices (usually open weekdays, 8am-5pm). Both allow you to sign an order form for power of attorney ("Matchtiging") for periodic automatic payments for such items as rent, utilities, newspaper, telephone bills, and the like. Both also use different checks for payment by mail and other type checks for paying in person. Your check sent by mail instructs your banker to pay the bank of the recipient who receives the payment from his own bank.

The Private Bank: The Dutch are well known for their banking acumen. Some major banks with branches throughout the country are AMRO, ABN, NMB, Bank Mees & Hope and RABO. They handle all types of financial transactions but their system is sometimes different than in other countries. There are several methods of paying for purchases:

1. A check for direct payment is a "betaalcheque" and is guaranteed by the bank for payment of Fl. 100 or less. This check has to be written in front of the "seller" who checks your "betaalpas" for I.D. This check is equivalent to cash and is accepted everywhere (shops, gas stations, restaurants, etc.). To withdraw cash, you may use up to three of these checks at any one time.

2. A beige-colored giro payment card ("accept girokaart") is frequently sent in place of a bill for purchases in another town such as for theater tickets, a subscription, monthly installments, tax payments or shop orders. You fill it in and sign it before sending it to your bank. A perforated stub serves as your receipt. This type of card can also be used for payments through the "postgiro" by sending it to the Giro Headquarters.

3. A bank giro is used for payment of an invoice ("rekening"). This flimsy, printed form with your name and address printed at the top is supplied by your bank. You fill in the amount to be paid, the payee's account number (bank or postgiro), name and town, indicate what the payment is for under "omschrijving" and then sign it. The top sheet is sent to your bank in an envelope supplied by the bank. You retain the copy in a small file "mapje" also provided by your bank. You can use this file to keep the daily statements of your account ("dagafschriften"). These indicate your original balance with additions or deductions and the final balance. Every statement is numbered consecutively, starting the calendar year with 1. Interest is paid on your account.

4. Bank checks can be used for payment of large sums such as when buying a car, furniture, TV. These are given out singly or loose in a folder to the account holder, not in a checkbook. The money necessary for making payment must be in the account before the bank will honor the check.

5. Your bank can also supply you with blue "Eurocheques" which are each valid for up to Fl. 300. The bank charges Fl. 10 per year against loss or theft of these checks. Unlike "betaalcheques," they are acceptable in most European countries. They can be used to make payments or to receive up to Fl. 300 in cash at any one time in any European currency. You will need to show a valid passport and the "Eurocard" and the bank will charge you Fl. 5 per check. Checks drawn abroad (i.e., in a currency other than Dutch) will be deducted from your account in guilders. When paying with a "Eurocheque," remember to write your card number ("Kaart-nummer") on the reverse of the check.

The Postgiro: Obtain an application at any post office. After completing it, submit it to your local post office. You will shortly receive an acknowledgment informing you that an account will be opened for you. This is followed by your account number, and a request that you deposit funds. At the same time, you will receive a folder containing giro forms used for paying your bills and a holder for your statements and envelopes addressed to the city in which your account will be administered. These envelopes need no postage. If you have requested checks for paying bills ("betaalkaarten"), you will be informed when and where to pick up your pass ("betaalpas") and checks.

A husband/wife account is made out in the name of both who are entitled to use the account individually and are each personally responsible for any deficits. AND/OR accounts are made out in the name of two private persons who may both use the account and are both responsible for any deficits.

A "giromaatpas" is used for identification when using checks or giro checks. To prevent theft, keep separately. Checks may be used at any post office to withdraw money from your account up to a total of Fl. 500.

After your account has been opened, you must apply for giro checks ("betaal-kaarten") which are used to pay shops, supermarkets, restaurants, theaters and railroad stations. You may also use them to withdraw money from your account at post offices throughout Holland and Europe. The highest amount you can receive on each paycard is Fl. 200.

If you need money when outside Europe, you may telephone your giro administrative office (the "deviezen" department) asking for funds which will be telegraphed to the post office where you are located within 24-48 hours. Girochecks may be cashed into local currency without problem throughout Europe on presentation of your Giropas and your passport.

Medical Care and Health Benefits

One of the first things a new resident in Holland should do is establish himself and his family with a family doctor—a "huisarts" (a general practitioner). The whole system of medical care is very well organized in the Netherlands and it is wise to have a little background on how this works in order to avoid trouble and frustration in case of an emergency.

First of all, one does not just go to an eye doctor, or a pediatrician, or a heart specialist because one decides he can't see or is going to have a baby or is having heart palpitations. You must go to your house doctor who will then refer you to the specialist you need—if he thinks you need it. Also, if you have not estab-lished yourself with a neighborhood doctor and you have an emergency illness in the family, it is sometimes difficult to get immediate attention.

Doctors work in certain regional areas of the city and will not take patients who live outside their area of responsibility. For instance, if a friend or business acquaintance has recommended Dr. X you may find that this doctor will not accept you as a patient if you live in Hillegersberg because he practices in the Blijdorp area. Doctors in Holland still make house calls in case of any serious illness—they also are responsible for government-insured patients (the bulk of their pratice) as well as private patients. Almost all segments of the local society are well covered by health provisions, therefore, everyone makes use of a doctor's services whenever the need arises. This results in all doctors having very busy schedules and explains the need for limiting the geographic area each doctor must cover. You will obviously want to find a doctor who practices in the neighborhood in which you live.

You can get help with finding a suitable doctor from the Municipal Medical Service (Gemeentelijke Geneeskundige Dienst), through your Embassy or Consulate, or you can look under "Artsen-Huisartsen" in the yellow pages of the telephone directory.

In addition to the Municipal Medical Service's overall public health duties, they will give shots, vaccinations and X-rays. School doctors fall under the supervision of this organization. The school doctor visits the school regularly, examines the children for general good health and warns the parents if he sees anything unusual in a child's growth development. He is in charge of dental health and in addition will give X-rays and other tests as needed.

Should a serious personal or emotional problem arise, or heaven forbid, a major crisis, referral to native English-speaking professional counselors is available through ACCESS, a multinational community service organization in The Hague that provides information, educational workshops and a counseling referral service, tel. (070) 558551, after 12/89, 355 8551. The Dutch equivalent, the Stichting Algemeene Christelijke Hulpdienst, has an SOS line open 24 hours a day. If whoever answers is not fluent in English, ask for someone who is to call back as soon as possible. SOS numbers are: The Hague, (070) 454500, after 12/89, 345 4500; Amsterdam (020) 161666; Rotterdam, tel. (010) 436 2244.

EMERGENCY TELEPHONE NUMBERS:

In case of emergencies during the night, on weekends, public holidays or vacations, one can call the following numbers for information as to which doctor or dentist is on duty. Police emergency numbers are given in Quick Reference.

Amsterdam: *Doctor's and Dentist's Help: tel. (020) 664 2111. Emergency: SOS Line (Distress) (020) 161666.*

The Hague: *Doctor's Help: tel. (070) 455300 or 469669 evenings. Dentist's Help: tel. (070) 654646 or 974491 weekends. Emergency: SOS (Distress) (070) 454500. After 12/89, add 3 prefix to all above local number (070).*

Rotterdam: *Doctor's Help: tel. (010) 420 1100 or 411 5504. Dentist's Help: tel. 455 2155 or 411 3500 (evenings). Emergency: SOS (Distress) (010) 436 2244.*

HOSPITALIZATION: Should you need to be hospitalized, your doctor or specialist will make the necessary arrangements and you will be notified when a bed is available—unless of course it is an emergency. It is important that your insurance company be informed of the date of hospitalization. This is often done directly by the hospital administration, so take your insurance card or information with you.

The type of insurance you have will determine the size of room you will occupy. Private rooms are usually only reserved for very serious or post-operative cases, so be prepared to share a room. You may ask for a telephone (slight charge), but will be supplied with a radio. Visiting hours vary from hospital to hospital, but you will be informed.

Your first visitor will be the department's intern, who will check your medical history, allergies, etc. If you need an operation, he will be followed by the anesthetist. Most doctors and nurses speak good English.

If your child has to go to hospital, you can be sure that he will receive kind attention. Ask to have him admitted to the children's section or directly to a children's hospital. (Available in Rotterdam, Amsterdam, The Hague, Utrecht and Zwolle.) Provided there are facilities available and your child's condition warrants your presence, you may be allowed to stay with him.

For minor accidents, remember that calling an ambulance may turn out to be very expensive, as it is not always covered by your insurance.

PREGNANCY: It is quite normal for family doctors or midwives (vroedvrouw) to handle prenatal, delivery and postnatal care. The midwife has three years' training before being qualified to deliver babies. Babies are delivered both at home and in hospitals. Complicated cases will be referred to an obstetrician (vrouwenarts), who will only deliver in a hospital to which he is attached. It is wise to discuss these possibilities with your house doctor and decide whom you want to look after your pregnancy. Exercise classes for pregnant women are given by local Cross Associations and are highly recommended even for non-Dutch speakers. (See Cross Associations.) They also organize "mother's helpers" for new mothers just out of hospital.

In the hospital you may stay either just 24 hours, being taken home by ambulance attendants, or eight to ten days after delivery. Whoever delivers the baby will want the birth to be as natural as possible; discuss the procedures with him well in advance. In Holland it is not a problem for husbands to be present when the baby is being born.

Three weeks after the baby's birth, the visiting nurse ("wijkverpleegster") will come to check you both. She will make an appointment for your first visit to the baby clinic. You may prefer to have all inoculations and vaccinations given by your doctor, but it is less expensive to use the local Cross Association baby clinic—if you don't mind a possible wait. In either case, you will be given a handy booklet in which all vaccinations will be recorded.

SEMI-PRIVATE HEALTH ORGANIZATIONS:

The cost of membership in a Cross organization is nominal and will vary depending on the township to which one belongs because such organizations are subsidized by the municipal government of the city they serve. They are associations of people who try to promote the health of the whole population. They employ their own doctors, nurses, midwives, technicians, social workers, and provide home care for the sick and elderly. The following Cross organizations serve our three major cities. For addresses of similar groups in other towns, contact the head office in Zoetermeer, tel. (079) 514021.

CROSS ORGANIZATIONS:

*Amsterdam: St. Amsterdamse Kruisverenigingen, Houtrijkstraat 116,
tel. (020) 868610.*

*The Hague: Het Groene Kruis, van Speijkstraat 31, tel. (070) 469799,
after 12/89, 346 9799.*

*Rotterdam: The Cooperating Rotterdam-Cross Associations (De Sticht-
ing Samenwerkende Rotterdamse Kruisverenigingen . . .
S.S.R.K.), Zomerhofstraat 71, tel. (010) 467 1122.*

SERVICES AVAILABLE THROUGH CROSS ASSOCIATIONS: Each branch of the Cross Associations may offer a slightly different service, but they will all provide medical equipment (on a loan basis) which might be needed, such as crutches, wheelchairs, etc.

It should be mentioned that a knowledge of the Dutch language would facilitate any relationship with these organizations since their office and technical personnel are not especially trained to service foreign residents. Still, the cost of membership is reasonable and families might find it well worth belonging.

1. Care for Mother and Child.

Prenatal care and gymnastics; lectures and courses to prepare the pregnant mother for the birth of her child.

Female help to come to the house for the first 10 days following the birth of the child. You have a choice of someone who stays all day or someone who will come twice a day to wash, feed, change the mother and child. If you desire this service, you are billed with a charge which is quite reasonable.

Postnatal care and general pediatric care for the baby until he/she reaches school age, at which time this service is taken over by the school doctor.

2. Household help in case the mother is ill. (Gezins Verzorging.)

There are two kinds of household help available: experienced help capable of running a household without direction in case the mother should be in the hospital; and a mother's helper who will come in and work under the direction of the mother when she is simply confined to bed. This is limited to a period of 6 weeks and is billed separately from the membership fee.

3. Care and Gymnastics for older people. A visiting practical nurse will come at regularly scheduled times to bathe and exercise old people confined to bed or wheelchair.

4. Services of a dietician are also available.

Note that you must have been a member for a minimum of six months in order to take advantage of the Cross Association services.

DENTISTS: Most insurance does not cover dental care and finding a dentist to suit your needs may also prove to be a problem. Some take only private patients and some accept no new patients. However, there are many up-to-the-minute dentists in Holland and one should inquire locally.

THE PHARMACY: Doctors' prescriptions are required for medicines. He will indicate if and how often this prescription may be renewed by the pharmacist. If you are privately insured, you will have to pay for the medication in the first instance, sending the invoice for reimbursement to your insurance company.

If your pharmacy is closed, a notice on the door will indicate which one is open. Similarly a tape-recorded telephone message will usually give you this information if you call—if not, the local VVV will know. Night service is listed in daily newspapers.

HEALTH INSURANCE: Most foreigners living in Holland are automatically insured by the company which employs them. It is wise to investigate the kind of coverage they give you and your family, both for sickness and life insurance. For those who are not automatically covered, health insurance falls into two main categories, National Insurance and Private Insurance.

National Insurance "Ziekenfondswet" applies to those earning less than Fl. 50,105 a year (in 1989). It provides the right to medical, pharmaceutical and dental care, hospital nursing and numerous other provisions.

Private Insurance should be taken out if your yearly earnings exceed the Fl. 50,105 above and if your place of employment does not take care of it. You should compare offers from several companies. If in need of information, contact the Dutch Consumers' Union (Consumenten Bond), tel. (070) 889377.

Churches

Churches of all faiths are well represented throughout the Netherlands. Those within the Randstad which hold foreign-language services are listed in the Quick Reference section just before the Index. Listings for Dutch churches are given in the newspapers and each town's informational pamphlet such as "This Week" in Amsterdam, or from the VVV.

Of special interest to Americans is the service commemorating the departure of the Pilgrims from Leiden to the United States held the last Thursday in November, American Thanksgiving Day, at Sint Pieterskerk, Pieterkerkchoorsteeg 17-A, Leiden. Included in the ecumenical service are a Catholic priest, Protestant ministers and a Jewish rabbi. For details, call the Leiden VVV.

A United Service for Peace usually held in late November/early December at the Scots Church in Rotterdam is a special service. A number of international churches are represented by their pastors, bishops and ministers participating in the service in their own language. Everyone is invited to the informal gathering which follows the service. Call the Church of Scotland, tel. (010) 412 4779 for details.

There are many seamen's organizations in Rotterdam but two which cater specially to seamen of any nationality: The Missions to Seamen, Pieter de Hoochweg 133, tel. (010) 476 4043, and Stella Maris, Willemskade 13, tel. (010) 413 3109.

Libraries

In Holland, there are both book and record lending libraries. Most of them charge a moderate subscription rate.

Avid readers will find their pennies vanish much too quickly if they must purchase all the books they want to read. Luckily, all large city libraries have a selection of English, French, German as well as Dutch books available for loan. They also carry foreign-language newspapers as well as a good selection of children's books in foreign languages. Two private libraries in our list below are the British Council Library in Amsterdam, and the American Women's Club Library in The Hague. Additionally, the Volksuniversiteit Library is available to the general public by applying for membership . . . a nominal fee is charged.

AMSTERDAM:

Amsterdam Centraal Bibliotheek, Prinsengracht 587, tel. (020) 265065, was opened in 1976 and is very modern, light and airy. It has an especially interesting collection of books on the history of Amsterdam and a large selection of English books, children's books, and foreign newspapers. They have the added service of computer rental. Membership cost is minimal. Open daily from

10am-5pm (except Sun. and Mon. mornings), and weekday evenings, 7-10pm.

The Universiteit's Bibliotheek, Singel 425, tel. (020) 525 9111, is open Mon.-Fri., 9:30am-midnight, Sat., 9:30am-1pm.

The British Council Library, Keizersgracht 343, tel. (020) 223644.

THE HAGUE:

Openbare Bibliotheek, the main public library, is on Bilderdijkstraat, tel. (070) 469235, after 12/89, 346 9235; open, Mon., noon-5:15pm and 7-9pm, Tues. and Thurs., 11am-5:15pm, Wed. and Fri., 11am-5:15pm and 7-9pm, Sat., 10am-1pm. This large pillared building in the heart of the city has a large selection of English books and a good children's section. Minimal subscription.

American Women's Club Library, Nieuwe Duinweg 25, tel. (070) 544171, after 12/89, 354 4171, has around 7,500 titles of English-language books. Join the library for about Fl. 45 per family per year without club membership.

ROTTERDAM:

The Central Gemeente Bibliotheek (Central Municipal Library), Hoogstraat 110, tel. (010) 433 8911, has many English-language books available. The "Leeszaal" has sections for English, French, German and Dutch novels. Local branches may also have a selection of foreign books. Library hours: Mon., 12:30-9pm, Tues.-Fri., 10am-9pm, Sat., 10am-5pm. The Central Youth Library is located in the same building and has the same hours. Opened in 1983, this modern Library is bright and cheerful with green plants hanging from various levels à la gardens of Babylon. There's a coffee café on the second floor and a library theater used for special events including an occasional foreign-language program. Most foreign newspapers are available.

The Rotterdam Reading Room (Rotterdamsch Leeskabinet) is worth investigating for scientific works, dictionaries, newspapers, journals and even such light relief as mystery thrillers and some children's books. A private enterprise with a long history, it is now located in the Erasmus University, Burgemeester Oudlaan 50, tel. (010) 452 5511, ext. 3159.

Record Lending Libraries

While this may be of equal interest to the younger generation, information on record lending libraries falls in the adult section because of the "responsibility" factor in being able to establish credit as a good risk. To become a member, bring your I.D. or a passport to verify your identity. Once approved for membership, you may take the records of your choice home for a week or longer and exchange them as often as you want. Membership fees are moderate. Their catalogue lists their complete collection and gives membership particulars.

AMSTERDAM:

Openbare Discotheek, Prinsengracht 587, tel. (020) 265065, has a vast collection of sheet music, an enormous selection of records to borrow, and laser discs

on classical and popular music themes. It also prides itself on its archive collection of records and video musical tapes (VHS) which can be enjoyed on the premises. They have tapes on jazz, Brazilian classical and modern music, opera, Holland Festival tapes, "Film International" tapes and a collection of special interest TV programs.

THE HAGUE:

Openbare Discotheek, Anna Paulownastraat 2, tel. (070) 459235, after 12/89, 345 9235, offers similar facilities and operates under the same general principles as that of Amsterdam. This library has an extensive collection of sheet music as well.

Discotheek Rijswijk, is part of the Rijswijk Library on Dr. Colijnlaan 343, tel. (070) 948808, after 12/89, 394 8808.

ROTTERDAM:

The Record Lending Libraries (Centrale Discotheek), Maritsweg 41, tel. (010) 412 0536 during regular office hours; is open Tues.-Fri., 10am-6pm, Sat., 10am-5pm, and on Thurs. and Fri. evenings, 7pm-9pm. The collection consists of 35,000 classical records; 90,000 nonclassical records, 50,000 LP's and 30,000 CD's—the largest collection in the Netherlands. There are also musical video tapes, children's records, pop music, folk music, jazz, the blues and much more. Radio and TV stations often use their services since they have records which are not available elsewhere. The library has a new discobus which goes to areas outside the center such as Pendrecht and Zuidwijk.

Social and Business Organizations

There are numerous social and business organizations of interest to foreign residents. It is not possible to list them all in this book but selections are given below, in Chapter 19 (The Younger Set), and in Quick Reference just before the Index. Below is a word about the National Society Organizations and the major Women's Clubs in the Randstad.

NATIONAL SOCIETY ORGANIZATIONS: Most foreign businessmen and women, in cooperation with their embassy officials, will promote such clubs as the Netherlands-America Institute, the Netherlands-Japan Club, and the Netherlands-England Society. There are similar clubs for other foreign nationals represented in Holland. The purpose of these groups is to meet socially and become better acquainted in order to promote matters of interest to the visitor and host countries. Call your appropriate embassy for details.

WOMEN'S SOCIAL ORGANIZATIONS: Providing friendship and one-on-one guidance if needed, the Women's Clubs organize group outings to introduce the Netherlands to their members; some operate community services; the American Women's Club in The Hague has a clubhouse with its own extensive library, etc.

Clubs in other parts of the country are listed, along with business and social clubs for men and women in the Quick Reference section.

AMSTERDAM:
The American Women's Club, write POB 70133, 1007 KC Amsterdam. This club includes the Hoorn, Leiden, Amersfoort triangle.
International Women's Contact, write POB 67, 1180 AB Amstelveen.
L'Amitie Club, contact Mme. N. le Cerf, tel. (020) 738175.

THE HAGUE:
(After 12/89, all code (070) numbers add a 3 prefix to the local number.)
The American Women's Club, Club House, Nieuwe Duinweg 25, 2537 AB The Hague, tel. (070) 544171.
The British Women's Club, Societeit de Witte, Plein 24, tel. (070) 461973.
The First International Ladies Luncheon and Dinner Club, Bloklandenplein 11, 2594 CK, The Hague.
International Women's Contact, write IWC, POB 84404, 2508 AK The Hague or tel. (070) 558863.
L'Amitie Club, call Mme. S. de Jong (070) 834433.
The Australian and New Zealand Women's Club, write POB 91445, 2509 EA The Hague.
The Canadian Women's Club, write POB 1022, 2240 BA Wassenaar.
The Japanese Club, see Rotterdam below.
Petroleum Wives Club, write POB 655, 2240 AP Wassenaar, Mrs. Schauerman, tel. (070) 551869.

ROTTERDAM:
American Netherlands Club of Rotterdam (ANCOR), write POB 34025, 3005 GA Rotterdam. International members welcome.
Pickwick, call Mrs. Thompson (010) 470 9937.
L'Amitie Club, contact Mme. M. Hoffman, tel. (010) 422 0896.
Japanese Club, call the Japanese Consulate-General, tel. (010) 430 3716.

Adult Educational Opportunities

Educational opportunities range from working for a university degree to taking art classes on the Riviera!

UNIVERSITY PROGRAMS: Attending a Dutch university is very difficult because the demand for space by Dutch students is so great that acceptance of foreigners is kept to a minimum. Information about higher educational opportunities for foreigners can be obtained through the Netherlands Embassy abroad or contact the Ministerie van Onderwijs en Wetenschappen, Voorlichting (Information), tel. (079) 531911. Following is a list of English-language universities offering degrees in the Netherlands.

Webster University, affiliated with Webster U. at St. Louis, Missouri, offers undergraduate courses in Business Management, Computer Studies and International Studies; graduate courses (leading to a BA, an MA and MBA) in Management, Marketing, Computer Resources, Management and International Relations. All courses are in English. This is the only accredited American University in the Netherlands. Contact Webster University, Boommarkt 1, 2311 EA Leiden, tel. (071) 144341.

The University of Maryland at Soesterberg Air Base, tel. (03463) 58963, offers associate and bachelor degrees in business and computer studies. Also BA in history and psychology through their Open University and weekend seminars.

The British Open University, contact the British Council Information Centre, Amsterdam, (020) 223644 or Dinah Bond, 55 rue Charles Quint, Brussels 1040, Belgium. Has fully accredited courses. Students receive correspondence packages throughout the year, work from set books and BBC TV programs. Credit is earned on the basis of completed written assignments and exams.

Erasmus University in Rotterdam, tel. (010) 408 1111, offers a program leading to a Masters of Business Administration . . . taught in English.

Volks-Universiteit Classes: This is a most unusual university—a folk or people's university—which offers lectures and courses in a wide variety of subjects such as photography, textile weaving, drawing, painting, spinning, etc., but also has an extensive language department. If you or your older children are interested in studying Dutch, there is a special course given regularly.

Amsterdam: Herenmarkt 93, tel. (020) 261626;
The Hague, Haagse Cultureel Trefpunt, Laan van Meerdervoort 16,
tel. (070) 636353; after 12/89, 363 6353.
Rotterdam, Westzeedijk 345, tel. (010) 476 1200.

MUSIC SCHOOLS: There are many Dutch schools of dance, music, art, drama, etc., but generally instruction is in Dutch so of minimal interest. The following music schools are a start in searching out the best possibilities. Registration is in April.

ROTTERDAM:
Stichting Rotterdamse Muziek en Dans School, Haverlandstraat 10-
12, tel. (010) 414 5518.

Rotterdams Conservatorium, Pieter de Hoochweg 122,
tel. (010) 476 7399.

THE HAGUE:
Stedelijke Muziekschool, Prinsengracht 25, tel. (070) 651848,
after 12/89, 365 1848.
Koninklijke Conservatorium, Juliana van Stolberglaan 1, tel. (070)
814251, after 12/89, 381 4251.
Muziekschool Wolthuis, Soestdijksekade 262, tel. (070) 237222, after
12/89, 323 7222.

AMSTERDAM:
Stichting Muziek-Lyceum, Jan Luikenstraat 27, tel. (020) 731470.
Stichting Muziekschool van het Amsterdams Conservatorium,
Bachstraat 5, tel. (020) 768242.
Volksmuziekschool Willem Gehrels, Nieuwekerkstraat 122,
tel. (020) 225082.
Sweelinck Conservatorium, Bachstraat 3, tel. (020) 730303.

DANCE SCHOOLS: From ballet to Scottish dancing! There are extremely helpful organizations to guide the newcomer. Four that have come to our attention are listed below.

Nederlands Instituut van de Dans, Herengracht 174, 1016 BR Amsterdam, tel. (020) 237541, has a list of recommended teachers and schools in all areas of the Netherlands.

They speak English and can also give any information required about dance instruction. All schools take pupils from six years up.

The Royal Academy of Dancing, Tongelresestraat 13, 5611 VJ Eindhoven, tel. (040) 113855 (contact Mrs. Emmy Moers, National Organizer RAD), can recommend studios for study in your area.

The English Dance Studio, Waverstraat 14, 1079 VL Amsterdam, tel. (020) 442431 (Pauline Holden), has been highly recommended.

Scottish Country Dancing is a great exercise and recreational form of complex folk dancing. Contact Pauline Cathcart, tel. (01751) 77816.

SPECIAL CLASSES, LECTURES AND GROUPS: The following list covers activities which are helpful in case of family problems, or for personal enhancement and fun. Some are a bridge to understanding the Netherlands.

ACCESS, tel. (070) 558551, after 12/89, 355 8551, offers educational workshops on cultural adaptation, human development and family life for the English-speaking community. All programs are in English, a minimum of three hours . . . nominal fee.

Alliance Francaise, an organization with activities to promote French culture. There are classes in French and meetings with films as well as regularly scheduled cultural groups from France: Contact, Alliance Francaise, Westersingel 14, Rotterdam, tel. (010) 436 0421; The Hague, tel. (070) 462578, after 12/89, 346 2578; Amsterdam, tel. (020) 261626.

Amateur and Semi-Professional Drama Groups (Little Theater). If you're a frustrated thespian, you might want to investigate the Anglo-American Theatre Group in The Hague, the American Repertory Theatre and the English-Speaking Theatre, both in Amsterdam. They meet regularly to produce English-language plays during the year . . . play readings are also organized.

Cordon Bleu Cooking Classes, at La Cuisine Francaise, Herengracht 314, Amsterdam, tel. (020) 278725, by Pat van der Wall Bake.

The Country We Live In, evening lectures sponsored by the City of The Hague, tel. (070) 636353, after 12/89, 363 6353; very worthwhile.

Drawing and Painting Classes are given weekly to a small international group in the Rotterdam/The Hague area . . . also workshops in France twice a year. Instruction in English; beginners welcome. Call (010) 422 9511 or 422 6399.

Museum Orientation and Educational Programs. Most large museums include an Education Department for the specific purpose of encouraging an appreciation of their collections. Dutch-speaking groups meet on a regular basis from small children to retirees. In addition, the Education Departments are very helpful and desirous of serving the entire community by arranging foreign-language tours and lectures. Three major museums to call are: Amsterdam, the Rijksmuseum, Stadhouderskade 42, tel. (020) 732121; The Hague, Gemeente Museum-Museon, Stadhouderslaan 41, tel. (070) 514181, after 12/89, 351 4181; Rotterdam, Boymans-van Beuningen Museum, Mathenesserlaan 18, tel. (010) 441 9400.

National Societies often have cultural lectures . . . contact your embassy for details.

NIVON (Netherlands Institute for Adult Education and Work Among Nature Lovers). They offer courses, study trips, camps and tourist trips to members. There are 17 "nature-lovers-homes" in Holland, P.C. Hooftstraat 163, 1071 BV Amsterdam, tel. (020) 766889 . . . also open to non-members.

Shopping

When spirits are low, the traditional female answer is to go shopping. Under these circumstances browsing through an open-air market can be as therapeutic as shopping in traditional stores and boutiques . . . and usually less expensive. These markets are indicated in the Provincial chapters under the appropriate towns. . . . they abound in all cities and especially in small towns during the summer months.

But shopping can be fun for all, including children if a quick stop in the toy department can be arranged. The problem arises in a foreign country of making oneself understood. Contrary to general belief, personnel in small shops do not always speak or understand English. In the big cities and in large department stores, there is a better chance you will have no trouble being understood than in small shops, greengrocers, bakeries, etc. The best answer is to take some Dutch language lessons. In department stores, you can usually get help by asking at the Information Booth or the Office.

Late Shopping: Most stores are open from 9am-5:30pm but one evening a week you may shop 'till 9pm. In Rotterdam this is on Friday; in Amsterdam and The Hague it's on Thursday. Major cities have several stores (mainly food and drink) that are open until late at night. Check your "Gouden Gids" (yellow pages of phone dirctory) under "Avondverkoop."

SUPERMARKETS: Albert Heijn, perhaps the best and biggest supermarket chain in the Netherlands has branches all over the country. They carry most things you will need from meats and groceries to household items and wines and liquors. And the beauty is, you can help yourselves without uttering a word to anyone. For the newcomer, the closest supermarket will be your easiest introduction to the types of food available, their names in Dutch, prices, etc.

DEPARTMENT STORES: There are two department store chains in the Netherlands where one can buy everything from a garlic press to a houseful of furniture, including large food departments. They each have large stores in Rotterdam, The Hague and Amsterdam—and one or the other has a branch in many other cities throughout the country as well. For the newcomer, they can facilitate shopping by offering a wide selection of goods under one roof. They also have a Charge Account Service and will exchange or refund merchandise which is not satisfactory if returned within a few days of purchase. Remember to keep your bill ("bon").

De Bijenkorf: Special departments for babies', young children's and teenagers' and adult clothes; toy department well stocked in Christmas season; sports equipment and clothing; books in English, French, German and Dutch; shoes, stockings, undergarments, furniture, drawing materials, photographic supplies; great food department and household articles.

Rotterdam: Coolsingel, tel. (010) 411 7400.
Amsterdam: Damrak 90a, tel. (020) 218080.
The Hague: Wagenstraat 32, tel. (070) 624991,
after 12/89, 362 4991.

Vroom and Dreesman: Special departments for babies', young children's and teenagers' clothes, toy department well stocked all year; foreign-language books; adult clothes and undergarments; sports clothes and equipment; records; photo supplies; baby furniture and supplies; food store; et cetera.

Rotterdam: Hoogstraat 185, tel. (010) 414 8844.
Vlaardingen: Veerplein 134, tel. (010) 434 2966.
Amsterdam: 201 Kalverstraat, tel. (020) 220171; 162
  Rokin, tel. (020) 220171.
The Hague: Spui 3, tel. (070) 924211, after 12/89, 392 4211;
  Leyweg 924, tel. (070) 669790, after 12/89, 366 9790.

SPECIALTY STORES: The following stores are also chains. Some can be found in other big European cities; however, they are more specialized in their merchandise than the department stores mentioned above.

C&A: Especially good for children's clothes from tiny tots to teenagers. You may return or exchange merchandise within a day or two of purchase if not satisfactory. Remember to keep your bill (bon).

Rotterdam: Coolsingel 80, tel. (010) 411 3250.
Amsterdam: Passage 1, tel. (020) 263132.
The Hague: Grote Marktstraat 59, tel. (070) 469410,
  after 12/89, 346 9410.

HEMA: For inexpensive clothing, good ham and cold cuts as well as miscellaneous household articles.

Rotterdam: Beursplein 2, tel. (010) 411 7950;
  Keizerswaard 103, tel. (010) 482 1722.
Amsterdam: Nieuwendijk 174, tel. (020) 247264.
The Hague: Grote Marktstraat, tel. (070) 659844,
  after 12/89, 365 9844.

Peek & Cloppenburg: Clothing primarily.

Rotterdam: Hoogstraat 200, tel. (010) 411 1780.
Amsterdam: Dam 20, tel. (020) 232837.
The Hague: Wagenstraat 16, tel. (070) 651822,
  after 12/89, 365 1822.

Perry Sports: Specializing in sports clothing; skiing supplies in winter, swimming outfits in summer, tennis and riding clothes, etc. Some sports and camping equipment available. For a large selection of boats, see their display center on the Kralingse Plas in Rotterdam.

Rotterdam: Lijnbaan 91, tel. (010) 411 9011.
Amsterdam: Overtoom 2-8, tel. (020) 189111.
The Hague: Spuistraat 20-22, tel. (070) 647840,
  after 12/89, 364 7840.

SHOPPING FOR HOBBIES: Stamp collecting, coin collecting, and crafts are only three of the many possible hobbies people enjoy. Where to obtain supplies for other hobbies can be located by asking at the department stores or from members of your social club who might have similar interests.

Stamp Collecting can take place in established stores but also at the open-air (covered) stamp exchanges which occur on regular days during the week.

> *Amsterdam trading takes place on the Nieuwezijds Voorburgwal opposite No. 280, Wed. and Sat., 1-4pm. Trams 1, 2 and 5.*
>
> *The Hague, a stamp market is held "Onder de Oranjeboom," corner Noordeinde-Paleisstraat, Wed. and Sat. mornings; at Amicitia, Westeinde 15, Sat. afternoon.*
>
> *Rotterdam, stamps are exchanged and/or sold every Sat. and Wed., 10am-5pm on the Schouwburgplein (opposite the Schouwburg Theater). Big dealers are present but so are the little men bringing their albums in shopping bags. Stamps can be purchased for 25 cents up!*

Coin Collecting: As a friend put it, "How Can You Afford It These Days?" Check with the VVV for their recommendations about reliable dealers.

Craft Shops and Painting Supplies: Try the larger department stores ... in particular Vroom and Dreesman and the Bijenkorf. You can also ask at the VVV or check the yellow pages of the telephone directory under "Schildersbenodigheden." There are many art supply shops these days.

SHOPPING FOR PARTIES! PARTIES!: Nothing can be more fun than putting together an unusual and imaginative party, whether it's for an adult dinner party or a special birthday celebration. The following addresses might be a help in getting you started.

Party Objects (Costumes, Hats, Garlands):

> *Amsterdam: Cladder, Utrechtsestraat 47, tel. (020) 237949; Serne & Son, Groeneburgwal 56, tel. (020) 245954.*

The Hague: Amusa, Passage 22, tel. (070) 460489, after 12/89, 346 0489. Het Masker, Vaillantlaan 129, tel. (070) 880498, after 12/ 89, 388 0498.
Rotterdam: Frans Moret, Vierambachtstraat 106, tel. (010) 477 2675.

Caterers (and where to rent party supplies):
Rotterdam: Kees-Jan van Dijk, J. Catsstraat 97a, tel. (010) 466 0779. Bobo Verhuur (Rentals), Pr. Hendrikstraat 33, tel. 422 2913.
The Hague: (After 12/89, add 3 prefix to local numbers following (070).) Taat en de Regt, van Gijnstraat 25, 2288 GB Rijswijk, tel. (070) 901011. De Haagse Traiteur, Spekstraat 10, tel. 647794. A.V.B. (Rentals), 35 Scheepmakerstraat, tel. 830236.
Amsterdam: La Cuisine Francaise, Herengracht 314, tel. (020) 278725. Special (Indonesian), N. Leliestraat 142, tel. 249707. Amsterdamse Verhuurinrichting (Rentals), Gerard Douwplein 21, tel. 799557. Butter Verhuurbedrijf, Ruysdaelkade 75, tel. 791196.
Veghel (North Brabant): Maison van den Boer, Marshallweg 4, tel. (04130) 62944. Among the best caterers in Holland, they deliver all over the country. Also have a beautiful party center in the Hulstkamp Gebouw in Rotterdam, tel. (010) 411 3100.

Pets

If you don't already have a pet, you might consider buying one after you are a bit settled. Once you add the new member to the family, you will want to know about Vets, pet grooming, and where to leave your pet when you go on holiday. And should they get lost or run away, you will need to contact Amivedi. But first, what's the best way to obtain a pet?

It is not recommended you buy large pets from a commercial shop; however, there are many listed in the yellow pages under "Dierenhandel." Be sure and ask for the animal's papers as protection and to know what sort of pet you are getting. Dogs sold by commercial shops are not controlled by the Kennel Club and there has been endless misery when animals are found to be in poor health. Unfortunately, this usually comes to light too late. If you are not looking for a pedigreed animal, you should consider making a visit to the local "pound," in Dutch it is called "Nederlandse Vereniging tot Bescherming van Dieren," where a variety of animals are just crying out for adoption.

Dutch Kennel Club: If you are interested in a pedigreed dog, contact the official Dutch Kennel Club, Raad van Beheer op Kynologisch Gebied van Nederland, Emmalaan 16, Amsterdam, tel. (020) 664 4471. This club will answer questions and give names and addresses of the various breed clubs who know which breeders may have puppies or adult dogs for sale. When contacting a breeder, it is advisable to mention whether you want a pet dog or a show specimen. Prices may vary and you will pay a lower price for an animal having a fault disqualifying it from being a show dog. Ask the secretary of the breed club for an indication of the average prices asked for your favorite breed.

Animal Rescue Organization, "de Dierenbescherming": This is a very reliable private organization that takes care of stray or unwanted and sick animals, commonly known as "de Dierenbescherming" and so listed in the telephone directory. Three "Dierenasiel" (pounds) are:

Amsterdam: Ookmeerweg 270, Osdorp, tel. (020) 106949.
The Hague: Schenkkade 1, tel. (070) 476018, after 12/89, 347 6018.
Rotterdam: R. Lankerakweg 22, tel. (010) 437 4211.

Here you can pick out a wonderful, healthy pet and only pay a small amount as long as you promise to give the animal a good home. For instance, you can get a nice cat for approximately Fl. 50 (it will have been spayed and have had its shots), or a dog from Fl. 125, depending on its size. The dogs have received their shots prior to being adopted—you will receive a certificate to this effect. In the case of a cat it is sometimes necessary to return in two to seven weeks (depending on the age of the animal) for it to receive its final shots. Animals are thoroughly examined by the vet before they are allowed to be taken away and if you have any questions, they will give you whatever information they have available. They usually can tell you if the cat is a house cat or if it is used to being out of doors part of the time; if the dog is used to children, etc.

If you leave the country and cannot take your pet, you may take it to the Asiel for readoption or to be put to sleep if no home can be found for it. If you find a stray animal, you may call them and they will take care of it. If your pet is lost, it may have been taken there. There are free clinics for those who cannot afford a doctor for their pet—however, you must pay for medicines.

Veterinarians (Dierenartsen): There are many excellent vets in all major cities and we would suggest you find the most conveniently situated one in your telephone book under "Dierenarts." Perhaps one or another of the official animal organizations listed above could also advise you.

PET EMERGENCIES:

The Police:
Amsterdam: (020) 222222.
The Hague: (070) 222222, after 12/89, 322 2222.
Rotterdam: (010) 41 41414.

Dierenasiel (Animal Pound):
Amsterdam: (020) 106869, 665 1888, and 936494.
The Hague: (070) 476018, after 12/89, 347 6018.
Rotterdam: (010) 437 4211.

Amivedi:
Amsterdam: (020) 185278.
The Hague: (Head Office), (070) 930212 before 6pm,
*   after 12/89, 393 0212.*
Rotterdam: (010) 483 5012 after 7pm (for dogs),
*   or 434 7352 (for cats and birds).*

Animal Ambulances:
Amsterdam: (020) 262121 and 261058, between 9am-3pm.
The Hague: (070) 674279 or 521238,
*   after 12/89, 367 4279 or 352 1238.*
Rotterdam: (010) 415 5666.

Amivedi is a special organization for the location of missing animals. It is a non-commercial enterprise of animal lovers whose aim is to bring owners and lost pets together. All stray animals reported to them are registered. Amivedi may also be called in cases of emergency where a pet urgently needs an ambulance to be taken to the nearest veterinarian, after a street accident for instance.

Grooming of Dogs: To have your dog properly groomed, stripped or clipped according to breed requirements, a number of grooming shops will be found in the yellow pages under "Hondenkapper," "Honden Kapsalon," "Hondentrim-salon," etc. The quality of the service may vary considerably. You should consult an authority such as the Raad van Beheer, tel. (020) 664 4471, who will give you the address of either the Kennel club closest to you, or the club of your breed of dog. They should be able to indicate a reliable professional.

Holiday Kennels: Leaving your pet behind when going on trips can be a painful experience; therefore, be sure that you are leaving it in expert hands. We strongly recommend you consult your local kennel club or veterinarian for reliable addresses. Be sure to book well in advance for such boarding kennels, particularly in the holiday season and around Christmas.

CHAPTER 17

THE GOOD LIFE: Out and About

Entertainment in the Netherlands is limited only by your interests and imagination. The choices can start with a simple movie date or staying home to watch TV; enjoying the cultural offerings such as the theater, symphony, ballet, opera or attending lectures; to dining out in high style and taking a fling at one of the casinos. Nightclubs aren't prevalent in the small towns but you have a wide choice in Amsterdam, The Hague, Rotterdam, Maastricht (just to name a few). Typical local pubs (Bruin cafés) and "Bodegas," cafés and terrace restaurants abound and are colorful places to relax and do some "people watching." Jazz clubs and theater cafés can also be found in the big cities. Get a list from the VVV.

The most frequent "entertainment" is eating out. This can range from a quick bite suitable for a family outing to the most expensive restaurant with a one-to-two star Michelin rating . . . for a special anniversary.

The following information hopefully will give you an idea about enjoying the "Good Life" . . .

WHAT'S GOING ON?: A non-Dutch reader need no longer have difficulty finding out what's going on. The newspapers list movies once a week. After a little practice, one will be surprised to find out how much one can actually understand even when you don't read Dutch. There is no Sunday edition, so both Saturday and Sunday TV programs are given in the Saturday paper. Movies are not listed in the daily papers as they are in the U.S. and other countries, but are listed in toto in the Thursday edition. So, if you're a movie-buff family, better save your Thursday movie section for use on the weekend.

In addition to the daily papers, there are other publications with updated information about what's going on:

"Roundabout." This monthly calendar in English of current entertainment (theater, review, sports events, etc.) fulfills a longstanding need for the foreign community. Previews of coming attractions come under the "Early Bird" section; "Dutch Treat" lists unique offerings as does "Kidstuff." Subscriptions, Fl. 25 for six months, write Roundabout, Prinsevinkenpark 31, 2585 HM The Hague.

In Amsterdam: A weekly publication "This Week" (Deze Week) lists movies, plays, concerts, cultural activities at museums, cabarets, special exhibits, etc. Available through the VVV and the Cultural Information Service (AUB).

In The Hague: The "Monthly Agenda" (only in Dutch) lists the activities and entertainment for the month . . . available at the VVV for Fl. 2.50. Also, "Info" which comes out every two weeks lists activities in English; free at the VVV.

In Rotterdam: Two monthly magazines, "Rotterdam This Month" (Deze Maand) and "Magazijn" (Fl. 2.50), are available through the VVV. They list theater offerings, musical and cabaret events, museum happenings and special events.

Most towns of any size will have their own version of the above.

MOVIES AND TV: Because Holland is a small country and it isn't worth the expense to dub movies and TV shows in Dutch, foreigners get a break in being able to see movies in the original language. English-speakers are especially fortunate since most of the programs are of English or American origin. Movies are generally not continuous and tickets for specific seats must be purchased. In the case of a very popular movie, it is wise to get seats ahead of time. This can be done in person a few hours before the performance, or by telephone. If you phone in a reservation, there will be a small charge (approximately Fl. .50 per ticket). The tickets will be held until a half hour before the show starts. Don't hesitate to call by phone to make inquiry as most of the movie personnel speak and understand English and will try to be helpful.

As indicated above, the newspapers list movie and television programs—once a week for movies but daily for TV.

Parents should know that in the Netherlands there is strict adherence regarding what movies children are allowed to see. Unlike in the U.S. where a parent can assume responsibility by accompanying his child, in Holland if the age limit for the movie is 16 years and your child is younger, he will not be allowed entry even if you are with him. For details, see "The Younger Set," Chapter 19.

CASINOS: French and American Roulette, Blackjack, One-Armed Bandits, Baccarat, can all be found at the casinos in Amsterdam, Groningen, Zandvoort, Valkenburg, Scheveningen and Rotterdam. Their locations and addresses are given in the Province chapter under the appropriate town. They are open from 2pm-2am daily . . . except Amsterdam which closes at 3am, is closed all day

May 4, and closes at 6pm on December 31. You can purchase entry tickets for a day, a month or a year . . . 1989 prices, Fl. 7.50, Fl. 20 and Fl. 125, respectively. Minimum age for entry is 18 years. A dress code is required. Minimum stakes for roulette vary with the table: Fl. 5, 10 and 20; for Blackjack, Fl. 5 and 10.

All casinos are air-conditioned, with a bar and restaurant.

AMATEUR THEATER: There are a number of "Little Theater" groups in the Randstad area which provide great satisfaction to the players and entertainment to the foreign resident who may be hungry for theater productions he can understand. Most Dutch plays are produced in Dutch, quite naturally. The amateur theater groups that have come to our attention are:

American Repertory Theater (ART), Kerkstraat 4, Amsterdam, tel. (020) 259495.

Anglo-American Theater Group (AATG), POB 85894, 2508 CN The Hague, tel. (070) 525029, after 12/89, 352 5029.

English-speaking Theater Amsterdam (ESTA), Leidsestraat 106, 1017 PG Amsterdam, tel. (020) 229742.

Leiden English-speaking Theater (LEST), Breestraat 165, 2311 CP Leiden.

ESTEC (International Theater), Keplerlaan 1, Noordwijk, has an English Theater Group (EIT), tel. (01719) 83400, Mrs. O. Melita, and a French Group (GEST), tel. (01719) 86555, Mr. Dauphin.

The Stadhouderij Theater Co., le Bloemdwarsstraat 4, Amsterdam, tel. (020) 262282.

THE PERFORMING ARTS

The whole range of performing arts is available in the Netherlands . . . the symphony, dance, opera, stage productions, circuses, ice-skating reviews, and more. We will deal with the more serious of these starting with how to get tickets.

BUYING SEASON TICKETS: Regular season tickets may be purchased through the box offices of the theaters where the performances are usually given and through the VVV reservations centers.

In Amsterdam, get in touch with the Amsterdams Uit Buro (AUB), Leidseplein, Mon.-Sat., 10am-6pm, or at the VVV Theater Bespreekbureau, Stationsplein, Mon.-Sat., 10am-4pm, tel. (020) 266444, or directly with the theater.

In the Hague, you can obtain tickets from the Bespreekbureau of the VVV, from the theater, or from Nederlands Theaterbureau, Zeekant 102, tel. (070) 543411, after 12/89, 354 3411.

In Rotterdam, a booklet entitled "Theater Seizoen" comes out in April or May giving details of the coming events and season series available. You must reserve before August 31, but for the best places you should reserve even earlier. If you elect to purchase a series with this group, you will have your reserved seats mailed to you in advance of box-office sales and you receive about a 10% reduction in price. The booklet is free and can be picked up at the ticket offices of the theaters and De Doelen. It can also be sent to you . . . call (010) 414 2911.

THE SYMPHONY IN THE NETHERLANDS: The Royal Concertgebouw Orchestra and the Netherlands Philharmonic of Amsterdam need no introduction. Their recordings are purchased worldwide and are known for their fine quality. Both orchestras have heavy schedules during the year including many tours abroad. The Royal Concertgebouw Orchestra's home is at the Royal Concert Hall where the first concert was held in 1888. The Netherlands Philharmonic performs at the Beurs van Berlage, Damrak 62a, formerly the Stock Exchange Building.

The Rotterdam Philharmonic Orchestra also makes many tours abroad and has carved out a fine reputation. It gives a series of concerts throughout the year at De Doelen, Rotterdam's Concert, Music and Conference Center with outstanding acoustics in the concert hall.

The Hague's "Residentie-Orkest" performs in the new Anton Philipszaal, home also of the Nederlands Dans Theater. From time to time, certain composers will be featured with a series of concerts dedicated to their works. For more information, contact the Anton Philipszaal or the VVV.

The Netherlands Chamber Music Orchestra (Nederlands Kamerorkest) performs at the Koninklijk Concertgebouw (Royal Concert Hall) in Amsterdam, the Anton Philipszaal in The Hague, and in De Doelen in Rotterdam.

THE DANCE IN THE NETHERLANDS: There are three major ballet companies in the Netherlands: Het Nationale Ballet (headquartered in the Muziek Theater in Amsterdam), the National Dance Theater in The Hague with its own hall in the Anton Philipszaal, and the Scapino Ballet in Amsterdam, the latter specializing in ballets appealing to children. Their repertoire consists mainly of narrative ballets, but also gradually leads to an understanding of the various forms of classical, modern and ethnic ballet. There are many smaller modern ballet groups.

These companies have a fine reputation and tour extensively throughout the Netherlands, Europe and the United States.

OPERA IN THE NETHERLANDS: The Netherlands Opera Foundation numbers about 100 voices and tries to use as many first-class Dutch artists as possible. They often have excellent visiting performers, directors and conductors—many from the United States. They perform in the Muziektheater in Amsterdam. For information, contact the Netherlands Opera Foundation, Waterlooplein 22, tel. (020) 551 8922.

Theaters and Auditoriums

In a country such as Holland with a long history of appreciation for the performing arts, some of the theater buildings are of some significance in their own right. And when the old buildings were no longer able to serve the theatergoing public's needs, innovative new—often avant-garde—architecture has resulted. The listing which follows gives the practical facts about the hall itself, a note about its history or unique features, and the type of performances usually given.

AMSTERDAM:

The Royal Concert Hall (Koninklijke Concertgebouw), Van Baerlestraat 98, tel. (020) 718345 . . . Trams 2, 5 and 16. The Royal Concert Hall has been recently modernized. In addition to 2,200 seats in the Main Hall and 492 seats in the Recital Hall, it boasts a most elegant foyer and a newly excavated basement where the Coral Room and the Artists' Foyer are located. Built in 1888, the Royal Concert Hall is known for its fine architecture and world-famous acoustics. Guided tours of the renovated Concertgebouw will be held daily from noon on, small admission. Box office is open Mon.-Sun., 9:30am-8:15pm; telephone reservations from 10am-3pm. Reservations can be made a month ahead; tickets available from the theater, the AUB Ticketshop and VVV, tel. 266444.

Muziektheater, Amstel 3, tel. (020) 255455 . . . Trams 4, 9, 14, 16, 24, 25, Buses 31, 56, and Metro Waterlooplein. The Muziektheater, part of the controversial Stopera building incorporating the new City Hall and overlooking the Amstel River, was opened officially in 1986. It houses the Dutch National Ballet, the Netherlands Opera and the Foundation "Het Muziek-theater." The latter group presents national and international visiting companies and will stage its own future productions as well. The box office is open Mon.-Sat., 10am-8:15pm, Sun., noon-8:15pm (non-performance days, open 'til 6pm). Reservations can be had one month in advance.

Theater Carré, Amstel 115-125 (east side of the Amstel River between the Nieuwe Prinsengracht and the Nieuwe Achtergracht), tel. (020) 225225 . . . Trams 4, 6, 7, 10 and Metro. There is a parking garage across from the Magere Brug (bridge). This famous theater was built in 1887 to stage circuses. Many diversified presentations are given such as operettas, variety groups, ballets,

369

theater-in-the-round, and musical comedies. Reservations can be made one month in advance at the VVV booking office in Amsterdam or at the theater box office from 10am-7pm; Sun., 1-7pm. For performances in progress, from 10am-5pm. Reservations can also be made by letter. Reservations by phone can be made seven days in advance through the VVV.

Stadschouwburg, Leidseplein 26 between Korte Leidsewarsstraat and Marnixstraat, tel. (020) 242311 . . . Trams 1, 2, 5, 6, 7, 10, or Buses 26, 65, 66 and 67. Built in 1894 in neoclassic style, this building was ultramodern and luxurious. The stage and the auditorium were equipped with electric light and central heating. The enormous chandeliers and decorative paintings on the ceiling came from Belgium. Ticket office operates Mon.-Sat., 10am-beginning of performance; Sun., only 1½ hours before a performance. Reservations by phone, 11am-6pm. Booking from one month in advance.

Nieuwe de la Mar Theater, Marnixstraat 404, tel. (020) 233462 . . . Trams 1, 2, 5, 6, 7, 10, Buses 26, 65, 66, 67. The theater has a rich tradition of cabaret which has given it an international reputation. Great cabaret artists and leading actors of the Netherlands perform here. After the performances, relax and enjoy the pleasant foyer of the theater. The box office is open Mon.-Sun., 11am-5pm; to reserve by phone, call between noon and 5pm; night box office, 6pm-8:15pm. Tickets may be obtained one week in advance . . . also through the AUB Ticketshop and the VVV.

Cannon Tuschinski Movie Theater, Reguliersbreestraat 26-28, tel. (020) 231510 (for tour reservations), offers regular guided tours to see this outstanding example of Art Deco, including influences from Jugendstijl and the Amsterdam School. The decorations include expressionist paintings, exotic woods, colored marble, Persian carpets, chandeliers and sculpture. Built on 1,200 ramming piles, its unique balance construction has no need for pillars allowing the moviegoer a clear view of the screen. The Wurlitzer Pipe Organ was brought from North Tonawanda in the U.S. to accompany silent movies . . . it is used for concerts as well. Movies are shown regularly. Guided tours are given Mon., Tues. and Wed. at 10:30am (approximately 75 minutes). Organ concerts are held during July and Aug., Sat., 11am.

Sonesta Koepelzaal, of the Sonesta Hotel, entry Kattengat 1 (nearby the Central Station), tel. (020) 212223 for reservations. This "theater" is famous for its coffee-concerts (offered with a brunch, etc.), and also for its Jazzclub and a variety of other performances given throughout the year. Sundays the doors open at 10:30am and theatergoers are treated to a free cup of coffee.

Beurs van Berlage, Damrak 62a, tel. (020) 271161, offers concerts in this skillfully converted Stock Exchange building. The Netherlands Philharmonic Symphony Orchestra performs here, amongst others.

English Church, Begijnhof 48, tel. (020) 249665 . . . concerts.

Diridas Poppentheater, Hobbemakade 68, tel. (020) 721588, Tram 16.

Kindertheater Circus Elleboog, Passeerdersgracht 32, tel. 269370, Tram 17.

Shaffy Theater, Keizersgracht 324, tel. (020) 231311, Trams 1, 2, 5, 13, 17.

The Vondel Park Open-Air Theater offers musical and theatrical performances during July and August, with specific days for theater, music, dance and mime, as well as special shows for children. Every Wednesday, there are mid-day classical lunch concerts as well as children's theater at 3pm. Thursday evenings there is folk music or jazz and Fridays, traditional theater, music or mime. Saturdays and Sundays offer pop concerts and experimental theater. All performances are free of charge. Check with Amsterdam VVV.

THE HAGUE AND SCHEVENINGEN:

After December 1989, add a 3 prefix to local numbers following (070) code. The magazine, "Info" lists all cultural events in The Hague . . . put out by the VVV every two weeks.

Nederlands Congresgebouw, Churchillplein 10, tel. (070) 548000 or 512851. This recently renovated congress center was built primarily to host international as well as local conferences. Activities such as political meetings, religious gatherings, automobile (and other commercial) shows, dance evenings, handicraft and antique fairs are held here as well as concerts, operettas, plays, and the North Sea Jazz Festival. The Tower Bar soars 200 feet above the center giving a bird's eye view over The Hague and Scheveningen. The underground garage has room for over 600 cars.

Dr. Anton Philipszaal, Houtmarkt 17, tel. (070) 609810, was inaugurated in 1988. Its modern architecture provides airy, elegant space, with independent "homes" for the Residentie Orkest and the Nederlands Dans Theater. Each has a performance hall, lounges for the public and space for study halls, dressing rooms, and such like for the performers. The building adjoins a modern hotel and an elegant Japanese restaurant for pre- or post-theater dining.

Koninklijke Schouwburg, Korte Voorhout 3, tel. (070) 469450, 11am-4pm . . . Trams 7, 8 or 9, or Buses 4, 18 and 22. The ticket office is open 9am-3pm. This theater first opened its doors to the public in 1804. The variety of its productions includes plays, concerts, cabarets, puppet shows, and specialty acts from Holland and abroad.

Diligentia Theater, Lange Voorhout 5, tel. (070) 464308 . . . Buses 4, 5 and 22, Trams 7, 8 and 9. The box office is open from 10am-1pm (closed Mon.). Many cabaretiers appear here but there are also concerts, plays and other programs which might appeal to non-Dutch-speaking audiences. Coffee and lunch concerts are held during the year.

Circus Theater, Gevers Deynootplein (near the Kurhaus in Scheveningen), tel. (070) 558800 between 11am and 4pm. Originally the location of a real circus, this building was converted some years ago into a theater-conference hall.

PUPPET THEATERS: Two puppet theaters of special interest are listed below. For a comprehensive list of puppet theaters, see Chapter 19.

Poppentheater Guido Van Deth and the Puppetry Museum, Nassau Dillenburgstraat 8, tel. (070) 280208, after 12/89, 328 0208, Bus 18. Museum open Sun. only from noon to 2pm. Conducted tours possible upon request. This theater seating 70 persons offers puppet shows for children on Sat. and Sun. at 2:30pm and adult shows on Fri. evenings, from October to March.

In 1971, the Puppetry Museum was officially recognized by the Ministry of Cultural Affairs, Recreation and Social Welfare. It is interesting to know that puppetry as a form of drama has existed for 5,000 years but that puppet shows for children only date from about 100 years. The museum has over 1,000 puppets and 500 prints in addition to a large library. There are many colorful and interesting puppets from France, Sicily, India, Germany, Java and Holland.

Poppentheater Frank Kooman, Frankenstraat 66, tel. (070) 559305, after 12/89, 355 9305, Trams 10, 11 and Buses 4, 65 and 89. Also check with the VVV for information.

Mr. Kooman is a happy man who needs no hobbies—his work is his full-time pleasure. A lucky man—but lucky, too, for young and old audiences who come to see one of his 300 performances per year. In one month, he may give 44 performances to a total of 10,000 children. Mr. Kooman makes his own puppets, writes the plays, composes the music and is all the voices of his characters. He stages adult plays as well as entertainment for children, and tries to learn about some of the audience members to surprise them with personal references. Adult plays are usually two hours; performances for children, one hour.

ROTTERDAM:

De Doelen (Music and Congress Center), Schouwburgplein 50, tel. (010) 413 2490; box office, weekdays, 11am-4pm, Sun., noon-4pm, evening of performances, from 7pm. Tickets may be purchased two weeks in advance. De Doelen is a modern concert center and the home of the Rotterdam Philharmonic Orchestra. Because of the theater's fine acoustics, many international artists come here for the pleasure of performing in this hall. Free lunchtime concerts are given in the main entry hall every Wednesday.

The Schouwburg Theater, Schouwburgplein 25, tel. (010) 411 8110, reopened in 1988, has been reconstructed in a controversial starkly modern fashion. Call for details on programs and ticket sales.

De Lantaren Theater, Gouvernestraat 133, tel. (010) 436 4998, is located in a rather rowdy area. Primarily of interest for the children's puppet theater on Sunday afternoons at 2:30pm.

Luxor Theater, Kruiskade 10, tel. (010) 413 8326, is right in the center of town. Many international artists perform in this theater which is also the main locale for the annual "Film International" festival.

Theater Zuidplein (South Rotterdam), Zuidplein 60-64, tel. (010) 481 5844 . . . metro stop "Zuidplein." The ticket office is open daily, 10am-4pm; sales for evening performances begin at 7pm. American and English companies often perform in this theater in plays, reviews, opera, operetta, variety shows, musicals, and concerts. Theater workshops are also offered.

Ahoy's Sport Complex (South Rotterdam), Zuiderparkweg 20-30, tel. (010) 410 4204, or 481 2144 (ticket office). This complex has a total of 130,000 square feet of space to host exhibitions of all kinds. Such international events as 6-day bike races, world tennis championships, ice hockey playoffs, and pop concerts take place here as well as circus performances, ice reviews and international dance groups. Special shows are booked for holiday periods such as "Holiday on Ice" and the "Christmas Circus."

DINING OUT

Chapter 1 describes some restaurant chains popular in the Netherlands and explains about Tourist Menu Restaurants. For the booklet which lists the latter throughout the country, contact the VVV, the NBT offices abroad, or write, "Tourist Menu," c/o Nederlands Bureau Voor Toerisme, Antwoordnummer 10140, 2260 WB Leidschendam, Holland . . . there's a small charge.

The VVV in all cities and most towns have a fulsome list of recommended restaurants which often give ethnic type, price, address, telephone number and how to get there. This listing is a good place to start giving you a chance to decide what suits your mood for the evening.

Reasonably priced meals can be had at "Eet Cafés" (some are listed in each of our major Randstad cities), at railway station and department store restaurants, at pancake restaurants, and at the well-known quick-food stops like McDonald's; many are mentioned throughout the book.

Eating out with children is a special experience . . . restaurants and foods they particularly like are discussed below as well as the best (and most expensive) places to dine out on special occasions.

In the provincial chapters (Section I), recommended restaurants are listed under "EATING OUT" followed by recommended places to stay overnight, if applicable. Hotels are not given for the Randstad area as these lists are easily available from the VVV, travel agents, and word-of-mouth. The list of "tried and true" restaurants in Amsterdam, The Hague and Rotterdam is too long to include in the provincial text so they will appear at the end of this chapter.

INDONESIAN RESTAURANTS: These are thicker than flies on honey in every town in the Netherlands. Due to the many years the Dutch were settled in Indonesia, this cuisine is almost a national dish in Holland. As it is not so familiar to newcomers as other international foods, a few words of description seem appropriate. Most Indonesian restaurants also serve Chinese cooking but if you're a purist, you may want to locate a restaurant which specializes in either one or the other.

The "rijstaffel" is the Indonesian specialty and consists of many small dishes such as chicken fixed in various ways, sateh (meat or chicken cooked over charcoal and served on a stick covered with a peanut sauce), rice, a soup-like sauce, vegetables prepared in different ways, and so on. It all goes in one dish to make a lovely mess but primarily to blend the flavors; there are sauces on the side for those who like their food especially hot.

These restaurants usually offer a choice of Two-Person Menu; Three-Person

Menu . . . Six-Person Menu, either emphasizing Indonesian or Chinese dishes and sometimes a combination of both. They are a good buy offering you a lot for your money. Chinese food is easier for children to like if they are not used to spicy foods and with a little bit of trial and error, you will find out which special dishes your children prefer. If you have a favorite Chinese dish and it is not listed, most waiters can speak a bit of English—or else they will find someone who can—and are most willing to be helpful. Don't forget—these restaurants always have a children's menu.

DUTCH TASTE TREATS: What are they? Portable "patat" (french fries) stands and the "Automatiek" dot the landscape in town as well as on the road in summertime. Students gravitate to these "eateries" for a quick snack any time of the day or night. Many of these Dutch specialties appeal to oldsters as well . . . try them to find your own favorites.

Patats—probably the most universally eaten food in the Netherlands . . . Known in the United States as "french-fried potatoes" and in England as "chips" and in France as "pommes frites." You must say if you want them with or without mayonnaise: "met" is "with" and "zonder" is "without." Dutch patats are in a class of their own and probably superior to any other variety.

Kroketten—(kroket in the singular)—known as rissoles in England and not known in this form in the U.S. Similar to timbales or croquettes, but with much less meat. Whatever there is, is in such small pieces that it is difficult to know whether it is there or not; children love these things.

Bitterballen—the same as kroketten but in small round balls. When offered as cocktail food, often served with mustard.

Frikandel—made of pure ground meat (usually beef and pork mixed) and shaped like a frankfurter or hot dog.

Worst—some are long; some are short; most are thin but some are fat. They can be the kind of sausage you will find in your green pea soup or the kind kids order from the patat stand— and there are lots of other kinds in between. We are interested here in the ones sold at the patat stand which are similar to the hot dog although the taste is different from its American cousin.

Hamburger—also different in flavor from the type Americans and Britons are used to due to the addition of some pork meat and seasonings, including nutmeg. McDonald's and Burger King come the closest to producing an American-style hamburger.

Gehakt Bal—a huge meatball which is made of ground meat (usually half beef and half pork), seasoned with nutmeg, salt and pepper, dipped in egg and bread crumbs and deep fried.

Slaatjes—potato salad, mixed salad or green salad.

Nasi Bal—this is an Indonesian food made of rice mixed with hot spices and meat, formed into a ball and fried in butter. These are too spicy for most children.

Bami Hapje—ditto above, but noodles are used in place of the rice.

Loempia—another Indonesian specialty which looks like a large bumpy pale yellow envelope filled with a mixture of meat, bean sprouts, vegetables and hot spices. The dough is a bit similar to the traditional Chinese spring roll covering,

374

although not so flaky. A meal in itself—plenty nutritious but it is sometimes quite spicy.

Oliebollen—like donuts, without the hole, these are traditional fare on New Year's Eve, eaten around midnight, and during winter markets and fairs.

Sandwiches and Saucijzebroodje: Many department store restaurants offer a wide variety of broodjes (sandwiches). In addition to the more traditional ham, cheese and salami fillings, you can get shrimp, smoked eel and herring as well! Saucijzebroodje is a flaky "puff" pastry with meat filling and is served warm or cold. They can often be found near one of the department store entrances. Small ones can be purchased from a bakery and reheated at home for a cocktail party.

Herring Stands: You may go in for this in a big way right from the start— OR, you wouldn't consider trying it for all the tea in China. Still, it is typically Dutch and should be tried at least once. To be properly traditional, the herring (raw fish) should be eaten whole (minus the head); you hold it by the tail, get under it and start eating at the headless end. They can be dipped in raw onion or eaten plain. The piece of tail left in your hand may be discarded! Try it and you'll become a fan . . . so they say.

Herring stands often include a choice of herring chopped in pieces on bread or toast; and shrimp sandwiches or smoked eel sandwiches for those not sold on herring. These may be had with or without mayonnaise and are very good. Incidentally, all herring stands also sell the most marvelous huge crispy pickles which can be enjoyed with or without herring.

The herrings are at their very best and most expensive (of course) from June (when the first "green" herrings are landed), to September. The Queen is presented with the first herring of the season, after which they are available to all comers.

Poffertjes: The Dutch love things in miniature and I wonder if poffertjes aren't an extension of that interest—they are the small version of the oversized pancake . . . almost anyway. Actually, they are made a bit differently. A batter is made up and put into a special griddle pan which has these little half-dollar (U.S.)-sized holes and it is cooked on top of the stove. As they brown, they are sort of tossed over for the other side to get done. You can have them absolutely dripping in butter and powdered sugar—the usual way—or, among other variations, as rum poffertjes which are especially nice for the adult palate. You cannot get poffertjes at just any restaurant; however, most tourist centers have a poffertjes stand or restaurant. Check with the local VVV.

Pannekoeken: These are a take-off on the French crêpes and not like the traditional American pancake at all. The difference is weight and size. Dutch pannekoeken are something like 14 inches across and are served on special plates to accommodate them. You can order them with a variety of toppings— apples, bacon, ham, stroop (a dark-colored syrup similar in taste to simple sugar syrup), and so forth. A list of well-established pancake restaurants is given below.

Some traditional Dutch dishes you can order out or try at home are:

Uitsmijter: The Dutch version of ham and eggs served on bread; a good luncheon choice.

Erwten soup: Old-fashioned split pea soup "à la Hollandaise" with pieces of fat bacon . . . a typical winter dish and a meal in itself.

Capucijners: Another winter dish, beans (similar to chick peas) cooked with onions, bacon and potatoes.

Blote Billetjes in het groene gras: A real mouthful meaning "naked bottoms in the green grass" . . . a combination of beans served with smoked sausages.

COOKIES AND CANDIES: Dutch cookies are terrific. It would seem every town in every province has its own special recipe for delicious eating. Even if we knew them all, we couldn't list them all.

Kruidkoek (pain d'epices, anise-flavored cakes and cookies) is a specialty of Friesland but this can be purchased throughout the land.

Suikerbrood, also from Friesland, a wonderful sugar cake, eaten at breakfast or whenever.

Blauwvingers come from Zwolle. These cookies with nuts are shaped in the form of ladyfingers.

Arnhemse meisjes can be had in Arnhem: literal translation,"Arnhem girls."

Sprits come from Utrecht . . . a small butter cookie.

Stroopwafels are a specialty of Gouda. Unusual cookies made in a waffle-patterned mold filled with a syrup similar to the syrup which is served with pancakes—a light sugar syrup.

Vlaaien are from Limburg and the south . . . these open-faced tarts are usually filled with seasonal fruits—apricot and cherry are favorites.

Korstjes come from the Eindhoven area . . . another version of the anise-flavored cookie only very hard.

Speculaas. Wherever they originated, they are available all over the Netherlands and come in small crunchy varieties as well as the 4- or 5-foot-tall cookies made in the form of Saint Nicholas during the holiday season . . . a lovely rich spicy flavor and delicious. The big ones keep for weeks.

Hopjes, Dropjes and Zuurtjes: There are special stores that sell ONLY hard candies which come in all shapes, colors and flavors. The most famous are perhaps the Haagse hopjes made by Raademakers in The Hague . . . nice coffee-flavored hard candies. Dropjes come in varying shades of black from light grey to pitch black and are based on licorice flavoring. Zuurtjes are the rest of the hard candies and come in all colors of the rainbow, including stripes, and in all flavors—the fruit-flavored ones are especially popular, called fruit (Dutch pronunciation please—"frowt") zuurtjes.

Muisjes and Hagelslag: Muisjes are anise flavored and Hagelslag is a chocolate-flavored grain-like topping. These soon become favorites with foreign children who quickly imitate their Dutch counterparts in sprinkling them on bread, in yogurt, etc. When a new baby is born, it is customary to offer visitors pink (for a girl) or blue (for a boy) muisjes on a rusk.

EATING OUT WITH CHILDREN: Do children have food favorites? Anyone who has a child knows perfectly well the answer is "yes." In some cases, it starts right from the cradle—more lovely Gerber's baby food has been spit out in all directions when the little charmer decides he/she will have none of it! Mum soon gets the message that it's easier to give baby what he likes as long as he gets his vitamins. So, when eating out with children why not make it a pleasant event for everyone and choose a place where they will get something they particularly like.

Holland is one of the most densely populated countries in the world—this means lots of children. They have come up with a highly civilized solution to the children-eating-out-problem—the kindermenu (children's menu). Kindermenus are available in most restaurants in the Netherlands with the exception of those which are definitely geared for adults only. No matter which restaurant you decide to patronize, the chances are ten to one that the children's menu will feature grilled chicken, patats and applesauce. I don't know who researched and discovered this magic formula, but somehow it works. The portions are child-sized and the whole thing is priced accordingly. Some restaurants even offer a choice of two or three children's menus . . . the second most popular will probably be the lunch or dinner featuring Kroketten.

In addition to eating out with Mum and Dad, the older children will want to go it alone at the local permanent or portable patat stand. See above for the special taste treats offered.

"On the road" sightseeing or in-town shopping, an easy stop with children is a McDonald's or Burger King. The Mexican palate has been appearing recently—check out the Tex Mex and Tex Taco places in The Hague and Scheveningen. Another quick stop is the Noordzee Quick restaurants which offer fish specialties at moderate cost; their open sandwiches, snacks, hot and cold plates to eat on the spot or take out are very popular.

For the youngest of the younger set in Amsterdam, you might want to try something different. Let the six- to twelve-year-olds do it themselves.

Kinder Kook Kafé (Children's Cooking Café), O.Z. Achterburgwal 193,

377

Amsterdam, tel. (020) 253257. (Reservations necessary—Saturdays between noon and 2pm.) Open only at weekends, you can deposit your 6- to 12-year-old at 3pm on Saturday or 11am on Sunday and return three hours later to a delicious three-course meal prepared and served by their own little hands. Delightfully inexpensive too and good for their Dutch! Arrangements can also be made for birthday or school groups.

PANCAKE RESTAURANTS: Generally informal and often in scenic or touristic places, they are usually a good choice when children are in tow and appeal to most people who aren't dieting! Don't forget, the Dutch pancake is not for the faint of heart. It usually measures 12"-14" across and is served on over-sized dishes. Our favorites in the Randstad include:

AMSTERDAM:
Pancake Bakerij, Prinsengracht 191;
Welcome, Prinsengracht 332;
Bedero on the O.Z. Voorburgwaal 224.
The "Boerderij Meersicht," an old farm restaurant in the Amsterdamse Bos, on the Koenenkade, with a playground, big terrace, and a Woods Museum (Bos museum). You can get there via the Haarlemmermeer museum tram—get off at the woods stop; open from noon-7pm daily.

DELFT:
Stads-Koffyhuis, Oude Delft 133, is an old favorite.

GOUDA:
Goudse Winkeltje, Achter de kerk 8.

LEIDEN:
Rotisserie Oudt Leyden with two restaurants, one is the Pannekoekenhuisje, Steenstraat 51 (also a top-notch first-class restaurant).
Leidse Hout, Houtlaan 100.
De Schaapsbel, Beestenmarkt 10.

THE HAGUE:
Maliehuisje, Maliestraat 10, or the
Malieveld Paviljoen on the Malieveld are well-known favorites.
Meyendell Restaurant in the Myenedell Park on Meyendelseweg 38 has the added attraction of lovely walks in the woods.

ROTTERDAM:
Pannekoekhuis de Big, Kralingseweg 20;
Pannekoekhuis, Kralingsezandweg 102;
Pannekoekhuis De Nachtegaal, Princes Beatrixlaan 11.
Janvier, Oud Binnenweg 126, tel. 412 8668.
Pannekoekhuis in Distilleerketel Mill at Delfshaven, Voorhaven 210, tel. (010) 477 9181.

Randstad Restaurants

The restaurants listed on the following pages start with some favorites—known and reliable—for Amsterdam, The Hague, Rotterdam and smaller towns in the immediate area. They are listed according to price categories, old Dutch atmosphere or unusual decor and atmosphere. Of the restaurants on our list not yet personally tried, we hope to eat our way through them as time and digestion permit. If you have other suggestions, don't hesitate to let us know.

Following is a special list primarily for those Outstanding Occasions of the best and most expensive places to dine according to recent reports. Many have a Michelin one-star rating (one or two have two stars), as well as accolades from other top Dutch and foreign gastronomic organizations.

AMSTERDAM RESTAURANTS:

"Eet Cafés" and Inexpensive Suggestions:
Brasserie van Baerle, van Baerlestraat 158, tel. (202) 791532 or 662 2090
Broodje van Kootje (sandwiches), at Leidseplein 20, tel. 232036 and Spui 28, tel. 237451.
Café Americain, Hotel American, 97 Leidsekade, tel. 245322.
Land van Walem, Keizersgracht 449, tel. 253544.
Molenpad, Prinsengracht 653, tel. 259680.
't Nieuwe Café, Eggertstraat 8, tel. 272830, on the Dam, built into the outer wall of the New Church opposite the Palace . . . ideal for coffee or reasonably priced lunches . . . terrific ice cream and pastries.

Rum Runners (Caribbean), Prinsengracht 227, tel. 274079.

Moderate-Priced:
Casa di David (Italian), Singel 426, tel. 425093.
de Oesterbar, Leidseplein 10, tel. 232988. Good fish.
't Haringhuis, 18 Oude Doelenstraat, tel. 221284. For the herring enthusiast!
Heineken Hoek, Kleine Gartmanplantsoen 1-3, tel. 230700. An informal, relaxing place to watch the passing parade.
Indonesia, Singel 550 (Muntplein), tel. 231758.
Mayur (Indian), Korte Leidsedwarsstraat 203, tel. 232142. Specializing in fine Indian dishes.
Piccolino Launge (Italian), Lange Leidsestraat 63, tel. 231495.

Expensive:
Christophe, Leliegracht 46, tel. 250807.
De Cost Gaet Voord De Baet Uyt, Oudebrugsteeg 16, tel. 247050.
De Kersentuin (French), Dysselhofplantsoen 7, tel. 664 2121.
De Prinsen Kelder, Dikker en Thijs, 444 Prinsengracht, tel. 267721.
De Trechter, Hobbemakade 63, tel. 711263.
Le Provencal (French), Weteringschans 91, tel. 239619.
't Swarte Schaep (French), 24 Korte Leidsedwarsstraat, tel. 223021. Dates from 1687.
Tout Court (French), Runstraat 13, tel. 258637.

Old Dutch/Medieval:
't Breugelhuys/De Compagnie van Verre (Medieval/party-theater), 20 Smaksteeg, tel. 244874. Fun with your own group or with the family. You can go for lunch ($6-8 approximately), or decide on a 3- or 4-hour evening feast on Saturday or Sunday. The Night of Breughel is a 4-hour event, Saturday evenings, 8-midnight . . . includes entertainment but drinks are separate. Approximate cost, Fl. 125 (1988). Sailor's Night at the Compagnie van Verre, also 4 hours on Saturdays costs approximately Fl. 145 including dinner, entertainment, beer, and wine. Reservations required.
Country House Boerderij Meerzicht (barbecue/grill), 56 Koenenkade, in the Amsterdam woods, tel 792744.
Die Port van Cleve, N.Z. Voorburgwal 178-180, tel. 244860. An old inn dating from 1887 specializes in native Dutch dishes . . . Thursday evenings in winter a winterdish buffet is offered. Other times, pea soup and T-bone steaks!
Hollands Glorie, 220-222 Kerkstraat, tel. 244764.

THE HAGUE RESTAURANTS: (Also Scheveningen and Wassenaar.)
After 12/89, local telephone numbers after code (070) take a 3 prefix.

"Eet Cafés" and Inexpensive Suggestions:
de Boterwaag, Grote Markt 8a, tel. 659686. Historic setting.
Café Hathor, Maliestraat 22, tel. 464081. Famous for a reasonable three-course lunch.
't Goude Hooft, Groenmarkt 13, tel. (070) 469713. A typical Dutch café/restaurant with a large pleasant terrace (also pancakes).

's Gravenhaagsche eet- en drinkinrichting, Hooistraat 1, tel. 468077 for the best sandwiches in town.

Haagsche Traiteur, Spekstraat 10, tel. 647794. Eat there or take away a pleasant lunch, also caters parties.

Montmartre, Molenstraat 4C, Tel. 656454. Croissanterie.

Park Lane, Parkstraat 37, tel. 653754.

Pizza Biffi, Denneweg 14, tel. 649497.

Schlemmer, on the Korte Houtstraat. Also do breakfasts and Sunday brunches.

Moderate Priced:

Aubergerie, Nieuwe Schoolstraat 17, tel. 648070. French cuisine and delightful atmosphere.

Bali (Indonesian), Badhuisweg 1, tel. 502434. Original restaurant is in downtown The Hague (atmospheric).

Los Gauchos (Argentine beef), Molenstraat 26, tel. 633154; also, Denneweg 71, tel. 651015.

Luden (French), Fredrikstraat 36, tel. 601733. Very reasonable menus.

Marco Polo, (Italian) Ketterinstraat 1b and 9, tel. (070) 652080 (2 places).

Le Mouton, Kazernestraat 62 (enter Nieuwe Schoolstraat), tel. 643263. Special monthly set menus as well as à la carte. Small, attentive service, fine linens and silver but rather smoky if you're allergic . . . moderate-expensive.

Perlier, Nieuwe Schoolstraat 13d, tel. 650807, very reasonable prices.

Tampat Senang, Laan van Meerdervoort 6, tel. 636787. An old favorite with intriguing decor; a lovely romantic garden section has been added. Depending on your order, can be expensive.

de Tijger, (Japanese). Prinsesstraat 10, tel. 642355.

Expensive:

Le Bistroquet, Lange Voorhout 98, tel. 601170. Nice bright atmosphere.

Restaurant Corona, Buitenhof, tel. 637930.

De Roberto, Noordeinde 196, tel. 464977. Also tops.

Jean Martin, Groenewegtje 114, tel. 802895. One of the best in The Hague.

Restaurant Julien, Vos de Tuinstraat 20, tel. 658602. A local favorite.

Saur, Lange Voorhout 47-53, tel. 461324. Another old favorite with outstanding fish specialties. Formal one-star Michelin restaurant upstairs is elegant and expensive; more fun is the bar-restaurant on the ground floor with chatty waiters and interesting patrons, many from the fields of film, art, music, politics.

Shirasagi, (Japanese) Spui 170, tel. 464700. Downtown by the Dans Theater.

Old Dutch Atmosphere:

Auberge de Kieviet, Stoeplaan 27, Wassenaar, tel. (01751) 79203. Country setting with French cuisine . . . expensive.

Wine Tasting:

Wijnkoperij de Gouden Ton, Denneweg 81, tel. (070) 462796. Great fun for wine lovers. Not a bar or restaurant; to encourage wine sales, the owner, Nico McGough, offers free wine-tasting on Thursday evenings between 7-9pm.

SCHEVENINGEN:
Ducdalf, Dr. Lelykade 5, tel. 557692. Fish specialties.
Kandinsky (overlooks the sea in the Kurhaus Hotel), Gev. Deynootplein 30, tel. 520052.
Les Pieds dans l'Eau (French), Dr. Lelykade, tel. 550040. Moderate, good fish.
Seinpost, Zeekant 60, tel. 555250.

ROTTERDAM RESTAURANTS: (Also, Delft, Delfshaven, Schiedam, Maassluis)

"Eet Cafés" and Inexpensive Suggestions:
De Admiraliteit, Admiraliteitstraat 17b, tel. (010) 413 4289.
De Ballentent, Parkkade 1, tel. 436 0462.
Big Ben, Stadhuisplein 3, tel. 414 9912.

Moderate-Expensive:
Beef-Eater, Stationsplein 45, tel. 411 9550. Carvery, good for families.
Central Park, Baden Powelllaan 10, tel. 436 5695. Intimate, modern, piano music on Sundays . . . owners are the cook and "Maitre d'."
Chalet Suisse, Kievitslaan 31, tel. 436 5062, on the edge of the Park situated overlooking the gardens . . . a lovely spot. Fondue is reasonably priced . . . other dishes more.
De Pijp, Geffelstraat 90a, tel. 436 6896. During WW II, this historic "speak-easy" served as a meeting place for the Underground. Some of the feel of that era is still evident. You should reserve ahead. Entrance is off the main street down a narrow alley. The interior is mostly dark brown, long bare tables where you sit family-style (no intimate tête-a-tête). This has traditionally been a students' hangout. Every September 5th, the restaurant is open to the new college (Erasmus University) arrivals and they are told stories of the past by the "oldtimers." When fraternities were forbidden by the Germans, students gathered secretly at the Pijp to cooperate with the resistance movement. That was when a closed-door policy was instituted which lasted until about ten years ago. Ninety years old in 1988, the Pijp's clientele is what makes it unique. Whole families gather here from grandparents, parents and teenagers. You might also run into Cabinet members, diplomats, mayors, professors and political figures of all kinds. Everyone talks to his neighbor . . . most speak English and this is one of the few places a foreigner can mix "at ease" without a formal introduction with local people. The last time we went, my neighbor told me her grandfather owned the distillery next door. He brought her father to the Pijp as a youngster, her father brought her and she has brought her children. Her grandfather's tie is one of the collection of ties hanging from the ceiling. Each tie is given a number and recorded in a book so one can always locate their tie or that of their relatives. In recent years a special Pijp tie has been instituted. When a customer becomes a "regular," he is presented with a Pijp tie and he gives the tie he is wearing to the Pijp collection.

Pancakes are on the menu but if you don't mind spending a bit more, the regular menu is extensive, including tournedos (Fl. 31), tongue, sweetbreads, chicken, veal, etc. You read the blackboard to make your choice. At midnight great gunnysacks of peanuts in the shell are distributed to all the tables—eat as

much as you like and throw the shells on the floor!
El Gaucho, van Vollenhovenstr. 58, tel. 414 1602. Steak and more steak.
Indonesia, Rodezand 34, tel. 414 8588.
Kam Sang, Freericksplaats 22a, Hillegersberg, tel. 422 9951. Very good with children.
Kalinka (Hungarian), Delfsestraat 12, tel. 414 1258.
Ocean Paradise (Chinese), Parkhaven opposite Euromast, tel. 436 1750 . A red and gold Chinese barge to rival those of Hong Kong. Long menu with great variety of dishes (including Indonesian). A perfect place to take the family; the large fishpond near the entrance fascinates the children. Try to get a table on the far side away from the quay where you can get a view of the Maas River traffic.
Popocatepetl (Mexican), Spaanse Poort 71, tel. 412 0364.
Portofino (Italian), Nieuwe Binnenweg 151, tel. 436 5163. You can see the cook throwing pizzas in the air 4 and 5 feet as he stretches the dough to the right size. Extremely popular so do reserve.
Singapore, Mauritsweg 52, tel. 404 6199.
Taj Mahal (Indian), Mariniersweg 18, tel. 412 0812.
Tropicana restaurants, Maasboulevard 100, tel. 402 0700. There are a number of restaurants to choose from in this swimming/sauna complex. The pancake restaurant is ideal for children (with a lego-table to keep them occupied), an Italian restaurant, La Gondola, with lovely view of the river . . . There is also a revolving French restaurant overlooking various swimming pools (expensive). Entry to restaurant and shop area is free . . . no need to swim.
Zochers, Baden Powelllaan 12, tel. 436 4249. Very different . . . mixed crowd from students to members of Parliament. Sometimes live classical music . . . "the" place for Sunday brunch while reading the Sunday newspapers . . . also lunches and dinners in elegant former residence.

Expensive:
Beau Rivage, Weissenbruchlaan 149, on the lake at Hillegersberg, tel. 418 4040. Outstanding cuisine in a restaurant overlooking a charming lake, about a quarter hour's drive from downtown.
Le Coq d'Or, Van Vollenhovenstraat 25, tel. 436 6405. Old-time restaurant with well-established reputation located downtown. Fine dining (French) upstairs; downstairs, informal with menu written on blackboard.
Park Heuvel, Heuvellaan 21, tel. (010) 436 0530. At the Maas River end of the Park . . . very modern and exclusive.
La Villette, Westblaak 160, tel. 414 8692. Very modern.

Old Dutch Atmosphere:
De Herberg, along a small canal, the Kleiweg 591, tel. 428 0993. Elegant setting with interesting collection of Dutch clocks . . . old-world service.
Kasteel van Rhoon (across the Maas River, south of Rotterdam), tel. (01890) 18896 (telephone for directions and information). The castle dates from 1433 . . . an established dining-out spot for family celebrations, business conference dinners, etc. There are tours with a light and sound performance in summer.
Old Dutch, Rochussenstraat 20, tel. 436 0344. Traditional Dutch food and

383

interior . . . sometimes there's dancing.

Den Rust Wat, Honingerdijk 96, tel. 413 4110. An atmospheric old inn dating from 1597 . . . good steaks.

De Zwetheul, Rotterdamseweg 480 (between Delft and Rotterdam), tel. (010) 470 4166. Fine cuisine, pleasant waterside terrace for summer drinks.

DELFSHAVEN:

Gasterie Deftshaven, Voorhaven 3, tel. 477 5181.

Oud Brugetje, Voorhaven 6, tel. 477 3449. Moderate-expensive.

Pannekoekhuis, in Distileerketel Mill, Voorhaven 210, tel. 477 9181.

SCHIEDAM: (West of Rotterdam)

La Duchesse, Maasboulevard 7, tel. 426 4625. Good reputation, attractive and cozy interior.

Hosman Frères, Korte Dam 8, tel. 422 4096. Charming intimate French atmosphere in a three-story building festooned with red awnings hugging the canal. Impeccable service in a well-appointed dining room . . . good wine list and excellent cuisine; the downstairs is moderate; upstairs is expensive.

Noordmolen, Nordwest 38, tel. 426 3104. Eat in a working windmill, illuminated at night and paddles turning . . . simple but nice family atmosphere; moderate.

't Oude Raedthuys, Schiedamseweg 26, Schiedam-Kethel, tel. 471 5800.

MAASSLUIS: (West of Schiedam)
Ridderhof, Sportlaan 2, tel. (01899) 11211. This 17th-century farmhouse has been converted into an extremely attractive restaurant. A reasonable meal is possible in the section of the farmhouse reserved for "plate service," and children can visit the animals in the nearby field.

DELFT:
Stadsherberg "De Mol," Molslaan 50, tel. (015) 121343. This former town orphanage dating from 1563 has been created into a 16th-century inn, trying to recapture its youth by inviting you to dine in medieval style. You will be attended by wenches in period dress, music, dancing, and meat roasting over an open fire. Telephone for specifics.

Fine Dining

A romantic anniversary or birthday dinner out on the town need not be a disappointment today! We can report good news. The variety of restaurants and the quality of the preparation of dishes in Holland's top category restaurants are hard to beat anywhere in Europe. This has not always been the case. Holland has been famous for its huge breakfasts, but its general cooking lacked finesse and imagination until about 10 years ago when a rapid metamorphosis occurred.

Price of course is a factor to be considered ... the best places are always expensive, but a number of starred restaurants offer two menus ... one more moderate than the full gourmet meal. There is no shame to inquire about the price of their "prix fixe" meals when calling to make reservations.

A list of some of the best regarded restaurants in the Randstad area follows as a convenience to readers for those special occasions. Restaurants preceded with an asterisk (*) indicate they have one Michelin star. These ratings vary from year to year, but the meal in such an establishment is rarely disappointing.

We regret to say that we have not had the pleasure of personal experiences with this entire list.

AMSTELVEEN:
*Molen de Dikkert, Amsterdamseweg 104a, tel. (020) 411378/459162.

AMSTERDAM:
Christophe, Leliegracht 46, tel. (020) 250807.
De Cost Gaet Voord De Baet Uyt, Oudebrugsteeg 16, tel. (020) 247050.
Dikker en Thijs, Prinsengracht 444, tel. (020) 258876/267721.
*De Kersentuin, Dysselhofplantsoen 7, tel. (020) 642121.
*De Trechter, Hobbemakade 63, tel. (020) 711263.
Le Provencal, Weteringschans 91, (020) 239619.
Tout Court, Runstraat 13, tel. (020) 258637.

DELFT:
De Zwetheul, Rotterdamseweg 480, tel. (010) 470 4166 . . . terrace.
THE HAGUE:
*Corona, Buitenhof 39-42, tel. (070) 637930.
De Roberto, Noordeinde 196, tel. (070) 464977.
Jean Martin, Groenewegje 115, tel. (070) 802895.
*Saur, Lange Voorhout 47-53, tel. (070) 463344.

LEIDEN:
*Rotisserie Oudt Leyden, Steenstraat 51-53, tel.(071) 133144.

NOORDWIJK AAN ZEE:
*De Graaf van het Hoogveen, Quarles van Uffordstraat 103,
tel. (01719) 12723/14323.

OEGSTGEEST:
*De Beukenhof, Terweeweg 2-4, tel. (071) 173188.

ROTTERDAM:
Beau Rivage, Weissenbruchlaan 149, tel. (010) 418 4040.
Parkheuvel, Heuvellaan 21, tel. (010) 436 0530.
*Le Coq d'Or, Van Vollenhovenstraat 25, tel. (010) 436 6405.
*La Villette, Westblaak 160, tel. (010) 414 8692.

SCHEVENINGEN:
*Seinpost, Zeekant 60, tel. (070) 555250.

SCHIEDAM:
Auberge Hosman Frères, Korte Dam 8-10, tel. (010) 426 4096.

SCHIEDAM-KETHEL:
't Oude Raedthuys, Schiedamseweg 26, tel. (010) 471 5800/471 5757.

WASSENAAR:
*Auberge de Kieviet, Stoeplaan 29, tel. (01751) 79403.

386

CHAPTER 18

SPORTS: Watching and Playing

There are those who enjoy watching and those who enjoy doing so we have divided this chapter into these two categories. Dutch "voetbal," or what we call "soccer," probably heads the list as the most popular spectator sport while sailing tops the list of favorites in active sports. Soccer has become increasingly popular in the U.S.; however, the Dutch game has many subtleties so we have tried to explain it in detail for those who don't already know it. The sports are listed alphabetically . . . not according to popularity.

Spectator Sports

The following does not attempt to include every man or woman's favorite spectator sport. Each town has its own offerings at different times of the year and many of these events have been noted throughout the book in the discussion of towns as well as under "Yearly Events," Chapter 20.

For the very sports-minded persons, the Monday editions of the local newspapers are highly recommended. They list the sports activities of the previous week with scores of winning teams, etc., and also the sports events for the coming week. The cost is minimal and the information is extensive. Obviously, written in Dutch, but not difficult to follow for enthusiasts.

BIKING AND CYCLING Holland couldn't be a more ideal country to enjoy biking and cycling . . . its generally flat terrain is perfect for enjoying these sports. One of the most exciting indoor cycle races is held at Rotterdam's Ahoy Hall in January . . . 6 days.

BOATING COMPETITIONS: While sailing is the most visual of the water sports, rowing meets, canoe competitions and speedboating are also popular. Canoe races are held in Zaandam (near Amsterdam) in March and International Speedboat races are held in Amsterdam in June. Canoeing is extremely popular in Groningen and Drenthe provinces. For more information, write the VVVs.

Rowing Meets: A rowing competition of national importance is held in September on the Bergse Voorplas, Rotterdam. Organized by the Nautilus Club, tel. (010) 413 8791.

Groningen has an important International Rowing Regatta on the Eemskanaal in mid-June. And Amsterdam holds its "Head of the River" races on the Amstel in April.

Sailing Races: Serious sailors participate in the North Sea Race which takes place at Whitsun. There are actually two races—the race between the Dutch boats from the Hook of Holland to Harwich (England), and the race from Harwich to the Hook of Holland with English and Dutch boats in competition. The latter race is the big race, of course. For exact dates, ask the VVV.

There are a number of sailing regattas throughout the country. A special event is the Regatta on the Frisian Lakes with "Skutsjes," historic commercial boats with nearby competitions of old-time sports such as pole vaulting, ring riding and flag waving. Then, there's the Harlingen-Terschelling Sailing Race about the end of May; "Vlaggetjesdag," a special fleet show in Urk, Flevoland, and another in IJmuiden (May/June); International Sailing Regatta in Veere, Zeeland; over Easter; "Deltaweek" international sailing contests of round and flat-bottomed boats at Colijnsplaat/Zierikzee, Zeeland, in July; International deep sea sailing races at Delfzyl, Groningen, over Whitsun; International Sailing competitions at Loosdrecht, South Holland, in July; the "Enkhuizer Klipperrace," Enkhuizen, in mid-September ("klippers" are a special type Dutch boat); and the International Sailing Competitions of round- and flat-bottomed boats in mid-September, also at Enkhuizen.

CAR AND MOTORCYCLE RACING: Exciting car races can be seen in the Scheveningen/Zandvoort area of South and North Holland as well as in the Province of Drenthe. For instance, motor car races are held on the Scheveningen beach early in the year. Zandvoort's Circuit (outside Haarlem) is a car and motorcycle racing track which attracts a lot of spectators. At Whitsun, there's a race for cars built before 1962 and in September, a regular car race festival is held. The current year's schedule can be obtained through the VVVs of Haarlem, The Hague, or Zandvoort.

The Province of Drenthe keeps its "Drenthe Circuit" from gathering moss by scheduling a number of events, starting with the National Motorcycle Championships on Ascension Day, then the European championship road races, quickly followed by the International Grand Prix Motor Races in Assen end of June . . . there is also a 4-day cycling tour in Assen in July. For information, contact the Assen VVV, tel. (05920) 14324.

HORSE SHOWS: Perhaps the second most important spectator sport held in Rotterdam is the Official International Horse Show (C.H.I.O.), the Concours Hippique, held yearly in August/September in the Kralingse Wood. Events are scheduled for five days with outstanding competitors from all over the world. It's a treat to see the fine horses from Argentina, Italy, England, etc., being put through their paces by riders who might be young girls or experienced military men. Members of the Royal Family usually attend the final event—if not oftener—and officiate at the closing ceremonies when the prizes are given. The more expensive seats are in a covered area—a blanket or pillow can soften the seating (wooden planks). There are food stands for sandwiches, hot and cold drinks, and even souvenir and other shops, especially erected for the pleasure of the customers.

"Jumping Amsterdam," a yearly indoor International Horse Show held in the R.A.I. Building the end of November or beginning of December, is widely advertised and well attended. The awards offered here are a special Netherlands Grand Prix, and an International Jumping Grand Prix. Tickets for these events are always at a premium so make your reservations well in advance.

Groningen is particularly known for its fine horses. At the end of December/beginning of January, horse show events for national riders can be seen in Veendam, and there are often trotting races in the Stadspark of Groningen. Check with the VVV.

Also, don't miss the Hague Horse Days in June in The Hague or the Breda Paard military horse show, mid-May in Breda. Also, keep in mind that in even years there's an International Concours Hippique in Denekamp, Overijssel.

Horseracing—Flat-racing and Trotting: From the middle of March through the middle of November, you can see flat-racing and trotting at Duindigt (tel. (070) 244427 for information; after 12/89, 324 4427) which is located at the edge of Wassenaar near The Hague. Take the children simply to see the races if you like, but for those who enjoy a little betting, this is also possible. On the last Sunday in June, there is the special international trotting race, the trophy being the Grand Prix of the Low Countries.

ICE HOCKEY, ICE SKATING RACES, AND FIGURE SKATING EVENTS: A relative newcomer to the scene of spectator sports in Europe, ice hockey is growing rapidly in popularity. The Netherlands Ice Hockey Team which is centered in The Hague has some Americans and Canadians on the team. Announcements of international ice hockey games held in de Uithof, The Hague or the Ahoy Hall in Rotterdam will be found in Info or Rotterdam "Deze Week," the sports section of the newspapers, or ask the VVV.

Most championship skating races are held in Eindhoven at the Kunst IJsbaan, tel. (040) 520483 or the VVV for details. See "active sports" for a list of ice skating rinks where competitions might be scheduled.

Although it is more and more rare to see the classic Eleven Towns Race due to lack of ice, races are held in the northern provinces, in particular at Deventer and Heerenveen. And if you should happen to be here during a good freeze, make sure you don't miss the traditional races on the canals . . . info from the Friesland VVV. Major figure skating events are held in The Hague.

SOCCER (VOETBAL): Dutch football or what we call "soccer," heads the list as the most popular spectator sport in the Netherlands. For addicts of American baseball or football, this is a good substitute. A description of the game and other specifics follow.

Football is probably one of the most popular ball games in the world. In England it is known as "soccer" but neither Dutch football nor soccer should be confused with American football which is more like English Rugby. Knowing something about Dutch football is very useful for young people living in Holland since it is THE national sport and the game will be played in the schools, and on weekends among amateur clubs, to say nothing about the professional games played by the Netherlands' formidable arch rivals, FEYENOORD of Rotterdam, AJAX of Amsterdam, or PSV of Eindhoven.

Every city, village and town in Holland has its own team and often more than one. Two best-known teams are AJAX of Amsterdam and FEYENOORD of Rotterdam. When these two clash, everything else in the two cities comes to a standstill. And the excitement of the supporters is so great that storeowners in Rotterdam and Amsterdam have been known to board up their windows as a protection against possible damage—the city where the game is played can literally be torn apart!

When Feyenoord plays at home there are special trains which go directly to the stadium in South Rotterdam and this may be the easiest way to get there or take bus 49, or metro.

The Ajax Stadium, Middenweg, Watergraafsmeer, is at the Southeast en-

trance to Amsterdam—Tram 9 is the best way to go. If you find you like the game and can stand the noise, season tickets are available.

And for the very talented, it is possible to play football by joining one of the amateur clubs of your choice. You must take a physical examination. Once pronounced fit, you will be assigned to one of the club's teams, depending on your ability. There are teams for boys under 12 years, they are called "aspiranten" (or beginners); 12-16 years are called juniors; and from 16 years on, they are seniors. Most Dutch boys join a private club and play on Saturday or Sunday during fall, winter and spring, with a training evening during the week.

Principles of the Game: Each professional team consists of eleven players inclusive of the Goal Keeper, plus two reserve players. Only two replacements are allowed per game. The play is timed with 45 minutes for each half making a total of 90 minutes to complete the game plus any injury time. The teams change sides at half-time. The game can only be stopped in case of injury, except for the 15 minute break at half-time. The ball may only be handled by the Goal Keeper. The other players may kick it, bounce it off their heads or their bodies, but they may not touch it with their hands or arms.

The large-size field is rectangular (130 yards x 100 yards). The long side is called the touch line; the wide side is called the goal line. The goal consists of two vertical posts spaced 24 feet apart and joined by a crossbar eight feet from the ground. The object of the game is to get the ball in your opponent's goal.

SWIMMING: Check with the Sports and Recreation Department of your City Hall (see below) to get the names of the major pools in your area. They would also be able to tell you of any swimming competitions of special interest, or ask the VVV or your swim club. A chilling event is the traditional New Year's Dive in the North Sea which takes place at Scheveningen and Zandvoort.

391

TENNIS: Tennis is an extremely popular sport in Holland. The ABN International Tennis Tournament is held in Rotterdam in mid-March in which all the top stars participate; another International Tennis Championship is held at Emmen (D) in July; and also the Dutch national championships are held in Hilversum (NH) in July.

Active Sports Opportunities

The greatest problem about listing various sports available in the Netherlands is missing someone's favorite! For full information about a sport which interests you and which is not mentioned below, contact your local Sports and Recreation Office:

Rotterdam: tel. (010) 417 2886.

The Hague: tel. (070) 808454, after 12/89, 380 8454.

Amsterdam: tel. (020) 511 0321.

For the younger set, activity sports courses are offered during school spring and summer vacations at the British School in Voorschoten; call Mr. Cook, (071) 769810 for particulars.

BASEBALL AND SOFTBALL: Baseball and softball are very popular with our Dutch hosts. In South Holland alone there are 24 associations which, we are told, would gladly welcome foreign members, both male and female, from age 8 on. Call the K.N.B.S.B., tel. (023) 390244 in Haarlem or (010) 451 2317 in Rotterdam for details.

The American Baseball Foundation (ABF): This organization was established by a group of sports-minded businessmen and educators to provide sports activities primarily for the American Community in Holland but open to all nationalities. The organization is governed by a formal Board of Directors and is fully incorporated under the Dutch Stichting laws. Some of the sports offered are baseball, basketball, bowling, flag football, soccer and softball. See Chapter 19 for more details.

In each sport, full intramural league competitions are held with championship awards to the winners and participation certificates for everyone. The teams are coached and refereed by interested men and women of the community. In addition, the baseball program for all but the Farm Leaguers (boys 7-10 years), includes regular participation in the District and National Dutch baseball leagues and tournaments. For information about participation, write to ABF, POB 133, Wassenaar, tel. (01751) 19067 weekends only.

BASKETBALL: The Netherlands Basketball Association is at Tollenstraat 7, 2282 BM Rijswijk.

BIKING: In the Netherlands, biking is a way of life but for most foreigners, it's a delightfully new or relearned experience. Why not pretend to be a real Dutch family and see the country from the seat of a bicycle? There are many organized or semi-organized tour groups which will lead you into some of the most beautiful Dutch landscapes for a day, a week or longer. Again, the VVV is your

392

best contact.

First, it is wise to learn some of the rules of the road:

BIKING RULES OF THE ROAD

1. *Learn the international traffic signs—they often apply to the bikers as well as the motorist.*
2. *Travel on the path reserved for bikers whenever there is one. These are well marked with signs saying "Fietspad" or sometimes "Rijwielpad." Incidentally, biking is not allowed on the sidewalks although very young children can get away with almost anything.*
3. *Signal when turning, but watch carefully that you are not cutting in front of an automobile. If you are turning, he has priority.*
4. *Have your bike in good working order including headlight, a back light, as well as wheel reflectors for the front and back wheels . . . this is compulsory. They are available from your local bike shop or department store sports department.*

A visit to the ANWB (Royal Touring Club) is recommended for serious bikers who want to get out into the country. The ANWB can suggest especially scenic routes; get you maps with bike trails marked; give you lists of hostels along the way; provide information about clubs or groups which meet and bike together or about the semi-organized area trips with the Netherlands Railways.

The VVV can also advise on local and national bicycle routes. They have brochures with routes for cycling in their cities and surrounding areas. For instance in Amsterdam, "Fietsen in Amsterdam," or "Holiday on Two Wheels," which covers the whole Netherlands including overnight stops, etc. There are bike tours through the dunes and the tulip fields. You can also bike in the Hoge Veluwe (free loan of bicycle). For information, contact the local VVV or Central Station.

Ena's Bike Tours, tel. (015) 143797 in Delft, will organize day tours from Amsterdam in small groups with a guide for the day to visit a windmill and cheese farm, take a boat ride and organize a picnic lunch (weather permitting) . . . tour departs, daily, at 10am, June-Oct. from the Amstel Station (Amsterdam); lasts about 7½ hours.

BOWLING: The Netherlands Bowling Federation is in Eindhoven, Hastelweg 11, POB 8032, Tel. (040) 520164. The Bowling Association, POB 87802, 2508 DE The Hague, is another contact. Some well-known alleys are:

Amsterdam: Bowling Centrum Knijn, Gelderplein 1.

Breda: Nassausingel 28 is a fine bowling alley.

Rotterdam: There is a large bowling alley at Lommerijk overlooking the lake in Hillegersberg, Straatweg 99; also at Batavier Kralingen, Eerste Jerichostraat 18, tel. (010) 414 5661; and at Hofplein Couwenburg 16, tel. (010) 465 5755.

Scheveningen: The Bowling Center at Scheveningen, Palace Promenade 990, is open from 10am until very late, even up to 3am on Saturdays. To reserve lanes, call (070) 543212, after 12/89, 354 3212.

CRICKET: The Royal Netherlands Cricket Association is the parent organization with which all reputable cricket clubs in the Netherlands are affiliated.

The V.O.C. (Rotterdamsche Cricket- en Voetbalvereniging), like its counterparts in other towns, is a private cricket and soccer club which offers boys from the ages of 8 and 14 an opportunity to play cricket in the summer season and soccer in the winter. Most of these clubs welcome foreign members and anyone interested should call the V.O.C. in Rotterdam, tel. (010) 418 9693; The Hague, H.B.S., tel. (070) 681950, and Quick H., tel. (070) 680323, after 12/89, 368 1950 and 368, 0323, respectively; in Amsterdam, A.F.C., tel. (020) 445575, V.R.A., tel. (020) 456615, A.C.C., tel. (020) 456068; Haarlem, Rood en Wit, tel. (023) 287085; and in Utrecht, Kampong, tel. (030) 514530.

FENCING: The address of the Netherlands Royal Fencing Association is Speulderbos 15, 2716 JW Zoetermeer, tel. (079) 212511. They can supply you with names and addresses of where you can join a group or take lessons. In our three cities, try:

Amsterdam: Call Mr. Visser, Sporthal Zuid, tel. (020) 158829 or 731314.

The Hague: Call Mr. C. Broer, tel. (070) 558112, after 12/89, 355 8112.

Rotterdam: Call Mr. Vandervoot, tel. (010) 411 0616 or 412 0801.

HOCKEY (field hockey): There are roughly 350 clubs of this popular sport in the Netherlands, most of them in the larger towns. All have a men's, women's and youth section. Much attention is given to the latter, especially the "minis" who begin at the age of 8 years. For information contact the Netherlands Royal Hockey Association, POB 455, 1180 AL Amstelveen.

HORSEBACK RIDING: There are many stables (maneges) in the Netherlands and choosing the right one for you depends to a great extent on finding one where the teachers do not object to speaking English. Call your local Sports and Recreation Office (Dienst voor Sport en Recreatie) for information.

ICE SKATING: Before coming to the Netherlands, you probably had a mental picture of a flat country with windmills, lots of water, and people in colorful clothes scooting here and there on their homemade Hans-Brinker-type skates! Well, it does happen that the lakes and canals will freeze and then suddenly, from out of nowhere, the children appear in multicolored woolen hats, scarves, and mittens, making bright spots against the ice. Unfortunately, this scene doesn't occur as often as it did— something about the winters being warmer and world temperatures changing and it's even possible that one day there will be a whole generation of Dutchmen who will grow up never learning to skate unless they learn on an artificial ice rink!

But let's assume that this is a good icy winter. If the freeze lasts long enough, of course, it is possible to ice skate almost anywhere . . . Lakes are tested for safety so before going out, be sure that the flag is up indicating that the ice is safe . . . a red flag means danger.

One of the traditional places to ice skate is Friesland, but closer to home perhaps, is Kinderdijk. Pile the family in the car, grab the skates and join the

394

many Dutchmen who have been skating here for years. This site of 19 windmills (in the immediate vicinity) is impressive any time but they stand out in sharp relief against a winter sky, their tops and arms snow-covered with icicles hanging here and there. People come from all over to skate on the frozen waters around the mills and to enjoy the beauty of these majestic structures.

In the good old days the popular "Koek en Zoopie" huts were everywhere to provide the chilly skaters hot steaming cups of anise milk (anijsmelk) and spice cake, or hot chocolate. Today, you can "do it yourself" by buying the anise-flavored sugar cubes (look for Smelta and De Ruijter brand names) and dropping them into the warm milk.

If there is a good freeze, the teenagers might like to participate in the five-lakes races or do the traditional skating tour from Rotterdam to Gouda, buying a Gouda pipe (and downing some Bols to keep the circulation going) and returning to Rotterdam with the pipe intact. For those who are not familiar with Gouda pipes, these are long, delicate white clay pipes. In the north of the Netherlands, there is the traditional Eleven Cities race with prizes for the winners and for those who have managed to stay in the race to the finish.

In addition to the canals and lakes which freeze naturally, there are tennis clubs which flood their courts and set up an "ice palace" where for a small entrance fee, you may join others of all ages and abilities skating to appropriate music. These ice rinks usually stay frozen longer than the lakes or canals. Amsterdam encourages its skaters in winter by "freezing" the section of the Leidseplein surrounded by cafés, from which it is almost as much fun to watch as it is to participate.

Those who do not want to depend on the whims of Father Winter can enjoy the facilities of artificial ice rinks throughout the Netherlands. For instance, in

Rotterdam, go to the Ahoy Hall, tel. (010) 812122, or to the Weena IJshall on the Weena; in Amsterdam, go to "Jaap Eden Hall," Radioweg 94, tel. (020) 949652, and in The Hague area there are two possibilities: IJsbaan "Uithof," Jaap Edenweg 10, tel. (070) 299066, after 12/89, 329 9066, or Prins Willem Alexander Sportcentrum, Oostwaards 23, in Zoetermeer, tel. (079) 411221. Other outdoor rinks are available in Assen, Deventer, Eindhoven, Utrecht and Groningen. The indoor rinks available are at Dordrecht, Eindhoven, Geleen, Groningen, The Hague, Heerenveen, 's Hertogenbosch, Leiden, Nijmegen, Tilburg and Utrecht. They open in October and close toward the end of March.

JUDO, JU JITSU, and KARATE: These Far Eastern sports are also popular in the Netherlands. Some cities have classes for children from eight years up. For information, contact the Netherlands Judo Association, Laan v. Meerdervoort 239, The Hague, tel. (070) 638926, after 12/89, 363 8926.

For other parts of Holland, check with the local Sports and Recreation Department.

RUGBY: There are now approximately 120 clubs spread over the Netherlands, each with two or three teams. Youngsters from the age of ten may join the junior teams. Rugby can be played in the following places: Amsterdam, Rotterdam, The Hague, Delft, Haarlem, Hoek van Holland, Gouda, Amstelveen, Noordwijk, Papendrecht, Sassenheim, Zoetermeer. For information call the Nederlandse Rugby Bond (Dutch Rugby Union), Schaepmanlaan 5, 1272 GJ Huizen, tel. (02152) 62656.

SAILING: Another outstanding Dutch sport which is open to all comers. In addition to the fine summer sailing camps available north and south, it is possible to take lessons through private clubs. For those in your area check with the Koninklijke Ned. Watersport Verbond, Van Eeghenstraat 94, Amsterdam, tel. (020) 664 2611. Often there are qualified young men interested in giving private sailing lessons who can be contacted through these clubs.

Incidentally, children are not usually taught to sail until they are twelve years old because they aren't considered strong enough to handle a boat under difficult weather conditions. For further information, contact:

Amsterdam: The Royal Rowing and Sailing Club the Hoop, Weesperzijde 65a, 1091 EH Amsterdam, tel. (020) 665 7844.

Rotterdam: The Royal Rowing and Sailing Club the Maas, Veerdam 1, 3016 DD Rotterdam, tel. (010) 413 8514, or Nautilus, Plantagelaan 3, tel. (010) 413 8791, 418 4429 . . . a good rowing club for beginners or recreation.

The Hague: The Netherlands International Yacht Club, located at Woubrugge near the beautiful Braassemeer lake (NIYC Secretary: Oostduinlaan 24, 2596 JN The Hague), is a family-oriented club whose major aim is to promote international entente. Members come from about a dozen different countries; there is a large British contingent as well as a few Canadians and Australians.

If you've ever dreamed of renting a traditional Dutch sailing vessel with crew, contact "Hollands Glorie," (010) 411 5880; departure points are Amsterdam for the north and Willemstad for the south. The VVV puts out a good booklet all about renting boats from 2-berths, motorized, to huge sailing ships, and there are many organizations which arrange special tour packages.

SQUASH: This sport is fast becoming more popular and clubs are springing up all over Holland. Contact the Nederland Squash Rackets Bond, POB 50, 2360 AB Warmond.

SWIMMING: Anyone living in the Netherlands can well understand why swimming is a required subject in school. There is water all around from little trickles to huge areas of land bordering monumental seas. Every community has access to an indoor pool, and sometimes an outdoor pool as well as fresh water swimming in lakes or natural pools. For specific information on pools in your city, check with the VVV or call the Dienst voor Sports en Recreatie. Also try the Royal NW Swimming Assn., Rembrandtlaan 25, 2251EV Voorschoten.

TENNIS: Teachers are fully booked which means arranging for lessons requires determination and persistence. While joining a tennis club is difficult, it may be possible to rent a court for a specific time period. For assistance in locating clubs, teachers, or courts for hire, contact your local VVV or Sports and Recreation Office, see above.

VOETBAL (SOCCER): Dutch voetbal is the MOST important sport in the Netherlands and you'd better bone up on the principles of the game. For activists, you will notice that children from eight years may apply to join one of the team clubs. We know of one foreign child who was accepted on a Feyenoord amateur team (affiliated with the professional team). Obtain information from the Royal Netherlands Football Assn., POB 43555, 2504 AN The Hague.

Private clubs in the main cities which welcome young foreign players are:

Amsterdam: AFC, Sportpark "Goed Genoeg," De Boelelaan, Buitenveldert, tel. (020) 445575 or Mr. de Bie, tel. 458850.

Haarlem: KHFC, Spanjaardslaan (Entrance Emauslaan), tel. (023) 287085 or Mr. Lagerwerf, tel. 260906.

The Hague: HBS, Evert Wytemaweg 3, (Daal en Bergselaan entrance), tel. (070) 681960, after 12/89, 368 1960, or Mr. Goldman, tel. 680249, after 12/89, 368 0249.

HVV, van Hogenhoucklaan 37-41, tel. (070) 248361, after 12/89, 324 8361, or Mr. ter Kuile, tel. 202055, after 12/89, 320 2055.

Quick H., Nieuw Hanenburg, Sav. Lohmanlaan, tel. (070) 680323, after 12/89, 368 0323, or Mr. Foortse, tel. 325 2138, evenings.

Rotterdam: VOC (Rotterdamsche Cricket- en Voetbalvereniging), Overschiese Kleiweg 499, tel. (010) 422 4918, or Mr. Bongers, tel. 418 6495, evenings.

Utrecht: Kampong, Laan van Maarschalkerweerd (behind Utrecht F.C. Stadium), tel. (030) 514530, and ask for Mr. Stokvis.

WALKING: It may surprise many foreigners that walking isn't done quite as casually in the Netherlands as in other countries. In the first place, before you

can walk in many scenic areas, you must have a special permit—a wandel-
kaartje. These may be obtained through local VVVs, the ANWB, or other places
like kiosks or restaurants on the spot.

In this country where there is so little woodland, and little variety of landscape, "Wandelterreinen" or "Walking Area" supply both, though in a somewhat regimented fashion. Duneland is often devoted to this purpose, other areas
being protected as Nature Reserves. There are six or eight different National
Conservation Societies, but the "Natuur Monumenten" publishes the most
compact and comprehensive booklet (Handboek)—available in Dutch only. For
yearly membership and a Handbook listing nearly all of the Netherlands nature
reserves and walking areas (also what plants, animals or birds are likely to be
found in each), write to the Vereniging tot Behoud van Natuurmonumenten in
Nederland, Noordeinde 60, 's Gravenland, tel. (035) 262004.

Especially recommended areas for walking are "the Wandelterreinen" and
Natuur Reservaten at Oostvoorne and Rockanje; the Staelduinse Bos, 's Graven-
zande (near Hook of Holland); Meijendel in The Hague; Schaap en Burg in
Hilversum and Duin en Kruidberg in Zandvoort.

Listed below are some carefully selected special walks showing the best of the
countryside in various areas which have been compiled by the Netherlands
Railways. Some of these allow access to areas which are otherwise restricted.

Dune walk at Castricum and National Park Kennemerduinen
Wood walk—Hulshorst—Nunspeet
Wood walk—Lunteren
Wood walk—Mastbos, Breda
Walk along the River Linge—Leerdam, Beesd
Thijse (nature) walk—Wolfhese, Westerbouwing
Wood walk—Oisterwijk (with small nature museum and café)
Beach walk—IJmuiden, Zandvoort

For further information contact the Nederlandse Wandelsport Bond, Pieters-
kerkhof 3512 JS, Utrecht, or the VVV.

MISCELLANEOUS: The list goes on and on. For instance:

Badminton: Fans should contact the Netherlands Badminton Association,
Marsmanhove 25, 2726 DA, Zoetermeer.

Fishing: You can fish in any canal that strikes your fancy, or in the lakes,
rivers or seas. Permits are purchased from the "Visakten" at the local post
office. Deep-sea fishing or sea angling is possible from the Scheveningen Pier
(Tower Island, lower gallery, approximately five guilders per day).

Flying: If you want to fly your own plane, take lessons, or what-have-you, you
can do so at Luchthaven Zestienhoven, Rotterdam. For information, contact the
KNVVL, Joz. Israelsplein 8, 2596 AS The Hague, tel. (070) 245457, after 12/89,
324 5457, or the airport at Zestienhoven, tel. (010) 374090. You can also take
flying lessons at Ben Air, Hilversum, tel. (01257) 1789 or 1201.

Golf: If this is your game, the Netherlands Golf Federation, Soestdijkers-
straatweg 172, 1213 XJ Hilversum, can give you a list of public and private golf
clubs in your area.

CHAPTER 19

THE YOUNGER SET

A child's life in Holland is something to be envied. Not that problems don't exist; it isn't easy to come to a new country, not know the language, enter a new school and have to make new friends. But there are so many compensations, once the newness has worn off, it's hard not to feel at home and become part of the scene. First off, most Dutch children do speak English so the communications barrier needn't be a serious one. Then, the international schools are top-drawer with a closely watched high level of teaching. Extracurricular sports, band/orchestra, art and music activities, and special school outings are there for the taking.

Sports are an important part of Dutch life. Soon, watching or playing soccer, hockey and international tennis, swimming, ice skating, and bike competitions replace those old favorites, baseball, football and basketball games. Distances are close and the whole country is peppered with great recreation parks, zoos, beaches, and museums both fun and educational.

Movies are usually in the original language; ditto TV. The air is great; the sense of security is good so you can get out on your own (at a reasonable age of course); transportation is plentiful and cheap; and the pace of life is relaxed allowing for old-time pleasures. Come and enjoy!

We'll start this chapter with baby-sitting, the needs of parents and children alike, followed by information on education, summer camps and schools, organizations of special interest, and entertainment in all its guises.

Baby-Sitting

The organizations listed below have a well-run baby-sitting service. Employees are screened thoroughly and are usually very well qualified—often they are college students. The agency also wants to make certain the prospective employer is a responsible person so their sitters come to no harm; therefore, you are usually requested to come into the bureau in person to register with the agency and pay your fees.

BABY-SITTING AGENCIES (OPPAS CENTRALEN):

AMSTERDAM:
   Kriterion Oppascentrale, tel. (020) 245848 between 5:30-7pm.
THE HAGUE:
   Kriterion Oppascentrale, Noordeinde 21, tel. (070) 469443,
   after 12/89, 346 9443, between 5 and 6:30pm, Sat., 3:30-6:30pm.
   ACCESS, In The Hague area: tel. (070) 558551, (after 12/89,
   355 8551), is a well-run organization to assist newcomers; they
   have a list of sitters.
ROTTERDAM:
   Oppascentrale Rotterdam, Statenweg 124a, tel. (010) 465 5115
   Oppascentrale Blijdorp, Statenweg 2a, tel. (010) 465 1136.

An effort is made to assign you a sitter who lives in your neighborhood to facilitate the problem of transportation. A sitter is responsible for his/her own transportation to your home but you are responsible to take them home at the end of the evening. In practical application, many sitters provide their own transportation home since they often come on their "bromfiets" or bicycle. If you keep them after midnight, or if you live in an isolated area, you must be prepared to return them home safely.

The minimum age of sitters may be either 18 or 21 years. Prices may vary according to the hours the sitter is required, and from agency to agency. They could range from Fl. 5.00 per hour between 7pm and midnight to double that amount for overnight stays.

Education

The Netherlands Ministry of Education (Ministerie van Onderwijs en Wetenschappen), POB 2500, 2700 LZ Zoetermeer, tel. (079) 531911 (ask for the Information Department), has information on all local schools, including foreign-language schools. They will send you pertinent booklets upon request.

In an effort to solve the high cost of international schools, the Ministry of Education can provide you with a complete list of government-subsidized schools with an English or International Stream education preparing students for the British IGCE, IGCSE, and/or the International Baccalaureate. These schools have become quite popular. One advantage is youngsters learn Dutch more easily and integrate better into the local communities. Some of these schools are:

THE HAGUE (South Holland):
   Het Nederlands Lyceum, Theo Mann-Bowmeesterlaan 75, 2597 GV The
   Hague, tel. (070) 244563, after 12/89, 324 4563.
HILVERSUM (Utrecht):
   Alberdingk Thijm College, Emmastraat 56 1213 AL Hilversum, tel. (035)
   214944 (Secondary school); Junior school, Violenstraat 3, 1214 CJ, tel.
   (035) 211703.

EINDHOVEN (North Brabant):
International Secondary School, Jerusalemstraat 1, 5625 PP Eindhoven, tel. (040) 413600 . . . infants and juniors, tel. (040) 519437.

GRONINGEN (Groningen):
Sint Maartenscollege, H.R. Holststraat 3, 9721 GS Groningen, tel. (050) 256113.

MAASTRICHT (Limburg):
Jeanne d'Arc College, Oude Molenweg 130, POB 4050, 6202 RB Maastricht, tel. (043) 612200.

OEGSTGEEST (South Holland):
Het Rijnlands Lyceum, Apollolaan 1, 2341 BA Oegstgeest, tel. (071) 155640.

ROTTERDAM: (South Holland):
Wolfert van Borselen School, Bentincklaan 280, 3039 KK Rotterdam, tel. (010) 466 0322 (Students 11-16 years).
De Blijberg, Gordelweg 216, 3039 GA Rotterdam, tel. (010) 466 9629 (Students 5-11 years).

CITY EDUCATION DEPARTMENTS: The City Education Departments can be helpful and will also have a complete list of local schools which they will send upon request:
AMSTERDAM: (020) 559 9111.
THE HAGUE: (070) 122507, after 12/89, 312 2507.
ROTTERDAM: (010) 417 3336 or 417 3195.

INTERNATIONAL SCHOOLS: The international schools are the best source for families who are only temporarily assigned to the Netherlands and want their children to continue in their "home" system. By writing directly to them, you can get their brochures giving ages covered, type of education provided, prices, time-schedules, transfer policies and more. In addition to the Randstad schools, there are several primary and secondary schools in other parts of the country, some of which offer boarding facilities. They are listed following the Randstad undergraduate schools.

PRE-SCHOOL: Nursery School, Crèches, Play Groups: Local international schools can offer help in locating nursery schools. The women's clubs are also a good source of information about support groups for parents with small children . . . some women's clubs have various play groups for small children. The ever-useful organization in The Hague, ACCESS, tel. (070) 558551, after 12/89, 355 8551, is also an excellent point of reference for lists of mother and young children's groups, even a support group of mothers of handicapped children.

KINDERGARTEN THROUGH HIGH SCHOOL: The title of the school tells the primary language of instruction and also the type of education offered. The larger schools are the American and British schools in The Hague and Amsterdam, and the Japanese school in Amsterdam. If English instruction is desired, it is recommended that all the schools located near one's residence should be

401

investigated in order to have the broad picture and make the right choice for your child.

AMSTERDAM:

The British Primary School, Van Eijkstraat 21, 1077 LG Amsterdam, tel. (020) 797840. Boys and girls from kindergarten through sixth grade.
Ecole Française d'Amsterdam, Uitenwaardenstraat 60a, 1079 CB, tel. (020) 446507. Elementary education.
International School in Amsterdam, A. J. Ernststraat 875, 1081 HL Amsterdam, tel. (020) 422227. Boys and girls from kindergarten through 12th grade.
The Japanese School in the Netherlands, Karel Klinkenbergstraat 137, 1061 AL Amsterdam, tel. (020) 118136. Boys and girls from 7-12 years.

THE HAGUE:

(All local numbers after (070) code to add a 3 prefix after 12/89.)
The American School of The Hague, Doornstraat 6, 2584 AM The Hague, tel. (070) 501051. Nursery through high school. Three schools: Elementary School, Rotterdamsestr. 66; Middle School, Haagsestraat 38; High School, Paulus Buysstraat 51. After August 1990: Rijksstraatweg 200 2241 BX Wassenaar. For info: U.S. Embassy, Community Liaison Officer, The Hague, tel. (070) 624911, after 12/89 362 4911.
The British School in the Netherlands, Tapijtweg 10, 2597 KH The Hague, tel. (070) 548911. Boys and girls from 3½ years to university. Locations: Kindergarten and Infant School, Granaathorst 2, tel. 477256; Junior School, Tapijtweg 10; Senior School, Jan van Hooflaan 3, 2252 BC Voorschoten, tel. (01717) 4492.
German School, Van Bleiswijkstraat 125, 1282 LB The Hague, tel. (070) 549454. Boys and girls 5 years to university.

ROTTERDAM:

The American International School of Rotterdam, Hillegondastraat 21, 3051 PA Rotterdam, tel. (010) 422 5351. Enrollment for ages 5-13 years.
Deutsche Schule von Rotterdam, Koraalstraat 17, 3051 VE Rotterdam, tel. (010) 418 8200. Boys and girls in the lower school only.

ENGLISH-LANGUAGE SCHOOLS OUTSIDE THE RANDSTAD:

ASSEN (Drenthe):
British School, PrincesIrenestraat 3, 9401 HH Assen, tel. (05920) 14684.
BERGEN (North Holland):
European School, POB 99, 1860 AB Bergen, tel. (02209) 2648.
BRUNSSUM (Limburg):
Afcentschool, Ferdinand Bolstraat 1, tel. (045) 278220. Primary and Secondary schools for children of NATO military personnel.
EINDHOVEN (North Brabant):
Regional International School, Humperdincklaan 4, 5654 PA Eindhoven,

tel. (040) 519437; International secondary school, tel. 733701.

OMMEN (Overijssel):
International School Eerde, 7731 PJ Ommen, "Kasteel Eerde," tel. (05291) 1452. Secondary school. Boarders and non-boarders.

UDEN (North Brabant):
American School, Aldetienestraat 21, 5402 ZC Uden, tel. (04132) 63667.

VILSTEREN (Overijssel):
International School, Vilsterseweg 16, 7734 PD Vilsteren, Ommen, tel. (05291) 8283. Primary school . . . boarders and non-boarders.

WERKHOVEN (Utrecht):
International School Beverweerd, Beverweerdseweg 60, 3985 RE Werkhoven, tel. (03437) 1341. Junior and Senior High School (grades 7-12) . . . International Baccalaureate.

MUSEUM ORIENTATION AND CREATIVE CLASSES: There are a number of extracurricular classes in the arts worth mentioning.

The Museum Orientation Programs offered by most major museums will appeal to some but not to others. There are programs geared for the youngest to serve primarily as a baby-sitting function while the parents tour the museum. For older children with a real interest in art, there are often imaginative and truly well-planned hands-on programs and guided tours related to the museum collection to spur the imagination of the young visitor. To find out what is available, check at the museum admission desk or telephone the Education Department of the museum of your choice.

The Volks-Universiteit (see Chapter 16 for addresses and telephone numbers) offers classes on Wednesdays when Dutch schools have the day off; therefore, their offerings may not be of use to children attending the international schools. However, if your child is free on Wednesdays, classes for children six to 12 years are given in drawing, painting, collages, puppet making, working with clay, fabric design, and so on. Instruction is in Dutch but most teachers speak English.

Dance, Drama and Music Groups are available for talented children (and adults too) who would like to take lessons in the creative arts. We personally know two American professional teachers who could be asked about private lessons: Mr. David Long, c/o the American International School in Rotterdam, tel. (010) 422 5351, is a superlative music teacher, and Mr. Albert Dolmans gives private art lessons to adults, but he might consider serious-minded older children . . . Mr. Dolmans takes a small group to paint in the south of France usually twice a year . . . a delightful experience, moderately priced, and fun for the art-oriented family; tel. (010) 422 9511. A discussion about music, dance and ballet schools is given in Chapter 16. Undoubtedly, there are teachers at other international schools who might be interested in giving private lessons or who would know qualified English-speaking persons in the community. For local Dutch teachers or groups, contact your VVV, City Information Bureau (Voorlichting), H.I.C. (help and information center) or one of the organizations listed below.

AMSTERDAM:
MAIC, J. van Brouwersplein 9, tel. (020) 799623.
Stichting Melkweg, Lijnbaangracht 234a, tel. (020) 241717.
Stichting voor Creativiteitsoutwikkeling, Leidsestraat 8,
tel. (020) 234144.

THE HAGUE:
Centrum voor Kunstzinnige Voorming, Juf. Idastraat 11, tel. (070) 924661,
after 12/89, 392 4661.

ROTTERDAM:
Kunst Stichting, Westersingel 20, tel. (010) 436 3111.

UNIVERSITY EDUCATION: An American, British or Japanese child will most likely decide to attend a university in his or her own country. The first place to seek advice about universities is your child's counselor, the school library, the American Women's Club Library and the following. In the beginning stages of your search, the special advisory service, Educational Futures, can be of help as well as the Counseling Office of the Fulbright-Hays Exchange Program between the Netherlands and the U.S.:
Educational Futures, contact Lora Schilder, Dorpstraat 49, 2900 LA Capella a/d IJssel, tel. (010) 458 8341, an advisory service for study in the U.S. offering testing evaluation and identification with the best possibilities for study and placement in universities and private schools.
Netherlands American Commission for Educational Exchange, (NACEE) Reguliersgracht 25, Amsterdam, tel. (020) 242435. This group administers the Fulbright-Hays Educational Exchange program between the Netherlands and the U.S. In addition to its basic program of exchange opportunities for research scholars, lecturers, teachers and graduate students, the Counseling Office gives information to Dutch students wanting to study in the U.S.
University Education in English: For the student who wants to remain in the Netherlands while pursuing an American education, there is one accredited American University; however, correspondence programs and part-time classes are given by the University of Maryland at Soesterberg Air Base (Utrecht), the British Open University in Brussels, and Erasmus University in Rotterdam . . . see Chapter 16 for details.
Webster University, Boommarkt 1, 2311 EA Leiden, tel. (071) 144341, is affiliated with Webster University of St. Louis, Missouri. It offers undergraduate courses as well as graduate classes leading to an MA and MBA.

STUDYING IN A DUTCH UNIVERSITY: This is not easy to arrange. Places for Dutch students are scarce and their needs would be considered first. However, if you wish to try, the consent of the Dutch Department of Education and Science is required for admission. Lectures are given in Dutch and a knowledge of Dutch is obligatory. Publications regarding study in Holland can be obtained from Dutch embassies and consulates abroad or from the Ministerie van Onderwijs en Wetenschappen, Voorlichting, tel. (079) 531911. Two organizations which supply information on studying in Holland are:

Foreign Student Service, (FSS) Oranje-Nassaulaan 5, 1075 AH Amsterdam, tel. (020) 715915. General information about studying in Holland including personal assistance in finding accommodations, giving insurance information, etc. They also organize a number of recreational activities and put out a monthy English-language bulletin.

Netherlands Universities Foundation for International Cooperation/Netherlands Center for International Academic Mobility, (NUFFIC-VISUM) POB 90734, 2509 LS The Hague, tel. (070) 510510, after 12/89, 351 0510, 1-4pm. This group supplies information and documentation on international higher education in Holland and the value of specific diplomas abroad. Its library has a large collection of university and college catalogues as well as periodicals in the field of higher education. Library is open Mon.-Fri., 9am-5pm.

Libraries

Many parents assume that because they are living in a foreign country, they must buy books for their children instead of belonging to a library. This is Holland and the normal rules don't always apply.

PUBLIC LIBRARIES: There are several good library sources with large children's sections in English, French and German in the main libraries in the Randstad, and even in other big city centers in the Netherlands. In addition, school libraries have many good "with it" books.

AMSTERDAM:
   The Amsterdam Central Library, Prinsengracht 587, tel. (020) 265065.

THE HAGUE:
   American Women's Club Library, Nieuwe Duinweg 25, tel. (070) 544171, after 12/89, 354 4171.
   Openbare Bibliotheek, Bilderstraat 1, tel. (070) 469235, after 12/89, 346 9235.

ROTTERDAM:
   Central Public Library (Centraal Gemeente Bibliotheek), Hoogstraat 110, tel. (010) 433 8911.
   Rotterdam Reading Room, Erasmus University, Burg. Oudlaan 50, tel. (010) 452 5511., ext. 3159.

RECORD-LENDING LIBRARIES: Separate from the book-lending outlets, but possibly of greater interest to little and big kids, are the record-lending libraries. A sample of their wares includes LP's, CD's, video tapes, children's records, pop, folk, jazz, blues music, etc. A more in-depth description is given in Chapter 16 as well as information about how one can become a member.

Cultural, Education and Work Exchange Programs

There are a number of organizations which provide helpful guidance to students sixteen years and older. They are a mixed bag offering a wide range of opportunities to study abroad or in Holland, take educational tours, participate in international exchange programs, get help in legal matters, and so on.

We have broken them down into four individual categories: Cultural Exchange, Legal Assistance, Travel, and Work Programs, but most of the organizations cover several programs.

CULTURAL EXCHANGE:

AFS (Inter-Cultural Exchanges), Keizersgracht 722, Amsterdam, tel. (020) 269481 or contact this group at 313 East 43rd Street, NY 10017, USA. They can arrange exchanges of Dutch and foreign students, 16-18 years, as well as language and further education courses for participants ... branches in 72 countries.

BIJK (Office for International Youth Contacts), POB 15344, 1001 MH Amsterdam, tel. (020) 264374. This government-subsidized organization gives information on student exchanges, holidays, and on practical and academic (as well as language training) programs.

Youth for Understanding, POB 25, 3645 ZT Vinkeveen, tel. (02972) 3120 ... in the U.S., 3501 Newark Street, N.W., Washington, DC 20016. They organize exchange programs for the 16-18 age group in host families between the USA and the rest of the world. Children may come to Holland for the summer, or for an entire semester. Students coming for one year are offered trips, general educational courses and a cultural program.

LEGAL ASSISTANCE:

JAC (Young People's Advisory Centre), exists all over the country. In Amsterdam, Amstel 30, 1017 AB, tel. (020) 24249; The Hague Social Unit, tel. (070) 655930, after 12/89, 365 5930; Rotterdam, 's Gravendijkwal 60, tel. (010) 436 0255; Utrecht, Oude Gracht 371, tel. (030) 313824. They give free and anonymous help in such fields as legal assistance, matters relating to foreigners, drugs, medical and pyschological problems.

EDUCATIONAL AND RECREATIONAL TRAVEL:

Holland Educational Program Foundation, Sweelinckplein 63, 2517 GR The Hague, tel. (070) 604838/469682, after 12/89, 360 4838/346 9682. Educational tours in Europe for individuals as well as groups ... study trips to industrial plants; arranges meetings with representatives of industry and commerce.

NBBS (Netherlands Foreign Students Relations Office), Head Office, Rapenburg 8, 2311 EV Leiden, tel. (071) 145757 ... branch offices also in Amsterdam, The Hague, Rotterdam, etc. This foundation organizes cheap trips—also educational ones—from and to Holland for everyone. Formerly only for students. Special facilities for group, school and faculty trips.

NJHC (Netherlands Youth Hostels Centre), Prof. Tulpstraat 4, 1018 GX Amsterdam, tel. (020) 551 3155. There are about 50 youth hostels in Holland available to local and international members. Courses, camps (sailing, gliding,

406

riding, etc.), conferences and school weeks are available. Addresses are available from the NJHC offices and the VVV.

YMCA-CJV (Young Men's Christian Association), POB 115, 3970 AC Driebergen-Rijssenburg, tel. (03438) 23233. This worldwide association organizes camping and travel for young people.

WORK PROGRAMS:

IJU (International Youth Exchange Foundation), Secretariat: Information Work Group, POB 501, 6800 AM Arnhem, tel. (085) 454649. This exchange program offers young people from 18 to 25 years the chance of gaining experience in work situations and practical work during a certain period abroad. They receive foreigners who come to spend a year in Holland and help in selecting young people leaving for a year.

RQ STICHTING (Foundation for International Student Work Camps), Willemstraat 7, 3511 RJ Utrecht, tel. (030) 317721. This group organizes three-week summer work programs in the Netherlands, Europe, Africa and Asia for the 18-30 age group.

Summer Camps and Schools

The summer camps and schools we list below are given as an aid in locating a good holiday experience among their peers for your child. They have been brought to our attention by reputable organizations or parents. Of course, we can offer no guarantees and each parent is strongly urged to thoroughly investigate personally the camps or schools before determining which—if any— your child will enjoy. Bear in mind that situations (and prices) vary from year to year.

Certain organizations are specifically designed to help you with brochures, lists, advice, etc.

Netherlands Children's Camping Association of the ANWB, Wassenaarseweg 230, The Hague, tel. (070) 141420, after 12/89, 314 1420. No camp can be listed until it has been in operation four years. Information on type of accommodations, reputation and suitability is given.

Netherlands Youth Hostels (NJHC), Prof. Tulpstraat 2-6, 1018 GX Amsterdam, tel. (020) 551 3155. The NJHC sponsors youth hostels all over the Netherlands and Europe. Minimum age, 14 years. At their hostels in Sneek, Grouw and Heeg (all in Friesland), and at Reeuwijk and De Kaag (South Holland), one-week yachting courses are given every summer. They also list

riding camps in various youth hostels and trips by covered wagon in Drenthe. **Social Advice Office (Maatschappelijk Advies en Inlichtingenbureau)** lists Dutch camps, international camps, youth hostels and youth congresses. In Rotterdam, tel. (010) 414 7780; in The Hague, (070) 631943, after 12/89, 363 1943; in Amsterdam, (020) 726644.

Scout Camps, for details write the Transatlantic Council, Boy Scouts of America, APO NY 09102; or Transatlantic Council, BSA, 6800 Mannheim 61, Autobahn Kaserne Bldg. 1002, Germany, tel. 09-49-(621) 471476; or the BSA District Office, Steenweg op Leuven 13, 1940 St. Steens-Woluwe, Belgium, tel. 09-32-(2) 720 9015.

VVV and Netherlands Board of Tourism both have brochures and information about youth camps, sailing and riding camps. Ask if they can find out which camp would be most suitable for non-Dutch speakers and if they have a "Kindervacantie" list which covers pony, camping and sailing camps. Addresses are given in Chapter 1.

SCOUT CAMPS: A number of regular Boy Scouts of America-operated scout camps can be found in Europe. For instance, there are Camp Freedom and Camp Dahn in Germany, Camp Kandersteg in Switzerland, Camp Tuscany in Italy, Camp Ole in Spain, with others in England, Greece and Turkey. For detailed information write the addresses given above.

RIDING CAMPS: Riding groups can be located all over the Netherlands and through them, you can obtain lists of suggested summer riding camps. Three organizations which we know about are:
Walter Eaton Children's Farm and Pony Center, Wuurde 112, Elst, Gelderland, tel. (08819) 1389. Open all year for children from 8-18. Affiliated with the Nederlandse Pony Club. They also offer windsurfing and canoeing.
IJslands Pony and Ruiter Centre, "Hesthagi," Family Ivaarde, Arnhemseweg 606, Beekbergen, tel. (05766) 1607.
Ponycentrum "De Burcht," Nederwoudseweg 25, Barneveld, Gelderland, tel. (03420) 13175.

SAILING SCHOOLS: For approved sailing camps and schools, contact the:
Nederlands Watersport Verbond, Van Eeghenstraat 94, Amsterdam, tel. (020) 664 2611. Other good contacts are the VVV offices for the provinces of South and North Holland, Friesland, Groningen, Flevoland and Zeeland, just to name the obvious places. Ask them which schools or camps they might recommend for English-speaking children. There are two schools in Rotterdam, one in Amsterdam and another in Enkhuizen which we list for "starters":
Kralingse Zeilschool, Kralingse Plaslaan 113, Rotterdam, tel. (010) 412 1098.
Royal Rowing and Sailing Club de Maas, Veerdam 1, Rotterdam, tel. (010) 413 8514.
Amstel Roeien Zeilvereniging, Hobbemakade 121, Amsterdam, tel. (020) 719105.
International Laser Sailing School, Jachthaven, Enkhuizen (North Holland), tel. (02280) 2778.

INTERNATIONAL SUMMER CAMPS: A newcomer is often at a loss about where to start looking for tried and true summer camps. The ones we list below have been in operation over many years and have excellent reputations. Start by writing the camp to find out about what they offer and their dates ... usually, they offer two-week programs but it would be possible to stay the entire summer if desired, although that might be a bit too long for younger children. Read their material carefully and get references if you can.

International Summer Camp Montana, La Moubra, CH-3962, Montana, Switzerland, tel. (027) 72384 or 72897.

International Summer Camp, at Pully and Vennes-Lausanne, Switzerland. Write, 7 Dynamostrasse, 5400 Baden, Switzerland, tel. (056) 23260.

Le Chateau des Enfants (a program of the American School in Switzerland). Write, Le Chateau des Enfants, the American School in Switzerland, 6926 Montagnola-Lugano, Switzerland.

International Ranger Camps, located at Camp Viking, Asserbo, Denmark, and Camp Lake Geneva, Switzerland. Write International Ranger Camps, 1854 Leysin, Switzerland.

Fun and Games

There are a lot of fun and games in Holland. Just think of the really outstanding amusement parks, safari parks, zoos and beaches which are discussed in Section I under the various cities ... you can also find them listed in the Index. Major zoos can be found in Amersfoort (U), Amsterdam (NH), Arnhem (G), Emmen (D) and Rotterdam (ZH). Beaches in the Randstad get an entire chapter to themselves ... Chapter 14. Thought has been given to the entertainment of the

409

littlest ones to teenagers and beyond. For instance, new arrivals might not be aware of the many special farms which exist in most towns called "Kinderboerderijen." This is the Dutch way to introduce children to all the common animals which would not be found in a zoo. Usually children can touch the animals right in the farm area, see the baby chicks at close range, feed the goats or whatever with approved fodder, and so on. Check with the VVV for the one nearest your home.

Scouting is international and needs no introduction. There are flourishing groups for boys and girls in Holland, including groups primarily with international members. If your child speaks Dutch, there are any number of Dutch groups to choose from. For information about the English-language groups, call the foreign schools or inquire at the embassies or consulates-general of the U.S. or the U.K. In addition, Scouting Nederland, Larikslaan 5, 3830 AE Leusden, tel. (033) 944814 can supply all information.

Once settled in a group, the scout must be outfitted. Scout shops all carry camping goods, English shoes, English books on scouting, song books, cook books, uniforms, shoes, knives, whistles, compasses, pennants and so forth. Anything of interest to the "open air" child from 7 years up (and including his parents) is available from the following shops:

AMSTERDAM: Comeniusstraat 509, tel. (020) 177164; Tues.-Fri., 9am-6pm, Sat., 9am-5pm, closed Mondays.

THE HAGUE: Medlerstraat 63, tel. (070) 934863, after 12/89, 393 4863; Mon., 1-5:30pm; Tues.-Fri., 8:30am-5:30pm, Sat., 9am-1pm.

ROTTERDAM: Heemraadssingel 129, tel. (010) 477 5911, Mon., 1-5:30pm and 7-9pm, Tues.-Fri., 10am-5:30pm, Sat., 9am-noon.

The American Baseball Foundation, (ABF), POB 133, Wassenaar, tel. (01751) 19067, weekends only. This private organization is composed of sports-minded businessmen and educators who have joined to provide sports activities primarily for the American Community in The Hague, but they welcome all nationalities. Sign-up for activities takes place in late August and early February. The programs are:

SEPT.-NOV.: Soccer for boys and girls, 5-15 years. Softball for girls and adults. Flag football for boys and girls, 8-14 years.

NOV.-JAN.: Bowling for boys and girls, 9-14 years.

JAN.-MARCH: Basketball for boys and girls, 9-14 years.

MARCH-JUNE: Baseball for boys 5-16 years. Softball for girls and adults. Soccer for boys and girls, 5-6 years.

Every child who registers gets a chance to play and will always be able to participate in any ABF program.

Entertainment and the Arts

Every child is going to be caught up in the movie and TV scene. Luckily for English-speaking children, Holland is a small country where it is uneconomic to dub the films in Dutch. As a consequence, movies made in foreign countries are shown with the original sound track. Usually the movie title will indicate the language of the film but when it is translated into Dutch, that can be a bit confusing.

Movies are listed in the Wednesday evening or Thursday morning editions of your daily Dutch newspaper. General films are given first followed by the special section of "Night Showings" (only for adults over 18 years), and then the "Kindermatinees," children's movies shown on Wednesday, Saturday, Sunday and holiday afternoons.

TV listings are given daily in the newspapers—after a little practice, one will be surprised to find out how much one can actually understand even when the newspaper is in Dutch. There is no Sunday edition, so both Saturday and Sunday TV programs are given in the Saturday newspaper.

Some theaters run a children's movie until about 7pm and then put on an adult film for the late show. Children of all ages are permitted in any evening movie which has an A.L. listing . . . see below.

KNT (Kinderen Niet Toegestaan) is the term used to describe "Parental Guidance." The Dutch abide very strictly to their KNT system which allows no latitude even if the parent accompanies the child and assumes responsibility. A rule is a rule in Holland and if the age limit is 16 years and your child is 14 or 15 years, he will not be allowed to enter the movie theater. Some indications are:

      A.L.: OK for all ages
      12: 12 years or over for admittance
      16: 16 years or over for admittance
      N: Dutch-language film
      E: English-language film
      F: French-language film
      D: German-language film

A.L. means the film is in Dutch and all ages are permitted; 12 E means children must be 12 years or older and the film is in English—got it?

For information about advance purchase of tickets, see Chapter 17.

THE CULTURAL SCENE: Before describing theater, symphony and ballet productions of interest to children, we'd like to explain about the Youth Cultural Passport, which gives young people (15 to 26 years) who are residents of the Netherlands reduced rates for concerts, the theater, films, museums, journals and magazines.

Youth Cultural Passport (Passport JEUGD). The organization is sponsored by the Art for Youth Foundation. Membership is nominal and includes a subscription to the local monthly program sheet. Application should be made at the Stichting Musische Vorming, Calandstraat 5-9, Rotterdam, tel. 436 1366, or from the VVV. In The Hague, ask at the Central Station VVV, and in Amsterdam from the VVV at Stationsplein 10 or from the AUB (Cultural Information Service) on the Leidseplein. Bring one passport photo for use on your membership card. They may also require proof of date of birth.

The Symphony and the Ballet welcome well-behaved children to any of their performances. Children from eight years on are often taken to the symphony or to the ballet in Holland. No one considers them a nuisance for the very reason that they are not. Here is a chance to introduce your child to the professional theater without it being prohibitive cost-wise. If you have a budding young ballerina on your hands, take her to see the Scapino Ballet—or if you have a determined drummer banging away on your third floor, a trip to hear the symphony orchestra of your choice might encourage a little more control. With the exception of opera and plays which are given in French, Italian, German or Dutch, there is a wide choice of evening performances which would appeal to children. The "Little Theater" productions in English are another introduction to the world of imagination. Teenagers, of course, will develop their own interests and artistic tastes and find many summer programs such as jazz festivals to enjoy.

Theaters that do attract the younger set are the puppet theaters ... again, usually, the language is universal; however, it never hurts to ask for an English synopsis. Ask the VVV about open-air puppet shows held in the summertime.

AMSTERDAM:

Diridas Poppentheater, Hobbemakade 68, tel. (020) 721588, Tram 16.

Kindertheater Circus Elleboog, Passeerdersgracht 32, tel. (020) 269370, Tram 17.

The Vondel Park Open-Air Theatre in Amsterdam is famous, attracting mostly young adults; however, on Wednesday afternoons at 3pm, there's a children's theater performance.

THE HAGUE:

(After 12/89, add 3 prefix to local number after code (070).)

Poppentheater Guido Van Deth and the Puppetry Museum, Nassau Dillenburgstraat 8, tel. (070) 280208, Bus 18. Conducted tours can be arranged upon request. For details about the theater and its history, see Chapter 17.

Poppentheater Frank Kooman, Frankenstraat 66, tel. (070) 559305, Buses 4, 65 and 89. See Chapter 17 for details about Mr. Kooman and the theater.

ROTTERDAM:

De Lantaren Theater, Gouvernestraat 133, tel. (010) 436 4998, has puppet shows in Dutch on Sunday afternoons at 2:30pm.

SUMMER STUDENT FESTIVALS take place all over Holland. Musicians, actors, or artists who might like to join some group can make inquiry through the Cultural Raad Zuid Holland, tel. (070) 245535, after 12/89, 324 5535. Your local VVV can also tell you where and when these events are scheduled.

CHAPTER 20

YEARLY SPECIAL EVENTS

The Dutch and foreign events discussed in this chapter are worth noting. They and other small local events are mentioned throughout the text, oftentimes described in detail. The Calendar was devised as a quick aid to planning a holiday whether one is visiting or living in the Netherlands. Some of these events occur yearly and are listed, but many are "spur of the moment" or a celebration only for that year commemorating a famous person or a national event. These latter are usually not listed. In order that you may look up the event in the appropriate chapters, the abbreviation for the province is given after the name of the town . . . each province is a chapter. Also, most towns are listed in the Table of Contents. We recommend — as always — you check with the NBT or the VVV when your plans are beginning to jell and you are keen on fitting in some special event into your tour schedule. The provincial abbreviations are:

ZH – South Holland	F – Flevoland	D – Drenthe
NH – North Holland	NB – North Brabant	O – Overijssel
U – Utrecht	Fr – Friesland	L – Limburg
G – Gelderland	Gr – Groningen	Z – Zeeland

Following the Calendar are explanations of Dutch special events and also a listing of foreign events that take place yearly organized by members of foreign organizations in the Netherlands.

The Calendar

DATE	LOCATION		EVENT
		JANUARY	
mid-January	Lisse	(ZH)	Midwinter flora, CBN Halls.
mid-January	Leiden	(ZH)	Leiden Jazz Week.
mid-January	Rotterdam	(ZH)	Six-day indoor cycling event, Ahoy Hall; World Indoor Soccer Championships.
end January/ February	Rotterdam	(ZH)	Rotterdam Film Festival — various cinemas.

DATE	LOCATION		EVENT
FEBRUARY			
beg. February	Apeldoorn	(G)	International Midwinter Marathon
beg. February	Utrecht	(U)	International Indoor Motorcross cycle races; Horse Inspection, Veemarkthallen.
February	All over		Carnival celebrations with parades. Especially Breda, Maastricht, 's- Hertogenbosch.
February/ March	Rotterdam	(ZH)	ABN World Tennis Tournament, Ahoy Hall.
mid-February	Bovenkarspel	(NH)	West Frisian Flora, flower show and home exhibit.
mid-February	The Hague	(ZH)	European Indoor Athletic Championships, Houtrust.
end February/ March	Amsterdam	(NH)	HISWA, international boat show, RAI.
MARCH			
March/ April	Leiden	(ZH)	Easter Cattle Show, Groennoordhallen.
mid-March	Amsterdam	(NH)	Blues Festival, Meervaart; International Chess Tournament.
mid-March	Maastricht	(L)	Pictura Fine Art and Antique Fair.
mid-March/ April	All over		Performances of Bach's St. Matthew's Passion. Also check Amsterdam, Haarlem, Maastricht, Den Bosch, Gouda, Leiden.
March	Breda	(NB)	International Art and Antiques Fair, Turfschip.
end March– May	Lisse	(ZH)	**Keukenhof** National Open-air flower exhibition. Bulbfields in bloom.
end March/ April	The Hague	(ZH)	Scheveningen City-Pier-City Run, Lange Voorhout (Half Marathon).
end March/ April	Zandvoort	(NH)	International Easter Motor Races.
end March– May	Vogelenzang	(ZH)	Tulip Show flowers in gardens and hothouses at Frans Roozen Nursery.
APRIL			
beg. April	Amsterdam	(NH)	Head of the River, rowing races, river Amstel.
April– September	Rotterdam	(ZH)	City tours in old tram plus tour of docks, Central Station.
April–October	Amsterdam	(NH)	Electrical Museum Tramline Amsterdam to Amstelveen every 20 mins. Haarlemmermeer Station.

DATE	LOCATION		EVENT
1 April	Brielle	(ZH)	Folkloric celebration of the trouncing of the Spanish by the "water beggars".
April	Gouda	(ZH)	Art Fair.
mid-April/ May	Amsterdam	(NH)	World Press Photo Exhibit, Nieuwe Kerk.
mid-April	Rotterdam	(ZH)	Rotterdam International Marathon.
mid-April– September	Alkmaar	(NH)	Cheese market with bearers in historic guild uniforms, craft demonstrations Fridays 10–12 noon.
mid-April	Haarlem to Noordwijk	(NH) (ZH)	**Flower Parade** in bulb-growing districts. Route: Haarlem-Bennebroek-Hillegom-Lisse-Noordwijk. Decorated floats on view at Hobaho Halls, Lisse the day before the parade or in Noordwijk the day after the parade.
April/ May	Tiel	(G)	Blossom Tour Route (fruit trees).
30 April	All over Holland		**Celebration** of the **Queen's birthday** and national holiday. Fairs (Kermis), organ-grinders, flags, and decorations, especially in The Hague.

MAY			
4 May	All over		**Dodenherdenking** — Remembrance Day of WW II dead.
May	Noordoostpolder	(Fr)	Bulb Route, Emmeloord.
May– September	Pieterburen area	(Fr)	Guided mud-flat walking to Schiermonnikoog and Ameland, Engelsmanplaat.
May– September	The Hague	(ZH)	Antique and bric-a-brac market, Thursdays 9 am–9 pm, Lange Voorhout.
May– September	Amsterdam	(NH)	Nieuwmarkt Antique market, Sundays 10 am–4 pm.
May–mid June	The Hague	(ZH)	Japanese Garden in full bloom, Clingendael Park, 9 am–8 pm.
2nd Saturday in May	Buren	(G)	Annual picturesque market in medieval walled village.
2nd Saturday in May	All over		**National Windmill Day** (windmills in action, many can be visited); and National Cycling Day.
May–June	Texel	(NH)	Migration of birds to breeding grounds. Guided Tours.
May–June	Tilburg	(NB)	Sheep-shearing festival.

415

DATE	LOCATION		EVENT
early May	Breda	(NB)	International Traditional Jazz Festival; street parades and open-air concerts.
beg. May	Amsterdam	(NH)	International Marathon, Dam.
mid-May	Breda	(NB)	**Breda Paard**, International Military Horse Show.
mid-May	Zandvoort	(NH)	International Easter Motor Races.
mid-May	Landgraaf	(L)	"Pinkpop" international open-air pop festival.
mid-May	Den Bosch	(NB)	**Jazz in Duke Town.**
mid-May	Leeuwarden	(Fr)	Frisian **Elfsteden** — Walking Tour along eleven towns.
end May	Amsterdam	(NH)	"Kunstrai," modern art exhibition in RAI and various galleries.
end May	Scheveningen	(ZH)	**Vlaggetjesdag**, festooned herring fleet opens the season, etc. Also Urk (F) and IJmuiden (NH).
end May	Harlingen	(Fr)	Harlingen-Terschelling Sailing Race.
end May	Delfzijl	(Gr)	**Neptune Festival**, fair and international deep sea sailing races.
end May	Veere	(Z)	International sailing regatta and folkloric costume show.
end May	Margraten	(L)	**Memorial Day Service**, last weekend in May.

JUNE

DATE	LOCATION		EVENT
June–August	Amsterdam	(NH)	Open-air theater, concerts etc., Vondelpark.
June	Major cities		**Holland Festival**, cultural and musical events.
June–August	Friesland		Most towns hold tilting competitions, old Frisian costumes (Bolsward) and "**Kaatsen**" handball competitions (Harlingen).
beg. June	The Hague	(ZH)	Equestrian Event, Lange Voorhout.
beg. June	Scheveningen	(ZH)	Air Show, stunt flying and demonstrations.
beg. June	Ede	(G)	Sheep shearing contest, old crafts, Ginkelse Heide.
beg. June	Apeldoorn	(G)	Jazz in the woods, international traditional and modern jazz.
beg. June	Texel	(NH)	"Ronde om Texel", catamaran race from De Koog.
mid June	Haarlem	(NH)	Barrel Organ festival.
mid June	Rotterdam	(ZH)	Poetry International, international poetry festival, Doelen.

DATE	LOCATION		EVENT
mid June	Groningen	(G)	**Martini Regatta**, international rowing competition, Eemskanaal.
mid June	Serroskerke	(Z)	Zeeland's Horse Day, Manege de Eendracht.
mid June	Scheveningen	(ZH)	International Kite Festival.
late June	Warffum	(Fr)	Op Roakeldais, costumed international folkdance festival.
late June	Amsterdam	(NH)	Dutch Open Championship, international rowing, Bosbaan.
late June	Assen	(D)	International Dutch Motorcycling TT Grand Prix.
late June	Wassenaar	(ZH)	International Trotting, Low Countries Grand Prix.
end June	Egmond aan Zee	(NH)	Jazz Festival.
end June	Hoorn	(NH)	Haartje Hoorn Market, folkdance groups and old crafts. Wednesdays 9 am–5 pm.
end June	Schagen	(Fr)	West Frisian Folk Market, procession of old Dutch carts, carriages, costumes, crafts. Thursdays 9 am–2 pm.
end June	The Hague	(ZH)	International Trotting Grand Prix, Duindigt.
end June	Wassenaar	(ZH)	Park Pop, International pop festival.
end June/July	Den Helder	(NH)	National Fleet Day in the new harbor area.
end June/July	Scheveningen	(ZH)	World Championship Catamaran Races.
June–August	Gouda	(ZH)	Old crafts, cheese and antique market, Thursdays 9 am–1:30 pm.
June–September	The Hague	(ZH)	**International Rose Show**, Westbroek Park. 20,000 roses of more than 350 species.

JULY

DATE	LOCATION		EVENT
all July	Rotterdam	(ZH)	Jeugdland (Youthland), indoor recreation facilities during school vacations, Ahoy Hall.
all July	Aalten	(G)	Folkloric festivities and Klompendag, demonstrations of wooden-shoe making (only on last Thursday).
beg. July	Amsterdam	(NH)	International Theater Festival, and Ballet Festival in Muziektheater.
beg. July	Zwolle	(O)	Art and Antique Market and International "Schnitger" Organ Recitals, St. Michael's Church.

DATE	LOCATION		EVENT
beg. July	Denekamp	(O)	Sheepshearers' traditional festival: market, handicrafts, pancakes.
July or August	Frisian Lakes Check VVV's	(Fr)	Regatta with Skutsjesilen. "Skutjes" are unique boats formerly used in commerce, with black or brown sails, a flat bottomed wide body with large wooden lee boards.
July/August	Friesland	(Fr.)	Fierljeppen pole vaulting across canals, ring riding. etc.
July/August	Bergen	(NH)	Open–air Art Fair, Fridays, 4 10 pm.
July/August	Hoorn	(NH)	Traditional Craft Market, Wednesdays 9 am–5 pm.
July/August	Barneveld	(G)	Balloon Fiesta. Also old Veluwse Market with folkdancing etc. Thursdays.
July/August	Kinderdijk	(ZH)	Windmill Days, mills operating — one open for viewing. Boat trips Saturdays 1:30–5:30 pm.
July/August	Purmerend	(NH)	Cheese Market, Thursdays 11 am–1 pm.
July/ August	Gouda	(ZH)	Cheese and crafts market, Wednesdays 9 am–2 pm.
mid-July/ August	Medemblik	(NH)	Romantic Market, products brought by barges; every Saturday.
mid-July	Warmond	(ZH)	International Sailing Week at De Kaag island.
mid-July	Middelburg	(Z)	Folklore Days, tilting at the ring, traditional costumes.
mid-July	Wassenaar	(ZH)	Horse Day, trotting races, Duindigt.
mid-July	Leiden	(ZH)	"**Leiden Lakenfeesten**", open-air folk festival.
mid-July	Emmen, Hoogeveen and Assen	(D)	Drenthe Four Day Tourist Cycling Event, 40, 60, 80 or 100 km; sportpark Houtlaan, Assen.
mid-July	Apeldoorn	(G)	International Four Day Walking Event.
mid-July	The Hague	(ZH)	**North Sea Jazz Festival:** Fridays– Saturdays 6 pm–4 am, Sundays 2 pm–1 am, Congress Center.
mid-July	Brunssum	(L)	Folklore Parade, performances by folk dance groups from all over the world.
mid-July	Nijmegen	(G)	International Four Day Walk. 30, 40 and 50 kms per day.
mid-July	Loosdrecht	(U)	Holland Week, International sailing competitions, and Loosdrecht Jazz Festival, Oud-Loosdrecht.

DATE	LOCATION		EVENT
mid-July	Hilversum	(U)	International Dutch Tennis Championships, Het Melkhuisje.
mid-July	Spakenburg	(U)	**Spakenburg Days**, local folk festival with crafts market etc.
end July	Hilversum	(U)	KLM Golf Open Championship.
end July	Chaam	(NB)	Chaam Eight, professional cycling circuit.
end July/ August	Enkhuizen	(NH)	Zuiderzee sailing event, Thursdays. Barrel Organ competitions on Organ Day.
end July	Joure	(Fr)	Re-creation of traditional Frisian farmer's wedding, horse-drawn carts, bareback-riding etc.
end July	Scheveningen	(ZH)	Swinging Scheveningen, street parades, jazz and Dixieland concerts.
end July	Voorschoten	(ZH)	Traditional horse market.
July–September	Vogelenzang	(ZH)	Summer Flower Show in gardens and greenhouses, Frans Roozen nursery.

			AUGUST
early August	Stellendam	(ZH)	Delta Flora, summer flower show, at the Visafslag.
early August	Rijnsburg	(ZH)	Flower Parade (Rijnsburg-Leiden-Noordwijk); Summer Flower Show in Auction Hall.
early August	Sneek	(Fr)	**Sneek Week**, international sailing competitions.
August	Amsterdam	(NH)	International Football Tournament, Olympic Stadium.
August	Rotterdam	(ZH)	International Football Tournament, Feyenoord Stadium. **CHIO Horse Show**, Kralingsebos.
August	Biddinghuizen	(F)	Flevofestival of Gospel Music, Flevohof.
August	Yerseke	(Z)	Mussel Festival, with Fair etc. Also at Breskens and Philippine (Z).
August	IJsselmeer	(NH)	Flevo Race and "Westwal Botterfestival" Races of traditional Dutch fishing boats.
mid-August	Scheveningen	(ZH)	International Firework Festival.
mid-August	Katwijk	(ZH)	Fishery Days and Flower Parade.
mid-August	Leersum	(U)	Central Holland Flower Parade.
mid-August	Zaanse Schans	(NH)	Annual Festival, traditional market, crafts etc.
mid-August	Vlissingen	(Z)	Weeklong street festival.

419

DATE	LOCATION		EVENT
mid-August	Heeze	(NB)	Brabant Days, cultural/historical events with parade on last Sunday.
mid-August	Delft	(ZH)	Jazz Festival and street parade.
mid-August	Winsum	(Fr)	"Fierljeppen" pole vaulting across canals; competitions.
mid-August	Ede	(G)	Heather Parade and Festival with various activities.
mid-August	Doorn	(U)	Castle tour with antique horse-drawn carriages.
end August	Breda	(NB)	National Tattoo, military and civic bands on parade, Breda Castle. "Orangerie" fair.
end August	Zeist	(U)	Antique Automobile Parade.
end August	Raalte	(O)	"Stoppelhaene", harvest festival.
end August	Valkenswaard	(NB)	International Motor Rally Cross Championships.
end August	Amsterdam	(NH)	Uit Markt, Museumplein, Amstel mime, cultural shows.
end August	Maastricht	(L)	"Preuvenemint"; Burgundian culinary festival, Vrijthof.
end August	Giethoorn	(O)	**Illuminated gondola trips**. (Also Oldeboorn (Fr.).)
end August	Harlingen	(Fr)	Fishery Day Celebrations: various events, costumes, old ships.
end August	Den Oever	(NH)	Fishery Day and Flower Festival.
end August	Amersfoort	(U)	"Keistadfeesten", various events, fair and tattoo.
end August	Rhoon	(ZH)	Sound and Light, Rhoon Castle, Saturdays 9:30 pm.
SEPTEMBER			
September	Amsterdam	(NH)	Prinsengracht concert. Piano concerts aboard barges. Prinsengracht.
September	Amsterdam	(NH)	Pictura, art and antique fair, RAI.
September	Amsterdam	(NH)	Gaudeamus Music Week, various theaters.
September	Rotterdam	(ZH)	Jazz Festival, various locations.
1st Saturday	Aalsmeer to Amsterdam	(NH)	**Annual Floral Parade**. Starts 9:30 am Aalsmeer Auction Hall, proceeds to Olympic Stadium, Amsterdam, 1 pm and on to the Dam where the Queen inspects the numerous floats, decorated cars, bands with drum majorettes, etc. Floats may be viewed in the Auction Hall the evening before the parade.

DATE	LOCATION		EVENT
beg. September	Gouda	(ZH)	Randstad Jazz Festival with street parade.
beg. September	Lelystad	(F)	Air Show.
beg. September	Zundert	(NB)	Flower Parade, market and street theater.
beg. September	Kinderdijk	(ZH)	Illumination of windmill complex with boat trip to view mills, 9–10:30 pm.
mid-September	Valkenswaard	(NB)	Flower Parade.
mid-September	Tiel	(G)	"Oogst en Fruitcorso", fruit and harvest parade, with exhibit in auction halls.
mid-September	Valkenburg	(ZH)	Oldest horse market in the Netherlands.
mid-September	All over		**Monument Day**, most monuments and museums are open free of charge.
mid-September	The Hague	(ZH)	**Prinsjesdag**. State Opening of Parliament by HM the Queen who rides in resplendent horse-drawn golden coach from her Palace to the Binnenhof, where she delivers the Throne Speech to members of parliament and foreign diplomats in the Hall of Knights.
mid-September	Middelburg	(Z)	City festival and fair.
mid-September	Ede	(G)	Airborne landing in commemoration of WW II parachute landings, Ginkelse Heide.
mid-September	Nieuw Niedorp	(NH)	Flower Mosaic Days.
mid-September	Enkhuizen	(NH)	"Enkhuizen Klipperrace", sailing competition of clippers.
mid-September	Breskens	(Z)	"Breskensweek", international sailing races of round and flat-bottomed boats.
mid-September	Oosterbeek	(G)	Tattoo and demonstration by paratroopers commemorating the 1944 airborne landings.
mid-September	Rotterdam	(ZH)	Jazz Festival. Also Open Harbor Day, Europort.
end September	Utrecht	(U)	Horse and cattle shows.
end September	Joure	(Fr)	Folklore Market.
end September	Zaanse Schans	(NH)	Eight active mills open with explanations from millers.
end September	Breda	(NB)	Four-in-Hand horse contest.
end September	Groningen	(Gr)	"Gronings Ontzet", commemoration of the relief of Groningen in 1672. Street festivities.

DATE	LOCATION		EVENT
			OCTOBER
Early October	Leiden	(ZH)	**Leidens Ontzet**. Liberation of Leiden celebrated with historic parade.
Early October	Laren	(NH)	Autumn flower and art show, Singer Museum.
Early October	St. Oedenrode	(NB)	Brabant Wooden Shoe Fair.
Early October	Alkmaar	(NH)	Alkmaar's Ontzet.
Early October	Gouda	(ZH)	Antique Fair.
mid-October	Delft	(ZH)	**Art and Antique Fair**, Prinsenhof.
mid-October	Oene	(G)	"Koefeest", horse and cattle market.
mid-October	Haarlem	(NH)	Antique Fair.
mid-October	Tilburg	(NB)	Wine Festival.
mid-October	Maastricht	(L)	Jazz Festival.
mid-October	Zandvoort	(NH)	International Windsurfing Event.
mid-October	Zuidlaren	(D)	Biggest Horse Market in Western Europe, Brink.
mid-October	Scheveningen	(ZH)	International Beach Motorcycle Races.
			NOVEMBER
Early November	Amsterdam	(NH)	**Jumping Amsterdam**, International Horse Show, RAI.
Early November	Zeist	(U)	"St. Hubertus Slipjacht" — hunting with horses. Also Den Treek, (U) and Someren (NB).
mid-November	Maastricht	(L)	International Motorcycle rally events.
mid-November	The Hague	(ZH)	International Figure skating competition.
mid-November	All over		**St. Nicholas Celebrations**. His official arrival.
last Thursday	Leiden	(ZH)	**Commemorative Thanksgiving Day** Service, St. Pieters Church.
			DECEMBER
December 2– January 6	Ootmarsum, Denekamp, etc.	(O)	Midwinter Horn Blowing — folkloric tradition announcing birth of Christ.
December 5	All over		St. Nicholas celebrations.
mid-December	Gouda	(ZH)	**Gouda by Candlelight**. Town hall and market candle-lit for ceremonial lighting of Christmas tree.
mid-December	Major cities		Tree-lighting ceremonies in Amsterdam, Rotterdam and The Hague on simpler scale.
mid-December	Voorburg	(ZH)	10,000 candles illuminate the old center of town.
mid-December	Groningen	(Gr)	European Youth Chess Tournament.
end December	Tilburg	(NB)	Antique Fair.
end December	Amsterdam	(NH)	Kerstflora — Christmas bulb show.
end December	Rotterdam	(ZH)	Christmas market and circus; Holiday on Ice; held at Ahoy Hall.

422

Yearly Dutch Events: An Explanation

January seems to be the month meant for resting from the series of holiday festivities which took place in December. Fireworks can be heard popping all over town on New Year's Eve and New Year's Day. In the larger cities, there are often City Hall receptions given by the Mayors for their constituents. January sixth is the normal date for taking down the Christmas trees and kids love collecting these for a common bonfire (supervised by adults, naturally). Also, mostly in the provinces of North Brabant and Limburg (small towns), you may be surprised to answer your doorbell on January 6th and find children dressed as the Three Kings serenading you. They go from door to door with their song and receive cookies and candy in exchange for their visit.

■ The **Queen's Birthday** is always celebrated on April 30th so this is a date you can count on if you are interested in participating in some very colorful events.

Most towns have a fair (kermis). The decorations in The Hague are especially colorful with great orange balls (for the House of Orange, remember?), hanging from the trees all along the Lange Vijverberg and Lange Voorhout. In all towns and cities of the Netherlands you will see the Dutch flag flying from private homes, office buildings, town halls, churches and windmills which are also bedecked with colorful bunting. Many of the commercial store windows are specially decorated as well. Birthdays of the other members of the Royal family are not national holidays but flags fly for each Royal birthday and the organ grinders will be out in full force. A special law allows the organ grinders to play whenever there is a Royal family birthday and happily, the members of the House of Orange are numerous so the organ grinders will not go into obscurity in the near future.

Folkloric markets and events are scheduled throughout the year but especially in June, July and August, the high tourist season. Every city and village turns itself inside out to attract visitors. A brand-new experience for visitors are these events based on folk tales giving an insight into Dutch history and humor. Some extraordinary happenings of true Dutch origin include "Op Roakeldais," a dance festival in Groningen; "kaatsen", handball competitions in Friesland; "Skotsploegh" performances in Frisian costumes; sheep-shearing in Loenen, Gelderland; Fierljeppen — pole-vaulting across canals in Friesland; "Skutsjes" boat races also in Friesland. "Skutsjes" are unique boats formerly used in commerce. The sails are black or brown and the body of the boat is flat and wide, and on each side, there are large wooden paddles or lee boards, which resemble butterfly wings, to insure stability). Each province has its own folkloric

423

event. Zeeland has a number of traditional games such as tilting for the ring on bare horseback, a very old and unusual tradition ... June–August in Middelburg and other villages; "Krulbollen", a type of bowling with wooden "balls" ... held in various towns; as well as archery competitions.

Also of interest are dates when **special interest events** are held such as garden shows, sports competitions, jazz festivals, art shows, boat regattas, walking tours throughout the country, and so on. One interesting experience is "mud-flat" walking to the Waddenzee Islands of Schiermonnikoog and Ameland from the mainland, see "Friesland". This is only possible when the sea level is low and takes place about the same time as the nesting season for the myriads of birds which come here to lay their eggs, approximately April 15–August 15. A very special experience for bird lovers. Not for the faint-hearted or unfit!

■ **"Prinsjesdag"** is another big event to schedule if possible. It takes place the third Tuesday in September in The Hague. The Queen goes from her palace to Parliament in her resplendent golden coach drawn by a team of Royal horses. She is accompanied by her family, some riding with her and others following in perhaps less splendid — but still very impressive — coaches. Foreign diplomats accredited to the **Netherlands have** reserved seats within Parliament itself, but the average townsperson must be content with coming early and standing by the side of the road. Sometimes, the waiting can seem long so this is not recommended for young children.

■ **"Leiden's Ontzet"** takes place on October 3. This festival and historical parade commemorate the day the Spaniards were routed from Leiden by opening the dikes and flooding the area. In their haste to retreat, the Spaniards left behind a pot of "stew" (hutspot) on the fire. The story goes the Dutch were strengthened by eating the stew, herrings and bread, and this fare is served

during this colorful event. Similar celebrations take place at Groningen and Brielle.

■ **Sinterklaas or St, Nicholas:** Christmas-time starts early in the Netherlands. December 5th is when Sinterklaas comes to town. St. Nicholas' Calendar Day, December 6th, is observed in most Roman Catholic countries, but only in the Low Countries — and especially in the Netherlands — is the eve of his festival celebrated nationwide by young and old, rich and poor, Christian and Jew alike, and without any religious overtones. Although Sinterklaas is always presented in the vestments of the bishop he once was, his status as a Saint, duly canonized by the Church, has played no part in the Dutch mind for centuries. Rather, he is a kind of benevolent Superman, whose feast on the evening of December 5th is the merriest and most beguiling event of the Dutch year.

St. Nicholas is based on historical fact. He did exist — he was born sometime in 271 A.D. and lived to December 6, 342 or 343. His fourth century tomb in the town of Myra, Asia Minor, has only recently been discovered by archeologists. That St. Nicholas' influence was especially strong in the Netherlands is primarily due to his role as patron saint of merchants and sailors. Once established, he soon became known as the benefactor of children. In the 14th century, choir boys of St. Nicholas Churches were given some money and the day off on December 6th. Somewhat later, the pupils of convent schools would be rewarded or punished by a teacher—a monk disguised as the venerable bishop, just as he is still presented today with his long white beard, his red mantle and mitre, and his gold crosier. Gradually, Sinterklaas became a household word. In due time, Sinterklaas came accompanied by his Moorish servant Piet, a grinning fellow with a birch rod, whose sack of goodies, when emptied, is large enough to carry away any naughty children.

While the American Santa Claus lives at the North Pole, the Dutch Sinterklaas is well known to live in Spain—how else would he have a Moorish servant? Sinterklaas arrives by boat, of course. So, in Rotterdam, for example, on a predetermined school holiday afternoon (usually the Wednesday afternoon before December 5th) Sinterklaas will arrive at Leeuwehaven and dispense his goodies on his way to his main rendezvous at the Stadhuisplein.

Now for the night of December 5th itself. The stores are jammed until closing with people frantically trying to get those last-minute "surprises". The streets are clogged with workers and shoppers who are hurrying home—many people leave the office early so that everyone is on the streets at the same time just to accentuate the congestion. Expensive gifts are definitely not necessary. It is the manner in which the gift is presented that counts. Small dime store articles, chosen with care and meaning are just what is needed, although nice presents are also sometimes given.

The really difficult part is writing the poem which must accompany each gift. Whether long or short, is entirely up to the rhyming talents of the giver, but it cannot be be left out. The poem should deal with the good points or the weaknesses of the recipient; just plain kidding is a must.

Another special aspect to this gift-giving is in the preparation of the packages, Here the imagination should be given free rein. Pretty gift wrappings are definitely out. The gifts should be carefully camouflaged and made to look like

425

something else. This requires careful planning and preparation. A big executive is not immune and can often be seen preparing a concoction of jello at the office within which he may have hidden a little package for his wife. Or gifts could be concealed in potatoes dressed as dolls; in a pudding made of colored starch; in a glove filled with wet sand, etc. Sometimes, there is a note in the pudding which says it's not here, look under the table, or some such. The greater the imagination, the greater the fun. Each surprise is addressed to the recipient and signed by Sinterklaas.

Sometimes both Sinterklaas and Piet arrive in traditional costume to deliver a few pertinent words to the friends and family who are assembled. He will say that young Susy has been too frivolous perhaps, or that John has been playing football instead of studying, or he will remark if one of the children has done something especially well during the year. If they have been very very bad, of course, they might be put in Piet's bag and taken off.

If Sinterklaas and Piet cannot appear in person, it is likely that the doorbell will ring loudly and Mother will answer, opening just wide enough to allow a black hand to throw in a lot of candies into the room for which the children make a dive. Now the fun begins. One present should be unwrapped at a time, the whole group watching while the embarrassed recipient reads his or her poem aloud.

Yearly Foreign Community Events

As indicated earlier, the foreign community sponsors a number of special events during the year. There are also events organized by the Dutch Government and

the international schools. Listed in chronological order are those of primary interest.

JANUARY: Model United Nations. This annual event is promoted by the international schools in The Hague area. Held in the Congresgebouw, more than 125 teachers and 1,200 students, from 20 countries take part from destinations as far flung as California, Caracas, Cairo, Amman and Stavanger. The opening and closing sessions are the most exciting times to attend. For information, call the American School of The Hague, tel. (070) 501051, after 12/89, 350 1051.

MARCH: The American Baseball Foundation sponsors an annual Sports Evening when team awards are presented. The evening is devoted to football and baseball films, celebrity speakers and sports personalities as guests. Contact ABF, POB 133, 2240 AC Wassenaar, tel. (0751) 19067, weekends only.

Easter Party — The Commonwealth Club sponsors an Easter Party which is usually held at the Mission to Seamen in Rotterdam. Easter eggs and games are the order of the day. Contact the Club Secretary at POB 85923, The Hague.

MAY: Memorial Day Ceremonies — Americans in particular might like to know about the special Memorial Day Ceremonies which are held at Margraten Cemetery, outside Maastricht, the last weekend in May. This is the largest American cemetery in the Netherlands and a beautiful place to visit any time of year. The Memorial Day Ceremonies are so colorful it is worth a special trip. The Queen's personal representative attends, as well as the American Ambassador, the American Consul General, leading military men, local mayors and other prominent citizens, Lots of ordinary folks come each year — some American, some Dutch, some other nationalities — and everyone is welcome. Dutch children from towns in the area participate by bringing their own bunches of flowers to put on the graves. There is usually a special salute by jet airplanes, speeches, wreaths are laid, and the grounds may be visited. It's a good three-hour drive from Rotterdam which makes this a long day trip. Valkenburg is a charming town (see Chapter 12) very near the cemetery which offers all sorts of hotel accommodations.

JUNE: A picnic is sponsored by the American Baseball Foundation in The Hague, usually on the closest weekend to the end of the school summer semester. It's an "All American-Day" with baseball games, children's games, plenty to eat, and so forth. For information about the exact date, tickets and venue, check with ABF, see March above, or the American Women's Club, tel. (070) 544171 (354 4171 after 12/89).

LATE OCTOBER–NOVEMBER: Many foreign churches and communities have annual charity bazaars at this time of the year. It's a great way to pick up special food items and little gifts for Christmas-giving. For information, check with individual churches or consulates.

NOVEMBER: Guy Fawkes Day (November 5th) Sponsored by the Commonwealth Club in The Hague. For details check with the British Embassy in The Hague, Tel (070) 645 800 or the Commonwealth Club. There is a film show followed by a big bonfire and fireworks display. The kids love the cartoon films. Held in Duinrell in Wassenaar.

Thanksgiving Day (Fourth Thursday in November) — A special Thanksgiving service is held in the historic St. Pieterskerk in Leiden. The American Community Council in The Hague organizes the event. For specifies about program, etc., telephone AWC The Hague, (070) 544171, after 12/89, 354 4171.

Annual United Service for Peace — Held at the Scots Church in Rotterdam at Schiedamsevest 119, tel. (010) 412 4779, 7:30 pm on a Sunday in November. Participants in the past have included representatives of the Dutch Gereformeerde Kerk, Eglise Wallonne, Church of England, The Finnish Church, The Russion Orthodox Church, the Deutsche Evangelische Gemeinde, the Roman Catholic Church, the Norwegian Church, St. Andrew's Church (Brussels), and the Nederlands Hervormde Kerk. The service is in all languages represented.

QUICK REFERENCE

The Royal Dutch Touring Club (AAA, AA and RAC equivalent)
Emergency Road Sevice "AA", tel. 06-0888 (for members; non-members can join "on the spot")
Head Office: Wassenaarseweg 220, The Hague, tel. (070) 314 7147
Amsterdam: Museumplein 5, tel. (020) 730844
Eindhoven: Elzentlaan 139, tel. (040) 118155
Groningen: Trompsingel 21, tel. (050) 184345
Maastricht: Koningsplein 60, tel. (043) 620666
Rotterdam: Westblaak 210, tel. (010) 414 0000
Utrecht: Van Vollenhovenlaan 277, tel. (030) 910333

CAR RENTALS:

Avis Rent a Car, Hogehilweg 7, 1100 DA Amsterdam, tel. (020) 564 1611; Schiphol Airport, (020) 604 1301; USA reservations, (800) 331-2112.
Budget Rent a Car, Kruisweg 823, 2132 NG Hoofddorp, tel. (02503) 17030; Schiphol Airport, (020) 604 1349; USA reservations, (800) 527-0700.
Diks Car Rental, Gen. Vetterstraat 51-55, 1059 BT Amsterdam, tel. (020) 178505; USA reservations, 800-223-5555.
EuropCar BV, Wibautstraat 224A, 1097 DN Amsterdam, tel. (020) 682111; Schiphol Airport, (020) 604 1566; USA reservations, (800) 328-4567; Canada reservations, (514) 878-2771.
Hertz, Saturnusstraat 25, 2132 HB Hoofddorp, tel. (02503) 34334; Schiphol Airport, (020) 601 5416; USA reservations, (800) 654 3131; Canada, (800) 263-0600.
InterRent, Kruisweg 607, 2132 NA Hoofddorp, tel. (02503) 34433; Schiphol Airport tel. (020) 601 5439; USA and Canada reservations, tel. (800) 421-6868.

CASINOS:

Amsterdam: Hilton Hotel, Apollolaan 138, tel. 789789.
Groningen: Kattendiep 150, tel. (050) 123400.
Rotterdam: Hilton Hotel, Weena 10, tel. (010) 414 7799.
Scheveningen (The Hague): Gevers Deynootplein 1, tel. (070) 543677 or 512621, after 12/89, 354 3677, 351 2621.
Valkenburg: Odapark, tel. (04406) 14600.
Zandvoort: Badhuisplein 7, tel. (02507) 18044.

CHURCHES:

The following churches offer services for foreigners in the Randstand. English-language services are indicated by an asterisk (*).
AMSTERDAM:
*****Baptist Chuch of Amsterdam,** Keizersgracht 676 or Kerkstraat 204, tel. (020) 423762.
*****Christ Church** (Church of England), Groenburgwal 42, tel. 248877; in Haarlem (the 1st and 3rd Sundays).

*Church of Jesus Christ of Latter Day Saints, Zaaiersweg 17, tel. 944990.

*Cross-Roads Christian Community (ecumenical), de Couserstraat 3, Buitenveldert, tel. 477333.

*De Goede Herder (Dutch Roman Catholic Church with English-language Mass, 9:30 am Sundays), 420 van Boshuizenstraat, tel. 420843.

Deutsche Evangelische Gemeinde, Viottastraat 44, tel. 732522.

*English Refomed Church (Church of Scotland), Begijnhof 48, tel. 249665.

*First Church of Christ Scientist, R. Wagnerstraat 32, tel. 662 7438.

*Friends Center (Quakers . . . services in Dutch but they translate as they go along), Vossiusstraat 20, tel. 794238.

Liberal Catholic Church, Deurloostraat 17, tel. 664 0854.

Liberal Jewish Community, Jacob Soetendorpstraat, tel. 423562.

Portuguese Synagogue, Mr. Visserplein 3, tel. 245451.

*St. John and St. Ursula, Begijnhof 30, tel. 221918.

Synagogues: Jac. Obrechtpl. Lekstraat, van Boechhorststraat 26, Buitenveldert, tel. 460046.

THE HAGUE:

NOTE: After 12/89 add a 3 prefix to all local numbers after code (070).

*American Protestant Church, Esther de Boer van Rijklaan 20, tel. (070) 244490.

Church of Christ of Latter Day Saints, Leersumstraat 11. tel. 237879.

Church of God of Prophecy, Hofcampweg 3, Wassenaar, tel. (071) 317113.

*Church of St. John and St. Philip (Anglican and Episcopal), Ary van de Spuiweg 1, tel. 555359, also services at the British School, Voorschoten, tel. (01717) 2762.

*English-speaking Roman Catholic Parish of The Hague, Ruychrocklaan 126, tel. 280816.

First Church of Christ Scientist, Andries Bickerweg 1, tel. 636652.

Liberal Jewish Congregation, Jan Evertstraat 7, tel. 656893.

Orthodox Jewish Community, Bezuidenhoutseweg 361, tel. 473201.

*Trinity Baptist Church, Bloemcamplaan 54, Wassenaar, tel. (01751) 16642.

LEIDEN:

Christian Evangelical Church, Holiday Inn, tel. (01717) 3860.

Unitarian Universalist Fellowship (every fourth Sunday), International House, tel. (03404) 57559.

St. Peter's Church (Dutch Reformed), Pieterkerkchoorsteeg No. 17-A. American Thanksgiving Day ecumenical services in English organized by the American Community Council . . . otherwise, services in Dutch.

ROTTERDAM:

Christian Science Society Rotterdam, Schiedamsevest 190, tel. (010) 421 5718

*Church of English-speaking Catholics, Robert Frimstraat 35, tel. 414 4577.

*Church of Scotland (Presbyterian), Schiedamsevest 119, tel. 412 4779.

Dansk Somanskirke, Coolhaven 1, tel. 476 4016
Den Norske Sjomanskirke Rotterdam, Drooglever Fortuynplein 4, tel. 436 5123
Deutsche Evangelische Gemeinde Rotterdam, 's Gravendijkwal 65, tel. 477 2070
Eglise Wallone de Rotterdam, Pierre Baleystraat 1, tel. 413 9847.
Le Foyer Français et Francophone (Catholique), Heemraadsingel 109,
    tel. 476 6689.
Greek Orthodox Church, Van Vollenhovenstraat 18, tel 436 1798.
Orthodox Synagogue, A.B.N., Davidsplein 4, tel. 466 9765
Russian Orthodox Church, Persijnstraat 16, tel. 477 1272
*St. Mary's Church (Church of England), Pieter de Hoochweg 133, tel. 476 4043
Suomen Merimieskirkko, 's Gravendijkwal 64, tel. 436 6164
Svenska Sjomanskyrkan, Parklaan 5, tel. 436 5461

CLUBS AND ORGANIZATIONS:
The following is a partial list of clubs of interest to foreign residents. For a list of
Women's Clubs in the Randstad, see Chapter 16; for Youth Clubs and Organi-
zations, see Chapter 17.
Alliance Française, Keizersgracht 708, Amsterdam tel. (020) 430 3716.
Alliance Française, Westersingel 14, Rotterdam, tel. (010) 436 0421.
American Association of the Netherlands (Business club), POB 9592, 25 AN
    The Hague.
American Baseball Foundation, (Athletic facilities and field in Wassenaar), POB
    133, Wassenaar, tel. (01751) 19067, weekends only.
American Chamber of Commerce, Carnegieplein 5, The Hague,
    tel. (070) 659808.
American Community Council, Doornstraat 6, 2584 AM, The Hague.
Amsterdam Business Club (Dutch/American), c/o U.S. Consulate General,
    tel. (020) 790321.
British Businessmen's Association, Raamweg 45, 2596 HN The Hague,
    tel. (070) 468888
British Club, Hildebrandlaan 23, 3768 GB Amersfoort (U).
British Club, St, Aagtenstraat 5, 2312 CA Leiden, (ZH).
British and English-Speaking Club, Hoofdstraat 91a, 2235 CD Valkenburg (L)
British NL Chamber of Commerce, Bezuidenhoutseweg 181, 2594 AH,
    The Hague, tel. (070) 478881, after 12/89, 347 8881.
British Society (for men and women), POB 7429, 1007 JK Amsterdam
Commercial Anglo-Dutch Society, Mr. H. van Engelen, tel. (020) 254414 . . .
    open to those interested in British-Dutch trade.
Commonwealth Club (for men and women), write POB 85923, 2508 CP
    The Hague; Branch in Rotterdam.
De Halve Maen, for info, telephone the Cultural Affairs Officer, U.S. Embassy.
    This organization is composed of alumni from universities in the U.S.:
    activities emphasize Dutch and American customs. Members include Dutch
    who have taught or studied in the U.S. and Americans living in Holland who
    are engaged in research, education or related fields.
English Speaking Club, Zegge 94, 1422 RC Uithoorn (NH)
International Round Table, Weesperzijde 65a, 1091 EN Amsterdam,

tel. (020) 665 7844
International Women's Club of Breda, Brederol 63, 4873 GH Etten Leur (NB)
International Women's Club of Eindhoven, POB 2390, 5600 CJ Eindhoven or tel. (040) 835166.
Irish Club of the Netherlands, Kethelweg 100, 3135 GN Vlaardingen, tel. (010) 435582
Irish-Dutch Friendly Society, Nassau Zuylensteinstraat 9, 2596 CA The Hague
Joint Committee Netherlands-American "Friendship Institutes", de Weide 32, 3993 DW Houten
Lions Club Administration, Multiple District 110 Dorpsstraat 11, POB 148, 3940 AC Doorn (U); also branches in The Hague and Rotterdam.
Nederlands-Amerika Institute Limburg, Proost de Beaufortstraat 8, 6231 EB Meersen (L)
Netherlands-England Society, contact Mrs. R. v.d. Wilden, Huis ter Hoornkade 19, 2282 JW Rijswijk, tel. (070) 984403, after 12/89, 398 4403. Branches throughout the Netherlands.
Rotary International Administration, Amstel 266, 1917 AM Amsterdam, tel. (020) 232405
Rotterdam Business Club, Mr. J. B. Kalkman, ETC, POB 4700, 3000 HK Rotterdam, tel. (010) 431 6380
Rotterdam Japan Club, c/o Japanese Consulate-General, tel. (010) 430 3716
St. Andrews Society of the Netherlands, Mrs. J. Mccoll, tel. (071) 173599, evenings.
Stichting Nederland-Verenigde Staten, Scheveningseweg 11, 2517 KS The Hague.
Women's International Network (business and professional women), POB 15692, 1001 ND Amsterdam.

EDUCATION:

Ministry of Education (Ministerie van Onderwijs en Wetenschappen), tel. (079) 531991.
The Foreign Student Service, de Blijberg, Gordelweg 216, 3039 GA Rotterdam, tel. (010) 466 9629.
City Education Departments: (They have a complete list of Government-subsidized schools approved for preparing students for the British CSE and CSSE as well as the International Baccalaureat examinations.)
Amsterdam: (020) 552 9111
The Hague: (070) 122507, after 12/89, 312 2507.
Rotterdam: (010) 417 3336 or 417 3195.

EMERGENCY TELEPHONE NUMBERS:
POLICE:
Amsterdam (020) 559 9111
The Hague (070) 104911, after 12/89, 310 4911
Rotterdam (010) 414 1414
FIRE:
Amsterdam (020) 212121

The Hague (070) 222 333, after 12/89, 322 2333
Rotterdam (010) 429 2929
MEDICAL EMERGENCIES: (see Chapter 16)
   Amsterdam (020) 555 5555
   Eindhoven 0611 (toll free)
   Groningen 0611 (toll free)
   The Hague (070) 222111, after 12/89. 322 2111
   Maastricht 0611 (toll free)
   Rotterdam (010) 433 3300.
   Utrecht 0611 (toll free)
MENTAL AND SOCIAL DISTRESS:
   Amsterdam (020) 161666
   The Hague (070) 454 500; also Access, (070) 558 551
   Rotterdam (010) 436 2244
PET EMERGENCIES:
   For lost pets, call Police or numbers in Chapter 16 under "Pets".
ANIMAL AMBULANCES:
   Amsterdam (020) 262121 and 261058, between 9am-3pm.
   The Hague (070) 521238 or 674279, add 3 prefix after 12/89.
   Rotterdam (010) 415 5666.
ROAD SERVICE
   ANWB 06-0888, Toll free.

HOLIDAYS:

Public Holidays (most shops are closed except on Good Friday morning): New Year's Day, Good Friday, Easter Sunday and Monday, Queen's Birthday (April 30), Ascension Day, Whit Sunday and Monday, Christmas Day, Boxing Day.
Remembrance Days (not a public holiday; most shops open): May 4—WW II Remembrance Day, May 5—Liberation Day.

LIBRARIES:

AMSTERDAM:
Amsterdam Centrale Bibliotheek, tel. (020) 265065
Universiteit Bibliotheek, tel. (020) 525 9111
British Council Library, tel. (020) 223644

THE HAGUE:
Openbare Bibliotheek, tel. (070) 469235; after 12/89, 346 9235
American Women's Club Library, tel. (070) 544171; after 12/89, 354 4171

ROTTERDAM:
Centraal Gemeente Bibliotheek, tel. (010) 433 8911
Rotterdam Reading Room, Erasmus University, tel. (010) 452 5511, ext. 3159

NBT (NETHERLANDS BOARD OF TOURISM):

Head Office: Nederlands Bureau voor Toerisme, Vlietweg 15, 2266 KA Leidschendam, tel. (070) 705705, after 12/89, 370 5705.

433

Offices Abroad: Great Britain, Ireland, Canada and United States offices are listed in Chapter 1. In addition, there are:
Australia: 5 Elisabeth St., Suite 302, Sydney N.S.W. 2000, tel. 276921.
Austria: Kärtnerstrasse 12/Kupferschmiedgasse 2, A-1010 Vienna 1, tel. 222 523525.
Belgium/Luxembourg: Ravensteinstraat 68, 1000 Brussels, tel. 02-512 4409.
France: 31/33 Ave. des Champs Elysees, 75008 Paris, tel. 1-4225 4125.
Italy: Via Paolo da Cannobio 33, 20122 Milan, tel. 280 56664.
Japan: No. 10 Mori Building, 1-18-1 Toranomon, Minato-ku, Tokyo, tel. 03-508 8015
Scandinavia and Finland: Styrmansgatan 8, 11454 Stockholm, tel. 09 46 860 8368.
Spain: Gran Via 55-4G, 28013 Madrid, tel. 341 241 5828.
Switzerland: Talstrasse 70, 8001 Zurich, tel. 01-211 9482.
West Germany: Laurenzplatz 1-3, 500 Cologne-1, tel. 0221-236 262.

NRC (NETHERLANDS NATIONAL RESERVATIONS CENTRE):

P.O. Box 404, Vlietweg 15, 2260 AK Leidschendam, tel. (070) 202500, after 12/89, 320 2500, FAX 202611. Hotel and other reservations handled by the NRC can be made locally from the above address or through the VVV offices listed at the end of this section. Visitors from overseas can make reservations for hotels, etc., through the overseas NBT offices listed above and in Chapter 1.

NETHERLANDS RAILWAYS (Spoorwegen or NS):

Toll free telephone: 06-899 1121.
  Information and Reservations:
Amsterdam: (020) 202266
Arnhem: (085) 451457
Breda: (076) 14386
Eindhoven: (040) 448940
Groningen: (050) 122755
Haarlem: (023) 323551
The Hague: (070) 471681, after 12/89, 347 1681
Hengelo: (074) 425667
Maastricht: (043) 214563
Nijmegen: (080) 222430
Rotterdam: (010) 411 7100
Schiphol: (020) 141959
Utrecht: (030) 332551

NEWSPAPERS:

International Herald Tribune, subscriptions, tel. (023) 322347
USA TODAY International, subscriptions, tel. 09.44.1. 831 2266

RANDSTAD

The Randstad is the area of greatest density of population formed by the cities of Amsterdam, Haarlem, The Hague, Rotterdam, Dordrecht and Utrecht. The
434

term is used often for quick identification. In this book, it relates especially to the land area encompassed by Amsterdam, The Hague and Rotterdam.

RELOCATION SERVICE:
Access, tel. (070) 558551; after 12/89 355 8551, The Hague
Crossroads Network, tel. (020) 477333, Amsterdam
Education for Relocation, tel. (04990) 77193, Eindhoven
EXPAT Advice, tel. (01751) 10143, Wassenaar
Formula Two, (020) 664 2759, Amsterdam
Relocation Services, tel. (01717) 4643 or (01751) 77330, Voorschoten/Wassenaar

SPORTS AND RECREATION OFFICES (Dienst voor Sport en Recreatie):
Amsterdam: (020) 511 0321
The Hague: (070) 808454; after 12/89, 380 8454
Rotterdam: (010) 417 2886

TELEPHONE ASSISTANCE:
Information: Dial 008 (for numbers within the Netherlands)
Information: Dial 06 0418 (for numbers outside the Netherlands)
Telegram: Dial 009
Customer Service: Dial 004

VVV and VVV-i OFFICES IN HOLLAND

VVV: Verenigingen voor Vreemdelingenverkeer—Local tourist assistance offices. All VVV-i offices are open at least from Monday to Friday, 9am-5pm and on Saturdays from 10am-noon. During the holiday season, they are often open in the evening and in some locations on Sunday afternoons also. They have much information on touring, will make hotel, theater, and tour reservations.

	Address	Telephone	Province
A			
Alkmaar	Waagplein 3	(072) 114284	North Holland
Almelo	De Werf 1	(05490) 18765	Overijssel
Almere	Spoordreef 20	(03240) 34600	Flevoland
Amersfoort	Stationsplein 28	(033) 635151	Utrécht
Amstelveen	Plein 1960, No. 2	(020) 452020	North Holland
Amsterdam	Stationsplein 10	(020) 266444	North Holland
Apeldoorn	Stationsplein 6	(055) 788421	Gelderland
Arnhem	Stationsplein 45	(085) 420330	Gelderland
Assen	Brink 42	(05920) 14324	Drenthe
B			
Bergen	Plein 1	(02208) 13100/12124	North Holland
Berlen op Zoom	Hoogstraat 2	(01640) 66000	North Brabant
Breda	Willemstraat 17-19	(076) 222444	North Brabant
Bussum	Wilhelminaplantsoen 6	(02159) 30264	North Holland

435

	Address	Telephone	Province
C-D			
Delft	Markt 85	(015) 126100	South Holland
Den Haag	(see "Hague")		
Den Helder	Julianaplein 30	(02230) 25544	North Holland
Deventer	Brink 55	(05700) 16200	Overijssel
Doetinchem	Walmolen-Ijsselkade	(08340) 23355	Gelderland
Dordrecht	Stationsweg 1	(078) 132800	South Holland
Drachten	Moleneind ZZ 71	(05120) 17771	Friesland
E			
Ede	Achterdoelen 36	(08380) 14444	Gelderland
Egmond a/zee	Voorstraat 82a	(02206) 2371/1362	North Holland
Eindhoven	Stationsplein 17	(040) 449231	North Brabant
Elburg	Juffersstraat 9	(05250) 1520	Gelderland
Emmen	Raadhuisplein 2	(05910) 13000	Drenthe
Enschede	Markt 31	(053) 323200	Overijssel
Epe	Past. Somstraat 6	(05780) 12696	Gelderland
G			
Gouda	Markt 27	(01820) 13666/13298	South Holland
Groningen	Naberpassage 3	(050) 139700	Groningen
H			
Haarlem	Stationsplein 1	(023) 319059	North Holland
Hague, The	Kon. Julianaplein 30	(070) 546200, after 12/89, 354 6200; Also see "Scheveningen" below	
Harderwijk	Havendam, 88	(03410) 12929	Gelderland
Heerlen	Stationsplein 4	(045) 716200	Limburg
Helmond	Markt 211	(04920) 43155	North Brabant
Hengelo	Enschedesestraat 45	(074) 919161	Overijssel
's-Hertogen-bosch	Markt 77	(073) 123071	North Brabant
Hilversum	Emmastraat 2	(035) 11651	North Holland
Hoek van Holland	Hoekse Brink 23	(01747) 2446/2456	South Holland
Hoogeveen	Raadhuisplein 3	(05280) 63003	Drenthe
I-J-K			
IJmuiden	Marktplein 42	(02550) 15611	North Holland
Katwijk aan Zee	Vuurbaakplein 11	(01718) 75444	South Holland
L			
Leeuwarden	Stationsplein 1	(058) 132224	Friesland
Leiden	Stationsplein 210	(071) 146846	South Holland
Lelystad	Agorahof 2	(03200) 43444	Flevoland
Lisse	Grachtweg 53a	(02521) 14262/15263	South Holland
Lochem-Laren-Barchum	Markt 24 (Lochem)	(05730) 1898	Gelderland
M			
Maastricht	Kleine Staat 1	(043) 252121	Limburg
Meppel	Kleine Oever	(05220) 52888	Drenthe

Address	Telephone	Province
N		
Noordwijk De Grent 8	(01719) 19321	South Holland
Nunspeet Stationsplein 1	(03412) 53041/2	Gelderland
Nijmegen St. Jorisstraat 72	(080) 225440	Gelderland
Nijverdal Grotestraat 61	(05486) 12729	Overijssel
O		
Oisterwijk De Lind 57	(04242) 82345/84973	North Brabant
Oosterhout Arendshof 42	(01620) 54459	North Brabant
Oss Burgwall 11	(04120) 33604	North Brabant
P-Q-R		
Roermond Markt 24	(04750) 33205	Limburg
Roosendaal Dr. Brabersstraat 9	(01650) 54400	North Brabant
Rotterdam Coolsingel 67	(010) 413 6000	South Holland
S		
Scheveningen Gevers Deynootweg 126	(070) 546200	South Holland
Schoonhoven Stadhuisstraat 1	(01823) 5009	South Holland
Sittard Wilhelminastraat 16	(04490) 24144	Limburg
T		
Texel Groeneplaats 9	(02220) 4741	North Holland
Tiel Stationsstraat 37	(03440) 16441	Gelderland
Tilburg Spoorlaan 416a	(013) 351135	North Brabant
U-V		
Utrecht Vredenburg 90	(030) 314132	Utrecht
Valkenburg Th. Dorrenplein 5	(04406) 13364	Limburg
Venlo Koninginneplein 2	(077) 543800	Limburg
Vlissingen Nieuwendijk 15	(01184) 12345	Zeeland
W		
Weert "Waag" Langpoort 1	(04950) 36800	Limburg
Winterswijk Torenstraat 3	(05430) 12302	Gelderland
X-Y-Z		
Zaandam Gedempte Gracht 76	(075) 162221/351747	North Holland
Zandvoort Schoolplein 1	(02507) 17947	North Holland
Zeist Steynlaan 19 A-B	(03404) 19164/18277	Utrecht
Zutphen Wijnhuis, Groenmarkt 40	(05750) 19355	Gelderland
Zwolle Grote Kerkplein 14	(038) 213900	Overijssel

VVV PROVINCIAL OFFICES: If you are interested in a specific province or region, you can apply in writing to one of the following VVV addresses:

Drenthe: P.O. Box 95, 9400 AB Assen
Flevoland: P.O. Box 548, 8200 AM Lelystad
Friesland: Stationsplein 1, 8911 AC Leeuwarden
Gelderland: P.O. Box 988, 6800 AZ Arnhem
Groningen: Naber passage 3, 9712 JV Groningen

Limburg: P.O. Box 811, 6300 AV Valkenburg
North Brabant: P.O. Box 90, 5260 AB Vught
North Holland: Rokin 9-15, 1012 KK Amsterdam
Overijssel: P.O. Box 500, 7600 AM Almelo
South Holland: Markt 85, 2611 GS Delft
Utrecht: Maliebaan 79, 3581 CG Utrecht
Zeeland: P.O. Box 123, 4330 AC Middelburg

RECOMMENDED READING

INTRODUCTION TO THE NETHERLANDS:

At Home in Holland, published by the American Women's Club of The Hague . . . a detailed book giving many answers to the problems of running a household.
Education for Relocation, by Elly Friedman, Graafschappad 38, 5691 LX Son (G).
Health Care in Holland, published by the American Netherlands Club of Rotterdam, POB 34025, 3005 GA Rotterdam, 1989.
Holland at Hand, by Lonnie Rodgers and Elly Friedman at Education for Relocation.
Inside Information, Gelderman-Curtis and Niks-Corkum . . . a complete orientation guide, POB 82058, 2508 EB The Hague, 1988.

BACKGROUND BOOKS:

The City of Erasmus, by L.W. Schmidt, published by "de Bezige Bij", Amsterdam . . . a look at Rotterdam before and just after WW II. (Look in a library).
The Dutch Puzzle, by Duke de Baena, L.J.C. Boucher, 1968. (Look in a library).
The Dutch Seaborne Empire: 1600-1800, by C.R. Boxer, published by Penguin, 1965.
The Dutch Today, by Frank E. Huggett, published by the Ministry of Foreign Affairs, 1974.
The Dutch Connection, by Frank E. Huggett, Ministry of Foreign Affairs, 1982.
Embarrassment of Riches, by S. Schama, U. of Calif. Press or Fontana, UK, 1988 . . . an interpretation of Dutch culture in the Golden Age.
History of the Low Countries, Pieter Geyl, Macmillan, London 1964. (Look in a library).
Holland, by A. Hopkins, published by Faber and Faber, UK, 1987.
The Kingdom of the Netherlands, published by the Ministry of Foreign Affairs . . . there are 25 booklets dealing with all aspects of the Netherlands: The Royal Family, Government, Business, Police, the Ministries, Development, etc.
The Netherlands: European Rendezvous, by Walter Imber/Bas den Oudsten, published by H.J.W. Becht, Amsterdam . . . a table-top picture book with English text.
Netherlands in Brief, published by the Ministry of Foreign Affairs every 3 years.
Netherlands in Perspective, by W. Shetter, published by Martinus Nijhoff.
Of Dikes and Windmills, by Pieter Spier, Doubleday & Co., Inc., New York.
A Short History of The Hague, Christine B. Weightman, published by Schie-Pers, Schiedam, 1974.

A Short History of The Netherlands, by Ivo Schoffer, published by Allert de Lange, B.V., Amsterdam, 1973 revised edition.

William and Mary, by Henri and Barbara van der Zee, published by Macmillan, London.

ART BOOKS:

Dutch Drawings from the Collection of Dr. C. Hofstede de Groot, J. Bolten, publishers A. Oosthoek, Utrecht . . . a table-top book with English text.

Naieve Schilders Zien Ons Land, published by Ploegsma, Amsterdam. A charming collection of works by Dutch Naif Painters . . . in color, text in Dutch.

Holland by Dutch Artists, by H.E. Gelder, Heinman publishers, 1959.

COOK BOOKS:

Cookin' in de Keuken, published by the American Women's Club, Amsterdam . . . American cooking with a Dutch accent.

Dutch Treats, compiled by Carol van-Klompenburg, Penfield Press, USA . . . recipes, folklore, proverbs.

Dutch Cooking, by A.M. Halverhout, published by Amsterdam/de Driehoek, 1972.

Dutch Oven Cooking by Ragsdale, published by Gulf.

Netherlands Cook Book, by A.M. Halverhout, published by Amsterdam/ de Driehoek, 7th edition.

GUIDE BOOKS:

De Nederlandse Musea, (and supplements), published by the Staatsuitgeverij, The Hague, 1982 . . . available through the ANWB. Text in Dutch, but listing all the museums in the Netherlands with facts such as contents, address, hours open and entrance fees. For the serious museum-goer.

Hotels, Motels and Restaurants in Nederland, Lasschuit's Officieel Adresboek (for the current year) . . in Dutch with explanations in English, French, Italian, German and Danish . . . photos and succinct data.

Hotels, (for the current year), published by the NBT . . . 67 pages.

Budget Hotels Holland, (for the current year) . . . 637 pages, four languages, available from NBT and VVV offices.

MAPS:

ANWB Noord, Zuid and Midden Maps to the scale 1:200 000 . . . clear, with indications to show interesting buildings, churches, convents, windmills, Megalithic tombs, castles, ruins, lighthouses, etc.

Grote Autokaart Nederland, one large map, scale 1:250 000 in four languages; by Shell.

Rotterdam Rijnmond, a Falk map in spiral bound form. Historical sketch in Dutch, German, English and French. Lists public buildings, consulates, museums, monuments, etc. Compact and easy to read; also gives trams, buses and metro information. Available for all major cities.

The Tourist Atlas of Holland, an Intermap bv Production, available from NBT or VVV offices . . . spiral form in English, German and Dutch editions . . . recreation and leisure in 20 maps.

NEWSPAPERS AND PERIODICALS (in English):

All foreign newspapers and magazines are available at newstands.

International Herald Tribune, subscriptions, tel. (023) 322347.

USA TODAY International, subscriptions, tel. 09.44.1. 831 2266.

Amsterdam Times, monthly magazine with lively articles on current events, calendar of events . . . available free from hotels as well as other outlets in Amsterdam and The Hague, tel. (020) 843804.

Holland Herald, a monthly magazine published in English by Media 2000 N.V., Amsterdam. Subscriptions: write Holland Herald, P.O. Box 696, Amsterdam.

Holland Life, a monthly magazine with articles of general interest. Subscriptions: write Holland Life, Keizersgracht 255, Amsterdam-C, tel. (020) 221301.

Roundabout, a monthly calendar of events focusing mainly on The Hague, but also listing special events in Amsterdam, Rotterdam and other major cities. Very useful if you want to keep up with what's going on in the Randstad . . . Prinsevinkenpark 31, 2585 HM The Hague.

Window, Rehong Publishers, Lange Voorhout 46, 2514 EG The Hague; monthly, with current events, etc.

VVV Publications distributed in hotels, VVV offices, etc. . . . mostly free.

In Amsterdam: *This Week*, magazine of events.

In The Hague: *Maand Agenda* and *Info*, Dutch and English text; monthly events in The Hague, Schveningen and Kijkduin.

In Rotterdam: *Magazijn*, covers films, theatrical and artistic events; *Deze Maand*, monthly events in Rotterdam in Dutch and English.

INDEX